# www.wadsworth.com

www.wadsworth.com is the World Wide Web site for Wadsworth and is your direct source to dozens of online resources.

At www.wadsworth.com you can find out about supplements, demonstration software, and student resources. You can also send email to many of our authors and preview new publications and exciting new technologies.

www.wadsworth.com
Changing the way the world learns®

# POLICE OPERATIONS: THEORY AND PRACTICE

## FOURTH EDITION

**KÄREN M. HESS, Ph.D.**
*Normandale Community College*

**HENRY M. WROBLESKI, LL.B.**
*Former Law Enforcement Coordinator*
*Normandale Community College*

THOMSON

WADSWORTH

Australia • Canada • Mexico • Singapore
Spain • United Kingdom • United States

**THOMSON**

**WADSWORTH**

Police Operations: Theory and Practice, Fourth Edition
Kären M. Hess and Henry M. Wrobleski

V.P., Editor in Chief: Eve Howard
Assistant Editor: Jana Davis
Editorial Assistant: Jennifer Walsh
Technology Project Manager: Susan DeVanna
Marketing Manager: Terra Schultz
Marketing Assistant: Gregory Hughes
Marketing Communications Manager: Stacey Purviance
Project Manager, Editorial Production: Matt Ballantyne
Creative Director: Rob Hugel
Art Director: Vernon Boes

Print Buyer: Barbara Britton
Permissions Editor: Kiely Sisk
Production Service: Shepherd, Inc.
Photo Researcher: Suzie Wright
Copy Editor: Amy Freitag
Cover Designer: Paula Goldstein
Cover Image: Copyright © Thinkstock/Getty Images
Cover Printer: Phoenix Color Corp
Compositor: Shepherd, Inc.
Printer: Courier Westford

Thomson Higher Education
10 Davis Drive
Belmont, CA 94002-3098
USA

**Asia (including India)**
Thomson Learning
5 Shenton Way
#01-01 UIC Building
Singapore 068808

**Australia/New Zealand**
Thomson Learning Australia
102 Dodds Street
Southbank, Victoria 3006
Australia

**Canada**
Thomson Nelson
1120 Birchmount Road
Toronto, Ontario M1K 5G4
Canada

**UK/Europe/Middle East/Africa**
Thomson Learning
High Holborn House
50-51 Bedford Row
London WC1R 4LR
United Kingdom

**Latin America**
Thomson Learning
Seneca, 53
Colonia Polanco
11560 Mexico
D.F. Mexico

**Spain (including Portugal)**
Thomson Paraninfo
Calle Magallanes, 25
28015 Madrid, Spain

Library of Congress Control Number: 2005929490

ISBN 0-534-63222-X

Dedicated to the hundreds of thousands of uniformed law enforcement officers, past and present, whose accomplishments have made such a difference in the quality of life in communities throughout the United States, and to those who are about to join them.

# Brief Contents

# Contents

## SECTION II

 GETTING THE JOB DONE:
BASIC POLICE OPERATIONS    97

### Chapter 4:  Patrol: The Backbone of Police Operations    99

**SECTION III**

# SPECIALIZED POLICE OPERATIONS  315

**Chapter 10: Criminal Investigation  317**

**SECTION IV**

 THE PERSONAL SIDE OF POLICE OPERATIONS   433

# Foreword

**Donald J. Clough,**
**Bloomington Police Department**

*P*olice Operations is a well-researched, comprehensive and up-to-date text that covers all major aspects of policing. It deals with what law enforcement leaders and researchers feel are the most critical issues facing law enforcement in the first decade of the twenty-first century. A theme running throughout *Police Operations* is that the motivated, professional uniformed officer can make a tremendous difference in how citizens are "served and protected."

The authors focus attention on what could be rather than on what has been in the past. They emphasize what the police responsibility is, the constitutional and statutory constraints under which police function and how the tasks to be performed can be accomplished responsibly and humanely within these constraints. Relevant landmark Supreme Court cases affecting police operations are presented throughout the text, giving students an understanding of case law and police procedures under varying circumstances.

Students are challenged to apply the information contained in each chapter to application exercises, critical thinking problems, InfoTrac College Edition assignments, Internet assignments and discussion questions. These exercises, problems and questions underscore the complexity of policing and the need for knowledge, skill and common sense in carrying out police operations. With such a base, police officers of the future will be able to find new ways to deliver police services fairly, equitably and effectively. They can, indeed, reshape approaches to some of the critical problems confronting law enforcement and may become the change agents of the future. The authors are to be congratulated on writing a text that not only covers all the basics of police operations, but does so in a way that students should find both interesting and challenging.

# Preface

## Purpose

Welcome to *Police Operations*. This text is *not* an introduction to law enforcement and the criminal justice system. It is intended to describe what police officers do and why. Therefore, it is short on theory and long on practical application, presenting the fundamentals of what policing is all about.

The basic reason modern society has police departments is summarized in the classic statement of police sociologist Egon Bittner*: "Something-ought-not-to-be-happening—about-which-something-ought-to-be-done-NOW!" This text goes beyond this reactive approach (which will always be an important and unavoidable part of policing), however, by also incorporating the techniques of proactive policing. Proactive policing is perhaps best illustrated in *community policing,* in which law enforcement partners with the citizens and organizations in a community to make the community safer for all. For such partnerships to work, law enforcement agencies must have carefully thought-through policies and procedures for dealing with crime and violence, both reactively and proactively. Community policing also emphasizes the need for individual officers on the street to be creative in their approaches to problems and to work with citizens as they solve these problems.

## Organization of the Text

The first section of *Police Operations* discusses the basics behind effective police operations, including the context in which services are provided and the skills required to provide these services (Chapter 1). Law enforcement officers must be thoroughly familiar with the citizens they are sworn to "serve and protect" (Chapter 2) as well as with the constitutional restraints within which they must operate (Chapter 3). They must be proficient in communication skills as well as in the numerous profession-specific skills required in law enforcement: conducting stops and frisks, making arrests, searching crime scenes and suspects, investigating crimes and assisting victims.

Section II discusses basic police operations, including patrol (Chapter 4); traffic (Chapter 5); crime, disorder and quality-of-life issues (Chapter 6); violence—domestic, school and workplace (Chapter 7); emergencies (Chapter 8) and terrorism (Chapter 9). The third section presents specialized police operations such as those performed by detectives in investigating crimes (Chapter 10), juvenile officers (Chapter 11) and officers who deal with gangs and drugs (Chapter 12). The final section discusses the personal side of law enforcement—what officers need to know about maintaining their physical and emotional well-being so they can continue in their chosen profession (Chapter 13) and what they need to know about protecting themselves from being sued and about acting not only legally but ethically as well (Chapter 14).

---

*From "Florence Nightingale in Pursuit of Willie Sutton: A Theory of Police," in *The Potential for Reform of Criminal Justice,* edited by H. Jacob. Beverly Hills, CA: Sage, 1974, p.30.

## New to This Edition

The Fourth Edition has added a chapter on terrorism (Chapter 9). All statistics and references have been updated, with the majority of the more than 500 new references having been published after 2000. In addition, the following changes have been made:

- Chapter 1—Police Operations in Context, 14 new references
- Chapter 2—Communication: PDAs, radio interference, interoperability, crisis intervention teams, police-based diversion programs for the mentally ill, certified forensic interviewer program, new guidelines for interviewing, avoiding contaminating an interview, consular rights warnings to foreign nationals, detecting deception, computer-assisted report entry, new terms, 49 new references, 4 new cases: *Daubert v. Merrell Dow Pharmaceuticals, Inc.* (1993), *Frey v. United States* (1923), *Hiibel v. Sixth Judicial District Court of Nevada et al.* (2004), *Kumho Tire v. Carmichael* (1999) and *Yarborough v. Alverado* (2004)
- Chapter 3—Operational Skills: Performing within the Law: de facto arrests, arguments against use-of-force continuums, anatomy of a lethal force event, reports on use of force, the new Taser × 26 and the Force Science™ Research Center, border searches, 2 new terms, 46 new references, 7 new Supreme Court cases: *Atwater v. City of Lago Vista* (2001), *Hiibel v. Sixth Judicial District Court* (2004), *Illinois v. Gates* (1983), *Kaupp v. Texas* (2003), *United States v. Banks* (2003), *United States v. Flores-Montano* (2004), *United States v. Ramirez* (1998)
- Chapter 4—Patrol: global positioning systems in vehicles, Segways, personal vertical takeoff and landing aircraft, 27 new references
- Chapter 5—Traffic: speeding in residential areas, curbing illegal street racing, decoy patrols, red-light running, no approach or call back car stop, sobriety checkpoints and saturation patrol compared, symptoms of road rage, 1 new term, 53 new references.
- Chapter 6—Crime, Disorder and Quality-of-Life Issues: expanded discussion of geographic information systems (GIS) and CompStat, quality-of-life issues, incivilities, responding to disorderly or troublesome people including panhandlers and prostitutes, dumping or police-initiated transport of troublesome persons (PITT), the Black Bloc, the operational triangle for responding to individuals who are mentally ill, 4 new terms, 48 new references
- Chapter 7—Violence: batterer intervention programs (BIPs), the controversial Duluth Model, categories of Internet sex crimes against minors, Munchausen syndrome by proxy, indicators of financial crimes against the elderly, a model to de-escalate juvenile aggression, 3 new terms, 65 new references
- Chapter 8—Emergency Situations: transfer of FEMA to the Department of Homeland Security; the Consensus Plan to eliminate police radio interference; the five biggest interview failures; Hurricanes Charley, Frances and Ivan in Florida; best practices following major critical incidents; technological advances in bomb disposal robots; 1 new term; 11 new references
- Chapter 9—Terrorism: an entirely new chapter. Highlights include the dual threat of domestic and international terrorism, asymmetric warfare, creation of the Department of Homeland Security and passage of the USA PATRIOT Act, initiatives in the fight against terrorism, role of the media in this fight, community policing and terrorism, The Intelligence Reform and Terrorism Prevention Act of 2004, two 2004 Supreme Court cases related to terrorism, 5 new terms, 82 new references

- Chapter 10—Criminal Investigation: the investigative process, cold cases, bait cars, 2003 Goldstein winner for excellence in problem-oriented policing, 5 new terms, 55 new references
- Chapter 11—Responding to Children and Juveniles: guidelines for determining whether a missing child is a runaway or has been abducted, curfews, truancy, underage drinking, rave parties, the 8% problem, a new problem-oriented policing case study, 4 new terms, 28 new references
- Chapter 12—Gangs and Drugs: gang impact teams, vertical and horizontal prosecution, special prosecution units, gang injunctions and ordinances, a five-pronged approach to gang reduction, the *National Drug Threat Assessment 2004*, *Pulse Check 2004*, *The National Drug Control Strategy 2004*, OxyContin®, combating prescription drug diversion, dealing with meth labs, an alternative to arrest for drug users, 2 new terms, 33 new references
- Chapter 13—Physical and Mental Health Issues: validation of physical fitness tests, interplay of stressors, addressing personal threat levels, the warrior attitude, responding to an emotionally disturbed person (EDP) call, countering a canine attack, safety advice from veteran officers, 25 new references
- Chapter 14—Liability and Ethics: police culture and the use of force, gray areas in police ethics, the deception continuum, 18 new references

## How to Use This Text (Pedagogical Aids)

*Police Operations* is more than a text. It is a learning experience requiring *your* active participation to obtain the best results. You will get the most out of the text if you first familiarize yourself with the total scope of law enforcement: read and think about the subjects listed in the Contents. Then follow five steps for each chapter to get *triple-strength learning.*

*Triple-Strength Learning*

1. Read the objectives at the beginning of each chapter, stated in the form of "Do You Know" questions. This is your *first* exposure to the key concepts of the text. The following is an example of this format:
   - What police operations are and what they include?
2. Review the key terms and think about their meaning in the context of law enforcement.
3. Read the chapter, underlining or taking notes if that is your preferred study style. Pay special attention to all information within the highlighted areas. This is your *second* exposure to the chapter's key concepts. The following is an example of this format:

 **Police operations** refers to activities conducted in the field by law enforcement officers as they "serve and protect," including patrol, traffic, investigation and general calls for service.

The key concepts of each chapter are emphasized in this manner. Also pay attention to all words in bold print. All key terms will be in bold print when they are first used.

4. Read the summary carefully. This will be your *third* exposure to the key concepts. By now you should have internalized the information.
5. To make sure you have learned the information, when you have finished reading a chapter, reread the list of objectives given at the beginning of that chapter to make certain you can answer each question. If you find yourself

stumped, find the appropriate material in the chapter and review it. Often these questions will be used as essay questions during testing.

6. Review the key terms to be certain you can define each. These also are frequently used as test items.

**A Note:** This text is designed to give you *triple-strength* learning *if* you (1) think about the questions at the beginning of the chapter before you read, (2) read the chapter thoughtfully for in-depth answers to these questions and then (3) read and reread the summary. Do not misinterpret triple-strength learning to mean you need only focus on three elements—the "Do You Know" items, highlighted boxes and summaries—to master the chapter. You are also responsible for reading and understanding the material that surrounds these basics—the "meat" around the bones, so to speak. The summaries are intended as a *review,* not as a shortcut or replacement to reading the entire chapter. If you read only the summaries, or focus only on the highlighted key concepts, you are not likely to understand or recall the content. Remember, not only your livelihood but your life is on the line in this demanding and rewarding profession. Begin your habits of self-discipline now.

## Exploring Further

The text also provides an opportunity for you to apply what you have learned or to go into specific areas in greater depth. To further strengthen your learning experience, the text includes discussion questions, application exercises in which you create policies and procedures related to the content of each chapter, and critical thinking exercises. Professional law enforcement officers should be able to create reasonable, legal, ethical and effective policies and procedures for the most common situations encountered in law enforcement. In addition, they should be able to approach each situation as a unique experience, perhaps requiring a more creative approach. Law enforcement officers must have good critical thinking skills. It is the intent of this text to provide a balance of both.

Finally, each chapter contains InfoTrac College Edition and Internet assignments allowing you to go into greater depth in areas of interest to you. Do as many of these assignments as your time permits.

Good reading and learning!

## Ancillaries

To further enhance your study of law enforcement and criminal justice, several supplements are available:

- **The Criminal Justice Resource Center http://cj.wadsworth.com**—An exceptional resource website containing links to over 3,000 popular criminal justice sites, jobs, news and other interesting and relevant links.
- **Careers in Criminal Justice 2.0 Interactive CD-ROM**—With this CD-ROM, students can view video profiles of actual testimonials from people in the field and link to the various career options in the criminal justice system while also learning about job requirements and salaries. Also included is FREE

access to the Holland personalized self-assessment test, designed to help students determine which careers best suit their interests, as well as tips on cover letters, resumes and interviews.

- *CNN Today* **Video Series**—Exclusively from Thomson/Wadsworth, the *CNN Today* Video Series offers compelling videos that feature current news footage from the Cable News Network's comprehensive archives. With offerings for Introduction to Criminal Justice, Criminology, Juvenile Delinquency and Corrections, each of these videotapes provides a varied collection of two- to ten-minute clips on such hot topics as police brutality, terrorism, high-tech crime fighting tools, registering sex offenders, juveniles behind bars, elderly inmates and much more. Available to qualified adopters, these videotapes are great lecture launchers as well as classroom discussion pieces.
- **Crime Scenes CD-ROM**—An interactive CD-ROM featuring six vignettes allowing you to play various roles as you explore all aspects of the criminal justice system.
- **Internet Investigator, Third Edition**—A colorful trifold brochure listing the most popular Internet addresses for criminal justice–related websites.
- **Careers in Criminal Justice and Related Fields: From Internship to Promotion, Fifth Edition**—This book provides specific information on many criminal justice professions, helpful tips on resumes and cover letters, practical advice on interview techniques and includes a free copy of the *Careers in Criminal Justice CD-ROM*, Release 2.0.

# Acknowledgments

We would like to thank Christine Hess Orthmann for her expert research and writing. We would also like to thank Waldo Asp for creating the *Exercises in Critical Thinking* found at the end of each chapter. We would like to thank the reviewers for the Fourth Edition: Sandra M. Hall Smith, Indiana University Northwest; Joe Morris, Northwestern State University; Becky Allen, Minot State University; Jeff Magers, Stephen F. Austin State University; and Steven Livernois, SUNY–Canton. Thanks are also due to the reviewers of the original manuscript and previous editions for their careful reading and constructive suggestions: James S. Albritton, Marquette University; David Barlow, University of Wisconsin–Milwaukee; Michael B. Blankenship, Memphis State University; William D. Braddock, Boise State University; Laura Brooks, University of Maryland; David L. Carter, Michigan State University; Robert Ives, Rock Valley College (Illinois); David A. Kramer, Bergen Community College; Floyd W. Liley, Jr., Mansfield University; Neal W. Lippold, Waubonsee Community College; James Malcolm, College of Lake County; James L. Massey, Northern Illinois University; Donald McLean, Oakland Community College; James E. Newman, Rio Hondo Community College— Police Academy (California); James T. Nichols, Tompkins Cortland Community College; Tom O'Connor, North Carolina Wesleyan University; Jerald L. Plant, Milwaukee Area Technical College; Carroll S. Price, Penn Valley Community College; Chester L. Quarles, University of Mississippi; James Sewell, Florida Department of Law Enforcement; B. Grant Stitt, University of Nevada at Reno; and Gary W. Tucker, Sinclair Community College. Any errors in the text are, however, the sole responsibility of the coauthors.

Finally, thanks to our editors at Wadsworth Publishing, Jay Whitney, Matt Ballentyne and Jennie Redwitz, for their outstanding advice, support and encouragement, and to Peggy Francomb, our production editor at Shepherd.

# About the Authors

Kären M. Hess, Ph.D., has written extensively in the field of law enforcement and conducts seminars on communication in law enforcement. She is a member of the English department at Normandale Community College and the president of the Institute for Professional Development. Dr. Hess is a graduate of the University of Minnesota, where she concentrated on educational psychology and instructional design.

Other Wadsworth texts Dr. Hess has coauthored are *Community Policing: Partnerships for Problem Solving*, Fourth Edition; *Criminal Investigation*, Seventh Edition; *Criminal Procedure; Introduction to Law Enforcement and Criminal Justice*, Eighth Edition; *Juvenile Justice*, Fourth Edition; *Management and Supervision in Law Enforcement*, Fourth Edition; *Private Security*, Fourth Edition; and *Careers in Criminal Justice and Related Fields: From Internship to Promotion*, Fifth Edition.

Henry M. Wrobleski, LL.B., is a well-known author, lecturer and consultant with 30 years' experience in law enforcement. Mr. Wrobleski is a graduate of the FBI Academy, was coordinator of the Law Enforcement Program at Normandale Community College and is now Dean of Instruction for the Institute for Professional Development. Other Wadsworth texts Mr. Wrobleski has coauthored are *Introduction to Law Enforcement and Criminal Justice*, Eighth Edition and *Private Security*, Fourth Edition.

# THE BASICS BEHIND EFFECTIVE POLICE OPERATIONS

Police operations deal with what officers do in the field as they "serve and protect." To fulfill their responsibilities, law enforcement officers have been given great power, power entrusted to them by the people they serve and defined by the laws of the land, state and municipality.

This section presents an overview of police operations starting with the context in which those services are provided. The society served, the laws it has enacted, the individuals entering law enforcement and the police organization itself have undergone great changes in the past decade—today's law enforcement uses mission statements, value statements, goals, objectives, policies, procedures and regulations to provide a basic structure within which officers normally function. Because law enforcement deals with such diverse problems, officers also must expect to use discretion while safeguarding citizens' constitutional rights (Chapter 1).

Law enforcement demands that its officers be multifaceted and well rounded. Officers must understand the complex communication process and the barriers that often exist within that process and within our diverse society. Officers also must be skilled in making field inquiries, interviewing and interrogating, and they must know how to do so while protecting the constitutional rights of victims, suspects and witnesses. Further, officers must record the information they have obtained in effective, reader-friendly reports, and they must know how to use the various records available (Chapter 2). Finally, officers need several profession-specific skills. They must understand and become skilled at conducting stops and frisks, making arrests, conducting searches and participating in undercover operations, all without violating anyone's constitutional rights (Chapter 3).

# CHAPTER 1

# Police Operations in Context

**DO YOU KNOW . . .**

- What police operations are and what they include?
- What changes have affected police operations?
- How our society has changed?
- How our law enforcement officers have changed?
- How the police organization may change?
- What community policing is?
- What a mission and a mission statement are?
- What the relationship is between goals and objectives?
- What police discretion is and what positive contributions it makes?
- What problems are associated with discretion?
- What balance presents a major challenge for law enforcement?

**CAN YOU DEFINE?**

| | | | |
|---|---|---|---|
| bifurcated society | dog shift | participatory leadership | procedures |
| broken windows metaphor | goals | police operations | racial profiling |
| community policing | mission | policy | regulations |
| discretion | mission statement | | selective enforcement |
| | objectives | | |

## Introduction

Just what do police officers do? What skills must they possess, and in what ways does the community rely on their services? Historically, police officers have been viewed as law *enforcement* officers, concerned with keeping the law from being broken and apprehending those who break it. This function, however, has broadened considerably, as evidenced in the label *peace officer* replacing *police officer* in many departments. No matter what priorities a law enforcement agency may have, certain basic police operations will be found.

**Police operations** refers to activities conducted in the field by law enforcement officers as they "serve and protect," including patrol, traffic, investigation and general calls for service.

Wuestewald and Wilds (2002, pp.138–139) note: "Today, law enforcement serves a more informed, diverse and sophisticated society than at any time in history.

Emerging new roles and missions have necessitated an unprecedented degree of adaptability from police organizations. The lexicon of contemporary policing has come to include terms like change management, community engagement, value-centered leadership, information management, cultural awareness, problem-oriented policing, conflict resolution and homeland security."

Before looking at specific police operations and the skills required to perform them effectively and efficiently, it is important to understand the *context* in which these operations occur. Although police operations have changed little over the last hundred years, the public served and the laws enacted by that public, the officers providing the services, the police bureaucracy itself and the community's involvement have changed and will continue to change.

This chapter begins by examining the various changes affecting police operations. This is followed by another important context affecting police operations: the department's mission and values, reflected in goals, objectives and tasks to be accomplished. Next the policies, procedures and regulations to fulfill the department's mission are discussed. The chapter concludes with yet another area greatly influencing operations—discretion; the discussion includes ethical decision making, the negative and positive sides of discretion and the interaction of discretion and critical thinking skills.

## Changes Affecting Police Operations

 Law enforcement is affected by a changing public and society, changing law enforcement officers, a changing police bureaucracy and a change in community involvement.

### A Changing Public and Society

The U.S. population is changing, and these trends will undoubtedly affect police operations:

- An aging U.S. population—Experts at the Population Division of the U.S. Census Bureau project by 2020, nearly 61 million Americans will be over age 65, and by 2040 that number will climb to 92 million. The increase is due not only to the aging of the baby boomers but to the increased life expectancy. When our country was founded, the average life expectancy was 35. In 2001 it was 77.1 years.
- An increasingly racially diverse population—In 1950 the U.S. population was 87 percent white; that percentage is projected to drop to 51 percent by 2050 (Miller and Hess, 2005, p.63). This trend is heavily influenced by a continuous influx of immigrants and the growing rate of interracial marriages.
- A growing number of single-parent households—One-parent families numbered 12 million in 2000 (32% of all family groups); single-mother families increased from 3 million (12%) in 1970 to 10 million (26%) in 2000, and single-father families grew from 393,000 (1%) in 1970 to 2 million (5%) in 2000 (Fields and Casper, 2001, p.7).
- A widening gap between the wealthy and the poor—A report from the Congressional Budget Office indicates incomes for the wealthiest Americans are rising twice as fast as those of the middle class. This economic disparity has led to a **bifurcated society**—the "haves" and the "have nots."

Our society is becoming older and has more minorities, more immigrants and more single-parent households, while the gap between the rich and poor continues to expand.

These trends underscore the need for those in the criminal justice field to be culturally sensitive to the public they serve, especially those who work as directly with that public as police officers do. Many theories have addressed how our existing system of laws and law enforcement affects and is affected by our evolving society.

Another major change affecting police operations is the type of officer performing them.

## A Changing Law Enforcement Officer

Historically, law enforcement has attracted young, white men out of the military. These men frequently had a high school education or less and were used to following orders without questioning authority. This is no longer true. Many people entering the field have no military experience. Furthermore, the ranks of today's police departments are less exclusively white men, as more women and minorities are being actively recruited. As noted in *Recruiting & Retaining Women* (n.d., p.21):

> In 1968 the Indianapolis Police Department made history by assigning the first two female officers to patrol on an equal basis with their male colleagues. Since that time, women have entered the field of law enforcement in increasing numbers and played a critical role in the development of modern policing. Yet, the number of women in law enforcement has remained small and the pace of increase slow. The most recent research shows that only 14.3 percent of sworn personnel are female, with an annual increase of only 0.5 percent over the last several years. At this rate, women will not achieve parity within the police profession for at least another 70 years, and many have cautioned that time alone is not sufficient to substantially increase their numbers.

*Police departments are achieving greater diversity, yet many departments are still not representative of the population they serve. Here San Antonio, Texas, police officers discuss plans for a street parade to be held later that day.*

James L. Shaffer

Jones (2004, p.165) suggests: "Research from the National Center for Women and Policing has shown that 'to successfully increase the number of women in policing, law enforcement agencies should develop a specific plan of action that targets women in the recruiting process and emphasizes the agency's desire to significantly increase the number of women in its ranks.'" In addition, according to Moore (2004, p.114): "Law enforcement has been slow to welcome women into its ranks. Although more women wear badges today than ever before, the attrition rate for female officers still stands much too high."

Lonsway and Campbell (2002, p.107) comment: "Credible research shows both that female officers are equally competent as their male colleagues, and that they bring a number of unique advantages to the field of law enforcement." Penny Harrington, Director of the National Center for Women and Policing, emphasizes the public appeal of women officers: "They get fewer citizen complaints than men do, and they are sometimes more compassionate about things such as sex offenses, children and rape victims" (Streit, 2001, p.71). As the number of women in law enforcement has increased, so too have the number of other minority officers:

> One of the main reasons it is important that various minorities are represented within a department is the department should reflect the make-up of the community that it serves. . . .
>
> When people within the community see a minority in uniform, it can make them more trusting of the entire department. They may feel that someone is there who will understand their problems and concerns (Streit, pp.70, 71).

Despite the gains made over the past several decades, women and minorities continue to be underrepresented among the ranks of the police. In addition to recruiting more women and other minority officers, departments are also progressively raising the educational standards for officer candidates. Traditionally, emphasis was placed on potential officers' physical strength, height, weight and such abilities as firearms skills. This focus began to change slightly during the 1920s and 1930s, when August Vollmer, considered by many as the father of professional policing, began advocating higher education for those entering law enforcement. In addition, the Wickersham Commission (1937) and the President's Commission on Law Enforcement and the Administration of Justice (1967) both recommended post–secondary education for law enforcement officers.

Research examining the effects of higher education on police officers' performance has produced varied and sometimes seemingly contradictory results. Some studies have found officers with more education perform more effectively and have a better capacity to handle the variety of tasks involved in modern policing, while other studies have concluded that higher-educated officers burn out more quickly and experience greater job dissatisfaction. Polk and Armstrong (2001, p.77) contend that higher education, regardless of any direct impact on officers' ability to perform their duties, is seen as beneficial by many agencies, who reward more educated officers with greater career advancement opportunities. Armstrong and Polk (2002, p.25) report: "Comparing officers with a bachelor's degree to those with no college, the time difference between being hired and the second promotion or assignment was 14 months less for those with the bachelor's degree."

Noting that the literature is mixed, Armstrong and Polk (p.25) list the following common advantages cited by supporters of higher education: "(1) The college experience allows for greater maturity. (2) The individual is exposed to other cultures and lifestyles. (3) College provides a broad base of knowledge that provides the officer with greater flexibility in the decision-making process. (4) College-educated officers are more receptive to change and new ideas. (5) The officer develops enhanced verbal and written communication skills."

It has also been noted that today's younger police officers come from a distinctly different cohort than previous groups—Generation X. This term was first used in 1979 to refer to the post–baby boomer market and includes those people born between 1963 and 1977. This segment of the population accounts for roughly 42 million (33.6 percent) of the nearly 125 million employed Americans and, as Messer (2001, p.14) notes: "This generation will be the new officer pool for the next 20 to 30 years." With this new generation come new challenges for police agencies:

> More than money is involved when it comes to recruiting Generation X officers. Money is definitely a major draw for Xers. However, there are some other, less traditional incentives that are attractive to the new Generation X officer. Above all other perks, Xers value training and self-building opportunities that will enhance their knowledge for possible promotions or outside opportunities in their futures. . . .
>
> Xers have a strong need for unique, stimulating jobs that allow for frequent personal contact and feedback from their supervisors. . . . Creative freedom and the power to plan their own work schedules will also stimulate interest with Generation X officers.

In addition to having different backgrounds and values from the "traditional" police recruit, police officers now are often called on to perform operations well beyond what traditionally has been provided.

 Today's police recruits include fewer people with military backgrounds and more women and minorities. New recruits have more education and place more value on job satisfaction than on material rewards. They also are expected to perform more diverse operations.

Given the changing needs of the public, the new type of person entering law enforcement and the growth of new services, it is logical that the bureaucracy directing police operations also must change.

## A Changing Police Bureaucracy

A basic principle held by Sir Robert Peel, often called the father of modern policing, was that the police must be organized militarily. The military model of the Metropolitan Police of London (established in 1829) was adopted in the United States and has been the model for our police departments since that time. Figure 1.1 illustrates this traditional pyramid of authority and organizational hierarchy.

This model, however, is now being questioned by many, partially because of the changes in police recruits and the trend toward community policing. Many police departments are moving away from the paramilitary model and adopting

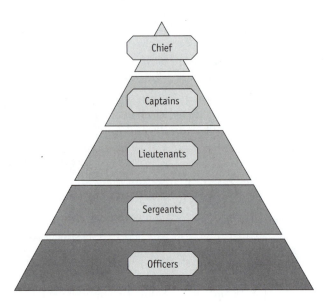

**Figure 1.1**  Traditional Pyramid of Authority and Organizational Hierarchy

a business or corporate model that flattens the organization and reduces the number of management and supervisory positions while increasing the number of officers. These officers are becoming better trained to act independently while providing more field services—that is, police operations.

 The police bureaucracy may become less militaristic and may move toward a team approach to providing services. This includes decentralization and a shift from management to leadership.

Kokkelenberg (2001, p.9) observes:

Bosses have subordinates, but true leaders have followers regardless of their rank or title. Historically, when individuals thought of leadership, they thought of rank. For rookies, it was the field training officer and for everyone else it was the level(s) above their rank. That perception, along with a top-down chain of command, caused a lot of people to believe that they cannot or should not do anything about recurring or organizational problems.

Many people, particularly Gen-Xers, no longer depend on the authority of somebody "above" them to dictate their opinions or control their actions. They are more independent, preferring to make up their own minds and accepting responsibility for their own actions. They still, however, need the support and guidance of a leader. Alsabrook et al. (2001, p.112) note: "The job of management is leadership, not supervision. . . . Police managers should lead by example."

Vernon (2004, p.60) observes: "Much is known about leadership. We live in a time when there are more books, films and videos about leadership than ever before. Amazon.com lists over 8,000 leadership titles." Many police organizations are undergoing a change from an authoritarian management style to a leadership style that focuses on teamwork. This style, called **participatory leadership,** allows officers to influence decisions affecting them and seeks to form a cohesive

**Table 1.1**  Authoritative versus Participative Styles

| Authoritative Manager | | Participative Leader | |
|---|---|---|---|
| **Approach** | **Results** | **Approach** | **Results** |
| Mandate (tell) | Communication is downward; little upward communication | Influence (tell and ask) | Greater upward and lateral communication |
| Position power | Tell-oriented | Personal power | Tell- and ask-oriented |
| Compliance (have to) | People do things because they "have to" | Commitment (want to) | People do things because they "want to" |
| Time | People put in their time but energy decreases | Time and energy | People put in their time and their energy |
| Produce | People produce to standard | Produce and perform | People perform more than "just the expected" |

SOURCE: Adapted from *Creating the High Performance Team,* Steve Buchholz and Thomas Roth. © John Wiley and Sons, Inc., 1987, p. 25. Used by permission of John Wiley & Sons, Inc.

team. The differences between the authoritative manager and the participative leader are summarized in Table 1.1.

Participatory leadership is usually highly motivating to all members of the team. In progressive police departments, the role of rank-and-file officers is elevated significantly, with their input being critical in decision making. It is further expected that rank-and-file officers will be in close contact with the citizens they serve and, therefore, can reflect citizen concerns as decisions are made and can provide leadership.

Stainbrook (2004, p.8) points out: "Every time you as a police officer put on that uniform and go into the field, people look to you to provide leadership. Whether it is solving their problems, saving them from a criminal or from themselves, or just by doing the right thing, you are the most visible representative of our government, our community and of a civil society." Concurring, Covey— author of the best seller *The Seven Habits of Highly Effective People*—suggests: "Leadership is simply the ability to influence others. That ability rests within each and every member of the law enforcement community, regardless of position, gender, rank, seniority, or sworn or civilian status. No one in policing is in a position to exercise greater influence than line-level deliverers of policing services. Dispatchers sending officers to the scene, officers resolving a domestic dispute, a DARE officer teaching fifth graders, an officer writing a traffic citation, or an investigator conducting an interrogation—they are all exercising their ability to influence others. That's leadership" (Covey, 2003, p.131).

This close contact with citizens is reflected in another major change in how police operations are conducted, that is, a change in community involvement marked by the adoption of a community policing philosophy.

## *A Change in Community Involvement: Community Policing*

When Peel established the London Metropolitan Police, he set forth a number of principles, one of which foreshadowed community policing: "The police are the public and the public are the police."

The Upper Midwest Community Policing Institute (n.d.) defines **community policing** as "an organization-wide philosophy and management approach that promotes community, government and police partnerships; proactive problem solving; and community engagement to address the causes of crime, fear of crime and other community issues." According to Brown (2001, p.56): "The essence of community policing is to return to the day when safety and security are participatory in nature and everyone assumes responsibility for the general health of their community—not just a select few, not just the local government administration, not just the safety forces, but absolutely everyone living in the community."

Miller and Hess (p.xix) suggest that community policing offers one avenue for increasing neighborhood safety: "Community policing is not a program or a series of programs. It is a philosophy, a belief that working together, the police and the community can accomplish what neither can accomplish alone. The *synergy* that results from community policing can be powerful. It is like the power of a finely tuned athletic team, with each member contributing to the total effort. Occasionally heroes may emerge, but victory depends on a team effort."

Community policing differs from earlier efforts such as team policing, community relations, crime prevention programs or neighborhood watch programs. Community policing involves a rethinking of the role of the police and a restructuring of the police organization. Rahtz (2001, p.57) describes how an officer operating under a traditional policing philosophy might spend his or her time:

> Reactive Jack's day is dictated by the radio. Anyone in the community who picks up the phone and dials 911 has more control over Jack than his supervisor does. Jack's workday is not informed by any serious analysis of the problems on his beat. Instead, he runs willy-nilly where the radio calls lead. He handles the calls as quickly as possible, and in the time between radio runs he cruises about with little purpose waiting for the next dispatch. For a lot of cops, that is the sum total of police work.
>
> For beat officers tired of the merry-go-round of reactive policing, for cops looking for a more intelligent approach to police work, community policing emphasizing problem solving will be a godsend.

Aragon (2004, p.66) observes: "Though patrolling and answering calls for service are highly important functions of officers, the absence of creative joint problem solving, empowering the residents of our neighborhoods and other community-based initiatives will not create long-term successes in a jurisdiction."

Community policing usually assigns specific officers to specific neighborhoods and actively involves them in helping the neighborhood solve its problems. Table 1.2 presents basic differences between traditional policing and community policing.

 Community policing is proactive, empowering citizens to help local law enforcement provide safer neighborhoods. It usually includes an emphasis on foot and bicycle patrol.

Community policing goes much further than traditional community relations programs or neighborhood watch programs, although it often includes these components. Community policing means that officers get to know the citizens in their assigned areas—those who are law-abiding and those who are not. It means

**Table 1.2** Traditional versus Community Policing: Questions and Answers

| Question | Traditional Policing | Community Policing |
| --- | --- | --- |
| Who are the police? | A government agency principally responsible for law enforcement. | Police are the public and the public are the police: the police officers are those who are paid to give full-time attention to the duties of every citizen. |
| What is the relationship of the police force to other public service departments? | Priorities often conflict. | The police are one department among many responsible for improving the quality of life. |
| What is the role of the police? | Focusing on solving crimes. | A broader problem-solving approach. |
| How is police efficiency measured? | By detection and arrest rates. | By the absence of crime and disorder. |
| What are the highest priorities? | Crimes that are high value (e.g., bank robberies) and those involving violence. | Whatever problems disturb the community most. |
| What, specifically, do police deal with? | Incidents. | Citizens' problems and concerns. |
| What determines the effectiveness of police? | Response times. | Public cooperation. |
| What view do police take of service calls? | Deal with them only if there is no real police work to do. | Vital function and great opportunity. |
| What is police professionalism? | Swift effective response to serious crime. | Keeping close to the community. |
| What kind of intelligence is most important? | Crime intelligence (study of particular crimes or series of crimes). | Criminal intelligence (information about the activities of individuals or groups). |
| What is the essential nature of police accountability? | Highly centralized; governed by rules, regulations and policy directives; accountable to the law. | Emphasis on local accountability to community needs. |
| What is the role of headquarters? | To provide the necessary rules and policy directives. | To [instill] organizational values. |
| What is the role of the press liaison department? | To keep the "heat" off operational officers so they can get on with the job. | To coordinate an essential channel of communication with the community. |
| How do the police regard prosecutions? | As an important goal. | As one tool among many. |

SOURCE: Malcolm K. Sparrow. *Implementing Community Policing: Perspectives on Policing.* Washington, DC: National Institute of Justice, November 1988, pp. 8–9.

they listen to the citizens and treat them as a business treats its customers. Community policing also capitalizes on people's natural tendency to subscribe to the NIMBY (Not In My Back Yard) philosophy. The closer to home police can get their message, the more likely they are to enlist community support.

A general philosophy behind community policing is explained by Wilson and Kelling (1982), who suggest that crime and social disorder are "inextricably linked" (p.31). They use a **broken windows metaphor** to describe the deterioration of neighborhoods. Broken windows that go unrepaired make a statement that no one cares enough about the quality of life in the neighborhood to bother fixing things that need repair. A study by Sampson and Raudenbush (2001), however, has recently challenged this classic theory as overly simplifying the link between crime and disorder:

> The capacity for neighbors to trust each other and intervene on each other's behalf for the common good plays a far greater role in the suppression of crime than do efforts to address signs of disorder, as posited in the "Broken Windows" theory. . . .
>
> It is the structural characteristics of neighborhoods, as well as neighborhood cohesion and informal social control—not levels of disorder—that most affect crime. While there is a correlation between disorder and crime . . . one does not provide a path for the other. A neighborhood's "collective efficacy," a combination of community cohesion and informal social control exerted by residents, can work as a mitigating factor. . . .
>
> "Broken Windows" says essentially that disorder in neighborhoods could be a direct cause of crime. If that were true, it might suggest a good strategy would be for law enforcement and other agencies to come in and clean up disorder as a way of reducing crime . . . [but] it's probably not that simple. . . . You can't just go into a neighborhood and impose order without the cooperation of citizens ("If It's Broken, Fix It," 2001, p.8).

Sampson and Raudenbush (p.5) acknowledge, however, that disorder is not entirely irrelevant to understanding crime: "Signs of physical and social disorder are highly visible cues to which neighborhood residents respond, and they potentially influence migration, investment, and the overall viability of a neighborhood."

Some confusion exists among community policing, community-oriented policing (COP) and problem-oriented policing (POP). Community policing and community-oriented policing are basically the same thing. POP uses a situational approach to policing, whereas community policing and COP focus on fostering working partnerships between the police and the community. These partnerships often employ POP; thus, POP can be considered as one strategy within the larger scheme of community policing or COP. The problem-solving element of community policing has been identified as an important motivator and source of job satisfaction for officers.

More and more departments are turning to community policing as the most effective way to set and achieve their goals. A study by the Bureau of Justice Statistics found: "Some 90 percent of all local law enforcement agencies serving populations of 50,000 or more helped facilitate community policing goals by giving patrol officers responsibility for specific geographic beats" ("Bottoms-Up! . . .," 2001, p.5).

Allender (2004, pp.18–19) provides an explanation of community policing that summarizes the preceding in a definition highlighting nine words: "Community policing is a *philosophy* of full service *personalized policing* where the same officers *patrol* and work in the same area on a *permanent* basis, from a decentralized *place*, working in a *proactive partnership* with citizens to identify and solve *problems*."

The philosophy of community policing and its effect on police operations will be found throughout this text as it is actually implemented in the field. This

*This trash-strewn, poverty-stricken, high crime, inner-city urban neighborhood in Brooklyn, New York, illustrates the disrepair and disorder described in Wilson and Kelling's broken window theory.*

text provides a chance to engage in some thought-provoking, critical thinking about important issues in police operations. To do so effectively requires an understanding of the basis for police operations. The functions undertaken by law enforcement officers should be viewed not as isolated activities, but rather as part of a master plan to accomplish the mission of the law enforcement agency.

## Mission and Values

Work should be meaningful. Officers who see themselves as serving an important function will be more productive and more satisfied in their profession than those who feel no sense of mission.

 An agency's **mission** is its reason for existence, its purpose. It is often embodied in a **mission statement.**

Mission statements should be short, believable, easy to understand, easy to remember and widely known. Consider the following example:

The Charlotte Police Department is committed to fairness, compassion and excellence while providing police services in accordance with the law and that are sensitive to the priorities and needs of the people.

Mission statements often are accompanied by the set of values on which they are based. These values must be shared by department members and the public served, or they will be meaningless. Ideally, these values also are consistent with the overall cultural values of the state and the nation. The values underlying the Charlotte Police Department mission statement are as follows. The Charlotte Police Department:

- Believes that the protection of life and property is its highest priority.
- Will respect and protect the rights and dignity of all people and conduct all citizen contacts with courtesy and compassion.
- Will strive for excellence in its delivery of police services and will utilize training, technology and innovation to achieve that goal.
- Recognizes its interdependent relationship with the community it serves and will remain sensitive to the community's priorities and needs.
- Will enforce the law impartially throughout the community.
- Recognizes the individual worth of each of its members.

Such value statements enhance officers' feelings of worth and importance and lend significance to the daily routine of police operations. As Berkow (2001, p.48) emphasizes, a mission statement and sense of values should guide day-to-day operations and not be just some "lofty sounding words framed and hung on the wall."

Mission and value statements are important to law enforcement agencies and should be the driving force behind police operations. They are, however, only the starting point. The next steps are to develop goals and objectives that will accomplish the mission and then to decide what specific tasks must be undertaken to accomplish the goals and objectives.

## Goals, Objectives and Tasks

Goals may vary from one police department to another, but they usually focus on the following:

- To preserve the peace.
- To protect civil rights and civil liberties.
- To prevent crime.
- To enforce the law.
- To provide services.
- To improve the quality of life in the community.
- To participate in partnerships to solve problems related to crime and disorder.

Although the words *goals* and *objectives* often are used interchangeably, most authorities agree that a goal is a more general term, referring to a broad, nonspecific desired outcome such as those previously listed. Goals are usually long range. Objectives, in contrast, are more specific outcomes, usually with a listing of specific tasks and a timetable attached.

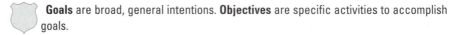 **Goals** are broad, general intentions. **Objectives** are specific activities to accomplish goals.

The distinction between goals and objectives is clarified in the California Council on Criminal Justice's *A Guide for Criminal Justice Planning:*

> Goal—A statement of broad direction, a general purpose of intent. A goal is general and timeless and is not concerned with a particular achievement within a specified time period.

*A police officer interacting with neighbors in a community policing program.*

Bob Daemmrich, Stock Boston

Objective—A desired accomplishment that can be measured within a given time and under specifiable conditions. The attainment of the objective advances the system toward a corresponding goal.

Goals give purpose to what may appear to be relatively unimportant tasks. An inscription carved in 1730 in a church in Sussex, England, proclaims: A vision without a task is but a dream, a task without a vision is drudgery, a vision and a task is the hope of the world.

Consider, for example, the differences in perspective of the following three bricklayers. In response to the question, What are you doing? the first bricklayer replies, "I'm making $15 an hour laying these stupid bricks." The second replies, "I'm building a wall." And the third says, "I'm part of a team that's building a cathedral so people can worship."

Or consider the difference in attitude between those police officers on the **dog shift** (typically, 11:00 P.M. to 7:00 A.M.) who see the drug pusher just arrested as nothing more than an annoyance and those officers who believe they have helped make the neighborhood safer, perhaps even saving a life.

Specific objectives or individual tasks in isolation may seem to accomplish little, but in combination they provide the direction needed to achieve the broad goals sought by the department. Common goals *are* important to team building.

How are objectives accomplished? Usually police departments establish policies that cover specific tasks that must be undertaken in basic police operations. They then create procedures to accomplish these tasks.

## Policies

Goals and objectives are more easily achieved with written policies guiding the police department's activities. A **policy** is a statement of principles that guide decisions. For example, our country's foreign policy guides our diplomats in their negotiations with foreign powers, just as the axiom "Honesty is the best policy" guides the conduct of most of us.

Policies not only provide guidance, they also help maintain organizational control and ensure accountability within an organization. In addition, they provide a basis for fair discipline. Written policies should be in those areas in which directions are needed, including public and press relations; personal conduct; personnel procedures and relations; and specific law enforcement operations with emphasis on such sensitive areas as the use of force, the use of lethal weapons, search and seizure, arrests and custody.

## Procedures

After policies are developed and put in writing, the next step is to identify procedures to carry out the policies, that is, guidelines for action or established methods. **Procedures** are step-by-step instructions for carrying out departmental policies.

Written procedures promote a uniformity of action that is especially important for ongoing calls for service or when a large number of officers perform the same services. Written procedures also may reduce civil liability. Figure 1.2 illustrates a directive containing a goal, a policy and the procedures for implementing the policy.

## Policies and Procedures Manuals

Martin (2002, p.116) stresses: "If a procedures manual is to have any credibility, it must be easy to comply with and easy to understand. If not, only minimal compliance can be expected. Keep in mind that short and concise documents are more likely to be read and understood than lengthy ones." Fulton (2001, p.118) suggests that policies be developed for sexual harassment prevention, pursuit, relief of duty and use of force, at minimum.

Sharp (2004, p.72) cautions that policies and procedures must be periodically reviewed: "According to a recent survey of 28 departments, they do update policies, but often as a reactionary procedure, rather than as a routine practice." Sharp (p.75) states: "The true test of the importance of policies and procedures manuals is not how professional they look or how many words may be misspelled. The key is to keep them as up-to-date as possible. While in the past they might have been a low priority for some agencies, they can be no longer. Currently, they are the first thing that opposing counsel asks for when something bad happens. The best way to be prepared for such events is to move policies and procedures revision to a high priority."

## Regulations

Regulations and procedures are similar and have the same intent: to guide conduct. **Regulations** are rules put out by a lower level of government, for example, a municipality, governing the actions of employees of the municipality, including police department personnel. These orders have the force of law for those people under their jurisdiction. Regulations are to a certain extent restrictive in that they force officers to adhere to certain codes of conduct. Like procedures, regulations should be in writing. Regulations help officers in decision making by eliminating discretionary action in certain areas.

## A Final Note and Caution

Police chiefs and supervisors cannot establish goals, objectives and policies in a vacuum. *All* officers, particularly those in the field, can contribute to under-

---

Mytown Police Department                    Date Issued: 01-01-06
                                            Page 1 of 1

Procedure Directive No. 06-0001

Effective Date: 01-01-06
Subject: Community Service Officer in Service Operations

---

**Goal:**

To provide community service officers with uniform procedures for in-service operations. The procedures will document community service officer (CSO) activities and provide reference material for a CSO training manual. The CSO in-service operation is new. As the CSO's tasks expand, additional procedures will be added to this directive.

**Policy:**

Community service officers will respond to calls only when directed by the dispatcher or supervisor or by the patrol officer's request. Community service officers will notify dispatch immediately when observing any criminal or suspicious activity. Community service officers will not respond to any call, emergency or not, as an emergency vehicle.

**Procedure:**

I. <u>Responding to Calls</u>

    A. When a CSO is responding to a call at the same time as a patrol officer, the CSO will stop or slow down to allow the patrol officer to arrive on the scene first. This will prevent a CSO from entering into a situation that is or could become dangerous.

    B. When a CSO is directed to a call where a patrol officer is not assigned or that a patrol officer has requested a CSO to handle, the CSO will call for assistance in any of the following circumstances:

        1. Any situation that the CSO determines on arrival as being dangerous or that could escalate into a dangerous situation.

        2. Any situation where a criminal violation has taken place and a suspect is still on the scene, leaving the scene or likely to return to the scene.

        3. Any situation in which the CSO has not had training or experience or that the CSO feels unable or not equipped to handle.

II. <u>Reports</u>

    A. The CSO will turn in all reports, including daily logs, to the report basket in the squad room unless otherwise specified.

    B. A supervisor will review and approve all reports and handle accordingly.

    C. A supervisor will place the CSO's daily report in the administrative in-basket.

---

John J. Doe
Chief of Police

**Figure 1.2** Sample Goal, Policy and Procedure Directive

standing problems and can assist in developing policies and procedures. Officers in face-to-face contact with community members usually are the best informed about problems in the field and potential solutions. These officers, in turn, will better identify and understand problems through direct contact and discussion with representative community members.

Goals, policies, procedures and regulations help make police departments efficient and effective. They are extremely important and deserve care in development and periodic evaluation. It must always be remembered, however, that not everything can be anticipated. Further, for every rule an exception usually can be found. Too many rules can be detrimental, limiting a department and its officers' flexibility. Flexibility is vital to law enforcement and includes the necessity for officers to use discretion.

# Discretion

**Discretion** is the ability to act or decide a matter on one's own. Police use discretion because no set of policies and procedures can prescribe what to do in every circumstance. The International Association of Chiefs of Police (IACP) "Police Code of Conduct" states: "A police officer will use responsibly the discretion vested in his position and exercise it within the law. The principle of reasonableness will guide the officer's determinations, and the officer will consider all surrounding circumstances in determining whether any legal action will be taken."

Discretion *must* be allowed for several reasons. One reason is that the law *overreaches,* seldom addressing exceptions that might arise. For example, although a highway may have a posted speed limit of 55 mph, a driver exceeding this limit may have very good reasons for doing so. Such a driver might be a volunteer firefighter on the way to a fire, an undercover police officer tailing a car, a parent taking a seriously injured child to the hospital or a man taking his wife who is in labor to the hospital. Technically, these people are speeding—but should they be given tickets? The law overreaches in each of these instances.

Another reason discretion is allowed is because human behavior is too varied and complex to be accommodated by inflexible legal rules, and in some cases the law may be better served by not being enforced. Consider the following explanations from motorists clocked at 50 mph in a 35 mph zone: "I've just come from my mother's funeral, and I'm very upset;" or "I just got fired;" or "I haven't ever received a speeding ticket in my life. I teach driver education at the high school."

Discretion makes enforcement of our laws *equitable,* that is, humanistic, considering the spirit rather than the letter of the law. Discretion also gives officers a sense of control over their jobs, which are, in many cases, primarily reactive.

Discretion allows for equitable enforcement of our laws and for police officers to grow morally and professionally.

Most officers appreciate the chance to work through a citizen's problem from beginning to end. They also appreciate the acknowledgment that they have something to contribute in the form of expertise, imagination and creativity, as well as problem-solving ability.

The ability to decide when to impose legal sanctions on those who violate the law, whether issuing traffic tickets or arresting someone, is known as **selective enforcement.** This type of discretion has only recently been recognized by police administrators and the general public as a proper aspect of officers' authority. While such discretion is acknowledged as a necessity for effective policing, it does have some drawbacks.

## *Problems with Officer Discretion*

Problems associated with officer discretion include:
- Lack of accountability.
- Unpredictability.
- Inconsistency and allegations of racial profiling.

Discretionary actions may also confuse citizens because they are not sure how they will be treated from one situation to the next. Discretion can be unpredictable from one officer to the next. For example, one traffic officer may allow up to 5 mph over the speed limit before stopping a motorist. Another may allow 10 mph over. The driver who gets a ticket for exceeding the limit by 5 mph when the driver who is going 10 mph over the limit does not get a ticket will see the situation as unfair.

Most importantly, discretion is often applied inconsistently. Equality under the law has always implied that people should receive similar treatment when they perform relatively the same acts. However, discretion lets officers treat different people differently. This may be seen as discrimination and, in fact, sometimes is. Some officers are harder on minorities, men or juveniles. This may be conscious or unconscious discrimination, but it does make for inconsistent enforcement of the laws. An example of such inconsistent, biased enforcement of laws is seen in **racial profiling,** when an officer uses a person's race to assess the likelihood of criminal conduct or other wrongdoing:

> The term "racial profiling" is a new label for a longstanding concern that policing is not practiced impartially. And while there is no way to accurately measure to what extent allegations are true or merely perceived, in fact, in some ways it doesn't matter. Both biased policing and the perceptions of biased policing are critical issues (Fridell, 2001, p.1).

Racial profiling is discussed in depth in Chapter 5. Officer discretion, while necessary, must also be limited.

## Limits on Discretion

 A major challenge facing law enforcement is finding the balance between a department's clear-cut goals, policies and procedures and its officers' discretionary actions.

Two factors must be kept in mind: (1) the primary goals of the department and (2) maintaining a balance between a need for clear policies and procedures and the accompanying need for discretion when exceptions arise. In addition, officers will be called upon to use critical-thinking skills in performing police operations.

## Discretion and Critical-Thinking Skills

To use discretion wisely, police officers need to develop their critical-thinking skills. Critical thinking includes a broad range of skills, such as problem solving, identifying perceptions, generating concepts from observations, applying concepts to police problems, designing systematic plans of action and approaching social problems from several different perspectives. As a result of learning to think critically, students and future police officers will:

- Learn to use their diverse backgrounds and those of others to resolve social problems in a more effective, acceptable manner.
- Learn specific ways to move from lower-order to higher-order thinking skills.
- Be better prepared to enter the world of police work and further their existing or future careers.

**SUMMARY**

Police operations are activities conducted in the field by law enforcement officers as they "serve and protect." Operations include patrol, traffic, investigation and general calls for service. Those engaged in police operations must take into consideration the important changes affecting them, including changes in the public and society served, the new law enforcement officers, the structure of the police bureaucracy and the involvement of the community.

Our society is becoming older and has more minorities, more immigrants and more single-parent households, while the gap between rich and poor continues to expand. Our law enforcement officers also have changed. Today's police recruits include fewer people with military backgrounds and more women and minorities. New recruits have more education and value job satisfaction more than material rewards. They also are expected to perform more diverse operations.

Another change is anticipated in the police bureaucracy itself. The police bureaucracy may become less militaristic and may move toward a team approach to providing services. This includes decentralization and a shift from management to leadership. Yet another change is the trend toward community policing. Community policing is proactive, empowering citizens to help local law enforcement provide safer neighborhoods. It usually includes an emphasis on foot and bicycle patrol.

Not only should those in law enforcement understand the context in which police operations are performed and the changes that have occurred; they also should understand the foundation for these operations. Most law enforcement agencies are guided by missions. An agency's mission is its reason for existence, its purpose. It often is embodied in a mission statement. This mission is accomplished most effectively by clearly stated goals and objectives. Goals are broad, general intentions. Objectives are specific activities to accomplish goals. The ways these objectives are to be carried out are frequently described in policies and procedures.

Officers need to follow policies, procedures and regulations, but they also need to use discretion. Discretion allows for equitable enforcement of our laws and for police officers to grow morally and professionally. Discretion is not without its problems, including a lack of accountability, unpredictability and the potential for inconsistency and allegations of racial profiling. A major challenge facing law enforcement is finding the balance between a department's clear-cut goals, policies and procedures and its officers' discretionary actions.

## APPLICATION

### GENERAL DIRECTIONS

When you complete each chapter, you will be asked to apply the information to develop suggested policies and procedures appropriate for your area. The Appendix on page 491 contains a form to use for this purpose. As with any other type of administrative writing, policies and procedures should be clearly written. Consider the following guidelines:

- Use short, simple words, avoiding police jargon.
- Use short, simple sentences: 10–15 words.
- Use short paragraphs: 2–3 sentences.
- Use lists when possible.
- Use active verbs, e.g., write *Clean the gun daily* rather than *The gun should be cleaned daily.*

- Use illustrations and diagrams for clarification.
- Have three or four individuals read and evaluate the policy and procedure.

Most important, keep things simple. Avoid the tendency to impress rather than to express, as illustrated by the young boy who, when asked to go to the whiteboard and write the answer to 2 + 2 =, wrote 4.0000.

### INSTRUCTIONS

Write a policy for writing policies, that is, outlining what policies should be written for. Then write at least five procedures to be used when writing policies.

## AN EXERCISE IN CRITICAL THINKING

At the end of each chapter you will be presented with exercises in critical thinking. These exercises were written by Waldo Asp, Normandale Community College, and are based on actual decisions of state appeals courts or state supreme courts throughout the country. Read each situation carefully. Then consider the alternative responses given and select the *most logical* statement based on what you have read in the chapter.

> On September 4, State Trooper Berg was on routine patrol when he stopped a car driven by Carl Lundberg for a traffic violation. Trooper Berg arrested Lundberg for breach of the peace and placed him in his squad car's back seat. Carl's brother, Allen Lundberg, went to the scene of the arrest and, without identifying himself, got into his brother's car with the apparent intention of driving it away.
>
> Trooper Berg got out of his vehicle, approached the as-yet-unidentified individual, and asked him to get out of the car and leave. Only after A. Lundberg got out of the car did he identify himself as the suspect's brother. Trooper Berg again asked A. Lundberg to leave the scene, but A. Lundberg persisted in questioning Trooper Berg as to why he could not take the car to avoid having it towed. Trooper Berg continued to insist that A. Lundberg leave the scene.
>
> The verbal sparring continued to escalate to such a point that it drew the attention of several individuals in the parking lot of a shopping mall across the street. Various witnesses testified that A. Lundberg yelled obscenities at Trooper Berg, "leaned over and pointed to his buttocks," and gave Trooper Berg "the finger." Witnesses also testified that Trooper Berg physically turned A. Lundberg around and "gave him a shove toward the parking lot," at which point A. Lundberg "kind of turned around and came close to hitting Trooper Berg's arm." That is when Trooper Berg told him he was under arrest.

1. While Trooper Berg was dealing with Allen Lundberg, Carl Lundberg (who was in the back of the squad car) managed to cause $500 damage to the squad's interior by kicking the door.
   a. This demonstrates that sometimes sticking to policies and procedures is not worth the trouble that is caused, for the general public will not accept impersonal execution of procedures.
   b. Officers need to understand the reasoning behind operations and be able to explain them to citizens, thereby possibly avoiding violent actions and breaches of the peace.
   c. In this case there was insufficient evidence to support a criminal conviction for obstructing legal process.
   d. Mere words (regardless of tone, loudness, agitation and word choice) cannot be used as a basis for a disturbing the peace charge.
   e. Only Carl Lundberg's actions should be prosecuted. Allen Lundberg should be released.

2. Officer involvement with the community would have helped Trooper Berg in what way?
   a. Witnesses might corroborate the yelled obscenities and other actions by A. Lundberg, as well as Trooper Berg's responses.
   b. Some community members could talk the Lundbergs into cooling off and also could assist Trooper Berg in physically escorting Allen away from the scene to prevent the escalation of anger.
   c. Many would enjoy the power and authority of becoming "assistant officers" with the rights of enforcing the law, as well as the status of being considered "officers and gentlemen."
   d. Fair, compassionate and excellent police service is possible only when responsibilities are not piled on one individual.
   e. With expanded opportunities for misconduct, more eyes are needed to keep watch for undesirable activity.

## DISCUSSION QUESTIONS

1. What purposes do goals serve in a police department?
2. What do you consider to be the most important goal for a police department?
3. What are the advantages of having written policies?
4. Do you feel that value statements are necessary? How can officers best be involved in developing a department's values?
5. Who should be involved in policy development?
6. Do you view discretion as more of an advantage or a disadvantage for police officers?
7. Have you observed police discretion in operation?

## INFOTRAC COLLEGE EDITION ASSIGNMENTS

- Use InfoTrac College Edition to answer the Discussion Questions as appropriate.
- Use InfoTrac College Edition to research articles and materials on *participatory leadership and management*. Be prepared to discuss the advantages and disadvantages of participatory leadership and/or management with the class.
- Read and outline "Community Policing: Exploring the Philosophy" by David M. Allender.

## INTERNET ASSIGNMENT

The U.S. Department of Justice's Bureau of Justice Statistics (BJS) website offers data, graphics and links to key facts. Before you use the website, take a tour by visiting http://www.ojp.usdoj.gov/bjs/tour/intro.htm. This will acquaint you with what is available. Once you know what is available, go to www.albany.edu/sourcebook/ and find materials that deal with policy options for juvenile offenders. Outline the positive and negative points of a controversial system continually in the forefront of discussion. Be prepared to share your outline with the class.

 **BOOK-SPECIFIC WEBSITE**

The book-specific website at http://cj.wadsworth.com/
wobleski_Hess_police_op4e hosts a variety of resources
for students and instructors. Many can be emailed to the
instructor. Included are extended activities such as Concept Builders - the 3 step learning module that reinforces
key chapter concepts, followed by a real-world applications and critical thinking questions. InfoTrac College
Edition exercises; Discussion Questions; interactive key-term FlashCards; and a collection of chapter-based Web
Links provide additional information and activities to
include in the curriculum.

### REFERENCES

Allender, David M. "Community Policing: Exploring the
Philosophy." *FBI Law Enforcement Bulletin*, March
2004, pp.18–22.

Alsabrook, Carl L.; Aryani, Giant Abutalebi; and Garrett,
Terry D. "Five Principles of Leadership." *Law and
Order*, May 2001, pp.112–115.

Aragon, Randall. "Excellence in Community Policing."
*Law and Order*, April 2004, pp.66–68.

Armstrong, David and Polk, O. Elmer. "College for Cops:
The Fast Track to Success." *The Law Enforcement
Trainer*, September/October 2002, pp.24–26.

Berkow, Michael. "Congratulations on Becoming Chief!
Now What Do You Do?" *The Police Chief*, June 2001,
pp.48–52.

"Bottoms-Up! COP Seen Giving More Officers Specific Beat
Responsibility." *Law Enforcement News*, February 28,
2001, p.5.

Brown, Jim. "Community Policing Reality Check." *Law
and Order*, April 2001, pp.55–58.

Covey, Stephen R. "Enhancing Public Trust: It's an Issue
of Character and Leadership." *The Police Chief*, April
2003, pp.128–133.

Fields, Jason and Casper, Lynne M. *America's Families and
Living Arrangements: Population Characteristics 2000.*
U.S. Census Bureau, Current Population Reports
(CPR), June 2001. (P20–537)

Fridell, Lorie. "New PERF Report Addresses 'Racial Profiling.'" *Subject to Debate*, June 2001, pp.1, 10.

Fulton, Roger. "Policy and Procedure Update." *Law
Enforcement Technology*, March 2001, p.118.

"If It's Broken, Fix It." *Law Enforcement News*, March 15,
2001, p.8.

Jones, Robin. "Recruiting Women." *The Police Chief*, April
2004, pp.165–166.

Kokkelenberg, Lawrence D. "Real Leadership Is More
than Just a Walk in the Park." *Law Enforcement News*,
February 14, 2001, p.9.

Lonsway, Kimberly and Campbell, Deborah. "Retaining
Women Officers." *Law and Order*, May 2002,
pp.101–111.

Martin, Jeff. "Revising Department Policy and Procedure
Manuals." *Law and Order*, July 2002, pp.114–116.

Messer, Matt. "Generation X: Ready to Rock and Roll?"
*Police*, January 2001, pp.14–20.

Miller, Linda S. and Hess, Kären M. *Community Policing:
Partnerships for Problem Solving*, 4th ed. Belmont, CA:
Wadsworth Publishing Company, 2005.

Moore, Carole. "Female Officers Benefit Departments."
*Law Enforcement Technology*, April 2004, p.114.

Polk, O. Elmer and Armstrong, David A. "Higher Education and Law Enforcement Career Paths: Is the Road
to Success Paved by Degree?" *Journal of Criminal Justice Education*, Spring 2001, pp.77–99.

Rahtz, Howard. *Community-Oriented Policing: A Handbook
for Beat Cops and Supervisors*. Monsey, NY: Criminal
Justice Press, 2001.

*Recruiting & Retaining Women: A Self-Assessment Guide for
Law Enforcement*. Los Angeles, CA: National Center for
Women & Policing, no date. http://www.womencops
@feminist.org.

Sampson, Robert J. and Raudenbush, Stephen W. *Disorder
in Urban Neighborhoods—Does It Lead to Crime?*
National Institute of Justice Research in Brief, February 2001. (NCJ 186049)

Sharp, Arthur. "Keep Policies and Procedures Updated."
*Law and Order*, June 2004, pp.72–75.

Stainbrook, Mark G. "Make Yourself a Leader." *Police*,
March 2004, p.8.

Streit, Corinne. "Recruiting Minority Officers." *Law
Enforcement Technology*, February 2001, pp.70–75.

Upper Midwest Community Policing Institute, brochure,
no date.

Vernon, Robert. "The Character of Leadership." *Law and
Order*, January 2004, pp.60–63.

Wilson, James Q. and Kelling, George. "The Police and
Neighborhood Safety: Broken Windows." *Atlantic
Monthly*, March 1982, pp.29–38.

Wuestewald, Todd and Wilds, Michael R. "Developing
Police Leaders: The University—Law Enforcement Partnership." *The Police Chief*, October 2002, pp.134–139.

# CHAPTER 2

# Communication: The Foundation of Police Operations

## Do You Know . . .

- What positive outcomes effective communication can produce?
- In what directions communication might flow?
- What special communication problems law enforcement officers may encounter?
- What special populations may pose especially challenging communication issues?
- When slurred speech may not be the result of intoxication?
- When police officers can stop a person to ask questions?
- What rights *Miranda v. Arizona* grants to suspects?
- What would make a confession inadmissible in court?
- What the four-domain model for detecting deception focuses on?
- What purposes written police reports serve?
- Who the likely audiences of police reports are?
- What the characteristics of effective police reports are?
- What two amendments police must balance when dealing with the media?

## Can You Define?

| | | | |
|---|---|---|---|
| absolute privilege | felony syndrome | interview | reader-friendly writing |
| admission | field inquiry | leading question | secondary victim |
| closed-ended question | grapevine | *Miranda* warning | statement |
| cognitive interview | informant | open-ended question | synchrony |
| conditional privilege | interoperability | primary victim | totality of |
| confession | interrogation | privileged information | circumstances |

## Introduction

Communication at any level is an inexact art. But misunderstood communication can have grave consequences in police work. Communication skills are critical to every aspect of effective police operations.

Communication is all around us. We are continually bombarded by spoken and written messages, yet most people give little thought to its importance, nor are they trained in communicating effectively.

 Effective communication can produce several positive outcomes and can be used to inform, persuade, diffuse, guide, motivate, reassure and negotiate.

In contrast, ineffective communication can result in confusion, false expectations, wrong conclusions, negative stereotypes, frustration, anger, hostility, aggression and even physical confrontations.

Police officers routinely communicate in every facet of their jobs, not only when they interview and interrogate individuals, but also during their interactions with the public, with coworkers in their departments and with professionals in other fields. Officers also may testify in court and fulfill public speaking assignments, especially those for school-age children and youths.

This chapter begins with a discussion of the lines of internal communication—horizontal and vertical as well as technological advances in communication and problems associated with using radios and cell phones to communicate. This is followed by a look at special populations that may pose especially challenging communication problems. A brief discussion of using language as a tool or a weapon follows.

The chapter then turns to communicating to obtain information: the field inquiry and the interview including interviewing and interrogating techniques. This is followed by a discussion of the role of informants and anonymous tips and the interrogation, including the use of the *Miranda* warning.

Next, report writing is discussed, including the importance of field notes as the basis of operational reports and how such notes might be supplemented by videotaping. This is followed by a discussion of written reports, including their purposes, audiences, ways to make them reader friendly and the content and characteristics of effective reports. Next is a brief look at computer-assisted report entry and records. The chapter concludes with a discussion on communicating with the media.

## Lines of Communication within an Agency

Communication within an agency may flow in different directions. It may flow vertically downward from the chief or upward from line officers. It may also flow outward or horizontally among those on the same "level" within the organization.

 Internal communication may be vertical (downward or upward) or horizontal (lateral).

In addition to the more formal lines of internal communication, informal channels also exist, called the **grapevine** or the "rumor mill." This powerful line of communication can help or hurt an agency. According to Moore (2004a, p.110), experts suggest that the grapevine can be used to disseminate information quickly, and it can be used to act as a barometer of what the workforce is thinking. Moore cautions: "Gossip is like crabgrass—even a small amount allowed to grow unchecked can overtake an otherwise well-cared-for lawn."

Communication between officers in the field, officers and headquarters, and officers and local, state and national data sources as well as information sharing among agencies has been enhanced greatly through advancing technology.

## Technological Advances in Communication

"The progression of law enforcement communications started with whistles and rattles and has advanced to hand-held radios and mobile data terminals

Ray Malace

*A Saginaw Township, Michigan, police officer uses his cell phone and a map to check a location. Using the cell phone avoids interrupting dispatch calls.*

mounted in patrol cars" (Dees, 2001, p.152). Cell phones are a common means of wireless communication. Rogers (2001a, p.88) reports: "Wireless emergency calls account for 20 to 25 percent of all calls to 911." Data from the Cellular Telecommunications and Internet Association (CTIA) reveal more than 51 million wireless emergency service calls were placed in 2000, equating to nearly 140,000 a day, or 96 calls per minute ("Wireless Calls Near . . .," 2001, p.9). Yet: "Statistics show almost none of the 911 calls generated daily from wireless phones provide location information to the 911 center that receives the call" (Rogers, 2001b, p.46). A technology being developed to augment the current capability of cell phones is Enhanced 911, or E911, which employs a geolocation feature to enable law enforcement to quickly trace where a wireless call is coming from.

Cell phones are able to relay more than just voices. Some also can send pictures. Many wireless devices can now display and send images of a crime scene or a suspect to hundreds of officers, using only a phone and a digital camera.

The trend toward community policing is bringing more officers out of the squad car to patrol on foot, bikes, motorcycles and horses. While this move puts officers closer to the citizens in the community, it also pulls them away from their vital link to real-time data—the vehicle-mounted laptop. Again, technology is available to assist such officers with their mobile police operations:

> PocketBlue is a handheld software application that is part of a fully integrated mobile data system for law enforcement, providing secure messaging and alarm capabilities connected to all mobile users . . . [thus giving] mobile officers the capabilities that in-vehicle users have. . . .
>
> Personnel on foot, bike or horseback can simply tap a button on the Palm to run NCIC [National Crime Information Center] queries or send secure messages.

When an officer receives a "hit" on a query, every mobile client . . . will be notified (Streit, 2001b, p.141).

Garand (2004, p.65) points out: "PocketBlue allows law enforcement professionals to check the status of vehicles, persons, boats, articles and guns without burdening a dispatcher, so they can stay focused on priority calls."

The potential applications to policing of these highly mobile, palm-sized devices are many, and officers nationwide expect to be using such personal digital assistants (PDAs) more frequently:

[One assistant police chief] visualizes PDAs working for SWAT teams, where digitized floor plans of a university campus could be uploaded in a command post; for school resource officers to query gang databases; for marine patrol perhaps with GPS; for investigators at a crime scene, etc. "It's not a complete replacement for full field reporting on a laptop," he says. "But you can't put a laptop on a bicycle" (Rogers, 2001c, pp.112–114).

Douglas (2003, p.44) notes: "Law enforcement software is now available for PDAs that can give you license plate information in 15 seconds while you are standing on the side of the road in the rain." Dees (2003, p.37) contends: "The versatility of the new cellular handsets may make traditional mobile computers an anachronism. These new phones and networks already offer capabilities that can serve most of the major functions of a mobile computer, and also replace additional equipment, such as the portable radio. . . . An officer running a driver's license query from the field might be able to see not only the status of the operator's license, but also the photo and signature associated with that license record—and all from a handheld device that doubles as his portable radio." Dees (p.38) notes: "Many of the new generation phones are also equipped with GPS receivers that report their location to the network."

As law enforcement officers become increasingly reliant on access to information while in the field, emerging technology will ensure they are automatically receiving the most current data.

Our society has become increasingly mobile, fueling an increase in technology to access information beyond that held at the local police station or in county records. Stanek (2004, p.167) points out: "Corporations across the globe can efficiently communicate with employees and subsidiaries in distant locations. But, in many cases, law enforcement agencies cannot electronically share information with a department in a neighboring city. With more than 18,000 individual criminal justice jurisdictions in the United States, the information sharing problems hindering law enforcement agencies are significant. In Minnesota we took a giant stride toward addressing these problems with the creation of CriMNet."

Streit (2001a, p.118) describes the benefits of CriMNet, an integrated system being developed in Minnesota that will allow law enforcement officials to track and share information throughout the state: "In the past, the only way to gain information on a suspect from another county was by physically calling that county and inquiring whether there is a record and then requesting the files be sent. This was not time efficient. With CriMNet, officials can get information in seconds, as well as photos and fingerprints for the suspect." Another benefit of this system is that, once fully implemented, it will create a completely integrated justice system, allowing courts, law enforcement and corrections to access each others' records (Streit, p.119):

In the past there was no threat to commit serious crime such as armed robbery, breaking and entering, battery, etc. Outside the county where the crime was committed, there would be no record of that offense. Officers would not know anything about previous offenses. A judge could impose or suspend a sentence because those other crimes would be kept in the dark. That person could be hired in a school without anyone knowing their complete criminal history.

Using CriMNet, police, prosecutors and courts will know a person's criminal history within seconds of his stepping into the courtroom or at the scene of a crime.

Police in Chaska, Minnesota, used CriMNet to find and arrest a career criminal who had burglarized a local business. Although he initially eluded capture, Chaska police used CriMNet's statewide probation information to track down the suspect's probation officer, who was able to help them locate him. While the police held the suspect on the Chaska crime, they found evidence in his home that connected him to more than 50 metro burglaries dating back to 2002 ("CriMNet Helps Police Nab Criminals," 2004, p.1).

Other areas are also recognizing the benefits of information-sharing networks. For example, the Regional Crime Information System (RCIS) implemented in Wisconsin tracks data not available on the state or federal government system: "The system covers five major areas: booking, juvenile crime, domestic violence, drugs and gangs, and general criminal activities, such as burglaries and stolen vehicles. RCIS is more flexible than state or federal systems and focuses on northwestern Wisconsin and the types of information participating sheriffs want to share" (Kanable, 2001, p.145). According to one sheriff: "The greatest benefit of the [RCIS] system is the master name search, being able to quickly find out who else has dealt with Jane Jones, in what jurisdiction and when" (p.147).

The FBI's National Crime Information Center (NCIC) 2000 system is an online real-time transaction processing database that maintains information on millions of records. Connecting to this system, patrol officers can run local, state and federal database checks ranging from driver's license and vehicle registration, to arrest reports, stolen/recovered property and even emergency phone numbers of business owners. The system handles over 2.5 million transactions every day and offers fingerprint matching capability, digital image data storage and a mobile imaging unit to electronically capture fingerprint and camera images and incorporate them into an NCIC database query (Harris website).

## Problems in Using Radios and Cell Phones to Communicate

    Special problems in communicating via radios and cell phones include keeping police communications secure, interference on the line and lack of interoperability.

### Communication Security

Many citizens have police scanners that allow them access to dispatcher-to-officer and officer-to-officer communications. Some criminals also use scanners, so security precautions must be taken.

Listening in on cell phone transmissions is prohibited under the Electronic Communications Privacy Act of 1986, but enforcing the law is next to impossible. And criminals seldom care about breaking this law. Therefore, conversations are not safe on mobile phones. As with cell phone conversations, wireless data transmissions are susceptible to interception.

While digital technology adds a level of security greater than the analog transmissions made over police radio frequencies, it is not totally secure. Consequently, data encryption, which "scrambles" transmitted data, is considered the best way to keep outsiders from accessing inside information. As more and more agencies go online, using the Internet to access and share data, keeping information secure in this medium has also become a challenge.

## Interference on the Line

As more people use wireless channels to communicate, the interference encountered has also increased. "The once-dependable police radio is literally being drowned out by a torrent of information-age services, such as wireless phones and instant messaging, that have made mobile communications available to millions of Americans" (Davidson, 2001, p.7):

> In Tigard, Oregon, recently, police twice were unable to radio for backup while facing armed suspects because of cell phone interference. . . .
>
> In Anne Arundel County, MD, police officers are plagued by eight "dead spots" where [commercial cellular phone services] have no towers. The problem came to a head when an officer stopped a speeding car and could not reach dispatch. As he wrote out a ticket, another officer stopped to warn him that the driver was a shooting suspect (p.40).

"Increasingly, our officers are being confronted with radio interference that either garbles or blocks their communications. To date, there have been nearly 1,000 reported cases of radio interference in 34 states on public safety radios operating in the 800-megahertz band. This interference occurs because radio channels assigned to public safety are intermingled among and adjacent to commercial channels such as cell phones."

Another problem occurs when the technology that is supposed to enhance communication experiences a glitch or "goes down." In the 1960s and 1970s, communication systems were relatively uncomplicated—emergency-service radios had a microphone and a speaker and users simply talked over them. Now, "the systems are full of controllers and microprocessors and software. There's a lot more to go wrong" (Davidson, p.43). The impact of this problem on police operations, according to Davidson (p.7), is unsettling: "The ongoing glitches have caused an untold number of close calls, at least a few injuries and may have contributed to the death of a police officer."

In July 2004, the Federal Communication Commission (FCC) unanimously approved the Consensus Plan (www.projectconsensus.org). Voegtlin (2004, p.8) explains: "Simply put, the Consensus Plan seeks to eliminate 800-megahertz interference by realigning the current jumbled licensing of 800-megahertz systems into two distinct blocks: one block for public safety and private wireless systems and one block for wireless carriers such as cellular service providers."

## Lack of Interoperability

Siegle and Murphy (2001, p.10) state: "Public safety wireless **interoperability** refers to the ability of public safety officials to communicate with each other seamlessly in real time over their wireless communications network."

Rogers (2002a, p.50) notes: "September 11th clearly brought into focus the need for multiple jurisdictions to be able to communicate." Garrett (2003, p.6) suggests: "In homeland security efforts, access to information is critical—the lives of officers, the public and even the country's welfare might be at stake. The Homeland Security bill has put provisions into place describing the types of information that should be shared and the methods that will be taken to protect that sensitive data, but little has been done to address the biggest hurdle of all: the technology that will be used to share it."

Garrett (2004, p.8) stresses: "We can't wait for another 9/11 to further the push for interoperable communications." Garrett contends that interoperability efforts have improved on a local scale, but much remains to be done on a broader scale. A study to which 192 mayors responded found that 49 to 60 percent of cities lack interoperable communications with various state agencies, including police, emergency management and emergency operations. Eighty-six percent lack such capabilities with state transportation departments. And percentages ranked in the high 90s for lack of communications interoperability among various critical infrastructures such as chemical plants, seaports and rail facilities.

McEwen (2004, p.146) points out: "As the law enforcement community is well aware, officers cannot perform their mission-critical duties when they lack interoperability. Police frequently are unable to share critical voice or data information by radio with each other, with surrounding jurisdictions, or with other public safety agencies. Whether in day-to-day operations or emergency response to large-scale incidents such as acts of terrorism and natural disasters, reliable mission-critical operable and interoperable communications are essential to protect the lives of officers and the public they serve." In short, as Ake (2003, p.20) observes: "Interoperability can improve public safety by making it easier for first responders to do their jobs."

Boyd, director of the Department of Homeland Security's SAFECOM program, notes the urgency of the situation: "In a war against terror . . . we cannot afford to put off, for two or five or 10 more years, taking the steps necessary to begin to achieve interoperability because we're talking about lives" (Kanable, 2004, p.12). Boyd states: "We're working with 50,000 public safety agencies. This is not going to happen overnight, but we think we can make it happen much more quickly than has happened in the Department of Defense" (Kanable, p.16). Says Boyd: "We believe that interoperability has to start at the local level and work up. More than 90 percent of the public safety wireless infrastructure in the United States is owned, operated and maintained by the state and local agencies" (Kanable, p.14).

Interoperability is a priority for law enforcement and is critical in large scale emergencies. However, much of the time law enforcement officers spend communicating is with individuals one-on-one, not only in trying to determine what problems exist in a community, but in investigating and solving crimes. Before looking at specific ways in which officers communicate with citizens and suspects, consider some of the problems officers might have in communicating with and understanding certain individuals.

# Problems in Communicating One-on-One

 Officers might have difficulty understanding the elderly, individuals who speak little or no English or who have different cultural backgrounds and those with disabilities or diseases that may impair their ability to communicate.

## *Communicating with the Elderly*

Jordan (2002, p.23) observes: "The criminal justice system and, in particular, law enforcement face the aging population as a special challenge for the 21st century." Hart (2001, p.1) reports: "The U.S. Bureau of the Census predicts that by 2030, the population over age 65 will nearly triple to more than 70 million people, and older people will make up more than 20 percent of the population (up from 12.3 percent in 1990)." According to population trends, older people (age 65 and up) will soon outnumber children for the first time in our country's history. Duncan (2001, p.75) notes:

> The unparalleled increase in the number of elderly persons living in the United States is having a major impact not only on the nation's health care and social service delivery systems but also on law enforcement. . . .
>
> More and more law enforcement officers are coming in contact with senior citizens on a regular basis. Criminals have learned that targeting the elderly and involving them in fraudulent schemes and scams is very lucrative.

Problems in communicating with the elderly can arise from the age differences between, and corresponding generational concerns of, senior citizens and law enforcement officers. However, perhaps the greatest challenge will be for officers to recognize when they are interacting with an elderly person who has Alzheimer's Disease. "With an estimated four million adults nationwide suffering from Alzheimer's Disease, and predictions of a virtual epidemic of the illness by mid-century, law enforcement agencies across the country have had to act quickly to learn the signs and symptoms of a condition that can turn ordinarily law-abiding senior citizens into menaces on the road and in their own homes" ("Cops Try Harder . . .," 2003, p.1).

Rickher (2003, p.9) explains: "Every day law enforcement officers respond to calls involving people with Alzheimer's Disease who are either lost, shoplifting or driving erratically. They may not remember where they live, or even their name." Rickher (p.12) notes: "People who have Alzheimer's Disease gradually lose their ability to communicate. As the disease progresses, they will be less able to express themselves or understand [officers]."

 An individual with Alzheimer's Disease may have slurred, incoherent speech resembling intoxication.

If Alzheimer's Disease is suspected, officers should look for an ID bracelet or other identification. Officers should identify themselves and explain what they will be doing, even if obvious. Officers should also maintain eye contact when speaking and try to keep a calm atmosphere. Physical restraints should be avoided if possible because they are almost certain to cause the person to lash out, verbally and physically. Rickher (p.9) suggests: "Create a soothing environment; reduce distractions; keep communication simple; and avoid restraints."

## Communicating with Non-English-Speaking Immigrants

The estimated number of illegal immigrants is growing at a rate of 100,000 to 300,000 a year. Often these non-English-speaking immigrants cluster together in relatively poor neighborhoods where crime rates are high.

In addition, many new immigrants come from countries where the police are feared rather than respected. The police in those countries keep secret files and have broad arrest powers. They may brutalize citizens, force confessions from them or simply imprison them without any "due process." In fact, due process may be a concept unknown to these new immigrants. Further, many new immigrants will become victims, especially of violent crimes. Again, their fear of the police will work against them as they are unlikely to report the crimes or to assist the police in investigating them.

One obvious way to enhance communication with non-English-speaking people is to recruit bilingual officers. Crank and Loughrin-Sacco (2001, p.194) note: "Criminal justice students reasonably recognize that language skills will enhance their employability. Language skills will help them deal with victims, witnesses and suspects in a legal environment. . . . A police officer, for example, may need a minimum of a basic set of commands for ensuring legal compliance and officer safety, and substantially more for obtaining witness testimony."

Traditional language classes are not necessarily effective because they include writing and "polite" conversation, not what police officers need. They need to master a small number of phrases with specific applications to street situations to maintain control until someone fluent in the target language arrives. Aware of the shortcomings of traditional avenues for language acquisition, some schools are implementing a program called Foreign Languages Across the Curriculum or FLAC (Crank and Loughrin-Sacco, pp.194, 207):

> [FLAC] is a national grants program designed to enhance the development of practical language skills across the professional programs in university settings. FLAC aims at the provision of professional terminology for students who already have a conversational knowledge of a foreign language and who want to extend their ability to apply those skills in a particular professional setting. . . .
>
> A series of FLAC courses will provide a student with a core terminology to participate in [their professional] environment, a set of materials that can be used to elaborate on the vocabulary, and a sensibility of the settings in which [a foreign language] facilitates justice system purposes (from field trips). It provides students with an awareness of the nature of the work on a day-to-day basis, and places the student into contact with materials that can provide specialized language skills.

One way to overcome language barriers is to compile a list of bilingual citizens in the community. This is easiest in large cities and those that have colleges and universities. Legal problems may arise, however, if confidential information is involved. Another approach to the language barrier is to subscribe to the *language line,* a translation service offered by AT&T that provides direct interpretation for police and other emergency service units responding to calls in over 140 languages. Technology is also available to help officers communicate with diverse populations, such as Point Talk Translators. Electronic voice translators that convey basic instructions in the subject's own language are also available.

## Communicating with Those from a Different Culture

Even when language is not a barrier, communication problems may result from customs and cultural differences in gestures, body language, body space expectations and the like. For example, the Asian custom of coin rubbing to cure children of diseases leaves marks on the skin that may be misinterpreted by teachers or police officers as signs of child abuse.

Another example: Unlike most Americans who know they should remain seated in their car if stopped by police, a Nigerian will usually get out of his car to show respect and may ignore a request to step back because it makes no sense to him. Furthermore, in Nigeria the distance for conversation is much closer, sometimes even less than 15 inches, and direct eye contact signifies deception, rudeness or defiance. These cultural differences could easily cause communication problems and conflict between an officer and an immigrant citizen.

## Communicating with Individuals with Disabilities or Conditions Affecting Speech

When people think of "cultural diversity," they typically think of racial, ethnic or even religious groups existing within mainstream America. Yet, in fact, the largest minority group in the United States, an estimated 49 million, consists of individuals with disabilities.

To ensure that people with disabilities are treated fairly, the Americans with Disabilities Act (ADA) was created. Yet, according to Colbridge (2001, p.23): "The Americans with Disabilities Act (ADA) is a difficult statute to understand and implement in the workplace. The statutory definition of a disability is confusing and subject to infinite variations. Determining who is disabled and, therefore, protected by the act, is difficult at best." Some disabilities are very obvious: paralysis and blindness, for example. Other disabilities, however, are not immediately apparent. Likewise, many conditions or diseases that impair speech are not immediately apparent and may be mistaken for intoxication or being under the influence of drugs. Nonetheless, officers must adhere to and abide by ADA requirements that prohibit discrimination against qualified individuals with disabilities in the delivery of government services, programs or activities.

Blindness and deafness are two of the most common disabilities officers may encounter. The *visually impaired* comprise over 11.5 million individuals, according to the National Society to Prevent Blindness. When interacting with people who are blind, police officers should not only identify themselves, but offer to let the people feel their badges as well. The *hearing impaired* are among those with "invisible" handicaps. Police officers will interact more effectively with citizens who are hearing impaired if they understand that most deaf people are not good lipreaders. In addition, the speech of individuals who have been deaf since birth may sound garbled and even unintelligible.

 The speech of a person who has been deaf since birth may be mistaken for that of one who is intoxicated or using drugs.

How deaf people communicate depends on several factors, including the type of deafness, the age at which the person became deaf, the individual's personality

*This officer's knowledge of sign language helps him communicate more clearly with a hearing-impaired person.*

and intelligence, speech and speech-reading abilities, general language skills and educational background. To communicate with an individual who is hearing impaired, officers should get the person's attention by gently tapping a shoulder or waving and speak slowly and clearly using short sentences. It is helpful to learn sign language. The services of a certified interpreter should be used whenever possible. In fact, several court cases have addressed when such services are required by law.

*People with epilepsy* also may present communication problems. Epilepsy is a disorder of the central nervous system in which a person tends to have recurrent seizures. It may alter behavior, movement, perception and sensation. Some seizures impair consciousness and may last from a few seconds to several minutes.

> An epileptic seizure can look like intoxication or the influence of street drugs, as all may involve impaired consciousness, incoherent speech, glassy-eyed staring and aimless wandering.

The person may be confused or need to rest after a seizure. A person having a seizure will generally regain their faculties within several minutes, whereas a drunk or high person will not.

## Communicating with Individuals Who Are Mentally Ill

Historically, mentally ill individuals were locked away from society in insane asylums. Long-term institutionalization or hospitalization was the norm. Likewise, mentally retarded individuals were placed into special schools, usually hidden away from society. In the mid-1960s, however, this changed, and a massive deinstitutionalization movement occurred, placing mentally disabled individuals into the community, but without the support they formerly had. The continuing trend of deinstitutionalization has had a direct impact on police, requiring them to acquire a new set of communication skills.

Deinstitutionalized mentally ill people may find it difficult to get to a clinic to receive follow-up service or ongoing outpatient care. They may even forget appointments or go off their treatment plan. As a result, they often stop refilling or taking needed medication, which eventually leads to behavior that brings them into contact with the law. Zdanowicz (2001, p.3) notes: "In recent years there has been a marked shift in responsibility for the untreated mentally ill from the mental health system to the criminal justice system. It is becoming increasingly clear that any hope of alleviating the burden of untreated mental illness rests with those who are impacted the most, our nation's law enforcement officials."

Engel and Silver (2001, p.226) contend changes in policing policies, such as implementation of community-oriented and problem-oriented policing, have increased officer contact with the community's mentally ill population: "A recent survey of a large metropolitan police department found that 89 percent of officers had contact with mentally disordered citizens in the previous year." According to Santoro (2001, p.23):

Sixteen percent of the total jail and prison populations are individuals suffering from mental illness, which is approximately seven times the number of people receiving care in state hospitals. . . .

For the seriously mentally ill who lack insight into their illness, the world can be a very confusing, cold and lonely place. Police officers are too often their only bridge to receiving emergency care or temporary shelter.

Scoville (2004, p.6) notes: "Confrontations with emotionally disturbed subjects put officers' lives at risk. . . . Unable to dispense psychotropic drugs or practice psychiatry, cops are sometimes confined to using force to prevent greater acts of violence. . . . Another problem is that in trying to defend himself or his partner, an officer may end up taking the very life he's trying to save."

To avoid or temper such situations, many departments have formed crisis intervention teams (CITs). Hill et al. (2004, p.18) explain: "Primarily, the purpose of a crisis intervention team (CIT) is to provide law enforcement officers with the skills they need to safely de-escalate situations involving people with mental illness who are in crisis, *not* to turn officers into mental health workers." Reuland and Margolis (2003, p.36) add: "This [CIT] approach employs specially trained uniformed officers to act as primary or secondary responders to every call in which mental illness is a factor." They also describe the mobile crisis team (MCT) approach: "Generally MCTs are composed of civilian personnel who are licensed mental health professionals. To ensure an effective, safe response, MCTs act only as secondary responders who are called out once law enforcement has secured the scene."

While many proclaim the inappropriateness of using the criminal justice system to handle situations involving mentally disordered individuals, few have focused attention on the appropriateness of using informal dispositions, including no police action, mediation, separation, lecturing and transports to homes or homeless shelters (Engel and Silver, p.246):

Reasons cited by officers for handling situations informally range from humanitarian (e.g., "the officer thought he did the right thing by taking the citizen to a place where he could take a shower and have a hot meal for free") to self-serving (e.g., "the officer did not want to transport the citizen because he was sweating profusely and he didn't want him in his take-home patrol car").

**Police-Based Diversion Programs**    Reuland (2004, p.3) reports: "Law enforcement agencies across the country have begun to change their practices and develop innovative partnerships with the mental health community to improve their responses to people with mental illness." She (p.12) suggests: "Access to additional services is also required to provide police officers with non-criminal justice system options for people who are in crisis but who do not meet the criteria for emergency evaluation." According to Reuland (p.14): "In most cases, if the call taker and dispatcher are sure the call involves a person with mental illness, they will dispatch directly to the CIT or police/mental health team." She (p.17) explains: "One reason for agencies to choose a CIT model or other police-based response over a mental health-based response, such as a mobile crisis team, is the importance of the police role in controlling potentially violent situations."

**Making Referrals**    Officers should know how to determine when someone needs referral to mental health professionals or a mental health court, how to access those resources and the procedures for formal commitment of individuals who pose a threat to themselves or others. However, a study by Cooper et al. (2004, p.295) highlighted police officers' frustration in handling mentally ill offenders and the lack of coordination in effort between police and mental health professionals.

## Communicating with Individuals Who Are Mentally Retarded or Autistic

Debbaudt and Rothman (2001, p.20) state: "Recent research concluded that the developmentally disabled are approximately seven times more likely to come in contact with law enforcement than others." As discussed, the ADA ensures that people with developmental disabilities, such as mental retardation or autism, remain a part of our nation's increasingly diverse workforce. To avoid future potential litigation, officers need to be able to communicate effectively with those who are developmentally disabled.

**Interacting with Individuals Who Are Mentally Retarded**    Recognizing mental retardation is the first step in dealing with it effectively. Often those who are retarded are adept at camouflaging their disability. When interacting with mentally retarded individuals, officers should try to find a quiet, private setting, be patient and speak slowly, using simple language and, if possible, visual aids, pictures or diagrams. Officers should be aware that people who are mentally retarded often try to please others and may, therefore, make untruthful statements thinking it is what the officer, or someone else, wants to hear.

**Interacting with Individuals Who Are Autistic**    Autism is a developmental disability that typically becomes apparent before a child reaches age three. According to Debbaudt and Rothman (pp.20–21):

> While some individuals with autism have mental retardation, autism is not retardation. It is a broad spectrum neurological disorder. . . . Estimates of persons having some form of autism exceed 500,000 nationally, becoming the third most common developmental disability in the United States. Autism affects the normal development of the brain relating to social and communicative interaction. Individuals with autism have difficulty appropriately communicating with, or relating to, others.

Some indicators that an individual may be autistic include the individual avoiding eye contact, lack of verbal response (50 percent of autistic people do not speak), speaking in monotone, repeating exactly what an officer says, engaging in repetitive physical actions, not responding to verbal commands or sounds, not understanding body language or recognizing a police uniform, dressing inappropriately for the weather and not asking for help or showing any indications of pain, even though physical injury may be obvious (Debbaudt and Rothman, p.23).

When responding to situations involving autistic individuals, officers should approach the person in a quiet, nonthreatening manner, avoid quick motions and talk in a moderate, calm voice. Instructions should be simple and direct, such as "stand up" or "go to the car now." They should understand that touching the autistic person may cause a protective "fight or flight" reaction (Debbaudt and Rothman, pp.22–23).

If a crime has been committed and an officer must take an autistic individual into custody, Debbaudt and Rothman (p.23) suggest: "Segregate the individual and never place them in the general incarcerated population before a mental health professional can evaluate them." Furthermore, use caution when considering an autistic suspect's statements: "Oftentimes, individuals with autism confess to crimes they did not commit because of their desire to please and willingness to accept an authority figure's version of events, even if untrue" (p.23).

## Communicating with the Homeless

The homeless, some three million people who are sleeping on the streets, constitute an ever-increasing social problem in the twenty-first century. They also pose a dual problem for police: some break the law, and some become victims. The homeless are frequently *victims* of crime and violence, and law enforcement is responsible for protecting the homeless from those who would take advantage of them. Another problem is that those who advocate for the homeless sometimes break the law—for example, taking over unoccupied private homes as well as unoccupied public buildings and demanding that these buildings be made into homeless shelters. On the other hand, countless citizens do not want people sleeping in their parks. They cite problems such as littering, stealing, drinking, doing drugs and public urinating and defecating.

In general, communities simply do not want the homeless around. Citizens clamor for their city councils to pass laws against sleeping in the street. And when city councils oblige, the social problem becomes a law enforcement problem.

The change in public attitudes toward the homeless is illustrated in cities that have toughened regulations on panhandling, sleeping in public places and other behavior associated with the homeless. Police may be asked to enforce regulations that prohibit lying down on benches in parks, panhandling, fighting, or disrobing and urinating or defecating outside toilet facilities. Because they have no home, most homeless people have lost the privilege of voting. Because they have no home, most cannot simply pick up the phone to call for help when needed.

Gary (2004, p.34) cautions: "Homeless people can be unpredictable due to mental illness and their learned survival instincts." He observes: "From a law enforcement perspective, the nightly ritual of dealing with sleepy transients in business doorways and public benches can be a troublesome speed bump on the way to fighting more serious crimes. After all, social work isn't a major goal of most law enforcement officers. Public safety is. . . . The more we can help law enforcement understand and prepare for homeless people, the safer everyone is."

Police must first see the homeless as individuals and as possible victims and then do all they can to protect them from victimization. Police should also be aware of what kinds of assistance are available for the homeless and make this information known, including helping them to obtain services.

## Communication as a Tool or a Weapon

Effective communication can be a powerful public relations tool and a means to implement community policing. A positive, service-type attitude begins with communication skills (Nowicki, 2001b, p. 21):

> The ability to effectively communicate with people is an absolute necessity for law enforcement officers and an often overlooked way to reduce the amount of force used. . . .
>
> The process of effective interpersonal communications is much more than using words alone. The proper body language, distance and voice inflection must be used to achieve the maximum desired results. Keep in mind the adage, "It's not what you say, it's how you say it."

Officers who use harsh, commanding words put people on the defensive. Most people, if pushed, will tend to push back. Recognizing this tendency to push back if pushed, officers must resist the temptation to engage in verbal confrontations and, instead, remain calm, using logic and reason in speaking with others. For example compare the command "Come here!" to the request "Excuse me, but I need to talk with you for a minute."

Nowicki (2001b, p.22) asserts: "Officers must be aware that their language has the potential to either incite or calm an incident." In any use-of-force transaction, officers must use professional language so their communication becomes a tool for controlling the situation instead of a weapon used against the officer should the incident go to review:

> Loud and professional verbal commands can be heard by the subject, the subject's friends or relatives, other officers and impartial witnesses. . . . At the use-of-force hearing, you want the witness to say the officer said, "Sir, stop resisting. Sir, get on the ground," not, "Put your face in the dirt, scum bag." Verbal skills are an important part of any use of force training program.
>
> Training in verbal skills teaches the officers to be assertive, not aggressive (Nowicki, 2001b, p.22).

An officer's ability to effectively communicate directly affects his or her ability to perform a vital function of policing—obtaining information.

## Communicating to Obtain Information

A tremendous amount of time is spent communicating during police operations. Although much information officers receive may seem irrelevant to the law enforcement mission, it is important to the person conveying the information and should be treated accordingly. Officers who listen empathetically to citizens' concerns will promote public relations, enhance the department's image and foster community policing. If they are truly "to serve and protect," officers must listen to their "clients."

The majority of officers' communicating time should be spent listening rather than speaking. Skillfully phrased questions can elicit a wealth of information. Active listening can greatly enhance the quality of the information obtained. This is true whether the communication involves a brief stop, a formal interview or an interrogation.

## The Field Inquiry

A **field inquiry** is the unplanned questioning of a person who has aroused a police officer's suspicions. It is not an arrest but could lead to one. Field inquiries are also referred to as *field contacts,* and a card on which the information is recorded is called the *field contact card.*

### The Authority to Stop

Law enforcement officers are expected to stop and question people acting suspiciously. If an officer stops someone for questioning (a field inquiry) and the officer believes the person may be armed, the officer can also pat down their outer clothing for weapons.

 The right to stop and question suspicious people was established in the landmark case of *Terry v. Ohio* (1968).

Briefly, this case involved Detective McFadden, an officer with 30 years of investigative experience, who observed three men who "just didn't look right" standing outside a jewelry store. After watching the men repeat a routine nearly a dozen times, McFadden suspected they were casing the store for a "stickup" and might be armed. Deciding to investigate their activity further, McFadden approached the men, identified himself as a police officer, asked for their names and then decided to act.

He turned one man, John Terry, around, and made a quick "pat down" of Terry's outer clothing and felt a pistol in one pocket. Keeping Terry between himself and the others, McFadden ordered all three men to enter the store, where he asked the store owner to call for police while he patted the outer clothing of the others. McFadden removed the revolver from Terry's pocket and another gun from the coat of a man named Chilton. Terry and Chilton were formally charged with carrying concealed weapons. When Terry and Chilton were brought to court, their lawyers moved that the guns could not be used as evidence, claiming they were illegally seized.

The trial judge disagreed, ruling that on the basis of McFadden's experience, he had reasonable cause to believe the defendants were conducting themselves suspiciously and some interrogation was warranted. For his own protection, the detective had the right to frisk the men whom he believed to be armed. The men were convicted, and both appealed their conviction to the U.S. Supreme Court. Before the Court's decision was handed down, Chilton had died. Therefore, the Court's review applied only to Terry.

The Court recognized Detective McFadden as a man of experience, training and knowledge, and certainly "a man of reasonable caution." And as a man of "*ordinary care* and prudence," he waited until he had strengthened his suspicions, making his move just prior to what he believed would be an armed robbery. Given these facts, the Court upheld the trial court verdict, adding that McFadden had to make a quick decision when he saw the three men gathered at the store, and his actions were correct.

A *stop* must be based on a *reasonable suspicion* that the person stopped is about to be or is actually engaged in criminal activity. For example, the person fits a description of a suspect, doesn't "fit" the time or place, is acting strangely, is known to associate with criminals, is loitering, runs away, is present at a crime scene and the area is a high-crime area. The stop may be all that occurs; it may lead to a patdown; or it may progress to an arrest, depending on the information received. The Supreme Court, in *Hiibel v. Sixth Judicial District Court of Nevada et al.* (2004), has upheld a Nevada law that makes it a crime for a person stopped for questioning, a *Terry* stop, to refuse to tell the police his name.

Ginn (2004, p.10) describes the issues in the *Hiibel* case: "The Court noted that asking questions is an ordinary and important part of any police investigation. The mere request for identification does not implicate the Fourth Amendment. Citing a series of Supreme Court decisions, the Court stated that it is 'clear that questions concerning a suspect's identify are a routine and accepted part of many *Terry* stops.' " As Rutledge (2004, p.76) asserts: "As long as police have a reasonable suspicion that would justify a temporary detention under *Terry v. Ohio*, a state statute could reasonably require a detained person to furnish at least his name." Rutledge (p.74) concludes: "A suspect's refusal to give his or her name can warrant an arrest."

Detaining a person for questioning is an important police function that easily generates hostility because people resent restriction of their freedom. Officers must be flexible. Some inquiries will be brief and simple; others extremely complex. To successfully obtain information, officers need to think in terms of six key questions: who, what, where, when, how and why.

## The Interview

The interview is another important type of routine communication used by police officers. It differs from the impromptu field inquiry in that an **interview** is the planned questioning of a witness, victim, informant or other person with information related to an incident or case. To be effective, interviews should be based on specific goals and objectives. As noted by Reece (2003, p.66):

> The quality of an investigation's interviews is often the deciding factor in its solvability and likelihood of a successful prosecution. A winning investigator typically presents prosecutors with well-documented and detailed interviews of not only the victim and suspect, but all witnesses who possess any information about the case and even those who don't.
>
> The rewards of a quality interview are numerous. It promotes the victims' and public's confidence in law enforcement and increases the likelihood of guilty pleas, reducing time spent testifying and saving tax dollars by reducing court costs and public defender fees. It reduces the man-hours often spent re-interviewing witnesses, due to an earlier officer's inexperience. It directs investigators to additional suspects, evidence of the crime, additional victims

and the recovery of property. A quality interview reduces the likelihood of false arrests and improves morale among the department and the investigating officer.

### The Certified Forensic Interviewer Program

The Center for Interviewer Standards and Assessment (CISA) has developed a Certified Forensic Interviewer (CFI) Program ("Certified Forensic Interviewer Program," 2003, p.42). It hopes the designation becomes comparable to a CPA for those in accounting. Benefits of obtaining a CFI include the following (p.44):

- Reduces exposure to liability.
- Helps establish credibility as an expert witness.
- Promotes officers with proven knowledge and training.
- Stands out when the next promotion comes around.
- Raises professional standards and accountability.
- Increases confession and conviction rates.
- Ensures consistent, predictable techniques.

### Guidelines for Interviewing

The National Institute of Justice has developed a guide for training officers to interview eyewitnesses: *Eyewitness Evidence: A Trainer's Manual for Law Enforcement* (2003). Their guidelines for interviewing eyewitnesses also apply to other types of interviewing (pp.10–12):

1. Establish rapport.
2. Inquire about the witness's condition.
3. Use open-ended questions (e.g., "What can you tell me about the car?") and augment with closed-ended questions (e.g., "What color was the car?"). Avoid asking leading questions (e.g., "Was the car red?"). An **open-ended question** allows for an unlimited response from the witness in his/her own words. A **closed-ended question,** in contrast, limits the amount or scope of information that the witness can provide. A **leading question** suggests an answer.
4. Clarify the information received.
5. Document information obtained in a written report.
6. Encourage the witness to contact investigators with any further information.
7. Encourage the witness to avoid contact with the media or exposure to media accounts concerning the incident.
8. Instruct the witness to avoid discussing the details of the incident with other potential witnesses.

Whether officers are seeking to comfort the victim of a crime while obtaining information or seeking to obtain a confession from a suspect, certain techniques can make interviews and interrogations more effective.

## Interviewing and Interrogating Techniques

Interviews and interrogations should be structured around the investigatory elements of the incident or crime. The need for careful planning and advance preparation cannot be overstated. In a preliminary interview at a crime scene, officers have extremely limited time for such planning. Consequently, they need to know their priorities in advance. They should obtain as much information as possible, identify and locate the offender(s), and broadcast the information or alert other officers and departments about the offense and identity of the offender(s).

Officers should not use police terminology when interviewing or interrogating people because it will increase the incriminating atmosphere of the questioning. For example, use *property taken* rather than *robbery*, *have sex* rather than *rape*, or *private use* rather than *embezzle*.

## Phrasing Questions

Evidence shows that the phrasing of questions can definitely influence answers. In one study, for example, observers who were asked, "How tall was the basketball player?" estimated his height to be, on average, about 79 inches. Those asked, "How short was the basketball player?" responded with an estimated average of about 69 inches.

To minimize the inadvertent biasing of memory, witnesses should give an uninterrupted narration before being asked specific questions. Interrogation should also take place as soon as possible so that misleading information from various sources does not become part of the remembered event.

Follow-up questions can reduce or eliminate confusion and clarify statements that seem to contradict previously stated facts. Contradictory statements by an individual may be innocent, due simply to an error in memory, or may indicate deception. Skilled questioning can uncover lies told as part of a witness's or suspect's statement. Navarro and Schafer (2001, p.9) acknowledge that while researchers in criminology and psychology have identified verbal and nonverbal behaviors that tend to indicate deception, detecting deception remains a difficult task: "In fact, multiple studies have found that lie detection, like a coin toss, represents a 50/50 proposition, even for experienced investigators."

## Avoiding Contaminating an Interview

Sandoval (2003, p.2) contends: "The objective of any interview should be to acquire accurate and complete information without contaminating the interview process." He (p.3) suggests: "Interviewing a subject on a noisy and busy city street with multiple onlookers is fraught with danger." Table 2.1 presents tips for avoiding interview contamination.

## Interviewing Witnesses: The Lifeblood of Criminal Cases

A witness is a person other than a suspect who is asked to give information about an incident or another person. A witness may be a victim, a complainant, an observer of an event, a scientific specialist who has examined physical evidence or a custodian of official documents.

Officers must take accurate notes on what witnesses see, smell or hear. They also must evaluate the witnesses' credibility on a number of intangible factors, such as their ability to articulate, their intelligence, their opportunity to observe, their sobriety and their stress level at the time of observation.

Officers must realize that a crime of violence can put witnesses in shock. A **primary victim** is one actually harmed. A **secondary victim** is not actually harmed but suffers along with the victim—a spouse or parent, for example. Therefore, witnesses to a criminal event may also be considered victims of the crime.

**Table 2.1**  Tips for Avoiding Interview Contamination

### Focus on Interview Environment

| *Questions to Consider* | *Strategies to Use* |
| --- | --- |
| Where should the interview take place? | A location free of distractions. |
| How should the room be configured? | Without barriers (e.g., desk or plants) between interviewer and subject. |
| Who should conduct the interview? | One interviewer builds rapport and engenders trust more easily. Two interviewers should use team approach; one asks questions and the other takes notes. |

### Focus on Interviewer's Behavior

| *Questions to Consider* | *Strategies to Use* |
| --- | --- |
| How can interviewers encourage subjects to talk? | Use an open and relaxed posture, facing the subject; lean forward, make eye contact, nod, and occasionally say "uh huh" and "ok." |
| How can interviewers encourage subjects to listen? | Speak slowly, softly, and deliberately; avoid stressing or emphasizing one word over another. |

### Focus on Interviewer's Questions

| *Questions to Consider* | *Strategies to Use* |
| --- | --- |
| What is a model for posing questions? | A funnel, with open-ended followed by closed-ended questions. |
| What are the benefits of open-ended questions? | Gather complete information, minimize the risk of imposing views on subject, and help assess subject's normal behavior. |
| What are the benefits of closed-ended questions? | Elicit specific details, ensure accuracy, and help detect deviations/changes in subject. |
| How can interviewers ensure thoroughness? | Address the basics of who, what, when, where, how, and why. |
| What are other cautions during questioning? | Never ask questions that disclose investigative information and lead the subject toward a desired response. |

SOURCE: Vincent A. Sandoval. "Strategies to Avoid Interview Contamination." *FBI Law Enforcement Bulletin*, October 2003, p.8.

*Officer distributing crime prevention material to youngsters.*

L. Kolvoord, The Image Works

*First Response to Victims of Crime* (2001, p.1) states: "By approaching victims appropriately, officers will gain their trust and cooperation. Victims may then be more willing to provide detailed information about the crime to officers and later to investigators and prosecutors, which, in turn, will lead to the conviction of more criminals." This document (pp.2–4) lists victims' three major needs: (1) the need to feel safe, (2) the need to express their emotions and (3) the need to know "what comes next" after their victimization.

Fritsch et al. (2004, p.389) point out: "Researchers have consistently cited lack of victim information regarding the availability of compensation and the application process as a significant reason why victims do not receive compensation." Their study found: "The police officers on the street do not need to be extremely well-versed in the intricacies of victim compensation—they need only to hand a small pamphlet to a victim of crime in which an injury-based loss was incurred." Fritsch et al. (p.390) conclude: "The information dissemination process involved in directing victims to sources of compensation should be as streamlined and simple as possible. There are well-trained and knowledgeable people on the other end of the phone numbers located on the pamphlets police officers should be distributing. There is no point in spending resources in training police officers on the intricacies of compensation. These funds would probably be better spent through in-service training in victimology and victim awareness, which might overcome some of the negative perceptions some officers have of victims."

Effective interviewing not only helps officers obtain needed information but also helps victims' and witnesses' future mental and emotional well-being. Officers should begin interviewing and questioning victims and witnesses only after establishing psychological and physical equilibrium. Insensitive questioning can compound the trauma. Sandoval and Adams (2001) suggest interviewers can enhance rapport building by "mirroring" how the interviewee acts and speaks, a technique known as Neuro-Linguistic Programming:

> Matching another person's body language or kinesics probably is the easiest and most obvious technique. . . . Interviewers should match another person's body language with subtlety and caution; otherwise, the person easily could become offended. People who develop rapport tend to match each other in posture and gestures. For example, individuals conversing together often adopt the same posture. . . .
>
> Successful investigators listen closely to the choice of words witnesses and suspects use. Then, they conform their language to match the interviewee, using similar visual, auditory, or kinesthetic phrases. . . .
>
> Matching another person's speech patterns, or paralanguage, constitutes the final, and perhaps most effective, way to establish rapport. Paralanguage involves how a person says something or the rate, volume, and pitch of a person's speech. . . .
>
> By matching interviewees' nonverbal behavior, the manner in which they say something, and even their choice of words, interviewers can increase rapport and enhance communication. As a result, the potential for gaining crucial information needed to help resolve investigations improves significantly.

Police officers should assure themselves that the witnesses they interview can and will testify. However, some information may be "off limits." **Privileged information** is information that need not be divulged to the police or the courts. Two kinds of privileges exempt witnesses from testifying: absolute and conditional. An **absolute privilege** permits no exceptions. For example, conversations about social, business and personal affairs are often private and privileged. Such conversations include communications between physicians and patients, lawyers and clients, husbands and wives or others under a special obligation of fidelity and secrecy. A **conditional privilege** usually takes the form of the "official information privilege." An example is asking the court to not disclose an informant's identity.

While witnesses may often be the only source of information available for solving a case, they are also fallible. One way to help witnesses recall events more accurately is the cognitive interview.

## The Cognitive Interview

The **cognitive interview** puts witnesses mentally back at the scene of an incident and encourages them to tell the whole story without interruption. According to Gillen and Thermer (2000, p.53): "The cognitive interview . . . is comprised of five phases and designed to elicit the maximum amount of reliable information from an eyewitness." They (pp.53–57) explain each phase:

*Phase 1—Introduction:* The interviewer seeks to control witness anxiety, establish rapport with the witness, ask the witness to generate information, request detailed factual information from the witness, and have the witness concentrate.

*Phase 2—Open-Ended Narration:* Given the phenomenon of memory association, the investigator seeks to:

- Recreate the context of the event.
- Request the witness to provide a narrative description.
- Make use of pauses. The power of the pause says "tell me more."

*Phase 3—Probing Memory Codes:* The memory of an event is not stored in a unified fashion. Rather, the memory is broken down into images stored in different areas of the brain. Based on a witness's narrative, an investigator can isolate moments where key information may have been stored as an image code. A series of steps helps the witness probe these codes:

1. Emphasize concentration.
2. Recreate the context.
3. Ask the witness to close his/her eyes.
4. Request a detailed description.
5. Avoid interrupting.
6. Take detailed notes.
7. Use a long pause before asking follow-up questions.
8. Ask open-ended questions.
9. Exhaust the witness image.
10. Probe the next image (repeat steps 1 through 9).

*Phase 4—Review:* When the investigator feels all important information has been harvested, a review is conducted. This allows the witness to confirm what the investigator recorded and may jog the witness's memory, providing additional information.

*Phase 5—Close:* The investigator obtains the witness's name, date of birth, address and other information—the background information generally collected first. It is put at the end of the cognitive interview to facilitate recall.

Del Torre (2001, p.6) emphasizes the importance of investing time in the interview: "One of the most crucial parts of an investigation takes place when the officer is obtaining the suspect description. Many officers are very conscious of the fact that if a good detailed description is obtained initially, the chance of capturing the suspect increases dramatically."

## Interviewing Children

"Historically, children were considered incompetent courtroom witnesses. However, legal barriers that once prevented children from offering courtroom testimony have been largely removed" (London, 2001, p.123). Officers may be particularly challenged when interviewing a child witness. Depending on the child's age, the witness may have a limited comprehension of what took place and/or may lack the vocabulary to adequately relate what was seen.

London (p.140) observes: "Interviewing children is a complicated endeavor. Recent psychological research has found that the quality of children's reports is dependent on the quality of the investigative interview."

In reviewing psychological research on interviews of children, London (p.132) concludes that interviewers should avoid leading questions, repeated interviews and linguistically confusing questions to minimize distortions in children's reports.

It is important the interview be conducted in a safe, child-friendly environment, preferably a room with child-sized furniture. Before the interview begins, however, the child and the adult who brought them should be introduced to the interviewer and any others who will be present. Then, the child should be taken on a brief tour of the building, pointing out where the restrooms are and where the accompanying adult will be waiting for the child.

The child should be praised indicating approval, for example, "You're doing a good job of telling me what happened." As with adult witnesses, officers should ask open-ended questions and avoid criticism.

London (p.139) advises: "It is imperative that police officers receive updated in-service training on interviewing children. Information about child interviews is changing quite rapidly; investigators trained in the 1980s would not be aware of the many new techniques. Even relatively recent training bulletins may suggest techniques that are discrepant with current research findings." London (p.132) reports on several techniques that research recommends interviewers *avoid:* leading questions, repeated interviews and linguistically confusing questions to minimize distortion in children's reports. London (p.133) says: "Interviewers should explain to children the goals and the general rules of the interview, including that they have the right to say, 'no.'" In addition (p.134): "Investigators should avoid wearing a police uniform or a gun." London (pp.135–137) also contends: "Open-ended questions should be used as much as possible during investigative interviews. . . . Police administrators should discourage the use of investigative aids such as AD dolls and drawings for interviewing children."

## Statements

If an interview yields important information, often a statement is taken. Bennett and Hess (2004, p.139) explain: "A **statement** is a legal narrative description of events related to a crime. It is a formal, detailed account. It begins with an introduction that gives the place, time, date and names of the people conducting and present at an interview. The name, address and age of the person questioned are stated before the main body of the statement." The body of the statement is the person's account of the incident. A clause at the end states that the information was given voluntarily. The person making the statement reads each page, makes any needed corrections, initials each correction and then signs the statement.

## Information from Informants

An **informant** is a person who provides information in a criminal action and whose identity must be protected. Due to an informant's residence, occupation, associates or lifestyle, that person may be in a better position than a police officer to obtain information about a particular crime.

Hendrie (2003) explains when an informant's information can give officers probable cause to make an arrest: "To be considered a concerned citizen informant by the courts, an informant must not be involved in the criminal milieu (p.12). If a concerned citizen's identity is known to the police, he is presumed credible (p.14). It is reasonable to believe that an informant has a motive to be truthful when he is expecting some leniency for pending charges (p.10). Often a tip given by an informant, along with some corroboration, can establish probable cause to arrest (p.18). The degree of corroboration necessary to establish probable cause is dependant upon the credibility and basis of knowledge of the informant" (p.20).

Often officers know the identity of the informant; in fact, some informants provide information to law enforcement regularly and are regarded as highly credible. Other times, however, police receive information about crime from individuals who refuse to identify themselves, calling into question the reliability of the tip.

## Anonymous Tips

Citizens are constitutionally protected through Fourth Amendment provisions from being forcibly detained by the government based solely on the false accusations of pranksters and those harboring grudges. Citing *Alabama v. White* (1990), Reak (2001, p.10) states: "The courts have long held that a tip from a known informant whose reputation can be assessed and who can be held responsible if his allegations are fabricated is generally more likely to be reliable than an anonymous tip." However:

> The United States Supreme Court has held . . . that an anonymous tip can provide the foundation for reasonable suspicion where the tip predicts future activities that the officer is able to corroborate, which makes it reasonable to think that the informant has inside knowledge about the suspect.

Officers must use sound judgment in how they respond to an anonymous tip, using court rulings as guidelines for what is legally allowed:

> On March 28, 2000, [in *Florida v. J.L.*,] the United States Supreme Court held that an anonymous tip that a person is carrying a gun is not, without more, sufficient to justify a stop and frisk of that person. . . . An officer must have a reasonable suspicion that a suspect is engaged in criminal activity and may be armed and dangerous. Whether a suspicion is reasonable depends upon both the content of the information possessed by the officer and its reliability (Reak, p.10).

# The Interrogation

The terms *inquiry, interview* and *interrogation* are often confused. In police terminology, *inquiry* usually refers to conversations held with citizens during routine patrol. *Interviews,* as just discussed, are planned questionings of people having information about incidents. In contrast, an **interrogation** is the questioning of a hostile witness or suspect from whom officers try to obtain facts related to a crime as well as an admission or confession. An **admission** contains some information about the elements of the crime but falls short of a confession. A **confession** is information supporting the elements of a crime given by a person involved in committing that crime.

Interrogations carry an implied suspicion of criminal knowledge or involvement and must be handled differently from interviews. The Police Executive Research Forum (PERF) has published *Model Procedures for Police Interrogation* (Caplan, n.d.), which states: "[An] interrogation occurs whenever an officer engages in conduct which he should know is likely to elicit an incriminating response from the suspect" (p.1). While interrogation is a vital law enforcement tool, it is susceptible to abuse and, consequently, is closely regulated by law. The landmark Supreme Court decision regulating police interrogation is *Miranda v. Arizona* (1966).

## *The* Miranda *Decision*

In *Miranda v. Arizona* (1966), 23-year-old Ernesto Miranda was arrested and interrogated about a rape and kidnapping. He confessed to the crimes but had not been told of his rights because police, aware Miranda had been arrested before, assumed he already knew his rights. The Court ruled (in a 5–4 decision) that the officers erred in not informing Miranda of those rights again:

> The Fifth Amendment privilege is so fundamental to our system of constitutional rule and the expedient of being given an adequate warning as to the availability of the privilege so simple, we will not pause to inquire in individual cases whether the defendant was aware of his rights without a warning being given. Assessments of the knowledge the defendant possessed, based on information as to his age, education, intelligence, or prior contact with authorities, can never be more than speculation; a warning is a clear-cut fact *(Miranda v. Arizona).*

 In *Miranda v. Arizona,* the Court established the following rights applied to custodial interrogations:
- The suspect has the right to remain silent.
- If the suspect gives up the right to remain silent, anything that the suspect says can be used in a court of law against him or her.
- The suspect has a right to speak to an attorney and to have an attorney present when being questioned by the police.
- If the suspect cannot afford one, an attorney will be appointed to represent the suspect *before* questioning begins.

In *Miranda* the Supreme Court held that these warnings are required *prior to custodial interrogation.* "Custodial" was defined as referring to the situation of a person who is "in custody" (under arrest) or *otherwise deprived of freedom of action in any significant way.* The test to determine if *Miranda* safeguards are triggered is whether a reasonable person in the suspect's position would conclude that he is not free to go (Caplan, p.2).

Many officers carry a card with the ***Miranda* warning** printed on it, clearly spelling out the suspect's rights, and read it verbatim to suspects. Of importance is whether the suspects understand each right. If, for example, a suspect speaks only Spanish, the warning might be read from a card bearing the warning in Spanish.

Another important facet of the *Miranda* decision is whether suspects are willing to give up these rights and talk to the police. If they do so, a signed waiver should be obtained. When reading *Miranda* rights to juveniles, special care should be taken to ensure the suspect understands the warnings. Furthermore: "Officers should honor a juvenile suspect's request to speak to a parent or guardian before waiving his rights" (Caplan, p.9). As a further precaution for police, Caplan (p.12) recommends: "In major felony cases, the notification of rights, the waiver and the subsequent questioning should be videotaped."

If at any time during an interrogation the suspect decides they want a lawyer, either by direct request or through a comment such as, "Maybe I ought to have a lawyer," all questioning must end until legal counsel has been secured. The court has even held that a suspect's question, "Do you think I ought to have an attorney?" was an assertion of rights requiring an immediate cessation of the interrogation.

It is not necessary to give a suspect the *Miranda* warnings if the officer does not intend to question the suspect, taking what is known as the *silent approach*. Other situations not involving "custodial interrogation" and, therefore, not invoking *Miranda* include brief on-the-scene questioning or investigatory questioning during a temporary detention, such as a *Terry* stop; roadside questioning following a routine traffic stop or other minor violation for which custody is not ordinarily imposed; routine booking questions attendant to arrest; nontestimonial identification procedures, such as fingerprinting, conducting a lineup, or taking voice, blood or handwriting samples; conducting a sobriety test; volunteered, spontaneous statements by a suspect, even if in custody; and questioning by a private citizen (Caplan, pp.2–7).

Two key elements when deciding if *Miranda* applies are (1) the *custodial* nature of the questioning (i.e., Would a reasonable person in the suspect's position conclude that he or she is not free to go?) and (2) the *authority* of the person asking the questions (e.g., A private citizen or an agent of the law?). *Miranda* applies only to custodial interrogation by police. However, when police engage the help of a private citizen to get around *Miranda* requirements, that citizen has effectively become an agent of the police. The situation of an undercover agent questioning a suspect illustrates how both elements are needed for *Miranda* to apply:

> The rule prohibiting the use of private individuals to circumvent *Miranda* also precludes interrogation by a "jail plant" or undercover agent while the suspect is in custody. *Miranda* prevents interrogation of custodial suspects by a "jail plant" in the absence of warnings and waiver, but it does not bar statements made by suspects while in custody that are overheard by undercover agents. Moreover, no rule prohibits an undercover agent from questioning to the fullest extent possible a suspect who is not in custody and who has not been charged. An encounter between an undercover agent and a suspect on the street is not custodial because the suspect does not know that he is dealing with a police officer and believes that he is free to leave (Caplan, p.7).

Judge (2004, p.10) points out that a recent Supreme Court ruling, *Yarborough v. Alvarado* (2004), held that the *Miranda* custody standard is the same for juveniles as it is for adults. Officers must be able to distinguish between a *Terry* "detention" and a *Miranda* "custody." While no bright-line rule exists for determining whether a particular police-suspect encounter is a *Terry* stop or an arrest, courts currently use the **totality of circumstances** test, that is, considering all relevant variables in a situation, including an individual's age, mentality, education and criminal experience. During an interrogation, it also includes whether the *Miranda* warning was given, if basic necessities were provided, the length of the questioning and the methods used during the interrogation.

## Waiving the Miranda Rights

If an individual waives his or her *Miranda* rights, special care must be taken with individuals who do not speak English well, who are under the influence of drugs or alcohol, who appear to be mentally retarded or who appear to be hampered mentally in any way. It is preferable to get the waiver in writing. Caplan (pp.9, 12, 14) suggests these interrogation guidelines for suspects who waive their *Miranda* rights:

- Officers should honor a juvenile suspect's request to speak to a parent or guardian before waiving his rights.
- In major felony cases, the notification of rights, the waiver and the subsequent questioning should be videotaped.
- Any direct request for counsel requires all questioning to end. A request to speak to someone other than an attorney, such as a parent, friend or even a probation officer, is not an assertion of the right to counsel.
- When a suspect attempts to reach an attorney but is not successful, most courts hold that he has asserted his right and cannot be questioned.

## Providing Consular Rights Warnings to Foreign Nationals

Clark (2002, p.23) notes: "Law enforcement officials must provide consular rights warnings to arrested or detained foreign nationals." He (p.24) explains: "A foreign national, including a lawful permanent resident alien, is anyone who is not a U.S. citizen." The State Department recommends the following notice be read to detained foreign nationals:

> As a non-U.S. citizen who is being arrested or detained, you are entitled to have us notify your country's consular representative here in the United States. A consular official from your country may be able to help you obtain legal counsel and may contact your family and may visit you in detention among other things. If you want us to notify your country's consular officials, you can request this notification now, or at any time in the future. After your country's consular officials are notified, they may call or visit you. Do you want us to notify your country's consular officials?

Under appropriate circumstances law enforcement must also notify the foreign nationals' consular officials. Clark (p.26) suggests that normally the state would expect notification to consular officials to have been made within 24 hours and certainly within 72 hours. He (p.28) also notes: "Notifying the consular official does not necessarily mean or include providing an explanation of the reason for the arrest or detention." Such notification does not apply to prisoners of war.

## Ethical Considerations in Interrogation

The use of deception during interrogations is highly controversial. Many interrogators feel it is a vital tool to elicit information, while others hold deception to be highly unethical. Many types of deception have been used during interrogations:

- Misrepresenting the nature or seriousness of the offense—for example, telling a suspect that the murder victim was still alive.
- Role-playing manipulative appeals to conscience—for example, projecting sympathy, understanding and compassion; using the good cop/bad cop routine.
- Misrepresenting the moral seriousness of the offense—for example, offering the suspect excuses, such as that a rape victim "asked for it."
- Using promises—for example, suggesting that a suspect's conscience will be eased.
- Misrepresenting identity—for example, pretending to be a reporter or a cellmate.
- Fabricating evidence.

Jayne (2001, p.14) asserts interrogation, out of necessity, relies extensively on duplicity and pretense:

> Trickery and deceit during an interrogation, therefore, occurs on a continuum. . . . The general guideline is that false verbal assertions are permissible, e.g., "The crime lab identified your DNA on the victim," but creating false evidence (typing up a fictitious crime lab report) is not.
>
> Courts recognize that falsely telling a suspect that his fingerprints were found inside the victim's house, for example, would not be apt to cause an innocent suspect to confess.

## Use of Force or Coercion during Interrogation

In addition to giving the *Miranda* warning, officers must avoid any force or coercion during interrogation, as any incriminating statements, admissions or confessions that result from such tactics are likely to be of little use in building a case against the suspect. In 1944 the Supreme Court ruled to exclude from evidence not only confessions obtained by beating, threats and promises, but also those obtained under conditions that were "inherently coercive."

 Confessions obtained by force or under "inherently coercive" conditions are inadmissible in court.

The Court measured what is or is not inherently coercive by reviewing the totality of circumstances in each case where the admissibility of the confession was at issue. Napier and Adams (2002, pp.13–14) note:

> Investigators move into clearly coercive territory when giving clear and substantial identification of end-of-line benefits to confession. The coercive aspect comes from investigators' statements that remaining silent will lead to greater penalties, but confessing to a minimized scenario will result in reward. Investigators may openly suggest that suspects will receive the most serious charge possible without a consent to the offered lesser interpretation of their actions. Many interviewers blatantly and precisely will state the suspect's expected penalty in unmistakable terms, such as the death penalty versus life imprisonment or life imprisonment versus 20 years. Similarly, investigators may threaten harm via investigation or prosecution of a third party, such as a

wife, brother or child, if suspects reject the lesser scenario. Some critics accurately have identified these tactics as being coercive enough to make innocent people confess to a crime that they did not commit.

## Detecting Deception

Dillingham (2004a, pp.49–50) suggests that lies are generally told for one of the following reasons:

- Prosocial: lying to protect someone, to benefit or help others
- Self-enhancement: lying to save face, avoid embarrassment, disapproval or punishment. These lies are not intended to hurt anyone; rather, they benefit the self.
- Selfish: lying to protect the self at the expense of another and/or to conceal a misdeed
- Antisocial: lying to hurt someone else intentionally or to gain an unfair/ unearned reward

Navarro (2003, p.23) thinks: "The detection of deception remains a difficult task. Interviewers can enhance their ability to detect deception by focusing on four domains—comfort/discomfort, emphasis, synchrony and perception management—rather than merely trying to detect traditional signs of deception, which, in some cases, may be misleading."

 A four-domain model for detecting deception focuses on comfort/discomfort, emphasis, synchrony and perception management.

Navarro (p.20) reports: "A person's *level of comfort or discomfort* is one of the most important clues interviewers should focus on when trying to establish veracity. Tension and distress most often manifest upon guilty people who must carry the knowledge of their crimes with them. Attempting to disguise their guilt places a distressing cognitive load on them as they struggle to fabricate answers to what otherwise would be simple questions."

In explaining *emphasis,* Navarro (p.21) says: "When people speak, they naturally incorporate various parts of their body, such as the eyebrows, head, hands, arms, torso, legs and feet, to emphasize a point for which they feel deeply or emotionally. This movement proves important to investigators because, as a rule, people emphasize when genuine. Liars, for the most part, do not emphasize with nonverbals. They think of what to say and how to deceive, but rarely do they think about the presentation of the lie."

The third component of the model, *synchrony,* means "in harmony" or "in sync." For example, in synchronized diving, the divers mirror each other's dive. Says Navarro (p.22): "In interviewing and detecting deception, synchrony plays an important role. Ideally, synchrony (e.g., harmony, congruence and concordance) should occur between the interviewer and the interviewee; between what is said vocally and nonverbally; between the circumstances of the moment and what the subject is saying; and between events and emotions, including synchrony of time and space."

Navarro (p.23) states: "*Perception management* occurs both verbally and nonverbally." Nonverbally, a deceptive suspect may yawn to show boredom or sit sloppily on a chair or couch to display their comfort with the situation. Verbally they may say such things as "I could never kill anyone" or "I am absolutely telling the truth." According to Navarro: "Other forms of perception management include attending the interview with someone of prominence in the community or a retinue of so-called close friends. Further, subjects may self-medicate through the use of alcohol or prescription drugs to appear placid and content. They may change their clothing or hair styles to appear more genuine or more socially conventional. In all of these examples, subjects attempt to manage the perception of the interviewer."

Many believe the ability to detect deception is greatly enhanced through use of technological instruments such as the polygraph and the Computer Voice Stress Analyzer (CVSA).

## The Polygraph and CVSA

A polygraph, which literally means "many writings," scientifically measures and records a subject's physiological reactions to specific questions in an effort to detect deception. As a polygraph operator asks a series of predetermined questions, changes in the subject's respiration, depth of breathing, blood pressure, pulse and electrical resistance of the skin are measured and graphed for analysis.

A polygraph might be used to clear suspects; confirm victim, witness and informant statements; or locate evidence. Polygraphs are sometimes used as part of an exploratory exam to further investigate the criminal involvement of someone already in custody for a different offense. Although the polygraph gives investigators another tool to use in their quest for information, the results are rarely admissible in court. Bennett and Hess (p.153) note: "Despite advances in technology, improved training of polygraph operators and claims of 95 percent accuracy, polygraph results are not now accepted by the courts."

Dillingham (2004b, p.48) notes: "The polygraph can only be allowed into evidence if the prosecution and the defense *both* agree to its admissibility. Naturally, it is not, as either side is sure to have an issue if the other desires the results to be admitted." The polygraph is not regarded as a valid scientific instrument as the Supreme Court ruled in *Frye v. United States* (1923), *Daubert v. Merrell Dow Pharmaceuticals, Inc.* (1993) and *Kumho Tire v. Carmichael* (1999).

Some contend polygraph results violate hearsay rules because it is impossible to cross-examine a machine. However, while polygraph results are not presently admissible in court, any confession obtained as a result of a polygraph test is admissible (Bennett and Hess, p.153).

Another type of truth detection instrument is the Computer Voice Stress Analyzer (CVSA), which is gaining popularity among law enforcement agencies. Furthermore, unlike the polygraph, the CVSA does not limit the subject to only "yes" or "no" responses; it can analyze any spoken word. No matter what type of technology is used, the results must always be used as an investigative aid, a supplement to a thorough investigation—never as a substitute for it.

## Documenting Confessions

A confession can be given orally or in writing, but it must always be voluntary to be admissible. Documentation of confessions is vital, as a properly documented confession increases the likelihood of swift and successful prosecution of criminals (Burke, 2001, p.18). Videotaped interrogations and confessions are becoming increasingly popular in law enforcement agencies nationwide to quell accusations of police brutality and reduce doubts concerning the voluntariness of confessions. Bennett and Hess (p.151) caution: "Even though a confession is highly desirable, it may not be true, it may later be denied, or there may be claims that it was involuntary. A confession is only one part of the investigation. Corroborate it by independent evidence." Usually the corroboration of independent evidence is contained in an officer's written report.

# Report Writing

Writing good reports is one of the most important skills law enforcement officers can possess. As O.W. Wilson and Roy C. McLaren wrote three decades ago: "Almost everything that a police officer does must be reduced to writing. What is written is often the determining factor in whether a suspect is arrested in the first place, and if he is arrested, whether he is convicted and sentenced. The contents of written reports, in fact, often have a great bearing in life-and-death situations. To say that officers need to be proficient in report writing is an understatement."

Well-documented police reports are more likely to encourage plea bargaining. In fact, it has been said that plea bargaining is often a trial by police report. Recognizing how well-written reports can protect officers from litigation, Nowicki (2001a, p.23) says:

> Surviving the streets is only one component of officer safety. Unfortunately, an often neglected component is report writing. The importance of this cannot be overestimated, particularly when it comes to justifying the legitimate use of force. Professional survival may depend on it. The officer must be able to write a truthful and complete report, one that is clear and concise.

Indeed, as our society becomes more complex, more litigious and more demanding of the criminal justice system, the greater will be the need for complete, accurate reporting by officers. An agency is only as good as its documentation. Operations budgets and overall department budgets depend a great deal on accurate documention of patrol activities. Unfortunately, many police officers are poor writers.

## The Importance of Field Notes

Effective field notes are the basis for all types of reports and for further investigation of cases and incidents. Notes should be taken as soon after an incident as possible and should be kept in a notebook. Most officers prefer loose-leaf notebooks because they are easily organized, and notes can be removed and used as needed for writing reports or for testifying in court.

The ABCs of effective field notes are accuracy, brevity, clarity and completeness. Accuracy is assured by repeating information, spelling names and verifying numbers. Brevity is accomplished by omitting the articles *a, an* and *the;* by omitting all other unnecessary words; and by using common abbreviations. However, even common abbreviations can be misunderstood. For example, many people hear *P.C.* and think *personal computer* or *politically correct.* Police officers, however, are likely to think *probable cause* or *penal code.* Context often helps make the meaning obvious.

Clarity includes legibility. Notes that cannot be deciphered a few weeks later because of sloppy handwriting are worthless. A clear picture of what happened during an incident or at a crime scene depends on careful, complete notes. The notes should contain answers to six basic questions: who, what, where, when, why and how. This is as true of misdemeanors as of felonies. Prosecutors contend that many police officers suffer from the **felony syndrome;** that is, they obtain complete information only on felony cases, deeming these to be "real" cases, with misdemeanors given much less time and attention. To the people involved, however, every incident or crime is important. Further, many more civil suits against police officers and departments arise from misdemeanor cases than from felony cases.

Field notes provide the basis for reports. Without good notes, officers cannot effectively perform one of their most important tasks—writing reports.

## Purposes of Reports

Police officers write many kinds of reports, including incident reports, continuation or supplemental reports, arrest reports, property and inventory reports, vehicle reports, missing-person reports, bias-motivated crime reports, domestic violence reports, police pursuit reports and accident reports, increasingly being called "crash" reports. These reports serve many important purposes.

Reports are used to:
- Permanently record facts.
- Provide details of a criminal incident to be used in a follow-up investigation.
- Provide a basis for prosecution.
- Provide data for federal and state crime reporting systems.
- Document the past and plan for future services.

It has often been said that a good report is more important than a good arrest. Cases can be made or lost on the officer's report alone. In addition, officers often are judged by their reports. A shoddy report makes the reader question the officer's intelligence, education or competence—or perhaps all three.

The most common problems in police reports include misspelled words; unfamiliar abbreviations; confusing or unclear sentences; missing information, such as elements of the crime; missing work addresses and phone numbers; extreme wordiness and overuse of police jargon; missing or incomplete witnesses' names and addresses; and use of assumptions.

## The Audience

A basic premise of effective writing is that it is reader based. All too often, writers try to *impress* their readers rather than to *express* their ideas clearly. They equate big words and long sentences with big brains and extensive education. WRONG. Reader-based writing avoids the tendency to impress.

The audience for police reports includes other officers, supervisors, other professionals within the criminal justice system and laypeople such as insurance investigators, social workers and reporters.

Hess and Wrobleski (2001, p.7) stress: "**Reader-friendly writing** avoids police jargon and abbreviations and communicates in plain, simple language. It is written as it would be spoken, and it considers its audience."

## The Effective Report

The basic content of a police report includes an introduction, the body and a conclusion. The information answers the questions who, what, where, when, why and how. Good reports have the same characteristics as good field notes as well as several additional characteristics.

 Effective reports are accurate, brief, clear, complete, legible, objective, grammatically correct and correctly spelled. Effective reports are also written in the past tense and in chronological order. They use verbs rather than nouns when possible, avoid sexist language and can "stand alone."

Some police departments have their officers tape their reports or use a dictating machine.

### *Computer-Assisted Report Entry*

Some police departments are using word processing packages for report writing, and others are going even further and using computer-assisted police report entry systems. Mobile technology is enabling officers to construct reports in the field, as information is obtained. Rogers (2002b, p.86) suggests: "The latest buzz is mobile field report writing software. Many agencies seem to be going toward an electronic reporting system, which is seen as a wunderkind that saves officers time and money." An officer from the Baton Rouge (Louisiana) City Police Department reports: "The typical officer used to spend about four hours a shift writing reports. Our new system has cut that time down to about 90 minutes a day" ("Software Helps Agency Work Smarter," 2002, p.96).

Before leaving the discussion of communication, one other important kind of communication should be considered—that between law enforcement and the media.

## Interaction and Cooperation with the Media

Moore (2004b, p.178) asserts: "The bottom line is that law enforcement needs the media and the media needs law enforcement." Rosenthal (2003, p.3), likewise, suggests: "The news media can be a pain. But they can also be law enforcement's single biggest force multiplier and a genuine asset in time of need. Cops can truly win with the media, if they only had the will to win and a little training on how to make that happen." According to Van Blaricom (2001, p.52):

> If an atmosphere of mistrust and hostility has developed between the news-makers and the news reporters, it will be reflected in how the news is reported. That is the nature of such a relationship. The solution to the status quo is to change the institutional attitudes. The police should start that potentially difficult process because they have the most to gain. The outcome can be more than worth the effort.
>
> When critically examined, it is hard to imagine two professions whose practitioners have more similar personalities. When either of them really wants to find out something, they will do everything within their power to learn the answer. And, the more difficult the search is made for them, the greater their competitive instincts become.
>
> Understanding this basic premise is the first step to good police-media relations. Every police department has interesting stories that portray police work as a positive force for good in the community. The media will tell those stories to the public, if the police will let them.

Keys to success in dealing with the media include:

■ Having a clear policy on what information is to be released to the press and what is not.
■ Treating all reporters fairly.
■ Being as sensitive to the need for the privacy of victims and witnesses as to the need of the public to know what is going on.

Covello, media expert at Columbia University, says the five biggest interview failures are: "Failing to take charge, failing to anticipate questions, failing to develop key messages, failing to stick to the facts and failing to keep calm" (Buice, 2003, p.26). In addition to knowing what to do and not to do, officers must also be aware of the public's "right to know" and the privacy rights of victims and witnesses.

 Police departments must balance the public's "right to know" and reporters' First Amendment rights to publish what they know with the police's need to withhold certain information and to protect the privacy of victims and witnesses—Sixth Amendment rights.

Some larger departments have a public information officer (PIO) who is the only one authorized to release information to the media. Other departments allow those officers involved in specific cases to be interviewed by reporters interested in the cases. Media organizations should be told who their contacts will be. Whether a department has a PIO or permits individual officers to talk with the media, the department should remember what Buice (2002, p.281) notes: "According to sociologists, 95 percent of what the public knows about law enforcement comes from the mass media. Thus, their opinions of and support for [an] agency are often directly linked to the amount of time and resources [an] agency spends on managing its message. In media relations, as in life, you truly do reap what you sow."

 **SUMMARY**

Effective communication can produce several positive outcomes. It can be used to inform, persuade, diffuse, guide, motivate, reassure and negotiate. Communication can be vertical (downward or upward) or horizontal (lateral).

Special problems in communicating include keeping police communications secure, interference on the line and lack of interoperability. Special populations that may pose especially challenging communication issues include the elderly, individuals who speak little or no English or have different cultural backgrounds and those with disabilities or diseases that may impair their ability to communicate, including blindness, deafness, epilepsy, Alzheimer's Disease, mental illness, mental retardation or autism. The speech of a person who has been deaf since birth or who has epilepsy or Alzheimer's Disease may be mistaken for intoxication.

Effective communication in the field is critical to successful police operations and includes field inquiries, interviews and interrogations. The right to stop and question suspicious people (field inquiries) was established in the landmark case of *Terry v. Ohio* (1968). In *Miranda v. Arizona,* the Court established the following rights applied to custodial interrogations:

■ The suspect has the right to remain silent.
■ If the suspect gives up the right to remain silent, anything that the suspect says can be used in a court of law against him or her.

- The suspect has a right to speak to an attorney and to have an attorney present when being questioned by the police.
- If the suspect cannot afford one, an attorney will be appointed to represent the suspect *before* questioning begins.

Confessions obtained by force or under "inherently coercive" conditions are inadmissible in court. A four-domain model for detecting deception focuses on comfort/discomfort, emphasis, synchrony and perception management.

In addition to verbal communication skills, police officers also need effective writing skills for both field notes and reports. Reports are used to permanently record facts, to provide details of a criminal incident to be used in a follow-up investigation, to provide a basis for prosecution, to provide data for federal and state crime reporting systems and to document the past and plan for future services. The audience for police reports includes other officers, supervisors, other professionals within the criminal justice system and laypeople such as insurance investigators, social workers and reporters.

Effective reports are accurate, brief, clear, complete, legible, objective, grammatically correct and correctly spelled. Effective reports are also written in the past tense and in chronological order. They use verbs, avoid sexist language and can "stand alone."

Police departments must balance the public's "right to know" and reporters' First Amendment rights to publish what they know with the police's need to withhold certain information and to protect the privacy of victims and witnesses—Sixth Amendment rights.

### APPLICATION

As head of the public relations department, you have noticed an increase in complaints against officers who have mistaken a disability or physical problem as intoxication. Officers have no guidelines on how to determine whether what appears to be alcohol- or drug-induced intoxication is indeed alcohol- or drug-induced intoxication.

### INSTRUCTIONS

Use the form in the Appendix to write a policy regarding communicating with individuals who *appear* to be under the influence of alcohol or drugs. Then write the procedures needed to carry out the policy.

### AN EXERCISE IN CRITICAL THINKING

On April 13, Joel Powell's car was stopped, and he and a companion were arrested a few miles away from, and a few minutes after, the burglary of a supper club. The burglary had been reported by an eyewitness whose descriptions of the event and the car involved were transmitted by radio to area police officers. Powell's car matched the description of the car in which the burglars left the scene. It was also traveling in the same direction on the same road. After Powell and his passenger had been taken into custody, the car was sealed, towed and searched. It contained two bank bags with about $500 in currency and coin, later identified as club property, and various tools, including pry bars, mauls, tire irons and a hacksaw.

1. Must the factual basis for stopping a vehicle arise from the officer's personal observation?
   a. When stopping a vehicle, officers must have a warrant when they do not personally observe a felony being committed.
   b. Arresting officers may rely on any communicated information when a possible felony is to be investigated.
   c. The basis for stopping a vehicle may be supplied by information acquired from another person as well as other law enforcement officials.
   d. Arresting officers must have personal knowledge of the facts constituting probable cause.
   e. Six factors must be taken into account:
      1. The particular description of the offender or the vehicle in which the offender fled.
      2. The size of the area in which the offender might be found.
      3. The number of people in that area.
      4. The known or probable direction of the offender's flight.
      5. Observed activity by the particular offender.
      6. Knowledge or suspicion that the offender has been involved in other criminality of the type presently under investigation.

   Not all of these factors were clearly or completely communicated, so the stop is not supported.

### DISCUSSION QUESTIONS

1. When you communicate with another person, are you aware of whether that person is really listening? How can you tell?

2. Do you feel the average citizen with whom you communicate is going to understand any legal language you may use to describe an offense?

3. What language barriers or other cultural barriers would you be likely to encounter in your community?

4. At night, you confront a suspicious man walking in an elite neighborhood. You stop to question the man, but he refuses even to give his name. What are you going to do? Elaborate and justify your decision.

5. How would you warn a suspect of his rights if, while you were interviewing this person, he suddenly said, "I committed the crime"?

6. What are some positive outcomes of good incident reports?

7. How do the media affect police operations?

### InfoTrac College Edition Assignments

- Use InfoTrac College Edition to answer the Discussion Questions as appropriate.

- Use InfoTrac College Edition to research articles on *deception*. List the difficulties in detecting deception. State and support your opinion on whether deception is a viable tool in interrogation.

- Use InfoTrac College Edition to find and outline one of the following articles:
  - "Subtle Skills for Building Rapport: Using Neuro-Linguistic Programming in the Interview Room" by Vincent A. Sandoval and Susan H. Adams
  - "When an Informant's Tip Gives Officers Probable Cause to Arrest Drug Traffickers" by Edward M. Hendrie
  - "The Montgomery County CIT Model: Interacting with People with Mental Illness" by Rodney Hill, Guthrie Quill and Kathryn Ellis
  - "Law Enforcement and the Elderly: A Concern for the 21st Century" by Lamar Jordan
  - "Strategies to Avoid Interview Contamination" by Vincent A. Sandoval
  - "Criminal Confessions: Overcoming the Challenges" by Michael R. Napier and Susan H. Adams
  - "Documenting and Reporting a Confession with a Signed Statement: A Guide for Law Enforcement" by Timothy T. Burke
  - "The Americans with Disabilities Act: A Practical Guide for Police Departments" by Thomas D. Colbridge
  - "Contact with Individuals with Autism: Effective Resolutions" by Dennis Debbaudt and Darla Rothman

- "Working with Informants: Operational Recommendations" by James E. Hight
- "The Psychological Influence of the Police Uniform" by Richard R. Johnson
- "Detecting Deception" by Joe Navarro and John R. Schafer
- "Offenders' Perceptual Shorthand: What Messages Are Law Enforcement Officers Sending to Offenders?" by Anthony J. Pinizzotto and Edward E. Davis
- "The Public Safety Wireless Network (PSWN) Program: A Brief Introduction" by Derek Siegle and Rick Murphy
- "A Four-Domain Model for Detecting Deception: An Alternative Paradigm for Interviewing" by Joe Navarro

 ### INTERNET ASSIGNMENT

Use the Internet to research *Miranda v. Arizona*, and outline what the Supreme Court told the police in this case. Be prepared to share your outline with the class.

 ### BOOK-SPECIFIC WEBSITE

The book-specific website at http://cj.wadsworth.com/wobleski_Hess_police_op4e hosts a variety of resources for students and instructors. Many can be emailed to the instructor. Included are extended activities such as Concept Builders - the 3 step learning module that reinforces key chapter concepts, followed by a real-world applications and critical thinking questions. InfoTrac College Edition exercises; Discussion Questions; interactive key-term FlashCards; and a collection of chapter-based Web Links provide additional information and activities to include in the curriculum.

### REFERENCES

Ake, George. "First Responder Communication across Jurisdictional Boundaries." *The Police Chief*, July 2003, p.20.

Bennett, Wayne W. and Hess, Kären M. *Criminal Investigation*, 7th ed. Belmont, CA: Wadsworth Publishing Company, 2004.

Buice, Ed. "PIO or Patrol?" *Law and Order*, September 2002, pp.280–281.

Buice, Ed. "Keys to Successful Media Interviews." *Law and Order*, September 2003, p.26.

Burke, Timothy T. "Documenting and Reporting a Confession with a Signed Statement: A Guide for Law Enforcement." *FBI Law Enforcement Bulletin*, February 2001, pp.17–22.

Caplan, Gerald M. *Model Procedures for Police Interrogation*. Washington, DC: Police Executive Research Forum, no date.

"Certified Forensic Interviewer Program." *Law and Order*, May 2003, pp.42–45.

Clark, M. Wesley. "Providing Consular Rights Warnings to Foreign Nationals." *FBI Law Enforcement Bulletin*, March 2002, pp.22–32.

Colbridge, Thomas D. "The Americans with Disabilities Act: A Practical Guide for Police Departments." *FBI Law Enforcement Bulletin*, January 2001, pp.23–32.

Cooper, Virginia G.; McLearen, Alix M.; and Zapp, Patricia A. "Dispositional Decisions with the Mentally Ill: Police Perceptions and Characteristics." *Police Quarterly*, September 2004, pp.295–310.

"Cops Try Harder to Get inside the Minds of Growing Ranks of Alzheimer's Sufferers." *Law Enforcement News*, October 15/31, 2003, pp.1, 8.

Crank, John P. and Loughrin-Sacco, Steven J. "Foreign Languages Across the Curriculum: A Model for the Delivery of Professional Language Training." *Journal of Criminal Justice Education*, Spring 2001, pp.193–211.

"CriMNet Helps Police Nab Criminals." *CriMNet News*, Winter 2004, Issue 3, p.1. Online www.crimnet.state.MN.us

Davidson, Paul. "Interference on the Line." Reprinted from *USA Today* in *American Police Beat*, May 2001, pp.7, 40, 43.

Debbaudt, Dennis and Rothman, Darla. "Contact with Individuals with Autism: Effective Resolutions." *FBI Law Enforcement Bulletin*, April 2001, pp.20–24.

Dees, Tim. "Aether PocketBlue." *Law and Order*, July 2001, pp.152–153.

Dees, Tim. "Cell Phones: They Aren't Just Phones Anymore." *Law and Order*, August 2003, pp.36–40.

Del Torre, Bob. "It's All in the Details." *American Police Beat*, March 2001, pp.6–7.

Dillingham, Christopher. "Pinocchio Part V: Why Does Pinocchio Lie?" *Police and Security News*, May/June 2004a, pp.49–51.

Dillingham, Christopher. "Pinocchio Part VI: Proxy Devices and the State of Lie Detection." *Police and Security News*, July/August 2004b, pp.47–51.

Douglas, Dave. "PDAs on Patrol." *Police*, February 2003, pp.42–45.

Duncan, Debra C. "Community Policing: Preserving the Quality of Life of Our Senior Citizens." *The Police Chief*, March 2001, pp.75–77.

Engel, Robin Shepard and Silver, Eric. "Policing Mentally Disordered Suspects: A Reexamination of the Criminalization Hypothesis." *Criminology*, 2001, pp.225–252.

*Eyewitness Evidence: A Trainer's Manual for Law Enforcement*. Washington, DC: National Institute of Justice, September 2003. (NCJ 188678) www.ojp.usdoj.gov/nij/eyewitness/188678.html

*First Response to Victims of Crime*. Washington, DC: Office for Victims of Crime, December 2001. (NCJ 189631)

Fritsch, Eric J.; Caeti, Tory J.; Tobolowsky, Peggy M.; and Taylor, Robert W. "Police Referrals of Crime Victims to Compensation Sources: An Empirical Analysis of Attitudinal and Structural Impediments." *Police Quarterly*, September 2004, pp.372–393.

Garand, Julie. "PocketBlue in Peabody, MA." *Law and Order*, August 2004, pp.64–65.

Garrett, Ronnie. "Sharing Info Begins with Interoperability." *Law Enforcement Technology*, January 2003, p.6.

Garrett, Ronnie. "Can We Talk?" *Law Enforcement Technology*, August 2004, p.8.

Gary, Charles. "How to . . . Police the Homeless." *Police*, June 2004, pp.30–34.

Gillen, Joseph J. and Thermer, Clifford E. "DNA-Based Exonerations Warrant a Reexamination of the Witness Interview Process." *The Police Chief*, December 2000, pp.52–57.

Ginn, Beverly A. "Stop-and-Identify Laws." *The Police Chief*, September 2004, pp.10–11.

Harris website. Government page: National Crime Information Center (NCIC) 2000. http://www.govcomm.harris.com/law/programs/ncic/

Hart, Sarah V. *Results from an Elder Abuse Prevention Experiment in New York City*. Washington, DC: National Institute of Justice Research in Brief, September 2001. (NCJ 188675)

Hendrie, Edward M. "When an Informant's Tip Gives Officers Probable Cause to Arrest Drug Traffickers." *FBI Law Enforcement Bulletin*, December 2003, pp.8–21.

Hess, Kären M. and Wrobleski, Henry M. *For the Record: Report Writing in Law Enforcement*, 5th ed. Bloomington, MN: Innovative Systems-Publishers, Inc., 2001.

Hill, Rodney; Quill, Guthrie; and Ellis, Kathryn. "The Montgomery County CIT Model: Interacting with People with Mental Illness." *FBI Law Enforcement Bulletin*, July 2004, pp.18–25.

Jayne, Brian. "They Don't Know That You Don't Know." *American Police Beat*, March 2001, p.14.

Jordan, Lamar. "Law Enforcement and the Elderly: A Concern for the 21st Century." *FBI Law Enforcement Bulletin*, May 2002, pp.20–23.

Judge, Lisa. "Is the Miranda Custody Standard Different for Juveniles?" *The Police Chief*, August 2004, p.10.

Kanable, Rebecca. "Agencies Form Regional Information Sharing System." *Law Enforcement Technology*, July 2001, pp.144–151.

Kanable, Rebecca. "A Roadmap for Interoperability: SAFECOM's Statement of Requirements Defines the Future for Communicating and Sharing Information." *Law Enforcement Technology*, July 2004, pp.10–19.

London, Kamala. "Investigative Interviews of Children: A Review of Psychological Research and Implications for Police Practices." *Police Quarterly*, March 2001, pp.123–144.

McEwen, Harlin R. "SafeCom." *The Police Chief*, April 2004, pp.146–149.

Moore, Carole. "If There Must Be Gossip, Use It for Good." *Law Enforcement Technology*, May 2004a, p.110.

Moore, Carole. "Encouraging Positive Media Relations." *Law Enforcement Technology*, June 2004b, p.178.

Napier, Michael R. and Adams, Susan H. "Criminal Confessions: Overcoming the Challenges." *FBI Law Enforcement Bulletin*, November 2002, pp.9–15.

Navarro, Joe. "A Four-Domain Model for Detecting Deception: An Alternative Paradigm for Interviewing." *FBI Law Enforcement Bulletin*, June 2003, pp.19–24.

Navarro, Joe and Schafer, John R. "Detecting Deception." *FBI Law Enforcement Bulletin*, July 2001, pp.9–13.

Nowicki, Ed. "Developing Good Reports." *Law and Order*, July 2001a, pp.23–24.

Nowicki, Ed. "Language and Voice Commands." *Law and Order*, May 2001b, pp.21–22.

Polisar, Joseph M. "IACP Support for the Consensus Plan." *The Police Chief*, July 2004, p.8.

Reak, Kevin P. "Recent Court Cases Shed Light on How to Deal with Anonymous Tips." *The Police Chief*, April 2001, p.10.

Reece, Hunter. "The Keys to Quality Interview Techniques." *Law and Order*, November 2003, pp.66–69.

Reuland, Melissa. *A Guide to Implementing Police-Based Diversion Programs for People with Mental Illness.* Delmar, NY: Technical Assistance and Policy Analysis Center for Jail Diversion, 2004.

Reuland, Melissa and Margolis, Gary J. "Police Approaches that Improve the Response to People with Mental Illnesses: A Focus on Victims." *The Police Chief*, November 2003, pp.35–39.

Rickher, Angela J. "Encountering Someone with Alzheimer's: Hands-On Tactics for Law Enforcement." *The Law Enforcement Trainer*, September/October 2003, pp.9–13.

Rogers, Donna. "Drive for E911 Picks Up Speed." *Law Enforcement Technology*, March 2001a, pp.88–92.

Rogers, Donna. "Project Locate." *Law Enforcement Technology*, July 2001b, pp.42–46.

Rogers, Donna. "Toy or Tool?" *Law Enforcement Technology*, July 2001c, pp.108–114.

Rogers, Donna. "Linking Communications for Interoperability." *Law Enforcement Technology*, August 2002a, pp.48–53.

Rogers, Donna. "Mobile Field Report Writing: Software for Mobile Reporting Is Not All Created Equal." *Law Enforcement Technology*, September 2002b, pp.86–92.

Rosenthal, Rick. "Training the Media." *ILEETA Digest*, October–December 2003, p.3.

Rutledge, Devallis. "Stop and Identify." *Police*, October 2004, pp.74–76.

Sandoval, Vincent A. "Strategies to Avoid Interview Contamination." *FBI Law Enforcement Bulletin*, October 2003, pp.1–12.

Sandoval, Vincent A. and Adams, Susan H. "Subtle Skills for Building Rapport: Using Neuro-Linguistic Programming in the Interview Room." *FBI Law Enforcement Bulletin*, August 2001, pp.1–5.

Santoro, Joseph. "Mentally Ill Pose a Grave Risk to Police Officers." *American Police Beat*, May 2001, p.23.

Scoville, Dean. "Mental Illness Can Kill . . . You." *Police*, January 2004, p.6.

Siegle, Derek and Murphy, Rick. "The Public Safety Wireless Network (PSWN) Program: A Brief Introduction." *FBI Law Enforcement Bulletin*, May 2001, pp.10–12.

"Software Helps Agency Work Smarter." *Law Enforcement Technology*, November 2002, pp.96–97.

Stanek, Rich. "CriMNet: Minnesota Catches Up with Criminals." *The Police Chief*, April 2004, pp.167–168.

Streit, Corinne. "Minnesota Gets Connected with CriMNet." *Law Enforcement Technology*, June 2001a, pp.116–119.

Streit, Corinne. "Technology in Your Pocket." *Law Enforcement Technology*, July 2001b, pp.140–143.

Van Blaricom, Donald P. "The Media: Enemies or Allies?" *The Police Chief*, April 2001, pp.52–56.

Voegtlin, Gene. "FCC Approves the Consensus Plan." *The Police Chief*, August 2004, p.8.

"Wireless Calls Near 140,000 per Day." *Law Enforcement Technology*, July 2001, p.9.

Zdanowicz, Mary. "A Shift in Care." *Community Links*, June 2001, pp.3–5.

## CASES CITED

*Alabama v. White*, 496 U.S. 325 (1990)

*Daubert v. Merrell Dow Pharmaceuticals, Inc.*, 113 S.Ct. 2728 (1993)

*Florida v. J. L.*, 529 U.S. 266 (2000)

*Frye v. United States*, (1923)

*Hiibel v. Sixth Judicial District Court of Nevada et al.*, No.03-5554 (2004)

*Kumho Tire v. Carmichael*, (1999)

*Miranda v. Arizona*, 384 U.S. 436 (1966)

*Terry v. Ohio*, 392 U.S. 1 (1968)

*Yarborough v. Alvarado*, 316 F.3d 841 (2004)

# CHAPTER 3

# Operational Skills: Performing within the Law

## Do You Know . . .

- What balance between freedom and order police officers must maintain?
- What two amendments restrict arrests and searches?
- What a stop and frisk involves?
- What constitutes an arrest?
- When officers may arrest someone?
- Why understanding and skill in making legal arrests are critical?
- How substantive and procedural criminal law differ?
- What the Exclusionary Rule is and its relevance to police operations?
- How officers arrest someone?
- How much force can be used in making an arrest?
- What three use-of-force tests are established in *Graham v. Connor?*
- When handcuffs should be used in conjunction with an arrest?
- What less-lethal weapons police officers have available?
- What police activity can be an obstacle to community policing?
- When a search can be conducted?
- How a search conducted with a warrant is limited?
- When a search warrant is *not* needed?
- How officers search a person and a building?

## Can You Define?

| | | | |
|---|---|---|---|
| arrest | exigent circumstance | mere handcuff rule | probable cause |
| compliance | frisk | observational | procedural law |
| continuum of contacts | functional equivalent | probable cause | stop |
| curtilage | good faith | patdown | stop-and-frisk |
| de facto arrest | "in the presence" | plain view | situation |
| due process of law | informational | positional asphyxia | substantive law |
| Exclusionary Rule | probable cause | | |

# Introduction

The basic skills discussed in this chapter—stopping and frisking, arresting and searching—may be needed in a variety of situations. Not only are these skills used often, but they are also strictly governed by law and usually by department policies and procedures as well.

Police officers are expected to be familiar with the basic rules of criminal procedure. It is not the intent of this text to go into the details of any of these basic rules but rather to remind the reader of their critical importance in police operations. Chapter 2 discussed the importance of obtaining information legally. This chapter focuses on making legal arrests and searches.

 Law enforcement officers must maintain a balance between "freedom to" and "freedom from."

In a democracy such as ours, law enforcement has the awesome responsibility of assuring that citizens have freedom *to* live, remain free, pursue happiness and have due process of the law. Law enforcement has also been charged with protecting society—that is, giving citizens freedom *from* crime and violence as well as *from* unreasonable search and seizure by the government. The conflict between these two competing responsibilities is sometimes referred to as due process versus crime control. Police officers must strike a balance not only between the rights of individuals and those of our country but also between the rights of law-abiding citizens and those of criminals. They must *act* to fulfill their responsibilities but always within the constraints of the law.

 Guarantees against unlawful arrests and searches are found in the Fourth and Fifth Amendments to the U.S. Constitution.

The Fourth Amendment states:

The right of the people to be secure in their persons, houses, papers and effects, against unreasonable searches and seizures, shall not be violated, and no warrants shall issue but upon probable cause, supported by oath or affirmation, and particularly describing the place to be searched, and the persons or things to be seized.

The Fourth Amendment protects the fundamental right to privacy that lies at its core. Its guarantees extend to arrest warrants as well as to search warrants. It does *not*, however, prohibit arrests or searches without a warrant.

The Fifth Amendment provides that no person shall be "deprived of life, liberty, or property without due process of law." Both the Fourth and the Fifth Amendments should be kept in mind throughout this text and, indeed, throughout an officer's career.

This chapter begins with an explanation of the common procedure of stopping and frisking someone acting suspiciously. Next, legal arrests are described, including when they can be made and the importance of assuring that they are legal. This is followed by a discussion of procedures for making legal arrests and the issues of handcuffing, excessive and deadly force, and the implications of the use of force for community policing. The chapter concludes with a discussion of legal searches, including procedures for searching both people and buildings. This chapter contains more court cases than other chapters simply because of the topic: acting within the law while making arrests and conducting searches. The principles (and cases) discussed in this chapter will have relevance throughout the remaining sections of this text.

## Stop and Frisk

Law enforcement officers are expected to stop and question people acting suspiciously, as discussed in the preceding chapter. If an officer stops someone for questioning (a field inquiry) and the officer believes the subject may be armed, the officer can also pat down the subject's outer clothing for weapons. This action *is* considered a search.

 A **stop-and-frisk situation** is one in which law enforcement officers:
- Briefly detain (*stop*) a suspicious person for questioning (this is *not* an arrest).
- And *if* they reasonably suspect the person to be armed, are allowed to pat down (*frisk*) the person's outer clothing (this *is* a limited search for weapons).

The right to stop and frisk suspicious people was established in the landmark case of *Terry v. Ohio* (1968), as presented in detail in Chapter 2. Recall that is how Detective McFadden, based on 30 years' experience as an investigator, stopped and frisked three men loitering outside a jewelry store because he suspected they were planning an armed robbery of the store. The frisk did, in fact, reveal two revolvers concealed in the men's coats, and when the case ultimately came before the U.S. Supreme Court, the detective's actions were upheld as legal. The stop, frisk and subsequent seizure of the weapons as evidence did not violate the suspects' constitutional rights.

The justification behind Detective McFadden's response in the *Terry* situation can be explained by considering the **continuum of contacts,** the almost limitless variation of contacts between the public and the police. Figure 3.1 illustrates how police action must correlate to an individual's actions to be constitutionally justified—police action becomes increasingly intrusive on individual freedom as the reasons for thinking criminal activity is afoot build. Harr and Hess (2005, p.176) state: "While the intent of the Constitution is to prevent the government from intruding on people's lives when they have done nothing wrong, this freedom, as with all constitutional rights, is not absolute. When police have lawful reason to act, it is expected they will, and they have the right to do so. The U.S. Supreme Court has clearly stated that police have a responsibility, in fact a duty, to act to prevent crimes and apprehend criminals and has shown continued support for law enforcement."

## *The Stop*

The stop is the first point on the continuum of contacts where police have the constitutional authority to interfere with a person's freedom. The **stop** in a stop and frisk must be based on a reasonable suspicion that the person detained is about to be or is actually engaged in criminal activity. The most common reasons for a stop were discussed in Chapter 2.

The Supreme Court ruled in *Illinois v. Wardlow* (2000) that unexplained flight from the police is pertinent in developing reasonable suspicion necessary for a stop and frisk. In this case, officers patrolling an area of Chicago known for heavy narcotics trafficking observed Wardlow standing on the sidewalk holding an

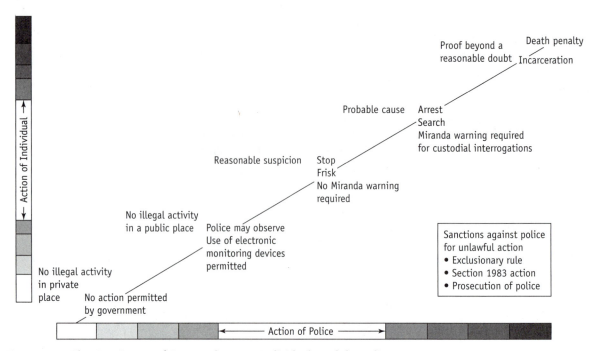

**Figure 3.1**   The Continuum of Contacts between Individuals and the Police

SOURCE: J. Scott Harr and Kären M. Hess. *Constitutional Law and the Criminal Justice System,* 3rd ed. Belmont, CA: Wadsworth Thomson Learning, 2005, p.176. Reprinted by permission.

opaque bag. Wardlow looked in the direction of the officers and immediately fled, causing the officers to give chase. When they caught him, one officer conducted a patdown for weapons based on his experience that guns were commonly present during drug deals. A hard object in the shape of a gun was felt in the opaque bag. When the officer opened the bag, he found a loaded handgun. Wardlow was arrested for a weapons violation.

The trial court held that the officer's actions were a lawful stop and frisk. Two appellate courts, however, reversed, and the case eventually came before the Supreme Court. Noting that the officers were bound by the *Terry* standard of reasonable suspicion, the Court ruled that while Wardlow's presence in a high-crime area was insufficient, in and of itself, to justify reasonable suspicion of criminal activity, it was a relevant fact the officers could consider. Wardlow's unexplained flight was another pertinent factor, as Justice Rehnquist rationalized: "Headlong flight—whenever it occurs—is the consummate act of evasion: it is not necessarily indicative of wrongdoing, but it is certainly suggestive of such." This consideration of multiple relevant factors continued the long-standing totality of circumstances test for officers in justifying reasonable suspicion.

In *Hiibel v. Sixth Judicial District Court* (2004) the Supreme Court ruled that police may properly request a person's name in a *Terry*-type stop. In this case, a Nevada rancher was stopped and asked for identification 11 times. He refused 11 times and was arrested and charged with the misdemeanor of refusing to identify himself. He was convicted and fined $250. The Nevada Supreme Court and the U.S. Supreme Court upheld his conviction (Greenhouse, 2004, p.A8).

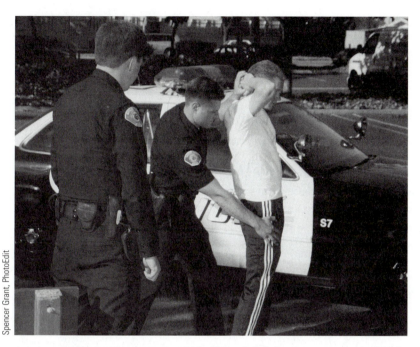

Spencer Grant, PhotoEdit

*A stop-and-frisk situation is one in which officers briefly detain a suspicious person for questioning, and if they reasonably suspect the person to be armed, they may pat down the person's outer clothing. The stop-and-frisk situation pictured here involves a known drug dealer.*

The stop may be all that occurs; it may lead to a patdown; or it may progress to an arrest, depending on the information received.

## The Frisk

The **frisk** or **patdown** in a stop and frisk is conducted for the officers' safety and also must be based on a reasonable suspicion that the person is armed. *Minnesota v. Dickerson* (1993) established that a frisk that goes beyond that authorized in *Terry* is invalid. The frisk cannot extend to a search for evidence. However, if during the frisk an officer feels what would reasonably be evidence, such as a packet of marijuana, the officer can retrieve the evidence under the "plain feel" doctrine discussed later in the chapter. If the stop turns into an arrest, a more thorough search can be conducted, also discussed later in the chapter.

In *United States v. Sokolow* (1989) the Court ruled: "In evaluating the validity of a stop such as this, we must consider the 'totality of the circumstances—the whole picture.' " In *Florida v. Bostick* (1991) the Supreme Court ruled that the location of a police-citizen encounter is only one factor to be considered in determining whether a seizure occurred: "In order to determine whether a particular encounter constitutes a seizure, a court must consider all the circumstances surrounding the encounter to determine whether the police conduct would have communicated to a reasonable person that the person was not free to decline the officers' requests or otherwise terminate the encounter." In an earlier case, *Alabama v. White* (1990), the Supreme Court ruled that reasonable suspicion is a less demanding standard than probable cause. Because the police made the stop on reasonable suspicion, it was legal.

Although a stop and frisk falls far short of an actual arrest and a full-blown search, it is *not* to be taken lightly, as the Court made clear in the *Terry* decision: "It is simply fantastic to urge that such a procedure [stop and frisk], performed in public by a police officer, while the citizen stands helpless, perhaps facing a wall with his hands raised, is a 'petty indignity.' " And, as noted, the stop might escalate into an arrest, depending on the specific circumstances.

## Legal Arrests

Making an arrest is one of the most important and extreme steps law enforcement officers take in their daily duties. The frequency of its occurrence, the nonserious nature of many offenses for which arrests are made, the poor character of many people subjected to it and their lower socioeconomic status must never lull officers into forgetting the lofty place arrest holds in our law. The police responsibility in arrests is clearly defined.

### Arrest Defined

The common meaning of *arrest* is simply "to stop." In a cardiac arrest, for example, the heart stops beating. Its meaning in the context of law enforcement is also generally known, that is, to seize and hold in jail or prison. The legal definition of *arrest* is somewhat narrower.

 An **arrest** is the official taking of a person to answer criminal charges. This involves at least temporarily depriving the person of liberty and may involve the use of force.

### When Arrests Can Be Made

The Fourth Amendment stresses the importance of having an arrest warrant when making an arrest (or conducting a search). The courts have, nonetheless, recognized other circumstances in which an arrest can legally be made.

 An arrest can legally be made:
- With an arrest warrant.
- Without an arrest warrant:
  - When any offense (felony or misdemeanor) is committed in an officer's presence.
  - When officers have probable cause to believe a person has committed a felony and no time is available to obtain a warrant.
  - For specifically enumerated misdemeanors, such as shoplifting in some jurisdictions.

**In the Presence**   "In the presence" does not refer to proximity, but rather to the officer's senses—that is, what the person making the arrest perceives through his or her senses. *Atwater v. City of Lago Vista* (2001) gave police the authority to arrest the driver of a vehicle for violations punishable only by a monetary fine, widening the authority of police in traffic-related stops (Walker and McKinnon, 2003, p.239). In this case, a police officer saw Atwater and her small children unrestrained in the front seat of her truck. The officer stopped the truck, confirmed that Atwater was in violation of the seat belt statute, handcuffed her and drove her to the police station. There she was made to surrender all her personal property, was photographed and placed in a jail cell for about an hour. Atwater sued the officer, the police chief and the city, claiming her Fourth Amendment right to be free from unreasonable seizures had been violated. In deciding the case, Justice Souter stated: "If an officer has probable cause to believe that an individual has committed even a very minor criminal offense in his presence, he may, without violating the Fourth Amendment, arrest the offender."

**Probable Cause**   Basic to lawful arrests is the concept of *probable cause*. **Probable cause** means it is more likely than not that a crime has been committed by the person whom a law enforcement officer seeks to arrest. An officer's *probable cause* to conduct an arrest depends on what the officer knew *before* taking action. An often-quoted definition of probable cause is from *Brinegar v. United States* (1949): "Probable cause exists where the facts and circumstances within the officers' knowledge, and of which they had reasonably trustworthy information, are sufficient in themselves to warrant a man of reasonable caution in the belief that an offense has been or is being committed."

In *Illinois v. Gates* (1983) the Supreme Court ruled that probable cause is a practical, nontechnical concept that should not be weighted in terms of "library analysis by scholars using tests." Rather, the court stated that the test for probable cause under the Fourth Amendment should be a "totality of the circumstances test" (Hendrie, 2002, p.24).

The law's ideal is for arrests to be made under an arrest warrant where a neutral magistrate stands between the person to be arrested and the arresting officer and calmly determines that probable cause exists for the arrest. But the law also recognizes that the practical necessities of keeping the public peace often demand that police officers make arrests without a warrant. Despite this admitted necessity, the courts will not relax the fundamental requirement of probable cause for arrest. Without this requirement, law-abiding citizens might be at the mercy of police officers' whims. The courts have made it clear that the requirements of arrest without a warrant are as stringent as those where warrants are obtained.

No precise formula for determining probable cause exists that can be applied to every case, just as no precise formula for determining reasonable suspicion for a stop exists. Both must be determined from the individual facts and circumstances of each case. Table 3.1 summarizes the basic differences between a stop and an arrest.

Probable cause can be either observational (what the officer sees) or informational (what the officer is told). **Observational probable cause** includes suspicious conduct, being high on drugs, associating with known criminals, the existence of a

**Table 3.1**   Stop versus Arrest

|  | *Stop* | *Arrest* |
|---|---|---|
| Justification | Reasonable suspicion | Probable cause |
| Warrant | None | Maybe |
| Officer's Intent | To investigate suspicious activity | To make a formal charge |
| Search | "Patdown" for weapons | Full search for weapons and evidence |
| Scope | Outer clothing | Area within suspect's immediate control |
| Record | Minimal—field notes | Fingerprints, photographs and booking |

SOURCE: J. Scott Harr and Kären M. Hess. *Constitutional Law and the Criminal Justice System,* 3rd ed. Belmont, CA: Wadsworth Thomson Learning, 2005, p.201. Reprinted by permission. All rights reserved.

criminal record, running away, presence in an unusual place or at an unusual time, presence in a high-crime area, presence at a crime scene, failure to answer questions, failure to provide identification, providing false information and physical evidence. The more factors present, the greater the probable cause. **Informational probable cause** consists of communications from official sources, such as wanted posters, statements from victims and information from informants.

## The Importance of Lawful Arrests

Because arrests deprive individuals of their freedom, it is crucial that law enforcement officers are skilled at making *lawful* arrests.

Skill in making arrests is critical because:
- Fundamental rights to personal liberty and privacy are involved.
- The law of arrest is strict and technical.
- Arrest is often the first step in criminal proceedings.
- Illegal arrests may taint crucial evidence of guilt.
- Police performance quality is judged by arrests.
- Arrests may lead to civil suits and criminal prosecution of officers.
- Arrests may endanger officers' lives.
- An arrest that may seem particularly brutal and inhumane can bring about immediate and violent community reaction, as in the 1965 Watts riot.

**Arrests Involve the Fundamental Rights to Personal Liberty and Privacy**   In every arrest, the right to personal liberty is involved. This is the fundamental right to come and go or stay when or where one may choose—the so-called right to freedom of locomotion. This right is embodied in the common law of England and is protected by our state constitutions and the U.S. Constitution.

Although the essential nature of the right to personal liberty cannot be denied, it is, nevertheless, not absolute. It is limited by the fact that people do not live in a vacuum, isolated from others. Their survival demands that they live and work in a society whose well-being is also vital. Therefore, when people commit offenses against society's law, their right to personal liberty can be restrained for the common good. In other words, they can be arrested, and their arrest is justified if made according to **due process of law,** that is, the fundamental principles of justice embodied in the Fifth and Fourteenth Amendments. The power of arrest is inherent in the right of society to defend itself. It has long been recognized that offenders may be arrested on criminal charges and be detained for trial even though they may ultimately be proved innocent of wrongdoing.

**The Law of Arrest Is Strict and Technical**   It severely limits the power of apprehension. It was formulated in England during the seventeenth and eighteenth centuries, when conditions were far different from those of today. The professional police officer was unknown, and the fate of those arrested for crimes was fraught with danger.

In that era, people arrested on serious charges were rarely granted bail. Prisoners awaited court action in jails overrun with disease and corruption and where the dreaded jail fever was common. They were kept in irons for the jailers' safety. If they escaped from the easily breached lockups, their wardens were held personally responsible. Because the jails were run for profit and fees were charged for almost every aspect of prison life, a poor person was in desperate straits.

This state of affairs led to the development of arrest laws greatly restricting the right to arrest. The courts, wanting a neutral judicial official to stand between the people being arrested and those doing the arresting, made it clear that an arrest was to be made only on the basis of a warrant issued by a magistrate. The courts also recognized the need to arrest without a warrant, but they spelled out the conditions under which such arrests could be made.

For example, they clearly distinguished between arresting without a warrant for a serious felony and arresting without a warrant for a minor misdemeanor. A warrantless arrest for a misdemeanor was limited to offenses committed in the arresting person's presence, whereas arrest for a felony without a warrant was not so limited. Obviously, there was less justification for arresting people without a court order for minor offenses and subjecting them to the attendant dangers than for doing so for serious offenses that affected the whole community.

The ironclad law of arrest has survived the conditions that brought it about. Modern statutes and court decisions have remedied some technicalities of former times, but the old common law still controls many aspects of arrest, despite the arrival of professional police officers and vastly improved detention facilities and procedures. Legislatures and judges have hesitated to change concepts and procedures where the rights to personal liberty and privacy loom so large.

**Arrest Is Often the First Step in Criminal Proceedings**    In the community's timeless attempt to keep the public peace through its criminal law, arrest by police officers is often the first step in criminal proceedings against wrongdoers. Despite the law's ideal that a court-issued warrant precedes an arrest, there is often no time in actual practice to apply for a warrant. The arrest must be made "now or never." Because police officers' duties often demand that they arrest people without the protection of a warrant, officers must know both the substantive and the procedural criminal law of their jurisdiction.

 **Substantive law** deals with content, or what behaviors are considered crimes. **Procedural law** deals with process, or how the law is applied.

Substantive law defines the elements of crimes and the punishments for each crime. For example, premeditation is an element in first-degree murder, and the punishment upon conviction might be life imprisonment or even death. Crimes and their punishments are decided by elected bodies such as Congress and state legislatures.

Procedural law governs how the law is enforced and is perhaps of greater importance to law enforcement officers than substantive law. Procedural law tends to be more controversial than substantive law. Although some laws are controversial (for example, those governing "victimless crimes" such as prostitution, gambling and use of marijuana), other laws, such as those allowing criminals to "get off" because of a technicality, are even more controversial. It seems to many people that the criminals have all the rights and that the rights of victims are ignored. This is in large part because the framers of our Constitution had, themselves, experienced life under rule of a tyrannical government and believed it was better to risk letting the guilty go free than to risk recreating a society where the innocent suffered injustice at the hand of an arbitrary, autocratic government.

Laws concerning crimes and arrest are complicated, and officers are allowed no margin of error in deciding whether the conduct, when not committed in the officers' presence, constitutes a felony and thus justifies arrest without a warrant. At one time, determining whether an offense was a felony or a misdemeanor was not difficult. The inherent seriousness or nonseriousness of the offense served as the guide. But this is no longer true. Legislatures have created felonies that are not inherently serious and misdemeanors that are. Officers must know the law.

The law will justify officers' actions if they proceed on the basis of probable cause or reasonable grounds. Yet, when they arrest without a warrant, they are responsible for exercising good judgment in hectic, fluid situations where mistakes are bound to occur.

**Illegal Arrests May Taint Crucial Evidence of Guilt**   Although illegal arrests will not immunize defendants against criminal prosecution, they may lead to the inadmissibility of crucial evidence of guilt. Physical evidence obtained by search and seizure incident to an illegal arrest, such as recovered stolen property or burglary tools, will be considered tainted and therefore suppressed under the Exclusionary Rule.

 The **Exclusionary Rule** established that the courts cannot accept evidence obtained in illegal searches and seizures, regardless of how relevant the evidence is to the case (*Weeks v. United States,* 1914).

*Weeks v. United States* applied only to federal cases. Nearly a half century later, *Mapp v. Ohio* (1961) established that the Exclusionary Rule applies to all state criminal proceedings under the due process clause of the Fourteenth Amendment. Verbal evidence, such as incriminating statements obtained in the immediate aftermath of an illegal arrest, may also be barred from the jury's consideration.

If officers are not aware that they are violating someone's constitutional rights, they are said to be acting in **good faith,** and the Exclusionary Rule may not apply. Harr and Hess (p.186) explain: "The good faith exception often comes into play when the government is executing arrest or search warrants. If such warrants are later found to be invalid, . . . the evidence obtained while executing the warrants is still admissible because the officers were acting in 'good faith.'"

*Massachusetts v. Sheppard* (1984) established that if police were relying on a search warrant that had been approved by a magistrate but later declared invalid, any evidence seized during that search would be admissible at trial. In a similar case, *United States v. Leon* (1984), the Court held: "Once the warrant issues, there is literally nothing more the policeman can do in seeking to comply with the law. Penalizing the officer for the magistrate's error, rather than his own, cannot logically contribute to the deterrence of Fourth Amendment violations."

In addition, *Murray v. United States* (1988) established that evidence initially seen by police during an illegal search could be admissible if later recovered under a valid warrant. Yet another ruling dealing with the Exclusionary Rule is *Arizona v. Evans* (1995), where the Supreme Court held that the Exclusionary Rule does not require suppression of evidence gained during arrests made on the basis of computer errors by clerical court employees. The exclusion was not required because court personnel were responsible for the computer's inaccurate records.

**The Quality of Police Performance Is Judged by Arrests**   The community's judgment of the quality of its police department frequently turns on the actions of officers in the more visible, dramatic areas of responsibility, such as apprehending felons. The public pays much less attention to officers' performance in the less colorful aspects of police work, even though extensive time and effort are necessarily required, for example, directing traffic.

**Arrests May Result in Civil Suits or Criminal Prosecutions**   An arrest may lead to a civil suit in state court against the officers for false arrest. It also may lead to a civil suit for deprivation of civil rights in federal court under an old post–Civil War federal statute, now codified as 42 U.S.C. § 1983. The hazard of lawsuits against police officers is discussed in detail in Chapter 14.

An arrest also may lead to a criminal prosecution against the officers for assault and battery on the grounds that an inordinate amount of force was used or to a criminal charge in federal court for deprivation of civil rights. The courts are conscious of the problems of law enforcement officers in this phase of their duty. For example, in the federal case of *Kozlowski v. Ferrara* (1954) the judge stated:

> The courts should bend every effort to insure the fearless and effective administration of the law by protecting their enforcement officers from vindictive and retaliatory damage suits. . . . Otherwise, as Judge L. Hand cautioned . . . to submit officials "to the burden of a trial and to the inevitable danger of its outcome, would dampen the ardor of all but the most resolute, or the most irresponsible, in the unflinching discharge of their duties."

**Arrest Is Extremely Dangerous and Sometimes Life Threatening for Police Officers**   Arrests put police officers in jeopardy every time they take this drastic step. The peril exists not only with hardened criminals where possible violence is an obvious, ever-present concern, but also with people who do not have criminal records. Ordinary people often lose all sense of emotional and mental balance when arrested. They can react to their loss of freedom and the danger to their reputation in unexpected ways and may resist fiercely rather than submit to the command of the apprehending officers.

## Procedures for Making Legal Arrests

The actual arrest is usually made by an officer stating to a person, "You are under arrest for . . . ." The person being arrested should be told clearly—not in police jargon or legalese—the reason for the arrest. Officers should always be on guard when making arrests. As noted, people can react violently to being arrested, even individuals who appear to be meek and incapable of violence.

Depending on the circumstances, the person may first be handcuffed for the officer's safety. The arrested person should be searched for weapons and destructible evidence, as discussed later in this chapter. If the arrested person is to be questioned, the *Miranda* warning must be given before any questions are asked.

In a typical arrest situation officers should:
- Announce the arrest and the reason for it.
- Handcuff the person if warranted.
- Search the arrested person for weapons and evidence.
- Give the *Miranda* warning if questions are to be asked.

## *De Facto Arrests*

A **de facto arrest** is a detention without probable cause that is factually indistinguishable from an arrest. In *Kaupp v. Texas* (2003) the Supreme Court held that without probable cause for arrest it is unlawful for law enforcement to transport a suspect against his will to the station for questioning. As Rutledge (2003a, p.77) puts it: "If police take someone from one location and transport him or her involuntarily to a police facility for investigation, this will be considered a de facto arrest. Without probable cause, that arrest will be unlawful, with predictable consequences for both evidence suppression and civil liability."

## The Use of Force in Making an Arrest

If the person being arrested offers no resistance, *no* force should be used in making the arrest.

 Guidelines for use of force when making an arrest:
- No resistance—use no force.
- Resistance—use only as much force as necessary to overcome resistance.
- Threat to officer's life—use deadly force.

The International Association of Chiefs of Police (IACP) defines *force* as "that amount of effort required by police to compel compliance from an unwilling subject" (*Police Use of Force in America 2001*, n.d., p.1). According to Williams (2003, p.71): "**Compliance** is, simply, a complete lack of physical resistance. It is a condition in which the suspect willingly, though perhaps not enthusiastically, moves in agreement with the conditions and lawful orders of officers."

*Police Use of Force in America 2001* (pp.i–ii) reports: "Police used force at a rate of 3.61 times per 10,000 calls for service. This translates to a rate of use of force of 0.0361 percent. Expressed another way, police did not use force 98.8639 percent of the time. . . . Physical force was the most common force used by officers, followed by chemical force and then impact." This document (p.iii) reports: "Arrests were the most frequent circumstance of use of force [39 percent]. . . . The next largest category was disturbance with 21 percent of use-of-force incidents and traffic stops with 14 percent." Figure 3.2 summarizes the circumstances in which officers used force. The IACP report (p.iv) also notes that 46 percent of all use-of-force incidents occurred where the subject was intoxicated or under the influence of drugs.

The Supreme Court acknowledged in *Graham v. Connor* (1989), the landmark case concerning police use of force:

> The reasonableness of a particular use of force must be judged from the perspective of a reasonable officer on the scene, rather than with the 20/20 vision of hindsight.
>
> The calculus of reasonableness must embody allowance for the fact that police officers are often forced to make split-second judgments—in circumstances that are tense, uncertain, and rapidly evolving—about the amount of force that is necessary in a particular situation.

Petrowski (2002a, p.26) explains: "An unreasonable use of force is one that no objectively reasonable law enforcement agent would have used." Gundy (2003, p.63) contends: "The objective reasonableness test is basically a balancing

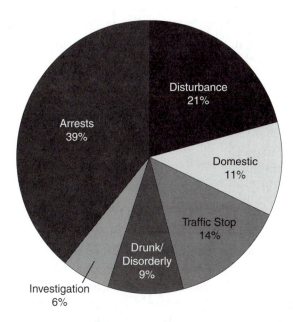

**Figure 3.2**    Percent Officer Use of Force by Circumstance of Encounter (1999–2000)

SOURCE: *Police Use of Force in America 2001*. Alexandria, VA: International Association of Chiefs of Police, no date, p.iii.

test that weighs the person's right to privacy and physical integrity against the government's legitimate interests in taking action against the person. Put another way, the more heinous the person's activities or threat level, the more force that an officer may justifiably use."

 *Graham* established a three-prong test for use of force: (1) the severity of the crime, (2) whether the suspect poses an immediate threat to the safety of law enforcement officers or others and (3) whether the suspect is actively resisting arrest or attempting to evade arrest by flight.

## Gender Differences in Use of Force

Several studies have examined whether a gender difference exists in police use of force, with the general consensus being: "Although men and women are equally likely to use force in their routine duties as law enforcement officers, women are less likely to engage in excessive force. Rather, female officers tend to emphasize communication and de-escalation of potentially violent situations, a style that is more in line with community policing ideals" (Lonsway, 2001, p.114).

## The Use of Force Model

Nowicki (2001c, p.35) asserts police use of force is more an art than a science because there are no use-of-force absolutes:

> Use of force applications must be broad enough to allow officers to have reasonable options to use in the field. Yet these options must be specific enough to provide parameters for officers to work within. . . . The "Use of Force Model" currently in use by the Federal Law Enforcement Training Center (FLETC) provides law enforcement officers with various options they may use as "Enforcement Electives."

As Nowicki (2001c, p.35) explains: "The FLETC Model categorizes the reasonable officer's perception to how a subject will or will not submit to arrest in one of five levels."

- Compliant Level—subject is cooperative and complies with the officer's commands.
- Resistive (Passive) Level—subject directs no physical energy to the arrest, yet does not follow the officer's commands.
- Resistive (Active) Level—subject directs energy and physical strength to resisting arrest but not directly at the officer. For example, a subject in a vehicle is told she is being arrested for DWI, and she then grabs hold of the steering wheel and refuses to let go. Compliance techniques officers may use include joint manipulation or restraints, leverage techniques, pressure points or even an OC [Oleoresin Capsicum or pepper] spray. Officers may also warn the subject prior to executing any of these techniques.
- Assaultive (Bodily Harm) Level—a direct, physical attack on the officer. Use-of-force options include striking with hands, fists, elbows and knees; kicking; baton strikes; and forcefully directing the subject to the ground.
- Assaultive (Serious Bodily Harm or Death) Level—an attack where officers reasonably believe that themselves or others would be subject to serious bodily injury or death. The appropriate officer response is deadly force.

### Use-of-Force Continuums

Aveni (2003, p.74) contends: "Force continuums have been evolving in the law enforcement community for more than three decades. These devices were, and remain for the most part, 'conceptualized tools.'" Figure 3.3 presents a use-of-force continuum that depicts the escalation from no force to extraordinary force.

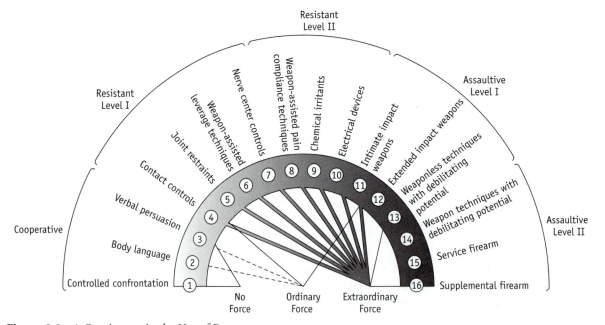

**Figure 3.3** A Continuum in the Use of Force

SOURCE: Adapted from Greg Connor. "Use of Force Continuum: Phase II." *Law and Order,* March 1991, p.30. Used with permission of *Law and Order* magazine.

Such force continuums are not without their critics. Aveni (p.75), for example, says: "Since little about policing is linear, non-linear force continuums would seem to be a better fit." Williams (2002, p.14) also criticizes such continuums: "Continuums require officers to escalate *progressively* from one level to another until they have control of the suspect. Then, once the suspect decreases resistance, officers must de-escalate their actions to an appropriate level of force. Rather than reflecting the real world of confusion, fear and sometimes an overwhelming sense of urgency that officers face in any violent confrontation with offenders, force continuums often represent an unrealistic, almost wishful ideal." More importantly, as Petrowski (2002b, p.24) notes: "Force continua perpetuate hesitation and exacerbate the natural reluctance of officers to apply significant force even when faced with a serious threat." He (pp.29–30) stresses: "Hesitation in using force is natural and inevitable. Policies and training must focus on overcoming hesitation, not encouraging it. There never can be bright-line rules. Every use-of-force situation is unique. . . . Officers must be trained to respond to the *threat* of violence and not to the *actual* violence itself. . . . Use-of-force training based on threat assessment will result in an escalating approach when it is appropriate and a timely response when it is not."

## Using Forcible Entry to Arrest

The right of law enforcement officers to use force to enter a building to make an arrest is almost 400 years old: "In all cases where the King is a party, the Sheriff, if the doors be not open, may break the party's house, either to arrest him, or do other execution of the King's process, if otherwise he cannot enter. But before he breaks it, he ought to signify the cause of his coming and to make request to open the doors" (*Semayne's Case*, 5 Coke, 918 [1603]).

The use of forcible entry to arrest was firmly established early on in common law, even though a fundamental liberty of people includes protecting their homes. The home as a sanctuary and place of refuge is embodied in the Fourth Amendment to the Constitution and in state constitutions and protects homes against unjustified invasion. Even under common law, officers' authority to break the doors of a house to arrest was eventually drastically limited. It had to be shown that officers had reasonable cause to break and enter to arrest. They had to justify such extreme and drastic actions.

**The Knock and Announce Rule**   As a general rule, before crossing the threshold of a house in such emergency cases, officers must identify themselves, make known their purpose, demand admittance and be refused. This requirement frequently is embodied in statutes. Devanney and Devanney (2003a, p.72) explain: "Modern courts have stated three general reasons for the rule, based on the Fourth Amendment's guarantee against unreasonable searches and seizures. First is the protection of the right to privacy of citizens. Second is the reduction of the risk of possible violence to both police and household occupants. Third is the prevention of unnecessary destruction of private property." Such notice is consistent with the presumption of innocence and lessens the danger arising from ambiguous conduct, bad information, mistaken identity and other practical hazards of everyday police work. It makes clear to those within a dwelling what the object of the breaking is and prevents them from justifiably considering it an aggression to be resisted.

Guidance on how long officers must wait after the announcement and using force to enter is provided in *United States v. Banks* (2003). Says Makholm (2004, p.64): "On December 2, 2003, the United States Supreme Court delivered a Christmas present to law enforcement officers throughout the U.S. via the Court's ruling in the case of *United States v. Banks.*" In this case, the Court ruled that 15 to 20 seconds between an officer's knock and announcement of a search warrant and actual forced entry was "reasonable," overturning a lower court ruling. The Court said: "The issue comes down to whether it was reasonable to suspect imminent loss of evidence after the 15 to 20 seconds the officers waited prior to forcing their way. . . . We think that after 15 or 20 seconds without a response, police could fairly suspect that cocaine would be gone if they were reticent any longer." In its unanimous ruling the Court announced it would continue to take a case-by-case "totality of the circumstances" approach to deciding the constitutionality of police searches.

Commenting on the unanimous decision, a police captain said: "I would have been shocked if it went the other way. The Court seems to appreciate the difficult challenges that law enforcement faces. This is a very common sense decision that promotes public safety by affirming a reasonable procedure the police use to fight crime" (Hopper, 2004, p.22).

Cerullo and Means (2004, p.10) caution: "After *Banks,* an officer executing a search warrant must still balance the knock, announce and wait requirements against both officer safety and evidence destruction concerns, and the entry must still conform to a reasonableness standard." Rutledge (2004b, p.75) suggests: "An audio or video recording of knock-notice announcements and entry provides good evidence of your compliance with knock notice, as well as the exact amount of time you waited before forcing entry. During the wait, keep repeating the knock and announcement over and over until someone responds, or until you go in."

**Level of Destruction**   If forcible entry is justified, the breaking must be done with the least amount of destruction. Only the slightest force is necessary to constitute a breaking. For example, pushing open an unlocked yet closed door constitutes forcible entry. Ramirez (2002, p.58) points out: "The courts are very cognizant of holding law enforcement officers accountable for excessive destruction of property." In *United States v. Ramirez* (1998) the Supreme Court held: "Excessive or unnecessary destruction of property in the course of a search will violate the Fourth Amendment, even though the entry itself is lawful and the fruits of the search are not subject to suppression."

## The Use of Handcuffs in Making an Arrest

"Used by [officers] for more than 200 years, handcuffs enable [officers] to restrict a prisoner's mobility, offering some degree of safety" (Meissner, 2002, p.30). Nowicki (2002a, p.14) suggests: "Officers need a handcuffing policy that addresses handcuffing for all arrestees, with adaptations for special occasions, such as for people with physical disabilities." Many law enforcement agencies have a policy stating: "In the interest of officer safety, all persons arrested and transported shall be handcuffed." This policy has been called the **mere handcuff rule.** But such a rule, making mandatory the application of a form of force in all arrests, conflicts with the Fourth Amendment's "objective reasonableness" standard for use of force.

Robert Brennen, PhotoEdit

*While handcuffing in some instances is vital to protecting an officer's life, to automatically handcuff every suspect arrested may leave the officer and the department open to a charge of objectively unreasonable handcuffing and a lawsuit.*

> Whether an arrested person should automatically be handcuffed while being transported is controversial. Officer discretion may be advisable.

While handcuffing in some instances is vital to protecting an officer's life, to automatically handcuff every suspect arrested may leave the officer and the department open to a lawsuit charging objectively unreasonable handcuffing.

Discretion might be used with the very young, the very old and the physically disabled, always remembering, however, that these individuals can still pose a threat to officers' safety. In some scenarios, officers must use "creative handcuffing" to address an individual's specific physical needs and limitations while protecting themselves.

In some instances officers go beyond handcuffs and use leg restraints or may even "hog-tie" extremely violent, unmanageable suspects. Be aware, however, this can pose an extreme hazard to the bound subject. **Positional asphyxia** may result if a person's body position interferes with breathing, as when a subject is in maximum restraints and placed prone on the ground or the back seat of the patrol car. Especially at risk of positional asphyxia are obese people whose weight can be displaced to the diaphragm, cutting off breathing; suspects who are acutely intoxicated from alcohol or drugs and, because of their state, may not realize they are suffocating; and suspects who have struggled violently before being restrained, making them susceptible to respiratory muscle fatigue.

## Excessive Force

As officers carry out their daily duties, moving up and down the continuum of contacts and making countless, on-the-spot decisions regarding how much force to use, one hazard is ever-present—the possibility of going a fraction beyond the amount of force necessary to achieve a legitimate police objective. Stepping over that invisible line puts officers knee-deep into the area known as *excessive force.* The IACP (*Police Use of Force* . . ., p.1) defines *excessive force* as "the application of an amount and/or frequency of force greater than that required to compel compliance from a willing or unwilling subject." As Flosi (2003, p.142) puts it: "Excessive force begins when the suspect's resistance ends."

Nowicki (2001a, p.29) contends: "Most officers would rather face a criminal with a firearm than an excessive force lawsuit." Of the hundreds of thousands of police-citizen contacts that occur every day, the only ones that seem to receive media attention are those involving charges of excessive force, estimated to be less than 0.5 percent of all calls for service. Despite their relative infrequency, police misconduct, brutality and excessive use of force do exist and are real problems for law enforcement:

> In the biggest settlement of a single police brutality claim in New York history, the city and the police union have tentatively agreed to pay $9 million to a Haitian immigrant tortured in a stationhouse bathroom. . . .
>
> [Abner] Louima was arrested in a brawl outside a Brooklyn nightclub in 1997 and was taken to the 70th Precinct stationhouse.
>
> Officer Justin Volpe—mistakenly believing Louima had punched him—sought revenge by sodomizing Louima with a broomstick.
>
> Volpe pleaded guilty to federal charges and is serving 30 years in prison. A jury found officer Charles Schwarz guilty of pinning Louima down during the assault; he and four other officers were convicted of lying about it ("NY Police, Louima . . .," 2001, p.A4). In this case, the officer's actions were clearly excessive. Being punched by a subject, even if it had happened, does not warrant a response of sodomy. Furthermore, this particular use of force was undoubtedly meant to cause the subject great physical pain and humiliation, neither of which is a legitimate police objective (Roane, 2001, p.28).

## The Use of Nonlethal or Less-Lethal Weapons in Making Arrests

"Less lethal is a degree or application of force used to control a situation. It is not designed to be fatal" (Bertomen, 2003, p.64).

 Less-lethal weapons for use with violent, combative suspects include tear gas and other chemical irritant sprays, impact weapons, the taser gun, foams, nets and K-9s.

Some of the most common nonlethal weapons are chemical irritant sprays, such as tear gas and oleoresin capsicum (OC), more commonly called pepper spray. According to Dallett (2004, p.10): "It is well documented that 97 percent of law enforcement officers carry some form of ASR [aerosol subject restraint]." Noting OC spray's effectiveness in 80–85 percent of the scenarios in which it is used, Nowicki (2001b, p.28) states: "Compared to other use of force options, OC sprays have reduced injuries to subjects and officers, reduced the number of excessive force complaints, and have cut down on workman's compensation claims." OC can be delivered in a cone-shaped spray, a fog, a directed stream, a splatter stream or a foam. Klugiewicz and Young (2003, p.66) contend: "The effectiveness of OC in a police operation is directly proportional to the competency of the officer using it."

Chemical irritants, in addition to being used in aerosol spray form, can be placed inside pellets and fired from a rifle, similar to paintballs. The PepperBall System, used by many police departments across the country, combines kinetic impact technology with OC pepper powder irritant. These devices are effective to about 30 feet but can also be deployed at point-blank range without causing great bodily harm: "The pain compliance in addition to the oleoresin capsicum has a synergistic effect in the apprehension of uncooperative or violent suspects. It's real hard to rub that "owie" on your chest or arm while it turns into a big red welt, while every mucus membrane you own feels like it has someone working it over with a blowtorch" (Douglas, 2001, p.27).

As with all other impact or extended impact systems, certain target areas are off limits. For example, officers are not allowed to hit in the neck or head with a PR-24, or straight stick, and the same applies for the PepperBalls.

Most conventional chemical agents work as either lachrymators, causing intense eye irritation and tearing, or respiratory irritants, which make it difficult to breathe. Other less-lethal devices that use directed kinetic energy in projectile form are impact weapons such as bean-bag rounds and rubber bullets.

Ijames (2001, p.17) notes: "The twelve-gauge pump shotgun and 'bean-bag' round is the most common less-lethal system on the streets of America today." The new DefTec 23 DS 12-gauge bean bag is a sock-style projectile filled with number nine birdshot. Four tails of fabric attached to the bean bag "head" allow for "drag stabilization," giving this projectile greater accuracy and range than flat or rolled bean bags. The 23 DS sock weighs only 1.4 ounces, has a velocity of 280 fps and a maximum effective range of 80 feet (Sanow, 2001, p.40). While death and serious injury rarely result from use of these less-lethal impact projectiles, death has occurred, often caused by improper shot placement. Certain areas of the body are very vulnerable to impact injury, whereas others are relatively resistant.

A less-lethal device that removes the need for accurate shot placement on a limited target area is the taser. An acronym for Thomas A. Swift Electric Rifle, the taser is a conducted energy weapon that fires a cartridge with two small probes that stay connected to the weapon by high-voltage, insulated wire. Nielsen (2001, p.57) explains: "When the probes contact the target, they transmit very short duration, high energy, electrical pulses along the wires to overwhelm the sensory nervous system, stunning the target." While prior generations of taser stun technology have had limited success in stopping extremely motivated subjects or those under the influence of drugs or alcohol, the advanced taser is able to incapacitate even the most focused combatants: "Over 800 human volunteers and suspects in the field have been subjected to the advanced taser. In all cases, there has been virtual 100% instant incapacitation" (Nielsen, p.61). Kester (2002, p.13) says: "Without a doubt the taser is becoming an extremely popular weapon, and is possibly the most effective less-lethal weapon currently on the market."

Nielsen (2004, p.164) describes the fourth generation of taser, the Taser X26, which is 60 percent smaller and lighter than the third generation. Nielsen suggests: "The Taser reduces injury to both suspects and officers, enhancing safety and reducing liability." He gives as an example the Orange County (Florida) Sheriff's Office who says officer injuries are down 80 percent since the taser was adopted, and lethal force use is down 78 percent.

Osborne (2004) reports that in Cincinnati during the first nine months of 2004 officers were assaulted 15 times. That compares to 55 incidents during the same period in 2003, a 73 percent drop since tasers came into use in their department. He also suggests the use of tasers has caused a major decrease in uses of other types of force, particularly chemical irritant spray and physical force. He notes that using physical force or chemical irritant spray on suspects can leave lasting injuries or effects while use of tasers leaves no effects after their five second electrical discharge is done.

Taylor (2004) notes that Taser International is developing an audio-video recording capability built into its taser. The audio-video capability, called a Video-Digital Power Magazine, will be built into the power supply module for the Taser X26 stun gun. It will be able to capture vital information before, during and after deployment of nonlethal force. The taser already contains tracking chips that record the time when the weapon was fired.

The taser is not without critics. Taylor notes that at least 50 people have reportedly died after having been shocked by the devices. However, Ederheimer and Cheney (2004, p.5) report that Taser International claims: "In over 30,000 actual field uses . . . there has never been a documented death . . . directly attributed to the Taser device."

Other less-lethal alternatives include a "sticky foam" that hardens like taffy and can effectively immobilize a person. Another alternative is an aqueous (water-based) foam similar to that used by firefighters that incapacitates suspects by filling the space so the person cannot see or hear, although they can still breathe. Air bags in the rear seat of squad cars offer a third option to immobilize combative suspects.

A "tool" long used by law enforcement that is now gaining acceptance as an alternative means of force is the K-9. Smith (2004, p.18) notes: "The courts have said the use of police service dogs can enhance the safety of officers, bystanders and the suspect. Police service dogs can also help prevent officers from having to resort to deadly force. I would argue that police service dogs should also be considered as less lethal." According to Devanney and Devanney (2003b, p.12): "Several federal courts . . . have already held that the use of properly trained police dogs does not constitute deadly force." Green (2004, p.39) notes: "An excellent source of K-9-related case law can be found on the Web site of Terry Fleck, an expert in the field of canine legalities (www.k9fleck.org)."

## The Use of Deadly Force in Making Arrests

Using deadly force is perhaps the hardest decision a law enforcement officer faces. The use of such force is prescribed by state and federal statutes and basically requires that deadly force be used only in self-defense or in defense of another. Until 1985, it was legal in many states for officers to use deadly force to prevent a felon from escaping. This practice, however, terminated following *Tennessee v. Garner* (1985), when the Supreme Court ruled that law enforcement officers cannot shoot "fleeing felons" unless they present an "imminent danger to life": "The use of deadly force to prevent the escape of all felony suspects, whatever the circumstances, is constitutionally unreasonable. It is not better that all felony suspects die than that they escape. Where the suspect poses no immediate threat to others, the harm resulting from failing to apprehend him does not justify the use of deadly force to do so."

Nowicki (2003, p.26) stresses: "When a deadly force situation presents itself, the officer must often act quickly and decisively. Any uncertainty in making that decision can cost the life of an innocent person or the life of the officer." Figure 3.4 illustrates the complexity of most lethal force events.

A nonprofit Force Science™ Research Center opened at Minnesota State University in Mankato in 2004. According to Remsberg (2004, p.10), this center, headed by Lewinski, "is dedicated to revealing the hidden truths about human dynamics so officers can be better trained, make better decisions and, ultimately, keep themselves and their communities safer." Research conducted at the center is attempting to define the limits of human performance and the parameters of danger. In answer to questions posed by Remsberg, Lewinski provided the following insights into "extreme encounters":

> [Research at the center showed that] males, especially, tended to use their hands and arms to assist them in turning. This often brought their gun up and forward, and could create the allusion that they were consciously pointing the gun at the officer. Actually this wasn't true because the suspect would continue rotating away from the officer to flee. But based on the split-second perception of threat, the officer could decide to shoot in self-defence . . . and by the time the bullet arrived, the suspect would be further turned and end up shot in the side or back. To someone who didn't understand the dynamics involved, it would look like the deliberate, illegal "execution" of a fleeing, nonthreatening subject. This would be disastrous for the officer. The bottom line: If an officer

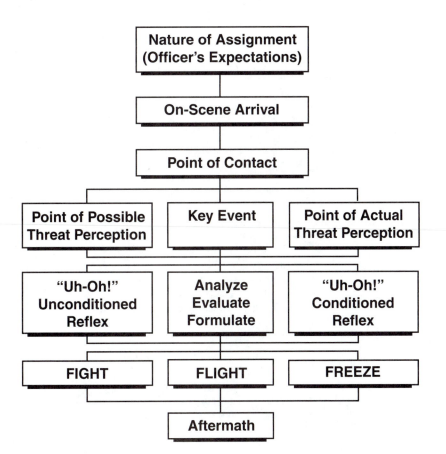

**Figure 3.4** Anatomy of a Lethal Force Event

SOURCE: Thomas J. Aveni. "The Force Continuum Conundrum." *Law and Order,* December 2003, p.75. Reprinted by permission.

dealing with a determined, armed suspect waits to shoot until he sees a gun pointed at him, it's too late (p.11).

In addition to keeping officers safer, a number of officers who have been charged criminally or sued civilly have been exonerated because of what we could reconstruct based on force science (p.12).

We've been able to document that when the average officer is shooting rapidly (as he would be in the adrenalized stress of defending his life), it takes him an average of two additional seconds to process the information and stop pulling the trigger once he perceives the threat has ended (p.13). . . .

Don't dismiss safety fundamentals. For instance, if you can't see a suspect's hands on a vehicle stop, you're casting your fate to the wind if you approach. Our studies have proved that wherever a suspect may have his hands hidden from sight in a car, he can reach a gun and shoot at you faster than you can react—even with your gun on target and your finger on the trigger (p.13).

## The Duty to Warn

If a felon is fleeing and an officer believes that felon is a significant threat to the officer or others, the officer should shout a loud warning, "Stop or I'll shoot!" before firing. The warning should be loud enough that in addition to the fleeing felon, *everyone* who might be a witness to both the fleeing and the use of deadly force will hear the warning. Lesh (2003, p.17) suggests that officers should provide a warning before using less-lethal devices as well. For example, "Drop the weapon or I'll release the dog." Table 3.2 summarizes when a warning is preferred or required in using specific types of force.

**Table 3.2**   Type of Force and Whether a Warning Is Required or Preferred

| *Type of Force* | *Is a Warning Required?* | *Is a Warning Preferred?* |
|---|---|---|
| Use of Deadly Force | Yes, if feasible, in all states. | A warning is required. |
| Use of less lethal shotguns and similar less-lethal device | A warning should be provided, if feasible, by officers in Alaska, Arizona, California, Guam, Hawaii, Idaho, Montana, Nevada, Oregon, Washington and the Northern Mariana Islands. | Yes, if feasible, in all states. Note that many manufacturers of less-lethal equipment now "require" that a warning be given before using their equipment against a suspect. |
| Batons | Probably not, unless the baton is being used in such a way as to be considered deadly force (such as with a blow to the head). | Yes, if feasible, in all states. |
| Canine deployment | Probably yes, at least in Alaska, Arizona, California, Guam, Hawaii, Idaho, Montana, Nevada, Oregon, Washington and the Northern Mariana Islands. | Yes, if feasible, in all states. |
| Oleoresin Capsicum | Probably not. | Yes, especially in those situations where the substance is used against a number of individuals such as during unlawful "protests." |

SOURCE: David N. Lesh. "The Duty to Warn." *The Law Enforcement Trainer*, March/April 2003, p.18. Reprinted by permission.

### Reports on Use of Force

Rutledge (2004a, p.59) urges: "The key to avoiding a finding of excessive force is being able to justify the kind and amount of force used. The accuracy and completeness of the force report are extremely important, not only for purposes of internal investigations, but also for criminal and civil liability and public relations purposes." In addition, Nowicki (2002b, p.26) cautions that officers need to be fluent in the language of force. He suggests, for example: "Agencies that use a Use of Force Report may want to consider changing the name of that document to Subject Resistance Report or Level of Resistance Report. Since all force that an officer uses is reactive, isn't the resistance of the subject more at issue than the force used by the officer?"

### Use of Force and Community Policing

An integral part of the community policing philosophy is that the police must become a part of the community rather than stand apart from it. This places police in a somewhat difficult position as they try to become a part of the very entity over which they must exercise power and authority. Facing the potential dilemma of having to use force against the very citizens with whom they are seeking to form partnerships, this arrangement also presents a paradox—the ability of police to use force to secure a peaceful community.

 Use of force can be a serious obstacle to the community policing philosophy.

Adding to this challenge is the seemingly disproportionate use of force against minorities and those of lower socioeconomic status. Miller and Hess (2005, p.42) observe:

> Because police-enforcement efforts focus on common criminals, who are frequently poor, the most use of force by the police will be directed against this part of the population.
>
> Citizens in white suburban areas . . . may never see a police officer use force. The most negative experience they are likely to have with a police officer is receiving a traffic ticket.
>
> When people from these widely separated communities talk about the police, it seems as though they are speaking of entirely different entities. On the one hand, police may be referred to as brutal, racist aggressors whereas others describe them as professional, helpful, efficient protectors.

The public must be educated about the legitimate use of force required to maintain peaceful neighborhoods. They might also have input into policies on the use of force as well as incidents involving alleged excessive use of force.

## Legal Searches

The Fourth and Fifth Amendments also restrict police officers in when they can search and for what. As with an arrest, a search usually should be conducted with a *warrant*. Procedures for obtaining and executing search warrants vary by locality, but generally search warrants may be issued if:

- The property was stolen or embezzled.
- Possession of the property is a crime.

- The property is in the possession of someone who intends to use it to commit a crime.
- The property was used in committing a crime.
- The items tend to show that a crime was committed or that a specific person committed the crime.

Three principal justifications have been established by the courts for the right to search.

A search may be legally conducted if:
- A search warrant has been issued.
- Consent is given.
- It is incidental to a lawful arrest.

## Search Warrants

Ideally, all searches would be conducted with a search warrant. To obtain a search warrant, officers appear before a magistrate and explain why they believe evidence might be found at a certain location (their probable cause). If the magistrate believes that probable cause exists, he or she will issue a search warrant.

*Wilson v. Arkansas* (1995) held that the "knock and announce" requirements are part of the reasonableness inquiry and that officers must knock and announce *before* they enter. As with an arrest warrant, officers seeking to search premises under the authority of a search warrant can break down a door to gain admittance if they are denied entrance. Even with a search warrant, however, the search must be limited.

A search conducted under the authority of a search warrant must be limited to the area specified in the warrant and for the items described in the warrant.

## Exceptions to the Search Warrant Requirement

Ten exceptions to the search warrant requirement are (1) execution of an arrest warrant, (2) frisks, (3) incident to arrest, (4) automobiles, (5) consent, (6) plain view/feel, (7) abandoned property, (8) open fields, (9) inventory and (10) exigent circumstances.

**Arrest Warrant Execution**   Officers can search for a suspect in the suspect's home to execute an arrest warrant if they have probable cause to believe the suspect is there. This exception applies *only* to the suspect's home. They cannot conduct a search of any other location even though they have the arrest warrant. For other locations, a search warrant is required. *Maryland v. Buie* (1990) established that officers may make a limited protective sweep of a home during an arrest if the circumstances warrant.

**Frisks**   As previously discussed, *Terry v. Ohio* established that officers can conduct a patdown of an individual they have stopped if they believe the person is armed and dangerous. This is a protective search for weapons only.

**Search Incident to Arrest**   *Chimel v. California* (1969) established that officers can search a person they have arrested for weapons and for evidence, but the search must be limited to the area within the arrested person's immediate control, sometimes referred to as the person's "wing span." It is entirely reasonable for the arresting officer to search for and seize any evidence on the arrestee's person to prevent its concealment or destruction and the area from within which the arrestee might gain possession of a weapon or destructible evidence.

*Maryland State Police make a random vehicle check at the entrance ramp to the Baltimore Washington International Airport. Earlier in the day, police were stopping all vehicles entering the terminal area as part of a security check.*

The area within a person's control includes women's purses, chairs suspects are sitting on at the time of arrest and the entire interior of an automobile if the person is in a car at the time of the arrest. (The trunk is not included in this exception.) *New York v. Belton* (1981) decided that an automobile's interior could be searched after a passenger was arrested.

**Automobile Exception**    *Carroll v. United States* (1925) established that because automobiles are mobile, officers may search them without a warrant if they have probable cause to believe the car contains evidence of a crime. This is the only exception allowing officers to search without a warrant even if they have time to get one. Probable cause alone supports the warrantless search. This exception includes the car's trunk, as well as suitcases within the trunk if the officers have probable cause to believe they contain evidence. Further, this exception applies to all kinds of motorized vehicles. *California v. Carney* (1985) declared that this exception applied to mobile campers.

**Consent**    The consent must be voluntary, and it must be given by a person who has the authority to do so. No threats can be used. The officers do not need to identify themselves as law enforcement officers. The consent can be withdrawn at any time during the search. Landlords cannot give consent to allow their tenants' apartments to be searched. Holcomb (2002, pp.25–26) notes: "Under the U.S. Supreme Court's totality of the circumstances test, the impact of everything that occurs during the course of an individual giving consent to search a particular person, place or thing must be considered when determining if the consent was voluntary." Holcomb (2004, p.29) stresses: "Officers meticulously should record statements made and actions taken during the entire time the officer has contact with the individual. Paying close attention to the details surrounding the consent search and clearly articulating the facts and circumstances of the search are critical in consent to search cases." In addition, says Holcomb (2003, p.27): "Officers who obtain written consent to search from an individual should document in detail the facts and circumstances under which the consent was given."

**Plain View**   If officers are performing their duties and come across evidence or contraband that is easily seen—that is, it is in **plain view**—they may seize it. As the Supreme Court explained in *Katz v. United States* (1967): "The Fourth Amendment protects people, not places. What a person knowingly exposes to the public, even in his own home or office, is not a subject of Fourth Amendment protection." According to Hunsucker (2003, p.10): "Anywhere a law enforcement officer has a right to be, he has a right to see—through the use of any of his unaided senses." Officers can use a flashlight, provided they have a right to be at the location in the first place. The question of whether officers using binoculars or telescopic devices can seize evidence they discover under the plain view exception is controversial. Some courts have allowed it; others have not.

Similar to not requiring an arrest warrant to allow officers to arrest someone they see committing a crime, a search warrant is not required for officers to seize contraband or other evidence that is in plain sight. Officers may not, however, act merely on reasonable suspicion and manipulate suspected evidence to determine its illegality. The evidence must be immediately recognizable as such.

In *Arizona v. Hicks* (1987) an officer, while conducting a lawful yet warrantless search of an apartment for a gunman immediately following a shooting, noticed several pieces of expensive-looking stereo equipment that seemed out of place in the otherwise poorly furnished room. Suspecting the items were stolen, the officer recorded the equipments' serial numbers, moving some of the pieces in the process. A later check on the serial numbers revealed the items were indeed stolen. A search warrant was obtained, and the equipment was seized.

Suspect Hicks was charged with and convicted of robbery. Upon appeal, however, the Supreme Court reversed, ruling: "Moving the equipment . . . did constitute a 'search' separate and apart from the search for the shooter, victims, and weapons that was the lawful objective of [the officer's] entry into the apartment." The Court held that probable cause, not merely reasonable suspicion, to believe that items seen are contraband or evidence of criminal activity is required for the items to be seized under the "plain view" exception to the warrant requirement.

**Plain Feel**   The *Minnesota v. Dickerson* case (1993) mentioned in the discussion of stop and frisk established the legitimacy of "plain feel" if probable cause is established. In this case, the Supreme Court ruled unanimously that a police officer may seize contraband discovered during a patdown search for weapons if it is immediately apparent to the officer that the object is an illegal substance. The officer may not, however, "manipulate" the object to determine whether it is actually contraband:

> To this Court, there is no distinction as to which sensory perception the officer uses to conclude the material is contraband. An experienced officer may rely upon his sense of smell in DUI stops or in recognizing the smell of burning marijuana in an automobile. The sound of a shotgun being racked would clearly support certain reactions by an officer. The sense of touch, grounded in experience and training, is as reliable as perceptions drawn from other senses. "Plain feel" therefore, is no different than plain view.

Despite this holding, the evidence against Dickerson was ruled inadmissible at trial because the police officer testified he had determined the lump contained cocaine only after squeezing, sliding and manipulating it. The Court said such manipulation was a search, not a limited patdown for protection.

**Luggage Searches**   The Court's reasoning in *Dickerson* has been applied to searches of luggage. In *Bond v. United States* (2000), the Court extended its "look, but don't touch" policy when it ruled police officers can visually inspect travelers' luggage but not squeeze or physically manipulate a bag to determine whether it contains drugs or other contraband. To do so would constitute a warrantless search, thus requiring probable cause.

**Thermal Imaging**   The use of technology that enables officers to see or hear into a subject's home has been heavily restricted by the law. While wiretapping, electronic surveillance and other sound-monitoring devices have been addressed by the court many times over the last few decades, a relatively recent issue involves the use of thermal imaging devices. In *Kyllo v. United States* (2001), the Supreme Court ruled the use of technology-enhanced surveillance equipment constitutes a "search" within the meaning of the Fourth Amendment if it reveals any information about the inside of a subject's home that police could otherwise know only by entering ("Use of Thermal Imaging . . .," 2001, p.186).

In this case, police were suspicious Kyllo was growing marijuana in his home, which was part of a triplex. Aware that indoor marijuana cultivation typically requires the use of high-intensity lamps, agents used a thermal imaging device to monitor the amount of heat emanating from Kyllo's unit. The scan showed Kyllo's garage roof and a side wall were relatively hot compared to the rest of the home and noticeably warmer than the neighboring units. This evidence, combined with an offer made by Kyllo to a police informant to supply marijuana, was used to obtain a search warrant. The search netted 100 marijuana plants, weapons and drug paraphernalia, and Kyllo was indicted on federal drug charges.

The lower court reasoned the thermal imaging technology did not reveal any intimate details about the activities inside the home, merely amorphous hot spots, and compared the level of intrusion to that involved in warrantless aerial surveillance. However, the majority of the Supreme Court disagreed, recalling the decision in *Katz v. United States* (1967) that individuals always retain the expectation of privacy in their homes: "To withdraw protection of this minimum expectation would be to permit police technology to erode the privacy guaranteed by the Fourth Amendment." Thus, police use of sense-enhancing technology constitutes a search that is presumptively unreasonable without a warrant ("Thermal Imaging of a . . .," 2001, p.13).

**Abandoned Property**   This applies to anything an individual throws away, including bags or purses discarded while being chased by the police. In *California v. Greenwood* (1988), the Court upheld the right of officers to search through an individual's garbage that had been placed on the curb. Some states, however, are more restrictive. New Jersey and Hawaii, for example, prohibit police from going through garbage without a warrant.

**Open Fields**   The house and the area immediately surrounding it, called the **curtilage,** cannot be searched without a warrant. The curtilage is basically a person's yard and is protected by the Constitution. Open fields, however, are not. *Oliver v. United States* (1984) held that open fields are not protected by the Constitution and that, even if they are posted with "No Trespassing" signs, police can search them without a warrant. In this case, police were headed for a marijuana patch.

**Border Searches**   Clark (2004, p.22) points out: "The need to safeguard U.S. borders has drawn more attention recently than ever before. The law traditionally has recognized that significant public safety interests are at stake when it comes to safeguarding America's borders. This has translated into a unique body of law that permits the government to exercise broad search authority at the border to safeguard the public." Clark also says: "A true border search can be made without probable cause, without a warrant, and, indeed, without any articulable [easily expressed or described] suspicion at all. The only limitation on such a search is the Fourth Amendment stricture that it be conducted reasonably." In *United States v. Flores-Montano* (2004), Chief Justice Rehnquist stated: "Time and again, we have stated that searches made at the border, pursuant to the longstanding right of the sovereign to protect itself by stopping and examining persons and property crossing into this country, are reasonable simply by virtue of the fact that they occur at the border."

Swarns (2004) reports that the Department of Homeland Security has given border patrol agents sweeping new powers to deport illegal aliens from the Mexican and Canadian borders without giving them the chance to make their case before an immigration judge. Until 2004 only officials at airports and seaports could deport certain groups of illegal immigrants without judicial oversight. In 2003 about 43,000 immigrants were swiftly deported without scrutiny from immigration judges. Swarns reports that homeland security statistics suggest that the new rules could nearly double that figure.

Routine searches are also allowed at places other than actual borders, under the functional equivalent doctrine. The **functional equivalent** doctrine refers to places other than actual borders where travelers frequently enter or exit the country, such as international airports. In addition, Clark (p.25) says: "All mail arriving from overseas certainly may be opened without a warrant at the postal facility in the United States."

**Inventory**   Most police departments will automatically conduct an inventory of impounded vehicles. An inventory search protects the owner's property, it protects the law enforcement agency against claims that property in its possession has been lost or stolen, and it uncovers any danger that may exist to police because of property in their possession, such as a bomb. Inventorying must be a standard department procedure for this exception to be used.

**Exigent Circumstances**   An **exigent circumstance** occurs when an emergency exists and there is no time for the officers to obtain a search warrant. That is, the evidence could be destroyed or gone by the time they obtained the warrant. This is a frequently used exception and also the most difficult to justify.

## Procedures for Legally Searching People

The least intrusive search is a patdown or frisk of a person's outer clothing as a protective search for weapons. In the case of arrest, the search is more thorough and also includes a search for weapons. According to Garner (2003a, p.47): "Anyone taken into custody for any reason must be searched. That's rule number one of the arrest process." In a search incident to arrest, certain basic guidelines should be followed.

 When searching a person, officers should:
- Handcuff the subject if warranted.
- Be on guard, keeping themselves at arm's length from the person being searched.
- Keep the subject facing away from the searching officer.
- Be aware of where the service revolver is and keep it as far from the subject as possible.
- Be systematic and thorough.
- Keep the person under control, preferably off balance.
- Use the back of the hand in the breast and crotch area when patting down or searching women.

The FBI and most police departments have a policy that individuals to be searched are handcuffed first for officer safety. If more than one suspect is to be searched, all except those currently being searched should be ordered to lie on the ground, facing away from the person being searched. If two officers are at the search scene, one conducts the search while the other officer stands guard.

## Procedures for Legally Searching Buildings

Officers often must search buildings in response to either alarms or calls from citizens. Such searches are fraught with danger and require extreme caution. As Garner (2003b, p.62) points out: "When it comes to searching buildings, there's no such thing as a 'safe' house."

*Chimel v. California* (1969) established that officers entering a structure to make a lawful arrest could look into areas within the arrestee's immediate control to deter the arrestee from obtaining a weapon or destroying evidence. In *Maryland v. Buie* (1990) the Supreme Court allowed the arresting officers to make a protective sweep of the immediately adjoining spaces where a potential assailant might be concealed. According to Rutledge (2003b, p.67): "This '*Buie* peek' does not require any suspicion that an assailant is present—but it is strictly limited to immediately adjoining spaces and does not permit a sweep through the entire premises."

Officers arriving at a building to search it should arrive as quietly as possible to preserve the element of surprise. To make certain that no one escapes from within the building, observation posts should be set up and maintained while the search is being conducted. A thorough search depends on having enough officers to not only visually contain the building but also thoroughly and systematically search the inside.

The building search itself must be carefully planned. If time permits, the owner of the building should be contacted to learn as much as possible about its layout and possible hiding places. The number of floors, including basements and attics, should be determined. Usually one door is selected as the entry/exit door for the search team. In some instances, however, officers enter the front and back of the building simultaneously.

Once inside the building, to avoid shooting officers, all officers must know what each is doing. Each should have a clear assignment and carry it out. A system of communication should be established to maintain contact. Should a suspect be located, assistance should be called for immediately. The search should continue, however, as more than one suspect might be in the building.

As officers search the building, they should use proven techniques. For example, when entering a room or a building, they should look into the structure from both sides of the doorway without exposing any more of the body than necessary. They should always keep low and move rapidly. If the building is dark, they should use a flashlight without becoming a target.

One of the most dangerous moments in searching a building occurs when officers come to a *corner*. An armed suspect could be around that corner. In such instances, mirrors and periscopes can be invaluable.

When searching a building officers should:
- Get as much information as possible before starting the search.
- Plan carefully. Set up an entry/exit point, learn the interior layout, assign personnel to cover each area.
- Arrive quickly and quietly.
- Set up containment positions around the building.
- Make sure enough personnel are available.
- Make use of solid cover during the search.
- Use proper search techniques.

Officers also should take safety precautions when searching to avoid coming into contact with material that is contaminated and could result in acquiring hepatitis B or HIV. The risk factor in this area is ever increasing. Protecting against such hazards is discussed in-depth in Chapter 13.

## Using K-9s in Searches

Dogs (K-9s) can be invaluable in conducting searches for suspects, evidence, drugs and bombs. According to Hamilton (2003, p.18): "Knowing that canines will save time and money is just common sense. A dog could search a building in 10 minutes while it might take two or three officers an hour to do that same search. . . . A dog's sense of smell is about 700 times greater than a human's." However, as Walker (2001, p.25) notes: "The use of dogs by officers implicates the Fourth Amendment." Numerous cases have addressed whether the use of detector dogs constitutes a search, with the court generally ruling that dog sniffs of inanimate items or in public locations are *not* searches.

For example, in *United States v. Place* (1983), the Supreme Court held that a dog sniff of lawfully detained luggage in a public place does not constitute a search. In *City of Indianapolis v. Edmond* (2000), the Court extended this principle to the dog sniff of the exterior of a vehicle to which police have legitimate access. Similarly: "Most courts addressing cases involving a dog sniff of the exterior of a warehouse or garage from a public location have found that it is not a search" (Walker, p.27). However: "While the Supreme Court has never directly addressed the issue, an examination of lower court case law indicates that a dog sniff of a person is generally considered a search" (p.31). Walker recommends: "Because courts are divided over when a dog sniff constitutes a search, and because state courts may find dog sniffs are searches under their own state constitutions, officers should consult with their legal advisors before using a dog to sniff items, locations or persons for the presence of contraband."

*An aerial view of four customs officers and a K-9 checking cargo for bombs and other threats. A dog frequently lessens the dangers associated with such searches.*

Despite the many benefits gained by using K-9s, officers must also be aware of some of the drawbacks and limitations:

> Dogs have good days and bad days. Sometimes a dog will miss dope. I mean, he'll go right over a large quantity of it, for whatever reason, and you wonder, "Why is this?" So it's not a 100% thing and it's probably the hardest thing to convey to people that you work with. They don't really understand.
>
> Another problem encountered in the K-9 unit happens when using bite dogs. When one is deployed, such as during a foot chase, everyone is told to stay behind the handler and the dog. Yet cops want to be the first ones in to catch the bad guy and if you try to do that ahead of the handler, you are going to get bitten. It happens regularly (Montoya, 2001, p.33).

## SUMMARY

While conducting police operations involving arrests and searches, law enforcement officers must maintain a balance between "freedom to" and "freedom from." The Fourth and Fifth Amendments to the Constitution restrict arrests and searches.

A stop-and-frisk situation is one in which law enforcement officers briefly detain (stop) a suspicious person for questioning (this is *not* an arrest) and, *if* the officers suspect the person is armed, are allowed to pat (frisk) the person's outer clothing (this *is* a limited search for weapons).

An arrest is the official taking of a person to answer criminal charges. This involves at least temporarily depriving the person of liberty and may involve the use of force. An arrest can legally be made with an arrest warrant, when any offense (felony or misdemeanor) is committed in an officer's presence or when officers have probable cause to

*(side) © Dennis Mac Donald/PhotoEdit*

believe a person has committed a felony and no time is available to obtain a warrant. Probable cause refers to a situation where it is more likely than not that a crime has been committed by the person whom a law enforcement officer seeks to arrest. An officer's probable cause to conduct an arrest depends on what the officer knew *before* taking action.

Skill in making arrests is critical because arrest involves fundamental rights to personal liberty and privacy. The law of arrest is strict and technical; arrest is often the first step in criminal proceedings; illegal arrests may taint crucial evidence of guilt; the quality of police performance is judged by arrests; arrests may lead to civil suits or criminal prosecution of officers; arrests may endanger officers' lives; and an arrest that may seem particularly brutal and inhumane can bring about immediate and violent community reaction, as in the 1965 Watts riot. An illegal arrest may result in evidence being excluded under the Exclusionary Rule, which established that the courts cannot accept evidence obtained in illegal searches and seizures, regardless of how relevant the evidence is to the case (*Weeks v. United States,* 1914).

To make lawful arrests, officers must know both substantive and procedural law. Substantive law deals with content, or what behaviors are considered crimes. Procedural law deals with process, or how the law is applied.

In a typical arrest situation, officers should announce the arrest and the reason for it, handcuff the person if warranted and then search the person arrested for weapons and evidence. The person should be given the *Miranda* warning if any questions are to be asked. Use of force when making an arrest is always an issue. If there is no resistance, no force should be used. If resistance occurs, only as much force as necessary to overcome the resistance should be used. If a threat to an officer's life exists, the use of deadly force is authorized in most departments. Handcuffing may be considered a use of force. Whether an arrested person should automatically be handcuffed while being transported is controversial. Officer discretion may be advisable.

Less-lethal weapons available for use with violent, combative suspects include tear gas and other chemical irritant sprays, impact weapons, the taser gun, foams, nets and K-9s. Use of force can be a serious obstacle to the community policing philosophy.

A search may be legally conducted if a search warrant has been issued, consent is given or it is incidental to a lawful arrest. A search conducted under the authority of a search warrant must be limited to the area specified in the warrant and for the items described in the warrant. Ten exceptions to the search warrant requirement are (1) execution of an arrest warrant, (2) frisks, (3) incident to arrest, (4) automobiles, (5) consent, (6) plain view/feel, (7) abandoned property, (8) open fields, (9) inventory and (10) exigent circumstances.

When searching a person, officers should handcuff the subject if warranted; be on guard, keeping themselves at arm's length from the person being searched; keep the subject facing away from the searching officer; be aware of where the service revolver is and keep it as far from the subject as possible; be systematic and thorough; keep the person under control, preferably off balance; and use the back of the hand in the breast and crotch area when patting down or searching women.

When searching a building, officers should get as much information as possible before starting the search, plan carefully, arrive quickly and quietly, set up containment positions around the building and make sure enough personnel are available. They should set up an entry/exit point, learn the interior layout and assign personnel to cover each area. They should also use available cover and proper search techniques.

## APPLICATION

You are a Bigtown patrol officer. You notice that transporting and booking a person arrested as a misdemeanant takes from one to three hours. This seems counterproductive because you are out of service during that time, not available for other calls, and the arrested person will usually be released from jail in a short time, often even before you finish the reports. You feel that issuing a citation to the person without formal procedures of arrest and booking would more than serve the purpose and would release you for more important duties. You approach your sergeant and pose your recommendations to her. She asks you to "put it in writing."

### INSTRUCTIONS

Use the form in the Appendix to make your policy and procedure. The policy will include the following:

> The policy of the Bigtown Police Department for releasing people from custody who have been arrested for a misdemeanor will change effective (date). Any person cited for a misdemeanor whom the officer feels will appear in court as promised may be given a written citation by the officer.
>
> *When a Citation May Be Issued.* Give several circumstances or conditions that may exist whereby officers could issue a citation to such a person who also has no previous criminal record.
>
> *Justifications for Not Issuing a Citation.* In completing this policy, you should insert what form is to be used when issuing a citation, what reports are necessary and also that issuing a citation means suspects should be entered in the arrest log and assigned a log number and a case number. You should indicate what needs to appear in the citation notification form.

### AN EXERCISE IN CRITICAL THINKING

At 7:40 A.M. on June 27, Officer Steve Sjerven was in the crossover preparing to turn south on Highway 65 to help the driver of an apparently disabled car. As he waited to turn, he saw a red pickup truck heading south on Highway 65 and made eye contact with the driver and sole occupant of the truck. The driver abruptly turned the truck right onto Tower Systems Road and appeared to immediately disappear. Not seeing the pickup truck or any dust that might be expected from a truck traveling down a gravel road, the officer concluded that the truck must have immediately pulled into a driveway. As the officer pulled up to assist the disabled car, he saw the pickup emerge and turn south onto Highway 65—a very short time after having turned onto Tower Systems Road. Inferring that the driver had turned off Highway 65 to avoid him, the officer motioned the driver of the pickup to stop. The driver did so, identified himself as Mark Johnson and admitted that his license had been revoked.

1. As the U.S. Supreme Court's decisions require only that an officer have a "particular and objective basis for suspecting the particular person stopped of criminal activity," what is your judgment of Officer Sjerven's approach?

   a. Since Johnson's action can be explained as consistent with lawful activities, Officer Sjerven should not stop him.

   b. The officer's suspicion, though nothing more than a hunch, was later verified by the stop.

   c. Sjerven stopped Johnson on mere whim, caprice or idle curiosity, and so should be disciplined for poor judgment in operational skills.

   d. Inferences and deductions might well elude an untrained person, but a trained police officer is entitled to draw inferences on the basis of "all of the circumstances."

   e. If the observed facts are consistent with innocent activity, then the stop is invalid.

### DISCUSSION QUESTIONS

1. The Fifth Amendment provides that no person shall be "deprived of life, liberty or property without due process of law." What does this really mean? Explain your answer as if you were giving a lecture to a high school class.

2. Substantive law is concerned with the content of the law. In criminal law it defines what behaviors are illegal and imposes punishments for engaging in them. Name five types of behavior the law does not tolerate.

3. When officers make an arrest without a warrant, they act at their own peril and are allowed no margin of error. Why is this statement written so stringently?

4. Describe a good example of "reasonable grounds of suspicion."

5. What search situations are officers likely to find themselves in? How can they best prepare themselves?

6. Discuss how you felt when you read about the Abner Louima case. Do you think this incident could have been prevented?

7. Do you feel that given the awesome power police hold, they can ever be true partners with citizens in community policing?

### INFOTRAC COLLEGE EDITION ASSIGNMENTS

- Use InfoTrac College Edition to answer the Discussion Questions as appropriate.
- Use InfoTrac College Edition to research recent incidents where *excessive force* was alleged against the police. Outline the characteristics that bring on alleged excessive force situations. Be prepared to share your outline with the class.

■ Use InfoTrac College Edition to find and outline one of the following articles:

- "Flight as Justification for Seizure: Supreme Court Ruling" by Michael E. Brooks
- "Reviewing Use of Force: A Systematic Approach" by Sam W. Lathrop
- "Using Drug Detection Dogs: An Update" by Jayme S. Walker
- "Deadly Force: A 20-Year Study of Fatal Encounters" by Larry C. Brubaker
- "U.S. Land Border Search Authority" by M. Wesley Clark
- "Inferring Probable Cause: Obtaining a Search Warrant for a Suspect's Home without Direct Information that Evidence Is Inside" by Edward Hendrie
- "Consent Searches: Factors Courts Consider in Determining Voluntariness" by Jayme Walker Holcomb
- "Obtaining Written Consent to Search" by Jayme Walker Holcomb
- "Consent Searches Scope" by Jayme Walker Holcomb
- "Use-of-Force Policies and Training: A Reasoned Approach" by Thomas D. Petrowski
- "Use-of-Force Policies and Training: A Reasoned Approach (Part Two)" by Thomas D. Petrowski
- "Force Continuums: A Liability to Law Enforcement?" by George T. Williams

 ## INTERNET ASSIGNMENT

Use the Internet to find and analyze five court cases that pertain to *reasonableness of arrests*. For each case, list what the court felt was fair and what the court saw as being unreasonable. Be prepared to share your lists with the class.

 ## BOOK-SPECIFIC WEBSITE

The book-specific website at http://cj.wadsworth.com/wobleski_Hess_police_op4e hosts a variety of resources for students and instructors. Many can be emailed to the instructor. Included are extended activities such as Concept Builders - the 3 step learning module that reinforces key chapter concepts, followed by a real-world applications and critical thinking questions. InfoTrac College Edition exercises; Discussion Questions; interactive key-term FlashCards; and a collection of chapter-based Web Links provide additional information and activities to include in the curriculum.

## REFERENCES

Aveni, Thomas J. "The Force Continuum Conundrum." *Law and Order*, December 2003, pp.74–77.

Bertomen, Lindsey. "The Less-Lethal Toolbox." *Law Enforcement Technology*, October 2003, pp.64–70.

Cerullo, Rob and Means, Randy. "U.S. Supreme Court Sharpens Police Drug-Fighting Tools." *The Police Chief*, February 2004, pp.10–12.

Clark, M. Wesley. "U.S. Land Border Search Authority." *FBI Law Enforcement Bulletin*, August 2004, pp.22–32.

Dallett, Kevin. "Training and Aerosol Subject Restraints." *The Law Enforcement Trainer*, January/February 2004, pp.8–11.

Devanney, Joe and Devanney, Diane. "An Analysis of the Knock and Announce Rule." *Tactical Response*, Spring 2003a, pp.72–74.

Devanney, Joe and Devanney, Diane. "Canine Case Law." *Law and Order*, September 2003b, pp.12–14.

Douglas, Dave. "Well Seasoned Suspects." *Police*, March 2001, pp.26–29.

Ederheimer, Josh and Cheney, Jason. "The Critical Issues in Policing Series: Police Use of Force and Police Management of Mass Demonstrations." *Subject to Debate*, November 2004, p.8.

Flosi, Ed. "Submission Recognition." *The Police Chief*, April 2003, pp.142–145.

Garner, Gerald W. "Search Patterns." *Police*, May 2003a, pp.44–50.

Garner, Gerald W. "Structure Searches." *Police*, September 2003b, pp.62–65.

Green, Bernie. "Well Trained and Reliable Canine." *Law and Order*, April 2004, pp.38–39.

Greenhouse, Linda. "Justices Rule Police May Properly Request a Name." *New York Times* as reported in the (Minneapolis/St. Paul) *Star Tribune*, June 22, 2004, p.A8.

Gundy, Jess. "The Complexities of Use of Force." *Law and Order*, December 2003, pp.60–65.

Hamilton, Melanie. "How to . . . Start a K-9 Unit." *Police*, February 2003, pp.18–23.

Harr, J. Scott and Hess, Kären M. *Constitutional Law and the Criminal Justice System*, 3rd ed. Belmont, CA: Wadsworth Thomson Learning, 2005.

Hendrie, Edward. "Inferring Probable Cause: Obtaining a Search Warrant for a Suspect's Home without Direct Information that Evidence Is Inside." *FBI Law Enforcement Bulletin*, February 2002, pp.23–32.

Holcomb, Jayme Walker. "Consent Searches: Factors Courts Consider in Determining Voluntariness." *FBI Law Enforcement Bulletin*, May 2002, pp.25–32.

Holcomb, Jayme Walker. "Obtaining Written Consent to Search." *FBI Law Enforcement Bulletin*, March 2003, pp.26–32.

Holcomb, Jayme Walker. "Consent Searches Scope." *FBI Law Enforcement Bulletin*, February 2004, pp.22–32.

Hopper, Joan. "Every Second Counts to the U.S. Supreme Court." *Law and Order*, January 2004, pp.22–24.

Hunsucker, Keith. "Right to Be, Right to See: Practical Fourth Amendment Application for Law Enforcement Officers." *The Police Chief*, September 2003, pp.10–13.

Ijames, Steve. "Impact in the Field." *Police*, July 2001, pp.16–20.

Kester, Don. "Less Lethal Technology Expands: Options Increasing for Law Enforcement Officers." *The Law Enforcement Trainer*, March/April 2002, pp.12–13.

Klugiewicz, Gary T. and Young, Dave. "Hot Shots." *Police,* October 2003, pp.58–66.

Lesh, David N. "The Duty to Warn." *The Law Enforcement Trainer,* March/April 2003, pp.16–18.

Lonsway, Kim. "Police Women and the Use-of-Force." *Law and Order,* July 2001, pp.109–114.

Makholm, John A. "Legal Lights." *The Law Enforcement Trainer,* January/February 2004, pp.64–65.

Meissner, Craig. "Ties that Bind." *Police,* December 2002, pp.30–33.

Miller, Linda S. and Hess, Kären M. *Community Policing: Partnerships for Problem Solving,* 4th ed. Belmont, CA: Wadsworth Thomson Learning, 2005.

Montoya, Hedy Liliana. "Dog Hair and Drool: Life in the Front Seat." *Police,* March 2001, pp.31–34.

"New York Police, Louima Reach Tentative $9 Million Deal." Associated Press, as reported in the (Minneapolis/ St. Paul) *Star Tribune,* July 12, 2001, p.A4.

Nielsen, Eugene. "The Advanced Taser." *Law and Order,* May 2001, pp.57–62.

Nielsen, Eugene. "The Taser X26." *Law Enforcement Technology,* October 2004, pp.164–169.

Nowicki, Ed. "Dealing with Litigation." *Law and Order,* April 2001a, pp.29–31.

Nowicki, Ed. "OC Spray Update." *Law and Order,* June 2001b, pp.28–29.

Nowicki, Ed. "Use of Force Options." *Law and Order,* February 2001c, pp.35–37.

Nowicki, Ed. "Handcuffing." *Law and Order,* March 2002a, pp.14–15.

Nowicki, Ed. "Language of Force." *Law and Order,* December 2002b, pp.26–27.

Nowicki, Ed. "Deadly Force: More than Firearms." *Law and Order,* June 2003, pp.24–26.

Osborne, Kevin. "Taser Use Gets Mixed Reviews." *The Cincinnati Post,* November 24, 2004. http://www.cincypost.com/2004/11/24/tasers112404.html

Petrowski, Thomas D. "Use-of-Force Policies and Training: A Reasoned Approach." *FBI Law Enforcement Bulletin,* October 2002a, pp.25–32.

Petrowski, Thomas D. "Use-of-Force Policies and Training: A Reasoned Approach (Part Two)." *FBI Law Enforcement Bulletin,* November 2002b, pp.24–32.

*Police Use of Force in America 2001.* Alexandria, VA: International Association of Chiefs of Police, no date.

Ramirez, Eugene. "Breaking and Entering." *Police,* May 2002, pp.58–61.

Remsberg, Charles. "New Force Science™ Center Unravels Vital Mysteries of Extreme Encounters." *The Law Enforcement Trainer,* Third Quarter, 2004, pp.8–13.

Roane, Kit R. "Brutality's Hefty Price." *U.S. News & World Report,* July 23, 2001, p.28.

Rutledge, Devallis. "Avoiding De Facto Arrests." *Police,* August 2003a, pp.74–77.

Rutledge, Devallis. "Officer Safety Searches." *Police,* November 2003b, pp.66–68.

Rutledge, Devallis. "Use of Force on Prisoners." *Police,* January 2004a, pp.58–59.

Rutledge, Devallis. "Knock before Entry." *Police,* February 2004b, pp.74–75.

Sanow, Ed. "New Use of Force Products." *Law and Order,* February 2001, pp.40–42.

Smith, Brad. "K-9 Use of Force Case Law." *Tactical Response,* Summer 2004, pp.18–21.

Swarns, Rachel L. "U.S. to Give Border Patrol Agents the Power to Deport Illegal Aliens." *New York Times,* August 11, 2004.

Taylor, Ed. "New Tasers Wired for Audio-Video." *East Valley Tribune* (Arizona), November 29, 2004. http://www.eastvalleytribune.com/index.php?sty=32307

"Thermal Imaging of a Residence Constitutes a Search." *NCJA Justice Bulletin,* June 2001, p.13.

"Use of Thermal Imaging Devices a Search, High Court Holds." *The Law Officers' Bulletin,* April 26, 2001, pp.186–187.

Walker, Jayme S. "Using Drug Detection Dogs: An Update." *FBI Law Enforcement Bulletin,* April 2001, pp.25–32.

Walker, Jeffery T. and McKinnon, Kristi M. "*Atwater v. City of Lago Vista:* Police Authority to Make Warrantless Misdemeanor Arrests." *Journal of Contemporary Criminal Justice,* May 2003, pp.239–252.

Williams, George T. "Force Continuums: A Liability to Law Enforcement?" *FBI Law Enforcement Bulletin,* June 2002, pp.14–19.

Williams, George T. "What Is Compliance?" *Law and Order,* December 2003, pp.70–73.

## CASES CITED

*Alabama v. White,* 496 U.S. 326 (1990)
*Arizona v. Evans,* 115 S.Ct. 1185 (1995)
*Arizona v. Hicks,* 480 U.S. 321 (1987)
*Atwater v. City of Lago Vista,* 532 U.S. 295 (2001)
*Bond v. United States,* 98-9349 (4/17/2000)
*Brinegar v. United States,* 338 U.S. 160 (1949)
*California v. Carney,* 471 U.S. 386 (1985)
*California v. Greenwood,* 486 U.S. 35, 36 (1988)
*Carroll v. United States,* 267 U.S. 132 (1925)
*Chimel v. California,* 395 U.S. 752 (1969)
*City of Indianapolis v. Edmond,* 121 S.Ct. 447 (2000)
*Florida v. Bostick,* 501 U.S. 429 (1991)
*Graham v. Connor,* 490 U.S. 386 (1989)
*Hiibel v. Sixth Judicial District Court,* 118 Nev. Adv. Op. No. 88 (2002); Supreme Court ruled June 21, 2004
*Illinois v. Gates,* 462 U.S. 213 (1983)
*Illinois v. Wardlow,* 120 S.Ct. 673 (2000)
*Katz v. United States,* 389 U.S. 347 (1967)
*Kaupp v. Texas,* 123 S.Ct. 1843 (2003)
*Kozlowski v. Ferrara,* 117 F.Supp. 650 (S.D.N.Y. 1954)
*Kyllo v. United States,* U.S. No. 99-8508 (6/11/2001)
*Mapp v. Ohio,* 367 U.S. 643 (1961)

*Maryland v. Buie,* 58 LW 4281 (1990)
*Massachusetts v. Sheppard,* 468 U.S. 981 (1984)
*Minnesota v. Dickerson,* 113 S.Ct. 2130 (1993)
*Murray v. United States,* 487 U.S. 533 (1988)
*New York v. Belton,* 453 U.S. 454, 462 (1981)
*Oliver v. United States,* 466 U.S. 170 (1984)
*Semayne's Case,* 5 Coke, 918 (1603)
*Tennessee v. Garner,* 471 U.S. 1 (1985)
*Terry v. Ohio,* 392 U.S. 1 (1968)

*United States v. Banks,* 124 S.Ct. 521 (2003)
*United States v. Flores-Montano,* No. 02-1794 (2004)
*United States v. Leon,* 468 U.S. 897 (1984)
*United States v. Place,* 462 U.S. 696 (1983)
*United States v. Ramirez,* 523 U.S. 65 (1998)
*United States v. Sokolow,* 490 U.S. 1 (1989)
*Weeks v. United States,* 232 U.S. 383 (1914)
*Wilson v. Arkansas,* 115 S.Ct. 1914 (1995)

# GETTING THE JOB DONE: BASIC POLICE OPERATIONS

It is in this section that most police operations books begin and end. But a law enforcement officer must never forget that the actual operations themselves are only half the job.

To perform police operations professionally, officers must always keep in mind the content of the first section. They must consider the context in which they operate—the citizens they serve as well as the colleagues with whom they work. Law enforcement officers are an integral part of this context, not a separate entity. They do not operate in a vacuum. Officers must use effective communications skills, and they must do so while staying within the law.

With this solid foundation, now focus on the actual operations law enforcement officers perform. At the heart of police operations is patrol, often called the backbone of the police organization (Chapter 4). Activities conducted during patrol often include other functions performed by officers, such as traffic enforcement (Chapter 5); responding to crime, disorder and quality-of-life issues (Chapter 6); deterring violence (Chapter 7); dealing with emergencies (Chapter 8) and securing our homeland (Chapter 9). The next section will focus on specialized police operations.

# Patrol: The Backbone of Police Operations

**DO YOU KNOW . . .**

- How patrol is typically described?
- What organizational contradiction is embodied in the patrol function?
- What functions patrol typically performs?
- How the majority of patrol time is spent?
- How crowds can be classified?
- What methods of patrol have been used and the advantages and disadvantages of each?
- What type of patrol has the most mobility and flexibility and is usually the most cost effective?
- What the Kansas City Preventive Patrol Experiment found?
- What most affects the possibility of on-scene arrests?
- What two basic causes account for delays in calling for service?
- What the SARA problem-solving process consists of?

**CAN YOU DEFINE?**

| | | | |
|---|---|---|---|
| differential police response strategies | impact evaluation | process evaluation | proximate |
| directed patrol | involvement crimes | proportionate assignment | response time |
| discovery crimes | problem-oriented policing (POP) | | |

## Introduction

Patrol has been one of the most widely discussed and controversial areas in law enforcement over the past several decades.

Patrol service has been described as the backbone of the police department.

Sweeney (2003, pp.89–90) contends: "Patrol officers remain 'master generalists' expected to handle competently a mind-boggling array of calls. . . . In addition to being varied, this master generalist's job is the most important in the police department." Theoretically, patrol officers are the most valuable people in the organization. To a certain extent, all activity radiates from them. But such a concept is not totally supported in fact by such measures as salary, working conditions and authority. In addition, according to Sweeney (p.90): "Challenging,

important and hazardous though patrol work may be, the laborious routine and onerous schedule prevent it from getting the prestige it deserves."

Usually the most complex, burdensome and dangerous aspects of police service are performed by uniformed patrol officers. The work may be carried out in an atmosphere emotionally charged with hostility—an environment that breeds distrust and danger—and in situations that require officers to be clergy, psychologists, therapists or many other types of professionals who deal with human problems.

This chapter begins with a discussion of the organizational contradiction embodied in patrol and the typical functions performed by patrol. This is followed by a look at the various methods of patrol, including foot, automobile, motorcycle, bicycle, mounted, air, water, all-terrain and K-9-assisted patrol. Next, patrol techniques and strategies are examined, including results of the classic Kansas City Preventive Patrol Experiment, area and shift assignment modification, response time, differential police response strategies and use of directed patrol. Then attention shifts to the critical role problem solving plays in patrol effectiveness. The chapter concludes with a discussion of patrol and community policing.

## An Organizational Contradiction— The Importance of Patrol

The fact is, the most crucial people on the law enforcement team are lowest on the totem pole. A police department's ability to carry out its mission of providing public service and controlling crime depends greatly on the uniformed patrol officers' capabilities.

 The fact that patrol officers, those who actually accomplish the department's goals, are lowest in status and in pay results in a serious organizational contradiction.

The reasons for the contradiction include the following. First, administrators might not truly believe in the importance of the patrol function. Second, they might not think that patrol is sufficiently stimulating, rewarding or challenging enough to keep the most able officers satisfied. Third, many officers want to be transferred because of the schedule. Patrol officers work nights, weekends and holidays. Such schedules can be especially troublesome to married officers whose spouses work normal hours. Many patrol officers seek transfers to other divisions or into management, not only to escape the hazards of patrol, but to have a better schedule, higher pay and increased status both inside and outside the department.

The majority of the country's police agencies are small, employing fewer than 20 officers. These departments assign almost all the officers to patrol, delegating additional special duties as needed. In a police agency with only one officer, that officer performs all roles from chief to records clerk, with the majority of the time spent serving a patrol function.

## Patrol Functions

Every patrol division performs different tasks, although some are common to all. Patrol duties are not usually described in great detail, except when officers answer specific calls for service. "Routine" patrol means different things to individual officers, supervisors and departments. For example, one officer on routine patrol may feel that if nothing is "happening," time can best be spent talking to citizens and getting to know the patrol areas. Another officer might feel the time should be spent looking into suspected gang activity. A third officer might feel this is the time to catch up on current events by reading the newspaper.

The police presence is intended to deter crime and give citizens a feeling of being protected. Officers not only help reduce racial tensions in large-city ghettos, but also often conduct educational programs and provide help to drunks, the mentally ill, street people or patrons of prostitution who may be at risk of robbery.

Among the important patrol functions are:
- Responding to noncrime calls for service.
- Controlling traffic.
- Assisting at the scene of a crime.
- Conducting preliminary investigations.
- Gathering intelligence.
- Making arrests.
- Patrolling public gatherings and special events.
- Assisting at the scene of a fire.
- Providing community service and general peacekeeping activities.
- Partnering with others to solve problems related to crime and disorder.

## Noncrime Calls for Service

*Responding to calls for service* is an important function of patrol officers. Many calls involve missing persons, damage to property, lost and found property, missing and stray animals, escort services, people locked out, licensing and inspections.

Television programs have made the *missing persons* function of the police department seem routine. In actuality, however, unless foul play is suspected or the person missing is retarded, mentally incompetent or in need of medication, the police do not become involved in missing person cases. If no crime has been committed and the missing person's safety is not in jeopardy, the police department performs an administrative function, recording the information to be used in helping to identify individuals who are unconscious, who are found wandering (senility) or who are found dead and have no identification on them. The National Crime Information Center (NCIC) includes a Missing Person File with four specific categories and criteria for entry: (1) disabled, (2) endangered, (3) involuntary (abducted, kidnapped) and (4) juvenile.

Citizens who experience *property damage* are likely to call the police. The first action of responding officers is to determine if any danger is inherent in the situation. If danger does exist, officers must act to remove the danger. For example, if a tree has fallen on power lines and hot wires are on the ground, police should rope off the area and call the power company. If no danger is inherent in the situation, officers should determine if the damage is the result of criminal or noncriminal actions. If it is criminal property damage, for example, the work of vandals, officers should conduct a thorough investigation. If it is a noncriminal (and nondangerous) situation, for example, a tree fallen on a home, police officers should advise the complainant of alternatives in taking care of the damage. The complainant usually should also be advised to notify his or her insurance agent.

The police department may also serve a *lost and found* function. People who find valuable property are likely to turn it in to the police department. Conversely, people who have lost items of value are likely to request assistance from the police department. In this situation, again, the police department plays primarily an administrative function, maintaining accurate records of lost or found property.

Some police departments also have the responsibility for *missing and stray animals,* especially unlicensed dogs. And they may be called on to deal with dangerous animals, such as bears, or with trapped animals, such as a raccoon up a chimney of a home.

Police may be called on to provide *escort service* to celebrities and other public figures who are either extremely popular or unpopular. They may also provide escort services for dangerous cargoes, such as those containing highly flammable materials, hazardous wastes and the like, or for oversized cargoes. In addition, police may be asked to provide escort services for funeral processions or for very valuable cargoes, such as large sums of cash. Little agreement exists on when escort services are appropriate or on how they should be provided; that is, should they include red flashing lights and sirens, or proceed as though on general patrol?

The police may also be called to assist *people locked out* of their cars or homes. In such instances it is usually preferable to have the civilian call a locksmith. If this is not possible, officers should check the identity of the person requesting assistance. Imagine the predicament of a police officer who assists a burglar in breaking and entering.

The police department is sometimes involved in *licensing* handguns. It is to the department's advantage to know who owns what kind of weapons in its jurisdiction. In addition, the police are in a position to investigate applicants for a license and to determine if such a license should be granted. They also may do background investigations on applicants for liquor licenses, taxi licenses and tow truck licenses. The police department is also involved in other types of licensing, such as issuing licenses for holding parades or for blocking off streets for community functions.

In addition, because officers routinely patrol the entire area over which the department has jurisdiction, many decision makers believe officers should be responsible for *inspections* to ensure adherence to fire codes, health codes and building codes. This is another area of controversy because such activities are extremely time consuming. They do present the advantage of familiarizing officers with the people and buildings on their beats. On the other hand, such activities take officers off the street and into buildings where they are no longer on preventive patrol but rather are serving functions that could easily be carried out by inspectors specifically hired for the jobs, usually at less cost.

In many areas, police are also responsible for checking the weight of trucks. Police are used in this capacity because they must be on the scene anyway to issue tickets to overweight trucks or to stop trucks that bypass the scales completely. Some contend, however, that the patrol officers in the vicinity could be called in for either of the preceding situations and that it might be more practical not to use patrol officers in this capacity.

 Between 80 and 90 percent of all calls for police service are of a noncriminal nature.

Whether police officers should spend time in all these activities is controversial. Yet, proposals to eliminate such social service functions fail to recognize the relationship between social-service-type calls and more serious crime. For example, a domestic disturbance can end in a serious assault or even homicide.

In addition, police are the only agencies available 24/7 for immediate help, which is one reason they are so often called to intervene in *domestic disputes.* Such disputes usually occur at night and commonly involve people who have been drinking. Police officers often are expected to defuse such situations without making an arrest. And they frequently are called to the same scene time and again. Such calls may lull officers into complacency, making them vulnerable should a normally routine call turn out to involve crazed, weapon-wielding individuals. Dealing with domestic disputes is discussed in detail in Chapter 7.

## Controlling Traffic

Patrol officers also serve a *traffic* function by directing traffic, responding to traffic crash calls, issuing tickets for traffic violations and the like, as discussed in detail in Chapter 5.

## Assisting at the Scene of a Crime

Responding to calls about *crimes in progress* or recently committed and conducting the *preliminary investigations* are other important functions of patrol officers. Because they are on patrol and readily available to respond, they are usually first on the scene. This is the type of call most officers consider to be "real" police work. On such calls, patrol officers are responsible for aiding injured victims, securing the scene, interviewing victims and witnesses and arresting any suspects present at the scene. "Research has indicated that the single most important factor in determining the success of a criminal investigation is information gathered by patrol officers at the time of the initial report" (T. Sweeney, p.101). In smaller departments, patrol officers may also continue the investigation and *gather intelligence.* In larger departments, the investigation may be turned over to the detective division. The investigative function is discussed in Chapter 10.

## Making Arrests

*Making arrests* is one of patrol officers' most awesome responsibilities, as discussed in Chapter 3. Officers have much discretion in this area, making decisions that can drastically change the futures of those engaged in unlawful activity. Officers can decide to arrest or not. Frequently, a simple warning is the best alternative. Not only do patrol officers deal with a wide variety of criminal and non-criminal situations; they also often deal with several such situations within a brief time.

## Special Events

Many functions performed by patrol officers can also be required in handling *special events.* Patrol officers are often an essential part of large public gatherings, including sporting events, rock concerts, parades, celebrations and political rallies. The presence of uniformed patrol officers helps assure peaceful assembly and prevents unlawful actions. Patrol officers also help expedite the traffic flow of both vehicles and pedestrians.

Because of the heavy demand placed by special events on police resources, the San Francisco Police Department created an *Events Management Manual.* This manual classifies crowds into specific types and subtypes and prescribes appropriate police responses for each. Table 4.1 summarizes the specific subtypes of crowds and the appropriate police reaction to each.

 Crowds may be classified as self-controlled, active or explosive.

Handling explosive crowds is discussed in Chapter 6.

**Table 4.1**   Appropriate Police Responses to Specific Subtypes of Crowds

| *Self-Controlled Crowds* | *Police Action* |
|---|---|
| Tranquil (e.g., shoppers and commuters) | No police action |
| Apprehensive (e.g., crowd forms because of an unanticipated event like a bomb threat) | Provide accurate information |
| Exuberant (e.g., outdoor concert goers) | Monitor |
| Competitive (e.g., sporting event or labor dispute) | Monitor closely |

Note: In all but the first case, an active police presence is assumed.

| *Active Crowds* | *Police Action* |
|---|---|
| Confused (e.g., traffic jam) | Give accurate information |
| Annoyed (e.g., a scheduled event doesn't start on time) | Provide accurate information |
| | Monitor closely |
| | Prepare control tactics |
| Displaying horseplay (e.g., throwing frisbees in a sports stadium) | Take immediate action to stop small group horseplay |
| Protesting (e.g., during the visit of an unpopular head of a foreign state) | Contact leaders of protest |
| | Establish rules for behavior |

| *Explosive Crowds* | *Police Action* |
|---|---|
| Crazed but not malicious (e.g., something desirable offered on a first-come, first-served basis) | Provide accurate information |
| | Set rules |
| | Use firm control techniques |
| Panicked (e.g., a fire at a crowded event) | Provide information |
| | Use control techniques |
| | Give avenues of escape |
| Vicious pranks (e.g., anarchists and skinheads mixed in with a group demonstration) | Remove disturbers immediately or place under close surveillance |
| | Consider dispersing the entire crowd |
| Disorderly (e.g., rioters) | Use full crowd-control techniques |

SOURCE: Reprinted from *The Police Chief*, Vol. LVI, No. 12, pages 29–36, December, 1989. Copyright held by The International Association of Chiefs of Police, Inc., 515 N. Washington St., Alexandria, VA 22314 U.S.A. Further reproduction without express written permission from IACP is strictly prohibited.

One trend is to hire off-duty patrol officers to perform the crowd-control function, particularly if the event is sponsored by private business or industry. Other alternatives include using volunteers or reserves to handle crowd-control problems.

## Assisting at the Scene of a Fire

The first action of police officers who come upon an *uncontrolled fire* is to call the fire department. Only then should any attempts be made to control or suppress the fire. Other functions the police may serve include traffic control, assuring that firefighting equipment can arrive quickly at the scene and helping search for and rescue people trapped by the fire. If children are trapped in a burning home, rescuers should check under beds and in closets because children frequently try to hide from the smoke and flames. Police officers can also provide crowd control, assist with first aid, transport injured people to the nearest medical facility and guard any personal property removed from the burning structure.

## The Community Service and Peacekeeping Function

In addition to their enforcement function, patrol officers also serve an important *peacekeeping function.* Although this function occupies the majority of the officers' time, it is largely unrecorded and unaccounted for. The public often misunder-

**Table 4.2** Patrol Officer Functions

| Function | Situations |
| --- | --- |
| Noncrime calls for service (80–90 percent of calls for service) | Noise and party calls<br>Domestic disturbances<br>Landlord/tenant disputes<br>Nuisance complaints |
| Traffic control | Traffic delays<br>Pedestrian problems<br>Crashes<br>Traffic violations<br>Drunken drivers |
| Preliminary investigations | Scene security<br>Emergency first aid<br>Evidence procurement<br>Victim/witness statements |
| Arrests | Warrants<br>Suspect transport<br>Court testimony |
| Public gatherings | Sporting events<br>Political rallies<br>Rock concerts<br>Parades<br>Special events |
| Community service | Speeches and presentations<br>Auto and home lockouts<br>Babies delivered<br>Blood transported<br>Home/business security checks |

stands this function. When they see officers driving around simply observing the area, citizens often criticize the police for not chasing criminals or for not finding the "jerks" who "ripped off" their apartment when they were gone. Further, the peacekeeping function is seldom included in police training. The tendency is to think that all officers need is a little common sense. Consequently, texts, manuals and training sessions seldom include this important patrol function, leaving officers to "play it by ear." Patrol functions are summarized in Table 4.2.

Partnering and problem solving were discussed in Chapter 3. To serve these various functions, officers have a variety of patrol methods from which to choose.

## Patrol Methods

The methods of patrol departments use vary, depending on local needs. Most jurisdictions use some form of foot patrol in combination with automobile patrol.

 Patrol methods include foot, automobile, motorcycle, bicycle, mounted, air, water, all-terrain vehicle and K-9 assisted.

### *Foot Patrol*

Foot patrol is the oldest form of patrol. Its primary advantage is close citizen contact. Other advantages include the enhanced rapport between officers and the citizens and its proactive, rather than reactive, nature, seeking to address neighborhood problems before they become crimes. Experiments with foot patrol conducted in Newark, New Jersey; Flint, Michigan; Oakland, California; Houston, Texas; and Boston, Massachusetts; have yielded similar results—foot patrol programs improve public relations between the police and the community but do not affect crime rates. However, Fuller (2004, p.63) contends: "An aggressive, street-smart police officer, working an active post, can develop as many (or more) quality cases and arrests working foot patrol as he can working motorized patrol." Fuller stresses: "If your agency claims to be focused on community policing (and who isn't these days?), getting your people out on foot to meet and greet people who live and work on their posts can be a huge plus. There is no better way to empower citizens and enhance community participation than to have your officers personally interact with the institutions and people they are sworn to preserve and protect."

One technique used during foot patrol is the *knock and talk,* where an officer knocks on a resident's door and asks if they can talk. It can be used to discover perceived problems or in investigations. According to Steffen and Candelaria (2004, p.85): "This underutilized (and sometimes controversial) technique can not only be used for narcotics investigations, but for other criminal investigations, as well."

Foot patrol is not without its disadvantages, however. It is relatively expensive and limits officers' ability to pursue suspects in vehicles as well as their ability to respond rapidly to calls for service in another area. Many studies show that although increasing the number of officers on foot patrol may not reduce crime, it does increase citizens' feelings of safety.

## *Automobile Patrol*

Automobile patrol reverses the advantages and disadvantages of foot patrol. Unlike officers on foot, officers in squad cars can pursue suspects in vehicles and can respond rapidly to service calls in other areas. They also can transport equipment needed to process crime scenes as well as suspects they have arrested. They can patrol a larger area in less time, or the same area as an officer on foot can, but more frequently.

Communication with the citizenry, however, is greatly reduced. In addition, the physical act of driving requires much of the officers' attention, diverting it from attention to subtle signs that criminal activity may be taking place. A further disadvantage is that automobiles are restricted in the areas they can access. In spite of these disadvantages, automobile patrol continues to be a mainstay of the patrol division.

 Automobile patrol has the greatest mobility and flexibility and is usually the most cost-effective patrol method.

To offset costs, many departments are buying refurbished highway patrol cars or using (and marking) vehicles seized from narcotics deals. In addition, given the rising costs of fuel, Sweeney (2004, pp.23–24) advocates that officers receive training on strategies to conserve gasoline; maintain their vehicles, including checking tire pressure; use directed patrol rather than driving aimlessly around; and make better use of aircraft and motorcycles.

Research on the effectiveness of the automobile patrol in preventing crime suggests that crimes prevented by a passing squad car are usually committed as soon as the police have gone.

**One-Officer versus Two-Officer Patrol Units**   Whether automobile patrol should have one or two officers per vehicle is controversial. Arguments can be made for either. One-officer units are more cost effective from a personnel point of view, allowing for twice the coverage and twice the power of observation. In addition, officers riding alone may be more careful and also more attentive to what is happening around them because they have no one to distract them with conversation.

Two-officer units are more cost effective in the number of patrol vehicles required and may increase officer safety. Some unionized departments' contracts stipulate that two officers be assigned to each patrol car. Some departments use two-officer units only in high-crime areas or only at night.

Efficient communication among one-officer units on patrol and a clear policy on when to call for backup is one way to increase the safety of single officers on patrol. Other ways include K-9-assisted patrol and vehicle-mounted video.

**In-Car Video (ICV)**   Increasingly popular are compact, high-resolution video cameras mounted by the squad car's rearview mirror. These cameras can record whatever happens in front of the car through a wide-angle lens. The camera is turned on and off by the officer and is supplemented by a lightweight, wireless microphone worn by the officer. The actual recording unit and tape are stored in a fireproof, bullet-resistant vault in the squad's trunk, inaccessible to suspects and officers alike. Therefore, any charges of tampering are avoided.

The cameras are used to document exactly what is said and done during a police stop, be it a traffic violation or a DWI. Such tapes help officers write their incident reports, assist in internal affairs investigations and help settle court cases. One such camera captured the murder of a Texas police officer and was key in gaining a conviction. Often people who are stopped and are acting belligerently will change their attitude completely when they learn they are being videotaped. In addition, the tapes serve a valuable training purpose.

Maghan et al. (2002, p.39) suggest: "Video technology could deter abuses by officers, limit frivolous complaints against officers about alleged abuses and help restore confidence in the fairness of police officers, streamline the truth-finding process by providing the best evidence and encourage the humane treatment of suspects and fairness and respect for civil rights and liberties." Westphal (2004, p.62) reports on a study by the International Association of Chiefs of Police (IACP) that found: "According to the 3,000 responses, video evidence captured by in-car cameras helped exonerate officers accused of wrongdoing 96.2 percent of the time. Complaints were sustained by the video recording 3.8 percent of the time."

**Global Positioning Systems (GPS)**   Rogers (2003, p.74) reports: "In the past two years, use of GPS technology has seen notable growth. . . . It may be used to track suspects, more efficiently monitor fleets or know the whereabouts of undercover surveillance officers, such as detectives or vice." According to Rogers (p.78): "The most obvious merit GPS offers is an advantage in officer safety."

**Facial Recognition for Patrol**   Whitehead (2004b, p.82) describes how facial recognition is being used in patrol cars in the Pinellas County (Florida) Sheriff's Office: "New digital cameras are being installed in 50 of the department's 550 marked patrol cars that will allow the officers on the street to photograph a subject with a digital camera, place the camera in a docking station in the patrol car, and, through a wireless communication to an image data base, conduct a face recognition search to determine if the individual has been previously arrested. And ultimately, give a name to the face—information that could be helpful in knowing how to handle the subject."

**Voice-Activated Patrol Car Equipment—Project 54**   Patrol vehicles have a broad array of high-tech radios, computers, GPS, video cameras, radars, lights, sirens and data bases available to field officers. Stockton (2004, p.148) notes: "The task of driving the car safely while effectively using the equipment can be daunting." However, technology is addressing this problem and promises to help officers be more efficient and safer during patrol operations. The technology is called Project 54, under development at the University of New Hampshire for the last five years. According to Stockton: "Over 200 police cars are currently on the road using Project 54, a technology that lets officers use their voice to activate patrol car equipment, run data inquiries and even change radio channels. Several more cars are added each week. Project 54 gets its name from the 40-year-old TV show *Car 54 Where Are You?*"

## Motorcycle Patrol

According to Kariya (2004a, p.24): "The motorcycle police officer has been an American icon for more than half a century." In fact, police motorcycle officers patrolled the streets of Pittsburgh, Pennsylvania, 100 years ago to enforce traffic regulations since their first appearance. Most police departments have their

David R. Frazier Photolibrary

*Motorcycles are a favorite of patrol officers because of their speed and maneuverability.*

motorcycles marked with the same insignia as their patrol cars. Motorcycle patrol has many of the same advantages as automobile patrol, especially speed and maneuverability. Motorcycles have greater access than automobiles to some areas and are better suited to heavy traffic, narrow alleys and rugged terrain.

Disadvantages include motorcycles' relatively high cost to operate; their limited use in bad weather; their inability to carry large amounts of equipment, evidence or prisoners; and the danger involved in riding them. Proper protective clothing and helmets are a must. A motorcycle also offers officers much less protection than a squad car should a person in a vehicle being pursued decide to start shooting.

## Bicycle Patrol

Bicycle patrol is not new. In the 1880s police in many large cities patrolled on bicycles. But automobile patrol displaced bicycle patrol for nearly 100 years until 1988 when bicycle patrol was reintroduced in Seattle, Washington.

Bicycle patrol is growing in popularity. Kariya (2004b, p.20) reports: "Today, more and more departments all over the world are adding bicycles to their arsenal of tools." Strandberg (2001a, p.102) suggests: "Bike patrols are on the cutting edge of community policing. Many cities have instituted these patrols, and their communities are better for it." Vonk (2002, p.92), likewise, notes: "The effectiveness of officers on bicycles in community policing roles has long been established." Vonk points out that bicycle patrol goes far beyond community policing; bicycle officers are effective in surveillance, night operations, traffic enforcement and crime detection as well.

Vonk (2003, p.85) notes: "Officers on bike patrol have pursued and caught armed robbers, home invasion criminals, car thieves, criminals breaking into cars and criminals in possession of stolen property. . . . They have assisted in searches for missing children. . . . Housing officers have used bicycles in the areas where both stealth and speed are essential, pursuing and arresting many

**Table 4.3**    Activities of Officers in Cars Compared to Officers on Bikes

| Officers Weekly Average | Officer in Car | Officer on Bike |
| --- | --- | --- |
| Hours on duty | 40.00 | 40.00 |
| Arrest—Felony | 01.00 | 02.25 |
| Arrest—Misdemeanor | 02.98 | 09.49 |
| Juvenile arrests & referrals | 00.88 | 02.11 |
| Field Interview Report (FIR) | 00.23 | 01.69 |
| Vice incidents | 00.48 | 04.67 |
| Property recovery incidents | 01.22 | 02.87 |
| Warrants served | 04.86 | 09.74 |
| Crimes discovered | 00.44 | 01.55 |
| Misdemeanor cleared/follow-up | 00.51 | 02.55 |
| Parking violation | 02.80 | 09.78 |
| Motorist assists | 00.64 | 06.57 |

SOURCE: Wesley Clark. "Electric Bicycles: High-Tech Tools for Law Enforcement." *Law Enforcement Technology*, November 2003, p.78. Reprinted by permission.

drug dealers, street thugs and trespassers." Clark (2003, p.78) reports on a study by the Cincinnati, Ohio, Police Department that compared activity of patrol officers on bikes to those in cars: "The study showed bike patrol officers reported significantly more activity in many categories, including arrests, crimes discovered, warrants served and motorist assists." The results of the study are summarized in Table 4.3.

In addition, Bellah (2001, p.78) notes: "The bicycle officer is an important public relations tool and is instrumental in bringing the citizenry closer to the police. An officer on bicycle, wearing the more casual 'uniform' of a polo-type shirt and shorts, is far more approachable than an officer zipping by in an air-conditioned cruiser with the windows up." Hicks (2003, p.89) reports on the success of the bike patrol at the University of Michigan Department of Public Safety: "When officers began patrolling the campus on mountain bikes, a new and fresh relationship developed between the police and the public. A rapport was easily established through the common ground provided by the mountain bike."

Like Vonk, Hicks (p.90) also reports: "UM's bike patrol has  .  .  .  proven to be a great crime prevention tool. It has enabled the department to target specific areas for regular enforcement or directed patrol. It has enhanced the safety of the students and the public during large-scale events. And it has become a source of great pride."

Heinecke (2004, p.81) observes: "One recent development for bicycle patrols is homeland security and disaster relief. On September 11, 2001, bicycle messengers, though not members of public service agencies, added to the relief effort by running messages, blood, first aid equipment and other supplies to and from Ground Zero."

Bicycle patrol is cost effective. For the cost of one police cruiser, 10 to 15 bicycle patrol officers can be outfitted (Bellah, p.78). Bicycles are also very maneuverable and good for enforcing bicycle, motorized scooter, rollerblading and

© Karl Weatherly/CORBIS

*Bicycle patrols are becoming more popular because of their ease in operation and their acceptance by the public, particularly children who view them as nonthreatening.*

skateboarding ordinances. On the Las Vegas strip where most of the elite casinos are located, all patrol is on bicycle: on the streets, in the parking areas and inside the casinos when officers respond to calls. Motor patrols go on the strip only when called for emergencies.

Additional advantages of bicycles include their stealth factor, allowing officers to sneak up on situations such as drug buys, and their green factor, referring to their environmentally friendly power source. This advantage, however, can turn into a disadvantage, as Strandberg (2001a, p.102) explains: "Riding a police bike up a huge incline on a hot summer day can result in an officer who's winded, exhausted and covered with sweat, who's not exactly arriving on the scene ready for anything." One answer to this is the electric bike. Equipped with a 36-volt battery, an e-bike can go up hills and go up to 18 to 20 mph on a straightaway.

Bicycles often are used in parks and on beaches and have many of the same advantages and disadvantages as motorcycles. Like motorcycles, bicycles leave the patrol officer extremely vulnerable. Officers should have the proper safety equipment and follow all basic safety practices while on bicycle patrol.

Mroz (2001, p.41), who has ridden a bicycle for 40 years and has been a recreational mountain bicyclist for nearly 15, cautions: "Bike patrol takes lots of practice and training." Recreational bicycling is a far cry from policing on a bicycle. For example, says Mroz (p.44): "Riding down stairs is a critical skill for police bicycle officers. It's not as hard as it seems, but the first time is an act of faith!" He also notes that during the final test after training for bicycle patrol, the last task was to "dump" the bike after a hard bike sprint and to run to handcuff a "suspect." Every officer nearly collapsed or fell as they started to run because of the change in muscle groups from biking to running: "Better not to learn this on the street."

*A Metropolitan Transportation Authority officer uses a Segway to patrol the Union Station in Los Angeles, California. Here he is giving directions to a family on vacation.*

AP/World Wide Press

Beck (2004, p.43) stresses: "Bike training is a high-risk, high-liability activity. As with training in firearms, defensive tactics and emergency vehicle operation, officers can get injured or even killed if the training activities aren't tightly controlled and properly supervised. Rarely is a bike class held in which someone doesn't fall. In fact, bike officers joke that there are two kinds of bike officers, those who have fallen and those who will."

### Segways

A new method of patrol is the Segway Human Transporter, commonly known as the "Segway HT" or simply a "Segway." Introduced in 2001, they are now being used by police departments throughout the country and for tasks ranging from patrol to HAZMAT.

Whitehead (2004a, p.24) explains: "They are the first self-balancing, electric-powered transportation. Segways are built similar to a children's scooter in that the rider must stand up on a platform with two wheels and hold onto a handlebar—but there, the similarities end. Segway is an extremely intelligent technology that has gyroscopes and tilt detectors that monitor the rider's center of gravity. When a rider leans forward, the Segway follows the shift in gravity and moves forward. And when a rider leans back, the Segway moves backward. Turns are made by twisting the handlebar. The harder the turn of the handlebar, the harder and tighter the turn of the Segway."

### Mounted Patrol

Fine (2001, p.6) recalls: "Folklore of the frontier lawman on horseback in the American Old West evokes an image of peace and justice. . . . That image of an officer on horseback remains a part of modern law enforcement. In the United States today, more than 600 organized mounted police patrol units form a visi-

*Mounted patrol serves important symbolic and practical functions. They are especially good for crowd control; one horse and rider is equal to 10 foot patrol officers in a crowd-control situation.*

A. Ramey/Photo Edit

ble pedestal and serve citizens throughout their jurisdiction. . . . An officer on horseback invites constructive community contact in its own unique way."

The greatest advantage is that officers on horseback are usually more acceptable than K-9s as crowd-control instruments and are much more effective at controlling a disorderly crowd than officers on foot or in any kind of vehicle (other than a tank). According to Slahor (2001, p.237): "The horse gives the police a more visible presence in a crowd, and the horse gives the officer a better view of problems." One horse and rider is equal to 10 foot patrol officers in a crowd-control situation.

Sherman (2003, p.55) notes: "Horse-mounted patrols are an economical adjunct to more sophisticated law enforcement technologies." According to Sherman (p.57): "One officer mounted on a horse can see as much as 10 to 15 officers on the ground." Mounted officers can often handle 911 calls and other emergencies with more speed and visibility than foot patrols. In addition, mounted patrol members can help search for evidence at crime scenes, round up stray animals after a truck has tipped over and search for lost children or bodies in tall corn or fields.

Mounted patrol is decreasing in the United States but is still used in some large cities for crowd and traffic control. Expense is one of the main disadvantages of mounted patrol. Nonetheless, as Fine (p.7) suggests: "Today, enhanced with modern practices, communication and technology, officers on horseback symbolize the original concept of American law enforcement—they provide protection, denote authority and strengthen community involvement."

## Air Patrol

Air patrol is the most expensive form of patrol, but it is highly effective when large areas are involved. For example, searching for a suspect, an escaped convict, a lost child or a downed aircraft can all be accomplished most efficiently by air. Small airplanes and helicopters are used as eyes in the sky not only to report traffic tie-ups but to work along with police cars to conduct criminal surveillance or to detect, clock and stop speeding vehicles. In addition, they can reduce the hazards and costs associated with high-speed pursuits.

Strandberg (2001b, p.20) notes: "Having police officers in helicopters, patrolling the city by air, results in quicker response times, safer methods of policing and overall better performance." Similar to mounted patrol, two officers in a helicopter can do the work of 10 to 15 officers on the ground (Strandberg, p.20).

Helicopters are valuable in rescue efforts during disasters such as fires in tall buildings, floods and earthquakes. Police aircraft and helicopters are also a cost-effective way to transport prisoners long distances. As mentioned, however, air patrol is quite expensive to operate and maintain. In addition to the high cost of buying, operating and maintaining aircraft, other disadvantages include citizen complaints about the noise and about being spied on.

## Personal Vertical Takeoff and Landing Aircraft

A promising new method of patrol is the personal vertical takeoff and landing (VTOL) aircraft, illustrated in Figure 4.1. Cowper (2004, p.36) says: "The VTOL aircraft bring with them capabilities that will allow the creation of new and innovative tactics vitally necessary for police to be successful in the future." He notes: "One of the safest and most effective means of vehicular pursuit is from the air." Cowper asks: "What if the majority of pursuits could be conducted by aircraft capable of following, monitoring and containing a suspect without disrupting traffic or further endangering innocent bystanders, helping to coordinate the deployment of ground units from a distance until the suspect could be safely cornered and captured?"

## Water Patrol

Water patrol units are extremely specialized and not in great use except in areas with extensive coasts or a great deal of lake or river traffic.

Like aircraft, boats are expensive to buy, operate and maintain. Further, those who operate them must have special training. Nonetheless, boats are the best means to effectively control violators of water safety regulations as well as to apprehend drug and gun smugglers. They are also valuable in rescue operations during times of flooding as well as in dragging operations for drowning cases.

A trend in water patrol is the use of personal watercraft (PWC) or jet ski, which has a very shallow draft, high maneuverability and stability. They are also easy to operate. The front compartment allows for storage of a ticket book, high-powered binoculars and a portable breath test. Many are equipped with public-address systems, sirens and lights.

In Miami Beach, Florida, officers on personal watercraft find they can approach areas not accessible to conventional patrol boats because of shallow water, low bridges or other impediments. The watercraft have been used in search and recovery, in recovering drowning victims, in deterring boating law violations

**Figure 4.1**  A Personal Vertical Takeoff and Landing Aircraft

(including reckless operation and DUI violations), in checking fishing licenses and catch limits and in improved public relations.

## *Special-Terrain Vehicles*

Police departments responsible for areas with extensive coastlines may also rely on jeeps or amphibious vehicles to patrol the beaches. This is also true of departments whose jurisdiction includes miles of desert. Those who must patrol where snow is common frequently rely on snowmobiles. Departments whose jurisdiction includes remote parts of the country may also use jeeps or all-terrain vehicles (ATVs). According to Strandberg (2004, p.18): "ATV use in law enforcement is here to stay and expanding every year."

An additional advantage of ATVs is that they can carry a substantial amount of support equipment. Streit (2002, p.17) says: "Some of the typical offenses found while patrolling are noise violations, fire hazards, illegal dumping, illegal shooting, trespassing with motor vehicles, illegal hunting, abandoning stolen vehicles and undocumented alien trafficking." Special-terrain vehicles are useful not only for routine patrol but also for rescue missions.

### K-9-Assisted Patrol

The K-9-assisted patrol is becoming more popular, with even smaller departments beginning to establish K-9 units. However, as Garrett (2001, p.26) stresses: "A K-9 program requires the right handler, the right dog and the right amount of training to be a success." The K-9 unit can be used to control crowds, break up fights, recover lost articles or find evidence. In addition, dogs can provide protection for a one-officer patrol.

Detector dogs are specially trained to sniff out narcotics, explosives or bodies (live and cadaver). Drug- and bomb-sniffing dogs are used extensively in international airports and border checkpoints. Tracker dogs can follow the scent of a fleeing suspect. Search and rescue K-9s were used after the Oklahoma City bombing and the September 11, 2001, terrorist attack on the World Trade Center to locate trapped or deceased victims.

Moore (2004, p.75) contends: "Dogs can do the work of three people . . . if you pit machines against dogs, the dog can do five times the work of the machine." According to Moore (p.79), dogs are being used extensively by border patrols: "In fiscal years 1993 to 2002 Border Patrol canine teams found 244,965 concealed persons, 3,407,464 pounds of narcotics and other drugs worth more than $2.7 trillion and seized more than $42 million in U.S. currency."

O'Hare International Airport in Chicago is using a Beagle Brigade to sniff out contraband plants, vegetables, meat and other items smuggled in from overseas. O'Hare's team has been credited with the seizures of 360 pounds of meat and 456 pounds of fruits and vegetables. Overall, Beagle Brigades at the nation's ports of entry were credited with identifying more than 75,000 prohibited agricultural items having cleared 50,173 flights ("Legal Beagles Sniff Out Edible Contraband," 2004, p.4). K-9 units are also an asset to public relations efforts. They can be used for demonstrations at state fairs or in local schools, showing how well trained and under control the animals are.

The German shepherd is the most frequently used dog for police work. Other popular breeds include Labrador retrievers, Giant Schnauzers, Rottweilers, Dobermans, Bouviers, Newfoundlands, Airedale terriers and Alaskan malamutes.

One dog trainer believes K-9 units can help revitalize communities: "Everybody loves a police dog. Other police officers call you to catch the baddest of the bad, but at the same time you get to take your dog to the nursing homes and the Boy Scout troop" (Hamilton, 2003, p.18).

Like other forms of specialized patrol, K-9-assisted patrol has disadvantages. Most police dogs work with only one handler. Should that handler become ill or disabled or be killed, the dog must be retrained. Further, if a K-9 handler is wounded, the dog may not allow emergency personnel near the officer to help. To counter such problems, many departments are cross-training their dogs to work with two handlers.

Another difficulty is that a K-9, like most dogs, is territorial, and its handler and its K-9 cruiser are part of its territory. It may become aggressive without being told to do so if its handler or cruiser is approached by strangers.

Training constitutes the greatest expense of K-9 units. The training usually takes 10 to 12 weeks and can cost one to two thousand dollars per team, in addition to the officer's salary during this time. Often the dogs are donated. The other expense is modifying the patrol car, removing the back seat and replacing it with a platform. Some units are equipped with a radio-controlled door or window opener that allows officers to release their K-9s from a distance. An alternative is for officers to leave a back window rolled down so the dog can get out of the car if called.

Another factor to consider when implementing a K-9 program is the potential increase in vulnerability to lawsuits, particularly in cases involving searches and use-of-force issues. Because law enforcement officers use K-9s to find people, clear buildings, sniff out bombs and locate evidence or contraband, their use implicates the Fourth Amendment. In *United States v. Place* (1983), the Supreme Court held that the exposure of luggage to a canine sniff in a public place did not constitute a search. However, as Walker (2001, p.31) cautions: "Because courts are divided over when a dog sniff constitutes a search, and because state courts may find dog sniffs are searches under their own state constitutions, officers should consult with their legal advisors before using a dog to sniff items, locations or persons for the presence of contraband." Courts have also ruled police use of K-9s as a use of force, some going so far as to deem it lethal force. However, as one officer stated in defending the "lethality" of his K-9: "I can recall the dog. I can't recall a bullet." As noted in Chapter 3 and echoed by Green (2004, p.39), an excellent source of K-9 related case law is the website of Terry Fleck, an expert in canine legalities (www.k9fleck.org).

### Combination Patrol

No single patrol method or combination of methods is best. Usually, the greater the variety of methods available, the more effective a department will be. Which methods of patrol to use will vary depending on the department's physical jurisdiction, the types of crimes occurring, the size of the department, the training of its officers and its budget. Once a department knows which methods it has available, it can determine effective patrol techniques.

## Patrol Techniques and Strategies

Patrol is, indeed, an essential function of law enforcement, yet it is not always as effective as it could or should be. To improve effectiveness, numerous patrol techniques and strategies have been tried and evaluated throughout the years, including routine patrol, rotating or fixed area and shift assignments, rapid response, differential police response and directed patrol. Perhaps the most classic study of patrol as it is traditionally performed is the Kansas City Preventive Patrol Experiment.

### The Kansas City Preventive Patrol Experiment

Although this study was conducted over three decades ago in 1972, it is still the most comprehensive study of the effects of routine patrol. In this experiment, 15 beats in Kansas City were divided into three groups, each with five beats:

*Group 1—Reactive Beats:* No routine patrol, responding only to calls for service.
*Group 2—Control Beats:* Maintained their normal level of routine preventive patrol.

*Group 3—Proactive Beats:* Doubled or tripled the level of routine preventive patrol.

 The Kansas City Preventive Patrol Experiment found that increasing or decreasing routine preventive patrol had no measurable effect on:
- Crime.
- Citizens' fear of crime.
- Community attitudes toward the police on delivery of police services.
- Police response time.
- Traffic accidents.

Says Klockars (1983, p.130), commenting on the findings of the Kansas City Experiment: "It makes about as much sense to have police patrol routinely in cars to fight crime as it does to have fire fighters patrol routinely in fire trucks to fight fire." However, Sweeney (2003, p.93) contends: "Despite nagging questions about the efficacy of uniformed patrols in preventing crime, the strategy of random mobile patrol continues to dominate daily operations in most police departments."

While the Kansas City Experiment demonstrated the limited effect increasing or decreasing the number of officers engaged in unstructured random patrol appears to have, other studies have found changing area and shift assignments can have a significant effect.

## Area and Shift Assignments

Patrol shifts typically divide the 24-hour period into three 8-hour shifts. One common division is 7:00 A.M. to 3:00 P.M., 3:00 P.M. to 11:00 P.M. and 11:00 P.M. to 7:00 A.M. (the dog shift). The municipality served by the department typically is divided into geographic areas on the basis of personnel available for patrol. Many departments rotate shifts or areas or both. Other departments assign permanent shifts, areas or both, feeling this allows officers to become more familiar with their assignments and, consequently, more effective in patrolling. A Bureau of Justice Statistics study (*Community Policing in Local Police Departments*, n.d.) found that 90 percent of all local law enforcement agencies serving populations of 50,000 or more helped facilitate community policing goals by giving patrol officers responsibility for specific geographic beats.

The shifts and areas new officers are assigned to depend on the supervisor's philosophy. Some departments assign rookies to high-crime areas and "fast" shifts to help them learn their new job more rapidly and to assess their performance. Other departments assign rookies to the slowest shifts and the lowest crime areas to allow them to ease into their new job. Two basic forms of shift scheduling are used. The first assigns equal numbers of patrol officers to each of the three shifts. The second assigns officers based on anticipated need.

As departments become more proactive, many are using *proportionate assignment,* which considers not only the number of calls but many other factors as well. In **proportionate assignment,** area assignments are based on the data available from requests for service, taking into account the amount and severity of crime occurring in various areas, population density, routes to the areas and any special problems that might be involved, such as large groups of non-English-speaking citizens. Boundaries of the patrol beat are determined by considering how rapidly a responding car can cover the area, and assignments are made so that in normal circumstances police can respond within three minutes.

## *Response Time*

Patrol effectiveness is frequently measured in **response time,** the time elapsed between when the call is received and when the police arrive on the scene. One obvious reason for rapid response is the opportunity to apprehend a person engaged in criminal activity. However, as Klockars (p.130) stresses: "Police currently make on-scene arrests in about 3 percent of the serious crimes reported to them. If they traveled faster than a speeding bullet to all reports of serious crimes, this on-scene arrest rate would rise to no higher than 5 percent."

Spelman and Brown (1991) replicated the citizen reporting component of the Kansas City Experiment response time analysis. They (p.164) found: "In the cities we studied, . . . *arrests that could be attributed to fast police response were made in only 2.9 percent of reported serious crimes.*" They attribute this low response-related arrest rate in large part to the fact that 75 percent of all serious crimes are **discovery crimes**; that is, they are completed before they are discovered and reported. This is in direct contrast to **involvement crimes,** in which the victim and suspect confront each other.

 Citizen reporting time affects the possibility of on-scene arrests more than police response time. Citizens delay calling the police because of decision-making problems or problems in communicating with the police.

After citizens decide to call the police, they may encounter other problems: no phone available, not knowing what number to call or not being able to communicate clearly with the person receiving the call. Response time is also increased when the department does not have enough patrol officers available for such duty at any particular time. Nonetheless, citizens *expect* a rapid response when they call. This expectation could be modified, however. The response may not need to be immediate, and it may not have to be made by a sworn officer. Many police departments are implementing differential police response strategies.

## *Differential Police Response*

**Differential police response strategies** vary the rapidity of response as well as the responder based on the type of incident and the time of occurrence. Differential police response strategies replace the traditional "first-come, first-served" and as-fast-as-possible response, depending on the type of incident and whether it is in progress, proximate or cold. Usually, if a crime is in progress, the response will be immediate and made by a sworn officer. If it is **proximate,** that is, recently committed, response to the call may be put ahead of other, less urgent calls. If the incident is "cold," that is, it happened several hours before, the response may be "as time permits" or even by appointment.

The most common alternatives used in differential response strategies include response by sworn or nonsworn personnel and whether it is immediate, expedited, routine or by appointment. Other alternatives for minor crimes include contact by telephone, mail, referral or no response. For example, a major personal injury would require an immediate response by sworn personnel, whereas a minor noncrime call might be handled by a referral. As long as callers are told what to expect and the reasoning behind the type of response selected, they usually are satisfied with the response, even if it is delayed up to several hours or scheduled as an appointment for the following day.

## Directed Patrol

If a department's goals are clear, and if the department has kept accurate records on calls for service and on crimes committed in the community, then based on this data, patrol time should be effectively structured to provide the best service and protection possible. It is usually much more productive to have officers' discretionary time directed toward accomplishing specific department objectives than to expect each officer simply to do his or her "thing." **Directed patrol** uses officers' discretionary patrol time to focus on specific department goals. These goals are often identified through problem-oriented policing.

# Patrol and Problem-Oriented Policing

**Problem-oriented policing (POP)**—that is, grouping calls for service to identify specific problems—was first formally introduced by Herman Goldstein in 1979. Based on 20 years of research, this approach suggests a fundamental shift in perspective, from reactive to proactive policing.

In this approach, police are trained to think not in terms of incidents but in terms of problems. According to Goldstein (1990, p.33): "In handling incidents, police officers usually deal with the most obvious, superficial manifestations of a deeper problem—not the problem itself." He contends that "incidents are usually handled as isolated, self-contained events. Connections are not systematically made among them, except when they suggest a common crime pattern leading to identifying the offender." What is needed, suggests Goldstein (p.33), is a different approach—problem-oriented policing:

> The first step in problem-oriented policing is to move beyond just handling incidents. It calls for recognizing that incidents are often merely overt symptoms of problems. This pushes the police in two directions: (1) It requires that they recognize the relationships between incidents (similarities of behavior, location, persons involved, etc.); and (2) it requires that they take a more in-depth interest in incidents by acquainting themselves with some of the conditions and factors that give rise to them.

The difference between incident-driven policing and problem-oriented policing is illustrated in Figure 4.2.

As noted by Eisenberg and Glasscock (2001, p.5): "Since the 1980's law enforcement agencies have applied the concept of problem-oriented policing to many community problems, such as alcohol-related crimes, burglaries, graffiti, sex offenses and trespassing. While POP has become a highly visible and utilitarian policing philosophy, the use of the SARA problem-solving technique has contributed greatly to its effectiveness."

## The SARA Problem-Solving Process

 The problem-solving process called SARA consists of four stages:

- Scanning—identifying the problem.
- Analysis—learning the problem's causes, scope and effects.

- Response—acting to alleviate the problem.
- Assessment—determining whether the response worked.

*Excellence in Problem-Oriented Policing* (2002, pp.2–3) describes each of these four stages:

**Scanning:**
- Identify recurring problems of concern to the public and the police.
- Prioritize problems.
- Develop broad goals.
- Confirm that the problems exist.
- Select one problem for examination.

**Analysis:**
- Try to identify and understand the events and conditions that precede and accompany the problem.
- Identify the consequences of the problem for the community.
- Determine how frequently the problem occurs and how long it has been taking place.
- Identify the conditions that give rise to the problem.

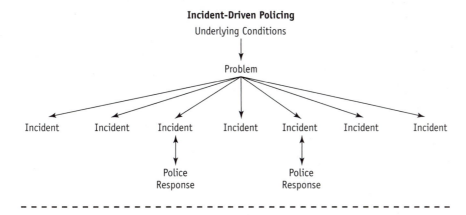

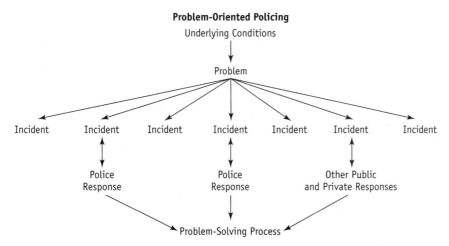

**Figure 4.2**   Incident-Driven and Problem-Oriented Policing Compared

SOURCE: John E. Eck and William Spelman. *Problem Solving: Problem-Oriented Policing in Newport News.* Washington, DC: Police Executive Research Forum, 1987, pp.xvi–xvii. Reprinted by permission.

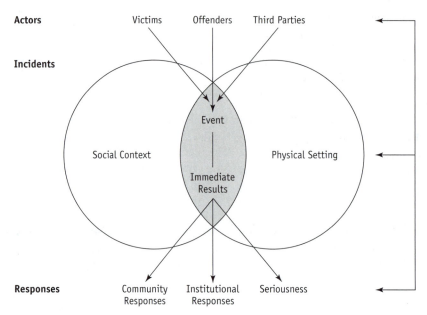

**Figure 4.3** Problem-Analysis Guide

SOURCE: John E. Eck and William Spelman. *Problem-Solving: Problem-Oriented Policing in Newport News.* Washington, DC: Police Executive Research Forum, 1987, p.55. Reprinted by permission.

- Narrow the scope of the problem as specifically as possible.
- Identify a variety of resources that may be of assistance in developing a deeper understanding of the problem.

**Response:**
- Search for what communities with similar problems have done.
- Brainstorm interventions.
- Choose among the alternative solutions.
- Outline a response plan and identify responsible parties.
- State the specific goals for the response plan.
- Identify relevant data to be collected.
- Carry out the planned activities.

**Assessment:**
- Determine whether the plan was implemented.
- Determine whether the goals were attained and collect pre- and postresponse qualitative and quantitative data.
- Identify any new strategies needed to augment the original plan.
- Conduct ongoing assessment to ensure continued effectiveness.

Figure 4.3 illustrates the areas that should be considered during problem solving, including the individuals involved, the incidents themselves and past responses. Table 4.4 illustrates potential sources of information available for identifying problems. Table 4.5 depicts the range of problems facing Newport News (Virginia) officers.

**Assessing Responses to Problems**    According to Eck (2002, p.6): "You begin planning for an evaluation when you take on a problem. The evaluation builds throughout the SARA process, culminates during the assessment and provides

**Table 4.4**   Potential Sources of Information for Identifying Problems

*Crime Analysis Unit*

Time trends and patterns (time of day, day of week, monthly, seasonal, and other cyclical events), and patterns of similar events (offender descriptions, victim characteristics, locations, physical settings, and other circumstances).

*Patrol*

Recurring calls, bad areas, active offenders, victim types, complaints from citizens.

*Investigations*

Recurring crimes, active offenders, victim difficulties, complaints from citizens.

*Crime Prevention*

Physical conditions, potential victims, complaints from citizens.

*Vice*

Drug dealing, illegal alcohol sales, gambling, prostitution, organized crime.

*Communications*

Call types, repeat calls from same location, temporal peaks in calls for service.

*Chief's Office*

Letters and calls from citizens, concerns of elected officials, concerns from city manager's office.

*Other Law Enforcement Agencies*

Multi-jurisdictional concerns.

*Elected Officials*

Concerns and complaints.

*Local Government Agencies*

Plans that could influence crimes, common difficulties, complaints from citizens.

*Schools*

Juvenile concerns, vandalism, employee safety.

*Community Leaders*

Problems of constituents.

*Business Groups*

Problems of commerce and development.

*Neighborhood Watch*

Local problems regarding disorder, crime, and other complaints.

*Newspapers and Other News Media*

Indications of problems not detected from other sources, problems in other jurisdiction that could occur in any city.

*Community Surveys*

Problems of citizens in general.

SOURCE: John E. Eck and William Spelman. *Problem-Solving: Problem-Oriented Policing in Newport News.* Washington, DC: Police Executive Research Forum, 1987, p.46. Reprinted by permission.

**Table 4.5** Newport News Officers' Range of Problems

|  | *Citywide* | *Neighborhood* |
|---|---|---|
| **Crime problems** | Domestic homicides | Personal robberies (Central business district) |
|  | Gas station driveoffs | Commercial burglaries (Jefferson Avenue business district) |
|  | Assaults on police officers | Vacant building (Central business district) |
|  |  | Residential burglaries (New Briarfield Apts) |
|  |  | Residential burglaries (Glenn Gardens Apts) |
|  |  | Larcenies (Beechmont Gardens Apts) |
|  |  | Thefts from autos (Newport News Shipbuilding) |
|  |  | Drug dealing (32nd and Chestnut) |
| **Disorder problems** | Runaway youths | Rowdy youths (Peninsula Skating Rink) |
|  | Driving under the influence | Shot houses (Aqua Vista Apts) |
|  | Disturbances at convenience stores | Disturbances (Marshall Avenue 7-Eleven) |
|  |  | Dirt bikes (Newmarket Creek) |
|  |  | Disturbances (Village Square Shopping Center) |

SOURCE: John E. Eck and William Spelman. *Problem-Solving: Problem-Oriented Policing in Newport News.* Washington, DC: Police Executive Research Forum. 1987, p.xxii. Reprinted by permission.

findings that help you determine if you should revisit earlier stages to improve the response." Figure 4.4 illustrates the problem-solving process and evaluation.

Eck (p.10) describes two types of evaluations to conduct: **process evaluation** that determines if the response was implemented as planned and **impact evaluation** that determines if the problem declined. Table 4.3 provides guidance in interpreting the results of process and impact evaluation. Eck (p.27) suggests several nontraditional measures that will indicate if a problem has been affected by the interventions:

- Reduced instances of repeat victimization
- Decreases in related crimes or incidents
- Neighborhood indicators: increased profits for legitimate businesses in target area; increased use of area/increased (or reduced) foot and vehicular traffic; increased property values; improved neighborhood appearance; increased occupancy in problem buildings; less loitering; fewer abandoned cars; less truancy
- Increased citizen satisfaction regarding the handling of the problem, which can be determined through surveys, interviews, focus groups, electronic bulletin boards and the like
- Reduced citizen fear related to the problem

**The SARA Model in Action** An example of problem solving in a situation facing most patrol officers is the Salt Lake City Police Department's approach to dealing with false alarms. Their solution, which used the SARA model received runner-up status in the Police Executive Research Forum's 2001 Herman Goldstein Award (*Excellence in Problem-Oriented Policing,* 2001).

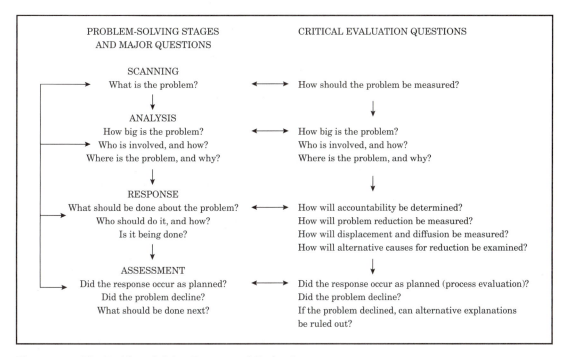

**Figure 4.4** The Problem-Solving Process and Evaluation

SOURCE: John E. Eck. *Assessing Responses to Problems: An Introductory Guide for Police Problem-Solvers.* Washington, DC: Office of Community Oriented Policing Services, 2002, p.6.

**Scanning**    Scanning revealed the following problems:

- False alarm calls were draining patrol resources, making up 12 percent of all dispatched calls, contributing to a significant backlog of calls for service.
- Average police response time to alarm activations was up to 40 minutes, well beyond when police could hope to apprehend an intruder.
- More than 99 percent of all alarm calls were false, making responding officers increasingly complacent, risking injury.
- Nearly $500,000 of the budget (1.2 percent) was attributable to false alarms, but only $150,000 in alarm fines were collected.
- False alarms had three main causes: user errors due to insufficient training; inadequate verification by alarm company monitoring stations; and improper installation, inferior equipment and application at the alarm site.

**Analysis**    Analysis revealed that past efforts to reduce the volume of false alarms through permits, warnings, fines and suspensions had only a modest effect. Examining other approaches tried elsewhere, from cost recovery to alarm industry regulation to outsourcing alarm administration, similarly proved only moderate effectiveness. Police response to alarms was most effective and efficient if the police had verification that an alarm activation indicated suspicious activity. Private security guards were ideally suited to make the initial verification. A legal opinion established that police were under no legal obligation to respond to all alarm activations.

**Response**    The police department proposed to the city council that a verified alarm response ordinance be required in all alarm activations and that eyewitness verification of suspicious activity be identified by alarm company personnel or a private guard before notifying the police department. A campaign was then conducted to inform the public, elected officials and the alarm industry about the purposes and advantages of verified response, and the police department conducted training for private security officers.

**Assessment** The police department experienced a 90 percent decrease in alarm-related calls for service during the first nine months, representing 6,338 fewer calls for service or the equivalent of five full-time patrol officers (valued at about $400,000). There are fewer backlogs of calls for service, and responses to high-priority calls for service have dropped from five to three minutes.

Alarm owners benefit by achieving a 6- to 15-minute alarm activation response compared to the 40-minute average the police provided. The alarm industry benefited by now providing customers with a valued quick response.

By using problem-oriented policing and no longer attempting to manage a private sector problem, the Salt Lake City's verified response alarm ordinance provides a long-term solution to a problem the department had struggled with for 20 years.

### Implementing Problem-Oriented Policing

Reuland et al. (2001, p.143) suggest: "Successful implementation [of problem-oriented policing] depends on quality staff who know their part within the organization, who have the tools to deliver, who are allowed to deliver, who want to deliver and who do deliver outputs and outcomes."

Dejong et al. (2001) used expectancy motivation theory to examine variations in police officers' problem-solving behavior. They looked at opportunity, skill, instrumentality (external incentives provided formally by the department) and reward-cost balance. Opportunity included self-directed time, shift, socioeconomic distress level of the beat and staffing level. Of these, only self-directed time and district staffing level were significant. Higher levels of district staffing were associated with more time spent on problem solving. Of the skill factors examined (college education, training in community policing and years of police experience) only the amount of experience was significant. Officers with fewer than 20 years' experience were more inclined to spend time problem solving.

Of the instrumentality variables, the most significant was the nature of the officer's work assignment: community policing officer versus patrol generalist. None of the reward-cost balance variables (belief that enforcing the law is most important, ambition for promotion, distrust of citizens, etc.) were significant. Dejong et al. (pp.58–59) conclude: "Especially powerful were the effects of giving an officer a specialized community policing job assignment. . . . It appears that the single most powerful thing a department can do to increase its problem-solving dosage is to assign more officers to these specialist jobs." An emphasis on problem solving is one distinguishing feature of community policing.

## Patrol and Community Policing

Patrol officers can be catalysts for joint police and community problem-solving endeavors. As Gerber (2001, p.40) suggests: "The face of law enforcement is changing from report-writing investigators who respond to emergencies and catch criminals to multi-faceted neighborhood workers tasked with affecting quality-of-life issues in the communities they serve. . . . Today's police officers must be part cop, part social worker, part paramedic, part teacher, part computer technician, part pastor, part parent and part politician."

Part of the evolution to community policing involves a shift in the patrol methods used, such as greater use of foot, bicycle, mounted and K-9-assisted patrol. Community policing also involves the redeployment of patrol officers from vehicles into small, decentralized police posts. In fact, some of the most effective community policing strategies used by patrol officers are quite simple and cost nothing. For example, the Burger King in Charles County, Maryland, was the first business in the country to set aside space as a "writing station" for officers. According to the owner, the main reason for setting up the writing stations was to help employees feel safer and to take an active part in community-police relations (Brown, 2001, p.18). Another example of a simple, no-cost strategy is New York City's Cab Watch. As Haldar (2001, p.13) explains:

> Cab Watch broadens the city's reach in law enforcement without spending a dime of tax money. With the help of the New York Police Department, Cab Watch trains cab drivers to report incidents and accidents without putting themselves or others at risk. Then, it outfits the drivers with 911-direct wireless phones, which are donated by Sprint PCS. More than 40 professionals have volunteered to help Cab Watch with management, accounting, public relations and graphic design. . . .
>
> In the last two years, Cab Watch has expanded from a 50-driver pilot program to more than 1,700 drivers outfitted with wireless phones and ready to dial 911 on the spot. Drivers have alerted police to hundreds of incidents, helping to lead to the arrest of suspects in slayings, hit-and-runs, burglaries, assaults, even incidents of pick-pocketing. The cabbies' quick calls also have helped save lives in car accidents and building fires.

Other strategies are more complex and involve numerous partnerships with patrol officers. One such strategy, the Model Neighborhood Program, used in West Valley City and modeled after the LAPD Model Neighborhood Program, is described by Kerstein (2001). The program's foundation is a partnership of city, county and federal agencies, the community and the local police department. The officer assigned to the area finds the names and addresses of each property's owners. Then HUD personnel, working with task force members of local police agencies, plan and conduct an area sweep serving arrest warrants, evicting problem tenants and identifying specific "hot spots" warranting extra attention. Coordination with local government agencies responsible for graffiti removal, impounding abandoned cars and trash pickup is also undertaken. At the same time, the local city attorney or ordinance enforcement officer works with the police to contact owners of neglected property and invites them to participate in the program by evicting problem tenants, renovating their properties and installing screening procedures for tenants. If owners are unwilling to join the program and improve their property, abatement procedures are begun to confiscate and raze the property.

Vernon (2004, p.66) notes that specific programs are not always necessary: "The observant officer who notices potential security issues at a residence or business, then takes the time to inform the owner/occupant and, further, makes the effort to offer solutions, has taken a major step not only toward potentially preventing a criminal act, but also in forging strong public relations within his assigned area, a cornerstone in community oriented policing."

## SUMMARY

Patrol service has been described as the "backbone of the police department." The fact that patrol officers, those who actually accomplish the department's goals, are lowest in status and in pay results in a serious organizational contradiction.

Officers on patrol serve many functions. Among the important patrol functions are responding to noncrime calls for service, controlling traffic, assisting at the scene of a crime, conducting preliminary investigations, gathering intelligence, making arrests, patrolling public gatherings and special events, assisting at the scene of a fire, providing community service and general peacekeeping activities and partnering with others to solve problems related to crime and disorder. Between 80 and 90 percent of all calls for police service are of a noncriminal nature. Patrol officers are often responsible for maintaining order with large groups of people. Crowds may be classified as self-controlled, active or explosive.

Methods of patrol include foot, automobile, motorcycle, bicycle, mounted, air, water, special-terrain vehicles and K-9 assisted. Automobile patrol has the greatest mobility and flexibility and is usually the most cost-effective method of patrol.

Different patrol techniques have met with varying degrees of success. The Kansas City Preventive Patrol Experiment found that increasing or decreasing routine preventive patrol had no measurable effect on crime, citizens' fear of crime, community attitudes toward the police on delivery of police services, police response time or traffic accidents. Regardless of the patrol strategy used, police effectiveness is greatly influenced by citizen involvement. Citizen reporting time affects the possibility of on-scene arrests more than does police response time. Response time is often lengthened because citizens delay calling the police. They often do so because of decision-making problems or problems communicating with the police.

The SARA problem-solving technique has contributed greatly to policing effectiveness and consists of four stages:

- Scanning—identifying the problem
- Analysis—learning the problem's causes, scope and effects
- Response—acting to alleviate the problem
- Assessment—determining whether the response worked

## APPLICATION

The local chamber of commerce has asked that you assign an officer to foot patrol in the business district because of numerous problems, such as vandalism, shoplifting, boisterous conduct by young people and general disruption of business because of gang activity.

You realize foot patrol is proactive, designed to prevent crime and deal with social problems before they become overtly criminal. The city council wants you to proceed; it will add an officer to your department to provide this service.

## INSTRUCTIONS

Write a policy and procedure that would offer guidelines to an officer and satisfy the business community's request. Keep in mind that foot patrol is an important assignment with many advantages over automobile patrol: more person-to-person contact, high visibility, enhanced public relations, the potential to be proactive and solve problems and increased community support.

Begin the policy with a statement of need. Consider that the officer, being highly visible, may need more supervision. Who will supervise the officer, and what will the officer's duties be? Some type of communication with the officer while on duty must be established, and a system of assignment decided on. Decide what parameters would be useful to officers on foot patrol when they employ the directed-patrol approach and problem-oriented policing. List expectations for the officer's conduct and responsibilities while serving this important function.

### AN EXERCISE IN CRITICAL THINKING

At 2:04 A.M. on a Friday, a burglar alarm went off at Prior Lake Marine, a business located on the outskirts of Prior Lake. Officer Ferderer of the Prior Lake Police Department, responding to the dispatcher's request at 2:07 A.M. for assistance in investigating a burglary in progress, drove toward the burglary scene. The only car he saw was a red 2000 Honda Accord with three men in it proceeding on a residential street just two blocks from Prior Lake Marine and headed away from that area. Ferderer turned and stopped the car about a mile from the scene at approximately 2:15 A.M.

Ferderer waited until Officer Gliniany of the Savage Police Department arrived to assist, then approached the car on foot. Another officer arrived a short time later. The three men in the car were all in short-sleeved shirts and jeans and were sweating heavily (their bodies were literally "soaked with sweat"). Although it was a warm night, the heavy sweating was obviously inconsistent with the men's having just been driving around. Ferderer could see that the driver and the rear-seat passenger were wearing tennis shoes and that the front-seat passenger was barefooted. In fact, as Gliniany testified, the front-seat passenger's feet were muddy.

After telling the men in the front seat to put their hands on the dashboard, Ferderer asked the driver, Terry Theis, what he was doing in the area. He said he had stopped to "take a leak" and that he, Rolland Moffatt and Gerald Moffatt were on their way to New Prague to visit a friend. Ferderer asked who the friend was, and apparently no name was given. Ferderer told the men there had just been a burglary in the area and he was checking it out. He did not tell the men they were suspects.

A decision was made to separate the men from one another by placing them in separate squad cars. Ferderer did this by removing each man, one at a time, frisking him for weapons and then placing him in a squad car.

After the three men were placed in separate squad cars, Officer Gliniany contacted Officer Brandt, who was with officers at the burglary scene, and asked Brandt if there were footprints at the scene. Brandt reported there were.

Under instructions radioed by a police sergeant at the burglary scene, the officers told each of the two men with shoes to take off one tennis shoe. At this point, Theis said

he asked one officer if he was unde[r] [arrest. The offi]cer said, "No, you're being detaine[d." The officers got a] third tennis shoe, that of the bar[efooted passen]ger, by reaching in and removing [it from the] front-seat passenger side, where it was [located. It] was then about 2:45 A.M. Officer Klegin o[f the] Police Department, who had been dispatched a[t] A.M.; drove to the scene of the stop, arriving about 15 minutes after the shoes had been seized, picked up the three shoes and drove them to the burglary scene. There he compared the distinctive treads of the tennis shoes, each a different brand, with the two different fresh tennis shoe footprints he found. He concluded that the pattern and size of each print had been made by two of the men.

Ten to fifteen minutes after Officer Klegin picked up the shoes, Sergeant McColl contacted the officers, then handcuffed the three men, told them that they were being taken into custody, gave them *Miranda* warnings and impounded the stopped car. This occurred at 3:16 A.M., 61 minutes after the car was stopped.

A search warrant was obtained, and the car was searched. Three pairs of gloves, a box of tools, a crowbar and other items were found in the trunk.

1. Did the police violate the Fourth Amendment rights of Rolland and Gerald Moffatt and Terry Theis in stopping their car a short distance from the burglary scene?
   a. Before receiving a search warrant, neither the stop, the limited investigation nor the seizing of shoes would be considered justified or proper.
   b. Police obtained probable cause to arrest shortly before 2:45 a.m., but before that time a stop would not be lawful.
   c. Observing the only car in the area moments after the report of burglary justifies stopping the vehicle.
   d. The observation that the three men were soaked with sweat and gave a lame reason for being in the area justified the stop.
   e. Actually, police have a right to stop any vehicle at any time as long as an officer has a hunch there is possible suspicious activity, so this stop was lawful.

2. Was the conduct of the police diligent and reasonable?
   a. There are no good reasons for placing each man in a separate squad car, and no such action should occur before they are given a *Miranda* warning and told they are under arrest.
   b. While conducting a limited investigation, officers must get all available information within half an hour, including any search. Further, confiscating the shoes so they could be taken to the burglary scene for comparison with footprints requires a warrant.
   c. Once the officers frisked for weapons and put the three men in the squad cars, they converted what

might have been a detention into an arrest for which there was no probable cause—no weapons were found.

d. This was diligent and reasonable police action because of the small police department and the facts that it was a burglary investigation (not just a petty offense) and there were three men involved; it was not in the interest of the police to release them quickly and allow them to get away with evidence of their guilt.

e. The 20-minute "bright line" rule by the American Law Institute, for the length of an investigative detention, makes this hour-long detention illegal.

## DISCUSSION QUESTIONS

1. Which of the following is the most complex objective of patrol: crime prevention, crime repression, apprehending offenders or recovering stolen property?

2. What factors should be considered when using K-9-assisted patrol? What restrictions should be placed on such patrol?

3. Which is the most effective method of patrol: foot patrol, bicycle patrol, one-officer patrol vehicle, two-officer patrol vehicle or some other method?

4. What factors should be considered in determining the most suitable patrol methods to use in a police agency? How do these factors affect the choice of patrol methods?

5. What are the relative strengths and weaknesses of foot patrol and automobile patrol? How can these two patrol methods be combined to enhance the effectiveness of patrol efforts?

6. Why does the patrol officers' behavior vary so widely from community to community?

7. How might the organizational contradiction embodied in the patrol function be reduced?

 **InfoTrac College Edition Assignments**

- Use InfoTrac College Edition to answer the Discussion Questions as appropriate.

- Use InfoTrac College Edition to research the *various incidents that occur on patrol* and *the various types of patrol* that agencies use. Can you determine a pattern or correlation in how the types of incidents handled influence the method of patrol used? Be prepared to share your findings with the class.

- Select one of the following articles to read and outline to share with the class:

  - "Looking Inward with Problem-Oriented Policing" by Terry Eisenberg and Bruce Glasscock

  - "Police on Horseback: A New Concept for an Old Idea" by John C. Fine

  - "Using Drug Detection Dogs: An Update" by Jayme S. Walker

 **INTERNET ASSIGNMENTS**

- Using the Internet, search for *patrol* and note the abundance of types listed. Select a law enforcement–related site and outline the information presented on the home page.

- Using the Internet, search for *community policing* and select two sites to review. Compare the types of programs and initiatives being used in each department and note reasons why they may be similar or different. How does the population, geography, socioeconomic climate and the like factor in? Be prepared to share your findings with the class.

 **BOOK-SPECIFIC WEBSITE**

The book-specific website at http://cj.wadsworth.com/wobleski_Hess_police_op4e hosts a variety of resources for students and instructors. Many can be emailed to the instructor. Included are extended activities such as Concept Builders - the 3 step learning module that reinforces key chapter concepts, followed by a real-world applications and critical thinking questions. InfoTrac College Edition exercises; Discussion Questions; interactive key-term FlashCards; and a collection of chapter-based Web Links provide additional information and activities to include in the curriculum.

## REFERENCES

Beck, Kirby. "The IPMBA Instructor Course." *Law and Order*, June 2004, pp.42–46.

Bellah, John. "Low-Speed Ahead." *Law Enforcement Technology*, October 2001, pp.76–82.

Brown, William. "Among the People." *Community Links*, March 2001, p.18.

Clark, Wesley. "Electric Bicycles: High-Tech Tools for Law Enforcement." *Law Enforcement Technology*, November 2003, pp.78–82.

*Community Policing in Local Police Departments, 1997 and 1999*. Washington, DC: Bureau of Justice Statistics, no date. (NCJ 184794) www.ojp.usdoj.gov/bjs/

Cowper, Tom. "Vertical Takeoff and Landing Aircraft for 21st Century Policing." *Law and Order*, September 2004, pp.36–41.

Dejong, Christina; Mastrofski, Stephen D.; and Parks, Roger B. "Patrol Officers and Problem Solving: An Application of Expectancy Theory." *Justice Quarterly*, March 2001, pp.31–61.

Eck, John E. *Assessing Responses to Problems: An Introductory Guide for Police Problem-Solvers*. Washington, DC: Office of Community Oriented Policing Services, 2002.

Eisenberg, Terry and Glasscock, Bruce. "Looking Inward with Problem-Oriented Policing." *FBI Law Enforcement Bulletin*, July 2001, pp.1–5.

*Excellence in Problem-Oriented Policing: The 2001 Herman Goldstein Award Winners*. Washington, DC: National

Institute of Justice, COPS and Police Executive Research Forum, 2001.

*Excellence in Problem-Oriented Policing: The 2002 Herman Goldstein Award Winners.* Washington, DC: National Institute of Justice, COPS and Police Executive Research Forum, 2002.

Fine, John C. "Police on Horseback: A New Concept for an Old Idea." *FBI Law Enforcement Bulletin,* July 2001, pp.6–7.

Fuller, John. "Rethinking Foot Patrol." *Police and Security News,* May/June 2004, pp.63–66.

Garrett, Ronnie. "Going K-9 Is Not as Easy as You Think." *Law Enforcement Technology,* September 2001, pp.26–31.

Gerber, Greg. "Local-Motive." *Law Enforcement Technology,* October 2001, pp.40–49.

Goldstein, Herman. *Problem-Oriented Policing.* New York: McGraw-Hill, 1990.

Green, Bernie. "Well Trained and Reliable Canine." *Law and Order,* April 2004, pp.38–40.

Haldar, Sujoy. "NYC Cabbies Extend Police Reach." *Community Links,* March 2001, p.13.

Hamilton, Melanie. "How to . . . Start a K-9 Unit." *Police,* February 2003, pp.18–23.

Heinecke, Jeannine. "Super Heroes Swooping In." *Law Enforcement Technology,* July 2004, pp.72–81.

Hicks, Gary. "Campus Bike Patrol." *Law and Order,* April 2003, pp.87–90.

Kariya, Mark. "Working on Two Wheels." *Police,* February 2004a, pp.24–30.

Kariya, Mark. "How to . . . Start a Bicycle Patrol Unit." *Police,* May 2004b, pp.20–24.

Kerstein, Alan. "Model Neighborhood Program Offers Effective Complement to Community Policing Efforts." *The Police Chief,* February 2001, pp.49–50.

Klockars, Carl B. *Thinking about Policing: Contemporary Readings.* New York: McGraw-Hill, 1983.

"Legal Beagles Sniff Out Edible Contraband." *Law Enforcement News,* July 2004, p.4.

Maghan, Jess; O'Reilly, Gregory W.; and Ho Shon, Phillip Chong. "Technology, Policing and Implications of In-Car Videos." *Police Quarterly,* March 2002, pp.25–42.

Moore, Carole. "Who Let the Dogs Out?" *Law Enforcement Technology,* September 2004, pp.74–80.

Mroz, Mike. "Cops and Bikes." *Police,* December 2001, pp.41–45.

Reuland, Melissa; Brito, Corrina Sole; and Carroll, Lisa. *Solving Crime and Disorder Problems: Current Issues, Police Strategies and Organizational Tactics.* Washington, DC: Police Executive Research Forum, 2001.

Rogers, Donna. "GPS Gains a Stronger Position." *Law Enforcement Technology,* September 2003, pp.74–80.

Sherman, Sue. "Police Units with Horse Sense." *Law Enforcement Technology,* September 2003, pp.55–59.

Slahor, Stephenie. "MEU: Mounted Units for Crowd Control." *Law and Order,* October 2001, pp.234–237.

Spelman, William G. and Brown, Dale K. "Response Time." In *Thinking about Police: Contemporary Readings,* 2nd ed., edited by Carl B. Klockars and Stephen D. Mastrofski. New York: McGraw-Hill, 1991, pp.163–167.

Steffen, George S. and Candelaria, Samuel M. "The Knock and Talk: What Is It and How Can You Use It Successfully?" *Police and Security News,* May/June 2004, pp.85–89.

Stockton, Dale. "Project 54: Ready for Prime Time Patrol." *Law and Order,* October 2004, pp.148–153.

Strandberg, Keith. "E-Bike Makes Biking a Breeze." *Law Enforcement Technology,* June 2001a, pp.102–107.

Strandberg, Keith. "Setting Up an Air Unit." *Law Enforcement Technology,* September 2001b, pp.20–25.

Strandberg, Keith. "Across Mountains and Beaches: All-Terrain Vehicles Are Extending Motorized Patrols." *Law Enforcement Technology,* February 2004, pp.16–18.

Streit, Corinne. "Patrolling in an Off-Road Environment." *Law Enforcement Technology,* July 2002, pp.16–20.

Sweeney, Earl M. "Maintaining Traffic Patrols in the Face of Rising Energy Costs." *The Police Chief,* August 2004, pp.23–24.

Sweeney, Thomas J. "Patrol." *Local Government Police Management,* 4th ed. Washington, DC: International City/County Management Association, edited by William A. Geller and Darrel W. Stephens, 2003, pp.89–133.

Vernon, Mick. "Observational Skills for Patrol." *Law and Order,* June 2004, pp.60–66.

Vonk, Kathleen D. "Beyond Community Policing: The Crime Fighting Effectiveness of the Police Cyclist." *Law and Order,* April 2002, pp.92–96.

Vonk, Kathleen D. "Bike Patrol Successes." *Law and Order,* April 2003, pp.82–86.

Walker, Jayme S. "Using Drug Detection Dogs: An Update." *FBI Law Enforcement Bulletin,* April 2001, pp.25–32.

Westphal, Lonnie. "The In-Car Camera: Value and Impact." *The Police Chief,* August 2004, pp.59–65.

Whitehead, Christy. "Segways and Community Interaction." *Law and Order,* August 2004a, pp.24–25.

Whitehead, Christy. "Facial Recognition for Patrol." *Law and Order,* September 2004b, pp.82–84.

**CASE CITED**

*United States v. Place,* 462 U.S. 696 (1983)

# CHAPTER 5

# Traffic: Policing in a Country on the Move

## DO YOU KNOW . . .

■ What three functional areas police traffic services include?

■ What the basic purposes of traffic enforcement are?

■ What syndromes are common in the driving public?

■ Who is responsible for traffic enforcement?

■ How the problem of speeding in residential areas can be addressed?

■ What the difference between aggressive driving and road rage is?

■ What the number one problem of traffic enforcement is?

■ What strategies are being used to deter DUI?

■ What issues should be addressed in a pursuit policy?

■ What a hazardous materials enforcement program should include?

■ What the responsibilities of officers responding to a crash scene are?

## CAN YOU DEFINE?

blood-alcohol concentration (BAC)

cruising

drug recognition expert (DRE)

drug recognition technician (DRT)

dual motive stop

enforcement index

implied consent law

pretext stop

pursuit

racial profiling

road rage

scofflaws

selective enforcement

traffic calming

## Introduction

Carrick (2003, p.44) notes: "Among the most common problems facing law enforcement today are those relating to traffic issues in their community. Citizens may call to complain about speeding cars in their neighborhood or voice concern over a nearby school crosswalk." Carrick (p.46) also points out: "The scope of traffic problems facing law enforcement is numerous and diverse. . . . When we think about the future of traffic safety, we can be certain that there will be more people, more cars and more congestion. All of these increases will equate into traffic management problems, increased frustrations for drivers and continued enforcement challenges."

The United States is truly a nation on the move. Citizens feel it is their right to drive cars and resent any limitations imposed on this "right." At the same time, they also expect city and state governments to keep the roadways in good

condition and the police to keep traffic moving. Besides simply keeping traffic flowing, officers involved in this important aspect of police work are also charged with helping at and investigating crashes involving vehicles. They also must deal with criminals who use vehicles in committing their crimes. This often involves high-speed chases. At the opposite end of the spectrum is law enforcement's responsibility to educate the driving public as to their responsibilities and the rules and regulations they must obey.

More officer time is spent on traffic patrol than any other police activity. Unfortunately, like patrol in general, traffic services are often perceived as unglamorous and rank low on the department's and community's priority list. However, according to Carrick (2004, p.20): "Traffic may not be the most glamorous part of police work, but it is arguably the most visible police function in our society today. Obviously, tremendous injury, damage and loss of life occur each day on our streets and highways. Since practically everyone uses the roads on a daily basis, a compelling quality of life issue is readily apparent."

 Police traffic services (PTS) are divided into three major areas:
- Traffic direction and control.
- Traffic enforcement.
- Crash investigation.

This chapter begins with a discussion of traffic direction and control. This is followed by a discussion of traffic enforcement and specific traffic violations, including failure to obey seat belt laws, speeding, red-light running, aggressive driving and road rage, and driving under the influence. Next the traffic stop is examined, including the use of automated citations and the issues surrounding pretext stops and racial profiling. This is followed by an in-depth look at recognizing and stopping drivers under the influence of alcohol and drugs. High-speed pursuits and hazardous materials enforcement are presented next. Then crash management and investigation are discussed. The chapter concludes with a look at the relationship between traffic, community policing and problem solving.

## Traffic Direction and Control

*Redirect traffic pattern in situation of crash.*
*1 + Control crashes.*
*2. Reduce traffic.*

"Traffic direction and control (TD&C) can be broadly thought of as facilitating the safe and efficient movement of vehicular traffic in hazardous conditions or special circumstances" (Rao, 2003, p.234). Traffic direction and control is a planned assignment and may take place regularly at such places as schools before and after closing, major sporting events, parades, rush hour and the like. It may also take place during unexpected or emergency events such as civil disturbances or natural disasters. In addition, TD&C is part of an officer's responsibility at crash scenes.

Traffic direction and control requires great skill in nonverbal communication. The tools officers normally use are their hands, eyes and a whistle. Seldom can verbal commands be issued. Officers get attention by short blasts on their whistles and by making eye contact with drivers. They provide direction with their hands, motioning drivers to stop, turn or go straight.

Officers engaged in traffic direction and control should plan carefully how best to position themselves, considering both their visibility to oncoming traffic and their personal safety. Safety precautions include wearing Day-Glo vests and,

*Directing traffic is a hazardous duty that officers must perform. Each year many officers are injured or killed by careless drivers.*

David R. Frazier Photolibrary

at night, using flashlights with cones attached. They must also consider how best to keep the traffic moving, including pedestrians, in the overall plan.

### The Cruising Problem

Since the 1950s, cruising has been a favorite pastime of teenagers and young adults. **Cruising**—driving around and around a predetermined, popular route, usually through the heart of a town or city—gives teenagers a chance to see who is going out together and what kinds of cars other teenagers are driving, to pick up dates and to spend their socializing hours in a relatively inexpensive way. When teenagers got out of hand in the 1950s and 1960s, police used existing curfew or loitering laws to send them home, a task easy to do in a small town.

By the 1970s, however, cruising had become a problem in major urban areas. Some cities passed cruising ordinances that prohibited a car from passing a specific point more than a certain number of times within a specific period. In addition, cruising is often associated with johns seeking prostitutes or with drug addicts seeking drug buys. Further, it has become associated with drive-by shootings, certainly of grave concern to any community and its police.

## Traffic Enforcement

A primary responsibility of traffic services is enforcing a municipality's and state's traffic rules and regulations, which are enacted for the safety of all citizens.

The two basic purposes of traffic enforcement are to control congestion and to reduce crashes.

Enforcement action taken against traffic violators serves a dual purpose. First, it allows the court to evaluate the propriety of a motorist's conduct and administer appropriate punitive sanctions directly against that driver. Second, it acts as a deterrent to other drivers in preventing future violations, as citizens who know that traffic laws are enforced are more likely to comply with the rules of the road.

Nonetheless, many drivers routinely break traffic laws, believing their minor infractions will not be noticed or result in tickets.

 The I-won't-get-a-ticket syndrome is common among the driving public.

A study by Chermak et al. (2001, p.365) found that citizens strongly support aggressive traffic enforcement practices and that implementing such strategies does not reduce their support. Nonetheless, perceptions of traffic enforcement are a mixed bag. Although most people respect the aims and efforts of police offi-cers in traffic enforcement as applied to *other* drivers, many motorists turn criti-cal of the same enforcement actions when they become the subject of a traffic stop. In fact, a common complaint of those ticketed for traffic violations is that the police should be focusing on catching real criminals instead of pulling peo-ple over for driving a little faster than the speed limit.

Even many police officers do not regard traffic enforcement as "real" police work, contending the writing of traffic citations could be done by nonsworn per-sonnel. Indeed, nonsworn personnel are helpful in many areas, such as parking violations. However, a crucial, frequently unrecognized aspect of traffic enforce-ment is the potential apprehension of wanted suspects.

Someone willing to commit a serious criminal act usually has little reserva-tion about breaking traffic laws. People who commit crimes are also the ones driving with revoked licenses, expired tags, or burned-out taillights or headlights. Sweeney (2003, pp.41–42) observes: "Traffic stops are crime-fighting tools. . . . Bank robbers don't case their targets and flee from the scene of the crime very far on foot; they soon jump into a motor vehicle to make their escape. . . . And the September 11 terrorists didn't hitchhike up and down the eastern seaboard for a year before they hijacked those airplanes on that fateful day; they drove." Hustmyre (2003, p.113) also notes: "All officers know America's highways are often haunted by criminals. They use them as escape routes, as a place to find victims and as a way to traffic their own nefarious brand of commerce—drugs, guns, stolen property and cash."

Thus, the potential for exposure of other crimes during the course of a traffic stop makes traffic enforcement a duty of all officers, not just those assigned to highway patrol or other specific traffic units.

 Even if a traffic enforcement unit exists, traffic enforcement is the responsibility of all officers.

A good example of the potential for a traffic stop to lead to a criminal appre-hension occurred when state trooper Charles Hanger stopped Timothy McVeigh's car because it lacked license plates. Trooper Hanger, unaware of the driver's involvement in the day's earlier terrorist bombing of the Alfred P. Murrah Build-ing, cited McVeigh for, among other things, the absence of license tags and carry-ing a concealed gun. While McVeigh sat in a jail cell being processed into the sys-tem for his offenses, investigators handling the bombing's aftermath were searching for suspects, including McVeigh. Their database search turned up a "hit," and the trooper was credited with apprehending the terrorist, McVeigh, who was later convicted and executed for his role in the bombing.

Most drivers stopped for traffic violations are not terrorist bombers or other such high-profile, wanted criminals—they will be average everyday people, the majority of whom, in all likelihood, are not necessarily actively refusing to conform to society's laws. They simply are not paying attention.

## *Traffic Violators and Violations*

Judging by the millions of traffic citations and parking tickets issued every year, operating a motor vehicle in compliance with all the laws is mastered by only a few motorists. Despite their good intentions and interest in community safety, hundreds of thousands of people—young and old, male and female, of all races, national origins, occupations and religions—violate traffic laws.

Violations range from failing to wear a seat belt or put children in the proper child safety seats, to changing lanes or turning without signaling, to ignoring "no parking" or "no turn on red" signs, to speeding or running red lights. The most serious traffic violations involve aggressive driving that may turn to road rage, or driving under the influence of alcohol and/or drugs. The reasons given for violations range from being late for an appointment; to "just keeping up with traffic;" to "getting away with something;" to being distracted by cell phones, radios, a steaming cup of coffee, screaming children or conversation with other passengers; to being daydreamers whose thoughts are far away from the responsibilities of driving a vehicle.

In fact, using a cell phone while driving has been determined so serious a distraction that it has become the subject of legislation. Horne (2001a, p.8) notes that lawmakers in 38 states introduced almost 90 bills in 2001 to restrict use of cell phones while driving. New York became the first state to enact legislation banning the use of handheld cellular phones by drivers (Horne, 2001b, p.10), and at least 10 local jurisdictions have passed such legislation. Critics, however, ridicule such bills as the solution to poor driving, arguing that if cell phones are banned because they distract drivers, then perhaps all vehicle radios should be removed, passengers should not be allowed to talk, and drivers should be prohibited from eating or drinking while behind the wheel. They urge law enforcement to focus on a driver's ability, or inability, to obey traffic laws, regardless of whatever else is occurring in the vehicle, noting how some drivers can observe the rules of the road while talking on the phone, especially when using hands-free equipment, while other drivers simply cannot chew gum and drive at the same time. One of the most prevalent motor vehicle violations is the failure to buckle up.

## *Seat Beat Laws*

In 1994, because safety belt use stood at only 12 percent, the New York legislature approved a bill creating the nation's first mandatory seat belt law. Also begun in 1994 was North Carolina's *Click It or Ticket Program* to increase use of seat belts. This program has "dramatically boosted safety belt use rates in eight states in the southeast" (Bolton, 2001a, p.181). The program uses heavy publicity and a solid public information and education campaign from mid-May to the beginning of June (Memorial Day). Ashton (2004a, p.66) points out: "Safety belts clearly save lives. Each percentage point increase in safety belt usage translates into 250 lives spared." Runge (2003, p.12) reports: "Our 2003 National Occupant Protection Use Survey (NOPUS) has shown a nationwide safety belt use of 79 percent as a result of the campaign [Click It or Ticket]. This is a historic high

*Traffic tickets are one way of gaining compliance with parking regulations. Here an officer debates whether to issue a ticket or order a tow truck for this violator.*

level of belt use, representing a 4 percent increase over 2002. This difference will result in saving at least 1,000 lives each year . . . and preventing more than 16,000 serious injuries . . . saving the U.S. economy an estimated $3.2 billion." All 50 states participated in the campaign and, according to Dewey-Kollen (2004b, p.12): "With more than 13,000 law enforcement agencies participating in the twice-a-year seat belt mobilizations, this effort to increase seat belt use ranks as one of the largest and most successful U.S. enforcement actions ever." In 2004 seat belt use reached a record 80 percent (Dewey-Kollen, 2004f, p.14).

Progress has also been made in child passenger safety says Dewey-Kollen (2004a, p.12): "Child passenger safety (CPS) is one area of traffic safety that has experienced an explosion of activity and positive results over the past 10 years." Among the key research findings reported by Dewey-Kollen are the following:

- Motor vehicle crashes are the leading cause of death for children in every age group from 2–14.
- Fifty percent of children under age 15 who were fatally injured in crashes were completely unrestrained.
- Child safety seats reduce the risk of fatal injury by 71 percent for infants and 54 percent for toddlers (1–4).
- Child safety seats are used incorrectly 80 to 90 percent of the time.
- A child's injury risk is reduced by 33 percent when moved from the front to the back seat.

However, according to Bolton (2003, p.70): "Too many children are still riding in the front seat of passenger vehicles." An estimated 15 percent of infants under age 1, 10 percent of those ages 1 to 3 and 29 percent of children ages 4 to 7 are still riding in the front seat (Bolton). "Child seat laws should be a daily part of an officer's patrol. Just as an officer or trooper is trained to observe license tags, inspection stickers and seat belt violations, it should be a part of standard patrol practice to notice if children are properly restrained inside vehicles" ("To Protect and Serve the Smallest Citizens," 2004, p.78).

In addition, Ashton (p.28) stresses: "Police officers responding daily to traffic crashes witness the reduction of serious injuries produced by buckling up, yet they sometimes fail to take advantage of the very occupant restraints for which they cite others." Another vital enforcement action that saves lives is getting drivers to slow down and obey the posted speed limit.

## Speeding

Speeding reduces the time drivers have to avoid crashes and lengthens stopping distances, increasing both the likelihood of crashing and the severity of the crashes that do occur (Insurance Institute for Highway Safety, 2001b).

According to the National Highway Traffic Safety Administration (NHTSA), speed is a factor in nearly 30 percent of all fatal crashes, killing an average of 1,000 Americans every month. The NHTSA estimates the annual economic cost to society of speed-related crashes to be $28 billion (*Traffic Safety Facts* . . ., 2001, p.1).

Many drivers, particularly younger ones, fail to anticipate hazards in the road and overestimate their ability to control their vehicle when the unexpected happens—another driver cuts in front of them, a dog runs across the street, a tire blows or they hit an icy patch in the road. Other drivers subscribe to the philosophy that it is safer to "go with the flow" of traffic, even if it is 10 miles an hour over the posted speed limit, than to obey the traffic law and make other drivers maneuver their speeding vehicles through numerous lane changes to get around slower traffic. Still others, lost in thought or conversation, are completely unaware of the speed at which they are traveling. Sometimes, compliance with the speed limit can be obtained simply by reminding drivers to check their speedometers. Other times, aggressive ticketing campaigns are needed to get drivers to slow down.

**The Problem of Speeding in Residential Areas**   Scott (2001, p.1) says that speeding in residential areas causes five basic types of harm: "(1) it makes citizens fear for children's safety; (2) it makes pedestrians and bicyclists fear for their safety; (3) it increases the risk of vehicle crashes; (4) it increases the seriousness of injuries to other drivers, passengers, pedestrians and bicyclists struck by a vehicle; and (5) it increases noise from engine acceleration and tire friction."

 Speeding can be addressed through engineering, education and enforcement responses.

*Engineering responses* include posting warning signs and signals as well as using traffic calming. As Scott (pp.9–10) explains: "**Traffic calming** describes a wide range of road and environment design changes that either make it more difficult for a vehicle to speed or make drivers believe they should slow down for safety." Some traffic calming measures are narrowing the road, putting bends and curves in the road, permitting parking on both sides of residential streets and timing traffic signals for vehicles traveling the desired speed.

*Education responses* include conducting antispeeding public awareness campaigns, informing complainants about actual speeds and providing realistic driver training. One effective educational campaign to combat speeding around schools, described by Dewey-Kollen (2003a), is "Keep Kids Alive Drive 25." This program posts signs in neighborhoods with the program's slogan. According to Dewey-Kollen (p.22) the program has reduced residential speeding and citizen complaints about speeding, made streets safer for pedestrians and provided a chance for neighborhoods to work with the police to take an active role in reducing speeding. She reports: "Cooperative KKAD25 programs have been effective in breaking the cycle of speeding complaints and police responses in cities across the United States."

*Enforcement responses* include enforcing speeding laws, using photo radar, using speed display boards, arresting the worst offenders and training citizen volunteers to monitor speeding. Dewey-Kollen (2004d) describes a program initiated by the Washington (state) Traffic Safety Commission (WTSC), law enforcement agencies and schools to reduce school zone speeding: doubling the fines. Says Dewey-Kollen (pp.12–13): "The fine, now $177, cannot be waived, suspended or reduced. Half the proceeds from the fine go to the WTSC for their School Zone and Pupil Transportation Safety Project and the remaining funds go to the state treasury. . . . Response to the state's School Zone Safety Project has been overwhelmingly positive, and eight years later the program is still going strong. Fines from school zone speed violations now fund more than $1.5 million in program activities biannually." Dewey-Kollen (p.14) notes: "While enforcement is critical to reducing speeding in school zones, engineering and education are important components as well."

Scott (pp.20–22) suggests several measures to reduce speeding in residential areas that seem to have *limited effectiveness:* reducing speed limits, increasing fines and penalties, erecting stop signs, installing speed bumps and rumble strips, and reengineering vehicles. However, these measures in conjunction with education and other engineering responses may prove to be effective.

**Curbing Illegal Street Racing**   Lowery (2003, p.51) describes how the Kent (Washington) Police Department partnered with state and local law enforcement agencies, private property owners, local businesses and the insurance industry to develop a high-profile enforcement action plan called Curb Racing and Achieve Safer Highways, or CRASH. He (p.54) offers the following suggestions for law enforcement agencies considering racing-related enforcement programs. First, have sufficient resources in place. "Dedicated race patrol teams must be deployed each weekend so that racers and spectators will anticipate their presence and avoid those identified patrol areas." Use undercover officers and vehicles. Videotape or photograph the racing activities. Develop interagency enforcement teams. Work with the media to keep the problem in the public eye. Develop an alternative site for street racing. And make Internet contact through street racing groups' websites and the department's own website. Information about the CRASH program is available on www.ci.kent.wa.us/.

**Using Decoy Patrols**   Carrick (2001, p.110) notes: "Over the years many jurisdictions have employed decoy officers in an effort to stem traffic violations. . . . Decoy patrol vehicles bridge the gap of police patrol and provide greater visibility. Let's face it, human nature causes everyone to slow down and check their driving when they see a marked police cruiser." Carrick reports that since deploying a decoy patrol in St. Johns County, Florida, the number of fatalities dropped by more than 80 percent.

**Speed Enforcement Technology** The conventional radar unit is the oldest electronic speed enforcement technology in use and is still the "tool of choice" for most traffic officers. Bowman and Fisher (2004, p.39) contend: "Today, motorists, prosecutors and judges can be assured that radar, when used in accordance with the manufacturer's instructions by properly trained officers, is a proven, valid and precise method of determining a vehicle's actual speed." A controversial new speed enforcement device is photo radar. Photo speed enforcement is also being used. Rao (p.215) suggests: "Photo radar programs are force multipliers for the police. They dramatically reduce the dangerous risks associated with speed enforcement for police and for drivers when the officer follows the offending vehicle into traffic. Cameras lead to consistent enforcement, which results in higher rates of compliance and, ultimately, in the reduction of injuries and deaths related to aggressive driving." These units are typically mounted in the rear of a sport-utility vehicle parked at roadside and aimed at a 22-degree angle at oncoming traffic. The radar detects a speeding car, records its speed, license number and the driver's face. It then generates a ticket that is mailed to the driver.

Many drivers use radar detectors in the hopes of avoiding speeding tickets. Fors (2004, p.30) reports that radar detector use in cars is legal in all states except Virginia, Washington DC and U.S. military installations, but its use in commercial vehicles was banned in all states by a directive of the U.S. Department of Transportation (USDOT) in 1995. He notes: "With heightened concern for domestic terrorism and potentials of 18-wheelers transporting terrorists or dirty bombs coupled with present realities of smuggling illegal aliens, illegal drugs, avoidance of safety inspections, speeding and outstanding warrants, detecting radar detectors in commercial vehicles is crucial for public safety. Now, the USDOT ban on radar detector use in commercial vehicles gives law enforcement probable cause for traffic stops when radar detectors are detected." Fors describes a radar detector chess game that has resulted from the development of devices that can detect the detector/detector. Many detectors added a new feature. According to Fors (p.32): "This feature detected the detector/detector before the detector/detector detected the detector . . . a radar detector/detector/detector."

Another type of speed enforcement is drone radar, which capitalizes on the fact that many motorists have radar detection units in their vehicles. Drone radar has the sole purpose of triggering these radar detection units, thereby slowing their drivers in most instances. The units can be connected with speed display signs that announce, "You are going X miles" to alert drivers they are speeding. Once drivers discover that a drone radar unit is operating and that no tickets are forthcoming, the effectiveness of the unit is lost, and the unit should be moved.

Radar trailers are also used to monitor and control speeds. The trailer shows the speed limit and the speed of approaching motorists. When people are in a hurry and are speeding or are distracted, they are also more likely to run red lights.

### Red-Light Runners

Bolton (2002, p.114) reports: "Red light running is the leading cause of urban crashes in the United States." The Insurance Institute for Highway Safety ("Yellow Lights . . .," 2001a, p.7) states more than one million crashes occur every year at U.S. intersections with traffic signals. A survey conducted in early 2001 of police chiefs from 60 departments across the country found 86 percent of respondents agreed red-light running was a problem for their department (Sharp, 2001, p.71). Bolton suggests that, as with deterring speeding, red light running might be deterred through education, engineering and enforcement.

He suggests that public awareness of the problems associated with red light running might be raised through press conferences, proclamations, billboards, posters, paycheck/bill stuffers and perhaps a radio station broadcasting from a high-crash location. Suggested engineering improvements include warning signs, pavement markings, skid resistance, bigger or brighter signs and signals, and timing of traffic signal phases. Another approach is to install automated red light cameras.

According to Helmick (2003, p.50): "Red light cameras are a low-cost, common sense way to reduce this problem." The Insurance Institute for Highway Safety has been studying the effectiveness of programs using cameras to photograph vehicles of drivers deliberately entering an intersection after the signal light has turned red and ticketing these violators by mail. Their study found that such programs reduce red light running by about 40 percent (2001b, p.24). Dewey-Kollen (2003b, p.30) notes: "The use of photo red light enforcement cameras necessitates explicit authorization by community or state legislative bodies." She (p.32) adds: "Numerous court cases . . . have held automated enforcement programs to be constitutional and not in violation of due process rights. . . . The use of red light camera enforcement was the focus of a highly publicized lawsuit brought in 2001 in San Diego, California. The Superior Court judge deciding the case upheld the constitutionality of the camera programs, but dismissed about 300 citations because of defects in how the program was operated, saying the city should exercise more oversight and replace the fee for citation payment arrangement. After San Diego suspended the use of red light cameras, red light crashes increased 14 percent citywide and 30 percent at intersections where red lights cameras had been operating."

For some people looking for faster ways to get from point A to point B, the red stoplight has become a personal nemesis, seen not as a device to enhance traffic flow and safety but as an enemy to be beaten. Getting "caught" at the light is more than an inconvenience; it's a mild form of defeat. Oldenburg (2004, p.E7) describes license plate sprays that are said to foil traffic cameras. He cites the owner of a company with eight delivery trucks who drew $1,300 in photo-radar fines a year, but none since the application of the clear glossy coating sprayed on the trucks' licenses. The spray is intended to bounce back the flash of the camera to overexpose the license plate. Sometimes it works; other times it does not. And it does not work if digital cameras are used, as they have no flash.

Another potential concern is the availability of signal-changing devices. A mechanism called a mobile infrared transmitter, or MIRT, is the trigger device in traffic preemptions systems: "The MIRT interacts with a receiving device mounted on a stoplight, and can change the light from a range of about 1,500 feet" ("Signal-Changing Device Raises Concerns," 2004, p.5). Although no cities have reported this as a problem, several cities are urging their legislators to pass legislation specifically banning the use of MIRTs by unauthorized individuals.

## Aggressive Driving and Road Rage

Aggressive driving has become one of the leading safety hazards on our highways and, according to several studies, is considered to be more dangerous than drunk driving or driving without seat belts. The NHTSA distinguishes aggressive driving from road rage, saying that behaviors of aggressive drivers include tailgating, making erratic or unsafe lane changes, exceeding speed limits or driving too fast for conditions, weaving in and out of traffic, and ignoring traffic control devices such as stop lights and yield signs. Aggressive driving often precipitates road rage. The NHTSA defines **road rage** as "an assault with a motor vehicle or other dangerous weapon by the operator or passenger(s) of one motor vehicle on the operator or passenger(s) of another motor vehicle and is caused by an incident that occurred on the roadway."

 Aggressive driving is a traffic violation; road rage is a criminal offense.

Porter (2004, p.46) gives the following symptoms of road rage:
- Mentally condemning other drivers or entertaining thoughts of violence against other drivers
- Verbally expressing condemnation of other drivers to passengers in your vehicle
- Violating traffic safety rules because you don't agree with them
- Engaging in aggressive and risky driving [as described above]

In an initiative called "Smooth Operator," more than 50 state and local law enforcement agencies have participated in four week-long waves of enforcement coupled with media coverage to remind motorists of the consequences of driving offensively. "Since its debut in 1997, the number of citations issued during the month that Smooth Operator is enforced has grown from 62,000 to 700,000" ("Aggressive Drivers Urged to Chill Out," 2003, p.6). Another serious traffic violation that may earn a driver some jail time is driving under the influence of alcohol or drugs.

## *Driving Under the Influence*

Whether called Driving While Intoxicated (DWI), Driving Under the Influence (DUI), Driving Under the Influence of Liquor (DUIL) or some other designation, those who do so are a critical problem for the community. Every 33 minutes, someone in this country dies in an alcohol-related crash. Law enforcement agencies take nearly 1.5 million drunk and drugged drivers off the road each year because of tougher laws, sobriety checkpoints and saturation patrols. And yet, an estimated 2,000 alcohol-impaired driving trips occur for every arrest.

A Mothers Against Drunk Driving (MADD) brochure states: "Those injured and killed in drunk driving collisions are not 'accident' victims. The crash caused by an impaired driver is a violent crime."

 Nationwide, DUI is the number one traffic law enforcement problem.

According to Bolton (2001b, p.73): "There is broad public support for getting impaired drivers off our streets and highways. In one study, 97 percent of respondents see impaired driving as a major threat to their safety or the safety of their families. Saturation patrols and checkpoints are favored as two means of attacking the problem, and more severe penalties for violations are also supported."

Yet police officers frequently simply issue a ticket and perhaps write a brief report, making prosecution extremely difficult. Those who do write complete reports may become frustrated at how the prosecutor treats DUI cases, often as just another traffic ticket. According to Robinson (2002, p.55): "Sixty percent of officers report that extensive paperwork discourages them from making a DWI arrest." Robinson (p.52) also notes: "Law enforcement officers have identified hardcore drinking drivers as a particular concern because they are difficult to detect and apprehend." Cahill (2004, p.86) contends: "While any impaired driver is a dangerous driver, the hardcore drunk driver poses a particularly difficult challenge to law enforcement. The hardcore drunk driver is someone who drives with a blood alcohol content (BAC) of 0.15 or more, does it repeatedly and is highly resistant to changing his or her behavior despite previous arrests or sanctions. Independent studies caution us that hardcore drunk drivers are responsible for over 58 percent of all alcohol-related deaths, even though on a typical weekend night they represent only 1 percent of all drivers on the road." Recognizing and stopping impaired drivers will be discussed in greater detail shortly.

### Selective Traffic Enforcement and the Enforcement Index

Officers cannot possibly stop and ticket every traffic violator. Consequently, most police departments rely on **selective enforcement.** As Rao (p.226) explains: "Selective traffic enforcement is part of a planned allocation of police personnel and equipment and is guided by a study of the kinds of violators and road conditions that contribute to collisions. The proliferation of computers has been a tremendous asset to target enforcement efforts, enabling police to track behaviors, locations, violations, types of drivers and types of vehicles."

Carrick (2004, p.20) describes the selective enforcement program "Operation Safe Ride" developed by the Florida Highway Patrol: "The concept is to simply concentrate all agency resources on a specific issue for two days each quarter. More than just another selective enforcement program, 'Safe Ride' gets everyone involved, including supervisors, command staff and even plainclothes investigators. Everyone goes into uniform during these two-day enforcement blitz periods, and everyone focuses on the problem identified."

Many police departments also use the **enforcement index,** a figure based on the ratio of tickets issued for hazardous driving violations to the number of fatal and personal injury crashes. The International Association of Chiefs of Police and the National Safety Council suggest that an index of between 1:20 and 1:25 is realistic for most cities, that is, for each fatal and personal injury crash, between 20 and 25 convictions for hazardous moving violations indicate effective traffic enforcement. For some cities, the ratio may be higher; for others, lower. The index provides only a starting point for setting traffic enforcement goals and evaluating results.

Given the wide array of traffic violations and violators, it is critical that traffic enforcement be conducted fairly and uniformly. Departments must have clear policies on when motorists should be stopped and on the appropriate action to take.

## The Traffic Stop

According to Onder (2001, p.26), traffic stops serve three primary purposes: (1) to stop a violation of the law for public safety, (2) to serve as a general deterrent to other drivers and (3) to modify the driver's future driving behavior.

Police encounters with citizens involving traffic infractions will almost always be emotional, and drivers' reactions will vary greatly, from anxiety to remorse, fear, surprise, anger or even hate. The first words officers say to violators set the tone for the rest of the contact. If officers are belligerent, the violators may be belligerent. If officers are pleasant, chances are the violators will be pleasant—but not always. Officers dealing with traffic violators should *never argue*. Motorists who want to debate their driving actions will never be convinced they are wrong and the officer is right. Further, officers should not try to justify the enforcement action, as this only adds to the drivers' preconceived idea that the officer is wrong, prejudiced or "picking on them."

Instead, officers should try to make the traffic contact an educational encounter for the driver, not a belittling or degrading experience. Motorists can be given information so they will be less likely to violate the law again. Studies have shown that many traffic stops by courteous, respectful officers have a positive effect on the citizens' perceptions of the police, even though a citation may be issued. Onder stresses: "Traffic enforcement offers agencies a way to build bridges to the community one traffic stop at a time."

Daniels et al. (2004, p.75) stress: "There is no such thing as a routine traffic stop. All officers know this, but some forget it at their peril." Ashton (2004b, p.29) observes: "Stopping on or near the roadway is one of the most dangerous facets of police work."

The stop should be made in a safe place, not necessarily the first available place. Dispatch should be notified of the stop and of the car's description and license number. After parking safely and leaving the light bar flashing, the officer should approach the car cautiously and stand clear of the driver's door, which could be swung open unexpectedly. Papenfuhs (2003, p.80) describes the inherent dangers in the traditional stop and suggests an alternative to approaching the car called the no approach or call back car stop:

> Sound tactical principles are never more often violated than during the execution of the routine car stop. In no other scenario are officers trained to leave cover and concealment, place themselves in a kill zone, minimize their distance from a threat and maximize themselves as targets. The tactical principles of cover, concealment, distance and escape routes are completely discarded as officers approach the driver of the vehicle.
>
> What is the option? Ask the driver of the stopped vehicle to exit his vehicle and approach the officer. . . .
>
> The call back car stop makes the vehicle stop much safer for the detained driver as well. Because of reaction time limitations, once an officer closes distance with a potential threat, and that threat makes a movement (such as raising a cell phone, which lead to a motorist's death in Chicago), the officer has no time to discern whether or not the item in the individual's hand is dangerous. The proper use of distance and cover adds to the officer's decision-making time, and minimizes the split second syndromes.

*Pennsylvania v. Mimms* (1977) established that police officers may order the driver of a vehicle to exit the vehicle during a stop for a traffic violation. In some states, officers may also use a handheld fingerprint scanner to identify wanted and missing people who are stopped. Officers can call into the National Crime Information Center (NCIC) database and remotely compare a suspect's fingerprints to that database.

Officers have great discretion in traffic enforcement. After making a stop, they usually do one of three things: (1) simply talk to the motorist and explain how they have violated the law, perhaps warning them verbally, (2) issue a warning ticket or (3) issue a citation. It is the third action that causes motorists to become irate, often acting illogically. Motorists have been known to make ridiculous and profane statements, to tear up tickets and to curse at officers. Sometimes such behavior stems from the fear of being discovered as "wanted" by the police and of being arrested on the spot, which can happen with a good communications system. Sharp (2004, p.70) reports: "The Legal Eagles, an organization dedicated to providing legal advice for citizens, notes on its Web site that there are an estimated 14 million traffic tickets issued per year in the United States. Only three percent of ticketed drivers, about 420,000 go to court to challenge the ticket through legitimate legal channels, although the number is growing."

## Automated Citations

Automated citations have simplified the traffic stop process. With handheld computers, which prompt officers for the information to be entered, citations can be issued on the spot and are legible and complete. Some handheld computers read the magnetic stripe on the driver's license in the same way magnetic tapes are read on credit cards. The information is saved and downloaded into the main processing unit at the end of the shift. In addition, these handheld computers can store and produce on command lists of stolen vehicles and revoked driver's licenses and can produce the daily logs that formerly required quantities of time and were tedious to complete. Says Miller (2003, p.78): "Electronic citations eliminate redundant data entry and can even be used in data analysis tools."

Handheld computers can also be used to deal with **scofflaws**—persistent lawbreakers. For example, when officers issue a parking ticket, they can run a check on the license and determine if other parking tickets are outstanding. If there are outstanding tickets, officers can have a boot put on one of the vehicle's tires so the vehicle cannot be moved before it can be towed to the impound garage.

An officer who issues a traffic citation accepts the obligation to pursue that action through the courts by preparing evidence, obtaining witnesses, testifying and performing the necessary functions to ensure a conviction.

## Pretext Stops

A **pretext stop,** also called a **dual motive stop,** is one in which an officer stops a vehicle not only for a traffic violation but also because the driver looks suspicious. For example, an officer sees a suspicious-looking driver and follows the vehicle, hoping a violation occurs to justify a stop. The officer may then use the stop as a pretext to investigate not only the violation but also the driver. Is such a stop legal? The states disagree. At the heart of the issue is the intent of the stop.

The question of pretext stops was clarified in *Whren v. United States* (1996). In this case, plainclothes officers patrolling a high-drug area in an unmarked vehicle saw a truck waiting at a stop sign for an unusually long time. The truck then turned suddenly without signaling and sped off at an "unreasonable" speed. The officers stopped the vehicle supposedly to warn the driver about the illegal turn and speed (traffic violations). When they approached the vehicle, they saw plastic bags of crack cocaine in the car and arrested the driver.

The motion to suppress the evidence (cocaine) was denied, with the Supreme Court ruling: "The temporary detention of a motorist upon probable cause to believe he has violated the traffic laws does not violate the Fourth Amendment's prohibition against unreasonable seizures, even if a reasonable officer would not have stopped the motorist absent some additional law enforcement objective." In other words, the validity and constitutionality of a stop does not depend on whether police officers "would have" made the stop but rather whether the officers "could have" made the stop. The real purpose of a stop, even if ulterior, does not render the stop and subsequent search invalid if there was, in fact, a valid reason for the stop, such as in this case traffic violations. Closely linked to the question of pretext stops is the issue of racial profiling.

## Racial Profiling

Batton and Kadleck (2004, p.31) define **racial profiling** as "the use of discretionary authority by law enforcement officers in encounters with minority motorists, typically within the context of a traffic stop, that result in the disparate treatment of minorities." The National Criminal Justice Association ("The Racial Profiling Controversy . . .," 2001, p.13) contends: "Racial profiling is a hot button issue for law enforcement today. Extensive media coverage of alleged use of racial profiling by police officers has not only caused many to believe the practice is deeply rooted, it has also helped to tarnish the minority community's trust in law enforcement."

Engel and Calnon (2004, p.49) examined the influence of drivers' characteristics during traffic stops and report: "The findings show that young black and Hispanic males are at increased risk for citations, searches, arrests and use of force after other extralegal and legal characteristics are controlled." Rojek et al. (2004, p.143) report similar findings: "The small but growing research literature on racial profiling has produced several common findings regarding race and ethnic differences in police stops, searches and arrests. Including the present study, the accumulated research indicates that Black motorists are more likely than Whites, and in some studies Hispanics, to be pulled over by the police. The racial difference in the probability of being stopped is small but consistent across local and national-level investigations employing different methods of data collection and analysis. In addition, Black and Hispanic drivers who have been stopped by the police are about twice as likely as Whites to be searched and arrested."

In explaining profiling, Tomaskovic-Devey et al. (2004, p.12) suggest: "The use of profiles in law enforcement is thought to increase the efficiency of officers and, consequently, the police organization as a whole. . . . The 'war on drugs' has certainly heightened the use of profiles in law enforcement."

In defending police actions that may appear to be racially biased, Labbe (2001, p.25) notes: "Police have a mandate to battle crime. They use the tools they know work and profiling is one of them." He (p.37) argues: "This nation's war on drugs is the No. 1 culprit behind the accusations of 'racial profiling.' It's an unpleasant fact that blacks are disproportionately involved in the drug trade. . . . Cops aren't out to get blacks so much as to get drug dealers, creating collateral damage for black motorists." Labbe concludes: "To allow political correctness to disarm police of an important law enforcement tool on the grounds of unfounded claims of racism is criminal." Along similar lines, Novak (2004, pp.65–66) reports: "Police officers have suggested disproportionate contacts between officers and citizens may be an unanticipated byproduct of the war on drugs, the get-tough-on-crime movement, zero-tolerance policing or perhaps efficient operational policies."

The issue of racial profiling has become more complicated since the terrorist attack on America on September 11, 2001. As Kinsley (2001, p.9) says: "Until recently, the term 'racial profiling' referred to the police practice of pulling over black male drivers disproportionately, on the statistically valid but morally offensive assumption that black male drivers are more likely to be involved in crime. Now the term has become virtually a synonym for racial discrimination. But if 'racial profiling' means anything specific at all, it means rational discrimination: racial discrimination with a non-racist rationale." He suggests: "We're at war with a terror network . . . planning more slaughter. Are we really supposed to ignore the one identifiable fact we know about them? That may be asking too much."

Nislow (2001, p.11) also notes: "After years of enduring harsh criticism and suspicion from the public for alleged racial profiling practices, law enforcement in the aftermath of the World Trade Center disaster has suddenly found itself on the high road, as some who once considered the practice taboo are now eager for police to bend the rules when it comes to Middle Easterners." Nislow reports on a *Los Angeles Times* poll taken after the September 11 attack, which found that 68 percent of those queried said they favored law enforcement "randomly stopping people who may fit the profile of suspected terrorists."

In October 2001 the Supreme Court refused to hear the only remaining case docketed for the year concerning an equal protection claim in a case where police officers stop people based primarily on racial or ethnic descriptions, in effect, upholding the ruling of the U.S. Court of Appeals for the Second Circuit in *Brown v. City of Oneonta*. As Spector (2002, p.10) explains: "The court held that where law enforcement officials possess a description of a criminal suspect that consists primarily of the suspect's race and gender, and where they do not have other evidence of discriminatory intent, they can act on the basis of that description without violating the Equal Protection Clause of the Fourteenth Amendment."

The court noted that subjecting officers to an equal protection strict-scrutiny analysis in making investigative detentions or arrests could hinder police work. Officers fearful of personal liability might fail to act when they are expected to. The court held: "Police work, as we know it, would be impaired and the safety of all citizens compromised. . . . The most vulnerable and isolated would be harmed the most. And, if police effectiveness is hobbled by special racial rules, residents of inner cities would be harmed most of all."

The Commission on Accreditation for Law Enforcement Agencies (CALEA) has added a prohibition against racial profiling to its list of more than 400 standards ("CALEA Takes Stand on Racial Profiling," 2001, p.5). Although conceding that profiling can be a useful tool in law enforcement, bias-based profiling is prohibited.

In 1999 Connecticut became the first state to pass racial profiling legislation, requiring every municipal police agency and the state police to collect race data for every police-initiated traffic stop. Since that time, measures dealing with racial profiling have been introduced in 24 states (Horne, 2001a, p.8). Cox (2001, p.61) notes: "A major concern voiced by critics of racial profiling legislation is that police officers will stop making traffic stops altogether out of fear of looking unfair or biased." He says, however, that no evidence supports this concern. Data collection is a large issue in many departments.

The Police Foundation's Institute for Integrity, Leadership and Professionalism in Policing has developed computer software for collecting and analyzing data on police officer-citizen contacts, including traffic stop data. The program, Risk Analysis Management System and the Quality of Service Indicator, produces detailed reports to help police managers make critical personnel and operational decisions. It is available online at www.policefoundation.org.

The Police Executive Research Forum (PERF) has produced a 160-page report, *Racially Biased Policing: A Principled Response* (Fridell et al., 2001), which reports on current theory and law enforcement efforts to combat racial profiling. It offers 50 recommendations in 6 key areas: (1) data collection, (2) accountability and supervision, (3) the establishment of a policy, (4) recruitment and hiring, (5) education and training and (6) minority-community outreach. More recently PERF has published *By the Numbers: A Guide for Analyzing Race Data from Vehicle Stops* (Fridell, 2004). The purposes of this Community Oriented Policing Services-supported document are: (1) to describe the social science challenges associated with data collection initiatives so that agencies and other stakeholders can be made fully aware of both the potential and limitations of police-citizen contact data collection, and (2) to provide clear guidelines for analyzing and interpreting the data so that the jurisdictions collecting them can conduct the most valid and responsible analyses possible with the resources they have."

Another area of traffic enforcement often associated with enhanced liability is officers' "public duty" to get drunken or drugged drivers off the road.

## *Recognizing and Stopping Drivers "Under the Influence"*

Most police officers are familiar with the common physical symptoms of the person under the influence of alcohol or drugs: slurred speech, bloodshot eyes, lack of coordination, staggering, smell of alcoholic beverage on breath or clothing, confusion, dizziness, nausea, exaggerated actions. Officers must be cautious, however, because many of these symptoms can be produced by medical conditions such as diabetes, epilepsy, heart attack or concussion. Driving actions that tend to indicate a DUI suspect include:

- Unusually slow or excessive speeds for driving conditions or posted limits.
- Erratic starts and stops.
- Weaving, drifting or straddling the center line.
- Failing to signal turns and lane changes.
- Problems making turns (either too wide or cutting across the curb).
- Repeated use of horn in traffic.

Any one of these actions by itself may indicate only carelessness or haste, but a combination of such actions provides probable cause for an officer to stop the car. The officer must then determine if the driver is "under the influence."

**Field and Chemical Tests for DUI**   Common standardized field sobriety tests (SFSTs) include the heel-to-toe straight line walk, the finger-to-the-nose test, a balance test and reciting the alphabet from a certain letter to another letter. One test used by some officers is the Horizontal Gaze Nystagmus (HGN) test, in which a thoroughly trained officer moves a pencil in front of a driver's face and watches the eyes. The trained officer can determine the motorist's level of intoxication from the manner in which the person focuses and how the eyes move. According to Rao (p.233): "The three recommended tests—walk and turn, one-leg stand and horizontal gaze nystagmus . . . have been shown to be almost 90 percent accurate in identifying persons with a BAC above 0.10 percent."

Chemical tests are also used. Because alcohol is absorbed directly into the bloodstream, its level of concentration can be tested. The **blood-alcohol concentration (BAC)** test represents the weight of alcohol in grams per milliliter of blood. A BAC of .08 represents 80 milligrams of alcohol per 100 milliliters of blood. (Some states use the term *blood-alcohol level [BAL]*.) States set specific blood-alcohol levels considered to indicate legal intoxication, the most common being .08. States that fail to comply with the national standard of 0.08 percent BAC lost 2 percent of their federal highway grants, starting in fiscal year 2004. That penalty increases to 5 percent in 2005, 6 percent in 2006 and 8 percent in 2007 (Horne, 2001a, p.8).

A driver's blood-alcohol concentration can also be revealed through a breath test, called a breath alcohol equivalent (BAQ) test. The same percentage should be obtained from both the breath and the blood test. Many squads carry a small, portable preliminary alcohol screening (PAS) device that can display a BAC level after a person suspected of drunken driving blows into it.

**Recognizing the Driver under the Influence of Drugs**    Often the symptoms of an individual impaired by drugs are very similar to those exhibited by an intoxicated person. This has given rise to a new specialty, the **drug recognition expert (DRE)** or **drug recognition technician (DRT).** These experts have over 80 hours of classroom training and 100 hours of field certification training, in addition to passing rigorous written and practical tests. People suspected of being under the influence of drugs or alcohol may be asked to take a blood, urine or breath test. If they refuse, the consequences can be extremely negative because of the concept of implied consent.

**Implied Consent**    The **implied consent law** states that those who request and receive driver's licenses must agree to take tests to determine their ability to drive. Refusal will result in license revocation. The implied consent law is based on the precept that driving an automobile is not a personal right but a privilege. Permission to drive a motor vehicle is given under whatever conditions and terms are considered reasonable and just by the granting state. Courts have uniformly upheld this principle.

In theory, no one is deprived of his or her constitutional rights by the implied consent law, nor is anything demanded of the driver that was not required before the law was enacted. The implied consent law gives drivers a choice:

> If you wish to drive an automobile on the public highways of this state, you shall be deemed to have consented to submit to certain prescribed circumstances and conditions (such as breath tests). If you fail to submit to such tests, your privilege to drive on the state's highways will be revoked.

**Videotaping Drivers**    Many police departments have made it standard practice to videotape individuals stopped for DWI. This does not violate the person's constitutional rights. *Pennsylvania v. Muniz* (1990) is the leading case on Fifth and

Sixth Amendment issues in videotaping drivers under the influence. The question before the Supreme Court was whether the police must give motorists suspected of DWI the *Miranda* warning before asking routine questions and videotaping them. The Court said, "No. The privilege against self-incrimination protects an accused from being compelled to testify against himself or otherwise provide the state with evidence of a testimonial or communicative nature, but not from being compelled by the state to produce real or physical evidence."

However, even though it is not a violation of a person's constitutional rights, videotaping a DWI stop may not be in the best interests of the prosecution. Unless the suspect is "falling down drunk," the videotape may actually work in the suspect's favor. Too often an officer's word appears to contradict what a jury sees on videotape. This is not because the officer has embellished the facts. It is because the jury is untrained at detecting intoxication at levels as low as .08 BAC in a defendant viewed on a video monitor.

## Strategies to Deter DUI

Traffic officers cannot do the job alone. Effective strategies to address the problem of impaired driving must include tougher laws, tougher judges and frequent and ongoing awareness campaigns to keep impaired drivers out of the driver's seat.

Cox (2004a, p.14) outlines current efforts to get impaired drivers off the road: "We have set in motion a national campaign of sustained enforcement of impaired-driving violations, including sobriety checkpoints and saturation patrols, punctuated by periodic high-intensity crackdowns and backed up by heavy public awareness campaigns stressing the message 'You drink and drive, you lose.'"

 Strategies to deter DUI include educating drivers through awareness campaigns and establishing sobriety checkpoints and saturation patrols. Additional efforts aimed at repeat offenders include using ignition interlocks and enacting vehicle forfeiture programs.

**Education and Awareness Campaigns**   Young people must be educated about not only the dangers of driving drunk but also the hazards of driving while high on pot, speed, cocaine, crack or various other drugs used today for recreation, escape and thrills. Two active national organizations committed to reducing drunk driving by raising awareness of the dangers it poses are Mothers Against Drunk Driving (MADD) and Students Against Drunk Driving (SADD). Founded in 1980, MADD's purpose, according to its brochure, is "to stop drunk driving and to support victims of this violent crime" ("Help Keep Families Together," n.d.). SADD programs have been organized in many high schools throughout the country to help new teenage drivers acknowledge the serious responsibilities that accompany a license to drive. Common SADD activities include designated driver programs for "special" events where underage drinking is likely, such as homecoming and prom, and staging mock crashes and funerals for students to "witness" the deadly consequences of irresponsible driving.

**Sobriety Checkpoints and Saturation Patrols**   Many states are using sobriety checkpoints to deter and detect drunk drivers. In *Michigan Department of State Police v. Sitz* (1990), the Supreme Court ruled: "Sobriety checkpoints are constitutional" because the states have a "substantial interest" in keeping intoxicated drivers off the streets and that the "measure of intrusion on motorists stopped at sobriety checkpoints is slight." The Court also cautioned against random stops, authorizing only well-conceived, carefully structured programs.

Greene (2003, p.2) explains that saturation patrols "constitute a vigorous tactic employed by law enforcement agencies to significantly impact an area known for a high concentration of alcohol-impaired drivers." He reports: "Research has indicated, however, that most impaired drivers never get arrested. Police stop some drivers, but often miss signs of impairment. Estimates revealed that as many as 2,000 alcohol-impaired driving trips occur for every arrest, and, even when special drinking-driving enforcement patrols are conducted, as many as 300 trips occur for each arrest." Greene stresses: "The key aspect in both sobriety checkpoints and saturation patrols rests with public awareness." Greene (p.5) concludes: "Both [saturation patrols and sobriety checkpoints] serve a significant purpose and, used together, can be effective in reducing the number of impaired drivers." He also reports: "It is proven that saturation efforts will bring more DUI arrests than sobriety checkpoints. If that represents an agency's goal and it has the resources, then it should use saturation patrols. If an agency's goal weighs heavier on the educational side, it should use sobriety checkpoints."

**Drug Checkpoints**   As noted by Makholm (2001): "Police 'checkpoints,' commonly known as 'road blocks,' have become an important part of modern policing in the United States, providing a powerful tool for the interdiction of drunk drivers and illegal aliens." However, in *City of Indianapolis v. Edmond* (2000), the Supreme Court ruled that police may not set up drug interdiction roadblocks because the Fourth Amendment generally requires that even a brief seizure of a motorist by the side of the road requires an individualized suspicion that the motorist committed a crime. As Justice O'Connor wrote: "We cannot sanction stops justified only by the generalized and ever-present possibility that interrogation and inspection may reveal that any given motorist has committed some crime."

**Dealing with Hardcore Drunk Drivers**   No matter how severe the consequences of drunk driving are, it seems some drivers are always willing to push their luck by continuing to get behind the wheel while intoxicated. The NHTSA's research shows that DWI offenders have usually committed between 200 and 2,000 unapprehended drunk driving violations before their first arrest and that an estimated 60 to 80 percent of people with suspended licenses continue to drive.

Hatch (2004, p.17) cautions: "In most cases, a driver who has been through the process [arrested for DWI] before will want to exercise their right to counsel before the testing decision and will have a specific attorney in mind. Officers can expect a chronic offender to try and get them to specifically state what constitutes a reasonable amount of time to contact an attorney." Hatch notes that this is a common stalling technique to allow the BAC to lessen.

*Ignition interlocks* are one solution aimed at the major problem of recidivism in DWI. As Garrett (2003, p.72) explains: "An ignition interlock helps offenders monitor how much they've drank; the vehicle simply won't start if they've had too much." An ignition interlock is a device that the person must blow into and register a satisfactory BAC on (usually .02 percent) before the car will start. To prevent someone other than the convicted DWI offender from using the system, a breath code is established. The Texas program provides installation, training in and periodic mandatory inspection of the ignition interlock device.

Several states have *vehicle forfeiture* legislation permitting the permanent confiscation of vehicles of repeat DUI/DWI offenders—drive drunk; lose your car.

### *Legal Liability*

The decision to arrest a drunk driver is not a discretionary one for police officers if the state has a law against drunk driving (which all states do). Arresting impaired drivers is an officer's *public duty,* a principle established in *Carleton v. Town of Framingham* (1993). In this case, an officer had spoken with an intoxicated driver inside a store but had put off taking him into custody, deciding instead to wait outside the store until the driver got into his car. When the officer then attempted a traffic stop for DUI, the intoxicated driver refused and continued driving, which resulted in a head-on collision and a lawsuit against the police.

**Investigating and Prosecuting Fatal Alcohol-Involved Crashes**   Dewey-Kollen (2004c, p.12) describes the approach used by Marion County (Indiana) in cases involving fatal alcohol-involved crashes. The prosecutor's office in Marion County boasts a 100 percent conviction rate from December 2002 to August 2004 for fatal crashes where a driver was operating a vehicle while intoxicated (OVWI). They attribute their success to the Marion County Fatal Alcohol CRASH Team (FACT). As Dewey-Kollen (pp.12, 14) explains:

> FACT blends cutting-edge investigations by specialists from traffic and homicide divisions of participating agencies with the legal resources of an on-the-scene OVWI prosecutor. . . . The OVWI fatality prosecutor position is based on a vertical prosecution model with one deputy prosecutor handling cases from initial investigation to conclusion.
>
> Police and sheriff's deputies across the county page this deputy prosecutor to come to fatal or hit-and-run crash scenes where alcohol involvement by a driver was suspected. In addition to becoming familiar with the crash scene, a benefit of the deputy prosecutor's direct involvement with on-the-scene investigation was the ability to work closely with officers to ensure that evidence was collected in accordance with current law.

## Enforcement and Pursuit

Pursuit is usually thought of as an officer in a police car pursuing a suspect in a vehicle; however, foot pursuits are also common and also hazardous. As Klugiewicz and Smith (2004, p.120) point out:

> Any officer who has ever had to run after a suspect knows that a foot chase is extremely hazardous. Running after a suspect can place you in a situation where you can be easily attacked, injured by accident or even have a heart attack. Real life is not a movie, and the decision to hoof it after the bad guy should never be made lightly. It can be a life and death decision. . . .

The message here should be stated in no uncertain terms: Never pursue a suspect on foot unless you absolutely have to.

Unfortunately, you sometimes have to do so. But you should know what you're getting into before you start sprinting after a suspect, and you should use every available and appropriate tactic to prevent a suspect from rabbiting.

The best way to end a foot pursuit is to prevent it from happening in the first place. . . .

One of the best tools you have to prevent a suspect from running is your voice.

As with foot pursuit, vehicle pursuits can be extremely hazardous. Nugent et al. (n.d., p.1) define a vehicle **pursuit** as "an active attempt by a law enforcement officer on duty in a patrol car to apprehend one or more occupants of a moving motor vehicle, providing the driver of such vehicle is aware of the attempt and is resisting apprehension by maintaining or increasing his speed or by ignoring the law enforcement officer's attempt to stop him." They suggest that the definition establishes four key points: (1) that the law enforcement officer is in a patrol car and, therefore, should be recognizable as a law enforcement officer, (2) that the driver is aware that the law enforcement officer is trying to stop him or her and resists the attempt, (3) that the reason for the pursuit may embrace traffic offenses, including speeding itself, and felonies, and (4) that the vehicle speed may vary.

Some departments have a "chase-them-all" policy. Others chase only those vehicles involved in felonies. And a few departments have a "no-chase" policy.

Issues that should be addressed in a pursuit policy include:
- Number of units actively participating.
- Use of roadblocks to end pursuits.
- Use of firearms during pursuit.
- Use of intentional contact.

Pursuit policies can take several forms. One type of pursuit management can be viewed as a continuum, as illustrated in Figure 5.1.

Sharp (2003, p.70) reports on the results of a survey of 30 randomly selected law enforcement departments of all specialities and sizes. Eighty-three percent restricted the circumstances under which officers are allowed to engage in vehicular pursuits. Ninety-three percent limited the number of cars that could be involved, usually two. Ninety percent reported that their safe-pursuit policies are becoming more restrictive. Sharp (p.72) also reports: "The most frequently mentioned conditions that must be taken into account in the decision to initiate, continue or terminate a pursuit were: nature of the suspect's violation (97 percent); weather (90 percent); presence of pedestrians on highway (97 percent); the benefits v. the dangers of chasing a suspect (87 percent); and officers' familiarity with the roads (70 percent)."

Daniels and Spratley (2003, p.85) contend: "The single most important concept to teach an officer is to think ahead. Throughout a pursuit, the officer should be thinking about and planning strategies for safely ending the pursuit. In situations where the only responsible decision is for the officer to halt the fleeing vehicle, he has to decide where, when and how to conclude the chase with minimum risk to the public, himself and the suspect." Daniels and Spratley (p.88) suggest:

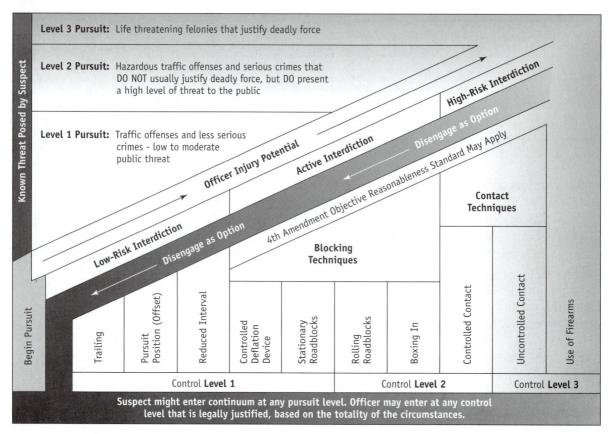

**Figure 5.1** Pursuit Management Continuum

SOURCE: Steven D. Ashley. "Pursuit Management: Implementing a Control Continuum." *Law and Order,* December 1994, p.60. Reprinted by permission of the author.

"Stop sticks, the box-in maneuver, stationary roadblocks and the PIT maneuver are the most common techniques used to bring a fleeing vehicle to a halt." The PIT maneuver refers to the Pursuit Intervention Technique in which the violator is spun to a stop.

Whenever pursuit does occur, if damage results, officers and/or their departments may face lawsuits. At issue is whether police officers violate the Fourteenth Amendment's guarantee of substantive due process by causing death through deliberate or reckless indifference to life in a high-speed automobile chase to apprehend a suspected offender. The Supreme Court, in *County of Sacramento v. Lewis* (1998), held: "In high-speed vehicle pursuit cases, liability in Section 1983 cases ensues only if the conduct of the officer 'shocks the conscience.' The lower standard of 'deliberate indifference' does not apply." Justice Souter noted that an officer's decision to pursue a fleeing suspect often is made in a "split-second . . . in circumstances that are tense, uncertain and rapidly evolving." Officers are forced to "balance on the one hand the need to stop a suspect and show that flight from the law is no way to freedom, and, on the other, the high-speed threat to everyone within stopping range, be they suspects, their passengers, other drivers or bystanders."

Bellah (2003, p.29) points out: "The real culprit [in a pursuit] is the rabbit. The motorist has the legal obligation to yield and stop when lawfully signaled by a police officer. The driver who fails to stop and elects to flee is the one responsible for placing his or her life in danger, placing the officers' lives in danger and is a menace to the civilian population."

An advance in technology that may be of help to officers engaged in pursuits is the DriveCam. This is a black box recorder that automatically records everything a driver sees, hears and feels for the 10 seconds before and after a crash, missed accident, abusive driving or other event of interest.

In many states, traffic enforcement also includes enforcing truck weight limits, enforcing bicycle and pedestrian regulations and regulating transportation of hazardous materials.

## Enforcement and Transportation of Hazardous Materials

Another area that is often overlooked in the traffic enforcement areas is transporting hazardous materials. Miller (2002, p.54) reports: "The U.S. Department of Transportation (DOT) estimates that 800,000 shipments of hazardous chemical, petroleum and other materials daily traverse the country. Of these, more than 50 percent may contain errors, including unlabeled loads, incorrect placard and marking identifiers and improperly segregated chemicals whose interaction can have potentially fatal consequences. Drivers falsify their logbooks, operate under suspended commercial licenses and transport hazardous materials without proper endorsements or shipping papers. And federal government officials have warned that terrorists could steal trucks loaded with explosives and use them as bombs." Most traffic codes do not include dealing with the transportation of hazardous materials (HM or HAZMAT).

A hazardous materials enforcement program should consist of:
- Terminal audits.
- Shipper and other audits.
- Road enforcement.
- Technical assistance and enforcement training.
- Emergency response.

Not only should the police conduct periodic audits at transporters' hazardous materials terminals to assure compliance with regulations, they also should conduct periodic audits of those who pack the materials to be transported. Police should conduct periodic inspections on the highway as well.

In addition, training should be made available to carriers and shippers, as well as to other law enforcement agencies in the state. Finally, law enforcement should have clearly established emergency response plans in case an accident or terrorist incident involving hazardous materials should occur. The emergency HAZMAT response is discussed in Chapter 8.

## Crash Management and Investigation

Rao (p.236) contends: "The loss of life and property from traffic collisions far exceeds that from all categories of crimes combined." Cox (2004b, p.15) reports: "Although the traffic fatality rate has dropped dramatically since the mid–1960s, traffic crashes account for 95 percent of all transportation-related deaths and 99 percent of transportation-related injuries. Traffic crashes are the leading cause of death for people ages 4 to 34. The total economic costs of motor vehicle crashes in the United States exceeds $230 billion annually." Cox also notes: "Traffic crashes are the leading cause of death in the line of duty for law enforcement officers. In 2003, 145 law enforcement officers died in the line of duty. Of these, 75 officers died in motor vehicle crashes." And yet the driving public often fails to perceive the hazards associated with driving.

 The a-crash-won't-happen-to-me syndrome is common among the American driving public.

When a crash does happen, people are frequently in shock or disbelief. They may be dazed or seriously injured. They may be hysterical. They may be belligerent.

 At a crash scene, officers are responsible for:
- Managing the scene, including protecting it, attending to injuries, keeping traffic moving and restoring normal traffic flow.
- Investigating and reporting the cause(s) of the crash.

It is worth noting that vehicle collisions were, until recently, called *accidents;* however, this term implied a rather random, causeless chain of events that resulted in the crash of one or more vehicles. Recognizing that many, if not most, such incidents happen because of some identifiable factor(s) or reason(s), not by chance or coincidence, these collisions are now referred to as *crashes.*

## *Responding to a Crash Call*

Officers called to the scene of a crash usually must proceed as rapidly as possible, treating it as an emergency. Once there they should park so as to protect the scene, but not so as to endanger other motorists coming on the scene. Once the scene is protected, the first responsibility is to attend to the victims. If injuries are serious, an ambulance or rescue squad should be called immediately. During this time, one officer should be keeping the traffic moving.

Crash scene management is critical because the more severe results of a crash can occur after the initial collision. This can include the injured not being properly or promptly cared for, other vehicles becoming involved in the crash, fires starting, hazardous materials leaking or other matters that increase the probability of injury or property loss and increase congestion.

Sweeney (2004, p.20) discusses the nationwide adoption of the National Incident Management System (NIMS) by the U.S. Department of Homeland Security and notes: "The traffic incident management system (TIMS) is a component of NIMS and adapts well to the control of traffic incidents." According to Sweeney (p.26), once an incident occurs, responsibilities of the incident commander include:
- Take immediate steps to stabilize the incident, provide for life safety and establish traffic control. A perimeter for the scene needs to be established and evacuate persons as required.
- Evaluate the situation and call for needed assistance.
- Triage the injured and provide appropriate field treatment and emergency care transportation.
- Extend the area of operation to ensure safe and orderly traffic flow through and around the incident scene.

- Provide for the safety, accountability and welfare of personnel, a responsibility that will be ongoing throughout the incident.
- Restore the roadway to normal operations after an incident has been cleared.

Sometimes problems arise at a crash scene when police, firefighters and emergency medical services (EMS) personnel converge on the scene. For example, firefighters often arrive on the scene with a fire truck and police officers feel it is simply in the way. The police may demand it be moved because it is obstructing traffic. What they should realize, however, is that fire trucks are brought to crash scenes for two very specific purposes: (1) the equipment officers may need is already on the truck, and (2) the truck provides good traffic control, protecting the crash scene and those responding to it. Such cooperation is important enough that it is mandated by the National Accreditation Association. Any police department seeking accreditation from this agency must meet the following guideline: "Command staff meetings will be held with the fire department command staff to exchange information and coordinate the public safety efforts."

## Crash Investigation and Reconstruction

After victims have been tended to, officers should turn their attention to the crash investigation phase. This usually begins with taking statements from those involved and from any witnesses. It has been suggested that officers not ask bystanders if they are witnesses to the crash, because they might not want to get involved. A better question is, What did you see happen?

After statements are taken, a physical examination of the vehicles involved and the scene is conducted. Officers should measure the location of skid marks, the final position of vehicle(s), roadway widths, distances to bridge abutments, utility poles and the like.

Photographs and careful notes are also critical in most serious crash investigations. A crash investigator should have a camera and be skilled in its use. Investi-

*Officers called to major crashes may sometimes be required to save drivers and passengers in dangerous situations.*

Dagmar Fabricus/Stock Boston

gators should photograph debris showing approximate point of impact—for example, broken glass, dirt from the underside of the vehicles and tire imprints or skid marks in soft material like mud, snow and sand. Also, photographs should be taken of more permanent evidence: roadside objects, view obstructions, traffic signs, vehicular damage, road and tire marks and the roadway environment.

In minor crashes, the so-called fender benders, a thorough investigation is seldom required. Officers should make certain the drivers involved exchange insurance information and complete the required forms. Many major crashes, including those involving disabling injuries and fatalities, are investigated by officers with specialized training. Such serious collisions often require a reconstruction of the crash.

Of assistance in accident reconstruction might be the "black box." "As the pre-crash data recorded by 'black boxes' installed in millions of American cars increasingly finds its way into accident investigations and criminal court proceedings, the issue of how unbiased the information is and who owns it is becoming a matter of increasing urgency for both prosecutors and privacy advocates" ("'Black Boxes' Change Nature of Crash Probes," 2004, p.4). These "black boxes" or Event Data Recorders (EDR) were designed to tell a car when to deploy its airbag, but the data contained has also been instrumental in determining the cause of a crash. In one case, a 2001 Corvette driven by a 55-year-old man ran off a winding road on a clear, dry day and crashed, instantly killing the driver. The car's EDR indicated the driver was not wearing a seat belt, did not brake, floored the accelerator and traveled at about 90 miles per hour in a 25-mile-per-hour zone. A comparison of the data with the physical evidence at the crash site and information from the driver's family that he was emotionally disturbed at the time of the crash led investigators to conclude the cause was likely suicide ("Black Boxes in Automobiles Aid in Crash Investigation," 2004, p.65). This article (p.66) also stresses: "Although retrieving information from the black box is a revolutionary development in crash investigation, the data must be compared with physical evidence at the scene before investigators draw any conclusions."

**Crashes Involving Pedestrians**    According to the National Safety Council (*Pedestrian Safety*, 2001): "Approximately 5,900 pedestrians are killed by automobiles every year [and] 84,000 suffer nonfatal injuries. Almost one-third of these victims are children under the age of 15 yet they represent only about 15% of the U.S. population."

Crashes involving pedestrians are very different from those involving only vehicles and, thus, require different investigative techniques. However, like vehicle crash investigations, photographs should be taken at all pedestrian-involved crash scenes, including photographs of the victim, the vehicle involved and the roadway.

## Fake "Accidents"

Staged auto crashes are always a possibility. Ambulance-chasing personal injury mills include a "capper" or "runner" who spreads the word that anyone involved in an auto collision can come to their agency for help. Some crashes are arranged for insurance fraud purposes. Figure 5.2 lists several indicators of insurance fraud.

1. Accident occurs shortly after a subscriber increases his coverage.
2. Accident occurs within a month of the vehicle being insured, or within a month of the policy's termination.
3. Attorney's representation letter is dated immediately after the accident.
4. Minor accident results in major medical costs, high demands for pain and suffering, and extensive lost-wage claims.
5. Minor accident results in excessive repair costs.
6. Major accident is documented through counter police report or no police report at all.
7. Rental vehicle may be used by claimants.
8. Targeted victims in swoop-and-squat accidents may be commercial vehicles or identified with company names.

**Figure 5.2** Insurance Fraud Indicators

### The Claimants

1. Three or more unrelated occupants in the "struck" vehicle claim to know very little about each other.
2. One or more claimants list a P.O. Box or hotel as his address.
3. Insured driver is eager to take blame for the collision.
4. Insured driver and/or claimants are difficult to locate.
5. Passenger/claimants are added after a police report has been completed.
6. Similar ethnic groups are involved, extending to attorneys and doctors.

### The Vehicles

1. Vehicles used by claimants are older and often have previous damage.
2. Claimant's vehicle carries no insurance.
3. Vehicles used may show previous salvage information.
4. Vehicles involved are not readily available for inspection.
5. Vehicle damage may be inconsistent with the facts of the accident and the statements of the parties involved.
6. All involved vehicles are taken to the same auto body shop.
7. No towing charges are incurred, despite major repair estimates.

### Medical Indicators

1. All claimants go to the same doctor.
2. Injuries to claimants are all soft-tissue type or subjective.
3. Injuries sustained to claimants far exceed the damage sustained to the vehicles.
4. The various injuries are always prescribed the same treatment.
5. Doctor's bills and reports are always the same, regardless of the accident or injury.
6. Patient speaks a foreign language with no explanation of how doctor and patient communicated.
7. Typed medical reports include no chart notes to substantiate findings.
8. Medical bills indicate routine treatment was provided on Sundays, holidays or doctor's day off.

It should be noted that the presence of several of these elements does not necessarily prove insurance fraud has occurred. They are merely indicators that further investigation may be warranted.

SOURCE: Nancy Dyer. "Staged Traffic Collisions and Automobile Insurance Fraud." *The Police Chief*, Vol. LXI, No. 7, July 1994, pp.51–54. Reprinted by permission. Copyright held by The International Association of Chiefs of Police, Inc., 515 N. Washington St., Alexandria, VA, 22314, U.S.A. Further reproduction without express written permission from IACP is strictly prohibited.

## Crash Reduction Strategies

One strategy to reduce crashes is use of decoy patrols as described earlier in the chapter. Carrick (2001, p.111) suggests that, as with any traffic enforcement and crash reduction effort, the first step is identifying a problem location. Actual placement considers visibility, safety and effectiveness. Decoys should not be placed where they might surprise unsuspecting drivers. Rather, they should be placed in a highly visible location for the desired effect. Carrick concludes: "Their use is innovative and demonstrates that more police on the streets is a good thing—even if they are dummies."

Another way to reduce crashes is through educational programs for beginning drivers. Dewey-Kollen (2004c, p.12) notes: "Teens and crashes—tragically these two words are linked together too often. Crashes are the leading cause of death for young people age 15 to 20." She recommends graduated driver license laws as lifesavers for teens: "Graduated driver licensing (GDL) is an approach to teen driving that helps young people gain independent driving skills in reduced risk situations. GDL consists of three distinct phases—learners permit, intermediate license, full licensure—and establishes a system whereby young drivers earn the privilege of an unrestricted license."

Redfern and Kwasnoski (2001, p.15) describe a series of interactive teaching tools that teachers can incorporate directly into math, physics, biology, health and driver education classes. *CRASH! The Science of Collisions* gives high school students a chance to test their knowledge about the operation of a vehicle and to understand and appreciate the consequences of driver error and impairment without the consequences of being involved in a crash. Descriptions of the activities can be found at www.legalsciences.com/crash.htm.

## Crash Reports

Complete and accurate crash reports are critical to selective enforcement and other traffic safety measures. Some agencies are one to two months behind in manually entering data from traffic incidents, making the data no longer "real time." To combat this problem, many agencies are turning to electronic report forms. As Galvin (2004, p.150) points out: "The quicker you can get accident data into the system, the more reliable your statistical data will be." Galvin (p.153) notes: "Another advantage to using electronic accident forms is the ability to integrate a diagram of the accident scene right into the diagram field on the report." In addition: "Using the templates cuts in half the time it takes to complete the report. And the report is a lot neater."

## Legal Liability

Crashes frequently result in lawsuits, so careful documentation of all facts is important. In addition, crash-scene management and investigation may also be the target of lawsuits, with the officers involved, their department and their city being named as defendants. Accurate, complete documentation not only helps should a lawsuit be initiated, but it also helps identify areas to be targeted for selective enforcement.

Legal liability in crash cases generally involves three areas of public duty: (1) to warn and protect other motorists, (2) to render assistance and (3) to secure the scene. Not all traffic services involve enforcement or crashes. Much of it deals simply with keeping the traffic flowing smoothly.

# Traffic and Community Policing

Sweeney (2003, p.43) asserts: "Police chiefs who have surveyed members of their communities to find out what they consider the most serious problems in their neighborhoods know that traffic problems are at the top of the list. This rating has been found in quiet residential communities and crime-ridden inner cities alike. Citizens want to see police on the street, and they don't want to see them ignoring traffic violations. Traffic enforcement is not at odds with community policing; in fact, it helps police satisfy important objectives of community-oriented police services—namely, increasing the visibility of officers and improving the quality of life for every member of the community."

An approach to safety on our roadways emphasizing partnerships and citizen involvement is the Safe Communities program, sponsored by the Department of Transportation. In the cover letter to a *Report to Congress,* Mineta (2001, p.1) writes:

> As the Secretary of Transportation, safety is my highest priority. . . . Safe Communities presents new challenges and opportunities for creating innovative partnerships to prevent and control transportation-related fatalities and injuries. It can bring together many new partners and implement a variety of programs such as Buckle Up America, You Drink & Drive You Lose, Operation Lifesaver, Red Light Running, and Prevention Through People to name just a few. Expanded partnerships with the health and business community are important, as is the development of new alliances among traditional transportation safety advocates. The Safe Communities approach enables communities to examine their data to determine their most significant injury issues by identifying specific causes of injuries and fatalities and their associated costs.

Increasing from a few sites in 1996 when the program began to 755 Safe Community Programs by December of 1999, the program is operating in every state, the Pacific Territories and Puerto Rico.

A more complex community policing strategy, but one that holds great promise, is being used in Utah. Here technology is enhancing traffic safety through a state-of-the-art partnership between the Department of Public Safety (DPS) and the Department of Transportation (DOT). This partnership has enhanced the mission of the Highway Patrol (UHP) through its Intelligent Transportation System (ITS), described by Knopp and Groustra (2001, pp.53–58). The Traffic Operations Center (TOC) houses the ITS technology as well as the command and control personnel from the DPS and DOT. The Center's technology includes computer-assisted dispatch (CAD) and the computerized traffic management system called CommuterLink. The Center connects dispatch personnel at the command consoles to police, fire and EMS agencies as well as the DOT transportation response teams. It also connects them to CommuterLink's many traffic control systems, incorporating synchronized traffic signals, highway signs, electronic weather and traffic sensors and some 200 closed-circuit TV cameras that cover every major roadway. As Knopp and Groustra (p.56) explain: "Because the dispatchers of all the services involved can see what is happening in real time, CommuterLink sends the right personnel and equipment in the correct direction to the exact location."

An integral part of the system is communicating with the motoring public. According to Knopp and Groustra (pp.56–57) the link to commuters includes broadcast media, cell phones, pagers, a website and e-mail. Thousands of commuters have signed up for e-mail traffic alerts that notify them within moments of any significant event so they can avoid driving into a major tie-up. In addition, commuters can access the website and click on a road map location to access the CCTV at that location and see in real time what the traffic situation is. The map shows green freeways if traffic is flowing, yellow if it is slow and red if there is a tie-up. Say Knopp and Groustra (p.57): "The benefits in traffic safety improvements, environmental pollution reduction, commuter time saved and financial savings realized during the first year of CommuterLink's operation has provided solid support for the integration of transportation and public safety technology and command and control operations." The partnership between the departments and the highway patrol, as well as the communication with the commuting public, is an excellent example of the community policing philosophy in practice.

## Traffic and Problem-Oriented Policing

The 2001 Winner of the Herman Goldstein *Excellence in Problem-Oriented Policing* was awarded to the California Highway Patrol (CHP) for its Corridor Safety Program: A Collaborative Approach to Traffic Safety (Helmick et al., 2001, pp.5–14). The program used the SARA model to address a high rate of fatal crashes on an infamous stretch of rural highway in California, the roadway where actor James Dean was killed in the late 1950s, dubbed "Blood Alley."

### Scanning

Scanning was rigorous, with 550 qualifying roadway segments examined. The selection process incorporated a variety of quantitative measures of the safety challenges on roadways throughout the state, along with more subjective information from traffic safety officials. Three years of collision and victim data were reviewed to minimize any statistical anomalies. Segments less than eight miles in length and those with an average daily traffic count of 1,000 vehicles or fewer were eliminated. Also, to be included in the selection pool, potential corridors had to pass through or be adjacent to an urban area and fall under the jurisdiction of the CHP. Segments with fewer than five deaths in three years were also eliminated. Based on statistical rankings and input from local experts, recommendations for corridor selection were presented to CHP's Executive Management who selected State Routes 41/46.

### Analysis

The CHP formed a multidisciplinary task force consisting of 31 members representing the CHP, Caltrans, local governments, fire departments, city police departments, state legislators, local public works departments and federal transportation officials. This task force studied the physical characteristics that might adversely affect safety: the adequacy of regulatory and advisory signage; the number of traffic or passing lanes; the presence of roadway shoulders and medians, and their size; the presence or absence of guardrails and other safety aids; the condition of the pavement; and the presence or lack of landscaping. The task force found that much of the corridor was quite remote, largely without cellular phone service and having too few call boxes. Call response times for emergency services depended on the EMS unit with jurisdiction over the area, sometimes not the closest unit. The roadway lacked adequate shoulders and medians, and existing signage was confusing and inadequate, as were existing passing and merging lanes. Being an east-west route, glare was a problem during sunrise and sunset. Various roadway curves also contributed to poor visibility.

The task force also looked at collision and traffic data and found that the primary collision factors spoke to the presence of aggressive driving and of impatient drivers who made unwise passing decisions when stuck behind large, slow-moving vehicles. The top five collision factors were unsafe turning, driving on the wrong side of the road, improper passing, driving under the influence and unsafe speed. The task force also found that collisions occurred most frequently on Friday, Saturday and Sunday between 1:00 P.M. and 6:00 P.M. Collision times and days reflected the presence of "weekend-warriors" who traveled to the coast on the weekends to escape the valley heat. It also suggested that many involved in collisions were local farm workers with limited English skills who were unfamiliar with California rules-of-the-road.

## Response

Proposed solutions fell into four categories: enforcement, emergency services, engineering and education.

**Enforcement**   Special enforcement operations were implemented and funded through federal traffic safety grants. Ultimately, officers worked 2,922 overtime hours, offered assistance and services to motorists 2,837 times and issued 14,606 citations.

**Emergency Services**   Additional emergency roadside call boxes were installed. A CHP helicopter was permanently assigned to the roadway, and agreements were reached with emergency service providers that the closest units should respond to collision scenes, without regard to jurisdictional boundaries.

**Engineering**   Several physical changes were made in the roadway. Raised-profile thermoplastic striping was installed where passing was allowed in one direction. In no-passing zones, a widened center median with rumble strips and thermoplastic striping was installed. Outside shoulders were treated with rumble strips. Several signing, striping and maintenance projects were completed. "Stop Ahead" warning signs were posted at key intersections, and chevron signs were installed to warn of impending curves.

**Education**   A variety of educational programs and materials involved the local media, businesses, government and residents in reminding motorists to drive safely. Two million color flyers emphasizing safe driving habits were printed and distributed through educational institutions, newspapers, local businesses, restaurants, recreational facilities and government agency offices. Large and small posters were posted in restaurants and in local businesses. In addition, three kick-off news conferences were held just before the Memorial Day weekend in three separate locations along the corridor.

## Assessment

The efforts were quite successful with fatal collisions reduced by 10 percent and injury collisions reduced by 32 percent. Over the five years of available data, it is estimated that the safety initiatives have saved 21 lives and prevented 55 injuries. As Helmick et al. (p.33) suggest: "Extraordinary traffic safety benefits can result from systematically identifying corridors, analyzing the causes of dangerous conditions, forming specific recommendations for action, and evaluating the resulting collision trends."

### SUMMARY

Police traffic services (PTS) are divided into three functional areas: traffic direction and control, traffic enforcement, and crash investigation.

The two basic purposes of traffic enforcement are to control congestion and to reduce crashes. Despite officers' efforts to maintain a high-profile, aggressive traffic presence, the I-won't-get-a-ticket syndrome is common among the driving public. Even if a traffic enforcement unit exists, traffic enforcement is the responsibility of *all* officers.

Some of the more challenging and hazardous motorist behaviors involve aggressive driving, road rage and driving under the influence. Aggressive driving is a traffic violation; road rage is a criminal offense. Nationwide, DUI is the number one traffic law enforcement problem. Strategies to deter DUI include educating drivers through awareness campaigns and establishing sobriety checkpoints. Additional efforts aimed at repeat offenders include using ignition interlocks and enacting vehicle forfeiture programs.

Another problem area for traffic officers is pursuit. Pursuit policies should address such issues as the number of units actively participating, use of roadblocks to end pursuits, use of firearms during pursuits and use of intentional contact. A frequently overlooked area in traffic enforcement involves transportation of hazardous materials. A hazardous materials enforcement program should consist of terminal audits, shipper and other audits, road enforcement, technical assistance and enforcement training and emergency response.

Dealing with motor vehicle crashes is another function of traffic services. Such crashes are the leading cause of death for people ages 1 to 33, yet the a-crash-won't-happen-to-me syndrome is common among the American driving public. At a crash scene, officers are responsible for managing the scene, including protecting it, attending to injuries, keeping traffic moving and restoring normal traffic flow. Officers are also responsible for investigating the cause(s) of the crash.

### APPLICATION

The chief of police of Ourtown receives a letter from the prosecutor stating that a serious problem exists in prosecuting DUI cases because there is no uniformity of procedures. To correct this, a policy must be written and instituted to successfully prosecute cases and to reinstate the faith of the public. This news comes as a shock to the chief, who immediately asks you, as supervisor of the traffic division, to take charge. The chief emphasizes that this is a problem demanding immediate attention. DUI cases must be thoroughly investigated so offenders can be successfully prosecuted.

### INSTRUCTIONS

Write a policy and procedure so officers who deal with DUI have direction, guidance and technical information. Include ways of detecting a driver under the influence, probable cause for stopping, observing the driver's condition, questioning the driver, giving the necessary field tests and invoking the implied consent law. Officers should mentally record the events as they occur as accurately as possible and make written notes at the earliest practical time. Witnesses should be interviewed to strengthen the case.

### EXERCISES IN CRITICAL THINKING

A. At 9:39 P.M. on June 14, Officer Morse investigated a motor vehicle crash. Firefighters extricated Janice Kostecky from her vehicle, which had rolled over. One firefighter who placed her in an ambulance informed Morse that Kostecky "reeked of alcohol." Morse did not speak to Kostecky or observe her closely at the crash scene. The other driver, who also had a strong odor of an alcoholic beverage on her breath, and several other witnesses indicated that Kostecky was not at fault for the crash.

Morse then spent 15 to 20 minutes with Kostecky at her bedside in the emergency room. She admitted she "had something to drink." Morse detected a moderate odor of an alcoholic beverage on her breath, but testified that his face was not close to hers. Morse also noted that her eyes were "glassy and runny-looking."

Morse concluded that Kostecky was under the influence of alcohol and arrested her for DUI. He read her the implied consent advisory and obtained a test, which disclosed an alcohol concentration of .10 or more. Kostecky's driver's license was revoked pursuant to the implied consent law.

1. Does Officer Morse have probable cause to believe Kostecky was under the influence of alcohol?
   a. No, because the officer's questioning of Kostecky amounted to a limited seizure, requiring a particularized and objective basis for suspecting her of criminal activity, and the other driver and witnesses indicated that Kostecky was not at fault for the accident.
   b. Yes, because Kostecky told the officer she "had something to drink," the officer detected a moderate odor of an alcoholic beverage on her breath and the officer noted that her "eyes were glassy and runny-looking."
   c. No, because merely "something to drink," a "moderate odor of an alcoholic beverage" and "glassy and runny-looking" eyes are not sufficient for probable cause to believe Kostecky was under the influence of alcohol.
   d. Yes, because any reasonable suspicion that an officer might have will be sufficient to believe someone involved in a traffic crash is under the influence of alcohol.
   e. No, because Kostecky was in a litter or bed in a hospital emergency room and was not able to perform field sobriety tests.

B. Just prior to 1:00 A.M. on February 10, Officer Janacek stopped Frank Pastuszak's vehicle for erratic driving. Pastuszak was 67 years old and claimed to have various physical ailments. Officer Janacek detected signs of intoxication, which Pastuszak claimed were due to his medical conditions. Pastuszak said he had not consumed any alcoholic beverages that evening. After Pastuszak became belligerent and profane, Officer Janacek arrested him and took him to the police station.

At the station, Janacek told Pastuszak to empty his pockets. His response was an obscenity. After again telling Pastuszak to empty his pockets and receiving the same response, the officer told him that, if necessary, his pockets would be emptied by force. Pastuszak then clenched his fists and raised his left hand. Officer Janacek and another officer then forcibly subdued Pastuszak, in the process fracturing his ankle.

Immediately after Pastuszak was forced to the floor, the officers started a video camera. Officer Janacek read the implied consent advisory, and when asked if he understood the test, Pastuszak did not respond. When asked to take an Intoxilyzer test, Pastuszak said, "I took one." When asked why he refused the test, Pastuszak responded with another barrage of profanity.

The officers did not arrange for a blood sample to be taken when Pastuszak was subsequently taken to North Memorial Hospital for surgery on his ankle.

2. Was Pastuszak reasonably justified in refusing to take an Intoxilyzer test?
   a. Pastuszak failed to meet his burden of showing that he could not have blown into the Intoxilyzer.
   b. The physical pain of multiple medical problems, compounded by the pain of a broken ankle, justified Pastuszak's behavior and refusal to take an Intoxilyzer test.
   c. The refusal to take an Intoxilyzer test places the burden of proof on the officers to arrange for a blood sample at a hospital.
   d. In the case of a senior citizen, officers should show respect even when verbal belligerence and abuse are experienced. Use of force is not justified in overpowering someone for a driving violation, even when he refuses to be cooperative.
   e. As there is no necessary reason for requiring Pastuszak to empty his pockets, considering the violation was simply for erratic driving, he has good reason for noncompliance. And without a blood test from the hospital, the courts will believe his claim about medical problems and his assertion that he had not consumed any alcoholic beverages.

## DISCUSSION QUESTIONS

1. What should be the top priority in a traffic program? Justify your selection.

2. Your municipality has an ordinance stating that it is against the law to drink and drive. Obtain a copy of that ordinance and bring it to class. What is the legal limit for intoxication? Do you feel the legal limit justifies the penalty if one is convicted? Would you suggest some modifications in the law as you see it enforced?

3. Three tests are usually given to determine if a person is under the influence of alcohol while driving: a breath test, a urine test and a blood test. From evidence that might be presented in court, which test would you favor if you were a police officer? What are the advantages and disadvantages in administering each test?

4. Is a pursuit policy justified in a police department, or should officers be allowed to make a discretionary decision to chase without the benefit of a specific policy?

5. Should officers expose those they are pursuing to hazardous roadblock conditions or be given permission to ram cars? If so, what restrictions should apply, if any?

6. Radar detectors used by motorists are a source of irritation to most traffic officers. Do you feel they should be declared illegal to possess and use, as they have been in some states?

7. Most warning tickets issued by officers are never formally recorded on a driver's record. Are such tickets an effective tool in obtaining compliance to traffic laws?

## INFOTRAC COLLEGE EDITION ASSIGNMENTS

- Use InfoTrac College Edition to help answer the Discussion Questions as appropriate.

- Use InfoTrac College Edition to research *road rage.* Write a brief (two- to three-page) report on the characteristics of this type of driver and the effects of aggressive driving. Be prepared to share your report with the class.

- Use InfoTrac College Edition to read and outline one of the following articles to share with the class:
  - "The Role of Race in Law Enforcement: Racial Profiling or Legitimate Use?" by Richard G. Schott
  - "Collecting Statistics in Response to Racial Profiling Allegations" by Karen J. Kruger
  - "High-Speed Police Pursuits: Dangers, Dynamics and Risk Reduction" by John Hill
  - "Alexandria CARES and BABY-1: Protecting the Future" by Dianne Gittins
  - "Battling DUI: A Comparative Analysis of Checkpoints and Saturation Patrols" by Jeffrey W. Greene

## INTERNET ASSIGNMENTS

Select one of the following assignments to complete.

- Use the Internet to find out what the DUI laws are in your state. Research adjoining states to see how the laws in your state compare to neighboring states. Be prepared to discuss your findings with the class.

- Go to www.nhtsa.dot.gov/safecommunities and see what materials are available to police departments to start a Safe Communities program in their city. Be prepared to share your results with the class.

- Download *Racially Biased Policing* at www.PoliceForum.org and outline one chapter of interest to you. Be prepared to present and discuss your outline with the class.

- Go to the National Traffic Enforcement Association's website http://www.trafficenforcement.org/ and select a topic to outline. This site features areas devoted to traffic enforcement, drug interdiction, crash investigation, DUI enforcement and more.

- Go to the website of the *CRASH!* program and outline the activities available through this curriculum: www.legalsciences.com/crash.htm.

## BOOK-SPECIFIC WEBSITE

The book-specific website at http://cj.wadsworth.com/wobleski_Hess_police_op4e hosts a variety of resources

for students and instructors. Many can be emailed to the instructor. Included are extended activities such as Concept Builders - the 3 step learning module that reinforces key chapter concepts, followed by a real-world applications and critical thinking questions. InfoTrac College Edition exercises; Discussion Questions; interactive key-term FlashCards; and a collection of chapter-based Web Links provide additional information and activities to include in the curriculum.

## REFERENCES

"Aggressive Drivers Urged to Chill Out." *Law Enforcement News,* May 15/31 2003, p.6.

Ashton, Richard J. "Saved by the Belt or Air Bag—Revisited." *The Police Chief,* March 2004a, p.66.

Ashton, Richard J. "Solutions for Safer Traffic Stops." *The Police Chief,* July 2004b, pp.28–33.

Batton, Candice and Kadleck, Colleen. "Theoretical and Methodological Issues in Racial Profiling Research." *Police Quarterly,* March 2004, pp.30–64.

Bellah, John L. "Cutting Out the Chase." *Police,* April 2003, pp.28–31.

"'Black Boxes' Change Nature of Crash Probes." *Law Enforcement News,* March 2004, p.4.

"Black Boxes in Automobiles Aid in Crash Investigations." *The Police Chief,* January 2004, pp.65–66.

Bolton, Joel. "Click It or Ticket Program Helps Increase Safety Belt Use." *The Police Chief,* October 2001a, p.181.

Bolton, Joel. "Getting the Impaired Driver off the Street." *The Police Chief,* November 2001b, p.73.

Bolton, Joel. "Red Light Running and Other Intersection Hazards." *The Police Chief,* August 2002, p.114.

Bolton, Joel. "Good News from NHTSA: Seat Belt Use Is Up." *The Police Chief,* May 2003, p.70.

Bowman, J. F. and Fisher, P. David. "Traffic Law Enforcement Technologies." *The Police Chief,* July 2004, pp.39–41.

Cahill, Patricia. "National Mobilization and Enforcement Campaign Begins in August." *The Police Chief,* June 2004, p.86.

"CALEA Takes Stand on Racial Profiling." *Law Enforcement News,* April 15, 2001, p.5.

Carrick, Grady. "Decoy Patrols: Dummies Reducing Traffic Fatalities." *Law and Order,* April 2001, pp.110–111.

Carrick, Grady. "Traffic Safety in the New Millennium." *Law and Order,* April 2003, pp.44–50.

Carrick, Grady. "Operation Safe Ride." *Law and Order,* August 2004, pp.20–22.

Chermak, Steven; McGarrell, Edmund F.; and Weiss, Alexander. "Citizens' Perceptions of Aggressive Traffic Enforcement Strategies." *Justice Quarterly,* June 2001, pp.365–391.

Cox, Otis. "NHTSA's Highway Safety Priorities." *The Police Chief,* April 2004a, pp.14–15.

Cox, Otis. "2003 Traffic Safety Data." *The Police Chief,* July 2004b, pp.15–16.

Cox, Stephen M. "Racial Profiling: Refuting Concerns about Collecting Race Data on Traffic Stops." *Law and Order,* October 2001, pp.61–65.

Daniels, Wayne and Spratley, Lynnette. "Brainpower Not Horsepower: Teaching Officers When and How to End Pursuits." *Law and Order,* July 2003, pp.85–89.

Daniels, Wayne; Spratley, Lynnette; and Ryan, James. "Traffic Stop Safety." *Law and Order,* July 2004, pp.74–80.

Dewey-Kollen, Janet. "Keep Kids Alive Drive 25." *Law and Order,* July 2003a, pp.20–22.

Dewey-Kollen, Janet. "Photo Red Light Enforcement." *Law and Order,* August 2003b, pp.28–32.

Dewey-Kollen, Janet. "Child Passenger Safety Week." *Law and Order,* February 2004a, pp.12–14.

Dewey-Kollen, Janet. "National Seat Belt Enforcement Mobilization." *Law and Order,* April 2004b, pp.12–14.

Dewey-Kollen, Janet. "Graduated Drivers License Laws." *Law and Order,* June 2004c, pp.12–14.

Dewey-Kollen, Janet. "School Zone Safety in Washington State." *Law and Order,* August 2004d, pp.12–14.

Dewey-Kollen, Janet. "Getting and Keeping Drunk Drivers Off America's Roads," *Law and Order,* September 2004e, pp.12–16.

Dewey-Kollen, Janet. "National Safety Belt Usage Now 80%." *Law and Order,* November 2004f, pp.16–19.

Engel, Robin Shepard and Calnon, Jennifer M. "Examining the Influence of Drivers' Characteristics during Stop with Police: Results from a National Survey." *Justice Quarterly,* March 2004, pp.49–90.

*Excellence in Problem-Oriented Policing: The 2001 Herman Goldstein Award Winners.* Washington, DC: National Institute of Justice, COPS and the Police Executive Research Forum, 2001.

Fors, Carl. "Detecting Detectors." *Law and Order,* April 2004, pp.30–32.

Fridell, Lorie A. *By the Numbers: A Guide for Analyzing Race Data from Vehicle Stops.* Washington, DC: Police Executive Research Forum, 2004.

Fridell, Lorie; Lunney, Robert; Diamond, Drew; and Kubu, Bruce; with Scott, Michael and Laing, Colleen. *Racially Biased Policing: A Principled Response.* Washington, DC: Police Executive Research Forum, 2001. www.policeforum.org

Galvin, Bob. "Accident Report Forms Go Electronic." *Law Enforcement Technology,* July 2004, pp.150–157.

Garrett, Ronnie. "Turning the Key on Drunk Driving." *Law Enforcement Technology,* May 2003, pp.72–75.

Greene, Jeffrey. "Battling DUI: A Comparative Analysis of Checkpoints and Saturation Patrols." *FBI Law Enforcement Bulletin,* January 2003, pp.1–6.

Hatch, Mike. "What to Expect from Chronic DWI Offenders." *Minnesota Police Chief,* Spring 2004, pp.15–19.

Helmick, D.O. "Spike." "Automated Red Light Cameras." *The Police Chief,* July 2003, pp.44–50.

Helmick, D.O.; Keller, John; Nannini, Robert; and Huffaker, Alice. "Corridor Safety Program: A Collaborative Approach to Traffic Safety." *The Police Chief,* July 2001, pp.32–35.

Horne, Jennifer. "State Legislatures Address Important Law Enforcement Issues." *The Police Chief,* June 2001a, p.8.

Horne, Jennifer. "It's a Wrap: State Legislators Conclude Their 2001 Session." *The Police Chief,* December 2001b, p.10.

Hustmyre, Chuck. "Catching Criminals on the Highway." *Law and Order,* September 2003, pp.113–117.

Insurance Institute for Highway Safety. "Yellow Lights: Small Changes in the Timing of Signal Lights Could Reduce Crashes at Urban Intersections." *Status Report,* April 28, 2001a, p.7. www.highwaysafety.org/srpdfs/sr3604.pdf.

Insurance Institute for Highway Safety, Highway Loss Data Institute. "Q & A: Speed and Speed Limits." Modified January 9, 2001b. www.highwaysafety.org/safety%5Ffacts

Kinsley, Michael. "When Is Racial Profiling Okay?" *Law Enforcement News,* October 15, 2001, p.9.

Klugiewicz, Gary T. and Smith, James G. "Think before You Run." *Police,* July 2004, pp.120–125.

Knopp, Martin and Groustra, Carol. "Utah's Intelligent Transportation Systems Pave the Way for Increased Public Safety." *The Police Chief,* July 2001, pp.52–58.

Labbe, J.R. "Get It Straight! Profiling Is Not Racism." *American Police Beat,* October 2001, pp.25, 37.

Lowery, Patrick J., Jr. "Curb Illegal Street Racing." *The Police Chief,* September 2003, pp.51–54.

Makholm, John A. "Legal Lights." *ASLET Law Enforcement Trainer,* January/February 2001.

Miller, Christa. "Enforcing Hazmat Transport: Responding to Hazmat Incidents." *Law Enforcement Technology,* August 2002, pp.54–60.

Miller, Christa. "That's the Ticket." *Law Enforcement Technology,* October 2003, pp.78–83.

Mineta, Norman Y. Cover Letter to the *Report to Congress: Safe Communities 1999.* Washington, DC: U.S. Department of Transportation, May 2001. (DOT HS 809258)

Mothers Against Drunk Driving (MADD). "Help Keep Families Together." (undated brochure).

National Safety Council. *Pedestrian Safety.* October 31, 2001. www.nsc.org/library/facts/pedstrns.htm.

Nislow, Jennifer. "Are Americans Ready to Buy into Racial Profiling?" *Law Enforcement News,* October 15, 2001, p.11.

Novak, Kenneth J. "Disparity and Racial Profiling in Traffic Enforcement." *Police Quarterly,* March 2004, pp.65–96.

Nugent, Hugh; Connors, Edward F.; McEwen, J. Thomas; and Mayo, Lou. *Restrictive High-Speed Police Pursuits.* Washington, DC: U.S. Department of Justice, no date. (NCJ 122025)

Oldenburg, Don. "Back at Ya: Sprays Said to Foil Traffic Cameras." *Washington Post* as reprinted in the (Minneapolis/St. Paul) *Star Tribune,* July 26, 2004, p.E7.

Onder, James J. "Tips for Conducting Professional Traffic Stops." *The Police Chief,* July 2001, pp.26–30.

Papenfuhs, Steve. "Tactically Sound Vehicle Stops: A Shift in Mind-Sets Can Save Lives." *Law and Order,* July 2003, pp.80–84.

Porter, Lowell M. "In Partnership with NHTSA: Washington State Patrol Focuses on Aggressive Drivers." *The Police Chief,* September 2004, pp.45–48.

"The Racial Profiling Controversy in America." *NCJA Justice Bulletin,* April 2001, pp.8, 13–15.

Rao, Angelo. "Transportation Services." In *Local Government Police Management,* 4th ed. edited by William A. Geller and Darrel W. Stephens. Washington, DC: International City/County Management Association, 2003, pp.207–238.

Redfern, Robert and Kwasnoski, John. "CRASH! The Science of Collisions." *Law and Order,* 2001, pp.15–16.

Robinson, Robyn. "DWI Enforcement: Solutions to Nine Common Problems." *The Police Chief,* July 2002, pp.51–58.

Rojek, Jeff; Rosenfeld, Richard; and Decker, Scott. "The Influence of Driver's Race on Traffic Stops in Missouri." *Police Quarterly,* March 2004, pp.126–147.

Runge, Jeffrey W. "Increasing Safety Belt Use: A National Priority." *The Police Chief,* December 2003, p.12.

Scott, Michael S. *Speeding in Residential Areas.* Washington, DC: Office of Community Oriented Policing Services Problem-Oriented Guides for Police Series No. 3, August 14, 2001.

Sharp, Arthur G. "Setting Cameras to Make Traffic Stops." *Law and Order,* May 2001, pp.71–74.

Sharp, Arthur G. "The Dynamics of Vehicle Chases in Real Life." *Law and Order,* July 2003, pp.68–74.

Sharp, Arthur G. "Fix 'Ticket Fixing.'" *Law and Order,* July 2004, pp.68–72.

"Signal-Changing Device Raises Concerns." *Law Enforcement News,* January 2004, p.5.

Spector, Elliot B. "Stopping Suspects Based on Racial and Ethnic Descriptions." *The Police Chief,* January 2002, pp.10–12.

Sweeney, Earl M. "Traffic Stops: Neglect Them at Your Peril." *The Police Chief,* July 2003, pp.38–43.

Sweeney, Earl M. "Managing Highway Incidents with NIMS." *The Police Chief,* July 2004, pp.20–27.

"To Protect and Serve the Smallest Citizens." *The Police Chief,* February 2004, p.78.

Tomaskovic-Devey, Donald; Mason, Marcinda; and Zingraff, Matthew. "Looking for the Driving while Black Phenomena: Conceptualizing Racial Bias Processes and their Associated Distributions." *Police Quarterly,* March 2004, pp.3–29.

*Traffic Safety Facts 2000: Speeding.* Washington, DC: National Highway Traffic Safety Administration, 2001. (DOT HA 809 333) www-nrd.nhtsa.dot.gov/pdf/nrd-30/NCSA/ TSF2000

## CASES CITED

*Brown v. City of Oneonta,* 221 F.3d 329 (2nd Cir.2000), cert. denied, 122 S.Ct. 44 (2001)

*Carleton v. Town of Framingham,* 615 N.E.2d 588 (Mass.App.Ct.) (1993)

*City of Indianapolis v. Edmond,* No. 99-1080 (2000)

*County of Sacramento v. Lewis,* 523 U.S. 833 (1998)

*Michigan Department of State Police v. Sitz,* 496 U.S. 444 (1990)

*Pennsylvania v. Mimms,* 434 U.S. 106 (1977)

*Pennsylvania v. Muniz,* 496 U.S. 582 (1990)

*Whren v. United States,* 517 U.S. 806 (1996)

# CHAPTER 6

# Crime, Disorder and Quality-of-Life Issues: Responding to the Call

### DO YOU KNOW . . .

- What the official sources of information about crime are?
- What the responsibilities of officers responding to a criminal action call are?
- What the preliminary investigation of a crime consists of?
- What issues may lead to civil disobedience in the twenty-first century?
- How police departments should be prepared to deal with demonstrations and violence?
- What the number one rule is when dealing with hostage situations, barricaded subjects or attempted suicides?

### CAN YOU DEFINE?

chain of custody
chain of possession
civil disobedience
collective efficacy
Crime Index
flashbangs
geographic
    information
    systems (GIS)

hot spots
incivilities
Part I (Crime Index)
    offenses
Part II offenses
preliminary
    investigation

property crimes
Stockholm syndrome
Uniform Crime
    Reports (UCRs)
violent crimes

## Introduction

Responding to calls about crime, disorder and quality-of-life issues is a basic function of law enforcement and has been a defining priority throughout the history of policing. In fact, many believe this is the only true function of the police and that in a perfect world, one free of all crime and disorder, police would be unnecessary. Of course, police operations involve more than just handling crime and disorder. By the same token, the response to crime and disorder is not new, nor has it always been solely the responsibility of law enforcement:

> English subjects of a thousand years ago could not wash their hands of crime. No looking the other way. No refusal to get involved. The English, beginning with the rule of Alfred the Great (870–901), were financially obligated to catch criminals. It was known as the "mutual pledge system." At the report of a crime, everyone in the community had to raise a "hue and cry." If the Crown's

subjects failed to catch an offender, the Crown's collectors would hit the incompetents with a royal fine. The intent was to force the entire realm to play cops.

Modern policing has returned to its roots, the legacy of Alfred the Great. The recent shift to community policing provides ample evidence of law enforcement relying on the public for help (Burns, 2001, p.18).

The FBI released crime figures for 2003 that showed that violent crime in the United States declined 3.0 percent and property crime decreased 0.2 percent from the estimated volume for 2002. Arrests are often used as a key measure of law enforcement's effectiveness in fighting crime. According to the UCR, in 2003 law enforcement in the United States made an estimated 13.6 million arrests for crimes committed, excluding traffic offenses. Law enforcement made 1.6 million arrests for property crimes that occurred in 2003, which represented 11.8 percent of the total arrests. Drug abuse violations accounted for nearly 1.7 million arrests, the most arrests for any offense type.

Figures released by the Bureau of Justice Statistics (BJS) from its National Crime Victimization Survey showed that the percentage of households experiencing crime, about 15 percent, did not change significantly between 2002 and 2003. About one in every 26 households in 2003 were either burglarized or had a member of the household age 12 or older who was a victim of a violent crime committed by a stranger. The BJS says crime remains at a 30-year low. Violent victimizations overall have declined by 55 percent during the past decade from 50 per 1,000 people in 1993 to 23 per 1,000 in 2003.

Many contend the added "eyes and ears" of the citizenry has contributed to the declining crime rate. Paradoxically, while crime rates are falling across the country, some citizens have grown increasingly fearful of crime and victimization. Some studies have found those who watched the most local television news reported the highest levels of fear of crime. Media accounts of crime usually focus on the most serious, sensational cases. The sensationalized media accounts may explain why the levels of citizens' fear of crime appears to be unrelated to the actual levels of crime in their neighborhood. Study after study shows that the media focuses on crime and violence to the neglect of other aspects of law enforcement. In one study of over 1,000 articles, the "overwhelming majority dealt with crime" (*Marketing Community Policing in the News: A Missed Opportunity?* 2003, p.3). As the adage states: "If it doesn't bleed, it doesn't lead."

Turner (2004, p.6) reports: "Acts of crime decrease, but fear of crime persists. Law enforcement agencies are improving their nuts-and-bolts approach to preventing and solving crime but may be falling behind on combating the psychological effects of crime. . . . Even after 9/11, most communities still list fear of street crime and robberies as their most pressing concern." Few agencies compile statistics on citizens' fear of crime, making it difficult to ascertain the actual extent of the problem.

Weitzer and Kubrin (2004, p.497) also suggest: "Many Americans report that they are fearful of crime. One frequently cited source of this fear is the mass media. The media, and local television in particular, often report on incidents of crime, and do so in a selective and sometimes sensational manner." Like Turner, they contend: "Fear of crime is a major problem in the United States."

Other surveys indicate the country as a whole appears to feel safer in their neighborhoods and homes today than they did several decades ago. A 1975 poll that asked: "Is there any area near where you live—that is, within a mile—where you would be afraid to walk alone at night?" found 45 percent of respondents replied yes, they were fearful of walking alone after dark. In answer to that same question in 2003, only 36 percent responded that they were fearful to walk alone at night (*Sourcebook . . .*, 2003, Table 2.35). Those reporting the most fear were minority females 50 years and older, with a high school education who earned under $20,000 in a clerical type job and lived in the Northeast (Table 2.36).

This chapter begins with a look at how crimes are classified and measured, including a discussion of the Uniform Crime Reports, the National Incident-Based Reporting System and the National Crime Victimization Survey. Next, crime mapping is presented, followed by a look at how police respond to calls about crimes and disorder. The chapter then examines the police response to disorder and civil disobedience; and crisis situations involving hostages, barricaded individuals and suicide attempts. The chapter concludes with a look at the relationship between crime, disorder and community policing.

## Classifying and Measuring Crime

The U.S. Department of Justice administers several statistical programs to measure the magnitude, nature and impact of crime in America. The Federal Bureau of Investigation (FBI) collects and disseminates crime statistics through its Uniform Crime Reports (UCR) Program and the National Incident-Based Reporting System (NIBRS). The Bureau of Justice Statistics (BJS) collects detailed crime information via its National Crime Victimization Survey (NCVS).

 The official sources of information about crime are the Uniform Crime Reports (UCR), the National Incident-Based Reporting System (NIBRS) and the National Crime Victimization Survey (NCVS).

While the UCR and NCVS programs each have unique strengths, they are conducted for different purposes and use different methodologies. Therefore, caution is needed in comparing crime trends presented by the UCR and NCVS because, as each examines the nation's crime problem from a unique perspective, their results are not strictly comparable. Nonetheless, the information they produce together provides a more comprehensive view of crime in the United States than either could produce alone.

### Uniform Crime Reports

The FBI gathers statistics on reported crimes from local, county and state law enforcement agencies throughout the country and reports the findings annually in their **Uniform Crime Reports (UCRs),** called *Crime in the United States.* According to the FBI (*Crime in the United States,* 2002, p.1), the law enforcement agencies active in the UCR Program during 2002 represented 17,000 law enforcement agencies serving 93.4 percent of U.S. citizens.

When the UCR Program was launched in 1929, seven offenses were chosen to serve as an index for gauging fluctuations in the overall volume and rate of crime reported to law enforcement: "Known collectively as the **Crime Index,** these offenses included the **violent crimes** of murder and nonnegligent manslaughter, forcible rape, robbery and aggravated assault and the **property crimes** of burglary, larceny-theft and motor vehicle theft. By congressional mandate, arson [a property crime] was added as the eighth Index offense in 1979" (*Crime in the United States*, p.1) [boldface added]. The UCR Program classifies these eight offenses as **Part I (Crime Index) offenses.** Arrest data is also collected for 21 additional crime categories classified as **Part II offenses,** a group which effectively includes all crimes not classified as Part I. A summary of the figures for the Part I crimes committed in 2003 is presented in Figure 6.1.

This graphic does not imply a regularity in the commission of the Part I offenses. Rather, it shows the annual ratio of crime to fixed time intervals. Figure 6.2 shows the distribution of the Part I offenses.

The Uniform Crime Reports program is undergoing major revision, moving from its current system of summary counts to a more comprehensive, detailed reporting system, the National Incident-Based Reporting System (NIBRS). This system is intended to replace the traditional eight offenses of the FBI Crime Index with detailed incident information on 46 offenses representing 22 categories of crimes.

# CRIME CLOCK

| Every 22.8 seconds | One Violent Crime |
|---|---|
| Every 31.8 minutes | One Murder |
| Every 5.6 minutes | One Forcible Rape |
| Every 1.3 minutes | One Robbery |
| Every 36.8 seconds | One Aggravated Assault |

| Every 3.0 seconds | One Property Crime |
|---|---|
| Every 14.6 seconds | One Burglary |
| Every 4.5 seconds | One Larceny-theft |
| Every 25.0 seconds | One Motor Vehicle Theft |

**Figure 6.1**   The Crime Clock

SOURCE: *Crime in the United States 2003*, Washington, DC: Federal Bureau of Investigation, 2003, p.6.

## National Incident-Based Reporting System

While the UCR counts incidents and arrests for the eight Crime Index offenses and arrests only for Part II offenses, NIBRS provides detailed incident information on 48 Group A offenses representing 22 categories of crimes. NIBRS also distinguishes between attempted and completed crimes.

Table 6.1 shows the NIBRS Group A offenses, comparable to the UCR Part I offenses. Table 6.2 shows the Group B offenses—the "other" offenses, or Part II offenses. Table 6.3 shows the data to be obtained for each offense.

According to McEwen (2003, p.402): "Compared with the summary UCR statistics, NIBRS provides more detailed data. Crime analysis is enhanced by having details on individual crimes that can then be analyzed and summarized in a variety of different ways. . . . The expansion to 46 crime classifications provides a means for police departments to analyze virtually every problem that might arise, including offenses related to domestic violence, use of guns, hate crimes and terrorism."

## National Crime Victimization Survey

Conducted by U.S. Bureau of the Census personnel and reported through the Bureau of Justice Statistics (BJS), the National Crime Victimization Survey (NCVS) is an ongoing survey of a nationally representative sample of approximately 49,000 households to collect information on crimes suffered by individuals and households, whether or not those crimes were reported to law enforcement.

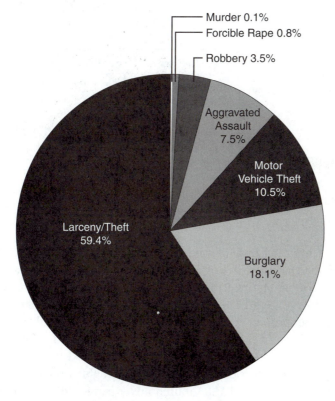

**Figure 6.2**   Percent Distribution of Part I Offenses

SOURCE: *Crime in the United States 2002*, Washington, DC: Federal Bureau of Investigation, 2002, p.11.

**Table 6.1** The NIBRS Group A Offenses

Arson
Assault offenses
   Aggravated assault
   Simple assault
   Intimidation

Bribery

Burglary/breaking and entering

Counterfeiting/forgery

Destruction/damage/vandalism of property

Drug/narcotic offenses
   Drug/narcotic violations
   Drug equipment violations

Embezzlement

Extortion/blackmail

Fraud offenses
   False pretenses/swindle/confidence game
   Credit card/ATM fraud
   Impersonation
   Welfare fraud
   Wire fraud

Gambling offenses
   Betting/wagering
   Operating/promoting/assisting gambling
   Gambling equipment violations
   Sports tampering

Homicide offenses
   Murder/nonnegligent manslaughter

Negligent manslaughter
Justifiable homicide

Kidnapping/abduction

Larceny/theft offenses
   Pocket picking
   Purse snatching
   Shoplifting
   Theft from building
   Theft from coin-operated machines
   Theft from motor vehicle
   Theft of motor vehicle parts/accessories
   All other larceny

Motor vehicle theft

Pornography/obscene material

Prostitution offenses
   Prostitution
   Assisting or promoting prostitution

Robbery

Sex offenses, forcible
   Forcible rape
   Forcible sodomy
   Sexual assault with an object
   Forcible fondling

Sex offenses, nonforcible

Stolen property offenses

Weapon law violations

SOURCE: Brian A. Reaves. *National Incident-Based Reporting System: Using NIBRS Data to Analyze Violent Crime.* Washington, DC: Bureau of Justice Statistics Technical Report, October 1993, p.1.

All household members age 12 and older (about 101,000 people) are interviewed every six months for three years. New households are continuously rotated into the sample.

Since its inception in 1973, the NCVS has been the primary source of information on the characteristics of criminal victimization and on the number and types of crimes *not* reported to law enforcement authorities. For example, data from the 2002 NCVS indicates only 48 percent of all violent victimizations and 38 percent of all property crimes were reported to police (Wald). About 16 million households experienced one or more of the victimizations measured by the NCVS. Theft affecting 1 in 10 households was the most frequent crime (Klaus, 2004, p.2). Klaus (p.1) reports the following highlights from the 2002 NCVS:

- In 1994 a quarter of all U.S. households experienced a violent or property crime. By 2002 the percentage of households victimized had dropped to 15 percent.

**Table 6.2**  The NIBRS Group B Offenses

Bad checks

Curfew/loitering/vagrancy

Disorderly conduct

Driving under the influence

Drunkenness

Liquor law violations

Nonviolent family offenses

Peeping Tom

Runaway

Trespassing

All other offenses

SOURCE: Brian A. Reaves. *National Incident-Based Reporting System: Using NIBRS Data to Analyze Violent Crime.* Washington, DC: Bureau of Justice Statistics Technical Report, October 1993, p.2.

- In 2002 a violent crime against a person age 12 or older occurred in 3 percent of U.S. households compared to 7 percent in 1994.
- About 4 percent of U.S. households in 2002 (half the 1994 percentage) were either burglarized or had a member who was a victim of a violent crime committed by a stranger.
- About 5 percent of households were vandalized at least once during 2002.

## From Measuring Crime to Predicting Crime—Becoming Proactive

These various data collection programs have created a documented history of crime problems throughout our country and have helped the national law enforcement community gain better insight into trends in criminal activity and victimization in the United States. As beneficial as these programs have been and continue to be, increasingly sophisticated computerized mapping tools now enable police at the local level to track and analyze crime directly affecting their community. In addition to real-time capabilities, this technology also has forward-looking capabilities, meaning it affords agencies a degree of predictability in forecasting future crime in their community, allowing the department to become proactive.

## Mapping Crime

Law enforcement's ability to understand the extent of crime and patterns to its occurrence is continuously evolving, and with it has come an enhanced capacity for police to tailor their response to suit a community's specific crime problems. Groff and LaVigne (2001, p.257) note: "Law enforcement officers and civilian crime analysts have been mapping crime with push pins and paper maps virtually since the time that police agencies were established." However: "The recent introduction of user-friendly mapping software, designed primarily for environmental

**Table 6.3**  NIBRS Data Elements

**Administrative Segment:**

1. ORI number
2. Incident number
3. Incident date/hour
4. Exceptional clearance indicator
5. Exceptional clearance date

**Offense Segment:**

6. UCR offense code
7. Attempted/completed code
8. Alcohol/drug use by offender
9. Type of location
10. Number of premises entered
11. Method of entry
12. Type of criminal activity
13. Type of weapon/force used
14. Bias crime code

**Property Segment:**

15. Type of property loss
16. Property description
17. Property value
18. Recovery data
19. Number of stolen motor vehicles
20. Number of recovered motor vehicles
21. Suspected drug type
22. Estimated drug quantity
23. Drug measurement unit

**Victim Segment:**

24. Victim number
25. Victim UCR offense code
26. Type of victim

27. Age of victim
28. Sex of victim
29. Race of victim
30. Ethnicity of victim
31. Resident status of victim
32. Homicide/assault circumstances
33. Justifiable homicide circumstances
34. Type of injury
35. Related offender number
36. Relationship of victim to offender

**Offender Segment:**

37. Offender number
38. Age of offender
39. Sex of offender
40. Race of offender

**Arrestee Segment:**

41. Arrestee number
42. Transaction number
43. Arrest date
44. Type of arrest
45. Multiple clearance indicator
46. UCR arrest offense code
47. Arrestee armed indicator
48. Age of arrestee
49. Sex of arrestee
50. Race of arrestee
51. Ethnicity of arrestee
52. Resident status of arrestee
53. Disposition of arrestee under 18

SOURCE: Brian A. Reaves. *National Incident-Based Reporting System: Using NIBRS Data to Analyze Violent Crime.* Washington, DC: Bureau of Justice Statistics Technical Report, October 1993, p.2.

and planning purposes, offers new tools for examining and predicting crime and criminal behavior" (p.257). Diamond (2004, p.42), likewise notes: "Crime-mapping technology gives agencies nationwide the intel to efficiently deploy officers and prevent crime." In explaining the benefits to mapping crime, LaVigne and Wartell (2001, pp.1–2) state:

> The case for mapping crime and criminal behavior is well founded in both research and practical applications. By and large, neither crime nor offending behavior is uniformly distributed across an environment. Rather, crime tends to cluster, forming "**hot spots**" in certain geographic areas. Hot spots can be

found within jurisdictions at a neighborhood level, often varying block by block. . . . Crime is also patterned in ways that relate to characteristics of the physical and social landscape. Mapping crime along with these characteristics can reveal relationships that suggest the underlying cause of crime problems, supporting more effective crime control and prevention measures.

At the most basic level, understanding where crime clusters in space helps local law enforcement allocate patrols to areas most in need of a police presence. . . .

Uncovering hot spots becomes an even more valuable tool when police can identify related factors that may be the underlying cause of a crime problem.

As Rogers (2001, p.66) tells: "In one case a young victim was beaten to death by a group of youth, in what the department called 'a swarming.' Several subsequent crimes were similar, and officers soon realized they had a pattern of swarming. Using a tool called Vertical Mapper, which presents a 3D image, they overlaid public transportation and elementary and secondary schools with the location of the beatings. They found these crimes were occurring after school and near certain schools and train stations."

According to Diamond (p.42): "Computers have revolutionized the art of crime mapping. Once just an exercise of sticking pins into a map glued to a bulletin board, crime mapping is now built on a foundation of '**geographic information systems,**' or GIS, a fancy term for creating, updating and analyzing computerized maps. The relevance of GIS to law enforcement is that these maps can be easily overlaid with strategic and tactical information such as recent burglaries." In addition, says Diamond (p.46): "A growing number of police agencies also use GIS to better protect their officers and deploy them more efficiently."

As Dees (2002, p.43) explains: "GIS applications can merge layers of information in visual form so that the relationships between places, times, events and trends become more evident than they would from analyzing the raw data. The layers can be added in, withdrawn or revised at will so that the user sees only the data that is relevant to the current analysis. Computers excel in manipulating large quantities of data, but people are still best at pattern recognition. GIS allows the strengths of computers and people to be combined for the best result."

Lutz (2003, p.118) notes: "With the advent of complex data networks and their associated databases, GIS is no longer just about making maps. It's about accessing data universally and rapidly over wide areas through a generic Web browser. . . . Intranets offer a cost-effective and powerful means of intra-departmental communications that computer mapping is just now beginning to exploit." Lutz (p.122) suggests: "Intranet mapping is not just about policing; it is also about community redevelopment and effectively coordinating governmental services and resources for both homeland security and economic development."

Some departments use crime mapping technology not only for long-term strategic planning but also to enhance their real-time response to crime: "The Toronto Police Department, the fifth largest force in North America with 5,000 sworn personnel, uses mapping to react more quickly to crime trends. It began as a simple project four years ago with the goal of simply speeding its reporting process up—it was taking up to three months to enter victim-reported occurrences, contact cards (individuals stopped by an officer) and arrests. Today, through a mapping process called Crime Management, officers have the data at their fingertips in 24 hours. Fresh data is available to every crime and intelligence analyst across the city, about 25 in total, most of whom are uniformed officers" (Rogers, p.66).

Another innovation in manipulating data is CompStat. As Schick (2004, p.17) explains: "CompStat, short for 'computer statistics' or 'comparison statistics,' is a multi-faceted system for managing police operations with a proven track record in several major metropolitan police departments tracing its roots back to 1994 in the New York City Police Department." According to McDonald (2004, p.33): "CompStat represents a sea change in managing police operations, and perhaps the most radical change in recent history." According to Walsh and Vito (2004, p.57): "CompStat is a goal-oriented, strategic-management process that uses information technology, operational strategy and managerial accountability to guide police operations. As designed by the New York City Police Department, the original model asserts that the primary police mission is the reduction of crime and the enhancement of a community's quality of life."

Shane (2004a, p.13) describes the "four crime-reduction principles that create the framework for the CompStat Process: accurate and timely intelligence, effective tactics, rapid deployment of personnel and resources, and relentless follow-up and assessment." Shane (2004b, p.12) suggests: "Coupled with these [four principles] are accountability and discretion at all levels of the law enforcement agency." Shane (2004c, p.20) concludes: "Law enforcement agencies can do well embracing the CompStat process. . . . Crime rates among the cities practicing CompStat reveal the program's true success. In New York City over the last 10 years, crime came down 64 percent; in Philadelphia, crime fell 23 percent between 1995 and 2002; in Baltimore, crime decreased 31 percent between 1995 and 1999; and in Newark, crime declined 51 percent between 1995 and 2001."

According to Weisburd et al. (2004, p.15): "Our study confirms what many police observers have noted: that CompStat has literally burst onto the American police scene." They report that 33 percent of large departments (100+ sworn officers) have implemented a CompStat-like program and another 26 percent are planning such a program. The results of this study are presented in Table 6.4.

As beneficial as this technology is for police operations, it has raised some legitimate concerns. For example, in light of communities' growing desire for access to timely information about crime and disorder in their neighborhoods, how much of this crime data should be made so readily available? While technically such data is public information, and citizens do have a right to know about

**Table 6.4**  Has Your Department Implemented a CompStat-Like Program?

| Department Size | Percent Yes | Percent No, But Planning | Percent No |
|---|---|---|---|
| Small (50–99 Sworn) | 11.0 | 29.3 | 59.8 |
| Large (100+ Sworn) | 32.6 | 25.6 | 41.8 |

Due to rounding, rows may not add to 100.

SOURCE: David Weisburd, Stephen D. Mastrofski, Rosann Greenspan and James J. Willis. "The Growth of CompStat in American Policing." *Police Foundation Reports*, April 2004, p.6. Reprinted by permission.

crime in their communities, how do law enforcement agencies address victims' right to privacy? Wartell and McEwen (2001, p.3) state:

> When a law enforcement agency posts a map of crime incidents on the Internet, it runs the risk of including too much or not enough data. For example, if a sexual assault victim's incident location is provided, then his or her identity can be determined, and his or her privacy has been violated. Yet if a sexual assault is not posted and subsequently an individual falls victim to a sexual assault, has the agency thwarted the public's legitimate interest?

Other concerns involve the possible revitalization of informal redlining methods used by some insurance and banking companies: "Whereas a neighborhood identified as a high-crime area could be targeted for various types of positive local interventions, it could also be flagged as undesirable, resulting in residential flight and ultimately causing more damage to an already problematic area" (Wartell and McEwen, p.3). Real estate agents and homeowners may become concerned about decreasing property values if crime maps lead to the perception their neighborhoods are unsafe.

## Responding to Calls about Crime and Disorder

How police officers respond to calls about committed crimes depends on several important variables:
- What specific crime is involved?
- Is the crime still in progress?
- How many suspects are involved?
- Are weapons involved?
- Is there a danger to the public?
- Could a hostage situation develop?
- How many officers are needed to respond?
- How many officers are available?
- Where are they?

Sometimes answers to all these questions are available. More often, however, responding officers lack much of this information.

Responsibilities of officers responding to a call regarding a criminal act include:
- Arriving as rapidly, yet as safely, as possible.
- Caring for any injured people at the scene.
- Apprehending any suspects at the scene.
- Securing the scene.
- Conducting a preliminary investigation.

### Arriving at the Scene

Whether the police arrive with red lights and sirens will depend on the nature of the information to which police are responding. The element of surprise may be important if the crime is believed to be still in progress. At other times, such as in assault cases, the siren may be desirable because it may frighten off the attacker. Each specific call must be assessed for whether the added speed of response available through the use of red lights and siren is an advantage. Recall the Kansas City Preventive Patrol Experiment, which showed that rapid response time did not greatly improve chances of making an arrest at the scene. In addition, the more rapid the response, the greater the likelihood of a crash en route involving the responding squad or citizens who happen to be in the way.

The National Institute of Justice (NIJ) has produced a guide for law enforcement officers (*Crime Scene Investigation* . . ., 2000, p.11) and states the following policy regarding initial response when arriving at a crime scene: "The initial responding officer(s) shall promptly, yet cautiously, approach and enter crime scenes, remaining observant of any persons, vehicles, events, potential evidence, and environmental conditions." Procedures listed in the guide for initial responders include noting or logging dispatch information (e.g., address/location, time, date, type of call, parties involved) and remaining alert and attentive.

The actual arrival may be fraught with danger; consequently, officers should make use of cover if it is thought the suspect might still be at the scene. If the element of surprise is important, officers should have a system of hand signals to coordinate their arrival and approach to the scene.

The next two responsibilities, attending to injured people and apprehending suspects at the scene, may occur in reverse order, depending on the situation.

## Attending to Injuries and Apprehending Suspects

Usually injuries and suspects at the scene are considered emergency matters to be attended to immediately upon arrival. If the injuries are not life threatening and the suspect is considered dangerous, apprehending that suspect will take precedence over attending to the injuries. The NIJ's general policy states: "The initial responding officer(s) arriving at the scene shall identify and control any dangerous situations or persons" (*Crime Scene* . . ., p.12). Control of physical threats ensures the safety of officers and others at the scene.

Once dangerous situations or people have been brought under control, "the initial responding officer(s') next responsibility is to ensure that medical attention is provided to injured persons while minimizing contamination of the scene" (*Crime Scene* . . ., p.13). The guide (p.14) also suggests: "Assisting, guiding, and instructing medical personnel during the care and removal of injured persons will diminish the risk of contamination and loss of evidence." As soon as emergency matters are tended to, the primary responsibility of the police is to secure the crime scene.

## Securing the Crime Scene

The first officer to arrive on the crime scene automatically incurs the critical responsibility of securing the crime scene from unauthorized intrusion or other contamination: "Controlling, identifying and removing persons at the crime scene and limiting the number of persons who enter the crime scene and the movement of such persons is an important function of the initial responding officer(s) in protecting the crime scene" (*Crime Scene* . . ., p.14). If more than one officer responds to the call, the scene can be secured immediately by one officer while the other officer handles any emergency situation.

Officers should consider any crime scene as highly dynamic and make the preliminary survey of the layout carefully. Lundrigan (2001, p.38) stresses the importance of preserving crime scene integrity:

The primary goal in crime scene assessment is to detect all traces that indicate a crime has been committed and establish any association between the crime and victim, or victim and perpetrator. . . .

All too often a crime scene is compromised by the presence of too many investigators. Items get moved, toilets get flushed and evidence is destroyed. Turning on a light switch, opening blinds or walking through a telling blood spatter pattern reduces the quality and quantity of recoverable evidence.

Sometimes securing the scene is as simple as closing a door, but other times it is more complex. In a bank robbery, for example, the entire lobby is usually secured and closed for business until the preliminary investigation is completed. Outdoor crime scenes are usually roped off or barricaded. Only those individuals with official business should be allowed into the crime scene. The NIJ (*Crime Scene* . . ., p.15) suggests setting well-defined, liberal and controllable boundaries is a critical aspect in preserving the integrity of evidentiary material: "Defining and controlling boundaries provides a means for protecting and securing the crime scene(s). The number of crime scenes and their boundaries are determined by their location(s) and the type of crime. Boundaries shall be established beyond the initial scope of the crime scene(s) with the understanding that the boundaries can be reduced in size if necessary but cannot be as easily expanded."

In some departments, this is where the responsibilities of the responding officers end. They keep the scene secure until investigators or detectives arrive to conduct the investigation, especially in crimes such as murder, as discussed in Chapter 10. The NIJ's policy regarding this "changing of the guard" states: "The initial responding officer(s) at the scene shall provide a detailed crime scene briefing to the investigator(s) in charge of the scene" and "Turn over responsibility for the documentation of entry/exit" (*Crime Scene* . . ., p.17). The *Crime Scene* guide (p.17) also notes: "All activities conducted and observations made at the crime scene must be documented as soon as possible after the event to preserve information. Documentation must be maintained as a permanent record." In other departments, the responding officers conduct the preliminary investigation and, perhaps, the entire investigation.

## The Preliminary Investigation

The more information and evidence that can be obtained immediately after a crime has been committed, the better the chances of identifying the person responsible and successfully prosecuting the case. Usually the officers responding to the call are in the best position to obtain this information and evidence.

 The **preliminary investigation** of a crime involves on-the-scene interviews of victims and witnesses, interrogation of suspects and a search of the scene itself.

The preliminary investigation is not so much an "investigation" in the traditional sense, where days, weeks, months, even years of tracking leads, developing suspects and refining theories go into the eventual solving of a crime. (The complete investigation itself is discussed in Chapter 10.) Compared to this level of examination, the preliminary investigation is a rather superficial on-site assessment and collection of evidentiary details observed by the first responding officer(s) and relayed by witnesses.

*Curiosity seekers can destroy valuable evidence at crime scenes, so it is necessary to cordon off the area.*

Dwayne Newman, PhotoEdit

In larger departments, if a suspect is apprehended at the scene, interrogation is usually done at the police department by experienced, trained investigators. Interviewing and interrogating were discussed in Chapter 2. Witnesses should be separated and their statements carefully recorded.

Officers arriving at the scene are often responsible for recognizing and gathering evidence as part of the preliminary investigation. Therefore, officers must know the elements of each crime and what evidence will prove them.

**Recognizing and Collecting Physical Evidence** The crime-scene search is, for certain offenses, the most important part of the investigation. A large part of the preliminary investigation centers around whether officers can obtain evidence that a crime has been committed and been committed by a particular person. Evidence may be the turning point determining whether a case can be made and a criminal convicted.

While some crimes, such as forgery, embezzlement and credit-card fraud, have no crime scenes and yield little to no physical evidence, many crimes do have crime scenes and provide physical evidence. The value of any physical evidence used in court to verify that a crime has been committed, to identify the person(s) who did it and to obtain a conviction often depends on the officers who arrive first at a crime scene. In most cases, the officers who protect and search a crime scene play a critical role in determining whether a case can be made.

Experienced officers anticipate finding certain types of evidence in specific crimes. In many offenses, criminals contact the physical surroundings and leave evidence linking themselves to victims and crime scenes. Violent crimes, for example, often involve a struggle and frequently yield evidence such as blood, hair, fibers, fingerprints and weapons. Property crimes, in contrast, commonly yield evidence such as tool marks on doors, windows, safes, money chests, cash registers and desk drawers, as well as fingerprints. Recognizing and collecting evidence are examined in greater depth in Chapter 10.

All preliminary investigations must be systematic and thorough. The finding of some answers does not mean that all answers have been uncovered. Likewise, the finding of some evidence does not mean that more may not exist. One is mindful of the question once considered the epitome of the obvious, Who's buried in Grant's tomb? Those who answer "General Ulysses S. Grant" are only half right. His wife, Julia, is buried with him. Professional police officers must get *all* the facts and information, not just the obvious.

When evidence is found, it must be carefully marked (often with the officer's badge number), placed in a secure container, sealed, tagged, recorded in the officer's notebook and, as soon as practical, placed in the property or evidence room. It must be kept secure until it is needed for trial. The **chain of possession,** or **chain of custody,** documents who has had control of the evidence from the time it is discovered until it is presented in court. Any time evidence is taken from the property room, it must be signed for. When it is returned, it is examined to be sure that it has not been altered in any way.

## Crime-Scene Units

Because the majority of local police departments have fewer than 20 sworn officers, they seldom have special teams of criminal investigators. In such cases, a crime-scene team consisting of patrol officers assigned crime-scene duty as a collateral duty is often of value.

The crime-scene unit, after a preliminary survey of the crime scene, determines the actual crime-scene perimeter and search area. They set the search objectives as well as the equipment and personnel needed and also develop a theory of the crime. In addition, they identify and protect transient evidence and prepare a narrative description of the scene.

In some departments, after these functions are performed, the work of the crime-scene unit is complete, and the case is turned over to an investigative or detective division. In smaller departments, however, the crime-scene unit may conduct the entire investigation.

Closely associated with the problem of crime is the problem of disorder and quality-of-life issues. When disorder occurs, police are expected to deal with it.

## Disorder and Quality-of-Life Issues

The *Law Enforcement News* 2003 Person of the Year was George Kelling, coauthor of the Broken Windows thesis. According to Nislow (2003, p.1): "'Broken Windows,' which broke onto the scene in 1982 in a cover story in *The Atlantic Monthly* coauthored by George L. Kelling and James Q. Wilson is rightfully considered, along with community policing and problem-oriented policing, as one of the three foremost ground-breaking ideas in criminal justice over the past two decades." Wilson and Kelling (1982, p.31) wrote:

At the community level, disorder and crime are usually inextricably linked, in a kind of developmental sequence. Social psychologists and police officers tend to agree that if a window in a building is broken *and is left unrepaired,* all the rest of the windows will soon be broken. This is as true in nice neighborhoods as in run-down ones. Window-breaking does not necessarily occur on a large scale because some areas are inhabited by determined window-breakers whereas others are populated by window-lovers; rather, one unrepaired broken window is a signal that no one cares, and so breaking more windows costs nothing. (It has always been fun.) . . .

The citizen who fears the ill-smelling drunk, the rowdy teenager or the importuning beggar is not merely expressing his distaste for unseemly behavior; he is also giving voice to a bit of folk wisdom that happens to be a correct generalization—namely, that serious street crime flourishes in areas in which disorderly behavior goes unchecked. The unchecked panhandler is, in effect, the first broken window (p.34).

Sampson and Raudenbush (2001) studied the link between disorder and crime, specifically, whether manifestations of social and physical disorder lead directly to more serious offenses. One key finding was that (p.2): "Disorder does not directly promote crime, although the two phenomena are related, and that collective efficacy is a significant factor in explaining levels of crime and disorder." They (p.1) define **collective efficacy,** as "cohesion among neighborhood residents combined with shared expectations for informal social control of public space" that inhibits both crime and disorder. They (p.2) found that disorder and crime both stemmed from certain neighborhood structural characteristics, notably concentrated poverty." They conclude: "Although reducing disorder may reduce crime, this happens indirectly, by stabilizing neighborhoods via collective efficacy."

Katz et al. (2001, pp.825–826) researched the impact of quality-of-life policing on crime and disorder noting: "Over the past two decades, police agencies across the nation have been adopting a variety of community policing strategies, including several that focus on the aggressive enforcement of disorder offenses. These aggressive strategies are popularly known as 'zero-tolerance,' 'order-maintenance' and 'quality-of-life policing'." They (p.827) point out that this movement has its roots in the "seminal essay" "Broken Windows." They (p.858) conclude: "The project [aggressive enforcement of disorder offenses] had a significant impact on disorder but a minimal impact on crime."

Weiss and Dresser (2001, p.117) contend: "Small things like reclaiming shopping carts, removing drunks from park benches, discouraging panhandling and advocating street lighting can reduce a city's crime rate, allowing it to regain its ambiance and beauty." Smith (2001, p.67) reports on a Blitz to Bloom initiative in Richmond, Virginia: "The City significantly increased its code enforcement efforts (building, environmental and fire), it employed its refuse collection department to haul away tons of trash and debris, and it used its public works department to repair street lights, replace signs and trim overgrown bushes and trees." Smith (p.60) reports: "A 92 percent reduction in reported crime occurred in the target area during the month-long crackdown period."

According to Miller and Hess (2005, p.55): "Broken windows and smashed cars are visible signs of people not caring about their community. Other less subtle signs include unmowed lawns, piles of accumulated trash and graffiti, often referred to as **incivilities.** Incivilities include rowdiness, drunkenness, fighting, prostitution and abandoned buildings." The community can be enlisted to deal with the physical incivilities. A more difficult challenge is responding to disorderly or troublesome people.

## Responding to Disorderly or Troublesome People

King and Dunn (2004, pp.339–340) contend: "Street-level interactions between police officers and various categories of disenfranchised, problematic or disorderly persons have long concerned observers of the police." Disorderly or troublesome people may include panhandlers, prostitutes and individuals who are mentally ill or homeless.

**Panhandlers**    Scott (2002, p.7) suggests the public holds two distinctly different views on panhandling: "The sympathetic view, commonly but not unanimously held by civil libertarians and homeless advocates, is that panhandling is essential to destitute people's survival, and should not be regulated by police. Some even view panhandling as a poignant expression of the plight of the needy, and an opportunity for the more fortunate to help. The unsympathetic view is that panhandling is a blight that contributes to further community disorder and crime, as well as to panhandlers' degradation and deterioration as their underlying problems go unaddressed. Those holding this view believe panhandling should be heavily regulated by police."

Scott (p.17) suggests: "Most researchers and practitioners seem to agree that the enforcement of laws prohibiting panhandling plays only a part in controlling the problem. Public education to discourage people from giving money to panhandlers, informal social control and adequate social services (especially alcohol and drug treatment) for panhandlers are the other essential components of an effective and comprehensive response."

**Street Prostitutes**    Scott (2001, p.1) reports: "Street prostitution varies with the type of prostitutes involved and their commitment to prostitution, the market size, the community's tolerance levels, the degree to which prostitutes are organized and the relationship of prostitution to drug use and trafficking. Street prostitution accounts for perhaps only 10 to 20 percent of all prostitution, but it has the most visible negative impact on the community." Surratt et al. (2004, p.55) studied street prostitution and found: "The marginalization of the women sex workers is further extended by the fact that nearly 45 percent of those in the sample are homeless, the majority have limited education and very few possess any sort of social or professional ties with the larger community. . . . Virtually all of the women encountered in this project indicated that prostitution is not a chosen career. Rather, for most it is *survival sex,* and for almost all it is the result of a drug habit combined with the lack of other skills or resources."

Scott (2001, pp.15–16) suggests: "Strategies that exclusively focus on arresting prostitutes are unlikely to be effective. Strategies that seek to reduce the harms caused by street prostitution rather than those that seek to eliminate prostitution altogether are more likely to work. At minimum, both prostitutes' and clients' conduct should be addressed. An effective strategy not only must force prostitutes off the streets and get them to stop their offensive behavior, but also must give them viable alternatives: either to get out of prostitution altogether, or to operate in less offensive locations, times or ways. This usually requires greater cooperation between the police and various service organizations."

**Individuals Who Are Mentally Ill**    Hill et al. (2004, pp.18–19) explain: "The term *mental illness* refers collectively to all diagnosable mental conditions characterized by alterations in thinking, mood or behavior (or some combination thereof) associated with distress or impaired functioning." According to Zdanowicz (2001, p.3): "In recent years there has been a marked shift in responsibility for the untreated mentally ill from the mental health system to the criminal justice system. It is becoming increasingly clear that any hope of alleviating the burden of untreated mental illness rests with those who are impacted the most, our nation's law enforcement officials."

Many agencies now provide Crisis Incident Team (CIT) training to help officers identify individuals who need mental health treatment, thereby preventing such individuals from ending up in jail for "disturbing the peace"—or dead. Some departments have specially designated CIT officers to respond to mental illness calls on a specific beat or area of responsibility. These officers often operate as part of a network to handle the community's mentally ill population. For example, as Hill and Logan (2001, p.31) describe: "In Montgomery County [Maryland], the police department's CIT program is an integral part of a multiagency partnership that includes the sheriff's office, the health and human services department, and the corrections and rehabilitation department . . . [as well as] the National Alliance for the Mentally Ill (NAMI) of Montgomery County, the National Mental Health Association, the Mental Health Association of Montgomery County, and the Springfield Hospital Center (the state mental hospital)." This program illustrates a community-based approach by partnering mental health practitioners from local government and private practice with local law enforcement to conduct officer safety and de-escalation training. In most departments, however, calls involving mentally ill subjects fall not only to a specialized unit of CIT officers but to all patrol officers.

Unfortunately, in some cases use of force is necessary. The courts have held that in certain situations police use of force against a mentally ill person is justifiable and necessary for the protection and safety of the officer and public. Ruiz and Miller (2004, p.364) note: "A lack of policy or guidelines in calls for service for persons with mental illness may tend to cause the responding officer(s) to handle these calls from a law enforcement perspective instead of a peacekeeper or helper."

Olson (2002, p.2) likewise stresses: "Public officials are under significant pressure to *do something* about individuals who have committed less serious crimes and are in contact with the criminal justice system usually because of inadequate treatment and support for their mental illness. The criminal justice system lacks the resources and expertise to properly respond to the overwhelming numbers of people with mental illness."

Van Blaricom (2004, pp.24–25) offers some guidelines for responding to individuals who are mentally ill: (1) Do not take risks. (2) Do SLOW DOWN and assess. (3) Do not shout orders or move in quickly too close. (4) Do continue trying to establish communication and rapport. (5) Do not prematurely introduce less-lethal weapons; they may not work and can provoke an attack. (6) Do take as much time as needed under the circumstances.

Gentz and Goree (2003, p.14) describe an operational triangle, shown in Figure 6.3, to respond to individuals with mental illness. They (p.14) emphasize: "The foundation of the operational triangle is safety. . . . Only after this is established and maintained should an officer focus on using communication skills to form an effective relationship with a subject." Communicating with individuals who are mentally ill was discussed in Chapter 2. Note that Van Blaricom, Gentz

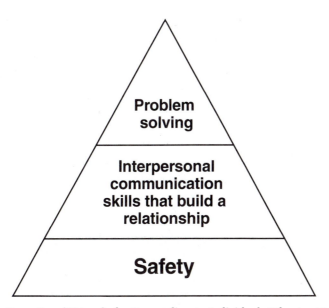

**Figure 6.3**   Operational Triangle for Responding to Individuals Who Are Mentally Ill

SOURCE: Douglas Gentz and William S. Goree. "Moving Past What to How—The Next Step in Responding to Individuals with Mental Illness." *FBI Law Enforcement Bulletin*, November 2003, p.15.

and Goree all stress safety as vital and also emphasize the importance of effective communication.

Reuland (2004, p.3) observes: "Law enforcement agencies across the country have begun to change their practices and develop innovative partnerships with the mental health community to improve their responses to people with mental illness." Many of those who are mentally ill are also homeless as a result of the deinstitutionalization that occurred in the 1960s and 1970s.

**The Homeless**   While it is not against the law to be homeless, many people living on the streets, by virtue of their lack of residence, do engage in illegal activity or otherwise contribute to a community's level of disorder. With no place to sleep, use the bathroom, keep their belongings, dump their trash, get drunk or take care of other private matters, the homeless have to conduct such "business" in public.

A large percentage of homeless adults are unemployed and, without income, many resort to panhandling or stealing just to be able to eat. National data indicate 20 percent of homeless people eat one meal a day or less. Addicts often turn to crime to support their habits or engage in crime while under the influence of alcohol and other drugs. Nearly half of all homeless people suffer from chronic health problems such as high blood pressure, arthritis, diabetes or cancer, and more than half lack medical insurance. Such health factors undoubtedly add to the stress of homelessness and may contribute to either the increased perpetration of crime by or vulnerability to crime of those afflicted. Victimization among the homeless is relatively common, with many reporting having had money or possessions stolen directly from them and having had money or possessions stolen while unattended.

Thus, while homelessness may begin as a social service issue, with entire families living on the streets or in cars, when it gets combined with the economic factor of unemployment, the medical factors of mental illness and/or substance abuse, and the increased risk of victimization, it can quickly become a criminal justice issue.

Some departments are providing sensitivity training to educate officers about the specific needs and concerns of homeless people. Other agencies have formed alliances between officers, city officials, local businesses, homeless shelters and human services outreach workers to provide a coordinated response to the multiple issues surrounding homelessness.

According to Gray (2004, p.34): "Homeless people can be unpredictable due to mental illness and their learned survival instincts. . . . From a law enforcement perspective, the nightly ritual of dealing with sleepy transients in business doorways and public benches can be a troublesome speed bump on the way to fighting more serious crimes. After all, social work isn't a major goal of most law enforcement officers. Public safety is." Gray (p.30) suggests: "Understanding the problems of people living on the streets can prevent violent encounters and costly repeated arrests. . . . When speaking with homeless people it's important to not invade their personal space, for reasons of courtesy and safety." He notes that in most jurisdictions, police can order help for homeless people who are endangering themselves, for example, someone living on the streets in dangerously cold weather. The operational triangle in Figure 6.2 could also be applied when responding to homeless people. Safety first, followed by communication to build rapport (as discussed in Chapter 2), concluding with problem solving.

**Dumping or Police-Initiated Transjurisdictional Transport of Troublesome Persons (PITT)**  King and Dunn (p.341) note: "Although the informal policy of transporting troublesome persons to another location—or police 'dumping' of problematic citizens—is generally acknowledged by police practitioners, it has rarely been discussed in the policing literature or systematically studied." King and Dunn (pp.341–342) define dumping or police-initiated transjurisdictional transport (PITT) of troublesome people: "Dumping or PITT is a low-visibility police activity that stands outside the legal and moral norms of policing. PITT occurs when a police officer interacts with a mentally disturbed person, a person who is homeless, a prostitute, a juvenile, a drunk or a person under the influence of drugs, the officer views this person as 'troublesome,' and the officer resolves the situation by transporting that troublesome person out of that officer's (or the department's) jurisdiction and releases that person into his or her own recognizance."

According to King and Dunn (p.342): "PITT is analogous to other punishments imposed by the criminal justice system, such as banishment. Some courts have used 'sundown parole' in which petty criminals were told to leave town or face imprisonment. PITT has also been referred to by a number of different terms. Transportation that involves buying troublesome people bus tickets to facilitate their removal has been called 'diesel therapy.' " The challenges to law enforcement when responding to troublesome people can be much greater when the situation is not one-on-one, as in facing a crowd bent on civil disobedience.

## Civil Disobedience

**Civil disobedience** consists of breaking a law to prove a point or to protest something. Civil disobedience occurs daily around the world, from the fight against apartheid in South Africa, to the quest for autonomy of ethnic groups in Europe, to demonstrations in Washington, DC, against racism or for a more responsive government. Our society, like many others around the globe, is filled with dissension. And law enforcement officers are the ones called on to control or suppress these demonstrations. For example, production of war materials during peacetime, violation of the environment, laboratory testing on animals, construction of nuclear power plants and lack of government interest in housing the homeless are all issues that have caused demonstrations requiring a police presence to control them.

The purpose in most cases of civil disobedience is to protest some governmental or institutional policy. While most protests start out lawfully and are relatively peaceful demonstrations, emotions may become inflamed, legal barriers are crossed, and a classic civil disobedience situation develops. A civilly disobedient person breaks the law to prove a point. The act is done openly. A law is violated because people feel the law violates their sense of what is right, and they are willing to accept punishment for their actions supporting their beliefs. In fact, the United States was born through the efforts of dissenters, as some of our greatest Americans, now regarded as heroes, were lawbreakers in their time. George Washington, Benjamin Franklin, John Adams and Alexander Hamilton were all civilly disobedient and considered traitors until success crowned their efforts.

Nonviolent lawbreaking begins when participants are willing to be punished by the courts for their lawbreaking. From there demonstrators may become violent lawbreakers, frequently disregarding the rights of others. The extreme result of this type of action is anarchy, chaos, revolution and bloodshed. The police generally agree that nonviolent protest is one thing to contend with, but violent protest infringes on the rights not only of others, but of police officers as well. This usually results in property damage, looting, personal injuries and, in some cases, death.

Violent dissent seems to be on the increase. An extreme desire for change often results in frustration and may be the reason for the radical switch in tactics seen in neighborhoods, on city blocks, as well as in organized demonstrations. Militancy and hatred spark riots. People will not condemn the violence because it seems to get faster results and, in some cases, seems to get the only results. However, violent dissent rarely succeeds in securing massive reform, especially where there are alternative ways to protest. Violence may bring quick recognition of a need in our society, but it seldom brings a quick remedy.

Ironically, various police actions have actually touched off riots or caused violent protests to escalate. In relatively mild protests and demonstrations, the presence of dogs, police officers' overreactions to demonstrators and rumors can cause conflagrations. These are not in keeping with the traditional nonviolent view of civil disobedience the police have had over the years.

Whether demonstrations are violent or nonviolent, police have been designated by our society as the correct vehicle for coping with the various kinds of demonstrations occurring in the twenty-first century.

## Issues Leading to Civil Disobedience

Rohr (2001, p.10) asserts: "The need to train law enforcement command and line officers to manage crowds and respond to civil disobedience has never been clearer. Large protests have accompanied such planned events as the World Trade Organization [WTO] meeting in Seattle, the national political conventions in

*During this anti-Iraq war demonstration in New York City, the presence of police officers helped keep an angry crowd under control.*

Joel Gordon

Philadelphia and Los Angeles, and the Group of Eight summit in Genoa, Italy." According to Winegar (2001, p.158):

> Every police agency must plan for crowd control and civil disturbance. It does not take a major occurrence like the WTO conference or the Republican National Convention to embroil the agency in a profound event. Consider the myriad reasons that have precipitated riots in recent history: sporting events, wedding receptions, labor disputes, social gatherings, college campus activities and police action. Even the smallest police agency can potentially be faced with an out-of-control crowd when rival high schools play a championship game. While some events may be spontaneous, many can be anticipated.

 Issues leading to civil disobedience include:
- Overt racism and bias.
- Human rights concerns.
- Environmental concerns.
- Animal rights concerns.
- Pro-life and pro-choice conflicts.

**Racism and Other Biases**   Historically, the Ku Klux Klan has been the epitome of violent racism. However, other groups are now contending for this dubious title. A group known as the skinheads poses a threat to minorities of several types, including homosexuals, Jews and "people of color," whom they call "mud people."

Skinheads get their name from their practice of shaving their heads, although some have let their hair grow out so as to not be so easily recognized by police. Acting in groups, they attack ruthlessly, often beating or stomping their lone victims. They often display patches bearing American flags, German swastikas and such slogans as "White Supremacy" and "WAR," an acronym for White Aryan Resistance.

Most states have enacted some type of hate crime penalty-enhancement statute allowing courts to issue more severe sentences for people convicted of criminal actions motivated by bigoted, prejudiced and hateful beliefs. Hate crimes are discussed in depth in Chapter 10.

**Human Rights Concerns**   Violent civil rights protests swept the country in the 1950s and 1960s and are being seen again. Gay rights issues, the rights of individuals with communicable diseases such as AIDS and the right to die are among the most hotly debated controversies.

**Environmental Concerns**   Environmental protest issues include nuclear waste disposal and logging versus forest preservation. Activist groups such as Earth First have forced not only municipal police but also rural police into thinking about dealing with protests and the unique circumstances they present. One key problem with the rural protests and demonstrations is that most of the law enforcement officers who have to deal with them know the protesters.

**Animal Rights Concerns**   Campaigns to protect certain species of animals have been around for decades and usually are confined to fund-raising efforts and massive informational mailings. However, one group, the Animal Liberation Front (ALF), has been described as a terrorist group because of the extreme measures they undertake for their "cause." For example, the ALF has been associated with more than 80 break-ins since 1977, including one that caused $3.8 million in damages to a University of California (Davis) animal research facility.

**Pro-Life and Pro-Choice Conflicts**   Conflicts between pro-life and pro-choice groups are common and often make headlines as groups of pro-lifers seek to shut down abortion centers and pro-choicers seek to stop them. What may begin as a relatively peaceful march around an abortion center or clinic may escalate rapidly into a violent, destructive confrontation resulting in property damage and personal injuries. Political careers have been made and destroyed on this single issue. The courts also have become involved in the controversy. And police officers are likely to have their own views on this highly personal issue.

Pro-life demonstrators and others involved in the harassment of doctors and patients feel it is their moral obligation to protest the taking of unborn human lives. They assert their First Amendment rights in such protests. However, the U.S. Supreme Court ruled in *Madsen et al. v. Women's Health Center Inc., et al.* (1994) that a Florida statute establishing a 300-foot zone around clinics to protect it from abortion protesters was constitutional. In addition, it was constitutional to restrict excessive noisemaking within the earshot of, and the use of images observable by, patients inside the clinic, and to create a 300-foot buffer zone around the residences of clinic staff.

**The Black Bloc**   Griffith (2003b, p.48) describes the Black Bloc as hard-core anarchists: "The Black Bloc isn't an organization so much as a school of thought and a form of protest . . . They're young, they're disaffected, and their trademark is property damage. Black Bloc activity at protests tends to start with a group of these hyper-violent, hyper-destructive anarchists breaking away from the main demonstration, roaming streets not covered by the protest permit, and wreaking havoc. Their favorite targets for bricks and firebombs are chain stores and restaurants that they view as symbols of corporate America."

## Responding to Demonstrations and Civil Disturbances

A key to responding to demonstrations is advance planning. Although officers may not know exactly when they may need to intervene, they can anticipate what types of intervention might be necessary depending on their locality. A police department responsible for a jurisdiction in which animal research is being conducted or in which an abortion clinic is located should be prepared for demonstrations that might turn violent.

To deal with demonstrations and possible violence, police departments should:
- Assess their risks.
- Develop contingency plans.
- Have a call-out system for off-duty officers.

Another key to effectively handling civil disorder incidents is a coordinated response among agencies, including police, fire and corrections personnel. Police departments should know what additional emergency medical personnel might be available and how to contact them. Police departments might also coordinate with corrections personnel regarding the handling and transportation of arrestees.

Some departments use a cross-arm carry to remove arrestees; others use stretchers. Whatever the method, departments must have a sound policy on use of force during demonstrations, and officers should use only as much force as is necessary to control the crowd. Rohr (p.10) states: "The usual circumstances in a crowd management or civil disturbance situation could call for reasonable use-of-force alternatives, including, but not limited to . . . nonlethal chemical agents such as oleoresin capsicum (OC), less-lethal impact munitions such as flexible or foam rubber baton rounds, compliance techniques, electrical control devices and other impact weapons, and mobile field force options." She adds: "There are no exceptions to the use-of-force policy. Even in a riot, only force that is objectively reasonable under the circumstances may be used to arrest violators and restore order."

Because many, if not most, demonstrations involve citizens' exercising their freedoms of speech and expression, any police action taken to reduce or stop that activity necessarily falls under court scrutiny. According to Rohr (p.11):

The U.S. Supreme Court has commented that the acceptable way of handling conduct intertwined with First Amendment activity is to punish it after it occurs, not to prevent the First Amendment activity from occurring in order to obviate the possibility of unlawful conduct. . . .

The U.S. Supreme Court has succinctly stated, "Freedom of individuals to oppose or challenge police action without risk of arrest is one of the principal characteristics by which we distinguish a free nation from a police state."

However, freedom of speech is not absolute. The U.S. Supreme Court has narrowed and clarified the extent of the "fighting words doctrine," which would justify police intervention, to those words which incite a breach of peace.

Griffith (2003b, p.50) describes the approach to crowd control used by one department when protesters were read the dispersal order and did not move: "Metro entered the scene like something from an epic movie. Down the hill came 25 mounted officers in a column of two, with helmets, face shields, the whole works. And behind them were four Suburbans with our guys on the side wearing tac vests, helmets and face shields, and carrying less-lethal weapons. They were followed by a big blue jail bus." Nyberg (2004, p.62) describes a similar approach to prepare for the Free Trade Area of the Americas (FTAA) demonstrations in Miami: "Anarchists came to the Sunshine State last fall planning to restage the Battle of Seattle, but local cops had another idea." Nyberg (p.64) noted: "Our Intel told us the Bloc was going to try to storm the Area grounds and set fires while blocking the traffic routes in and out of the Port. . . . Our department, Miami-Dade, was going to commit almost one-third of its entire sworn force of about 1,100 to this effort to supplement the City of Miami Police. There would also be help from the Florida Highway Patrol and a few other small departments." Their formidable show of force worked, and the "savage attacks that the Black Bloc promised never came close to fruition" (p.66).

Slackman and Baker (2004) describe how the New York City Police Department kept demonstrators outside the 2004 Republican National Convention orderly:

> Plainclothes police officers on stylish Italian motor scooters herded bicycle-riding demonstrators into thick orange nets stretched across intersections. Airborne spy cameras on blimps and helicopters monitored the crowd. Digital video cameras were used to tape arrest scenes and collect evidence for later use in court. A military-inspired sound device was ready to disperse crowds with shouted orders or painful blasts of noise.
>
> After more than a year of planning and training, the New York Police Department oversaw yesterday's giant protest march by combining traditional methods of crowd control—from undercover officers who infiltrated the crowd to a huge show of force—with a variety of new techniques that clearly took some of the protesters by surprise.

Videotaping the demonstration and the police response can counter any claims of police brutality. If a demonstration gets big enough and violent enough, a jurisdiction may call on the National Guard for help. This request usually has to be made by the sheriff to the governor.

In addition to the challenge of demonstrations and civil disobedience, police sometimes face the challenge of large celebratory crowds. Oldham (2002, p.113) cautions: "It is vitally important that any action taken by law enforcement be seen as reasonable by those in the crowd who are true celebrants or witnesses to the celebration. If, in the back of their minds, the crowd as a whole sees the actions of the police as measured and necessary for public safety they will be supportive. If however they see those actions as heavy-handed many may instantly become part of the disruptive hardcore and will multiply the problems that law enforcement will encounter." Oldham (p.116) concludes: "Law enforcement agencies of all sizes continue to be confronted by large gatherings and will need to be able to contend with a wide range of crowd control issues. It is vital that plans be laid to deal with any contingency and the proper training, equipment and support be in place prior to any such event so that order is maintained and public safety preserved."

Butterfield (2004) notes: "The death of a 21-year-old college student outside Fenway Park on October 21, the night the Red Sox beat the Yankees for the American League pennant, is only the latest reminder that crowd control has reemerged as one of the toughest challenges for the police."

Another form of disorder law enforcement officers must be prepared to deal with is that accompanying crisis situations. Frequently, negotiation techniques are called upon to prevent such crises from escalating to violence.

## Crisis Situations

Terestre (2004, p.32) suggests: "State-of-the-art police command vehicles can be invaluable tools for crisis negotiators. These vehicles are equipped with multiple phone lines, multi-frequency radios, satellite TV, and even bathrooms and kitchens."

In some critical incidents Special Weapons and Tactics (SWAT) teams may be used. As Ramirez (2003, p.58) explains: "A SWAT team is a designated unit of law enforcement officers who are specifically trained and equipped to work as a coordinated team to respond to critical incidents, including, but not limited to, hostage taking, barricaded suspects, snipers, terrorist acts and other high-risk incidents."

Scoville (2003, p.28) notes: "SWAT teams have been a part of the public consciousness since 'S.W.A.T.' made its television debut in 1975. The images of their real-life counterparts are also embedded in our memory: shooting it out with the Symbionese Liberation Army, descending onto the grounds of a Colorado high school campus; deploying at a North Hollywood bank robbery. To the appreciative hostage whose life they have saved, SWAT team members are knights in shining ballistic armor. To their critics, they are gung-ho macho men, prone to wrong house entries and preemptive shootings. Somewhere between the images, the perceptions and accusations lies a truth: if ever an entity embodied the philosophy of 'hope for the best, but plan for the worst,' it is the SWAT unit."

According to Griffith (2003a, p.46): "Well over 90 percent of all critical incidents that involve tactical police response are resolved without a gunfight. The bad guy looks out the window, sees the SWAT team, knows that tear gas and maybe armed assault will follow, and decides that further resistance is futile. So he throws down his gun or turns it on himself." Crises police officers may face include hostage situations, barricaded individuals and suicide attempts.

### Hostage Situations

When police respond to a call about a crime in progress or a terrorist group in action, they may encounter a hostage situation. Kaluta (2004, p.12) contends: "A large metropolitan police department responds, on average, to two hostage situations a week." The FBI and most domestic police departments divide hostage-takers into four distinct categories: (1) the criminal trapped at the crime scene or escaping from the crime scene who uses bystanders as shields or bargaining tools, (2) terrorists, (3) prisoners and (4) mentally unstable individuals. Category 1 is considered the "traditional" hostage situation.

It is important to recognize which type of hostage situation is involved because the negotiation process is directly affected. The most dangerous hostage situation is usually one involving terrorists; terrorists are usually willing to die for their cause and have little problem killing others. The most prevalent and usually least dangerous hostage situation involves the mentally disturbed.

Pearson (2001, p.44) states: "The first two hours of any hostage incident are the most dangerous. Tension, stress and anxiety are all extremely high in the hostage-taker, hostage and rescue personnel. As time progresses, the hostage and his captor have the opportunity to emotionally bond and, in general, calm down." This phenomenon is called the **Stockholm syndrome** and involves the process of transference, in which hostages feel positive toward their captors and negative toward the police, and the captors return these positive feelings. Steele and Sanow (2004, p.56) note that law enforcement and the media often misunderstand the Stockholm syndrome: "Virtually everyone in the media gets it wrong. Far from being a negative thing for law enforcement, the onset of the interpersonal bonding, called the Stockholm syndrome, makes it less likely for the hostage taker to harm the hostages or victims."

Because the first few hours of a hostage incident are so volatile, it is important for those responding to the high-anxiety situation to *slow everything down*. Beyond allowing time for captors and hostages to calm down, other benefits to stalling include having enough time to adequately contain and isolate the scene and being able to call in the appropriate personnel for the response.

 The number one rule in hostage situations is to slow things down.

If a strategy that involves negotiation of some type is selected, it is critical that someone skilled in hostage negotiations should be available to talk with the hostage holder. The FBI hostage negotiator course emphasizes "negotiators don't command; commanders don't negotiate." To have the person in command of the containment of the situation also conduct the negotiations is usually not the best approach. The commander at the scene should devote full attention to the entire situation. In addition, if the hostage-taker knows the negotiator is also the person in command, the hostage-taker also knows that individual has the authority to grant requests. With the commander as negotiator, the advantage of stalling while waiting for authorization is lost.

Because the majority of hostage situations involve mentally unstable captors, many hostage negotiation teams include mental health professionals. In addition to mentally disturbed hostage-takers, police may need to deal with those under the influence of alcohol.

SWAT members may attempt to facilitate the victim's rescue and the perpetrator's apprehension by distracting the hostage holder so a tactical plan can be implemented. In hostage situations and also in some high-risk entries, some police departments have used **flashbangs,** devices that explode with a loud bang and emit a brilliant, temporarily blinding light. Flashbangs should not, however, be used when the elderly or small children are a part of the situation because they may panic. Flashbangs also may create a lot of smoke, reducing visibility, and

*Armed police officers wearing bulletproof vests take up position behind a car outside a small branch of the Bankers Trust office, which was being held up by a lone gunman. The gunman, who was holding six hostages, demanded 10 million dollars in gold and the release of several Symbionese Liberation Army members.*

UPI/Bettmann/Corbis

they may set off smoke alarms. Ijames (2004, p.42) describes both the positive and negative side of flashbangs: "When properly deployed they reduce the risk of death or serious injury to officers and suspects alike. They have also directly contributed to fatalities, catastrophic injuries and significant property damage in more than a few cases." Many techniques used in hostage situations are also appropriate when responding to a situation in which an individual is barricaded or threatening suicide.

## Barricaded Individuals and Suicide Attempts

Police departments need clear guidelines on how to handle life-threatening situations such as those involving barricaded individuals and those who are threatening suicide. Of prime importance are the lives of those involved. If no danger exists for the police or the public, it is often best to talk the situation out or simply wait it out.

 The number one rule in barricaded-individual or suicide-attempt situations is to slow things down.

If officers respond to a successful suicide, they must secure the scene and conduct a thorough investigation, keeping in mind that, to many people, suicide is a stigma. Family members may hide or destroy evidence of a suicide, including a note that may have been left. This may be done so that insurance can be collected. Sometimes those intent on dying set up a situation in which they get the police to pull the trigger, a phenomenon known as victim-precipitated homicide or, more commonly, suicide by cop.

**Suicide by Cop** Honig (2001, p.89) states: "As any officer can attest, confrontation with a suicidal person is often dangerous and can frequently turn deadly." She reports on a study of officer-involved shootings in which suicide by cop (SBC) was found to account for nearly 25 percent of such shootings. According to Parent: "In recent years a majority of the people killed by police officers were suicidal. . . . For those with suicidal tendencies, being killed by police can be more appealing than committing suicide, which comes with a 'loser' stigma" ("Officer's Research Shows . . .," 2004, p.15).

Gallo (2004, p.14) suggests: "The suicide-by-cop scenario is one in which police officers are most victimized while being most manipulated. As one officer asserted: 'It's not enough that we put our lives on the line when we protect them. Now they expect us to assume the responsibility of killing them, too.'"

Honig (p.93) suggests several steps for officers responding to a potential SBC incident:

- Contain the area, while remaining aware that too close a containment may allow the precipitator [the person trying to force a shooting] to provoke a deadly confrontation.
- If time and circumstances allow, make a clear demand for compliance—a demand that will usually be ignored.
- Ask the person what he or she wants (specifically, ask if they are trying to die).
- If family, friends or acquaintances of the subject are present, ask if they are aware of the subject's mental health history, chemical dependency or any criminal record.
- Remain a good listener, while avoiding making promises or committing to anything.
- Use a less-than-lethal weapon only as a diversionary tactic before making a planned attempt to apprehend but never as a stand-alone tactic, as the use of such devices without an immediate attempt to apprehend may in fact escalate the situation.

Honig (p.90) stresses using caution if less-than-lethal options are introduced, noting in nearly a quarter of all officer-involved shootings later identified as SBC incidents, officers had initially used less-lethal weapons to subdue the subject. However, when such tactics failed and the situation escalated, police were left with little option other than to shoot.

As with other crisis incidents, officers should attempt to slow down the situation when possible. However, the pacing of the event ultimately rests in the hands of the subject. Honig (p.93) states: "No matter how tactically sound the response may be, a suicide-by-cop incident may turn into a deadly force encounter due to the actions of the precipitator. In 70 percent of the incidents studied, shootings occurred within 30 minutes. Thirty-seven percent of the shootings occurred within five minutes of officers arriving on scene."

A final step for officers involved in an SBC incident that ends in the subject's death is for the officer to recognize the range of emotions that may follow the shooting and to receive timely critical incident stress debriefing. Officers involved in SBC shootings have reported feeling angry at and used by the perpetrator, guilty for shooting someone who was not necessarily dangerous but in dire psychological pain, and a sense of failure for not recognizing the "set up." When officers do not work through these emotions, their ability to respond effectively to future incidents is severely compromised, making the officer vulnerable to potentially fatal errors in judgment and leaving the department susceptible to lawsuits. The mere instant it takes an officer to second-guess a course of action is all the time a subject needs to pull the trigger. Furthermore, officers unable to resolve the incident in their own minds may succumb to overwhelming feelings of guilt and failure and become, themselves, suicidal.

While some suicidal individuals come to police attention through an acute episode of crisis behavior, others are suffering from the more chronic condition of mental illness. Santoro (2001, p.23) reports: "Ten to fifteen percent of individuals suffering from schizophrenia or manic-depressive illness . . . commit suicide," sometimes with an officer's unwitting assistance. Zdanowicz (p.4) adds: "More than one million people with schizophrenia and manic depressive illness are not being treated on any given day. They are more likely to experience homelessness, suicide, incarceration, victimization and violence."

Williams (2003, p.67) suggests that sometimes what looks like a suicide-by-cop is better described as death by indifference: "While the individual shot by police may have committed a suicidal act, he may not have been suicidal. In fact, the offender's physical survival probably did not enter his thought processes at the moment he made his fateful decision. Instead, this person was, momentarily indifferent to the consequences of his threatening behavior. Rather than suicide by cop, he committed 'death by indifference.'"

## Crime, Disorder and Community Policing

An effective police response to crime and disorder requires community mobilization and active citizen involvement as, in the long run, vibrant neighborhoods are the best defense against crime. The law enforcement community has recognized this principle in embracing community policing and seeking to address and solve local problems through partnership with residents.

As discussed, since the advent of community policing, many departments across the country have focused on the aggressive enforcement of disorder offenses. These aggressive strategies are popularly known as "zero-tolerance," "order-maintenance" and "quality-of-life" policing. Following their seminal article, "Broken Windows," Wilson and Kelling (1989, p.49) contend: "Like it or not, the police are about the only city agency that makes house calls around the clock. And like it or not, the public defines broadly what it thinks of as public order, and holds the police responsible for maintaining order. Community-oriented policing means changing the daily work of the police to include investigating problems as well as incidents. It means defining as a problem whatever a significant body of public opinion regards as a threat to community order. It means working with the good guys, and not just against the bad guys."

Some agencies, such as the San Diego (California) Police Department, have taken community policing "up a notch," to a strategy called neighborhood policing. As Stewart-Brown (2001, p.17) explains, neighborhood policing resembles the traditional style of policing in that police are at the forefront of solving community problems but differs in the process used to identify crime and quality-of-life problems that are priorities for police response:

> The more traditional forms of neighborhood policing focus on communication but no interactive problem solving. Usually, residents identify community problems that they see as a priority. Then, law enforcement targets these problems for resolution. Although this strategy of policing has been effective

in appeasing community residents and solving some crime and quality-of-life problems, it remains similar to the old style of policing—it puts the bulk of responsibility for problem resolution on law enforcement.

The City Heights Neighborhood Alliance in San Diego, California, has taken the concept of community policing to the next level. It promotes a wrap-around, problem-solving approach where police and community residents work in a true partnership to solve crime and quality-of-life issues. This nontraditional neighborhood policing strategy promotes resident action. It empowers community residents with the knowledge, tools, and guidance to solve crimes and quality-of-life problems. By actively involving the individuals who live among, experience and commit the crimes, the San Diego Police Department has created an effective and efficient alliance that can solve many of the problems that once required law enforcement intervention.

Numerous examples of communities coming together to deal with problems of crime and disorder using problem-oriented policing are available.

## Crime, Disorder and Problem-Oriented Policing

"Designing Out Crime: The Chula Vista Residential Burglary Reduction Project"* is one of the 2001 Herman Goldstein Award winners for excellence in problem-oriented policing.

Although residential burglary rates had declined in Chula Vista in the mid-1990s, the number of burglaries was still unacceptably high in 1996, when more than 900 of 52,000 households were victimized. The program used the SARA model to address the problem.

### Scanning

A resident survey reinforced the need to focus on residential burglary: 82 percent of respondents indicated that they were concerned about burglary, making it the second-highest ranked crime or disorder problem in the city after the problem of speeding vehicles. It was imperative that potential buyers and builders saw Chula Vista neighborhoods as safe places to live, as 30,000 new housing units were scheduled for construction over the next 20 years.

### Analysis

To better understand the dynamics of the burglary problem, project staff carefully examined all sides of the crime triangle—victim, offender and location. The police department undertook an extensive study of the factors that attracted burglars to specific homes, as well as those protective devices that were most effective at preventing burglaries. Researchers and sworn police staff interviewed more than 250 victims and 50 burglars, conducted more than 100 street-view environmental assessments, and reviewed over 1,000 incident reports of burglaries committed against single-family homes. Key findings from the analysis phase included:

*Source: Adapted from "Designing Out Crime: The Chula Vista Residential Burglary Reduction Project." In *Excellence in Problem-Oriented Policing: The 2001 Herman Goldstein Award Winners.* Washington, DC: National Institute of Justice, Community Oriented Policing Services and the Police Executive Research Forum, 2001, pp.27–37.

- Doors without deadbolt locks were targeted.
- Windows with single-paned glass were targeted.
- Windows with simple stock latches were easily defeated.
- Sliding glass doors without specialized pin locks were easily rocked off their tracks.
- Homes that appeared unoccupied were targeted.
- A relatively frequent and highly preventable type of burglary, particularly in newer neighborhoods, was the open garage door burglary.
- In 94 percent of the burglaries, points of entry other than the front door were hidden from the street, either by high shrubbery or solid wood fencing.

An additional review of police department data revealed during the previous 18 months, 569 single-detached homes had reported a burglary or attempted burglary. Analysis indicated 70 percent of the residential burglaries had occurred during daylight hours, but only 58 percent had occurred during weekdays. (If burglaries were occurring randomly, 71 percent should have occurred on weekdays.)

### Response

Chula Vista police developed an array of solid, practical responses based heavily on crime prevention through environmental design (CPTED) principles and, to a lesser extent, public education efforts. Environmental protections were thought to be especially appropriate for Chula Vista, which lacked the around-the-clock surveillance provided by a strong Neighborhood Watch program—particularly in newer residential areas.

Police also focused on changing construction standards for new homes, realizing if they could negotiate built-in burglary prevention features, it would achieve target hardening and make such homes less attractive to would-be burglars. They developed a mutually beneficial, collaborative relationship with the new housing development and building industry. Such "burglar-resistant" features would not only lower the incidence of burglary but would also provide an attractive selling point to home buyers.

Project staff approached home development executives about partnering in the effort to prevent burglaries. Developers agreed to several design modifications of new homes, including installing deadbolt door locks on vulnerable garage service doors, using only windows that met strict forced-entry resistance standards and installing pin locks on all sliding glass doors. Developers agreed to distribute a safety and security brochure spelling out ways to prevent burglary and a brochure on antiburglary landscape ideas. Developers also required that garage doors be kept shut, in accordance with homeowners' association rules. Finally, developers agreed to task each newly created homeowner's association with setting up and maintaining a permanent Neighborhood Watch program.

### Assessment

Although the long-term impact of the antiburglary project will not be felt for some time, the initial results are very promising. Residential burglary rates in Chula Vista dropped 29 percent in 1999. Burglaries declined 13 percent in National City, which borders Chula Vista to the North, and 16 percent in the City of San Diego, which borders Chula Vista to the South.

In assessing the effectiveness of antiburglary home design modifications, police found that a home in a new-construction neighborhood where the developer had agreed to install burglary prevention features was 37 percent less likely to be burglarized than a home in the adjacent mixed-age neighborhoods.

The department was able to conclude that the use of their collaborative problem-solving model led to a win-win situation that will continue to provide a payoff for all members of the Chula Vista community well into the twenty-first century.

## SUMMARY

The official sources of information about crime are the Uniform Crime Reports (UCR), the National Incident-Based Reporting System (NIBRS) and the National Crime Victimization Survey (NCVS). One major function of law enforcement is to respond when a crime has been committed. Responsibilities of officers responding to a call regarding a criminal act include arriving as rapidly, yet as safely, as possible; caring for any injured people at the scene; apprehending any suspects at the scene; securing the scene; and conducting a preliminary investigation.

The preliminary investigation involves on-the-scene interviews of victims and witnesses, interrogations of suspects and a search of the scene itself. First responding officers may discover evidence on the scene and will need to initiate the chain of possession, or custody, which documents who has had control of the evidence from the time it is discovered until it is presented in court.

In addition to dealing with crime, police officers are also often called upon to deal with situations involving disorder and civil disobedience. Civil disobedience consists of breaking a law to prove a point or to protest something. Issues leading to civil disobedience include overt racism and bias, human rights concerns, environmental concerns, animal rights concerns and pro-life and pro-choice conflicts. To deal with demonstrations and possible violence, police departments should assess their risks, develop contingency plans and have a call-out system for off-duty officers.

Sometimes when police respond to a call regarding a crime, a hostage situation develops. The number one rule in hostage situations, as well as in situations involving barricaded individuals or those threatening to commit suicide, is to slow things down.

### APPLICATION

The chief of police of the Bigtown Police Department notices there is no policy or written procedure to guide patrol officers when they receive a call to a crime scene. Past analysis of reports indicates that many officers have made their own policies as to what their responsibilities are. No uniformity exists. The chief calls you in as the head of the patrol division and instructs you to formulate a policy and procedure for all officers when responding to a crime.

### INSTRUCTIONS

Use the form in Appendix A to make the policy and procedure. The overall policy of how such calls are to be regarded and the specific procedures to be followed, including priorities, should be addressed.

### AN EXERCISE IN CRITICAL THINKING

In the early afternoon of July 3, Walter Skramstad recognized Officer John McArthur driving a police car ahead of him. Skramstad closed in on McArthur, allegedly to ask him whether there would be either a dance or a demolition derby during the holiday weekend. The testimony conflicts as to whether Skramstad tried to run McArthur off the road or flag him down. Thereafter, both cars pulled over to the side of the road. Officer McArthur maintains that Skramstad got out of his car with his fists clenched. Using profanity, Skramstad vehemently threatened McArthur. A scuffle ensued in which McArthur broke Skramstad's jaw. Officer McArthur subsequently arrested Skramstad.

After arriving at the Law Enforcement Center, Skramstad told McArthur, "The next time I come after you, I'll put you in intensive care. I'm going to kill you. I'm going to get your family. I know where you live." As a result of these events, Skramstad was charged with making terroristic threats.

1. If you were to back up Officer McArthur and you had approached the scene just as the scuffle broke out, what would be your first actions?
   a. Make careful observations so that you could collect physical evidence and record exactly what was said and done by both parties.
   b. Look to see if other witnesses might be present so that you could interview them for corroboration.
   c. Secure the crime scene so that evidence was preserved and no one else got involved.

d. Prepare to attend to the injuries each had sustained.

e. Arrive as rapidly, yet as safely, as possible, and assist in apprehending the suspect.

2. Approximately a week before this incident, Skramstad and McArthur had met at a gas station, where they had engaged in a heated argument during which Skramstad challenged McArthur to a fight and threatened to "get" McArthur's family.

a. Because physical safety has been threatened, use of violence on July 3 is justified.

b. If Skramstad had a prior conviction for aggravated assault, an officer would have the right to shoot to prevent Skramstad's escape.

c. An officer should first threaten, then give an order and try other sophisticated verbal interventions, and finally resort to distraction so that suspects see the consequences of their behavior.

d. Because Skramstad operates in a John Wayne style, officers can best communicate with him in the same style.

e. Physical violence is not justified, and courts will not support officers who use violence in cases of threats like Skramstad's.

3. As testimony is conflicting about whether Skramstad tried to run McArthur off the road or flag him down to ask information, how might you proceed to gather evidence as part of the preliminary investigation?

a. Refer to departmental databases to discover previous Skramstad incidents.

b. Call for a crime scene unit to set the objectives, develop a theory of the crime and prepare a narrative description of the scene.

c. Seek and interview witnesses.

d. Look for fingerprints, blood, hair, bite marks, shoe and tire impressions, tool fragments and marks, glass fragments, paint marks, fibers, firearms and other tangible evidence.

e. Photograph the scene and draw diagrams to show the positions of cars and people.

### DISCUSSION QUESTIONS

1. What forces spark crime and disorder in our streets?

2. Select a recent popular movie you have seen that contains scenes of crime, disorder or quality-of-life issues. Compare your reactions with those of other students. Discuss its effects on the general population who may see it.

3. Does your community have more or less crime and disorder than average? On what do you base your opinion?

4. Have you ever participated in a demonstration? If so, what was the cause? How did you feel about participating? Was it peaceful?

5. Is homelessness a problem in your community? If so, how does your police department deal with it?

6. Have there been any instances of the police having to interact with the mentally ill in your community? Were they handled well by the police?

7. Have there been instances of suicide by cop in your community? If so, what were the circumstances and were the police justified in using deadly force?

### INFOTRAC COLLEGE EDITION ASSIGNMENTS

■ Use InfoTrac College Edition to help answer the Discussion Questions as appropriate.

■ Use InfoTrac College Edition to find and outline one of the following articles:

• "Community Mobilization: The Foundation of Community Policing" by Recheal Stewart-Brown

• "Moving Past What to How—The Next Step in Responding to Individuals with Mental Illness" by Douglas Gentz and William S. Goree

• "The Montgomery County CIT Model: Interacting with People with Mental Illness" by Rodney Hill, Guthrie Quill and Kathryn Ellis

• "CompStat Design" by Jon M. Shane

• "CompStat Implementation" by Jon M. Shane

• "Law Enforcement's Response to People with Mental Illness" by Michael Klein

• "Hostage/Barricade Management: A Hidden Conflict within Law Enforcement" by Gregory M. Vecchi

• "Crisis Negotiation Teams: Selection and Training" by Chuck Regini

• "Negotiation Position Papers: A Tool for Crisis Negotiators" by Vincent A. Dalfonzo and Stephen J. Fomano

• "Too Close for Comfort: Negotiating with Fellow Officers" by Sandra D. Terhune-Bickler

### INTERNET ASSIGNMENTS

Select two of the following activities, and be prepared to share your assignments with the class.

■ Go to the Bureau of Justice Statistics' website at http://www.ojp.usdoj.gov/bjs/abstract/cvusst.htm and outline what the site has to say about *crimes reported and not reported* to the police as well as *police response time* for reported crimes.

■ Go to the FBI's website at www.fbi.gov and find *Crime in the United States,* the Uniform Crime Reports. Outline the chapters in this report.

■ Go to the Ford Foundation's website at www.ford-found.org/ and find the report "Crime Control by the Numbers" by David C. Anderson. Outline the report.

■ Go to the National Institute of Justice's website at http://www.ncjrs.org/nij/mapping/ to find the guide, *Mapping Crime: Principle and Practice.* Outline one chapter of interest to you.

■ Go to the National Institute of Justice's website at http://www.ncjrs.org/txtfiles1/nij/188739.txt to find the document "Privacy in the Information Age: A Guide for Sharing Crime Maps and Spatial Data." Outline the potential privacy concerns that may arise from sharing mapping data.

 ### BOOK-SPECIFIC WEBSITE

The book-specific website at http://cj.wadsworth.com/ wobleski_Hess_police_op4e hosts a variety of resources for students and instructors. Many can be emailed to the instructor. Included are extended activities such as Concept Builders - the 3 step learning module that reinforces key chapter concepts, followed by a real-world applications and critical thinking questions. InfoTrac College Edition exercises; Discussion Questions; interactive key-term FlashCards; and a collection of chapter-based Web Links provide additional information and activities to include in the curriculum.

### REFERENCES

Burns, Ronald. "Amber Plan: Hue and Cry." *Community Links*, September 2001, p.18.

Butterfield, Fox. "Student's Death Returns Crowd Control to the Fore." *The New York Times*, November 1, 2004.

*Crime in the United States 2003: Uniform Crime Reports.* Washington, DC: Department of Justice, Federal Bureau of Investigation, 2003. www.fbi.gov/ucr/cius_02/html/web/index.html.

*Crime Scene Investigation: A Guide for Law Enforcement.* Washington, DC: Department of Justice, National Institute of Justice, January 2000. (NCJ 178280)

Dees, Tim. "Understanding GIS." *Law and Order*, August 2002, pp.42–46.

"Designing Out Crime: The Chula Vista Residential Burglary Reduction Project." In *Excellence in Problem-Oriented Policing: The 2001 Herman Goldstein Award Winners.* Washington, DC: National Institute of Justice, Community Oriented Policing Services and the Police Executive Research Forum, 2001, pp.27–37.

Diamond, Joe. "Connecting the Dots." *Police*, April 2004, pp.42–47.

Gallo, Gina. "Decedent as Perpetrator, Killer as Victim." *Law Enforcement News*, January 2004, pp.13–14.

Gentz, Douglas and Goree, William S. "Moving Past What to How—The Next Step in Responding to Individuals with Mental Illness." *FBI Law Enforcement Bulletin*, November 2003, pp.14–18.

Gray, Charles. "How to Police the Homeless." *Police*, June 2004, pp.30–34.

Griffith, David. "Outgunned." *Police*, March 2003a, pp.46–51.

Griffith, David. "Policing Dissent." *Police*, August 2003b, pp.44–50.

Groff, Elizabeth R. and LaVigne, Nancy G. "Mapping an Opportunity Surface of Residential Burglary." *Journal of Research in Crime and Delinquency*, August 2001, pp.257–278.

Hill, Rodney and Logan, Joan. "Civil Liability and Mental Illness: A Proactive Model to Mitigate Claims." *The Police Chief*, June 2001, pp.29–32.

Hill, Rodney; Quill, Guthrie; and Ellis, Kathryn. "The Montgomery County CIT Model: Interacting with People with Mental Illness." *FBI Law Enforcement Bulletin*, July 2004, pp.18–25.

Honig, Audrey L. "Police-Assisted Suicide: Identification, Intervention, and Investigation." *The Police Chief*, October 2001, pp.89–93.

Ijames, Steve. "Negative Outcomes with Flash Bangs." *Tactical Response*, Summer 2004, pp.42–47.

Kaluta, Roman W. "Interoperability for Day-to-Day Operations." *The Police Chief*, September 2004, p.12.

Katz, Charles M.; Webb, Vincent J.; and Schaefer, David R. "An Assessment of the Impact of Quality-of-Life Policing on Crime and Disorder." *Justice Quarterly*, December 2001, pp.825–876.

King, William R. and Dunn, Thomas M. "Dumping: Police-Initiated Transjurisdictional Transport of Troublesome Persons." *Police Quarterly*, September 2004, pp.339–358.

Klaus, Patsy A. *Crime and the Nation's Households, 2002.* Washington, DC: Bureau of Justice Statistics, February 2004. (NCJ 201797)

LaVigne, Nancy G. and Wartell, Julie. *Mapping across Boundaries: Regional Crime Analysis.* Washington, DC: Police Executive Research Forum, 2001.

Lundrigan, Nicole. "Crime Scene Priorities." *Law and Order*, May 2001, pp.38–42.

Lutz, William. "The Powerful Combination of Intranets and Mapping." *Law Enforcement Technology*, June 2003, pp.118–122.

*Marketing Community Policing in the News: A Missed Opportunity?* Washington, DC: National Institute of Justice Research for Practice, July 2003. (NCJ 200473)

McDonald, Phyllis P. "Implementing CompStat: Critical Points to Consider." *The Police Chief*, January 2004, pp.33–37.

McEwen, Tom. "Information Management." In *Local Government Police Management*, 4th ed. edited by William A. Geller and Carrel W. Stephens. Washington, DC: International City/County Management Association, 2003, pp.391–421.

Miller, Linda J. and Hess, Kären M. *Community Policing: Partnerships for Problem Solving*, 4th ed. Belmont, CA: Wadsworth Publishing Company, 2005.

Nislow, Jennifer. "LEN Salutes Its 2003 Person of the Year." *Law Enforcement News*, December 15/31, 2003, pp.1–2.

Nyberg, Ramesh. "Backing Down the Bloc." *Police*, March 2004, pp.62–68.

"Officer's Research Shows that Suicide by Cop Incidents on the Rise in North America." *Police*, February 2004, p.15.

Oldham, Scott. "Madness of March: Dealing with Large Celebratory Crowds." *Law and Order,* September 2002, pp.112–116.

Olson, Robert K. "Law Enforcement Response to People with Mental Illness." *Subject to Debate,* March 2002, pp.2–3.

Pearson, Cecil. "What to Do If You Are Taken Hostage." *Police,* January 2001, pp.44–45.

Ramirez, Eugene P. "SWAT and the Law." *Police,* May 2003, pp.58–60.

Reuland, Melissa. *A Guide to Implementing Police-Based Diversion Programs for People with Mental Illness.* Delmar, NY: Technical Assistance and Policy Analysis Center for Jail Diversion, 2004.

Rogers, Donna. "The Rap on Mapping." *Law Enforcement Technology,* June 2001, pp.64–68.

Rohr, Carol Ann. "Training for Managing Crowds and Responding to Civil Disobedience." *The Police Chief,* October 2001, pp.10–11.

Ruiz, Jim and Miller, Chad. "An Exploratory Study of Pennsylvania Police Officers' Perceptions of Dangerousness and Their Ability to Manage Persons with Mental Illness." *Police Quarterly,* September 2004, pp.359–371.

Sampson, Robert J. and Raudenbush, Stephen W. *Disorder in Urban Neighborhoods—Does It Lead to Crime?* Washington, DC: National Institute of Justice Research in Brief, February 2001. (NCJ 186049)

Santoro, Joseph. "Mentally Ill Pose a Grave Risk to Police Officers." *American Police Beat,* May 2001, p.23.

Schick, Walt. "CompStat in the Los Angeles Police Department." *The Police Chief,* January 2004, pp.17–23.

Scott, Michael S. *Street Prostitution.* Washington DC: Office of Community Oriented Policing Services, Problem-Oriented Guides for Police Series No. 2, August 6, 2001.

Scott, Michael S. *Panhandling.* Washington, DC: Office of Community Oriented Policing Services, Problem-Oriented Guides for Police Series No. 13, January 29, 2002.

Scoville, Dean. "How to Start a SWAT Team." *Police,* March 2003, pp.28–33.

Shane, Jon M. "CompStat Process." *FBI Law Enforcement Bulletin,* April 2004a, pp.12–21.

Shane, Jon M. "CompStat Design." *FBI Law Enforcement Bulletin,* May 2004b, pp.12–19.

Shane, Jon M. "CompStat Implementation." *FBI Law Enforcement Bulletin,* June 2004c, pp.13–21.

Slackman, Michael and Baker, Al. "With Restraint and New Tactics, March Is Kept Orderly." *The New York Times,* August 30, 2004.

Smith, Michael R. "Police-Led Crackdowns and Cleanups: An Evaluation of a Crime Control Initiative in Richmond, Virginia." *Crime & Delinquency,* January 2001, pp.60–83.

*Sourcebook of Criminal Justice Statistics, 2003.* Washington, DC: Bureau of Justice Statistics, December 2003. (NCJ 190251) www.albany.edu/sourcebook

Steele, David and Sanow, Ed. "FBI's Crisis Negotiation Course." *Tactical Response,* Summer 2004, pp.48–57.

Stewart-Brown, Recheal. "Community Mobilization: The Foundation for Community Policing." *FBI Law Enforcement Bulletin,* June 2001, pp.9–17.

Surratt, Hilary L.; Inciardi, James A.; Kurtz, Steven P.; and Kiley, Marion C. "Sex Work and Drug Use in a Subculture of Violence." *Crime & Delinquency,* January 2004, pp.43–59.

Terestre, David J. "Talking Him Down." *Police,* March 2004, pp.26–33.

Turner, Lisa M. "Crime Falls, Fear Holds On." *Community Links,* August 2004, p.6.

Van Blaricom, D. P. "Preventing Officer-Involved Deaths of the Mentally Ill." *The Law Enforcement Trainer,* Third Quarter 2004, pp.22–25.

Walsh, William F. and Vito, Gennaro F. "The Meaning of CompStat." *Journal of Contemporary Criminal Justice,* February 2004, pp.51–69.

Wartell, Julie and McEwen, J. Thomas. *Privacy in the Information Age: A Guide for Sharing Crime Maps and Spatial Data.* Washington, DC: Institute for Law and Justice, July 2001. (NCJ 188739)

Weisburd, David; Mastrofski, Stephen D.; Greenspan, Rosann; and Willis, James J. "The Growth of CompStat in American Policing." *Police Foundation Reports,* April 2004.

Weiss, Jim and Dresser, Mary. "Cleaning Up the City." *Law and Order,* June 2001, pp.117–118.

Weitzer, Ronald and Kubrin, Charles E. "Breaking News: How Local TV News and Real-World Conditions Affect Fear of Crime." *Justice Quarterly,* September 2004, pp.497–520.

Williams, George T. "Death by Indifference." *Law and Order,* December 2003, pp.66–69.

Wilson, James Q. and Kelling, George L. "Broken Windows: The Police and Neighborhood Safety." *The Atlantic Monthly,* March 1982, pp.29–38.

Wilson, James Q. and Kelling, George L. "Making Neighborhoods Safe." *The Atlantic Monthly,* February 1989, pp.46–52.

Winegar, Scott. "Crowd Control: Planning for Civil Disobedience." *Law and Order,* October 2001, pp.158–162.

Zdanowicz, Mary. "A Shift in Care." *Community Links,* June 2001, pp.3–5.

**CASE CITED**

*Madsen et al. v. Women's Health Center, Inc., et al.,* No. 93–880. Argued April 28, 1994, decided June 30, 1994.

# CHAPTER 7

# Violence: At Home, in the Classroom, on the Job

**Do You Know . . .**

- Who is at risk of being a victim of domestic violence?
- What law enforcement's responsibility is when domestic violence occurs?
- How dangerous police response to a domestic violence call is?
- What the Minneapolis experiment established?
- What *Thurman v. City of Torrington* (1984) established?
- What the Broward Batterer's Intervention Program found?
- Whether incidents of school violence can be anticipated or are always a surprise?
- What three-pronged approach is an effective response to the issue of school violence?
- What controversial measures have been taken to make schools safer?
- What similarities exist between school and workplace violence?
- If warning signs typically precede incidents of workplace violence?

**CAN YOU DEFINE?**

battered woman
   syndrome
battering
bullying
child abuse
elder abuse

expressive violence
instrumental violence
lockdown
Munchausen
   syndrome by proxy
   (MSBP)

osteogenesis
   imperfecta
stake-in-conformity
   variables
zero-tolerance policies

## Introduction

Violence has accompanied every stage of our country's existence from its birth to the present and is often involved in ensuring law and order. Indeed, one of the great ironies of police authority is the ability to use force to achieve a peaceable society. Violence is connected with some of the most positive events of U.S. history: independence from England through the Revolutionary War, the emancipation of slaves and preservation of the Union following the Civil War, and the expansion and stabilization of frontier society via vigilante violence. Some of the nation's most violent criminal figures, such as Al Capone, John Dillinger, Jessie James and Bonnie and Clyde, were popular folk heroes. Even today, our nation is drawn into a violent fight for the preservation of its values, including the freedom to live in peace. In fact, a statement made by Martin Luther King, Jr., nearly

40 years ago seems eerily prophetic in light of recent events: "The choice today is no longer between violence and nonviolence. It's between nonviolence and nonexistence."

Many fear violence is becoming a way of life in the United States, and there exists among the public a common perception that violent crime is spinning out of control. True, violence occurs throughout the United States and directly touches the lives of millions of people. However, the reality is that violent crime is down, as discussed in Chapter 6. Bureau of Justice Statistics (BJS) statisticians Rennison and Rand (2003, p.1) report findings from the National Crime Victimization Survey (NCVS): "Between 1993 and 2002 the violent crime rate decreased 54 percent, from 50 to 23 victimizations per 1,000 persons age 12 or older." According to the 2003 NCVS data, the number of victims of violent crimes for 2003 decreased further to 22.6 percent (Wald, 2004).

The dominant expression of violent behavior in the United States involves acts of *interpersonal* violence that occur nearly everywhere, every day. Domestic violence is a major challenge for law enforcement. In addition, barroom brawls, street fights, beatings, slashings, stabbings and shootings are the types of violent transactions most likely to require a police response. These "garden-variety" acts of violence require police officers to possess excellent communication skills. They may also have to resort to violence themselves.

Children are also demonstrating an increased capacity for violence, which has crept into our schools and made students fearful of victimization by their classmates. Metal detectors, surveillance cameras and drug- and weapons-detector dogs are a growing presence on school campuses nationwide. When the final bell rings and the class day is over, the violence is carried over onto the extracurricular activities fields, where kids are taught to compete and win at all costs. Aggression is rewarded and even modeled by the parents who, in front of their own children, shamelessly hurl more than words at coaches, umps and parents of the opposing team.

Workplace violence also captures headlines, as the media report more murder-suicide stories involving disgruntled employees who return to the office seeking vengeance against the "higher ups" who wronged them. Stress at home, in the classroom and on the job moves with people as they go from point A to point B, sometimes manifesting as road rage. Drivers run each other off the road, assault each other during postcrash confrontations and shoot each other for zipping into the parking spot they had been waiting for.

While reading this chapter, keep in mind that because the police have a monopoly on the *legitimate* use of force, they have the authority to impose themselves on conflicts as third-party agents of social control. Therefore, police-citizen encounters are *always* potentially coercive relationships. This is a particularly important factor when considering the role of the police in controlling "typical" violent encounters. The dangers implicit in this for both the police and the citizens involved are thoroughly documented in research on violence.

This chapter begins with an overview of domestic and family violence and the various forms of partner abuse, including battered women, battered men and gay domestic violence. Next is a look at the police response to calls of domestic violence and the challenges presented by incidents of stalking. The section on domestic and family violence concludes with a discussion of child abuse and neglect, often referred to as maltreatment, abuse of the elderly, and community policing and domestic violence. Next the chapter examines the increasingly publicized issue of school violence and how police are expected to respond in efforts to keep our nation's students and teachers safe. The final domain of violence presented in this chapter concerns that found in the American workplace. The chapter concludes with problem-oriented policing and violence.

## Domestic and Family Violence

It seems contradictory that the social unit people depend on for love and support can also foster violence. But this is true in thousands of homes. While people who live together usually form close relationships, they may also take their hurts and frustrations out on others within the family. In fact, violence is often taught by parents who use physical force to discipline their children. Some parents even say, while administering a spanking or beating, "This hurts me more than it hurts you." They truly believe it is their responsibility to punish their children physically when the children misbehave. Many parents also teach their children to defend themselves and to "fight their own battles." Children come to learn that "might makes right."

Kingsnorth and Macintosh (2004, p.301) note: "During the last 25 years, social definitions of domestic violence have evolved from private wrongs to acts meriting an aggressive response from the criminal justice system. The change reflects the impact of the women's movement, civil liability lawsuits, changing criminal justice system ideology and academic research." Johnson (2002, p.65) contends: "Today, domestic violence is acknowledged as a serious, violent crime and as a scourge on society that greatly harms women [and men], increases the amount of child abuse, drains medical resources, and endangers the lives and welfare of officers." Felson et al. (2002, p.617) point out: "Victims of domestic violence are less likely than victims of other types of violence to call the police because of their privacy concerns, their fear of reprisal, and their desire to protect offenders, but they are more likely to call for self-protection and because they perceive domestic assaults as more serious."

According to Rennison (2003, p.1): "1,247 women and 440 men were killed by an intimate partner in 2000." *Law Enforcement News* suggests: "Controlling behavior, stalking and enforced social isolation may be precursors of lethal domestic violence" ("Domestic Homicide Tipoffs May Be Missed," 2004, p.9). Turner (2002, p.81) contends: "When a gun is involved in a domestic dispute, it is 12 times more likely that the violence will end in death."

Domestic violence knows no bounds. It occurs in families of all races, ethnicities and religions and across all socioeconomic and educational levels, although it is more likely to involve law enforcement at the lower economic levels. Researchers Van Wyk et al. (2003, pp.433–434) confirmed that: "Partner violence was more than twice as likely to occur in highly disadvantaged neighborhoods than in neighborhoods that are relatively well-to-do." The tensions of our complex society, the prevalence of drug and alcohol abuse, and the fact that people are living longer, often creating an emotional and economic strain on their children, all contribute to the problem of domestic violence.

 Wives, husbands, significant others, children, elders—in fact, anyone within a family unit—may be at risk of becoming victims of domestic violence.

## Partner Abuse

Sherman (n.d., p.1) speculates "family" violence is the most widespread form of violence in the country. However, domestic violence is often viewed by others, including those in law enforcement, as a family matter. Even victims may hold this perception, agonizing over the decision to report abuse to authorities. The victim wrestles with feelings of fear, loyalty, love, guilt and shame; often there is a sense of responsibility for other victims in the household. The victim also knows that reporting is a risk. All too often police or prosecutors minimize or ignore the problem, and the victim is left alone to face an attacker who will respond with anger at being reported or incarcerated.

Victims often do not want to press charges and do not want the victimizers to be put in jail. A victim may not only fear retaliation, but also not want to give up the abuser's income or companionship. All victims want is for the violence to stop. It seldom does, however, and instead continues on in an increasingly frequent and severe three-stage cycle of abuse shown in Figure 7.1.

Garrett (2001b, p.120) cites research supporting this pattern of abuse, noting with the average domestic violence call, prior to police involvement, there had been 30 incidents of domestic violence that had never been reported.

Not only does such violence tend to be self-perpetuating; it can also be passed from one generation to the next. The National Coalition Against Domestic Violence (NCADV) cautions that 60 percent of boys who witness domestic violence will grow up to batter and 50 percent of the girls who witness such abuse will grow up to be battered women.

### *Battered Women*

Under English common law, a woman was her husband's property, and he could beat her with a stick as long as the stick was no larger in diameter than his thumb, hence the well-known phrase "rule of thumb." Unfortunately, many modern-day relationships suffer under this archaic concept, but today it is called **battering—**

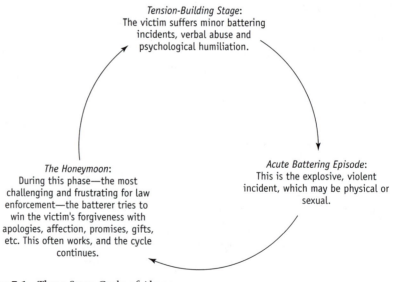

**Figure 7.1** Three-Stage Cycle of Abuse

the use of physical, emotional, economic or sexual force to control another person. Whether the batterer is consciously applying his "rule of thumb" to keep "the little woman" in line, or whether he is merely continuing a cycle of abuse witnessed as a child that later came to define how relationships "worked," the behavior of battering is about power and control. It is violence, and it can take many forms. It happens among married and unmarried couples. It may surface after a once-happy relationship takes a wrong turn, or battering may have actually been an element of a relationship as it was forming.

Rennison (p.1) reports: "Intimate partner violence made up 20 percent of violent crime against women in 2001." Of the reported 691,700 cases of intimate partner violence, 85 percent involved violence against women. Simple assault was the most frequent violent act (72 percent), followed by aggravated assault (14 percent), robbery (7 percent) and rape/sexual assault (7 percent).

Batterers are not only violent; most are also extremely jealous, suspicious and possessive. They generally have very traditional ideas about the relationship between men and women and often try to isolate their wives or girlfriends from family and friends. Battering tends to worsen over time, sometimes ending in death. Websdale et al. (2001, p.66) note: "Research suggests that a large number of women who commit suicide do so because of their violent victimization at the hands of an intimate male partner. . . . Studies show abuse as a factor in as many as 44 percent of female suicide attempts."

While many believe violence between intimates is more prevalent in relationships where partners have not taken wedding vows, surveys from the United States and Canada indicate domestic violence occurs in 28 percent of all marriages, likely a conservative estimate considering most domestic violence incidents are unreported ("What Every Congregation . . .," 2001). Furthermore, leaving an abusive marriage does not guarantee the battering will end. Women separated from their husbands experience intimate partner violence at rates significantly higher than married, divorced, widowed or never married women, and divorced women are victimized by an intimate partner at the second highest rate among the marital categories.

*Violence against Women: Identifying Risk Factors* (2004, p.ii) reports on two research studies whose findings were remarkably similar: "Being sexually or physically abused both as a child and as an adolescent is a good predictor of future victimization. Child sexual abuse on its own, however, did not predict adult victimization. Women who were victims of both sexual and physical abuse before adulthood were more likely to become adult victims of physical or sexual abuse than women who had experienced only one form of abuse or women who had not been early victims of abuse."

Women living in poverty also face increased risk of domestic violence: "According to data from the Justice Department, women in families where the household income is less than $10,000 a year are five times more likely to experience domestic abuse than those in families with incomes of more than $30,000" ("Suit Targets Wholesale . . .," 2001, p.10). A report from the NCJRS found that violence against women occurs more in disadvantaged neighborhoods: "For women, having financial problems in their intimate relationships and living in an economically distressed neighborhood combine to create greater risk of injury and violence" (*When Violence Hits Home* . . ., 2004).

Several types of "special needs" victims of domestic violence have been identified. Battered *immigrant women* face the triple threat of being held in isolation by their batterers, being isolated by language barriers and often being fearful and distrusting of the police and government in general. An estimated 17 percent of *pregnant women* are battered, with the abuse either beginning or intensifying during pregnancy.

*Women with disabilities* are also more vulnerable to physical, emotional and sexual abuse. Physical disabilities resulting from injury (e.g., paralysis, amputation), disease (e.g., multiple sclerosis) or a congenital condition (e.g., cerebral palsy) can prevent victims from escaping violent situations. Abusers may also withhold mobility-assisting apparatuses, such as prosthetic devices or wheelchairs. Sensory disabilities, such as vision and hearing impairments, may severely hinder abused women's ability to seek help because, while they may be able to physically escape the violent environment itself, they often face communication and mobility challenges once outside. Mental impairments, including mental retardation, mental illness and cognitive disabilities caused by head trauma, also increase a woman's risk of abuse because they may limit victims' ability to physically defend themselves and diminish their problem-solving capacity such that they do not know how to seek or where to go for help.

Finally, *women married to police officers* face the difficulty of seeking help from their abuser's colleagues, some of whom may even be the batterer's close friends. According to Gallo (2004a, p.132): "Research suggests violence may occur more frequently in police families than among the general public." Gallo (2004b, p.60) contends: "Domestic violence in police families has always been one of the original 'don't ask, don't tell' issues—alternately ignored, hidden or denied, firmly protected by the blue wall of silence." A *Law Enforcement News* interview with Griggs, founding director of the National Police Family Violence Prevention Project explains why this may be partially true: "At some point I have to be able to assume that because we wear the same badge and the same uniform, we're also at the same consciousness. So if you're not a bad guy' cause I'm not a bad guy—I have to be able to trust you. So I don't necessarily see my colleagues with the same lens that I'm using when I deal with people on the street" ("The LEN Interview: Renae Griggs  . . .," 2004, p.9).

Lonsway and Conis (2003, p.133) point out: "Victims of domestic violence involving an officer are uniquely vulnerable because the officer who is abusing them holds all the cards. Perhaps most obvious, the officer who is perpetrating the violence has a gun and all the authority of a position within law enforcement to use against his victim. If the victim tries to escape or seek help, the officer knows the location of battered women's shelters and many of the people involved in the system. Of course, the officer also knows how to manipulate the system to avoid detection and accountability, and abusive officers are often masters at shifting blame to the victim and creating the impression that the victim is the one who is crazy or perpetrating the abuse." Despite officers' sworn duty to uphold the law, they are susceptible to the same stresses that spark abuse in others' relationships, perhaps even to a greater degree.

The abused intimate may also struggle with the added consequence of a complaint leading to the officer's loss of employment. A 1997 federal law known as the Lautenberg Amendment to the Gun Control Act prohibits any person with a misdemeanor domestic violence conviction from possessing or purchasing a firearm. Unable to carry a weapon, officers are not likely to keep their jobs. Thus, a victimized police spouse wishing only to have the violence stop, not to get the batterer fired, may choose not to report the abuse.

## Battered Men

Although not as prevalent as wife battering, husband or boyfriend battering does exist. Of the instances of intimate partner violence reported in 2001, 15 percent were committed against men. The most common type of violence was simple assault (49 percent), followed by aggravated assault (35 percent) and robbery (16 percent) (Rennison, p.1).

Some women are much larger and stronger than their husbands or boyfriends and may beat them at will. Others are physically inferior to the men in their lives, but the men, when hit, will not hit back. Further, women tend to use weapons as equalizers; therefore, the physical harm may be greater. Husbands and boyfriends can also be emotionally abused through belittling, name-calling, ridiculing in public and the like. In extreme cases, some battered women use their abuse as justification to kill their batterers, a phenomenon known as **battered woman syndrome,** which is now recognized as a defense by the courts. Movies such as *The Burning Bed* have helped to publicize the predicament of women who are beaten by their husbands and the lengths to which they may go to end the abuse.

Some studies suggest a trend in young women becoming more aggressive in domestic relationships. Research by Moffitt et al. (2001) studied 360 couples recruited through the Dunedin (New Zealand) Study, a project begun in 1972 in which research participants are part of a life-long investigation of health and behavior issues. Moffitt et al. (p.23) report:

> A survey of the full Dunedin cohort showed that many young women believe they can hit male partners with impunity; significantly more young women than young men believed that their hitting would not injure their partner, that the police would not intervene, and that their partner would not hit back. However, these beliefs are misguided, as women's abuse does have consequences. . . . Women inflict a substantial minority of domestic injuries and deaths, . . . women make up as many as one-quarter of police arrests for abuse in some jurisdictions, . . . and men do abuse women who abuse them.

Men are more likely to not report acts of violence against them by their intimate partner. As noted by Kingsnorth and Macintosh (p.307): "In a society that defines masculinity in terms of self-reliance, stoicism and control, males are likely to encounter serious emotional costs when they seek validation of their victim status." Migliaccio (2001, p.208) contends: "Men who have been abused may be cognizant of the possible negative reactions of others and may choose not only to refuse to report any incidents of abuse, but also to deny both to themselves and others that the abuse even exists."

While calls involving battered men are generally not considered the "traditional" type of domestic call, police responding to calls of domestic violence between gay or lesbian partners may find themselves in even more unfamiliar territory. Nonetheless, partner abuse among the gay community does exist and is increasingly being brought to the attention of law enforcement.

## Gay Domestic Violence

Noting the preponderance of research devoted to domestic violence in heterosexual relationships, Burke et al. (2001, p.1) assert the topic as it relates to the gay community has been grossly neglected despite the fact it does exist. A study conducted over a decade ago found nearly 500,000 of the estimated 12 million gay adult males were victims of domestic violence, and it is presumed those numbers have risen proportionately through the years. Research also suggests that domestic violence ranks third among the major health problems facing gay men, preceded only by substance abuse and AIDS (Burke et al., p.1). Data also indicate gay domestic violence homicides are more likely than deaths resulting from gay bashing (p.1). A survey by Burke et al. (p.5) of 73 self-identified gay adults found:

- 28 percent of respondents report having been threatened with physical harm by a partner.
- 31 percent of respondents report actually being physically harmed by a partner.
- 22 percent of respondents report experiencing vandalism or property destruction at the hands of a partner.
- 19 percent of respondents report being pressured into sexual activities by a partner.

In addition, when survey participants were asked if they feared becoming victims of same-sex domestic violence, 38 percent responded "yes" (p.5). The survey also indicated many of those who had been victimized did not report their victimization to the police, the reasons given being fear of retaliation, fear of loss of emotional support, a desire to avoid embarrassment or shame, fear of being "outed," a distrust of law enforcement and lack of confidence in the courts. Finally (p.5): "A majority of all respondents (80%) replied 'strongly disagree' to the statement, 'domestic violence is not a real crime.'"

Burke et al. (2002, p.233) cite research reporting that about 47 percent of gays and lesbians have been victims of violent domestic relationships. And that, taken as a whole, same-sex domestic violence is comparable in prevalence to heterosexual domestic violence. They (p.242) suggest that the two most common forms of domestic violence were verbal harassment and prohibiting social contacts (40 percent).

The police response to calls of domestic violence must be unbiased and executed without regard to the victim's gender or the gender of their abuser.

## Responding to Domestic Violence Calls

Legislative bodies have placed the burden of settling domestic disputes largely on the shoulders of the police. The domestic dispute requires special skills, especially communications and negotiating skills, on the part of law enforcement. Family violence has a strong tendency to repeat itself, and officers often are called back several times—sometimes in the same evening. It also tends to escalate. Effective handling of the first few calls can greatly decrease the number of further calls.

In most crimes, the responsibilities of the responding officers are clear-cut: gather evidence supporting the elements of the crime, determine who is responsible and make an arrest. Responsibilities in domestic violence calls are much less clear-cut. Often it is not at all obvious who is responsible. Frequently both parties are at fault, but the violence must still be ended. Even if one party is clearly to blame, it is usually a mistake for officers to take sides in a domestic dispute. They must maintain their objectivity.

Police responding to a domestic violence call involving a fellow officer may find it particularly challenging to remain objective, yet they must adhere to department policy regarding the handling of such calls, not only because of ethical and professional obligations but because the integrity of the policing profession and the community's trust are at stake.

Police responding to a call in which the man claims to be the victim often have difficulty believing a woman can physically abuse a man. Officers may downplay the seriousness of the call and may actually blame the man for being weak or cowardly. As with any other assault, one involving a woman battering a man must be investigated thoroughly. If probable cause exists to believe an assault has occurred and the woman did it, she should be arrested. It may also be difficult to sort out who the primary aggressor is when police respond to a domestic call and find both partners disheveled, bruised and hostile.

Responsibilities at the scene of domestic violence include:

- Stop the violence.
- Separate those in conflict.
- Administer medical assistance if required.
- Determine if assault has occurred.
- If no probable cause for an arrest exists, mediate the situation. Get them to talk it out, to stop shouting and fighting and to start talking and thinking about their situation.
- If mediation is not possible, order the abusive spouse out of the house.
- Suggest possible solutions and sources of assistance to the abused person.
- If probable cause supporting the crime of assault does exist, make an arrest.

 Police officers responding to a domestic violence call are responsible for investigating it thoroughly as an assault and for making an arrest if probable cause exists.

## The Danger of Domestic Calls

It is commonly thought that a domestic call can be one of the most dangerous calls police officers receive. Indeed, some calls are extremely dangerous, even fatal, for the responding officer(s). Garner (2002, p.46) notes how the response to domestic violence has changed over the years: "But one part of the domestic violence scenario that remains unchanged is its extreme danger for the law enforcement officer sent to restore order out of mayhem." He suggests: "Many domestic violence scenes are made more hazardous by the presence of alcohol, drugs and deadly weapons." Garner (p.47) recommends that officers never go on a domestic violence call alone.

 Responding to a domestic violence call is hazardous, but not as hazardous as is often thought.

Websdale et al. (p.70) suggest: "Greater awareness of the events in relationships and communities that precede domestic homicides can improve police policies, inform police intervention, and lessen the likelihood of officer injury and death."

*A hearse carrying the body of fallen Capitol Police Officer John Gibson turns off Memorial Drive and into Arlington Cemetery in Arlington, Virginia, during his funeral procession. Officers who are called upon to deal with violence can become victims of that violence themselves.*

AP Photo/Stephan Savoia

### *Documenting Evidence of Domestic Violence*

After the abuser has been arrested and removed from the scene, a thorough investigation is needed, including comprehensive interviews with the victim and any witnesses. Information should be obtained about the frequency and intensity of the domestic violence as well as any previous police contacts.

In examining how law enforcement may improve the chances of domestic violence cases making it to court, Dawson and Dinovitzer (2001, p.593) note: "When prosecutors perceive a victim to be cooperative, the odds that a case will be prosecuted are seven times higher than if a victim is not perceived to be cooperative. . . . The two most important determinants of victim cooperation are the availability of videotaped testimony and meetings between victims and victim/witness assistance workers." In examining how one jurisdiction implemented this practice, Dawson and Dinovitzer (p.604) assert:

> [Their] goal is to have a videotaped statement recorded immediately after the incident, or at least within 24 hours. The police are responsible for taping victims' testimony; generally these informal interviews are held at the police station. In extreme circumstances, the police may videotape victims' testimony outside the police station. In one case, for example, the police videotaped the victim's statement in her hospital room. . . . Prosecutors may use this videotape in lieu of victims' testimony in cases where victims cease to cooperate

with the prosecution. Prosecutors are committed to pursuing the admission of this evidence more actively at trial.

Photographs should be taken of injuries and of indications of the level of violence, such as tipped-over or broken furniture, smashed objects and the like. Any evidence of the violence should be properly collected. Keep in mind bruises often do not show up until several hours after a battering, perhaps even a day or two later. Furthermore, many victims change their minds within 24 hours of filing a complaint of abuse and try to drop charges against their batterer. As with videotaping statements, photographing evidence may be necessary insurance in cases where victims are uncooperative in seeing the case through to prosecution and can also help remind victims why they must stand firm in pressing charges.

## Arresting Batterers

Traditionally, the police response to a domestic call regarding wife battering has been to try to mediate the situation or to simply get the batterer out of the house for the night. Unless the police were threatened or actually assaulted, arrests seldom were made. Today, arrests are not made because often the police do not have the legal authority to do so unless they actually witness the assault or unless the victim presses charges. Sometimes, making an arrest only adds to the violence as the batterer seeks to avoid being arrested. Other times, the victim changes her mind and refuses to cooperate with the police. In addition, such cases are often not prosecuted vigorously.

Felson and Ackerman (2001) examined how a suspect's relationship to an assault victim affects whether the police make an arrest. Their (p.655) results indicate:

> In cases of minor assaults the police are less likely to make an arrest when the suspect is an intimate partner of the victim than when the suspect is an identifiable stranger. However, the police are not as lenient when the suspect is an intimate partner as they are when the suspect is someone else the victim knows. Intimate partner suspects avoid arrest in part because they are less likely to commit their crimes in front of witnesses. In addition, victims who know the suspect in any way are reluctant to sign complaints, and this reluctance inhibits arrest.

For several decades, researchers have sought to assess the effects of arrest on intimate partner violence and how such a response compares to more informal, therapeutic intervention methods such as on-scene counseling and temporary separation. While many studies throughout the years have produced inconsistent findings, researchers have now come to a general consensus about the benefit of arrest.

**The Minneapolis Domestic Violence Experiment**    In 1981 the National Institute of Justice (NIJ) and the Minneapolis Police Department conducted what many now consider one of the most influential social science studies ever completed. The study, led by Lawrence W. Sherman (Sherman and Berk, 1984), examined three police responses to domestic violence calls and their effects on reducing future abuse:

- Arrest the suspect.
- Give only advice to the suspect.
- Order the suspect to leave the premises.

Instances of repeat violence were examined through a review of police records and interviews with the victims. Although the effectiveness of advising compared to separating is inconclusive from this study, the effectiveness of arrest is clear.

 In the Minneapolis experiment, arrest was clearly more effective in reducing future violence than advice or sending the suspect away.

The finding—that police should arrest suspects in domestic violence cases, as opposed to giving them on-the-spot counseling or other types of more lenient treatment, because arrests reduce recidivism—affected police policies nationwide and led Congress to fund grant programs encouraging law enforcement agencies to establish "pro-arrest" policies ("New Study Confirms . . .," 2001, p.6).

Follow-up studies replicating the Minneapolis Experiment, however, yielded less conclusive results. In fact, in some cases, offenders who were arrested had higher levels of recidivism than those who were not arrested. Such findings led some, including Sherman, to call for the repeal of mandatory arrest laws. After further research examining the dynamics between socioeconomic status, domestic violence and the likelihood of repeated abuse, Sherman developed a community-specific law enforcement policy advocating mandatory arrest of batterers in neighborhoods with low unemployment and discretionary arrest in those with high unemployment ("Arresting Development in . . .," 2001, p.1). His reasoning was based on findings that arrest increased recidivism among unemployed suspects by 52 percent but reduced subsequent violence by 37 percent among batterers who were employed. Sherman's conclusion: officers should be allowed discretion in deciding whether to make an arrest.

Results of the most recent study on the effects of police action in domestic violence has found "good evidence" that arrest of batterers is consistently and directly, though modestly, related to reduced subsequent aggression against female intimate partners (Maxwell et al., 2001, p.9). Maxwell et al. (2002, p.51) report: "These results lend limited support for policies favoring arrest over informal police responses to intimate partner violence. However, the analyses also show that despite police intervention, a minority of suspects repeatedly victimize their partners and that factors other than formal sanctions play larger roles in explaining the cessation or continuation of aggressive behavior between intimates."

Research by Finn et al. (2004, p.565) found: "Dual arrests in family violence cases have increased following passage of proarrest laws." Their research found: "Officers who believed that their department would support arrest of both parties were more likely to arrest both parties. Officers who perceived that their department encouraged arrest of the primary aggressor only are more likely to arrest the husband only. When both parties were injured, officers were likely to arrest both. Experienced officers were more likely than novice officers to use dual arrest."

In formulating a response, police might consider the difference between **instrumental violence** (that used to control) and **expressive violence** (that resulting from hurt feelings, anger or rage). Arrest may work best for batterers who use instrumental violence, but other methods, such as learning to mediate differences, may work better with batterers who use expressive violence.

**"Failure to Protect" Lawsuits**   In many states, officers who have evidence that an assault has occurred have no choice but to make an arrest. The case largely responsible for this change in approach is *Thurman v. City of Torrington* (1984), in which Tracey Thurman, over a period of eight months, contacted Torrington police on at least 11 separate occasions to report threats upon her life and the life of her child made by her estranged husband, Charles Thurman.

Between October 1982 and June 1983, Charles's threatening behavior became more violent, and after he smashed Tracey's windshield while she was inside the vehicle, he was placed on probation and ordered to stay away from her. However, Charles, ignoring the conditions set for his probation, continued to threaten Tracey, and the police continued to respond to her calls with their "oh, no, not again" attitude. On May 6, 1983, she obtained a court-issued restraining order forbidding Charles from assaulting, threatening and harassing her. And on June 10, 1983, when Charles went to her house demanding to see her, Tracey called the police asking he be picked up for violating his probation. About 15 minutes later, expecting police to arrive shortly, Tracey went outside to talk to Charles, who then stabbed her 13 times in the chest, neck and throat. Ten minutes later (25 minutes after her call), a single officer arrived on the scene to witness Charles drop a bloody knife and kick Tracey in the head as she lay on the ground. Thurman sued the police department for "failure to protect."

At the trial, the department defended its "hands off" response as a means of promoting domestic harmony by refraining from interference in marital disputes. The jury, however, decided the police response had been less than adequate, evidencing a pattern of deliberate indifference on the part of the police department to the complaints of the plaintiff Tracey Thurman and to its duty to protect her. The court added an officer may not "automatically decline to make an arrest simply because the assaulter and his victim are married to each other."

Tracey was awarded $2.6 million dollars. The department appealed, and Thurman later settled out of court for $1.975 million. The case resulted in the passage of the Family Violence Protection and Response Act in Connecticut and has resulted in more than 60,000 arrests. The message in the law is clear: domestic violence is a crime.

 *Thurman v. City of Torrington* (1984) established that domestic violence is an assault rather than simply a family affair. Officers and departments can be sued for "failure to protect."

Police departments that develop and implement proarrest policies in domestic assaults can substantially reduce the risk of being sued for federal civil rights violations alleging discrimination. Another way to reduce liability and exposure to lawsuits is to require officers responding to domestic assault calls to document when and why no arrest was made—for example, there was a lack of probable cause because no injuries were visible on the victim, no signs of a struggle, and the like.

## Batterer Intervention Programs

Jackson (2003, p.1) explains the origin of batterer intervention programs: "With the establishment of proarrest policies in the 1980s, increasing numbers of batterers were seen in criminal courts across the country. Initially, they were sentenced to jail. Some victims, however, began to say that although they wanted the battering to stop, they did not want their partners incarcerated. To respond to these requests while still holding the batterers accountable, offenders were referred to batterer intervention programs (BIPs, also known as spouse abuse abatement programs or SAAPs)." Jackson, program manager in NIJ's Office of Research and Evaluation, reports: "Although early evaluations suggested that BIPs reduce battering, recent evaluations based on more rigorous designs find little or no reduction. The methodological limitations of virtually all these evaluations, however, make it impossible to say how effective BIPs are." Jackson notes that most of the programs studied were based on the Duluth Model (described later in the chapter).

Gordon and Moriarty (2003) report on the BIP used in Chesterfield County, Virginia, which found only limited support for court-ordered treatment for batterers. Feder and Forde (2003, p.12) report on the Broward, Florida, BIP, based on the Duluth Model, and state: "The results of this study show that counseling had no clear and demonstrable effect on offenders' attitudes, beliefs or behavior." This study did find that the batterer's "stake-in-conformity" was the most significant factor in the rehabilitation process. **Stake-in-conformity variables** include marital status, employment, residential stability and age—all variables offenders might lose if convicted for a repeat offense.

 The Broward batterer intervention program found that marriage, home ownership and steady employment led to fewer violent offenses after an offender completed a batterers' intervention program.

The NIJ Report *Batterers' Intervention Programs: Where Do We Go from Here?* notes that most BIP programs are based on the Duluth Model. The report concludes that the programs in Broward County, Florida, and Brooklyn, New York, show little or no effect on reoffense rates, and no impact on batterers' attitudes about domestic violence (Jackson et al., 2003).

**The Controversial Duluth Model**   Pence and Paymar (2004, p.376) explain: "The Duluth Model was designed in 1981 as a coordinated community response of law enforcement, the criminal and civil courts and human service providers working together to hold offenders accountable for the behaviors and to make communities safer for victims." The goal of the program, according to Pence and Paymar, is "to help offenders understand that their beliefs about women, men and marriage contribute to their abusive behavior; that violence is intentional and a choice; that most violence is designed to control an intimate partner; that the effects of abusive behavior damage the family and that each abuser has the ability to change." They note: "The Duluth Model has been mischaracterized as a counseling program." They also criticize the findings of the NIJ stating: "The NIJ recognized the methodological shortcomings in their own research."

Sanow (2003, p.4) cites the findings of the NIJ study of BIPs and their conclusions and then puts forth other shortcomings of the Duluth model: "The Duluth Model has two glaring weaknesses: (1) Since the batterers' motivations for violence differ, the same type of program may not work with all batterers. (2) The Duluth Model, based on white feminist theories, doesn't work with minority populations." Sanow points out that alternative programs such as Emerge, Amend and Choice exist and should be considered because: "These alternative programs have also been reviewed to see if they work. In 21 out of 24 controlled studies, the reoffense rates were lower."

## *Helping Victims Deal with the Assault*

Besides arresting the abuser, officers responding to calls of domestic assault can help battering victims by making them aware of the many resources available to them. Support groups, counseling programs and shelters have been established throughout the country to help victims of domestic violence. Other strategies that also may effectively address the problem include establishing programs to rehabilitate those who commit domestic violence, and using protective and restraining orders and assuring that such orders are adhered to.

**Restraining Orders**   A civil restraining order, also called a Temporary Restraining Order (TRO), is a legally enforceable document that limits physical contact between abuser and abusee. Furthermore, a TRO is valid anywhere a victim might go within the country. Article IV, Section 1 of the U.S. Constitution contains the phrase, "Full faith and credit shall be given in each state to the public acts, records, and judicial proceedings of every other state." It is this provision that allows such things as marriage licenses and driver's licenses to have nationwide validity, regardless of which state issued them.

Despite a federal law requiring officers to honor out-of-state protection orders, many agencies remain ignorant of this provision and how to handle such orders. According to the Office for Victims of Crime (*Enforcement of Protective Orders*, 2002, p.1): "Whereas all states have enacted laws authorizing the issuance of civil or criminal protective orders, available enforcement tools vary from state to state."

While orders of protection are a primary weapon in the fight against domestic violence and have been effective in reducing or stopping violence in some domestic relationships, they are only as good as the enforcement of them and the soundness of an officer's discretion. Newspaper reports of women who had restraining orders having been killed are all too common. A two-frame editorial cartoon lampooning the effectiveness of orders of protection shows, in one frame, a man's fists, feet, a gun, a knife and a baseball bat. The other frame showed a woman's hand holding a piece of paper containing the words *Restraining Order*.

Another type of domestic violence requiring an enhanced awareness by and response of law enforcement is stalking, as Burgess et al. (2001, p.309) assert: "Compared to battering, stalking behavior appears to have an added level of dangerousness."

# Stalking

If the goal of domestic abuse is to exert power and control over a victim, often through fear, stalking certainly qualifies as such abuse. The Office for Victims of Crime (OVC) defines stalking as "the willful or intentional commission of a series of acts that would cause a reasonable person to fear death or serious bodily injury and that, in fact, does place the victim in fear of death or serious bodily injury" (*Strengthening Antistalking Statutes*, 2002, p.1). Stalking is a crime in every state.

Most stalking cases involve a male offender and a female victim who had a prior intimate relationship with each other. In addition to this primary category of intimate or former intimate stalking, two other categories exist: acquaintance stalking, where the stalker and victim may know each other casually and may even have dated once or twice but were never intimate; and stranger stalking, commonly found in cases involving celebrities and other public figures, where no prior relationship between the stalker and victim exists.

A study by Burgess et al. (p.309) identified two basic types of batterer stalking patterns: "In the Ambivalent Contact Pattern, estranged partners tended to contact their partners at home, at work and in public places; send flowers or contact partners' friends or family; and send letters and watch their partners surreptitiously. In the Predatory Contact Pattern, they made hang-up calls, threatened to cause harm, threatened to kill their partners, entered their partners' homes without permission, followed their partners' cars and physically harmed their partners." Burgess et al., while admitting the relationship between battering and stalking behaviors is not yet fully understood, suggest the identification of predatory stalking behaviors can be a valuable tool to law enforcement officers when attempting to assess when stalking behavior is likely to lead to an escalation of violence.

## The Police Response

Wood and Wood (2002, p.4) suggest: "In particular, law enforcement personnel should look for signs of behavior that are sinister, disjointed, bizarre or extremely unreasonable." They (p.5) suggest: "Because stalking may precede violent crimes against persons or property, early recognition of these phenomena may provide opportunities for early intervention to prevent subsequent violence. Threat assessment is the term used to describe the set of investigative and operational techniques that can be used by law enforcement professionals to identify, assess and manage the risks of target violence and its potential perpetrators. Threats are not necessarily predictive in the sense that individuals being stalked always will become victims of violence; however, threats obviously may require further investigation."

When officers conduct threat assessments, Wood and Wood (p.6) suggest they consider that victims are more at risk when stalkers corresponded with them for over one year; sought face-to-face contact; formed detailed, plausible plans; stated specific times, dates and places that contact would occur; telephoned and wrote their victims; and sent them letters originating from more than one location."

Wood and Wood also suggest that the following factors were not predictive. Stalkers who communicated anonymously were not more dangerous than those who signed their communications. In addition, no link has been established between stalkers who harassed their targets with or without accompanying threats. And no predictive value has been found between those stalkers who threatened their victims and those stalkers who approached their targets.

## Cyberstalking

*Cyberstalking*—the repeated use of the Internet, e-mail or other electronic communication device to harass or threaten another person—presents another challenge for law enforcement due to the anonymity afforded offenders. Hitchcock (2003, p.18) contends: "Cyberstalking is an escalated form of online harassment directed at a specific person that causes substantial emotional distress and serves no legitimate purpose. The action is to annoy, alarm and emotionally abuse another person." According to D'Ovidio and Doyle (2003, pp.11–12): "When compared to other cybercrimes, cyberstalking has been the most prevalent crime reported to and investigated by CITU [Computer Investigation and Technology Unit of the New York City Police Department] since the unit's inception."

The U.S. Justice Department has urged law enforcement agencies to provide officers the computer training they need to investigate cyberstalking: "Citing reports that some victims have been told by local police simply to change their telephone numbers or turn off their computers, the Justice Department said that such responses are 'not acceptable'" ("Police Agencies Lack . . .," 2001, p.7).

D'Ovidio and Doyle (p.15) likewise suggest: "Administrators should prioritize technical training that provides investigators with the knowledge needed to perform e-mail-related forensics." They (p.14) note: "The global reach of the Internet and the instantaneous nature of computer-mediated communication present law enforcement with jurisdictional issues that could negatively impact the investigation and the subsequent prosecution of computer crimes."

Another form of domestic violence challenging police officers is child abuse.

## Child Abuse

Hess and Drowns (2004, p.552) define **child abuse** as: "Any physical, emotional or sexual trauma to a child for which no reasonable explanation, such as an accident, can be found. Child abuse includes neglecting to give proper care and attention to a young child." Parents who deny their children the food, clothing and nurturing they require are guilty of neglect, which can be just as damaging to the child as physical abuse. The Administration for Children and Families (ACF) (2001) defines child abuse and neglect as, at minimum: "Any recent act or failure to act on the part of a parent or caretaker which results in death, serious physical or emotional harm, sexual abuse or exploitation; or an act or failure to act which presents an imminent risk of serious harm."

According to *Child Maltreatment* (2004):
- An estimated 896,000 children were determined to be victims of child abuse or neglect in 2002.
- Children ages birth to 4 years had the highest rates of victimization.
- An estimated 1,400 children died due to abuse or neglect; 76 percent of those killed were younger than four.
- More than 80 percent of perpetrators of maltreatment were parents.

Why parents abuse their children is perplexing. Sometimes it is out of frustration. Sometimes it is from unrealistic expectations. Often abusing parents feel their children "have it coming" because of words or actions. And sometimes it is simply, and sadly, the only way a parent knows to treat their children, having been raised in an abusive home themselves.

Frequently, child abuse and neglect occur together, although either one alone constitutes *maltreatment,* a term that encompasses all variations of abuse (physical, emotional, sexual) and neglect (physical, emotional, educational). The younger the victim, the more likely the perpetrator is to be a family member.

Children who are abused or neglected may grow up with poor self-images and view the world as hostile and violent. They tend to perpetuate this dysfunctional behavior in the relationships and families they form as adults. Finkelhor and Ormrod (2003, p.1) assert: "The impact of [child abuse and neglect] on young victims can be devastating, and the violent or sexual victimization of children can often lead to an intergenerational cycle of violence and abuse." Underscoring the link between child abuse and delinquency, English et al. (2002) report: "Our findings strongly support the relationship between child abuse and neglect and delinquency, adult criminality and violent criminal behavior. Abused and neglected children are 48 times more likely to be arrested as juveniles, 2 times more likely to be arrested as an adult and 3.1 times more likely to be arrested for a violent crime than matched controls." These findings replicate earlier studies. Loeber et al. (2001) contend that being victimized may lead youths to engage in illegal activities, associate with delinquent peers, victimize other delinquents and avoid legal recourse in resolving conflicts. In addition, Kilpatrick et al. (2003, p.1) note the emotional consequences that youths experience because of victimization, including psychological disorders as well as substance abuse and dependence.

Data from the Office of Juvenile Justice and Delinquency Prevention (OJJDP) indicates as many as 10 million children have been witness to or victims of violence in their homes or communities (Streit, 2001, p.50). In addition (p.50): "The OJJDP has also found that approximately 2 million adolescents, ages 12 to 17, appear to have suffered from post traumatic stress disorder, stemming from violent experiences in their past." Such a history may send these youths down a future course of repeated and increasingly serious run-ins with law enforcement.

Adolescence is a difficult time for many youths as they experience physical and emotional changes. Their emerging sexuality and growing independence can be extremely difficult to live with. They may become involved with drugs or alcohol. They may join gangs. At the same time, their parents may be entering middle age and facing their own personal crises. Adolescents who are abused have an option not available to younger children—they can simply run away. Many become part of the homeless population and often turn to prostitution or crime to support themselves.

Even when children are not themselves the direct targets of abuse, they may become "invisible victims" through continued exposure to other abusive relationships. According to Streit (p.50): "Children who witness domestic violence experience higher levels of behavioral, social and emotional problems than those who live in a caring environment." Osofsky (2001, p.3) echoes: "Both research and clinical work have shown that witnessing community and domestic violence has a consistently negative impact on children's emotional, social and cognitive development, although it affects children of different ages in different ways."

Educators are the most common source of reports of abuse and neglect to child protective service agencies. And as Finkelhor and Ormrod (p.2) note:

> Child abuse can come to the attention of police in a variety of ways: from victims and their families, from concerned community members, from professionals such as teachers and doctors, and from other authorities such as child welfare agencies. Professionals in all States, and even ordinary citizens in some States, are mandated to report child abuse to responsible authorities. In some States, police are considered to be the responsible authority for reporting purposes, and in many States, statutes now require child welfare authorities to share all child maltreatment reports with law enforcement. Child welfare

investigations substantiate or confirm about one-third of all child maltreatment reports. In some States, these investigations are conducted jointly by child welfare and police; in a few jurisdictions, responsibility for investigation lies with law enforcement only. Thus the police have become increasingly involved in child abuse cases, but their role in reporting and investigating child abuse can vary quite a bit from jurisdiction to jurisdiction.

## *The Police Response*

Historically, as with spousal abuse, law enforcement agencies were reluctant to pursue reports of child abuse with the same vigor as calls involving other, more traditional offenses. Today, however, there is no denying the responsibility of the police in regard to abused children: "When parents assault or molest their children, it is conventionally thought of as child abuse and, therefore a child welfare problem. However, these acts are also crimes, and a substantial portion of child abuse cases are investigated and adjudicated by the criminal justice system" (Finkelhor and Ormrod, p.1).

When police are called about child abuse, their first responsibility is to the child. In many states, if it appears the child is in danger, police may take the child into protective custody. In addition, officers responding to a domestic call involving adults must remain aware of the "invisible victimization" suffered by children who witness violence in the home and tend to these young victims as well. Whatever the exact nature of the call, Streit (p.51) offers several guidelines for officers approaching a scene where children are involved:

- Officers should travel in pairs to the highly charged and potentially dangerous scene and remain calm when they arrive which, in turn, will help those involved at the scene stay calm as well.
- Officers must look for the children when surveying the scene to ensure they are safe. Children often hide when they are frightened, making it sometimes difficult for officers to determine their presence.
- Officers must make sure the children and any other apparent victim stays safe. This may mean officers have to take the victim with them when they leave the scene.

As one detective stated: "In the past . . . children's names wouldn't even be documented as being at the scene of a domestic situation. They were left with the other parent or a caring guardian to get help. The police didn't get involved. Today, things have changed" (Streit, p.51). Officers may help mitigate the effects of experiencing or witnessing abuse just by talking with children. Streit (p.54) states:

> Although officers may not realize it, they help tremendously by simply reassuring children that things can get better and that they are available if help is needed. "I can think of a number of times when children were given a message that the officer or detective was going to do what they could to keep that child safe," says [one counselor]. "This message of hope and safety are crucial first steps in helping children begin to believe that their lives might be 'normal' or at least the abuse will stop."

Police should also be alert to children who are present when adults are arrested. Often additional charges of *endangering children* should be made, and those children should also be taken into protective custody. Harris (2004, p.8) notes the danger posed by adults who expose children to toxic meth lab operations, firearms, pornographic material and criminal activity: "Methamphetamine abuse and production have become major factors in the increase of child abuse and neglect cases. Estimates have indicated that children are found in approximately one-third of all seized meth labs. Of those children, about 35 percent test positive for toxic levels of chemicals in their bodies. In other areas, those numbers have proven even higher. More alarming, however, is the possibility that 90 percent of all meth labs go undetected, leaving many children to suffer needlessly."

Officers' next responsibility is to thoroughly investigate the situation. Interviews with family members, medical records, reports from welfare workers and interviews with neighbors can all help determine if a charge of child abuse is warranted. Police must be especially careful when charges of child sexual abuse are involved, as such allegations can do much damage and destroy reputations, even if unfounded. The interviews also can provide information as to whether the child can be returned to the home or should be placed in a foster home.

Interviewing child victims and witnesses requires much sensitivity and adherence to certain protocol. Streit (p.51) notes: "In the past after the abused child was removed from the scene, the child would be interviewed multiple times. Interviews were first done by a counselor, then police, detectives, social workers, medical examiners, therapists and finally the district attorney in court. 'By the time it got to trial, the child didn't want to talk about what happened,' [one detective] says. This caused a lot of undue trauma to the kids, and forcing them to talk about it over and over was actually hurting them more."

Two Supreme Court decisions affect children's testimony in abuse and neglect cases. The Court held in *Maryland v. Craig* (1990) that the Sixth Amendment "right to confront witnesses" does not always mandate face-to-face confrontation between a defendant and a child abuse victim-witness at trial, if the child victim-witness will be emotionally traumatized by testifying in the defendants' presence. In *Idaho v. Wright* (1990), the Court ruled that an out-of-court statement by an alleged child sexual abuse victim is not automatically deemed trustworthy nor guaranteed to be admitted at trial, but also ruled that an out-of-court statement may be admitted if it is determined the child making the statement is likely to be telling the truth.

States vary in the standard of proof required to substantiate allegations of child abuse and neglect, ranging from a case worker's judgment, to some credible evidence, or a preponderance of evidence. However, some cases of abuse are obvious. For example, in a well-publicized 1996 case, a Chicago couple faced multiple charges of child abuse after their four children told authorities their parents had fed them a "regular diet" of boiled rats and cockroaches and had repeatedly raped and drugged them for the past four years. And in 1999, $2^1/_2$-year-old Miguel Arias-Baca spent the final moments of his short life getting slammed against the floor. He died slowly and painfully, his brain swelling with blood and his face smeared with his own feces, after his drunken foster father returned home from a Super Bowl party to find the toddler with a dirty diaper.

Sometimes these fatal tragedies result from a single violent episode. Most often, however, they are the culmination of months, even years, of abuse that somehow went unnoticed or fell through the cracks of the child protective and criminal justice services.

## Special Challenges Related to Child Abuse Investigations

Some cases of child abuse present special challenges to responding officers, including child sexual abuse cases and cases involving "brittle bone disease" or Munchausen syndrome by proxy.

**Child Sexual Abuse Cases**   As with other forms of neglect or abuse, the sexual victimization of children can have devastating effects on the victims and can lead to an intergenerational cycle of violence and abuse. The media have reported several instances of child sexual abuse by Catholic priests. Such reports might lead to the conclusion that this crime is on the increase. However, statistics show a decline in child sexual abuse cases. Finkelhor and Jones (2004, p.1) report: "The number of sexual abuse cases substantiated by child protective service (CPS) agencies dropped a remarkable 40 percent between 1992 and 2000, from an estimated 150,000 cases to 89,500 cases."

Complicating the challenge of investigating allegations of child sexual abuse is the fact that the Internet has entered the picture. According to Wolak et al. (2003, p.1): "Law enforcement at all levels made an estimated 2,577 arrests during the 12 months starting July 1, 2000, for Internet sex crimes against minors." They suggest that because Internet sex crimes against minor include a diverse range of offenses, cases sharing crucial common elements in terms of challenges posed for law enforcement investigators should be grouped into categories such as those shown in Figure 7.2.

The second category involved undercover operations in which officers went on Internet chatrooms posing as minors, usually in the age range of 13 to 15, and waited to be contacted by adults seeking sexual encounters. The undercover officers were careful not to initiate any conversations about sexual topics, and they kept logs of all their online conversations to be used as evidence in court. The online relationships culminated in face-to-face meetings where the offenders were arrested and charged with attempted sexual assault or other offenses. According to the study by Wolak et al., the vast majority of offenders were non-Hispanic white males older than 25.

Whether the youthful victim of sexual abuse is contacted via the Internet or in some other way, in some rare cases the result is the ultimate form of abuse: a sex-related child abduction homicide. Geberth (2004, p.32) reports: "Although the data indicates that these incidents are statistically rare [between 100 to 200 cases annually], they are horrendous crimes." He (p.33) stresses: "Delays in reporting missing children become critical. Consider the fact that a little under half of the children are murdered within one hour of being abducted, three quarters are dead within three hours, and nine out of 10 are often killed within 24 hours. Any delay can make a difference in whether the victim is found alive."

Officers should conduct a neighborhood canvass in the area of the victim's last known location, the victim/killer contact site, the body recovery site and any other site determined to be important to the investigation. According to Geberth (p.36): "The majority of suspects in these cases are white males, averaging 27 years old, single, living with someone else, unemployed or under employed if working, considered strange by others, with a history of past violent crimes against children."

Another challenge related to investigations of child abuse is when a medical condition mimics the signs of physical abuse.

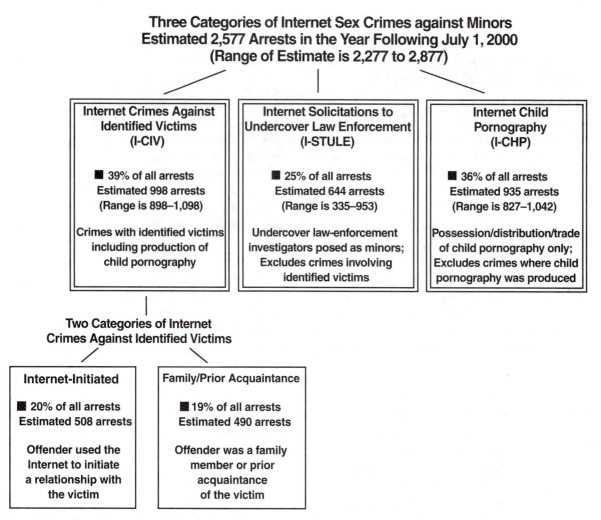

**Figure 7.2**    Three Categories of Internet Sex Crimes against Minors

SOURCE: Janis Wolak, Kimberly Mitchell and David Finkelhor. *Internet Sex Crimes against Minors: The Response of Law Enforcement*, Washington, DC: National Center for Missing and Exploited Children, 2003. Reprinted by permission.

**Osteogenesis Imperfecta (OI)**    More commonly known as "brittle bone disease," **osteogenesis imperfecta** is a medical condition characterized by bones that break easily. Because child abuse is also characterized by broken bones, false accusations of child abuse may occur in families with children who suffer from OI. Unfortunately, when false accusations of child abuse occur, families become victimized. Consequently, it is critical for responding officers to be aware of such conditions and to not automatically discount a parent's denial of child abuse. A thorough investigation will include interviews with social services staff and medical professionals. Cases in which parents are found to have a history of often changing the hospitals or physicians who treat their children *may* indicate an attempt to hide child abuse. In other instances, children who are frequently admitted to the hospital may be the victims of a form of abuse known as Munchausen syndrome by proxy.

**Munchausen Syndrome by Proxy**    As Chiczewski and Kelly (2003, p.20) explain, **Munchausen syndrome by proxy (MSBP)** is a "bizarre psychiatric ailment that leads a person to fabricate a child's illnesses to fulfill their own needs for attention and sympathy." They stress: "Law enforcement personnel and EMS providers need to know the significance of behavioral artifacts in the recognition, investigation and prosecution of MSBP offenders. Chiczewski and Kelly (p.22) offer the following guidelines to help identify a case of MSBP:

- A described medical problem that does not respond to the normal course of treatment
- Multiple responses to the same location for the same patient with similar complaints or a variety of illnesses
- A family history of similar incidents with siblings, including multiple SIDS [sudden infant death syndrome] within the family
- Signs and symptoms disappear upon the child's removal from the parent
- Attempts by a caregiver to convince others of illness even in the absence of signs and symptoms

Children themselves may become perpetrators of family violence, when they are grown and turn abusive to their elderly parents. Thus, the elderly may be as vulnerable to violence as children are.

## Elder Abuse

Jordan (2002, p.23) suggests: "The criminal justice system and, in particular, law enforcement face the aging population as a special challenge for the 21st century." In 1900 the average life expectancy of U.S. residents was only 47 years. A century later, that figure has nearly doubled, and the elderly, those age 65 and up, will soon outnumber children for the first time in our country's history. The U.S. Bureau of the Census projects that by 2030, the U.S. population over age 65 will number about 70 million, more than double the number of seniors in 1998 (Garrett, 2001a, p.56). Census data also reveals the fastest-growing segment of the elderly population is occurring among Americans age 85 and older. Duncan (2001, p.75) asserts: "The unparalleled increase in the number of elderly persons living in the United States is having a major impact not only on the nation's health care and social service delivery systems but also on law enforcement."

With the increasing number of elderly comes an increasing number of elder abuse cases. **Elder abuse** includes the physical and emotional trauma, financial exploitation and general neglect of a person aged 65 or older. Elder abuse affects people of all races and ethnicities, religions, socioeconomic groups and educational levels. According to Garrett (2001a, p.57): "Elder abuse today is at the level of awareness that child abuse was in the '60s and domestic abuse was in the '80s and '90s". Payne and Berg (2003, p.439) report: "The 1990s witnessed the criminalization of elder abuse. This criminalization included the creation of mandatory-reporting legislation, increased penalties for elder abusers, and modification in criminal procedure for older victims."

Just as it is difficult to understand how parents could abuse their children, it is difficult to understand how adult children could abuse their elderly parents. Literature suggests multiple causes of abuse and that most instances are not intentional and preconceived but are the result of the accumulation of stress and limited knowledge and resources for the person providing care. Elderly victims, however, often allow the abuse to continue, being either unwilling or unable to report it. For example, an elderly parent being "cared for" at home by a grown child may fear that reporting the abuse will lead to the caretaker's arrest and incarceration, thus forcing the elderly victim into a nursing home. On the other hand, if the elder reports the abuse and the caretaker is not arrested, the elder may end up in an even more violent situation with an abusive caretaker seeking retaliation for being "told on." Elderly parents may choose not to report abuse because they feel guilty, ashamed and embarrassed that their own children are mistreating them. Sometimes elderly parents either do not know who to report abuse to or are physically unable to report it, perhaps because they are bedridden with no access to a telephone or they have no visitors. Other times, the abused elders are so disoriented, confused or otherwise impaired they do not recognize their mistreatment as abusive.

Elderly residents in nursing homes also have been abused, physically and sexually, by caregivers and sometimes even by other residents. As with the elderly parents living with their children, nursing home residents may have no way to contact help and may fear retribution if they claim they are being abused.

Many other elderly people are not physically abused; they are simply neglected, deprived of all but the most basic necessities. Still others are financially exploited, targeted by unscrupulous scam artists and bilked out of their life savings, or defrauded by caregivers or relatives. Johnson (2004, p.7) divides financial crimes against the elderly into two categories: stranger and relative/caregiver. Johnson describes types of fraud perpetrated on the elderly such as phony prizes and sweepstakes, investment scams, solicitations for nonexistent charities, predatory loans and mortgages, bogus insurance and confidence games; and telemarketing, mail and face-to-face contract schemes.

## Indications of Financial Crimes against the Elderly

Johnson (2004, pp.23–24) provides indicators of financial abuse, including:

- A recent acquaintance expresses an interest in finances, promises to provide care or ingratiates him- or herself with the elder.
- A relative or caregiver has no visible means of support and is overly interested in the elder's financial affairs.
- A relative or caregiver expresses concern over the cost of caring for the elder, or is reluctant to spend money for needed medical treatment.
- The utility and other bills are not being paid.
- The elder's placement, care or possessions are inconsistent with the size of his or her estate.
- A relative or caregiver isolates the elder, makes excuses when friends of family call or visit, and does not give the elder messages.
- Checking account and credit card statements are sent to a relative or caregiver and are not accessible to the elder.
- At the bank, the elder is accompanied by a relative or caregiver who refuses to let the elder speak for him- or herself, and/or the elder appears nervous or afraid of the person accompanying him or her.
- The elder is concerned or confused about "missing money."

## The Police Response

Domestic elder abuse should be defined and documented as a crime separate from assault, battery, burglary, murder or some other category. This would accomplish two purposes: raise awareness of the problem and help outline a proper police response to the problem. Garrett (2001a, p.57) contends: "Law enforcement must play a critical role in a three-fold response to elder/disabled issues within the community." The first step is prevention and an effort to empower the elderly by providing information about abuse that will protect them from victimization. The second step is to identify the at-risk population such as those elderly dependent on others for some or all of their basic daily needs. The third step is for law enforcement to recognize and understand why the elderly are abused and develop a comprehensive strategy to meet the needs of these victims.

Because physical evidence of assault or neglect is vital to establishing a charge of elder abuse, officers responding to a call where physical abuse is suspected should examine the elderly victim for indicators such as fractures, bruises, burns, lacerations and punctures. Officers should look for the presence of old and new wounds and be alert to difficulties the elderly victim has with walking or sitting, recognizing that mobility impairment is also a normal part of aging.

Evidence of psychological abuse is more difficult to detect but may manifest as depression, a change in personality, a loss of interest in themselves and their surroundings, anger or agitation.

Law enforcement must also respond to financial abuse of the elderly, as Duncan (p.75) notes: "Criminals have learned that targeting the elderly and involving them in fraudulent schemes and scams is very lucrative." Financial abuse includes stealing, embezzling or misusing money or possessions, savings or stocks, misusing the person's property or other resources and denying the elderly a home.

Sometimes the grown children are responsible for financially exploiting their elderly parents. Garrett (2001a, p.58) states: "An important consideration is that in many cases the elderly victim is the financial stronghold to the abuser's lifestyle. This is in contrast to what . . . many first responders believe to be true. 'First responders tend to see the elderly as below the poverty level,' [says one officer], 'but by the time we get called into an elder abuse situation, the abuser has stripped the financial resources of the elderly person to where they are destitute.' " Elder abuse also includes neglect that may take the form of abandonment or denial of food, shelter, clothing, basic hygiene practices and medical attention. Often abusers rely on over-medicating their victims to control them.

While interviewing abused elders directly is a preferred police response, often the victim is confused or unable to grasp what has happened. Elderly victims may have impaired mental abilities or memories. In such instances, information provided by other people becomes extremely important. If elderly victims live at home, all those who have contact with the victims should be interviewed. If elderly victims live with one of their children, all family members should be interviewed. If elderly victims live in a nursing home, other residents of the home as well as the care providers should be interviewed. The past record of the institution should be looked into, including any violations of licensing standards reported to the state department of human services or whatever agency issues licenses to nursing homes.

## Cooperative Efforts

As with other areas of domestic violence, cooperative efforts in responding to elder abuse are critical and can include social workers, mental health workers, elder protective services, hospital workers, shelters for the elderly and transportation services.

According to Garrett (2001a, p.59): "It takes more than just a desire to help to provide meaningful services for seniors. It takes a multi-jurisdictional approach. . . . Starting a TRIAD within a community can be a logical way to begin providing needed services. . . . TRIAD is a collaborative effort of police and senior organizations throughout the nation. . . . TRIAD surveys the community to determine what seniors view as needed and then the various agencies work together to ensure these services are provided."

## Community Policing and Domestic Violence

As stressed throughout this text, multiagency partnerships and a focus on community policing have been shown to increase the effectiveness of police response to crime. The application of such collaborative efforts to the issue of domestic violence is as promising as it is to any other police operation, yet it faces the same challenges found with other areas involving partnerships. Giacomazzi and Smithey (2001, pp.99–100) state: "Traditionally, law enforcement agents, the criminal justice system at large, religious organizations, health care providers and society in general have reinforced the idea that family violence is a family problem. This perception has led to a long history of criminal justice noninterference in family assault cases in the United States." However, these are the very community elements crucial in forming a multiagency collaborative response to domestic violence. Giacomazzi and Smithey (p.117) contend:

> If police agencies are to embrace collaborative problem-solving efforts, police culture, attitudes and practices must change to begin the process of a meaningful response to family violence. This change must embrace a sense of community, with the necessary conditions for collaboration in place. Although this change is easier said than done, the community-policing context— one that encourages these conditions (intraownership, democratic self-management, education, and a true sense of membership)—certainly appears to be a ripe environment for necessary changes to take place that would enhance collaborative efforts.

Osofsky (p.16), likewise, stresses:

> From a law enforcement perspective, community-oriented policing that builds trust and relationships with both juveniles and family members and that is primarily proactive than reactive will go a long way toward preventing juvenile crime and child victimization. Programs to help children cope with trauma must be able to address the issues of domestic violence and trauma to parents or caregivers. By incorporating these elements into future prevention and intervention programs and continuing to study effective strategies, practitioners can help break the cycle of violence by minimizing youth victimization and exposure to violence.

These same collaborative efforts might be used to address school violence.

## School Violence

As Small and Tetrick (2001, p.3) note: "Crime and violence in schools are matters of significant public concern, particularly after the spate of tragic school shootings in recent years." And, as Pollack and Sundermann (2001, p.13) contend: "More than anything else, the school shootings of recent years have taught us that school safety is not about any one method of control: metal detectors, surveillance systems or swift punishment. . . . We now understand that safe schools require broad-based efforts on the part of the entire community, including educators, students, parents, law enforcement agencies, businesses and faith-based organizations."

As noted earlier, educators are commonly the ones who detect and report to authorities incidents of suspected child abuse or family violence. Educators may also, however, be first-hand witnesses to and, on occasion, victims of violence, as the aggression experienced at home by some children finds its way onto school grounds. A variety of elements may lead police in a certain jurisdiction to have to respond to incidents of school violence.

While incidents of school violence are to be taken seriously and have received much media attention in recent years, such publicity has also generated a widespread, baseless fear that today's schools are teeming with youths more valueless and violent than ever before. In fact, in *Indicators of School Crime and Safety*, DeVoe et al. (2003, p.iii) report: "Indicators demonstrate that sizable improvements have occurred in the safety of students: between 1992 and 2001, the violent crime victimization rate at school declined from 48 violent victimizations per 1,000 students in 1992 to 28 such victimizations in 2001. Even so, violence, theft, bullying, drugs and firearms are still prevalent."

Researchers Brown and Benedict (2004, p.372) report: "Almost half of the students [in Brownsville, Texas] reported having seen other students carry knives at school, roughly 1 in 10 reported having seen other students carry guns at school, and more than 1 in 5 reported being fearful of weapon-associated victimization at school." They (pp.372–373) suggest: "Contrary to media presentations of school violence as an epidemic, most official data indicate that juveniles are less likely to be violently victimized while at school than while away from school. In fact the chance of a child being violently killed at school is less than one in a million."

For many, the words "school violence" bring to mind images of gun-wielding youths, sprays of bullets and unfathomable carnage. Hoang (2001, pp.18–19), however, states: "The definition of school violence, an unacceptable social behavior ranging from aggression to violence that threatens or harms others, goes beyond highly publicized incidents of mass bloodshed to include acts such as bullying, threats and extortion. Therefore, school violence spans a broad range of antisocial behavior that law enforcement must address." One of these behaviors—bullying—is very common on school playgrounds, in neighborhoods and in homes throughout the country and, as Ericson (2001, p.1) observes, "has long been considered an inevitable and, in some ways, uncontrollable part of growing up." However, bullying has very real links to school violence and can sometimes become deadly.

## *Bullying*

"Bullying among school children is a very old and well-known phenomenon" says Olweus (2003, p.12). While some parents, other adults and even students tend to dismiss schoolyard bullying as a "rite of passage," a simple cycle of the big kids "picking on" the little kids, who in turn grow up to be the big kids who pick on the little kids, and so on, the U.S. Department of Education asserts

**bullying** is more than just big versus small: "Bullying involves intentional, repeated hurtful acts, words or other behavior. There is a real or perceived power imbalance between bully and victim" (Peterson, 2001, p.18). Cooper and Snell (2003, p.23) explain: "People who bully take advantage of an imbalance of power, such as greater physical size, higher status or the support of a peer group." Bullying may be:

- Physical—hitting, kicking, spitting, pushing, punching, poking, hair-pulling, biting
- Verbal—name-calling, taunting, gossip, malicious teasing, making threats
- Psychological/Emotional—rejection, humiliation, ostracism, intimidation, extortion, spreading rumors, manipulating social relationships, berating personal characteristics such as perceived sexual orientation
- Sexual—harassment and actual abuse

Ericson (p.1) adds: "Males tend to bully and be bullied more frequently than females. . . . Bullying generally begins in the elementary grades, peaks in the sixth through eighth grades, and persists into high school." Research has shown an estimated 1.6 million children in grades 6 through 10 in the United States are bullied at least once a week, and 1.7 million children bully others as often (Ericson, p.1).

Bullying is a serious concern in the issue of school violence because of its far-reaching and long-lasting impacts beyond a specific "episode" between bully and victim. Sampson (2002, p.1) contends: "Perhaps more than any other school safety problem, bullying affects students' sense of security." In addition, according to Olweus (p.16): "Most students in a classroom with bully/victim problems are involved in or affected by the problem." Ericson (p.1) expands on the effect of bullying: "Bullying can affect the social environment of a school, creating a climate of fear among students, inhibiting their ability to learn, and leading to other antisocial behavior . . . such as vandalism, shoplifting, skipping or dropping out of school, fighting, and the use of drugs and alcohol." Bullying can also lead to criminal behavior later in life: "Pioneering research by Professor Dan Olweus . . . [found] 60 percent of males who were bullies in grades 6 through 9 were convicted of at least one crime as adults, compared with 23 percent of males who did not bully; 35 to 40 percent of these former bullies had three or more convictions by age 24, compared with 10 percent of those who did not bully" (Ericson, pp.1–2).

According to Ahmed and Braithwaite (2004, p.288): "Tackling school bullying is a multidimensional exercise: parents, teachers and children are all important players. Children who are impulsive, who perceive their school as unable to control bullying and whose families appear to be enmeshed in conflict are at greater risk of becoming bullies."

Williams (2004, p.35) asserts: "Antibullying programs only work at a child's early stage of development. At a later stage, the programs must be supported by legislation, for bullies do not grow out of it; rather they grow into criminals. Falcon (2004, p.380) describes a program aimed at decreasing bullying: "Adopt-A-Bully focuses attention on the problem-maker more than on the victim and dovetails nicely with the mandate of the school liaison partnership." In this program the school liaison officer (SLO) and school administrators meet daily to pool information on bullying activities. Once a bully or potential bully is identified, he or she is assigned a mentor, either the SLO or one of the administrators. The program is a combination mentorship for troubled students and a bullying deterrent.

Attention must also be paid to victims of bullying. Some victims of bullying suffer such humiliation and loss of self-esteem they become violent toward themselves. As one professor of social work puts it: "Suicide is bullying's quiet little secret. It's one kid at a time, so it doesn't catch our attention" (Piazza, 2001, p.68). He estimates, however, based on suicide statistics released by the Centers for Disease Control and Prevention, the number of bully-related suicides by children under age 19 or what he calls "bullycides," is in the triple digits. The effects of bullying can also lead its victims to turn their anger and frustration outward.

## School Shootings

According to Garrett (2004, p.6): "School-associated violent deaths jumped to 43 during the 2003–2004 school year, exceeding the number of school deaths over the past two school years combined and totaling more than any other individual school years since before the Columbine shootings." Consider the following excerpt from a 15-year-old boy's journal: "I hate being laughed at. But they won't laugh after they're scraping parts of their parents, sisters, brothers and friends from the wall of my hate."

These words were written by Kip Kinkel, who later killed both of his parents and then went on a shooting spree at his high school in Springfield, Oregon, killing two students and wounding two dozen more. A year later came the tragedy at Columbine High School in Littleton, Colorado, where two shooters killed a dozen students and a teacher and wounded 23 others before turning their guns

© John Gress/Reuters/CORBIS

*On March 22, 2005, police forensic vans sit outside Red Lake Senior High School in Red Lake, a northern Minnesota Indian reservation. The day before a student shot and killed nine people and then turned the gun on himself.*

on themselves. Further investigation revealed the shooters had been plotting for a year to kill at least 500 and blow up their school. As investigators delved into the factors contributing to these and other instances of school violence, one commonality emerged: "The students who fired the guns were picked on. Bullied. Teased. Harassed" ("Bullying, Teasing and . . .," 2001, p.1). As shown in Table 7.1, school shootings have occurred throughout the United States, from Alaska to Florida, from Pennsylvania to California.

Despite the geographic spread, a common thread seems to pull a majority of these events together: "Many of the recent shooters have felt put upon at school. Even the Secret Service worries about bullying. A study run by its National Threat Assessment Center found that in about two-thirds of 37 school shootings over the last 25 years, the attackers felt 'persecuted, bullied, threatened, attacked or injured' " (Peterson, p.17).

Following traditional law enforcement protocol, many have tried profiling the shooters and victims involved in school violence, searching for a pattern that may help predict or prevent similar events in the future. Reporting on the Santana High School shootings in Santee, California, Maran (2001) states: "The shooter is a boy again—this time he's 15, a freshman—and once again, he's a kid who got picked on at school all the time. . . . He [fits] the increasingly familiar profile of the schoolyard gunman—a white teenage boy, a misfit, in a large suburban high school." Pedersen (2002, p.33) adds: "A convincing commonality in the history of perpetrators of school violence is their propensity to animal cruelty. Inquiries into such behaviors should not be overlooked, nor evidence of such behavior minimized."

Teachers and others should avoid relying on profiles or checklists of danger signs to identify the next youth likely to bring lethal violence to a school. According to Wen (2004): "Researchers keep looking for the portrait of a teenage killer, but to little avail." A study by the Secret Service found some school shooters were socially isolated while others were quite popular. Some were bullied, some were not. They came from both intact and broken families, and academic performance ranged from excellent to failing (Peterson, p.19). Echoing the attitude of other experts on student violence: "U.S. Secret Service Assistant Special Agent Matt Doherty stresses the need for law enforcement officers to disregard profiles and make behavior-based assessments when evaluating students for threat potential. 'Look at the individual's behavior,' he says" (Pedersen, p.30).

Wattendorf (2002, p.11) asserts: "In 75 percent of the 37 shooting incidents studied, school shooters disclosed their plans in advance to classmates."

 School violence almost never occurs without warning.

Garrett (p.6) describes this occurrence at Columbine: "In the time leading up to the Columbine massacre, Eric Harris and Dylan Klebold, described by their peers as loners, dorks and outcasts, told others about their desire for revenge and their plans for violence. The kids who heard these things told no one. Had they felt comfortable sharing this information with just one adult—perhaps even a police officer—the lives of 13 people might have been spared." Wen, likewise, notes: "Researchers say the discovery that teenage killers tend to scheme over time and spill secrets can be used to the advantage of educators and police if they stay in touch with students."

**Table 7.1**   Summary of School Shootings in the United States, February 1996–March 2001

| Date | Location and Estimated Population* | Number Killed | Number Wounded | Shooter(s) |
|---|---|---|---|---|
| February 2, 1996 | Moses Lake, WA (16,300) | 2 students, 1 teacher | 1 | Barry Loukaitis, 14 |
| February 19, 1997 | Bethel, AK (6,500) | 1 student, principal | 2 | Evan Ramsey, 16 |
| October 1, 1997 | Pearl, MS (23,600) | 2 students | 7 | Luke Woodham, 16 |
| December 1, 1997 | West Paducah, KY (25,800) | 3 students | 5 | Michael Carneal, 14 |
| December 15, 1997 | Stamps, AR (2,400) | 0 | 2 | Colt Todd, 14 |
| March 24, 1998 | Jonesboro, AR (52,500) | 4 students, 1 teacher | 10 | Mitchell Johnson, 13<br>Andrew Golden, 11 |
| April 24, 1998 | Edinboro, PA (6,800) | 1 teacher | 2 students | Andrew Wurst, 14 |
| May 19, 1998 | Fayetteville, TN (7,500) | 1 | 0 | Jacob Davis, 18 |
| May 21, 1998 | Springfield, OR (50,700) | 2 students | 22 | Kip Kinkel, 15 |
| June 15, 1998 | Richmond, VA (199,300) | 0 | 1 teacher, 1 guidance counselor | Male, 14 |
| April 20, 1999 | Littleton, CO (41,300) | 14 students (including 2 shooters), 1 teacher | 23 | Eric Harris, 18<br>Dylan Klebold, 17 |
| May 20, 1999 | Conyers, GA (8,500) | 0 | 6 | Thomas Solomon, 15 |
| November 19, 1999 | Deming, NM (14,900) | 1 student | 0 | Victor Cordova, Jr., 12 |
| December 6, 1999 | Fort Gibson, OK (3,800) | 0 | 4 students | Seth Trickey, 13 |
| February 29, 2000 | Mt. Morris, MI (3,100) | 1 (6-year-old) | 0 | Male, 6 |
| May 26, 2000 | Lake Worth, FL (29,000) | 1 teacher | 0 | Nathaniel Brazill, 13 |
| March 5, 2001 | Santee, CA (53,900) | 2 | 13 | Charles Williams, 15 |
| March 7, 2001 | Williamsport, PA (29,900) | 0 | 1 | Elizabeth Bush, 14 |
| March 22, 2001 | El Cajon, CA (90,200) | 0 | 5 | Jason Hoffman, 18 |
| March 21, 2005 | Red Lake Indian Reservation, MN (5,162) | 1 teacher, 1 security guard, 7 students and 1 shooter | 10 | Jeff Weise, 17 |

SOURCE: Adapted from Borgna Brunner, editor. *The Time Almanac, 2002*, p.362.

*Population data from the U.S. Bureau of the Census

**Early Warning Signs**   Although use of profiles and checklists is strongly discouraged, early warning signs of violent behavior have been recognized that, when presented in combination, might aid in identifying and referring children who may need help.

Such early warning signs include social withdrawal; excessive feelings of isolation or rejection; being a victim of violence; feelings of being picked on; low school interest and poor performance; expression of violence in writings and drawings; uncontrolled anger; patterns of impulsive and chronic bullying; discipline problems; past history of violent and aggressive behavior; drug and alcohol use; affiliation with gangs; possession of firearms; and threats of violence. None of these signs alone is sufficient for predicting aggression and violence.

## The Police Response

As the nature of school violence has changed over the years, so too has law enforcement's response to such incidents. According to Sanders (2001, p.100):

> The tragic shootings in Littleton, CO, changed the entire landscape of police tactics and training. . . . Gone are the days when the first police officers at the scene of an active shooter were expected merely to contain the scene and call SWAT. . . .
>
> Large and small agencies are accepting they must be adequately prepared at the patrol level to handle such time critical, mega-violent incidents as school shootings. Hard experience has proven these events are not a strictly urban problem, nor can they wait for a traditional SWAT response. Patrol staffs and tactical teams nationwide are expanding their traditional roles, blurring the lines somewhat in a trend toward training and equipping officers at all levels to quickly and decisively put an end to such incidents.
>
> Another trend, particularly among smaller departments, is toward more cross-training and pooling of resources. A comprehensive, step-by-step discussion of police response to school violence is beyond the scope of this text; however, several publications focus in their entirety on this subject. A particularly useful document published by the International Association of Chiefs of Police (IACP), based on the input of more than 500 experts and 15 focus groups with a diverse range of disciplines addressing school violence, is the *Guide for Preventing and Responding to School Violence,* available online at www.theiacp.org.

# In Search of Safer Schools

 An effective three-pronged approach to school security encompasses crisis planning, security technology and school/law enforcement/community partnerships.

## Crisis Planning

Every agency and institution affected or involved during an episode of school violence must decide in advance how they plan to respond, knowing that no two situations will be exactly the same and even the best-laid plans will require on-the-spot, last-minute adjustments. For police, the first step is generally to obtain blueprints or floor plans and to conduct walk-throughs of local schools. Pedersen (p.32) suggests: "Most experts agree that all schools should have a violence prevention plan available for law enforcement officers; one that identifies access points, dark hallways and architectural considerations that will affect physical safety."

Some departments stage mock disasters to test their emergency preparedness for acts of school violence and to identify areas that need improving. Such drills often highlight the importance of collaboration and communication with other agencies to an effective response.

Rosenbarger (2001, p.30) describes such an exercise: "The Benton County, IN, Sheriff's Department's mock shooting at the county's sprawling rural high school involved: tactical teams from four different sheriff's departments; patrol officers from more than a dozen police and sheriff's departments; negotiators from the state police; EMS from three locations; emergency management, paramedics and a moulage team from the regional medical center; electronic and print media from three counties; and a MedEvac helicopter." He (p.36) concludes: "The overall lesson from this training is the same lesson that happens so frequently. Teams cannot train for just one piece of the police response to an emergency and expect the pieces to all fit together seamlessly during the real emergency. At some point, every aspect of the response, from the patrol response to the tactical response, to the command response to the EMS and MedEvac response, must be brought together for a realistic test."

Law enforcement in San Diego County has the dubious distinction of having responded to two high school shootings only 17 days apart, both in March 2001. They credit much of their success in resolving these incidents to the regional communications system (RCS), a network "which provided us with the interoperability we needed to talk with all of the agencies dispatched to the call and coordinate their work at the scene" (Zoll and Munro, 2001, p.55).

Hemmer (2004, p.1) describes the plan devised by the Prince William County (Virginia) Police Department to prevent school shootings: "All sworn members of the Prince William County Police Department are trained in a quick-response method for dealing with school violence that involve an efficient and speedy entry using overwhelming response tactics." He (p.3) notes: "Police officers in the years before Columbine were trained to not go in, but to establish a perimeter and obtain more information before acting. . . . The current thinking [is] to use an overwhelming response—especially in terms of personnel—as soon as possible to limit opportunities for more shootings." Weiss and Davis (2004, p.119) also suggest this approach: "Uniformed on-duty officers or sheriff's deputies are the major or key players; they are the front line." Hemmer (p.1) notes: "The officers are also trained to think for themselves rather than wait for command. . . . Once five officers arrive they just form quickly into a team." In addition to having a plan, many schools are using security technology to enhance school safety.

## Security Technology

A second prong in the effort to achieve safer schools involves security technology, such as weapons screening programs, entry control systems and video cameras. According to Dorn (2001, p.32):

> Currently, students who carry weapons to school are caught only on very rare occasions. Based on student surveys, [a] conservative estimate is that students carry guns to school 18 million times each year. Less than 4,000 student gun expulsions are reported to the United States Department of Education each year. Even after factoring for underreporting, it's estimated that only one gun is recovered for every 4,500 times that a gun is carried to school. For knives and other types of weapons, the rate of carry is even higher, and the recovery rates are lower.

In addition, research by Schreck et al. (2003, p.460) found: "The attempts of schools to protect students through target-hardening strategies (e.g., metal detectors and security guards) were consistently unsuccessful."

Recognizing that a significant proportion of school violence is perpetrated by those who neither attend nor work at the school, many districts are implementing entry control systems, such as photo ID cards, to make it easier to spot outsiders. Video cameras are also being installed as a way to curb school violence. According to Sanchez (2003, p.19): "Remote viewing through surveillance cameras is the wave of the future." Most cameras are not actively monitored but, rather, tape on a continuous loop and are reviewed only when an incident is reported. When a high school in Washington State became beset by bullying problems, the school put the issue under the microscope and gathered as much data as they could. According to Smith-LaBombard (2001, p.10): "Through police incident reports and student surveys, I identified the lunchroom as the center of bullying and harassment. [The] school resource officer had to spend a disproportionate amount of time in the lunchroom to keep a lid on aggression. Students most often mentioned the lunchroom when they talked of feeling unsafe in school." She (p.9) also reports incidents of bullying, harassment and intimidation decreased, in part, as a result of surveillance video cameras being placed in the lunchroom.

While many other schools have found positive benefits in using video cameras and other security devices, technology cannot replace the human factor.

## *Partnerships*

In cannot be emphasized enough that, as with so many other areas of police operations, partnerships are a vital component in an effective response to school violence. As Dorn (p.31) states bluntly: "A school without a law enforcement partnership is as outdated as a school without electricity." While partnerships to address the issue of school violence can take many forms and involve numerous entities, one of the most effective approaches has been to station officers directly on school campuses as school resource officers (SROs).

**School Resource Officers (SROs)**   According to Girouard (2001, p.1): "Part Q of Title I of the Omnibus Crime Control and Safe Streets Act of 1968, as amended, defines the SRO as 'a career law enforcement officer, with sworn authority, deployed in community-oriented policing, and assigned by the employing police department or agency to work in collaboration with school and community-based organizations.' "

Dorn (2004, p.16) notes: "School resource officers serve as important liaisons between police departments and local schools." He (p.18) also notes: "School resource officer programs have had considerable success in reducing violence. SROs have even successfully thwarted a number of planned school shootings and bombings."

Atkinson (2001, p.55) states: "Demand for [SROs] has increased dramatically with heightened public concern about school safety." The reason for this can be understood by looking at the Safe Schools Pyramid developed by the Center for the Prevention of School Violence and illustrated in Figure 7.3.

The pyramid "reflects the importance of the community policing concept in school safety. The community sits at the pyramid's base because the school environment often mirrors what's happening in the community. Community problems can disrupt the school environment and impede learning. The school resource officer (SRO) is the first level of the pyramid itself, depicting the SRO's function as an integral connection between the school and the community.

While SROs have traditionally served to educate students about topics such as pedestrian safety and the dangers of substance abuse, Scott (2001, p.69)

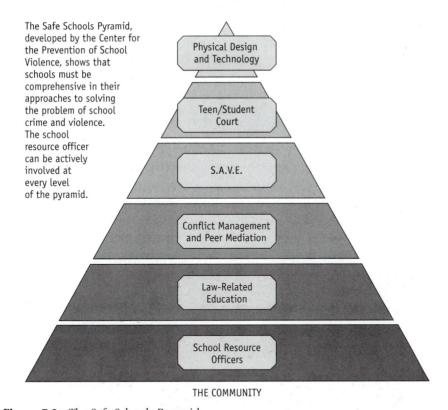

The Safe Schools Pyramid, developed by the Center for the Prevention of School Violence, shows that schools must be comprehensive in their approaches to solving the problem of school crime and violence. The school resource officer can be actively involved at every level of the pyramid.

Physical Design and Technology

Teen/Student Court

S.A.V.E.

Conflict Management and Peer Mediation

Law-Related Education

School Resource Officers

THE COMMUNITY

**Figure 7.3** The Safe Schools Pyramid

SOURCE: Ronnie L. Paynter. "Policing the Schools." *Law Enforcement Technology.* October 1999, p.35. Reprinted by permission of the Center for the Prevention of School Violence.

notes: "More recently the role of the school liaison program has changed as local law enforcement agencies are attempting to defuse potentially violent student situations in light of shootings at high schools across the country in recent years." He adds: "They have realized the need to impact children at an earlier age to help stop a potential problem down the road. The real goal is to keep kids out of the prison system and help them to establish a variety of values early on."

According to a survey by the National Association of School Resource Officers (NASRO), 99 percent of the nearly 700 SROs surveyed report that their program has improved school safety and prevented crime and violence (Lavarello and Trump, 2001, p.63). More specifically, the survey found:

> Two-thirds of the 689 SROs who responded to the NASRO survey indicated that they have prevented a faculty or staff member from being assaulted by a student or someone else on campus. More than 90 percent said that they prevent from 1 to 25 violent acts on campus every year, and most of those reported preventing 11 or more per year. An even larger number of SROs, 94 percent, indicated that students have reported incidents to them in which the student believed that a violent act was imminent. . . .
>
> The survey shows that more than 97 percent of SROs carry firearms. But 83 percent of the respondents replied that they have never had to remove their gun from its holster. Almost all SROs favored being armed.

Miller (2001, p.166) reports: "About 73 percent of police departments with 100 or more sworn employees have SROs on their payrolls." However, communities with large police forces are not the only ones in need of these professionals. Refer again to Table 7.1 and note the estimated population sizes of communities that have experienced weapon-related school violence since 1996. These communities range in size from 2,400 residents to nearly 200,000 residents, and more than one-third of the affected communities had populations less than 10,000. Dorn (p.31) acknowledges that, while full-time SROs are not required at every school, every school should have an effective collaboration with law enforcement.

**Operation CleanSWEEP**   San Bernardino County, California, has developed its own three-pronged approach to school safety through Operation CleanSWEEP (Success With Education/Enforcement Partnership), a triple partnership between the office of the superintendent of schools, the sheriff's department and the court system. Using juvenile citations, security assessment and special projects, this triumvirate tackled the problem of school crime and violence perpetrated by youths who previously had received neither genuine punishment nor rehabilitative guidance. As Penrod (2001, p.21) explains:

> Operation CleanSWEEP is a system that, among many different efforts, places students into *other* programs—programs designed to stymie their unacceptable behavior. For many teenagers, this program represents their first encounter with the concept of personal accountability, and it intends to have them feel the sting of a collective societal reprimand for their actions. At the same time, CleanSWEEP seeks to avoid criminalizing offending students (no permanent criminal record exists for cited students). Moreover, by keeping offenders in the classroom, the program avoids disrupting their education and also helps the school not lose attendance funding due to suspended or expelled students.

He (p.22) concludes: "School resource officers have reported that as offenders have gone through the court system and told other students about their experiences, students have begun to realize that the consequences for personal misbehavior are becoming unavoidable. All in all, Operation CleanSWEEP has had a tremendous impact. Not only have measurably fewer fights and acts of disruption and defiance occurred on participating school campuses but educators and students alike feel safer in their learning environment."

## Other Efforts to Prevent School Violence

Some schools have supplemented their violence prevention efforts with programs, policies and procedures aimed at problematic student behavior. Intervention and behavior modification programs have proven successful in some jurisdictions. For example, a high school once plagued by bullying, harassment and intimidation resolved such issues through a multifaceted effort involving:

- Increased staff presence in identified problem areas, such as the lunchroom.
- Mandatory participation in Harassment Awareness Training class for student harassers.

- A Big Brothers/Big Sisters mentoring program that paired high school and middle school students to help prevent bullying among freshmen.
- Workshops that brought together student athletes (identified as the group primarily involved in bullying), victimized students, school staff, victim services advocates and police officers. Parents, counselors and other community members concerned about violence issues were also allowed to attend (Smith-LaBombard, p.9).

Saulny (2004) reports on a program instituted in 12 of New York City's most dangerous schools. The program concentrates on the small, quality-of-life things such as clean restrooms and lack of graffiti on the walls. This sends an unequivocal message that order is the order of the day. Such attention to detail combined with an influx of police officers, school safety agents, and other disciplinary and support staff are making a difference. School officials report a 48 percent decrease in major crimes such as assault and grand larceny. The problems were easy to see before institution of the program: students gambling in the cafeteria, wearing head coverings with gang colors, running through the halls, kicking classroom doors, ignoring teachers and disciplinarians. One principal resigned citing "work-related stress." But now, at the main doors, students waiting to pass through metal detectors stand in orderly, quiet lines. One deputy inspector said: "What you're seeing is people actually engaging with students, telling them what the expectations are before they even get through the door."

One veteran math teacher said: "I've been here since the 1980s, and I would say that this is first time in 12 years I can teach in the morning with my door open. I locked the door for good reason. I almost got killed four years ago. Somebody knocked, I opened the door and a kid swung a skateboard at my head. That's how wild the halls were." Perhaps most telling is the statement of an 18-year-old senior about the changes that have occurred bringing something invaluable—peace of mind: "I don't worry about getting shot anymore."

Another approach to preventing school violence is for those involved with students, particularly law enforcement officers, to have the skills to de-escalate juvenile aggression. Golden (2004, p.32) describes three key differences between adult and juvenile aggression: "First, adults have a much greater ability to control their aggression. . . . Second, juveniles tend to exhibit emotional aggression, whereas adults tend to exhibit deliberate aggression. However, juveniles can exhibit either form. . . . [Third], juvenile aggression is much more volatile and unpredictable than adult aggression. Therefore, it can be significantly more dangerous." He presents a model to de-escalate juvenile aggression, shown in Figure 7.4.

Golden (p.32) describes the difference between emotional and deliberate aggression: "Emotional aggression is usually an out-of-control act that is often annoying and loud. . . . Deliberate aggression is often a criminal act with specific intent to do harm to a person or property."

 Some schools have adopted controversial measures to prevent school violence, including zero-tolerance policies or school security procedures known as lockdowns.

Most such policies and procedures focus on the possession of weapons and other contraband on school property. And while it seems to make good sense that schools, in fulfilling their duty to maintain a safe learning environment,

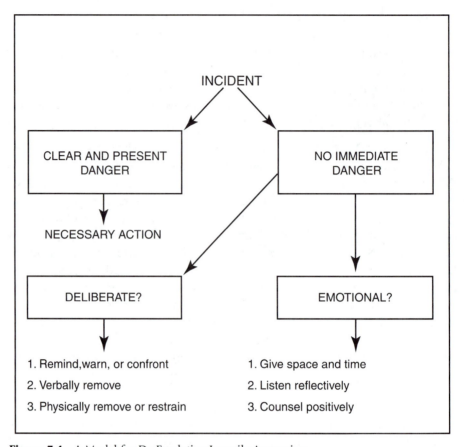

**Figure 7.4** A Model for De-Escalating Juvenile Aggression

SOURCE: Jeffrey S. Golden. "De-Escalating Juvenile Aggression." *The Police Chief*, May 2004, p.34. Reprinted by permission.

should restrict what students are allowed to carry on campus, policies and procedures aimed at achieving the goal of safety are not without controversy.

## Zero-Tolerance Policies

Holloway (2001/2002, p.84) notes: "**Zero-tolerance policies,** those school policies that mandate predetermined consequences or punishments for specific offenses, have become a popular disciplinary choice."

Criticism of these policies is expressed by Heck (2001, p.9), who cautions: "Schools across the nation have adopted zero-tolerance policies hoping that they will lessen the chances that a violent incident will occur. However, while such policies might prove useful in some situations, school administrators must use them with discretion and common sense; otherwise, a net-widening effect may result, which can place additional strain on students, teachers, parents, law enforcement, and the juvenile justice system." Consider, for example the following case from Fort Myers, Florida:

A high school honor student who will graduate next week was sent to jail and will miss the ceremony because a kitchen knife was found in her car. [According to a report,] school officials saw the knife on the floor of the passenger's side of [her] car while she was in the school. [The girl], 18, spent Monday in jail on a felony charge of possession of a weapon on school property. . . .

"They're taking away my memories," [she] said, as she walked out of the Lee County Jail . . . after posting $2,500 bail. "I'm so angry. I won't get to graduate with my friends because of a stupid kitchen knife." The knife, which has a 5-inch blade, had been left in the car after [she] moved some possessions over the weekend, she said. Her family claims the arrest is a case of political correctness run amok. But [the] principal said, "A weapon is a weapon is a weapon" ("Florida Honor Student . . .," 2001, p.A13).

Another controversial effort aimed at preventing school violence is the planned but unannounced lockdown.

## Proactive Lockdowns

Some schools are taking a **lockdown** approach not as a reactive response to a crisis, but rather as a proactive step to avoid a crisis. Guy (2001, p.7) describes how these efforts aim at deterring school violence:

Students in McMinn County, Tennessee, have one more reason against mixing drugs, guns, and school. They know that at any time they will face a surprise lock down. Then the school hallways will not be filled with students and teachers, but with police dogs and SWAT teams.

During a lock down, high school students are detained in classrooms while police and dogs scour the campus, searching for contraband or any danger to a safe educational environment. It is a new, controversial approach to keeping schools safe. So far, the results are positive.

Numerous legal issues must be considered when planning such a lockdown, and thus, collaboration with the district attorney's office is required with this approach. While part of the lockdown team searches the campus for contraband, another part meets with students to discuss what is occurring (Guy, p.8):

In the classrooms, officers explain about "amnesty time," which allows students to turn over illegal narcotics, unlawful prescription medications, inhalants, knives or firearms in their possession without fear of prosecution. Students are also given the opportunity to list such items in their cars and lockers. To provide some degree of anonymity, teachers and officers leave the classrooms for several minutes while students put their lists and illegal items in an amnesty box.

While some criticize such lockdowns as being frightening or intimidating to students, and some students complain they feel threatened when their day is interrupted by the police, this approach has, thus far, not been challenged in court or before a school board (Guy, p.8). Furthermore, beyond curbing the possession of drugs and weapons in the public schools, these lockdowns emphasize "the essential partnership between law enforcement and the school system. They provide the community with tangible evidence that government agencies are cooperating to prevent drug abuse and violence in schools and to provide a safe educational environment for students and teachers" (Guy, p.8).

While proactive lockdowns may be effective in locating and securing weapons that might be used in incidents of school violence, they are employed very infrequently in very few schools. Zero-tolerance policies fall dangerously short in their effectiveness if students believe any prohibited items they bring to school will go unnoticed. In fact, many weapons are discovered only after they have been used in a violent episode. Metal detectors, again, are used rather infrequently, especially in smaller schools and in smaller communities, despite statistics showing these jurisdictions are also vulnerable to fatal school violence.

So while these efforts are seen as nice luxuries for those schools able to afford the fiscal and human resources needed to implement them, they cannot be relied on alone and are no substitute for the power of partnerships between students, teachers, officers, parents and other members of a community. Indeed: "While metal detectors and security guards can spot guns in book bags, adults and students must work together to deal with bullying, teasing and harassment before they escalate to one more Columbine" ("Bullying, Teasing . . .," p.5). Dorn (p.31) adds: "The problem of weapons violence in our schools is complex. No single strategy will show lasting success. If used as stand-alone solutions, school resource officer programs (SROs), metal detectors, peer mediation programs and bullying programs will fail to produce a truly safe school environment. When a wide range of protective measures are integrated into a comprehensive strategy, dramatic improvement can result. This strategy should involve a community-based approach tailored to fit the needs and resources of the community."

## Workplace Violence

The third major setting for violence for which law enforcement must prepare a response is the workplace. A survey of Fortune 1000 companies found violence in the workplace and the damaging trauma caused by such events to be, for the third straight year, the leading concern of security managers at America's largest corporations ("Violence in the Workplace . . .," 2001, p.42). Rudewicz (2004, p.41) reports: "Incidents of workplace violence accounted for 14 percent of all work-related fatal occupational injuries in 2002, and according to the Department of Labor, violent acts continue to rank among the top three causes of workplace fatalities for all workers." According to the National Institute for Occupational Safety and Health website: "Each week, an average of 20 workers are murdered and 18,000 are assaulted while at work or on duty. Nonfatal assaults result in millions of lost workdays and cost workers millions of dollars in lost wages."

Crawford (2002, p.22) reports: "Workplace violence, according to one study, can cost businesses as much as $4.2 billion annually. The Workplace Violence Institute reports an estimated 16,400 threats are made, 723 workers are attacked and 43,800 are harassed during an average workday. According to the Occupational Safety and Health Administration (OSHA), more than 1,000 workers are victims of homicide at work each year. The U.S. Department of Justice estimates nearly 2 million assaults and threats occur each year in the workplace." The vast majority (82 percent) of workplace homicides were caused by firearms, followed by stabbings (8 percent); hitting, kicking or beating (5 percent); and "other methods" (5 percent) (Duhart, 2001, p.10).

Similar to other violent crime trends, workplace violence has experienced a decline in recent years. However, it should be recognized that workplace violence may be the result of the presence of gang members in the workforce. According to Witkowski (2004, p.95): "Having gang members in the work force increases the potential for violence on the job, as research has shown gang members have greater access to weapons and are more likely to use them in the commission of a crime."

Workplace violence may also be a spillover of domestic violence. Paziotopoulos (2003, p.104) notes: "Domestic violence does not stay home when its victims go to work. It can follow them, resulting in violence in the workplace. . . . Any mid-to-large sized company has employees struggling with domestic violence. This includes prosecuting offices and police departments. Just as victims of domestic violence can be officers or prosecutors, all workplaces are vulnerable and should have policies that address these situations."

While the problem of domestic violence creeping into the workplace is to be taken seriously, according to Duhart (p.8): "Workplace violence victims were more likely to be victimized by a stranger than by someone they knew. In more than half of all workplace victimizations [55.6%], a stranger was the perpetrator. About 1% of all workplace crime was committed by a current or former boyfriend, girlfriend, or spouse—an intimate—of the victim." In 39.4 percent of workplace violence incidents, the offender was a casual acquaintance of the victim. Furthermore: "Law enforcement employees were victimized by a stranger more than any other occupation; about three-quarters of all law enforcement victimizations were committed by a stranger" (p.8). The exceptions to this general finding: "Workers in the mental health field and teachers were the only occupations more likely to be victimized by someone they knew than by a stranger" (p.8).

## Similarities between School and Workplace Violence

Researchers have noted some striking similarities between school and workplace violence.

 Similarities between school and workplace violence include the perpetrators' profiles, the targets, the means and the motivation.

The perpetrators are frequently loners with poor social skills, often obsessed with violence and weapons. The targets include authority figures and peers who are in conflict with them. The perpetrators often bring an arsenal of weapons and kill all who get in their way. The common motive is revenge, believing they have been treated unjustly. Most are suicidal and feel they have nothing left to lose. School and workplace violence also tend to provide early warning signs before acts of violence.

The caution issued previously regarding the hazards of profiling perpetrators of school violence also applies to attempts at identifying those at risk of committing workplace violence. Ferguson (2001, p.50) warns that by focusing exclusively on the employee, little attention may be given to two other situation factors identified as key components in workplace violence incidents: "Experts in workplace violence prevention underscore the importance of three key factors in such incidents. In addition to the personality of the perpetrator, . . . the particular stress and the specific setting must also be considered. The stress is the precipitating event that causes the violence to erupt, and the setting might be the factory or office and its perceived environment." Precipitating events for workplace violence might include missed promotions and terminations (Jaeger, 2001, p.74).

### Early Warning Signs

"Eight Must-Recognize Warning Signs of Workplace Violence" (2002, p.4) presents behaviors that could indicate potential for violence identified by the federal Office of Personnel Management (OPM):

- Direct or veiled threats
- Intimidating, belligerent, harassing, bullying or other inappropriate and aggressive behavior
- Numerous conflicts with supervisors and other employees
- Bringing a weapon to the workplace, brandishing a weapon in the workplace, making inappropriate references to guns, or fascination with weapons
- Statements showing fascination with incidents of workplace violence, statements indicating approval of the use of violence to resolve a problem or statements indicating identification with perpetrators of workplace homicides
- Statements indicating desperation (over family, financial and other personal problems) to the point of contemplating suicide
- Drug/alcohol abuse
- Extreme changes in behavior

According to the article: "Each of these behaviors is a clear sign that something is wrong. None should be ignored." Jaeger (p.74) also notes: "Many employees who have committed fatal attacks gave clear, early warning signals that were not adequately addressed by their employers."

 As with school violence, workplace violence rarely occurs without warning.

Paziotopoulos (pp.107–108) states: "When a serious incident of workplace violence occurs, many people tend to say that the individual just snapped. It is well recognized among threat assessment professionals that people don't just snap and that there are pre-incident indicators that suggest the potential for violence."

### The Police Response

The threat of workplace violence can be either internal or external—the violent employee or the victimized employee. How a company addresses the issue of violence on the premises will depend, in large part, on whether the threat comes from inside or outside the workplace.

While no two incidents of workplace violence are exactly the same, a general multipronged approach of prevention and control is used as a starting point for most cases. McDonald (2001, p.7) identifies several steps a crisis response team may take in implementing a successful violence prevention program, including constructing violence risk profiles for the workplace, developing policies and procedures to guide the team, training team members and supervisory staff, arranging access to medical and mental health expertise, and announcing clear disciplinary rules. Part of an emergency preparedness effort should include steps to make blueprints or floor plans of the premises available to law enforcement, should an episode of workplace violence turn into a barricaded subject incident or one where hostages are involved.

Officers can work with a company's crisis response team to train staff in how to detect signs of violence and procedures for reporting them to the threat management team. Prescreening programs are also strongly recommended. Noting how workplace violence can strike anywhere, anytime and anyone, Lewis (2001, p.71) suggests: "Preventing the unthinkable requires a proactive approach. . . . Thorough background checks are your first line of defense and are the most proactive." He identifies three benefits to this policy: "Applicants with something to hide often decide not to complete the employment application when they are advised of a pending background check. . . . Another added benefit is that applicants with past records become very honest during the interview. . . . A third benefit comes into play when an applicant has a record of minor crimes, which may not preclude hiring. Many times, it is not the felony hits, but the small, tell-tale signs that uncover an applicant's tendencies towards workplace violence."

According to Jaeger (p.74), information derived from background checks can present a double-edged sword for employers:

> Employers can face extraordinary potential liability when they don't manage and eliminate the potential for violence in the workplace. A legal wrinkle that employers must acknowledge is the apparent contradiction of two federal mandates: the Americans with Disabilities Act (ADA) and the Occupational Health and Safety Act (OSHA). OSHA decrees employers must provide a safe working environment for its employees. But the vaguely worded ADA can make it legally difficult for a company to take strong action against an employee with a mental or emotional instability. . . .
>
> Though companies must be vigilant to the early warning signs of potential violence, they also must be aware of a legal limitation imposed by ADA. The act severely restricts "profiling" of employees through observation of traits presumed to be potentially violent.

As Bahls and Bahls (2001, p.98) explain: "Employers might be tempted to screen out mentally unstable job applicants by asking whether they have histories of mental illness or drug abuse. [However,] that would violate the ADA, which prohibits discrimination against people with physical or mental disabilities, real or perceived."

So what can employers and law enforcement do when the law seems to tie their hands in how they prevent workplace violence? The answer is to take the same approach as that done with school violence—focus on behavior-based assessments. Other preventive measures include a no-weapons policy, drug and alcohol testing, and alternative dispute resolution (ADR) programs.

Access control is another area businesses may consider when addressing the issue of workplace violence. Some companies have developed scripts and step-by-step instructions for on-site security personnel for managing violent employees and visitors, including how to summon and advise law enforcement. In cases where an abuser enters the workplace to victimize an employee, security or another member of the crisis management team must call police immediately.

In taking a community-policing approach to the problem of workplace violence, officers may also educate and inform local businesses of resources available to help employees who are victims of domestic violence.

## Problem-Oriented Policing and Violence

"The South Euclid School Bullying Project"* is one of the 2001 Herman Gold-stein Award winners for excellence in problem-oriented policing.

Attention to tailor-made, individual responses in a broader, more holistic fashion is [an] attribute of successful projects. In South Euclid, Crime Prevention through Environmental Design (CPTED)–style modifications were paired with better teacher supervision of "hotspots." Role-playing training for teachers in conflict resolution was paired with antibullying education for students and parents. Combining physical prevention with social and managerial prevention strategies is called "2nd Generation CPTED." It represents the most advanced form of crime prevention.

### *Scanning*

Unchecked disorderly behavior of students in South Euclid, Ohio, led the school resource officer (SRO) to review school data regarding referrals to the principal's office. He found that the high school reported thousands of referrals a year for bullying, and the junior high school had recently experienced a 30 percent increase in referrals for bullying. Police data showed that juvenile complaints about disturbances, bullying and assaults after school hours had increased 90 percent in the last 10 years.

### *Analysis*

All junior high and high school students were surveyed. Interviews and focus groups were also conducted with students—identified as victims or offenders—teachers and guidance counselors. Finally, the South Euclid Police Department purchased a Geographic Information System to complete crime and incident mapping of hotspots within the schools. The main findings pointed to four main areas of concern: the environmental design of school areas, teachers' knowledge and response to the problem, parents' attitudes and responses, and students' perspectives and behaviors.

#### Environmental Design Findings
- Locations in the school with less supervision or denser population (primarily the hallways, cafeteria and gymnasium) were more likely to have higher rates of bullying.
- Students avoided certain places at school because of fear of being bullied (for example, students avoid hallways near lockers of students who are not their friends or who are not in their classes).
- Race and ethnicity was not a primary factor in bullying.
- A vast majority of students reported witnessing bullying or being bullied in the classroom during class.

#### Teacher Issues
- Although bullying occurred frequently, teachers and students infrequently intervened.

*Source: Adapted from "The South Euclid School Bullying Project." In *Excellence in Problem-Oriented Policing: The 2001 Herman Goldstein Award Winners.* Washington, DC: National Institute of Justice, Community Oriented Policing Services and the Police Executive Research Forum, 2001, pp. 55–62.

- When students were asked what would happen if they told a teacher about an incident of bullying, more than 30 percent said "nothing."
- In interviews, students said they wouldn't tell teachers about bullying incidents because they were afraid of further retaliation, they expected the teacher to "do nothing," or were afraid the teacher wouldn't believe or support them, especially if the bully was popular or well liked by the teacher.

### Parent Issues

- Students who reported being physically disciplined at home were more likely to report that they had been bullied.
- More than one-third of parents who had talked to their kids about bullying had instructed them to fight back. Students said they would not tell a parent if they are bullied because they believed their parents would "overreact."

### Student Issues

- Students who reported that they engaged in bullying typically perceived their own behavior as "playful" or "a normal part of growing up." They said that everyone gets picked on but some "don't know how to take it," "take things too seriously" or "just don't know how to fight back."
- Victims of bullying did not perceive this behavior as "fun" or "normal."
- Victims viewed bullies as "popular."
- Only 23 percent of students were likely to tell their parents they were a victim of bullying.
- Students were more likely to seek adult help for someone else who was bullied than for themselves.
- Students with lower grade point averages were significantly more likely to physically hurt someone else.
- Students who were secure in a peer group were more likely to intervene in bullying and less fearful of retaliation.
- Students suggested that involvement in school activities helped them to form a niche where they felt safe, supported and free from victimization.

## *Response*

The SRO, collaborating with a social worker and university researchers, coordinated a Response Planning Team to respond to each of the areas identified in the analysis. Environmental changes involved modifying the school bell times and increasing teacher supervision of hotspot areas. Counselors and social workers conducted teacher training courses in conflict resolution and bullying prevention. Parent education included mailings with information about bullying, an explanation of the new school policy, and discussion about what they could do at home to address the problems. Finally, student education focused on classroom discussions with homeroom teachers and students, and assemblies conducted by the SRO. The Ohio Department of Education also contributed by opening a new training center for "at-risk students" to provide a nontraditional setting for specialized help.

## *Assessment*

The results from the various responses were dramatic. School suspensions decreased 40 percent. Bullying incidents dropped 60 percent in the hallways and 80 percent in the gym area. Follow-up surveys indicated there were positive attitudinal changes among students about bullying and more students felt confident teachers would take action.

The overall results suggested that the school environments were not only safer, but that early intervention was helping "at-risk" students succeed in school.

## SUMMARY

Wives, husbands, children, elders—in fact, anyone within a family unit—may be at risk of becoming a victim of domestic violence. Police officers responding to a domestic violence call are responsible for investigating it thoroughly as an assault and for making an arrest if probable cause exists. Responding to a domestic violence call *is* hazardous, but not as hazardous as is often thought. In the Minneapolis experiment, police officers responding to domestic violence calls found that arrest was clearly more effective than advice or sending the suspect away. *Thurman v. City of Torrington* (1984) established that domestic violence is an assault rather than simply a family affair. Officers and departments can be sued for "failure to protect." The Broward batterer intervention program found that marriage, home ownership and steady employment led to fewer violent offenses after an offender completed a batterers' intervention program.

School violence is of growing concern to law enforcement and almost never occurs without warning. An effective three-pronged approach to school security encompasses crisis planning, security technology and school/law enforcement/community partnerships. Some schools have adopted controversial measures such as zero-tolerance policies or school security procedures known as lockdowns.

Similarities between school and workplace violence include the perpetrators' profiles, the targets, the means and the motivation. As with school violence, workplace violence rarely occurs without warning.

### APPLICATION

As the officer in charge of the records bureau, you have noted an extraordinary increase in family violence. The officers' reports show that dispositions have been erratic and, in some cases, officers' actions have caused more serious violence. You bring this to the chief's attention and are instructed to formulate a policy and procedures to handle family violence calls. The need statement should include that family violence is a serious crime and that victims of such violence are not receiving the maximum protection the law and those who enforce the law can provide.

### INSTRUCTIONS

Write the need statement first. Then state the purpose of the policy establishing procedures in family violence cases. Make sure the policy and procedures do not interfere with officers' individual discretion when it is needed. This should be stated in the policy.

In the procedures, provide guidelines on how officers should proceed when the family dispute is a misdemeanor and how they should proceed when it is a felony. Cite the state law or city ordinance governing these procedures. Also state when an arrest should be made. If necessary, contact your local police department or sheriff's office for examples of a policy and procedures that would be useful as guidelines.

### EXERCISES IN CRITICAL THINKING

A. On November 22, Officers David Miller and Peter Kelly were called to investigate a disturbance of the peace at 1131 Selby Avenue, St. Paul, Minnesota, reported by Jeanne McDowell, a neighbor. In the past month, several domestic disturbances had been reported and investigated at this address, which officers knew was the residence of Eddie and Donna Konkler.

While approaching 1131 Selby, the officers heard a loud male voice shouting obscenities, the sound of breaking glass, two loud thumps and the muffled sounds of children crying. Officer Miller knocked loudly on the door and called out to Eddie, who opened the door. He held a revolver in his right hand, and his breath smelled of an alcoholic beverage. Donna was sitting on the floor leaning against a wall. She had a bloody nose and several red marks on her face. Broken glass was scattered around the room.

Officer Miller was successful in talking Eddie into relinquishing the revolver and in quieting him, but for 15 minutes, Eddie and Donna continued shouting and cursing at each other and at the officers. During this time, Officer Kelly assisted Donna in stopping the bleeding, and she became subdued. Eddie continued his verbal abuse, so the officers requested that Eddie leave the house until he became calm. Eddie then told the police he was sorry and would not cause any more trouble. The officers gave suggestions for possible agencies that could help and suggested specific places where Donna could receive assistance if future repetitions of abuse were to occur.

1. What mistake did Officers Miller and Kelly make?
   a. Because of the cold weather in Minnesota, Eddie should not be removed from his residence; a firm warning and threat of arrest would be sufficient.

b. Police should not approach a domestic disturbance by letting an abusive person know who they are. The abuser should not be given a chance to then draw a dangerous weapon.

c. Police should not allow the parties to refuse to talk to one another—make the two stop fighting and shouting, and then insist that they talk and think about their situation so that mediation can bring about a solution to their problem.

d. Repeated domestic abuse and an assault involving the display of a dangerous weapon justifies an arrest for second-degree assault.

e. The officers should issue a ticket for disturbing the peace, but cases of domestic problems do not involve an arrest for criminal sexual conduct, kidnapping, terroristic threats or second-degree assault.

B. William Mosby, age 34, had known the mother and family of N.D., age 7, for seven years. Immediately before the events in question, Mosby had lived with N.D.'s family for three weeks. At the end of the third week, N.D.'s mother gave permission for N.D. to go grocery shopping with Mosby while she went to work.

After going to the cleaners, grocery store and liquor store, Mosby took her back to the apartment building. There Mosby had N.D. scrub a shower stall. He gave her a robe to change into, saying he would wash her clothes with his laundry. N.D. reported that Mosby, who had been drinking beer, had N.D. sit on his lap. N.D. reported that Mosby said, "I want to have a baby by you." But N.D. said she was not ready for that. After taking a shower, Mosby came and stood naked in front of N.D. He then put on some boxer shorts, sat on the bed and asked N.D. to comb his hair. Mosby then told her to lie down and asked if she "ever had a dicky before." He then put his finger in her vagina and touched her chest. N.D. began crying and Mosby slapped her, telling her to shut up, and tried to get the robe off. When she ran to unlock the door, Mosby told her to lock the door, or he was going to beat her. However, N.D. unlocked the door and ran screaming to the caretaker's apartment.

The caretaker testified that Mosby, wearing only boxer shorts, came running after N.D. and asked the caretaker if he believed N.D. N.D. told the caretaker to look at her, opened the robe, and said, "Look at what I've got on." Mosby kept closing the door to the caretaker's apartment, and the caretaker kept opening it. A next-door tenant came and said she had called the police. Mosby looked excited, jumped up and left the apartment building. The next-door tenant took N.D. to the tenant's apartment. N.D. threw up while there. The police let N.D. go home without being given a medical examination.

2. What is the responsibility of the police who arrive on the scene?
a. Having made sure that physical violence has ceased, the police are responsible to advise the mother on her rights and responsibilities.

b. Police should require the caretaker to notify them if Mosby returns and again causes trouble.

c. Police must interview all witnesses, determine if there is a substantial basis for finding probable cause for criminal sexual conduct, procure an arrest warrant and go out to search for Mosby.

d. As no probable cause for arrest exists, mediate so that emotions can calm down, and help the mother and N.D. start talking about their situation by suggesting possible solutions and sources of assistance.

e. Instead of letting N.D. go home without being given a medical examination, medical assistance should be sought.

3. Why are cases of domestic violence or criminal sexual conduct difficult to prosecute?
a. Evidence is usually insufficient to establish beyond a reasonable doubt that one is guilty of domestic violence or criminal sexual conduct in either the first or second degree.

b. Testimony is insufficient to establish sexual penetration.

c. Victims have tendencies, due to emotional trauma, to fabricate charges resulting in evidence of dubious credibility which, upon close examination, is filled with discrepancies.

d. Victims are fearful of future retaliation and continue to hope the offender will change his ways.

e. Adult males are more believable than children or women.

4. If N.D.'s mother obtains an order for protection (OFP),
a. The police can arrest Mosby even if he had done nothing to her or her child *if* he comes to her home after having been ordered to stay away, and she calls the police.

b. Mosby can have no further contact with the victim at her home but can make contact only at her place of work or other neutral ground.

c. Police can and should make an arrest only if additional assault or threat of bodily harm is made.

d. A police officer will be assigned to protect her for 24 hours.

e. It will be voided if she lets the abuser into her home or allows visitation with her children.

### DISCUSSION QUESTIONS

1. Before reading this chapter, did you know about the extent of domestic violence? If yes, what have you read, seen or known about the problem?

2. Do you think parents have the right to discipline their teenage children? What do you think about hitting, slapping, yelling, restricting youths to their rooms, imposing monetary penalties and the like?

3. Much controversy exists in the schools regarding punishing children through the use of physical force.

What is your position on allowing school officials to use physical force against students?

4. What do school and workplace violence have in common?

5. Why should law enforcement be knowledgeable about workplace violence?

6. What has been your experience with bullying?

7. Does your local police department have an SRO? If so, in what schools does the officer work?

### INFOTRAC COLLEGE EDITION ASSIGNMENTS

■ Use InfoTrac College Edition to help answer the Discussion Questions as appropriate.

■ Use InfoTrac College Edition to find articles on *violence*. There are over 35 categories of violence you should be aware of. Scroll through until the article, "The Latest School of Thought: A Special Focus on School Security," appears. Outline what has been working for school security and the areas that have been evaluated for further protection. Be prepared to share and discuss your outline with the class.

■ Use InfoTrac College Edition to find the article "Murder at Work" by Jane McDonald. List what factors security experts consider as contributors to violence-prone workplaces and what their solution to this problem includes. Be prepared to discuss your findings with the class.

■ Use InfoTrac College Edition to read and outline one of the following articles to share with the class:

• "Violent Crimes among Juveniles: Behavioral Aspects" by William Andrew Corbitt

• "The School Shooter: One Community's Experience" by William P. Heck

• "Bomb Threat Assessments (Focus on School Violence)" by Ronald F. Tunkel

• "Addressing School Violence: Prevention, Planning and Practice" by Francis Q. Hoang

• "Safe Harbor" by Steven C. Bahls and Jane Easter Bahls

• "Murder at Work" by Jane McDonald

• "A Study on Cyberstalking: Understanding Investigative Hurdles" by Robert D'Ovidio and James Doyle

• "Munchausen Syndrome by Proxy: The Importance of Behavioral Artifacts" by Deborah Chiczewski and Michael Kelly

• "Suicide Risk and Hostage/Barricade Situations Involving Older Persons" by Arthur A. Slatkin

• "Operation CleanSWEEP: The School Safety Program that Earned an A+" by Gary S. Penrod

• "Stalking-Investigation Strategies" by George E. Wattendorf

• "Stalking the Stalker: A Profile of Offenders" by Robert A. Wood and Nona L. Wood

• "Law Enforcement and the Elderly: A Concern for the 21st Century" by Lamar Jordan

• "Drug-Endangered Children" by Jerry Harris

 ### INTERNET ASSIGNMENTS

■ Go to www.ojp.usdoj.gov/bjs/abstract/iscs01.htm and select a chapter from *Indicators of School Crime and Safety, 2001* to read and outline. Be prepared to discuss your outline with the class.

■ Go to www.theiacp.org and find *Guide for Preventing and Responding to School Violence*. Find information on one of the following topics:

• Physical security at school buildings and violence prevention

• Warning signs of violence and the consequences of failing to recognize and respond to those signs

• Police training on school violence

• Threat assessments and crisis planning

• Legal considerations and legislative issues

Read and summarize the information. Be prepared to share your findings with the class.

■ Go to www.ed.gov/offices/OSERS/OSEP/earlywrn .html and select one chapter from *Early Warning, Timely Response: A Guide to Safe Schools*. Read and outline the chapter, and be prepared to discuss your outline with the class.

### BOOK-SPECIFIC WEBSITE

The book-specific website at http://cj.wadsworth.com/ wobleski_Hess_police_op4e hosts a variety of resources for students and instructors. Many can be emailed to the instructor. Included are extended activities such as Concept Builders - the 3 step learning module that reinforces key chapter concepts, followed by a real-world applications and critical thinking questions. InfoTrac College Edition exercises; Discussion Questions; interactive key-term FlashCards; and a collection of chapter-based Web Links provide additional information and activities to include in the curriculum.

### REFERENCES

The Administration for Children and Families. "What Is Child Maltreatment?" Washington, DC: U.S. Department of Health and Human Services, April 2001. www.calib.com/nccanch/pubs/factsheets/childmal.cfm.

Ahmed, Eliza and Braithwaite, Valerie. " 'What, Me, Ashamed?' Shame Management and School Bullying." *Journal of Research in Crime and Delinquency*, August 2004, pp.269–294.

"Arresting Development in Latest DV Research." *Law Enforcement News*, October 31, 2001, pp.1, 6.

Atkinson, Anne J. "School Resource Officers: Making Schools Safer and More Effective." *The Police Chief*, March 2001, pp.55–63.

Bahls, Steven C. and Bahls, Jane Easter. "Safe Harbor." *Entrepreneur*, April 2001, p.98.

Brown, Ben and Benedict, Wm. Reed. "Bullets, Blades and Being Afraid in Hispanic High Schools: An Exploratory Study of the Presence of Weapons and Fear of Weapon-Associated Victimization among High School Students in a Border Town." *Crime & Delinquency*, July 2004, pp.372–394.

"Bullying, Teasing and Harassment in School." *American Association of University Women in Action*, Summer 2001, pp.1, 5.

Burgess, Ann W.; Harner, Holly; Baker, Timothy; Hartman, Carol R.; and Lole, Christopher. "Study Provides Tools to Assess When Stalking Behaviors Will Lead to Escalation of Violence." *Journal of Family Violence*, Vol.16, No.3, 2001, p.309.

Burke, Tod W.; Jordan, Michael L.; and Owen, Stephen S. "A Cross-National Comparison of Gay and Lesbian Domestic Violence." *Journal of Contemporary Criminal Justice*, August 2002, pp.231–257.

Burke, Tod W.; Owen, Stephen S.; and Jordan, Michael L. "Law Enforcement and Gay Domestic Violence in the United States and Venezuela." *ACJS Today*, May/June 2001, pp.1, 4–6.

Chiczewski, Deborah and Kelly, Michael. "Munchausen Syndrome by Proxy: The Importance of Behavioral Artifacts." *FBI Law Enforcement Bulletin*, August 2003, pp.20–24.

*Child Maltreatment 2002: Summary of Key Findings*. Washington, DC: National Clearinghouse on Child Abuse and Neglect Information, April 2004.

Cooper, Doug and Snell, Jennie L. "Bullying—Not Just a Kid Thing." *Educational Leadership*, March 2003, pp.22–25.

Crawford, Jay. "When Employee Stress Turns Violent." *Access Control & Security Systems*, February 2002, pp.22–24.

Dawson, Myrna and Dinovitzer, Ronit. "Victim Cooperation and the Prosecution of Domestic Violence in a Specialized Court." *Justice Quarterly*, September 2001, pp.593–622.

DeVoe, Jill F.; Peter, Katharin; Kaufman, Phillip; Ruddy, Sally A.; Miller, Amanda K.; Planty, Mike; Snyder, Thomas D.; and Rand, Michael. R. *Indicators of School Crime and Safety: 2003*, Washington, DC: National Center for Educational Statistics, October 2003. (NCJ 201257)

"Domestic Homicide Tipoffs May Be Missed." *Law Enforcement News*, February 2004, p.9.

Dorn, Michael. "Preventing School Weapons Assaults." *Police*, May 2001, pp.30–35.

Dorn, Michael. "How to . . . Start an SRO Program." *Police*, October 2004, pp.16–24.

D'Ovidio, Robert and Doyle, James. "A Study on Cyberstalking: Understanding Investigative Hurdles." *FBI Law Enforcement Bulletin*, March 2003, pp.10–17.

Duhart, Detis T. *Violence in the Workplace, 1993–99*. Washington, DC: Bureau of Justice Statistics, Special Report, December 2001. (NCJ 190076)

Duncan, Debra C. "Community Policing: Preserving the Quality of Life of Our Senior Citizens." *The Police Chief*, March 2001, pp.74–77.

"Eight Must-Recognize Warning Signs of Workplace Violence. *The Supervisor's Guide to Workplace Security*, 2002, p.4.

*Enforcement of Protective Orders*. Washington, DC: Office for Victims of Crime, Legal Series Bulletin #4, January 2002.

English, Diana J.; Widon, Cathy Spatz; and Ford, Carol Brand. *Childhood Victimization and Delinquency, Adult Criminality and Violent Criminal Behavior: A Replication and Extension*. Washington, DC: National Institute of Justice, 2002. (NIJ 192291)

Ericson, Nels. *Addressing the Problem of Juvenile Bullying*. Washington, DC: Office of Juvenile Justice and Delinquency Prevention, June 2001, Fact Sheet #27.

Falcon, Melanie. "Adopt-A-Bully Program." *Law and Order*, February 2004, pp.380–382.

Feder, Lynette and Forde, David R. "The Broward Experiment." In *Batterer Intervention Programs* by Shelly Jackson, Lynette Feder, David R. Forde, Robert C. Davis, Christopher D. Maxwell and Bruce G. Taylor, Washington, DC: National Institute of Justice, June 2003, pp.5–13. (NCJ 195079)

Felson, Richard B. and Ackerman, Jeff. "Arrest for Domestic and Other Assaults." *Criminology*, August 2001, pp.655–676.

Felson, Richard B.; Messner, Steven F.; Hoskin, Anthony W.; and Glenn, Deane. "Reasons for Reporting and Not Reporting Domestic Violence to the Police." *Criminology*, August 2002, pp.617–642.

Ferguson, Harv. "Looking Beyond the School Shooter Profile." *The Police Chief*, May 2001, pp.48–52.

Finkelhor, David and Jones, Lisa M. *Explanations for the Decline in Child Sexual Abuse Cases*. Washington, DC: OJJDP Juvenile Justice Bulletin, January 2004. (NCJ 199298)

Finkelhor, David and Ormrod, Richard. *Child Abuse Reported to the Police*. Washington, DC: Office of Juvenile Justice and Delinquency Prevention, May 2003. (NCJ 187238)

Finn, Mary A.; Blackwell, Brenda Sims; Stalans, Loretta J.; Studdard, Sheila; and Dugan, Laura. "Dual Arrest Decisions in Domestic Violence Cases: The Influence of Department Policies." *Crime & Delinquency*, October 2004, pp.565–589.

"Florida Honor Student Tripped Up by Zero-Tolerance Policy." Associated Press, as reported in the (Minneapolis/St. Paul) *Star Tribune*, May 24, 2001, p.A13.

Gallo, Gina. "Airing Law Enforcement's Dirty Laundry." *Law Enforcement Technology*, June 2004a, pp.132–137.

Gallo, Gina. "The National Police Family Violence Prevention Project Helps Departments Address Domestic Abuse in Police Families." *Law Enforcement Technology*, July 2004b, pp.60–64.

Garner, Gerald W. "Behind Closed Doors." *Police*, May 2002, pp.46–51.

Garrett, Ronnie. "The Graying of America." *Law Enforcement Technology*, October 2001a, pp.56–61.

Garrett, Ronnie. "Software Defines Risk in Domestic Violence Cases." *Law Enforcement Technology*, September 2001b, pp.120–123.

Garrett, Ronnie. "Keep an Eye on School Safety." *Law Enforcement Technology*, May 2004, p.6.

Geberth, Vernon. "Sex-Related Child Abduction Homicides." *Law and Order*, March 2004, pp.32–38.

Giacomazzi, Andrew L. and Smithey, Martha. "Community Policing and Family Violence against Women: Lessons Learned from a Multiagency Collaborative." *Police Quarterly*, March 2001, pp.99–122.

Girouard, Cathy. *School Resource Officer Training Program*. Washington, DC: Office of Juvenile Justice and Delinquency Prevention, March 2001, Fact Sheet #05.

Golden, Jeffrey S. "De-Escalating Juvenile Aggression." *The Police Chief*, May 2004, pp.30–34.

Gordon, Jill A. and Moriarty, Laura J. "The Effects of Domestic Violence Batterer Treatment on Domestic Violence Recidivism: The Chesterfield County Experience." *Criminal Justice and Behavior*, Vol. 30, No.1, 2003, p.118.

Guy, Joe D. "Lock Down." *Community Links*, September 2001, pp.7–8.

Harris, Jerry. "Drug-Endangered Children." *FBI Law Enforcement Bulletin*, February 2004, pp.6–11.

Heck, William P. "The School Shooter: One Community's Experience." *FBI Law Enforcement Bulletin*, September 2001, pp.9–13.

Hemmer, Alex. "Preventing School Shootings: Prince William County's Success Story." *Subject to Debate*, August 2004, pp.1, 3.

Hess, Kären M. and Drowns, Robert W. *Juvenile Justice*, 4th ed. Belmont, CA: Wadsworth Publishing Company, 2004.

Hitchcock, J.A. "Cyberstalking and Law Enforcement." *The Police Chief*, December 2003, pp.16–27.

Hoang, Francis Q. "Addressing School Violence: Prevention, Planning, and Practice." *FBI Law Enforcement Bulletin*, August 2001, pp.18–23.

Holloway, John H. "The Dilemma of Zero Tolerance." *Educational Leadership*, December 2001/January 2002, pp.84–85.

Jackson, Shelly. "Batterer Intervention Programs." In *Batterer Intervention Programs: Where Do We Go from Here?* by Shelly Jackson, Lynette Feder, David R. Forde, Robert C. Davis, Christopher D. Maxwell and Bruce G. Taylor, Washington, DC: National Institute of Justice, June 2003, pp.1–4. (NCJ 195079)

Jackson, Shelly; Feder, Lynette; Forde, David R; Davis, Robert C.; Maxwell, Christopher D.; and Taylor, Bruce G. *Batterer Intervention Programs: Where Do We Go from Here?* Washington, DC: National Institute of Justice, June 2003. (NCJ 195079)

Jaeger, Sandy. "The Age of Rage." *Security Technology and Design*, February 2001, pp.6, 74.

Johnson, Kelly Dedel. *Financial Crimes against the Elderly*. Washington, DC: Office of Community Oriented Policing Services, Problem-Oriented Guides for Police, Problem-Specific Guides Series No. 20, August 4, 2004.

Johnson, Richard. "Changing Attitudes about Domestic Violence." *Law and Order*, April 2002, pp.60–65.

Jordan, Lamar. "Law Enforcement and the Elderly: A Concern for the 21st Century." *FBI Law Enforcement Bulletin*, May 2002, pp.20–23.

Kilpatrick, Dean G; Saunders, Benjamin E.; and Smith, Daniel W. *Youth Victimization: Prevalence and Implications*. Washington, DC: National Institute of Justice, April 2003. (NCJ 194972)

Kingsnorth, Rodney F. and Macintosh, Randall C. "Domestic Violence: Predictors of Victim Support for Official Action." *Justice Quarterly*, June 2004, pp.301–328.

Lavarello, Curtis and Trump, Ken. "Police in Schools Improve Safety, Prevent School Violence; Largest Survey of School Officers Says Many School Crimes Go Unreported." *The Law Enforcement Trainer*, November/December 2001, p.63.

"The LEN Interview: Renae Griggs, Founding Director of the National Police Family Violence Prevention Project." *Law Enforcement News*, January 2004, pp.9–10.

Lewis, Mark. "Lurking Danger: Workplace Violence—How Safe Is Your Business?" *Security Products*, August 2001, pp.70–73.

Loeber, Rolf; Kalb, Larry; and Huizinga, David. *Juvenile Delinquency and Serious Injury Victimization*. Washington, DC: OJJDP Juvenile Justice Bulletin, August 2001. (NCJ 188676)

Lonsway, Kim and Conis, Pete. "Domestic Violence." *Law and Order*, October 2003, pp.133–140.

Maran, Meredith. "Deadly Ambivalence." March 6, 2001. www.salon.com/news/feature/2001

Maxwell, Christopher D.; Garner, Joel H.; and Fagan, Jeffrey A. *The Effects of Arrest on Intimate Partner Violence: New Evidence from the Spouse Assault Replication Program*. Washington, DC: National Institute of Justice Research in Brief, July 2001. (NCJ 188199)

Maxwell, Christopher D.; Garner, Joel H.; and Fagan, Jeffrey A. "The Preventive Effects of Arrest on Intimate Partner Violence: Research, Policy and Theory." *Criminology and Public Policy*, November 2002, pp.51–80.

McDonald, Jane. "Murder at Work." *Risk Management*, March 2001, p.7.

Migliaccio, T. "Marginalizing the Battered Male." *Journal of Men's Studies*, September 2001, pp.205–226.

Miller, Christa. "The Small-Town School Resource Officer: Prudent Investment or Prohibitive Cost?" *Law Enforcement Technology*, October 2001, pp.166–174.

Moffitt, Terrie E.; Robins, Richard W.; and Caspi, Avshalom. "A Couples Analysis of Partner Abuse with Implications for Abuse-Prevention Policy." *Criminology and Public Policy*, November 2001, pp.5–36.

National Institute for Occupational Safety and Health Website. *Violence in the Workplace.* www.cdc.gov/niosh

"New Study Confirms Benefit of Domestic Violence Arrests." *Criminal Justice Newsletter*, September 19, 2001, pp.6–7.

Olweus, Dan. "A Profile of Bullying." *Educational Leadership*, March 2003, pp.12–17.

Osofsky, Joy D. *Addressing Youth Victimization.* Washington, DC: Office of Juvenile Justice and Delinquency Prevention, Action Plan Update, October 2001. (NCJ 186667)

Payne, Brian K. and Berg, Bruce L. "Perceptions about the Criminalization of Elder Abuse among Police Chiefs and Ombudsmen." *Crime & Delinquency*, July 2003, pp.439–459.

Paziotopoulos, Pam. "Workplace Domestic Violence." *Law and Order*, August 2003, pp.104–109.

Pedersen, Dorothy. "Student Threats: Benign or Malignant?" *Law Enforcement Technology*, January 2002, pp.30–33.

Pence, Ellen and Paymar, Michael. "Defense of the Duluth Model." *Law and Order*, February 2004, p.376.

Penrod, Gary S. "Operation CleanSWEEP: The School Safety Program that Earned an A+." *FBI Law Enforcement Bulletin*, October 2001, pp.20–23.

Peterson, Karen S. "When School Hurts." *The Law Enforcement Trainer*, July/August 2001, pp.17–19.

Piazza, Peter. "Scourge of the Schoolyard." *Security Management*, November 2001, pp.68–73.

"Police Agencies Lack Experience Investigating Cyberstalking." *Criminal Justice Newsletter*, October 30, 2001, pp.6–7.

Pollack, Ira and Sundermann, Carlos. "Creating Safe Schools: A Comprehensive Approach." *Juvenile Justice*, June 2001, pp.13–20.

Rennison, Callie Marie. *Intimate Partner Violence, 1993–2001.* Washington, DC: Bureau of Justice Statistics Crime Data Brief, February 2003. (NCJ 197836)

Rennison, Callie Marie and Rand, Michael R. *Criminal Victimization, 2002.* Washington, DC: Bureau of Justice Statistics National Crime Victimization Survey, August 2003. (NCJ 199994)

Rosenbarger, Matt. "Multi-Jurisdictional Mock School Shooting." *Law and Order*, December 2001, pp.30–36.

Rudewicz, Frank E. "The Road to Rage." *Security Management*, February 2004, pp.41–49.

Sampson, Rana. *Bullying in Schools.* Washington, DC: Office of Community Oriented Policing Services Problem-Oriented Guides for Police Series No. 12, March 22, 2002.

Sanchez, Tom. "High-Tech Crisis Plans: Tools for School Safety." *The Police Chief*, April 2003, pp.18–20.

Sanders, John R. "A Model Approach to School Violence." *Law and Order*, August 2001, pp.100–101.

Sanow, Ed. "Goodbye, Duluth Model." *Law and Order*, November 2003, p.4.

Saulny, Susan. "City Adapts a Police Strategy to Violent Schools." *The New York Times*, October 19, 2004.

Schreck, Christopher J.; Miller, J. Mitchell; and Gibson, Chris L. "Trouble in the School Yard: A Study of the Risk Factors of Victimization at School." *Crime & Delinquency*, July 2003, pp.460–484.

Scott, Mike. "School Liaison." *Law and Order*, September 2001, pp.68–70.

Sherman, Lawrence W. "Domestic Violence." In *Crime File Study Guide*, National Institute of Justice. Washington, DC: U.S. Government Printing Office, no date.

Sherman, Lawrence W. and Berk, Richard A. *The Minneapolis Domestic Violence Experiment.* Washington, DC: Police Foundation Reports, 1984.

Small, Margaret and Tetrick, Kellie Dressler. "School Violence: An Overview." *Juvenile Justice*, June 2001, pp.3–12.

Smith-LaBombard, Halley. "Bullies Find No Refuge in Oak Harbor." *Community Links*, September 2001, pp.9–10.

Streit, Corinne. "Preventing Child Abuse in Your Community." *Law Enforcement Technology*, October 2001, pp.50–55.

*Strengthening Antistalking Statutes.* Washington, DC: Office for Victims of Crime Legal Series Bulletin #1, February 2002. (NCJ 189192)

"Suit Targets Wholesale Domestic-Violence Evictions." *Law Enforcement News*, September 15, 2001, p.10.

Turner, Nancy. "Domestic Violence and Firearms: Recognizing the Danger." *The Police Chief*, February 2002, pp.81–83.

Van Wyk, Judy A.; Benson, Michael L.; Fox, Greer Litton; and DeMaris, Alfred. "Detangling Individual-, Partner- and Community-Level Correlates of Partner Violence." *Crime & Delinquency*, July 2003, pp.412–438.

*Violence against Women: Identifying Risk Factors.* Washington, DC: NIJ Research in Brief, November 2004. (NCJ 197019)

"Violence in the Workplace Still Number One Security Threat for Fortune 1000 Corporate Security Managers." *Security Products*, July 2001, p.42.

Wald, Matthew L. "Most Crimes of Violence and Property Hover at 30-Year Lows." *The New York Times*, September 13, 2004.

Wattendorf, George E. "School Threat Decisions Demonstrate Support for Early Action." *The Police Chief*, March 2002, pp.11–12.

Websdale, Neil; Moss, Heather; and Johnson, Byron. "Domestic Violence Fatalities Reviews: Implications for Law Enforcement." *The Police Chief*, July 2001, pp.65–74.

Weiss, Jim and Davis, Mickey. "School Crisis: Israeli-Style." *Law and Order*, June 2004, pp.116–121.

Wen, Patricia. "Accused Teen Fits No Single Profile: School Violence Defies Stereotype." *The Boston Globe*, October 10, 2004.

"What Every Congregation Needs to Know about Domestic Violence." Minnesota Center Against Violence and Abuse, 2001. www.vaw.umn.edu

*When Violence Hits Home: How Economics and Neighborhood Play a Role.* NIJ website http://www.ojp.usdoj.gov/nij/pubs-sum/205004.htm

Williams, Dan. "Bullying: A New Approach." *The Police Chief*, May 2004, p.35.

Witkowski, Michael J. "The Gang's All Here." *Security Management*, May 2004, pp.95–99.

Wolak, Janis; Mitchell, Kimberly; and Finkelhor, David. *Internet Sex Crimes against Minors: The Response of Law Enforcement.* Washington, DC: National Center for Missing and Exploited Children, November 2003.

Wood, Robert A. and Wood, Nona L. "Stalking the Stalker: A Profile of Offenders." *FBI Law Enforcement Bulletin*, December 2002, pp.1–7.

Zoll, Tom and Munro, Curt. "Regional Communications System Plays Vital Role in Resolving Two High School Shootings." *The Police Chief*, November 2001, pp.55–59.

## CASES CITED

*Idaho v. Wright*, 110 S.Ct. 3139 (1990)

*Maryland v. Craig*, 110 S.Ct. 3157 (1990)

*Thurman v. City of Torrington*, 595 F. Supp. 1521 (D CONN 1984)

# CHAPTER 8

# Emergency Situations: When Disaster Strikes

### Do You Know . . .

- What emergencies a police department should plan for?
- What the four phases of an emergency usually are?
- What should be included in a predisaster plan?
- What FEMA's mission is?
- What two major difficulties police face during disasters?
- What the "pulse" of the government's response to an emergency is?
- What posttraumatic stress disorder is and why it is important to police officers who respond to emergency calls?
- Who should conduct a critical-incident stress debriefing and when, and who should attend?
- What emergency conditions require special considerations and contingency planning?
- What the prime consideration in any emergency is?
- What the two postemergency "killers" may be?
- What the policy of most police departments is regarding the handling of suspected bombs?

### Can You Define?

critical-incident stress debriefing (CISD)

emergency operations center (EOC)

FEMA

firewall

HAZMAT incident

posttraumatic stress disorder (PTSD)

predisaster plans

triage

## Introduction

Emergencies may be natural or caused by people. Natural emergencies include floods, fires, tornados, hurricanes, typhoons, tidal waves, landslides, avalanches, volcanic eruptions, extreme temperatures, blizzards, leaking natural gas and earthquakes. People-caused emergencies include civil disturbances; industrial and transportation accidents; hazardous-materials spills; water contamination; radiological and arson incidents; explosions; biological, chemical and nuclear attacks; and terrorist attacks. Emergencies may involve individuals, neighborhoods, communities, counties or even larger areas.

Every police department is expected to deal effectively and efficiently with all types of emergencies. Heal (2002, p.1) points out, after a disaster, things never get back to what was normal before the crisis. He notes that after the Northridge earthquake in Los Angeles County in 1994: "The aftershocks and aftereffects continued for months, even years—bridges down, roads impassable, traffic patterns altered, buildings condemned and boarded up, houses unlivable, and people's lives forever changed." It almost goes without saying that after September 11, 2001, the United States itself is forever changed. Terrorism and homeland security are the focus of Chapter 9. Those departments not prepared to handle emergencies not only may fail to protect property and life, but also may face expensive, time-consuming lawsuits as well as adverse political decisions.

 Police departments should have predisaster plans for those emergencies likely to occur within their jurisdictions.

This chapter begins with a look at the four phases of an emergency, followed by a discussion of predisaster plans and incident command systems. Next, the guidelines for dealing with emergencies are examined, including how to deal with posttraumatic stress following large-scale disasters and the importance of critical-incident stress debriefings. The chapter then focuses on special considerations in dealing with specific kinds of natural and person-made emergencies. The chapter concludes with a brief look at the relationship between emergency situations and community policing.

## The Four Phases of an Emergency

 Most emergencies happen in four phases: (1) the *warning* period, (2) the *impact* period, (3) the *immediate reaction* after impact and (4) the period of *delayed response*.

Usually as much *warning* as possible is desirable. Sometimes, however, warnings are impossible, as is the case, for example, with earthquakes and train derailments. In addition, advanced warning might have an adverse effect on some individuals, who may panic and become totally helpless, as though the emergency had already occurred. Their panic may spread to others. For example, this reaction sometimes occurs following the posting of a hurricane warning when the eye of the storm is projected to make landfall over a heavily populated area.

During the *impact period,* when the emergency is actually happening, different people will react differently. For many it will be stunned inactivity, a paralysis of sorts, with people unable to act effectively. Others, fueled by adrenaline, may act with determination, purpose and strength. Some report going "on automatic pilot." The period *immediately following the disaster* is the most crucial from the standpoint of rescue operations. Effective performance can save property and lives. A *delayed response* may occur once the immediate danger is past. Those who were functioning effectively may cease to do so, and vice versa.

## Predisaster Plans

Every department should have a carefully formulated, periodically updated emergency plan, the contents of which will depend on the types of emergencies to be anticipated for a jurisdiction. Jurisdictions in the North, for example, would need to include responses for blizzards, while those along the coast would include hurricane responses. *Unanticipated* emergencies should, however, also be included. For example, blizzard-like conditions can paralyze southern states precisely because such weather is not expected there.

**Predisaster plans** should include:

- What emergencies to prepare for.
- What needs to be done in advance (supplies on hand, agreements with other agencies, etc.).
- What specific functions must be performed during the emergency and who is responsible for performing them, including outside organizations and agencies that might help.
- How to keep the media informed.
- What steps need to be taken to restore order after the emergency is ended.
- How the response is to be evaluated.

The plan should be developed *not* solely by top management, but also by those who would be involved in implementing it, including government officials, fire department personnel, health care personnel and the like. Jurisdictions may seek assistance in developing their predisaster plan from the Federal Emergency Management Agency, or **FEMA,** an independent federal agency founded in 1979 and charged with building and supporting the nation's emergency management system. FEMA is staffed by more than 2,600 full-time employees and nearly 4,000 standby disaster assistance employees available to help after disasters.

The mission of FEMA is to reduce loss of life and property and protect our nation's critical infrastructure from all types of hazards through a comprehensive, risk-based, emergency management program of mitigation, preparedness, response and recovery.

On March 1, 2003, FEMA became part of the Department of Homeland Security. It has three strategic goals:

1. Protect lives and prevent the loss of property from natural and technological hazards.
2. Reduce human suffering and enhance the recovery of communities after disaster strikes.
3. Ensure that the public is served in a timely and efficient manner (FEMA website).

FEMA recommends communities address the following functions in disaster plans: (1) communication, (2) transportation, (3) public works, (4) firefighting, (5) intelligence efforts to assess damage, (6) mass care for those people displaced from their homes, (7) resource support (contracting for the labor needed to assist in a disaster), (8) health and medical, (9) search and rescue, (10) hazardous materials, (11) food or feeding and (12) energy. Communications should be the number one priority.

The emergency plan should also identify the levels of emergencies that might occur and the level of response required. Many jurisdictions use a three-level approach, with Level 1 including minor events that can usually be handled by on-duty personnel. A Level 2 event is a moderate to severe situation that requires aid from other agencies and perhaps other jurisdictions. A Level 3 event refers to catastrophes in which a State of Emergency is proclaimed and county, state and even federal assistance is requested. In such instances, the National Guard is often called for help.

Historically, many police departments have placed low priority on emergency management, believing that mass disasters were unlikely to happen in their jurisdictions. However, this is no longer a realistic approach. Every agency should have a plan for responding to an emergency and that plan should be practiced. Axt (2003, p.51) suggests: "Drills are to security as dress rehearsals are to Broadway; they are the only way to ensure success for the real performance."

 Lack of communication and coordination are the major problems during disasters.

## Communication, Coordination and Interoperability

Siegle and Murphy (2001, p.10) describe the Public Safety Wireless Network (PSWN) program, a joint effort sponsored by the U.S. Departments of Justice and the Treasury: "Public safety wireless interoperability refers to the ability of public safety officials to communicate with each other seamlessly in real time over their wireless communications network. Whether by voice or through data transmissions, interoperable communications can mean the difference between life and death for citizens and public safety personnel and often holds the key to minimizing loss of property when disasters occur." The PSWN officials recognize that setting up a national system may be beyond our present capabilities, but stress the possibility of regional networks.

Other efforts are being directed at getting the E-911 system for cellular phones in place nationally. "While the push has been ongoing to get wireless communications providers to implement an industry-wide tracking system for cellular phones, the need for such technology was given new urgency in the wake of the World Trade Center disaster" ("Now More than . . .," 2001, p.6). E-911 or enhanced 911 has geolocation capabilities allowing the person receiving the call to locate the caller to within 50 to 100 meters. As Rogers (2001a, p.88) reports: "It's [E-911's] happening in hundreds of communities, but it's still behind schedule." She (2001b, p.42) suggests: "This problem is further compounded by the fact that every year cell phone usage goes up. Approximately 115,000 wireless emergency calls to 911 are placed to our nation's Public Safety Answering Points (PSAPs) each day. Estimates are that wireless calls account for as many as 50 percent of all 911 calls received." It is vitally important that the geographic location of the person making the call be automatically available to PSAP personnel.

Another communication consideration is that during emergencies, phones and wireless systems can become overloaded. According to the *Criminal Justice Newsletter:*

> Major law enforcement groups are supporting a plan to overhaul the licensing of certain radio frequencies in order to make public safety communication more reliable.
>
> Currently, officers' lives are at risk because of radio interference that results in garbled, fuzzy or blocked calls over police radios, the law enforcement groups said. The police groups have endorsed a plan by the Federal Communications Commission (FCC) to reallocate frequencies, saying the plan would solve the problem. But some wireless telephone companies are opposing the plan saying it would create disruption in their operations.

The problem stems from the fact that radio channels assigned to law enforcement, firefighters and other public safety agencies are intermingled among channels for commercial purposes, such as cell phones. The plan backed by law enforcement, called "the Consensus Plan," would create a separate block of frequencies for law enforcement, and that would virtually eliminate interference, the law enforcement groups said.

On July 8 the FCC unanimously adopted a compromise set of reforms that includes elements of the Consensus Plan. But the issue is not yet settled; some wireless telecommunications have said they intend to file challenges to the FCC action ("Law Enforcement Groups Applaud Plan to End Radio Interference," 2004, p.6).

## Planning for Evacuation

In any disaster requiring evacuation, traffic control becomes a major challenge. The National Incident Management Coalition (NIMC) is an alliance representing the U.S. government, motorist clubs, the trucking industry and highway safety organizations whose purpose is to spread the "Incident Management" idea throughout the country. Its incident management approach has four parts: detection, response, clearance and recovery.

## Planning to Protect Computers

Spranza (2001, p.18) notes: "Protecting computers and networks from viral assault, data loss and physical damage is of paramount concern to keep computer operations healthy." He suggests that virus protection software and firewalls should be in place to protect against accidental or intentional sabotage of computers and networks. A **firewall** is a security measure intended to prevent unauthorized Internet users from accessing private networks connected to the Internet.

A good intrusion-detection system can analyze network traffic for intrusions and intrusion attempts as well as examine events and compare them to patterns identified as indicators of misuse.

The National Institute of Justice (NIJ) and the National Cybercrime Training Partnership conducted a study in 1998 to assess the needs of state and local law enforcement agencies to combat electronic crime and cyberterrorism. Although they identified more than 100 needs, they narrowed the list to the "Critical Ten" identified needs (Stambaugh et al., 2001, p.x): (1) public awareness, (2) data and reporting, (3) uniform training and certification courses, (4) on-site management assistance for electronic crime units and task forces, (5) updated laws, (6) cooperation with the high-tech industry, (7) special research and publications, (8) management awareness and support, (9) investigative and forensic tools and (10) structuring a computer crime unit.

Finally, risks can be reduced by having duplicate back-ups or a fully redundant communications system.

## Planning to Interact with the Media

According to Rosenthal (2001, p.16): "The single biggest key to successful management of any critical incident is planning. The first and perhaps most basic principle of any such media management plan is that law enforcement bosses should decide right now that they will work with the media to the maximum extent possible during a crisis."

Police and media representatives should meet and draw up agreements that respect the presses' First Amendment right to freedom of the press, but also the Sixth Amendment rights of others to privacy as well as law enforcement's need for safety and successful management of critical incidents. As Buice (2001, p.58) notes: "Just as the time to buy a fire truck is not on the way to the fire, the time to establish sound message management is not when the news hits the fan. Successful police chiefs and PIOs [public information officers] realize that effective message management is a journey, not a destination, and they understand that the journey is a long one."

Effective message management must be built on mutual trust. Hilte (2001, p.22) suggests such trust can be built over time for the price of a few cups of coffee, an occasional lunch and periodic visits at the local radio, television and newspaper offices. He (p.27) notes: "The law enforcement media mega-event is dynamic and fast paced. There is no foolproof blueprint for success. There are, however, certain actions a PIO can take to prepare. The time spent in preparation is well worth it."

Guidelines to prepare for the media onslaught certain to occur during a crisis include the following (Slader and Wilds, 2001, pp.127–131):

- Policies should be proactive, not reactive.
- Officers should be trained to expect to be caught on candid camera.
- A written statement should be prepared before any news conference.
- A news conference should be scheduled as early as possible.
- Officers need to know what information is protected by law.
- Information should be dispensed to the media at regular intervals.
- The phrase "no comment" should be avoided.

According to Covello, media professor at Columbia University: "The five biggest interview failures are failing to take charge; failing to anticipate questions; failing to develop key messages; failing to stick to the facts; and failing to keep calm" (Buice, 2003, p.26). Staszak (2001, p.10) cautions: "The overwhelming search for news should warn law enforcement that the media will get their story one way or another. Cooperating with the media remains the most reasonable avenue for PIOs to take." Van Blaricom (2001, p.53) offers another caution for PIOs: "Never mislead. Regardless of the circumstances, misleading the media will never be forgiven or forgotten." Finally, as Tyler (2001, p.51) points out: "We should remember that the media always has the last word."

## The Emergency Operations Center

During times of disaster, it is imperative that government continues to function in a coordinated way. A key to effective emergency management is the emergency operations center (EOC).

 The **emergency operations center (EOC)** is the "pulse" of the government's response to an emergency and helps reduce the problems of lack of communication and coordination.

Of course, sometimes the incident will dictate the location of such a center. Often an existing site in a government building works well. Ideally, the center is located close to police, fire and government officials. Douglas (2001, p.33) suggests the EOC be staffed by all departments within jurisdictions responsible for critical services, including law enforcement, fire, emergency medical services, power and gas, streets or highways department, water services, sewer, government (city manager or governor's office) and the press.

## Guidelines for Dealing with Emergencies

Every emergency will present a unique challenge to responding officers. Nonetheless, several guidelines can help assure the most effective response possible at each phase of the disaster.

### *Before the Emergency*

- Be prepared. Be proactive. Anticipate the immediate problems and the personnel needed to deal with them.
- Identify the equipment and resources required, and make certain they are either available or immediately accessible. To deal with disasters, departments should have, at minimum, lighted traffic batons, barricades, reflective signs for vehicles, safety vests for traffic officers and special vehicle-mounted lights and sirens.
- Establish and maintain good relationships with the media. They are among the first on the scene of emergencies and have a job to do. They can be invaluable in getting messages out to the general public and keeping panic to a minimum. They can also be a terrific liability if a good relationship does not exist.
- Establish a system so that police officers can know that their own families are safe during an emergency.

*The needs of officers are met by an efficient and effective emergency operations center. Here officials from various law enforcement agencies work in the New York Police Department Emergency Operations Center preparing for the Republican National Convention held in New York City in August 2004.*

## During the Emergency

- Take time to assess the situation. Do not make the situation worse by acting without thinking.
- Make saving lives a top priority. Establish a **triage** area where surviving victims can be separated according to the severity of their injuries. Those with critical medical needs should be tended to immediately and, once stabilized, transported to medical facilities. A morgue area for those who have died in the crisis should also be established.
- Do not broadcast a general call for help. Carefully but quickly assess what is needed and call for that.
- Keep the channels of communication open and the information flowing as required to those who need it.
- Keep as many options open as possible. Avoid either/or thinking.
- Do not get sidetracked by personal, individual requests for help, but rather focus on the big picture, routing individual requests to the appropriate source of assistance.
- Accept the fact that the police cannot do everything. The emergency manager must prioritize and delegate responsibilities quickly. Mistakes will probably happen.
- Involve key personnel as rapidly as possible. Do not let other agencies shirk their responsibilities.
- Keep top city officials fully informed of progress and problems.
- Ensure that someone is tending to normal business.

## After the Emergency

- Get back to normal as soon as possible.
- Expect that victims of the disaster or emergency may have very emotional reactions, including posttraumatic stress disorder. This is also true of the officers who have dealt with the disaster or emergency.
- Also expect that lawyers will get into it. *Document* everything that was done.

Evaluate the response after the situation has returned to normal. Look upon "mistakes" as the "least effective alternatives" as well as learning opportunities. Modify emergency-preparedness plans as needed based on what has been learned.

**Posttraumatic Stress after Large-Scale Disasters**   According to the American Psychiatric Association, **posttraumatic stress disorder (PTSD)** refers to the development of characteristic symptoms following a psychologically traumatic event generally outside the range of human experience. The symptoms include:

- Reexperiencing the event, either while awake or in recurrent dreams.
- Detachment and lack of involvement, diminished interest in formerly important activities, detachment from other people.
- At least two other of the following symptoms not present before the event:
  - Hyperalertness.
  - Sleep disturbance.
  - Guilt about surviving when others did not.
  - Memory impairment or trouble concentrating.
  - Avoiding activities that remind the person of the event.

Not only do many disaster victims experience PTSD, but so do many of those involved in helping them, especially if deaths have been particularly gruesome or have involved children. Police officers *are* susceptible to PTSD and should have support groups available to them.

 Posttraumatic stress disorder (PTSD) is a debilitating stressful reaction to a traumatic event; PTSD may last for months or years. It can be experienced not only by victims, but also by those who help the victims.

The likelihood that PTSD will occur in responding police officers can be reduced by having contingency plans that require them to mentally rehearse probable disaster situations, thus lowering their anxiety. It can be reduced further by practicing these plans, assigning each officer a specific task, maintaining order during the emergency, requiring that officers get some break periods during the emergency if it lasts longer than 10 hours and having a thorough debriefing following the emergency.

**The Critical-Incident Stress Debriefing**   An important consideration following a disaster is to conduct a **critical-incident stress debriefing (CISD)**, proven to be a powerful tool in preventing posttraumatic stress disorder.

 A CISD should be conducted by a professional mental health practitioner 24 to 48 hours after the incident and should be mandatory for all personnel involved in the incident.

One conducted before 24 hours has passed is likely to be ineffective as the full impact may not yet be felt. These debriefings should be mandatory to avoid anyone's feeling it is not macho to attend. The FEMA search and rescue teams located throughout the country are trained to do debriefing if an agency needs assistance in this area.

**Best Practices for Coping with Major Critical Incidents**   Sheehan et al. (2004, p.3) note: "Law enforcement professionals do not have the luxury of sitting back and theorizing when confronted with catastrophes." They (p.4) suggest: "Reviewing the evolving practices of uniquely experienced organizations, commonly referred to as an analysis of best practices, can prove informative." They studied several organizations' approach to crisis intervention, including the Bureau of Alcohol, Tobacco, Firearms and Explosives' Peer Support Critical Incident Stress Management Program; the FBI's Employee Assistance Unit; the Federal Law Enforcement Training Center (FLETC) Critical Incident Stress Management Program; the National Fraternal Order of Police (FOP) Critical Incident Stress Management Program; the New York City Police Organization Providing Police Assistance (POPPA); the Oklahoma City Critical Incident Workshop; the U.S. Marshals Service (USMS) Critical Incident Response Team (CIRT); and the U.S. Secret Service Critical Incident Peer Support Team.

Sheehan et al. (p.8) suggest: "Five best practices emerged from the many practical, empirically field-tested strategies used to deal with large-scale critical incidents. They almost are universal, and agencies should consider them in any organizational approach to effective critical incident stress management":

1. Early intervention—early psychological intervention for those officers responding to critical incidents.

2.  Complete care—use of a phase-sensitive, multicomponent crisis intervention system as part of an overall continuum of care.
3.  Peer support—a virtual imperative to a successful law enforcement program.
4.  Specialized training—specialized training in crisis intervention/emergency mental health is important before implementing such programs.
5.  Tactical intervention—including the ability to perform one-on-one small- and large-group crisis intervention and family support services, as well as the ability to access spiritual support assistance and treatment resources.

Sheehan et al. (pp.8–9) also identified five core competencies as features of a best practices model:

1.  Assessment and triage—agencies need to rapidly evaluate affected officers and provide them with assistance consistent with the resources at hand.
2.  Crisis intervention with individuals—mass critical incident care is not a one-size-fits-all proposition.
3.  Small group crisis intervention—peers supporting each other in a group setting can be highly effective and efficient.
4.  Large-group crisis intervention—a town meeting provides another way for people to process the tumultuous events engulfing them.
5.  Strategic planning—the process is strategic because it involves preparing the best way to respond to the circumstances of the organization's environment, whether or not the circumstances are known in advance.

They (p.10) note: "No group is more affected than those who impose order upon the chaos resulting from a major critical incident." They (p.11) suggest: "In an era of incipient terrorism, agencies must provide proactive training." Sheehan et al. (p.12) conclude: "Regardless of the size of the department, the men and women who have dedicated themselves to protect their communities will benefit from adopting these best practices."

**Identifying Fatalities**   A comprehensive disaster plan should include how fatalities will be identified. Help in identifying fatalities is available through the FBI Identification Division's Disaster Squad, which has aided in such disasters as the volcanic eruption of Mount St. Helens, in the 1978 mass murder-suicides at Jonestown, Guyana, and in the 1986 space shuttle explosion. It also provided assistance during Operation Desert Storm. Its free identification services are available 24/7. In addition to cost-free fatality identification services offered by the Disaster Squad, the FBI provides assistance to law enforcement and civic agencies in formulating emergency response plans.

**Restoring Order**   When emergencies have been controlled and their urgency has diminished, police services are still needed. The constant threat of looting and malicious damage will continue until the area again becomes functional and the residents return to their homes or emergency workers are no longer present. When extra police are required following an incident, supervisors should conduct a gradual phase-out rather than allowing an abrupt return to normal duty.

Also, following any emergency situation, there is usually a steady flow of curiosity seekers that will tend to taper off as interest diminishes and the area returns to normal. This process may take several hours, days or weeks, depending on the emergency's magnitude. Some emergencies are so severe they are declared disasters. Eldridge (2004, p.18) explains: "By its definition, a disaster is when some type of natural or man-made event causes regional damage. This could include tornados, flooding, civil unrest, forest fires and the like. It can also include less damaging but equally severe situations, such as droughts, extreme cold and heat waves, an economic collapse, a crime snap or toxic substance release."

# Natural Disasters

Just as general guidelines can be specified for emergencies, general guidelines and considerations can be made in advance for specific kinds of natural emergencies, reducing the loss of property and lives.

> In addition to general predisaster plans, contingency plans should be made for such natural disasters as floods, explosions, fires, cyclones and earthquakes. In all such emergencies, saving lives is of top priority.

## *Floods*

A flood, although damaging and usually predictable, demands a coordinated response and implementation of a previously thought-out plan. Normally, police will assist residents and merchants in the affected areas to evacuate their homes and their businesses. As soon as a police department receives notice of an impending flood, the regular and reserve officers are usually called to duty. In some instances, they may be put on alert or on standby in case they are needed.

During an evacuation and while the emergency is in progress, the police must seal off the affected area to prevent looting and vandalism. Special passes can be

*A Putnam County, Florida, deputy sheriff uses his walkie talkie for an update on an emergency.*

Joel Gordon

issued to residents who have legitimate business in the area. All others not living or having business in the flood area should be excluded.

## Explosions

Explosions may be accidental or purposeful. Accidental explosions may result from earthquakes, natural fires, plane or train crashes or natural gas leaks. Purposeful explosions include those caused by arsonists, discussed later in the chapter, and by terrorists, discussed in Chapter 9. Department policies and procedures should be developed for dealing with all types of explosions.

## Fires

Fires are usually the fire department's primary responsibility, although some police departments have a combined public safety service. Such departments have trained officers to assist firefighters. One police responsibility is to protect firefighters from harassment. Some sections of cities are plagued with spectators who taunt firefighters and try to disrupt firefighting. In these cases, police officers must protect firefighters and also control spectators, protect fire equipment and regulate traffic drawn to the scene.

When the Bandelier National Park Service started a "controlled burn" west of Los Alamos, New Mexico, in 2000, high winds spread the fire eastward, destroying structures in Los Alamos and threatening the Los Alamos National Laboratory. The area's 18,500 residents were evacuated without a single death or serious injury. The police department had long had a plan in place because of the sensitivity of the work at the National Laboratory, which conducts classified nuclear weapons development.

Utility agencies shut off gas and water. A reverse 911 system notified many residents by telephone, delivering instructions on the evacuation. The local radio station switched to 24-hour coverage of the evacuation, and loudspeaker announcements from emergency vehicles reached residents who had not heard the news. To prevent looting, National Guard personnel patrolled the town along with state and local police. In addition, the police held two press briefings a day to accommodate the hundreds of media people on the scene.

## Cyclones: Hurricanes and Tornados

In strict meteorological terminology, a cyclone is an area of low atmospheric pressure surrounded by a wind system blowing, in the Northern Hemisphere, in a counterclockwise direction. When this weather system develops over water, it is called a hurricane or, in the western Pacific, a typhoon. Cyclones occurring over land are tornados. Many of the emergencies already discussed may also occur during a hurricane or tornado, including flooding, fires and explosions, accompanied by looting and vandalism.

A hurricane is a very strong tropical cyclone involving heavy rains and sustained winds over 74 mph. It may also be accompanied by a strong storm surge, with large waves causing extensive damage to coastal property and near-shore structures. Barnett (2004, p.41) describes the devastation in Florida caused by Hurricane Ivan while Florida was still reeling from Charley and Frances, two severe hurricanes that came ashore just three weeks apart in late August and early September of 2004. According to the FEMA website, damage from the three hurricanes is about 1.7 billion dollars.

In addition to the tragic loss of life and damage to property, those responding to the disaster may face communication and mobility problems. Regular phone lines may be down, two-way radio communications may be unavailable due to damaged repeaters, and cellular communications networks may be overwhelmed by ongoing use. Getting around may be difficult because road signs and other landmarks may be gone, street lights may be out, and many roads may be blocked by such obstacles as fallen trees, live utility wire and other debris. Some low areas may be flooded and impassable. Highways and other main travel arteries may become gridlocked during the evacuation efforts, and debris scattered across roadways may cause numerous flat tires and other traffic mishaps, involving not only citizens but first responders as well.

Eventually, things will come under control, but time, and perhaps lives, may be saved if a predisaster plan is in place. Citizens should be educated on the steps to take, such as evacuating if advised to do so, boarding up windows or closing shutters if not evacuating, and having ample potable water and flashlights or candles available.

Other parts of the country are threatened by tornados—dark, funnel-shaped clouds containing violently rotating air that twists, rises and falls, and where it reaches the earth causes great destruction. A tornado's diameter can range from a few feet to over a mile, with winds circulating between 200 and 300 mph. The length of a tornado's path on the ground varies from under a mile to several hundred miles. In an average year in the United States, some 800 tornadoes injure more than a thousand people. Again, preparedness is the key to limiting the amount of destruction. Tornado warning systems are an integral part of preparedness, as is education of the public as to steps to take, where to seek shelter and the like.

In the aftermath of such natural disasters, many departments find their most significant problem is not, as might be expected, the cleanup but rather the quick depletion of their yearly overtime budgets and completion of the massive amount of paperwork required by FEMA in order for the jurisdiction to be reimbursed for expenses resulting from the disaster.

 Postemergency "killers" may be overruns in overtime and excessive paperwork.

## Earthquakes

While floods and hurricanes usually can be predicted, earthquakes strike with no warning. Areas in which earthquakes are likely to occur must have preestablished plans to deal with such emergencies. Included within these plans should be measures to deal with collapsed buildings and bridges, downed power lines, fires, explosions, injuries and deaths. As in other kinds of emergencies, traffic problems, vandalism and looting must also be anticipated.

## Accidental or Intentional Emergencies

Jurisdictions must also be prepared for catastrophic accidents and deliberate acts that can lead to loss of life or injury and destruction of property.

 Contingency plans also must be made for other emergencies such as plane crashes, hazardous materials spills, bomb threats, actual bombings and terrorist attacks involving chemical, biological and nuclear weapons of mass destruction. Regardless of cause, in all such emergencies, saving lives is the top priority.

While plane crashes and hazardous materials spills are often accidental, terrorists may intentionally cause such disasters in their efforts to cause death and fear as discussed in Chapter 9.

## Plane Crashes

The 1996 crash of TWA Flight 800 off Long Island into the Atlantic, the terrorist hijacking and subsequent crash of United Flight 93 into a rural Pennsylvania field on September 11, 2001, and the November 2001 crash of American Airlines Flight 587 into a residential neighborhood in Queens, New York—all highlight the extreme destruction and tragedy such an emergency can cause. A plane crash carries very heavy responsibilities because loss of life usually is associated with the crash. Upon notification of a plane crash, the police department must notify the Federal Aviation Administration (FAA), which has jurisdiction over and responsibility for such investigations. The National Transportation Safety Board (NTSB) also has jurisdiction if a death is involved. In the case of a military aircraft, the military service involved must be notified. The security of the aircraft and its scattered parts then becomes the responsibility of the military police.

The initial responsibility of the police department is to seal off the area surrounding any parts that may have been separated from the plane. Frequently, other jurisdictions may become involved, as parts of the aircraft may be found several blocks or miles away from the main crash site. If large numbers of people are injured, the ambulance services and the fire department rescue units may become overburdened. When this occurs, the hospital may send several of its staff members to the scene to assist. Police officers must provide easy access to and from the scene for those hospital personnel.

## Hazardous Materials (HAZMAT) Incidents

Some emergencies to which police are called may involve hazardous materials **(HAZMAT incident)** and other dangerous goods: derailed trains, overturned chemical-laden tank trucks, incidents at industrial plants or other scenes where toxic substances are present. Modes of transportation of hazardous materials include truck, rail, pipeline, water and air, and each mode presents its own unique challenges to HAZMAT responders. According to the U.S. Department of Transportation ("Hazardous Materials Shipments," 2002): "Hazardous materials traffic levels in the U.S. now exceed 800,000 shipments per day and result in the transport of more than 3.1 billion tons of hazardous materials annually." In 2000 the USDOT received reports of 17,514 HAZMAT incidents resulting in 13 deaths, 246 injuries and more than $72 million in damages.

The USDOT asserts: "Human error is the probable cause of most transportation incidents and associated consequences involving the release of hazardous materials." An example of an accidental HAZMAT emergency was the derailment in North Dakota of a train with four cars carrying anhydrous ammonia that leaked following the crash. One person died and hundreds were evacuated, with many requiring hospitalization. HAZMAT events may also be intentional, such as the dispersal of anthrax using the U.S. mail system. The law enforcement response to such deliberate releases involves not only actions directed toward the HAZMAT incident itself but also to the follow-up criminal investigation. Whatever the origin, the increasing number of hazardous materials in commercial use has significantly raised the likelihood of law enforcement officers being called to a spill, and they must be trained to respond appropriately.

Some law enforcement agencies have their own HAZMAT teams, but others have a regional team. Strandberg (2001, p.18) describes the various kinds of HAZMAT training offered by the Emergency Response Training Center located outside Pueblo, Colorado. As part of the course, law enforcement personnel go through technician training that meets OSHA's requirements for responding to HAZMAT incidents. According to Conlon, director of marketing: "Law enforcement agencies benefit from the training because it helps them understand what the people who wear the protective clothing and are plugging the leaks are going through" (Strandberg, p.20).

Czarnecki (2002, p.13) describes the training law enforcement officers should be receiving, including an introduction to the WMD [weapons of mass destruction] concept, local and federal organizations responding to WMD incidents, review of past NBC [nuclear, biological, chemical] weapons, overview of NBC agents, dissemination devices, how to recognize NBC incidents, responder actions, containment, decontamination, triage, first aid, protective equipment and how to activate the local emergency response plan.

Short of any specialized training, officers should know some basic guidelines for responding to HAZMAT emergencies. When hazardous cargo is being transported, federal law requires the hauler to carry a manifest specifically detailing what they are carrying, how much and the shipment destination. Many manifests also provide an MSDS, or material safety data sheet, with information on handling, containing and neutralizing the hazardous materials or dangerous goods in the event of a spill, leak or other inadvertent release. Haulers are also required to display a colored placard and symbol identifying the hazardous nature of their shipment. The most familiar warnings are the colored placards on the sides and rear of the trailer or shipping container, generally visible from a greater distance than the symbol, thereby, allowing first responders to tailor their approach accordingly. The standard placard colors and what they represent are:

- Flammable—red
- Corrosive—black and white
- Explosive—orange
- Poison—black and white
- Nonflammable gas—green
- Oxidizer—yellow

Officers should have binoculars in their vehicles so they can read placards and markings on trucks or railroad cars involved in accidents. Robinson (2004, p.64) suggests: "If the fire department has a ladder truck, [officers] might be able to set it up at a distance, raise the ladder and use binoculars to read the placard on the side of an overturned tanker." Because the danger of explosion, fire or toxic fumes is always present, officers should stay as far away as possible but also try to identify what the truck or railroad car was transporting.

The USDOT stresses: "The scene of an incident can be chaotic, so the right actions may not always be obvious." General safety precautions and other basic guidelines for first responders to a HAZMAT accident scene include:

- Respond upwind and upgrade, when possible, and anticipate changes in wind direction.

- Park vehicles heading away from the incident, then approach on foot.
- The first priority is to isolate and secure the scene. Use barrier tape, traffic cones or barricades, *not* flares.
- Keep contaminated, ill or injured people away from others.
- If necessary, initiate an evacuation.
- Do not eat, drink or smoke at any hazardous materials incident.
- Do not touch any container, and avoid contact with liquids or fumes.
- Treat all hazardous materials as if they were toxic or explosive. Always consider the possibility of more than one hazard being present.
- Latex (surgical type) and leather gloves are *not* adequate protection against most hazardous materials.
- Keep your dispatcher informed of any/all actions you take at the scene.

The *2000 Emergency Response Guidebook* (ERG2000) was developed jointly by the U.S. Department of Transportation, Transport Canada and the Secretariat of Communications and Transportation of Mexico for use by firefighters, police and other emergency services personnel who may be the first to arrive at the scene of a transportation incident involving a hazardous material. It is primarily a guide to aid first responders in (1) quickly identifying the specific or generic classification of the material(s) involved in the incident and (2) protecting themselves and the general public during this initial response phase of the incident. The ERG is updated every three years to accommodate new products and technology. Free copies are available to public emergency responders in the United States through their state DOT coordinator. Included in the *2000 Emergency Response Guidebook* is a "Table of Initial Isolation and Protective Action Distances," suggesting distances useful to protect people from vapors resulting from spills involving dangerous goods considered poisonous or toxic by inhalation (TIH). The table also provides first responders with initial guidance until technically qualified emergency response personnel are available. Distances show areas likely to be affected during the first 30 minutes after a HAZMAT spill and could increase with time. For more information, go to http://hazmat.dot.gov.

Another useful resource is CHEMTREC, the Chemical Transportation Emergency Center, established in 1971 by the chemical industry as a public service hotline for firefighters, law enforcement and other emergency responders. An integral part of the American Chemistry Council (formerly known as the Chemical Manufacturers Association), CHEMTREC maintains a state-of-the-art communication center and a high-end MSDS document storage and retrieval system, containing nearly 2.8 million MSDSs. These documents enable CHEMTREC to supply information on a product's known hazards and what to do and not do in case of a spill, a fire or exposure to the substance.

CHEMTREC can also provide immediate advice by telephone for the on-scene commander at a HAZMAT emergency. Its personnel will promptly contact the shipper of the hazardous material(s) involved in the incident for detailed assistance and relay an appropriate response back to the on-scene incident commander. In some situations, a segment of the chemical industry or even a company may have a HAZMAT team that will respond. CHEMTREC can alert such teams if they exist. CHEMTREC's 24-hour Emergency Call Center, located in Arlington, Virginia, may be accessed toll-free by first responders at (800) 424-9300.

## Bombs and Bomb Threats

Any business or establishment can be the victim of a bomb threat or bombing. Among the most common targets are airlines, banks, educational institutions, government buildings, hospitals, industrial complexes, military installations, office buildings and utilities. According to the ATF, the top three motivating factors for bombings are vandalism, revenge and protest (Weiss and Dresser, 2002, p.75).

The February 26, 1993, bombing of the World Trade Center in New York, which killed six and injured more than a thousand, and the April 19, 1995, bombing of the Alfred P. Murrah Federal Building in Oklahoma City, which left 169 people dead and nearly 500 injured, were not just disasters resulting in loss of life but were also major crime scenes—the sites of the mass murders of innocent civilians.

According to Smith (2003, p.43): "The average law enforcement officer will never encounter an actual bomb during his career. However, it is very probable that he will have to deal with suspicious packages, bomb threats and found explosives." Although 98 percent of bomb threats are hoaxes, the threats are costly and emotionally charged, and may be dangerous if people panic. Having a well-established procedure to handle a bomb-threat call is imperative. It should be written, kept in plain view of those who answer the phone and practiced. If a threat is received, the person who receives it should know exactly what to do. Receivers of bomb threats should:

- Keep the caller talking as long as possible.
- Try to learn as much as possible about the bomb, especially when it will go off and where it is located.
- Try to determine the caller's sex, age, accent and speech pattern, and whether he or she is drunk or drugged.
- Listen for any background noises.
- Immediately notify the appropriate person(s) of the call.

Some organizations have forms such as that shown in Figure 8.1 to be completed by any individual who receives a telephoned bomb threat. It is critical that individuals who answer telephones know who to report a bomb threat to. This person then determines what action to take. Alternatives include ignoring the threat, searching for the possible bomb or evacuating the premises. No matter what alternative is selected, the police should be called.

A command post should be established as soon as the decision is made to treat the bomb threat as real. The entire building should then be diagrammed and areas crossed off as they are searched. A system of communicating among searchers must be established, but it must not involve the use of portable radios, as they may detonate the bomb. All searchers should be cautioned not to turn on lights, as this might also detonate the bomb. Searchers should move slowly and carefully, listening for any ticking sounds and watching for trip wires.

Sometimes metal detectors are used to assist in the search. Many police departments are using bomb-sniffing dogs with great success. Such dogs are trained to move quietly and to not bark when a bomb is located, but rather to simply "point" to it. Explosives-detecting dogs are especially valuable in searching cluttered or inaccessible areas. Laska (2002, p.52) stresses that those who respond to bombs (threatened or actual) should have available bomb suits, HAZMAT protection and robots.

---

## BOMB THREAT INSTRUCTIONS

### Place this card under your telephone

**Questions to ask:**
1. *When is the bomb going to explode?*
2. *Where is it right now?*
3. *What does it look like?*
4. *What kind of bomb is it?*
5. *What will cause it to explode?*
6. *Did you place the bomb?*
7. *Why?*
8. *What is your address?*
9. *What is your name?*

### *Exact wording of the threat:*

_____

_____

_____

_____

_____

_____

*Sex of caller:* _____ *Race:* _____

*Age:* _____ *Length of call:* _____

### Additional information on reverse.

---

Number at which call is received: _____

Time: _____ Date: ___/ ___/___

*Caller's Voice:*
☐ Loud   ☐ Soft   ☐ High   ☐ Deep
☐ Intoxicated   ☐ Disguised   ☐ Calm   ☐ Angry
☐ Fast   ☐ Slow   ☐ Stutter   ☐ Nasal
☐ Distinct   ☐ Slurred   ☐ Accent (*type:* _____)

Other Characteristics: _____

_____

If voice is familiar, who did it sound like? _____

*Background Sounds:*
☐ Voices   ☐ Quiet   ☐ Animals
☐ Street Traffic   ☐ Office Machinery   ☐ Airplanes
☐ Trains   ☐ Factory Machinery   ☐ Music
Other: _____

*Threat Language:*
☐ Foul   ☐ Well spoken (educated)
☐ Taped   ☐ Message read by threat-maker
☐ Irrational   ☐ Incoherent

*Remarks:* _____

_____

_____

Report call immediately to: _____
Phone number: _____

Date: ___/ ___/ ___
Name: _____
Position: _____
Phone Number: _____

**Figure 8.1** Sample Bomb Threat Instructions

SOURCE: International Association of Chiefs of Police. *Project Response: The Oklahoma City Tragedy.* Alexandria, VA: IACP, 1995, p.10. Reprinted by permission.

Areas that are usually unlocked and unwatched are the most common sites for bombs, for example, restrooms, lobbies, lunch rooms, elevators and stairs. Officers should look for anything out of place or foreign to the area, for example, a briefcase in the restroom. Bombs can be hidden in lunch pails, briefcases, shopping bags, candy boxes and any number of other types of containers. According to the ATF, the most common types of containers used are pipe bombs and bottles. Dynamite sticks, cans, boxes, pressurized cartridges and grenade hulls are also used but not as frequently (Weiss and Dresser).

Bombings with potentially disastrous effects are remarkably simple to perform. Several underground newsletters give detailed instructions on how to make bombs using common materials such as lead pipe filled with black powder, caps screwed on both ends and a fuse. Haber (2004, p.13) notes: "Pipe bombs and other improvised explosive devices (IEDs) pose a serious threat to federal, state and local government facilities, considering how easily and inexpensively they can be put together. Schools, shopping malls, stadiums and other public places people can freely walk around and through are potential targets."

Many indicators should alert law enforcement officers to suspicious packages: lopsidedness, protruding wires, oily stains on the wrapper, a strange odor, no return address, excessive weight, titles only, no names, incorrect titles, visual distractions, foreign mail, air mail, special delivery, restrictive markings such as confidential or personal, postage not canceled, excessive security tape or string and handwritten or poorly typed addresses (Weiss and Dresser, p.75). Officers should be suspicious of any plastic bottle emitting a gas or causing the ground around it to discolor.

If a bomb is found, the police should be prepared to deal with it themselves or know who to call to deal with it.

 The policy of most police departments when dealing with a suspected bomb is *do not touch*—move the people away from the bomb, not the bomb away from the people. A 300-foot radius is a good general rule to follow.

It is usually not necessary for officers to act immediately other than to evacuate the immediate area and to then call the fire department or a bomb disposal unit who are better equipped to handle such situations. If a military installation is close by, its bomb demolition team may help. When a suspicious object or bomb is located, doors and windows in the area should be opened, and all fire extinguishers should be readied and in position to combat any fires caused by the explosion. The bomb should be surrounded with sandbags or similar shock-absorbing objects. Valuable and irreplaceable documents, files, computer disks and other items should be removed from the vicinity and, if time allows, so too should highly flammable material.

Laska (p.55) suggests: "Although it's an expensive piece of equipment, a robot is a versatile machine that greatly enhances the safety of personnel on incidents. On many calls, a robot may perform all operations on a device, protecting the technician from hazard. It also is a valuable responder for hazardous materials incidents, including chemical, radiological and biological devices, making a technical worker impervious to the effects of such devices." Page (2002, p.136) suggests:

> Police bomb disposal and hazardous duty robots are becoming less like remotely controlled machines and more like curious little humans. . . .
>
> Government researchers at Sandia National Laboratories in Albuquerque, New Mexico, have taken a remote-controlled wheeled police robot and given it an embryonic brain. This allows the bomb 'bot to make many "how to" decisions on its own, without human control. It also frees up operators' time so they can make more critical "what to do next" decisions during potentially dangerous bomb disablement or other law enforcement missions.
>
> The purpose of the upgrade is to substantially improve police explosive ordinance disposal (EOD) operations, mainly through enhanced controllability of the manipulator arms. Certain characteristics inherent in robots are ideal for the tense work of disarming bombs—they don't get tired, and they are immune to smoke, toxic fumes and emotional stress. Giving them a better memory is the next step.

Cox (2004, p.106) describes another technological advance, the enhanced EOD, the recoilless disrupter: "A disrupter is a device that uses gunpowder to fire a jet of water or a projectile at a particular component of an explosive in order to render it safe."

As with other emergency responses, collaboration among many agencies is generally required during and immediately following a bombing. As was the case in Oklahoma City, bomb technicians and special investigators worked side by side with clean-up crews, around the clock, seven days a week, sifting through hundreds of tons of debris. The army of response and rescue workers included law enforcement officers, firefighters, sheriff's deputies, dog handlers, emergency medical teams, hospital personnel, engineers, heavy equipment operators, chaplains, National Guard members, Red Cross staff and volunteers and social service workers from across the country.

## Emergencies and Community Policing

One difficulty frequently encountered by departments seeking to implement community policing is that no sense of community exists. This is noted by Miller and Hess (2005, p.60): "It is extremely difficult to maintain community policing when the values of groups within a given area clash." In times of crisis, such as that following the terrorist attacks of September 11, this "sense of community" may either be strengthened or weakened.

On the "up-side" of emergencies and disasters, be they natural or not, is how the community often pulls together for survival, support and recovery. Walls come down, the circle of trust expands and people look past their differences to focus on their common ground—as Americans in need of help from one another. The flip side to this, of course, is that some people may react just the opposite— walls go up, trust in others diminishes, and suspicion and fear grows toward citizens who share any characteristics with those deemed responsible for the crisis.

### SUMMARY

Police departments should have predisaster plans for those emergencies likely to occur within their jurisdictions. Such plans should include what emergencies to prepare for; what needs to be done in advance (supplies on hand, agreements with other agencies, etc.); what specific functions must be performed during the emergency and who is responsible for performing them, including outside organizations and agencies that might help, how to keep the media informed, what steps need to be taken to restore order after the emergency is ended and how the response is to be evaluated.

Jurisdictions may seek assistance in developing their predisaster plan from the Federal Emergency Management Agency, or FEMA, an independent federal agency charged with building and supporting the nation's emergency management system. The mission of FEMA is to reduce loss of life and property and protect our nation's critical infrastructure from all types of hazards through a comprehensive, risk-based, emergency management program of mitigation, preparedness, response and recovery.

Lack of communication and coordination are the major problems during disasters. These problems can be reduced by having an emergency operations center (EOC), which is considered the "pulse" of the government's response to an emergency. Any particularly devastating event can have long-range emotional effects, including posttraumatic stress disorder (PTSD), a debilitating stressful reaction to a traumatic event. PTSD may last for months or years. It can be experienced not only by victims, but also by those who help the victims. A powerful tool in preventing posttraumatic stress disorder is the critical-incident stress debriefing (CISD), which should be conducted by a professional mental health practitioner 24 to 48 hours after the incident and should be mandatory for all personnel involved in the incident.

In addition to general predisaster plans, contingency plans should be made for such natural disasters as floods, explosions, fires, cyclones and earthquakes, as well as other person-made emergencies such as plane crashes, hazardous-materials spills, bomb threats and actual bombings, and terrorist attacks. In *all* such emergencies, saving lives is of top priority. Common postemergency "killers" include overruns in overtime and excessive paperwork.

The policy of most police departments when dealing with a suspected bomb is *do not touch*—move the people away from the bomb, not the bomb away from the people. A 300-foot radius is a good general rule to follow.

### APPLICATION

As your department's emergency management officer, you have been directed to establish a policy and procedure to respond to a natural disaster likely to threaten your jurisdiction. Include the roles of local, state and federal agencies in your policy and procedure.

### AN EXERCISE IN CRITICAL THINKING

On July 8 at 3:35 A.M., two police officers received a call reporting a multiple-car crash on the eastbound lanes of Interstate Highway 94 three miles east of Twin Lakes at the crossing of the Kinnickinnic River. There were patches of fog approaching the area, reducing visibility in the location of the collisions to 100 feet. Seven vehicles had collided. Four were in the ditch to the right side of the road; one was on the left shoulder facing toward the ditch; one was on the right shoulder with the front left tire four feet into the right lane; and one vehicle was straddling the two lanes with its front tire in the right lane and its back tires in the left lane.

1. As no headlights of approaching traffic can be seen,
   a. Both officers should leave their squad cars, with lights flashing as warnings, and survey damages to vehicles and personal injuries.
   b. One officer should stop all approaching traffic at a point west of the patches of fog while the other officer surveys the scene to call for the appropriate assistance.
   c. One officer should act as an emergency manager and prioritize and delegate responsibilities.
   d. Immediately broadcast a general call for help—obtain ambulance and medical help, wreckers and clean-up assistance, then stand aside to direct traffic.
   e. The first to arrive on the scene should attempt to give first aid to individuals requesting help, and the second should begin an investigation to see if gross misdemeanors for aggravated driving violations are in order.
2. If one person is observed leaving the scene of the crash,
   a. The second officer to arrive should pursue and arrest that individual and place him or her in the back seat of the squad car for later interrogation and sobriety tests.
   b. The first officer to arrive should call for K-9 backup to track down the individual for interrogation.
   c. Both officers should ignore this departure unless the individual appears to pose a threat to others. After the initial traumatic shock, this person will probably recover emotional balance and return without coercion.
   d. Action should be taken only if the emergency manager assesses it to be necessary and timely.
   e. Officers should request an ambulatory survivor who is physically able to chase down this individual and bring him or her back to the scene of the crash.
3. In addition to three injured people who were removed in ambulances and two who were given medical attention but not hospitalized, Reginald Jones was found slumped behind the wheel of the vehicle found in the middle of the highway. Others testified that they had braked and swerved to miss his vehicle, which along with the poor visibility had caused the onset of the multiple-vehicle collision. One officer walked up just as Jones was about to be removed from the vehicle by ambulance attendants. The attendants turned Jones over to the officer, who noticed indications of intoxication. Jones refused to take field sobriety tests, stating the officer had no right to ask him because an acquaintance named "Arel" had been driving the car all evening until it stalled at the spot where police found it. Jones did not request an attorney.
   a. Jones should be arrested for an aggravated driving violation.
   b. Insufficient evidence exists for Jones to be tested or arrested.
   c. Only if other witnesses can corroborate that no other person was in the vehicle with Jones should he be interrogated.
   d. If Jones can give "Arel's" full name and address, then he should be released; otherwise, he should be arrested and interrogated.
   e. As Jones is the prime suspect who has caused the entire emergency, he should be arrested, searched, handcuffed and taken to police headquarters for interrogation.

### DISCUSSION QUESTIONS

1. What types of emergencies are most likely to occur in your community? Least likely?
2. Assume that the potential for flooding exists in your community. What type of training would you recommend for the police department?
3. What should be the foremost concern of police officers when dealing with a natural disaster?
4. In dealing with a bomb threat, what are the most important considerations?
5. How might the media be of help during an emergency situation?
6. Have you ever been involved in an emergency situation yourself? How well was it handled? What could have been done differently?
7. Does your local law enforcement agency have an emergency preparedness plan? If so, what does it consist of?

### INFOTRAC COLLEGE EDITION ASSIGNMENTS

- Use InfoTrac College Edition to answer the Discussion Questions as appropriate.
- Find and read the article "The Manageable Future" by Charles S. Heal. Pay special attention to the two figures. Summarize what each figure graphically depicts, and be prepared to share your summary with the class.
- Find and read the article "Nationwide Application of the Incident Command System" by Michael D. Cardwell and Patrick T. Cooney. Write a brief report explaining what the acronym FIRESCOPE stands for, what it is intended to do and why the authors suggest it should be adopted nationwide. Again, be prepared to discuss your report with the class.
- Law enforcement is faced with many emergencies during any given year. Check on bomb threats and note who is conveying the threats and who is receiving them. Can the police effectively deal with the number of threats shown? Discuss your findings with the class.
- Read and outline one of the following articles to share with the class:
  - "Nationwide Application of the Incident-Command System: Standardization Is the Key" by Michael D. Cardwell and Patrick T. Cooney
  - "The Manageable Future: Envisioning the End State" by Charles S. Heal
  - "The FBI's Critical Incident Stress Management Program" by Vincent J. McNally and Roger M. Solomon
  - "The Public Safety Wireless Network (PSWN) Program: A Brief Introduction" by Derek Siegle and Rick Murphy

- "Media Trends and the Public Information Officer" by Dennis Staszak

### INTERNET ASSIGNMENTS

Select two assignments to complete:
- Go to FEMA's website at www.fema.gov and find their detailed list of steps to create an emergency management plan. Outline the basic steps, and be prepared to share your outline with the class.
- Go to the Transportation Technology Center Inc., (TTCI) website at www.ttci.aar.com and outline the courses in HAZMAT training offered that might be of interest to law enforcement officers. Be prepared to discuss your findings with the class.

### BOOK-SPECIFIC WEBSITE

The book-specific website at http://cj.wadsworth.com/ wobleski_Hess_police_op4e hosts a variety of resources for students and instructors. Many can be emailed to the instructor. Included are extended activities such as Concept Builders - the 3 step learning module that reinforces key chapter concepts, followed by a real-world applications and critical thinking questions. InfoTrac College Edition exercises; Discussion Questions; interactive key-term FlashCards; and a collection of chapter-based Web Links provide additional information and activities to include in the curriculum.

### REFERENCES

Axt, David A. "Places Everyone." *Security Management*, June 2003, pp.51–58.

Barnett, Megan. "A Stormy Season's Heavy Toll: Furious Hurricane Ivan Claims Lives and Disrupts the Economy." *U.S. News & World Report*, September 27, 2004, p.41.

Buice, Ed. "Leadership Principles for Effective Message Management." *The Police Chief*, April 2001, pp.58–60.

Buice, Ed. "Keys to Successful Media Interviews." *Law and Order*, September 2003, p.26.

Cox, Jennifer. "Recoilless Disrupter Enhances EOD Technology." *Law Enforcement Technology*, February 2004, pp.106–109.

Czarnecki, Fabrice. "NBC's of First Response." *American Police Beat*, January/February, 2002, pp.1, 12–14.

Douglas, Dave. "Emergency Management and Emergency Operations Centers." *Police*, November 2001, pp.32–36.

Eldridge, Christopher. "Preparing for a Super Disaster." *Law Enforcement Technology*, August 2004, pp.18–27.

Haber, Grant. "Facing the Threat of Improvised Explosives." *Law Enforcement News*, May 2004, p.13.

"Hazardous Materials Shipments." U.S. Department of Transportation, February 2002. http://hazmat.dot.gov

Heal, Charles S. "The Manageable Future: Envisioning the End State." *FBI Law Enforcement Bulletin*, January 2002, pp.1–6.

Hilte, Ken. "Preparing for the Media Mega-Event." *The Police Chief*, April 2001, pp.22–27.

Laska, Paul R. "Bomb Disposal Equipment in the Era of the War on Terrorism." *Law Enforcement Technology*, January 2002, pp.52–55.

"Law Enforcement Groups Applaud Plan to End Radio Interference." *Criminal Justice Newsletter*, August 2, 2004, p.6.

Miller, Linda S. and Hess, Kären M. *Community Policing: Partnerships for Problem Solving*, 4th ed. Belmont, CA: Wadsworth Publishing Company, 2005.

"Now More than Ever, E-911." *Law Enforcement News*, October 15, 2001, p.6.

Page, Douglas. "Get Smart: A Bomb 'Bot with Know-How." *Law Enforcement Technology*, July 2002, pp.136–142.

Robinson, Patricia A. "The Leaking Tanker." *The Law Enforcement Trainer*, May/June 2004, pp.59, 64.

Rogers, Donna. "Drive for E911 Picks Up Speed." *Law Enforcement Technology*, March 2001a, pp.88–92.

Rogers, Donna. "Project Locate." *Law Enforcement Technology*, July 2001b, pp.42–46.

Rosenthal, Rick. "Media Relations: Your Critical Incident." *Law and Order*, November 2001, pp.16–17.

Sheehan, Donald C.; Everly, George S., Jr.; and Langlieb, Alan. "Current Best Practices: Coping with Major Critical Incidents." *FBI Law Enforcement Bulletin*, September 2004, pp.1–13.

Siegle, Derek and Murphy, Rick. "The Public Safety Wireless Network (PSWN) Program: A Brief Introduction." *FBI Law Enforcement Bulletin*, May 2001, pp.10–12.

Slader, Richard and Wilds, Michael. "Eye of the Storm: Dealing with the Media after a School Crisis." *The Police Chief*, October 2001, pp.124–131.

Smith, Jim. "How to Conduct a Bomb Search." *Police and Security News*, September/October 2003, pp.43–46.

Spranza, Francis. "Warding Off Computer Viruses." *Law Enforcement Technology*, April 2001, pp.18–24.

Stambaugh, Hollis; Beaupre, David S.; Icove, David J.; Baker, Richard; Cassaday, Wayne; and Williams, Wayne P. *Electronic Crime Needs Assessment for State and Local Law Enforcement*. Washington, DC: National Institute of Justice, March 2001. (NIJ 186276)

Staszak, Dennis. "Media Trends and the Public Information Officer." *FBI Law Enforcement Bulletin*, March 2001, pp.10–13.

Strandberg, Keith W. "Hazmat Training." *Law Enforcement Technology*, January 2001, pp.18–21.

*2000 Emergency Response Guidebook*. Washington, DC: U.S. Department of Transportation, 2000. http://hazmat.dot.gov/pubs/erg2004/gydebook.htm.

Tyler, Gary K. "Four Ways to Improve Your Media Relations." *The Police Chief*, April 2001, pp.48–51.

Van Blaricom, D.P. "The Media: Enemies or Allies?" *The Police Chief*, April 2001, pp.52–56.

Weiss, Jim and Dresser, Mary. "Bomb Threat Recognition." *Law and Order*, January 2002, pp.75–79.

# CHAPTER 9

# Terrorism: Securing Our Homeland

**DO YOU KNOW . . .**

- What most definitions of terrorism include?
- What three elements are common in terrorism?
- How the FBI classifies terrorist acts?
- What motivates most terrorist attacks?
- What domestic terrorist groups exist in the United States?
- What methods terrorists may use?
- What federal office was established as a result of 9/11?
- What the lead federal agencies in combating terrorism are?
- How the USA PATRIOT Act enhances counterterrorism efforts by the United States?
- What the first line of defense against terrorism in the United States is?
- What the three-tiered model of al Qaeda terrorist attacks consists of?
- What four obstacles to intelligence effectiveness are?
- What a key to successfully combating terrorism is?
- What the Community Protection Act authorizes?
- What two concerns are associated with the current "war on terrorism"?
- What balance law enforcement must maintain in the "war on terrorism"?

**CAN YOU DEFINE?**

| | | |
|---|---|---|
| asymmetric war | cyberterrorism | *jihad* |
| bioterrorism | deconfliction | sleeper cell |
| contagion effect | ecoterrorism | terrorism |

## Introduction

"The terrorist attacks of September 11, 2001, sounded a clarion call to Americans: our nation must prepare more vigorously to prevent and, if necessary to manage the consequences of man-made disasters" (McDonald and McLaughlin, 2003, p.14). Lesce (2001, p.99) states: "The airline attacks of September 11, 2001, provided incontrovertible proof of America's vulnerability to terrorism, even low-tech threats using edged weapons. . . . Nuclear, chemical and biological threats have been known for decades, acceptance that the threats are real has been sluggish and preparations lacking." Oldham (2001, p.94) also notes: "While there had been a building momentum within the law enforcement community to prepare for weapons of mass destruction (WMD) [prior to September 11], those

events seemed years in the future or unrealistic. As a result, many of those preparations were pushed to the back burner of financial, tactical and logistical planning. After the 11th that movement has become a torrent of agencies scrambling to make up for the years of neglect in planning, equipment and training."

An excerpt from the 9/11 Report (2004) reads: "The 9/11 attacks were a shock, but they should not have come as a surprise. Islamist extremists had given plenty of warning that they meant to kill Americans indiscriminately and in large numbers. . . . The most important failure was one of imagination. We do not believe leaders understood the gravity of the threat. The terrorist danger from bin Laden and al Qaeda was not a major topic for policy debate among the public, the media or in the Congress."

The Terrorism Research Center outlined the effects of this attack: "The President of the United States made it very clear in his September 20th speech to the Congress, the nation and the world, that this threat has not achieved its objectives of fear. Rather, it has galvanized the United States into action." President George W. Bush said: "Tonight we are a country awakened to danger and called to defend freedom. Our grief has turned to anger, and anger to resolution." The horrific events of September 11 did pull together and unify the American people in a way most had never seen. Patriotism was immediately popular. Thousands of volunteers helped search for victims and donated blood and money. The American flag flew everywhere.

In addition to galvanizing the nation, the events of that tragic day had other ramifications. Reuland et al. (2004, p.5) suggest: "The events of September 11, 2001, forever changed the nation's view of our security if faced with a large-scale terrorist attack." Peed and Wexler (2004, p.vii) point out: "Local, state and federal law enforcement agencies are still feeling the effects of September 11, 2001. In the years that have passed since those tragic events, law enforcement professionals have been working to redefine their roles as they continue traditional crime-fighting efforts while also taking on tremendous new counterterrorism activities." But the threat remains.

In June the State Department reported: "Significant acts of terror world-wide reached a 21-year high in 2003" (Schweid, 2004, p.A1). In 2002, 205 terrorist incidents occurred compared to 208 in 2003. Fewer people were killed in 2003, 625 compared to 725 killed in 2002. However, many more were injured in 2003, 3,646 compared to 2,013 injured in 2002. Thirty-five U.S. citizens were killed in international terror attacks in 2003. The deadliest was a suicide bombing in Riyadh, Saudi Arabia, which included 9 Americans among the 26 victims (Schweid). The department's report did not include U.S. troops wounded or killed in Iraq as they were directed at "combatants."

This chapter begins by defining terrorism and classifying terrorism as domestic or international. Next is a look at the various motivations for terrorism, the new type of war that law enforcement is engaged in and the methods used by terrorists. This is followed by a look at the federal response to terrorism, including the formation of the Department of Homeland Security and passage of the USA PATRIOT Act. Next is a discussion of the critical role of local law enforcement in responding to terrorism and efforts to detect, prepare for, prevent, protect against, respond to and recover from terrorist attacks. Then initiatives to assist in the fight against terrorism and the role of the media in this fight are discussed, followed by two major concerns related to that war: erosion of civil liberties and retaliation against people of Middle Eastern descent. The chapter concludes with a discussion of community policing and homeland security.

## Terrorism Defined

The Terrorism Research Center defines **terrorism** as "the use of force or violence against persons or property in violation of the criminal laws of the United States for purposes of intimidation, coercion or ransom."

 Most definitions of terrorism have common elements, including the systematic use of physical violence, either actual or threatened, against noncombatants to create a climate of fear and to cause some religious, political or social change.

Carter and Holden (2003, p.300) suggest: "Terrorism may be seen as a tactic, strategy, philosophy or pejorative label to describe the activities of one's enemies." They contend: "The most useful definition of terrorism is a form of political or religious militancy that uses violence or the threat of violence in an attempt to change behavior through fear." According to McVey (2002, p.174): "Terrorist acts can be identified as being criminal in nature, symbolically targeted

*A shell of what was once part of the facade of one of the twin towers of New York's World Trade Center rises above the rubble that remains after both towers were destroyed in a terrorist attack Sept. 11, 2001. The 110-story towers collapsed after two hijacked airliners carrying scores of passengers slammed into the twin symbols of American capitalism.*

Shawn Baldwin/AP World Wide Photos

and always aggressive. They seek to achieve political goals and communicate a message."

 Three elements of terrorism are: (1) it is criminal in nature, (2) targets are typically symbolic and (3) the terrorist actions are always aggressive and often violent.

# Classification of Terrorist Acts

 The FBI categorizes terrorism in the United States as either domestic or international terrorism.

## *Domestic Terrorism*

The 1995 bombing of the Murrah Federal Building in Oklahoma City and the pipe bomb explosions in Centennial Olympic Park during the 1996 Summer Olympic Games highlight the threat of domestic terrorists. They represent extreme right- or left-wing and special interest beliefs. Many are antigovernment, antitaxation and engage in survivalist training to perpetuate a white, Christian nation. The right-wing militia or patriot movement is a law enforcement concern because of the potential for violence and criminal behavior. Some states have passed legislation limiting militias, including types of training they can undergo. In October 2002 the Washington, DC area was terrorized by a sniping spree. The sniper mastermind, John Allen Muhammad was sentenced to death by a judge who called the shootings that left 10 people dead "so vile that they were almost beyond comprehension" (Barakat, 2004, p.A3). His teenage accomplice, Lee Boyd Malvo, was sentenced to life without parole (Jackman, 2004, p.A3).

Brinkley (2004, p.43) presents what he describes as "undeniable facts" about terrorism:

1. We as a country will be attacked again.
2. Residents and/or citizens of this country will carry out these attacks.
3. Car bombings will become a tool of choice to be used against us.
4. Threat groups will practice a greater level of organization and sophistication in technologies and weapons.
5. Only by practicing due diligence and using sound and consistent enforcement practices can meaningful safety and security be achieved.

Domestic terrorism is examined in-depth under the discussion of motivation for terrorism.

## *International Terrorism*

International terrorism is foreign-based or directed by countries or groups outside the United States against the United States. The FBI divides international terrorism into three categories: (1) foreign state sponsors of international terrorism using terrorism as a tool of foreign policy, for example Iraq and Afghanistan; (2) formalized terrorist groups such as Osama bin Laden's al Qaeda; and (3) loosely affiliated international radical extremists who have a variety of identities and travel freely in the United States, unknown and undetected by law enforcement or the government.

HO/AFP/Getty Images

*This combo image from the FBI Internet site shows "Assam the American" believed to be Adam Gadahn, a missing California man and a follower of Osama bin Laden. Gadahn, now 26, converted to Islam at age 17 and attended a mosque in Orange County, California.*

### The Dual Threat

As Pitcavage (2003, p.35) stresses: "As America goes forward in its war on terrorism, those who wage that war must always remember that there are fronts. Even as the United States seeks to eradicate international terrorist groups such as al-Qaeda, it must never forget to protect its citizens from those among them who would like nothing better but to tear it apart and recast it in their own, warped image. America's police officers are on the front lines of that battle." Garrett (2002, p.22) also urges: "In the war against terrorism, it's important that all law enforcement—local, state and federal—keep as close an eye on domestic terrorists as they do on the international variety." One approach to understanding terrorism is to examine the motivations that produce it.

## Motivations for Terrorism

 Most terrorist acts result from dissatisfaction with a religious, political or social system or policy and frustration resulting from an inability to change it through acceptable, nonviolent means.

Religious motives are seen in Islamic extremism. Political motives include such elements as the Red Army Faction. Social motives are seen in single-issue groups such as antiabortion groups, animal rights groups and environmentalists. According to Brinkley (2004, p.43): "A wide range of groups on the left and right, including environmentalist groups, pose specific challenges and threats to law enforcement operations and the officers who run them."

Garrett (2004a, p.88) asserts: "While not every activist is an extremist, law enforcement should pay attention to those who are." She (p.90) suggests: "The high profile crimes—the $50 million arsons—tend to occur two to three times a year in this country. But if you include crimes such as smashed windows; death threats; small, Molotov Cocktail-type arsons; you're talking several times per week." Garrett (p.92) cautions: "If you don't take care of the little problems, bigger problems will grow out of them."

 Terrorist groups within the United States with specific motivations include white supremacists, black supremacists, militia groups, other right-wing extremists, left-wing extremists, pro-life extremists, animal rights activists and environmental extremists.

## White Supremacists

Scoville (2003, p.48) notes: "One of the oldest American terrorist organizations is the Ku Klux Klan. Formed by Confederate veterans following the Civil War, the goal of the original Klan was to terrorize freed blacks and exert political influence over the Reconstruction south. . . . The Klan is still out there. Members of local and regional Klan groups have been blamed for church burnings, intimidation and harassment of minorities and minority advocates, and other crimes." Neo-Nazi groups also espouse white supremacy. Skinheads, discussed in Chapter 12, fall into this category.

## Black Supremacists

The Black Panther Party for Self-Defense was established in 1966 during a time of racial turmoil. According to Scoville (p.46): "Today, a newly reconstituted Black Panther Party for Self-Defense has been organized, and it qualifies as a hate group. These contemporary Panthers are heavily armed, advocate violence against whites, and like their 1960s predecessors, see cops as the enemy."

## The Militia Movement

According to White (2003, p.228), most militia groups are heavily armed and practice their sharpshooting skills. Many militia members are frustrated, overwhelmed and socially unable to cope with the rapid pace of change in the modern world. Commonly militia groups provide the rhetoric for violence.

## Other Right-Wing Extremists

The preceding groups might also be described as right-wing extremists. According to White (2003, p.223): "The appearance of right-wing extremism came to fruition around 1984 and has remained active since that time." He (p.224) cites three issues that rejuvenated the extreme right: the Brady Bill, Ruby Ridge and Waco.

The Brady Bill caused militia groups to fear federal gun control legislation. The Ruby Ridge incident involved an attempt to arrest Randy Weaver, a white supremacist charged with selling illegal firearms to undercover ATF [Alcohol, Tobacco and Firearms] agents. A shootout ensued, resulting in the death of a U.S. Marshal and Weaver's young son. The FBI laid siege to Weaver's Ruby Ridge cabin and killed his pregnant wife before Weaver surrendered.

White (p.225) describes the third galvanizing incident, the federal siege of the Branch Davidian compound near Waco, Texas:

In 1993, ATF agents attempted to serve a search warrant on the compound, but they were met with a hail of gunfire. Four agents were killed, and several were wounded. After a three-month siege, FBI agents moved in with tear gas. Unknown to the agents, the compound was laced with gasoline. When the FBI moved in, the Branch Davidians burned their fortress, killing over 70 people, including several young children held inside the compound.

### Left-Wing Extremists

Brinkley (2003, pp.33–34) explains: "The left wing believes in a Pro-Marxist stance where the rich must be brought down and the poor elevated. Presently the largest groups of supporters for this cause are Anarchists. . . . This group believes that one receives according to one's needs."

### Pro-Life Extremists

Although many pro-life, antiabortion advocates stay within the law in promoting their beliefs, some groups do not. One such group is an active terrorist organization called the Army of God. According to Scoville (p.48): "Abortion clinics and their staffs are common Army of God targets, with zealots committing crimes, ranging from arson, to assault, to assassination."

### Animal Rights Activists

As Scoville (p.46) notes: "One of the most active domestic terrorist groups is the Animal Liberation Front (ALF). This clandestine and decentralized group has claimed credit for attacks on meatpacking plants, furriers and research labs. Founded in England in 1976, ALF's influence spread to the United States in 1982. The succeeding two decades have seen the group cause millions of dollars in damages and medical research setback through its acts of vandalism, arson and the 'liberation' of laboratory animals."

### Environmental Extremists

Environmental extremists are often referred to as ecoterrorists, with *eco* being derived from *ecology*—the study of the interrelationships of organisms and their environment. **Ecoterrorism** seeks to inflict economic damage to those who profit from the destruction of the natural environment. According to Nilson and Burke (2002, p.1): "Ecological-terrorism is used as a tactic to stop companies, institutions, organizations and governments from damaging or altering the environment."

One such group is the Earth Liberation Front (ELF), often working with the Animal Liberation Front (ALF). Arson is a favorite weapon, responsible for tens of millions of dollars of property damage, including a U.S. Department of Agriculture building, a U.S. Forest Service ranger station and a Colorado ski resort. The group claims responsibility for releasing 5,000 mink from a Michigan fur farm, 600 wild horses from an Oregon corral and burning the Michigan State University's genetic engineering research offices. In 2000 they claimed responsibility for torching a $2 million home in Colorado. In 2002 ELF claimed responsibility for arson at a research lab under construction on the St. Paul campus of the University of Minnesota to protest genetic engineering on plants (Sanow, 2002, p.5).

Nilson and Burke (p.3) contend that ecoterrorists commit many criminal acts in their fight to save nature, including equipment vandalism, package bombs or pipe bombs, destruction of research data, arson of buildings, obliteration of experimental plants and animals and the like. According to the FBI, ELF was responsible for more than $43 million in property damage from 1996 to 2002.

Although motivations for terrorists both within the United States and outside our borders may differ, they have in common the tactics they use, that being an entirely different type of warfare.

## A New Kind of War—An Asymmetric War

The Terrorism Research Center declared: "The attack of September 11 will be the precipitating moment of a new kind of war that will define a new century. This war will be fought in shadows, and the adversary will continue to target the innocent and defenseless." This new kind of war has been called an asymmetric war.

An **asymmetric war** is one in which a much weaker opponent takes on a stronger opponent by refusing to confront the stronger opponent head on. As Choudhury (2002, p.183) explains: "The weaker side selects as its main axis of battle those areas where the adversary does not expect to be hit and where the attack will cause a huge psychological shock. The use of asymmetrical measures is conceived of as creating power for the powerless and rendering the stronger adversary unable to use its conventional resources."

Lasky (2002, p.4) suggests: "An asymmetric foe is an Osama bin Laden, international terrorist group, drug cartel or Mafiosi-type. We've recently found our military in other asymmetrical situations like those in Somalia, Kosovo and Lebanon where rogue states have disintegrated into such anarchy that conventional military parameters disappear. But this is now the reality of warfare." As Page (2004, p.86) suggests: "Terrorism has caused a blurring of war and crime." This has drawn law enforcement directly into the war. Page (p.87) notes: "Local law enforcement will be expected to handle complex tactical situations such as chemical, biological and nuclear events." These are among the arsenal of methods terrorists use.

## Methods Used by Terrorists

Terrorists may use arson; explosives and bombs; weapons of mass destruction (biological, chemical or nuclear agents); and technology.

The use of arson has already been discussed.

Reuland and Davies (p.5) state: "The term 'CBR' is used by law enforcement agencies as shorthand to include all potential terrorist threats that can have consequences for the health of large numbers of people. These threats include chemical agents (C), biological agents (B) and radiation exposure (R)." They present the most likely to least likely terrorist threats (see Figure 9.1) and the level of impact by the weapon used (see Figure 9.2).

### Explosives and Bombs

From 1978 to 1996 Theodore Kaczynski terrorized the country as the Unabomber, through a string of 16 mail bombings that killed three people apparently in a protest against technology. Ramzi Ahmed Yousef, found guilty of

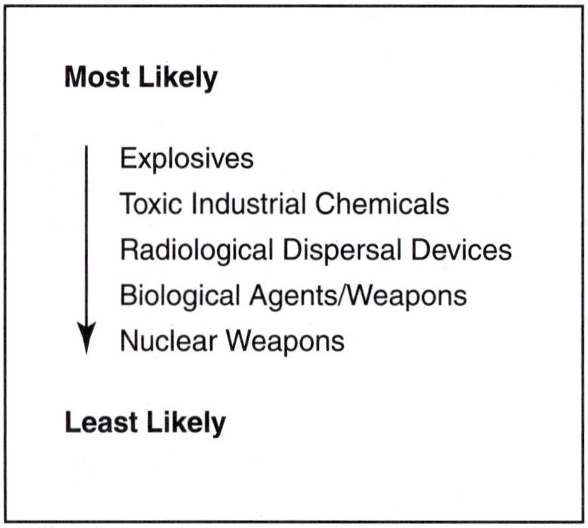

**Most Likely**

Explosives
Toxic Industrial Chemicals
Radiological Dispersal Devices
Biological Agents/Weapons
Nuclear Weapons

**Least Likely**

**Figure 9.1**   Terrorist Threats from Most Likely to Least Likely

SOURCE: Melissa Reuland and Heather J. Davis. *Protecting Your Community from Terrorism: Strategies for Local Law Enforcement. Volume 3: Preparing for and Responding to Bioterrorism.* Washington, DC: Community Oriented Policing Services Office and the Police Executive Research Forum, September 2004, p.7. Reprinted by permission of the Police Executive Research Forum.

**Greatest Impact**

Biological Agents/Weapons
Nuclear Weapons
Toxic Industrial Chemicals
Radiological Dispersal Devices
Explosives

**Least Impact**

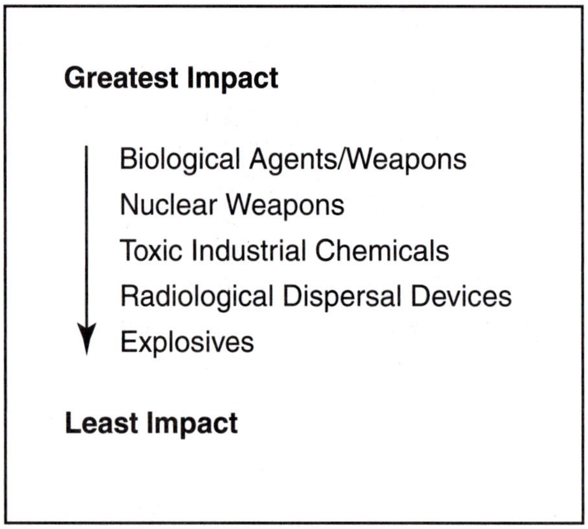

**Figure 9.2**   Level of Impact by Weapon Used

SOURCE: Melissa Reuland and Heather J. Davis. *Protecting Your Community from Terrorism: Strategies for Local Law Enforcement. Volume 3: Preparing for and Responding to Bioterrorism.* Washington, DC: Community Oriented Policing Services Office and the Police Executive Research Forum, September 2004, p.8. Reprinted by permission of the Police Executive Research Forum.

masterminding the first World Trade Center bombing in 1993 declared that he was proud to be a terrorist and that terrorism was the only viable response to what he saw as a Jewish lobby in Washington. The car bomb used to shatter the Murrah Federal Building in 1995 was Timothy McVeigh's way to protest the government and the raid on the Branch Davidians at Waco. In 2002 Lucas Helder terrorized the Midwest with 18 pipe bombs in mailboxes in five states, leaving antigovernment letters with the pipe bombs. Six exploded, injuring four letter carriers and two residents. And the most horrific act of terrorism against the United States occurred on September 11, 2001, when two airplanes were used as missiles to explode the World Trade Center and another plane was used as a missile to attack the Pentagon. A fourth plane crashed in a Pennsylvania field before it could reach its intended target.

Gips (2003, p.16) describes one terrorist tactic, using a secondary explosive device after a first one is set off. This tactic was used in Bali, Indonesia, in October 2003 when a hand grenade was tossed into a nightclub, causing patrons to flee to the streets where they encountered a Jeep bomb. The attack, which killed almost 200 people, was attributed to Muslim extremists in Indonesia with links to al Qaeda. According to Moore (2003, p.24): "Regardless of the group responsible, the destruction highlights the effectiveness of the car bomb—one of terrorism's more deadly tools."

"The Shape of Things to Come" (2003, p.20) reports: "Car and truck bombings will continue to be the principal modus operandi for terrorists, with the main targets being U.S., British and Israeli military and diplomatic facilities. But also at risk are businesses popular with expatriates, including shopping malls, restaurants, bars and supermarkets."

**Suicide Bombers**   According to "Suicide Terrorism" (2003, pp.20–21): "Terrorists are ever willing to sacrifice themselves for their cause." Most believe the act makes them martyrs and assures them a place in their version of heaven. Their families are usually held in reverence and taken care of. Suicide bombers try to kill as many people as possible. "Confronting the Suicide-Bomber Threat" (2003, p.16) contends: "Although the United States has yet to be plagued by the type of routine belt-bomb suicide attacks that Israel experiences, many experts believe that it is only a matter of time before this tactic makes its way across the Atlantic."

**Prevention Strategies**   Levine (2004, p.30) describes the challenge of trying to stop the terrorists' low-tech, lethal weapon of choice, the car bomb: "The simplicity and stealth of these weapons make them a complex foe. It's virtually impossible to screen all the cars and trucks that rumble past critical buildings. So authorities now use simple tools, such as restricting parking and traffic and putting up concrete median barriers and security checkpoints.

Moore (p.24) stresses: "A successful line of defense against car bombs would rely heavily on police-civilian coordination." He (p.28) explains: "Terrorists may unwittingly give away their bombing plans by their actions or behavior." According to Moore (p.29): "Beyond standard security that entails intelligence, static physical security [CCTV] and active detection methods, there are unique measures to apply that can lessen the car bomb threat: (1) use vehicle registration to conduct background checks for terrorist connections, (2) engage in rigorous registration enforcement and (3) restrict the type and size of vehicles imported." Moore (p.31) contends: "Vehicle registration may discourage terrorists from relying on car bombs because the car may be traced to the owner after the fact."

"Confronting the Suicide-Bomber Threat" (p.16) suggests that among the warning signs revealing a suicide bomber are unseasonable garb, obvious disguises (such as a police uniform with a security badge), and profuse sweating, a well-dressed, perfumed individual who has prepared to meet his maker.

## *Weapons of Mass Destruction (WMD)*

Symonds (2003, p.19) suggests: "Weapons of mass destruction (WMD) are not the result of any recent technological developments. Biological WMDs have actually been in use since the 1300s. The advent of the 20th century brought with it the first use of artificially produced WMDs—or chemical agents— during World War I. Today the world faces the major problem of how to get the genie back into the bottle. The means and recipes for the development of nuclear, radiological, biological and chemical weapons are well known and documented."

Guida (2002, p.54) suggests: "Terrorism through the release of biological, chemical and radiological agents is predicated upon use of the environment as a medium or weapon of mass harm and destruction. As a group, such acts can be referred to as enviroterrorism (this term should be distinguished from ecoterrorism, which has frequently been used to describe crimes committed allegedly to protect the environment)."

Nuclear, biological or chemical agents are also referred to as NBC agents in the literature. "Safety on the Scene" (2002, p.6) notes that at NBC scenes, telemetry— "data transmission to a remote location via radio, satellite, wireless or other communication"—can assist responders in several ways:

- It can relay weather data (including wind direction and speed, barometric pressure, relative humidity, etc.) to incident command (IC), allowing IC to assess the hazard's spread and to plan evacuations.
- It also can be combined with robotic detection and identification technology to warn IC of NBC agents' presence and strength.
- It can work with global positioning systems (GPS) to transmit the coordinates of an NBC release relative to the position of IC responders, residential or other civilian centers or other critical location information.
- It can track vehicles charged with transporting NBC materials to and from the site.

Some experts suggest that bioterrorism is the third most likely terrorist act to occur. Incendiary devices and explosives are most likely to be used because they are easy to make. Chemical devices are next in likelihood because the raw materials are easy to get and easy to use.

**Biological Agents**    **Bioterrorism** involves such biological weapons of mass destruction (WMD) as anthrax, botulism and smallpox. Raffel (2003, p.1) notes: "Many countries and terrorist groups have the capability to mass produce lethal viruses and distribute them throughout the human population." Hanson (2004b, p.18) cautions: "The potential for a bioterrorist attack in the United States has become an unfortunate reality following the events of 9/11 and the anthrax scares." In referring to the anthrax attacks, Czarnecki (2002, p.1) says: "The real question is whether they are isolated acts of terrorism or the beginning of a series of nuclear, biological and chemical (NBC) attacks from an organized and highly sophisticated network of terrorists, possibly backed by one or several hostile countries." As of December 13, 2001, postal inspectors nationwide have arrested 53 individuals for anthrax-related hoaxes and threats. The $1,250,000 reward being offered for information leading to the arrest and conviction of the anthrax mailer who sent contaminated letters to television news anchor Tom Brokaw

(NBC), Senators Leahy and Daschle, and the *New York Post* generated over 600 calls to *America's Most Wanted* (Esposito, 2002, p.58).

A survey of 2,000 hospitals conducted by the U.S. General Accounting Office (GAO) found that although 80 percent had written emergency response plans for large-scale infectious disease outbreaks, fewer than half had conducted training related to bioterrorism ("Bioterrorism," 2003, pp.24–25).

Hanson (2004a, pp.10–11) observes: "Since the incubation for most biological agents is days instead of hours, much of the actual crime scene—when finally discovered—will be greatly degraded from an evidence standpoint. And, if the agent involved is a transmissible disease, it may have already spread to others beyond the original site, making the initial target site appear larger than it really is and complicating the search for meaningful trace evidence. . . . And because of the lengthy incubation period for many agents, officers may be dealing with individuals who are carrying an infectious and transmissible agent, but not outwardly showing any signs of illness. In this arena, law enforcement personnel must take adequate steps to protect themselves during all phases of the investigation. Doing this involves education and training, and that education begins with knowing what biohazards exist." Especially susceptible to bioterrorism are the nation's food and water supply, which might also be attacked using chemical agents.

**Chemical Agents**   Nason (2003, p.44) notes: "The Aum Shinrikyo event in the Tokyo subway in 1995 initially focused the security industry's efforts on detecting and mitigating chemical agent threats. That incident confirmed what all of us in this industry had long feared. A non-state entity could manufacture a viable chemical agent and deliver it in a public location." As White (2003, p.240) explains: "Members of a religious cult, the Aum Shinrikyo released a poisonous gas, sarin, into the crowded subway system. The act involved criminal terrorism for psychological gratification, but it had a deadly twist. . . . The terrorists were members of an organized religious cult trying to destroy the Japanese government." Unfortunately, anyone with access to the Internet can obtain the chemical formula for sarin in less than 40 minutes through a web search and can produce it inexpensively.

According to White (2003, p.251): "Chemical agents are not as lethal as biological agents, and they are easier to control." The four common types of chemical weapons are nerve agents, blood agents, choking agents and blistering agents. One agent, ricin toxin, is both a biological and a chemical weapon. According to Hanson (2003, p.16), ricin is more than 1,000 times more poisonous than cyanide. He (p.18) notes: "In its purest form, an amount of ricin toxin no bigger than a grain of table salt can kill an adult." Hanson also states: "According to a recent Monterey Institute of International Studies report, detailed procedures for ricin extraction and use were found in al Qaeda's military manuals seized in safe houses and caves in Afghanistan."

**Nuclear Terrorism**   Stanton (2002, p.156) warns: "The United States finds itself at greater risk of an attack by nuclear-based weaponry today than at the height of the Cold War." According to the U.S. Nuclear Regulatory Commission (NRC) an average of approximately 375 devices of all kinds containing radioactive material are reported lost or stolen each year. Stanton reports: "Analysts say that this new nuclear threat will never be eliminated, only minimized. They point to the quantities of lost or stolen (called 'orphaned') radioactive waste in the United States and around the world that would be easy for terrorist groups to obtain. They also point to the arsenal of loosely guarded Russian tactical nuclear weapons (TNWs), some of which are also already missing." According to Stanton: "The successful detonation of a low-yield nuclear device or RDD [radiological dispersion device] would far surpass the aftermath of the terrorist attacks on September 11, 2001." Such devices are also called "dirty bombs." However, as Hughes (2004, p.32) suggests: "The primary destruction and disruption from a dirty bomb detonation will be caused by public panic, not radiation."

**A WMD Team**   Hughes (2003) advocates that local law enforcement agencies select and train officers to form a WMD team. The officers' time is not devoted solely to the unit, but is ready if a need for their skills arises. According to Hughes (p.21): "A WMD unit trains together and is tasked with responding to, assessing and resolving the crisis portion of any Weapons of Mass Destruction event. . . . Responders to a WMD incident must be capable of assessing any agents or products disseminated as well as how rapidly they are spreading and be equipped to contain and neutralize them. These tasks require an above-average knowledge of chemistry, meteorology, physics and tactics, not to mention immediate access to some fairly specialized equipment. HazMat is not enough."

### Technological Terrorism

White (2003, p.273) notes: "Technological terrorism is one of the more frightening scenarios one can imagine. Modern societies are susceptible to two methods of technological terror. The first is the employment of mass destruction weapons or the conversion of an industrial site—for example, a chemical plant—into a massively lethal instrument through sabotage. The other method is to attack a source that supplies technology or energy. The results of either type of attack could be catastrophic. Technology looms as a potentially sinister partner in the evolution of terrorism."

White (p.244) suggests: "The United States is the most technologically advanced superpower in the world. . . . The irony of U.S. success with technology is that the country has become vulnerable to attacks on technology and by technology." White (p.247) notes: "The United States relies on energy to support its technology, and the interruption of energy supplies could be construed as a national security threat. If a nation or terrorist group could shut off U.S. energy, it could close down major portions of the economy. Secure energy production, transportation and storage are all critical to the United States."

**Cyberterrorism** is defined by the FBI as "terrorism that initiates, or threatens to initiate, the exploitation of or attack on information systems." Uner (2003, p.26) cautions: "The threat of cyberterrorism is real; it's only a matter of when." White (p.255), however, suggests: "Cyberterrorism is probably a misused term. Terrorists may use computers in terrorist acts. Such acts include the disruption of services, attacks on infrastructures including the defense system and placing cyberbombs in selected information systems." Damage to our critical computer systems can put our safety and our national security in jeopardy. Each of the preceding types of terrorism poses a threat to our national security.

## The Federal Response to Terrorism

In 1996 the FBI established a Counterterrorism Center to combat terrorism. Also in 1996 the Antiterrorism and Effective Death Penalty Act was passed, including several specific measures aimed at terrorism. It enhanced the federal government's power to deny visas to individuals belonging to terrorist groups and simplified the process for deporting aliens convicted of crimes.

In 1999 then–FBI Director Louis Freeh announced, "Our No. 1 priority is the prevention of terrorism." The FBI added a new Counterterrorism Division with four subunits: the International Terrorism Section, the Domestic Terrorism Section, the National Infrastructure Protection Center and the National Domestic Preparedness Office. But this was not enough to avert the tragic events of September 11. It took a disaster of that magnitude to make the war on terrorism truly the first priority of the United States. One of the first initiatives was establishing the Department of Homeland Security.

## The Department of Homeland Security

On October 8, 2001, President Bush signed Executive Order 13228 establishing the Department of Homeland Security (DHS) to be headed by Governor Tom Ridge.

 As a result of 9/11 the Department of Homeland Security was established, reorganizing the departments of the federal government.

How the establishment of this department reorganized the federal government was explained in Chapter 1. The mission of the Department of Homeland Security is "to develop and coordinate the implementation of a comprehensive national strategy to secure the United States from terrorist threats or attacks."

 At the federal level, the FBI is the lead agency for responding to acts of domestic terrorism. The Federal Emergency Management Agency (FEMA) is the lead agency for consequence management (after an attack). The Department of Homeland Security serves in a broad capacity, facilitating collaboration between local and federal law enforcement to develop a national strategy to detect, prepare for, prevent, protect against, respond to and recover from terrorist attacks within the United States.

The DHS has established a five-level color-coded threat system used to communicate with public safety officials and the public at large: green represents a low level of threat, blue a guarded level, yellow an elevated level, orange a high level and red a severe level. To learn what the DHS is doing to keep America safe, go to http://www.ready.gov/.

In addition, the Office for Victims of Crime (OVC) has available the Terrorism and International Victims Unit (TIVU) to help victims of terrorism and mass violence (*Terrorism and International Victims Unit*, 2002). This organization provides training and technical assistance to first responders. It provided support to Oklahoma City in 1995 following the bombing of the Murrah Federal Building. After the attack on America September 11, 2001, TIVU played a key role in OVC's response to victims and their families in New York. Another effort to enhance national security was passage of the USA PATRIOT Act.

## The USA PATRIOT Act

On October 26, 2001, President Bush signed into law the Uniting and Strengthening America by Providing Appropriate Tools Required to Intercept and Obstruct Terrorism (USA PATRIOT) Act, giving police unprecedented ability to search, seize, detain or eavesdrop in their pursuit of possible terrorists. The law expands the FBI's wiretapping and electronic surveillance authority and allows nationwide jurisdiction for search warrants and electronic surveillance devices, including legal expansion of those devices to e-mail and the Internet.

 The USA PATRIOT Act significantly improves the nation's counterterrorism efforts by:
- Allowing investigators to use the tools already available to investigate organized crime and drug trafficking.
- Facilitating information sharing and cooperation among government agencies so they can better "connect the dots."
- Updating the law to reflect new technologies and new threats.
- Increasing the penalties for those who commit or support terrorist crimes.

**Using Tools Already in Use in the War on Drugs**    Baveja (2002, p.36) suggests that the war the United States has waged on illicit drugs may provide lessons in the current fight against terrorism:

> Despite their differences, terrorism and illicit drug activity have several commonalties in their delivery and control, making a compelling case for exploring further to decipher any shared lessons. For example, drugs and terrorism involve covert illegal activities that call for sophisticated undercover enforcement operations. Both terrorism and drug activity do have a domestic component, but the threat from the organized and international component of these activities is far more devastating. In addition, there is evidence to suggest that terrorist cells and networks have structures similar to those of drug cartels.
>
> Further, both counterterror and counterdrug strategies require coordination among various law enforcement agencies, and strategic cooperation and information sharing with other partner countries. Finally, an overall policy for both these problems involves careful weighing of different strategies that reach beyond U.S. borders and span the globe.

**Facilitating Information Sharing**    The importance of this provision of the act can be seen in the case of an al Qaeda cell in Lackawanna, New York:

> This case involved several residents of Lackawanna, who traveled to Afghanistan in 2001 to receive training at an al Qaeda-affiliated camp near Kandahar. The investigation of the "Lackawanna Six" began during the summer of 2001, when the FBI received an anonymous letter indicating that these six individuals and others might be involved in criminal activity and associating with foreign terrorists. The FBI concluded that the existing law required the creation of two separate investigations in order to retain the option of using FISA [Foreign Intelligence Surveillance Act]: a criminal investigation of possible drug crimes and an intelligence investigation related to terrorist threats. Over the ensuing months, two squads carried on these two separate investigations simultaneously, and there were times when the intelligence officers and the law enforcement agents concluded that they could not be in the same room during briefings to discuss their respective investigations with each other.
>
> The USA PATRIOT Act, however, took down the "wall" separating these two investigations by making clear that the sharing of case-sensitive information between these two groups was allowed. As a result of key information shared by intelligence investigators, law enforcement agents were able to learn that an individual mentioned in the anonymous letter was an agent of

al Qaeda. Further information shared between intelligence and law enforcement personnel then dramatically expedited the investigation of the Lackawanna Six and allowed charges to be filed against these individuals. Five of the Lackawanna Six pleaded guilty to providing material support to al Qaeda, and the sixth pleaded guilty to conducting transactions unlawfully with al Qaeda. These individuals were then sentenced to prison terms ranging from seven to ten years (*Report from the Field: The USA PATRIOT Act at Work*, 2004, p.3).

## Updating the Law to Reflect New Technologies and New Threats

Before the passage of the USA PATRIOT Act, applications for orders authorizing electronic surveillance or physical searches under FISA had to include a certification from a high-ranking Executive Branch official that the purpose of the surveillance or search was to gather foreign intelligence information. As interpreted by the courts and later the Justice Department, this requirement meant that the "primary purpose" of the collection had to be to obtain foreign intelligence information rather than evidence of a crime. Over the years, the prevailing interpretation and implementation of the "primary purpose" standard had the effect of limiting coordination and information sharing between intelligence and law enforcement personnel. Because the courts evaluated the government's purpose for using FISA at least in part by examining the nature and extent of such coordination, the more coordination that occurred, the more likely courts would find that law enforcement, rather than foreign intelligence, had become the primary purpose of the surveillance or search (*Report from the Field: The USA PATRIOT Act at Work*, 2004, p.3).

In defending the viability and constitutionality of "roving wiretaps," Attorney General Ashcroft stated: "We are not asking the law to expand, just to grow as technology grows. . . . Terrorist organizations have increasingly used technology to facilitate their criminal acts and hide their communications from law enforcement. Terrorists are trained to change cell phones frequently, to route email through different Internet computers in order to defeat surveillance" ("Congress Debates Terror . . .," 2001, p.3).

**Increasing the Penalties for Terrorism**   The PATRIOT Act also includes money laundering provisions and sets strong penalties for anyone who harbors or finances terrorists. Senate Banking Committee Chairman Paul Sarbanes calls the PATRIOT bill the most significant money laundering legislation "since money laundering was first made a crime" in 1986, adding: "Osama bin Laden may have boasted 'Al-Qaeda includes modern, educated youths who are as aware of the cracks inside the Western financial system as they are aware of the lines in their hands,' but with [the PATRIOT legislation], we are sealing up those cracks" ("Congress Debates Terror . . .," p.3).

The 1984 Act to Combat International Terrorism (ACIT) established a monetary reward program for information involving terrorism. And as Kash (2002, p.27) points out: "The recently enacted PATRIOT Act amended the reward program's authority by increasing the amount of money offered or paid to an informant." The PATRIOT Act also establishes new punishments for possessing biological weapons and makes it a federal crime to commit an act of terrorism against a mass transit system.

**Controversy Over the USA PATRIOT Act**    According to Boyter (2003, p.17):

> The law [the PATRIOT Act] has come under increasing attack from groups across the political spectrum. Some members of Congress and civil liberties groups say the act has given federal agents too much power to pursue suspected terrorists, threatening the civil rights and privacy of Americans.
>
> Attorney General Ashcroft has defended the law, arguing that repealing it would endanger lives and aid terrorists. He said that any attempt to strip law enforcement agents of their expanded legal powers could open the way to further terrorist attacks.
>
> He said that the law had been essential in preventing another terrorist attack in the United States. Expanding the powers of federal agents to use wiretaps, surveillance and other investigative methods and to share intelligence information "gives us the technological tools to anticipate, adapt and outthink our terrorist enemy," he said.

*Report from the Field* (p.1) states: "Since the USA PATRIOT Act was enacted, the Department of Justice—ever cognizant of civil liberties—has moved swiftly and vigorously to put its new tools into practice. As of May 5, 2004, the Department has charged 310 defendants with criminal offenses as a result of terrorism investigations since the attacks of September 11, 2001, and 179 of those defendants have already been convicted." The act is due to expire in 2005 unless Congress renews it.

The Justice Department has launched a website, www.lifeandliberty.gov, devoted to the PATRIOT Act to dispel some of the myths about the act. As Devanney and Devanney (2003, p.10) explain: "The intent of the Patriot Act, when it was passed in 2001 as an immediate response to the 9/11 attacks, was to provide *federal* law enforcement with better means to defend against terrorism" (emphasis added). They note: "Even in the first days after 9/11, federal officials recognized the importance of local officers in defense against terror. In October 2001, President Bush signed executive Order 12321, which called for federal agencies to reach out to state and local agencies." The concern about local involvement was later incorporated into the Homeland Security Act (HSA) in November 2002. But again, this act focused on reorganizing 22 agencies to defend against terrorism. Devanney and Devanney suggest: "At present, the exact relationship between these local entities and the federal government is still evolving, particularly as it concerns funding issues." Unquestionably, the efforts of local law enforcement agencies are critical in the fight against terrorism.

## The Critical Role of Local Law Enforcement in Homeland Security

Bodrero (2002, p.43) notes: "Every terrorist event, every act of planning and preparation for that event (if conducted inside the United States) occurs in some local law enforcement agency's jurisdiction. No agency is closer to the activities within its community than the law enforcement agency that has responsibility and jurisdiction for protecting that community." The importance of partnerships between law enforcement agencies at all levels cannot be overstated as they apply to the war on terrorism:

- The officer in the field, perhaps by transmitting the details of a seemingly routine traffic stop to a centralized data system, could potentially help avert a national disaster (Hickman and Reaves, 2002, p.83).
- It is vital that patrol officers correctly see themselves as the country's first line of defense against terrorist attacks (Gardner, 2003, p.6).
- When it comes to homeland security, every law enforcement officer can play a vital role. . . . A single law enforcement officer can indeed foil a devastating terrorist attack (S. Wexler, 2003, p.30).
- The 600,000 American law enforcement officers could become the eyes and ears of intelligence agencies, the first line in homeland defense (White, 2004, p.5).

 The first line of defense against terrorism is the patrol officer in the field.

According to Berger (2002, p.6): "The 16,000 state and local law enforcement agencies in the United States—and the 700,000 officers they employ—patrol the streets of our cities and towns daily and, as a result, have an intimate knowledge of those communities they serve. . . . This unique relationship provides these agencies with a tremendous edge in effectively tracking down information related to terrorists."

Berkow (2004, p.25) suggests: "American policing is well into the new post-September 11 era of new duties. Before the attacks, the world of counterrorism, site security and intelligence gathering were generally restricted to either the largest of police agencies or those departments that were responsible for specific identified threats. Most police agencies in the United States were neither trained to carry out these tasks nor focused on them. Since the attacks, every agency in the United States regardless of size or location has accepted these new homeland security missions to some degree. Every agency has now added a counterterrorism mindset to their regular mission and is focused on building and enhancing that capability."

Pedersen (2002, p.6) recalls how firefighters sometimes call police officers the "blue canaries," a reference to the caged canaries miners used to take underground with them, and whose death warned of gas accumulation, thus allowing the miners time to escape the fatal fumes. He suggests the events of September 11 have forced law enforcement to change its mindset when responding to disasters. As was seen in this disaster, police officers, firefighters and others rushed to help those still inside the burning and heavily damaged structures—a rush that, while saving some victims, proved fatal for many responders. Sometimes it is more prudent to assess the situation and the risks involved with rushing in to help.

Savelli (2004, pp.65–66) points out: "Keep in mind, any law enforcement officer can potentially come in contact with a terrorist at any time, whether investigating an unrelated crime, conducting normal duties or responding as a back-up for another law enforcement officer. Also, keep in mind how many of the 9-11-01 hijackers had contact with law enforcement officers in various parts of the country and how many unsuspecting law enforcement officers, in any capacity, may have such contact with terrorists today or in the future." Savelli (pp.65–66) provides the following examples:

- Sept. 9, 2001 Ziad Jarrah, hijacker of the plane that crashed in Shanksville, Pennsylvania, was stopped by police in Maryland for speeding. He was driving 90 mph in a 65 mph zone. He was issued a ticket and released.

- August 2001 Hani Hanjour, who hijacked and piloted the plane that crashed into the Pentagon, killing 289 persons, was stopped by police in Arlington, Virginia. He was issued a ticket for speeding and released. He paid the ticket so he would not have to show up in court.
- Mohammed Atta, who hijacked and piloted the plane that crashed into the north tower of the World Trade Center, was stopped in Tamarac, Florida, for driving without a valid license and issued a ticket. He didn't pay the ticket so an arrest warrant was issued. A few weeks later he was stopped for speeding but let go because police did not know about the warrant.

Bridges (2002, p.35) lists 14 issues that the new war and Operation Enduring Freedom present to local law enforcement: (1) security at major events; (2) tactical actions (executing search and arrest warrants); (3) nuclear, biological and chemical threats; (4) investigations; (5) intelligence; (6) bomb threats; (7) suspicious packages; (8) suspicious people; (9) hate crimes; (10) civil unrest (protestors against military action taken against terrorists); (11) critical facility security; (12) dignitary protection; (13) regional coordination of intelligence gathering and antiterrorism efforts; and (14) balancing civil liberties and security.

A survey of 192 mayors of U.S. cities found that between September 11 and the end of 2001, the cities increased security-related spending by $87.6 million, with the largest portion (43 percent) going to overtime. New equipment was a close second at 31 percent. Expenditures included surveillance cameras, security gates, bulletproof glass, filters for building ventilation systems, security badges, outdoor lighting, gas respirators, concrete planters, body armor, biohazard suits, metal detectors, fences, motion detectors, caller-ID technology, alarms, vehicle-tracking systems, electronic door locks, guardhouses and bomb-sniffing dogs ("Cities Pondering Wide Array . . .," 2002, p.6). However, according to Garrett (2004c, p.6) in a recent poll conducted by the International Association of Chiefs of Police (IACP), 71 percent of the 4,500 agencies that responded to the survey reported being 'not at all prepared' or 'somewhat unprepared' to prevent terrorism. A mere 1 percent claimed that they were 'adequately prepared.' " An important step in preparedness is learning about the enemy.

## Understanding the Enemy

DeMuro (2003, p.32) emphasizes the need for "focused terrorism awareness training for law enforcement." S. Wexler (p.35) likewise stresses:

> The only way to successfully fight terrorism in the United States is for law enforcement to gain a clear understanding of the adversary and to establish meaningful inroads with the Arab community. Local law enforcement has to be brought up to speed as to who the adversary is, their thinking processes, their tactics and their mindset. . . . Local law enforcement must try to establish a good foothold in the Arab and Muslim communities so that they can obtain assistance in developing assets that can root out these individuals. It's not going to be done by the INS, the FBI or NSA satellites. It's going to be done by local law enforcement.

**The Criminal versus the Terrorist** The importance of knowing one's enemy cannot be overemphasized. One critical dimension of this knowledge is differentiating the street criminal from the terrorist. Polisar (2004, p.8) observes: "Suddenly agencies and officers who have been trained and equipped to deal with more traditional crimes are now focused on apprehending individuals operating with different motivations, who have different objectives and who use much deadlier weapons than traditional criminals." Table 9.1 summarizes the most basic differences.

It should be recognized, however, that terrorists also engage in criminal behavior.

**Crimes Associated with Terrorists**   Savelli (pp.21–36) identifies the following crimes as commonly associated with terrorists: mail theft, coupon fraud, sale of illegal cigarettes, identity theft, credit card scams, ATM fraud, counterfeit food products and postage stamps, money laundering and video/audio piracy.

**Terrorist Indicators**   Savelli (p.16) also notes: "Law enforcement officers should be aware of terrorist indicators. Awareness of these indicators will give the law enforcement officer a strong basis to recognize terrorist related information upon being exposed to it. Such indicators are: negative rhetoric, excessive physical training, anti-American literature or a disregard for US laws. Terrorists and their supporters tend to act similar since many of them have trained in the same terrorist training camps and share the same negative ideology."

**Valuable Targets for a Terrorist Attack**   Mariani (2003, pp.106–107) suggests the following as valuable targets: a high-occupancy structure or any site where a significant number of human lives are affected; a structure containing dangerous substances or articles; any vital, high-use object comprising infrastructure; an item of significant historical, symbolic, strategic, defensive or functional value to the nation; a structure or item with high replacement cost; and a structure holding highly sensitive, rare, historical or irreplaceable artifacts, documents or other such content.

**The Typical Stages in a Terrorist Attack**   Mariani (p.97) provides additional insight into terrorist attacks by explaining the typical stages. The first stage is research, including surveillance, stakeouts and local inquiries. The second stage is planning, usually conducted behind closed doors. The third stage is execution, the actual attack and possible escape. Mariana suggests: "Of these three main

**Table 9.1**   Differences in the Street Criminal and the Terrorist

| Typical Criminal | Terrorist |
|---|---|
| Crimes of opportunity | Fighting for political objective |
| Uncommitted | Motivated by ideology or religion |
| Self-centered | Group-focused—even berserkers or lone wolves |
| No cause | Consumed with purpose |
| Untrained | Trained and motivated for the mission |
| Escape-oriented | On the attack |

SOURCE: Adapted from D. Douglas Bodrero. "Law Enforcement's New Challenge to Investigate, Interdict and Prevent Terrorism." *The Police Chief*, February 2002, p.44.

stages, local law enforcement in general and the patrol officer in particular can best serve the counter-terrorism effort with stage one. It is at this stage that the terrorists are out in the open . . . mingling amongst us, driving, traveling, shopping, dining out . . . watching us, studying us, noting our habits, discovering our vulnerabilities and reporting back to their handlers with prospective targeting data to begin the planning stage."

In addition to the preceding general information regarding terrorists, law enforcement officers should become familiar with the training received by members of al Qaeda and the tactics they use.

**Understanding al Qaeda**   Cid (2003, p.33) urges: "The al Qaeda training manual should be required reading for anyone with counterterrorism responsibilities at any level of law enforcement." White (2004, pp.99–101) describes the lessons taught in the al Qaeda manual seized by the Manchester Constabulary in the United Kingdom (available online at www.fbi.gov).

The first lesson is a general introduction beginning with a lamentation on the state of the world and ending with a call to holy war (*jihad*). Other lessons focus on the qualities of al Qaeda members; forgery; safe houses and other hiding places, including instructions for establishing a clandestine terrorist network; secret transportation and communication; training and security during training; and weapons, one of the keys to terrorism, including building an arsenal and safely storing explosives. The remaining lessons discuss secrecy and member safety, emphasizing the need to maintain family and neighborhood ties in the operational area; security, emphasizing planning and operations (secrecy is constantly stressed); reconnaissance, including methods for clandestine spying and capturing prisoners; intelligence gathering; tips on handling recruited agents and dealing with counter measures; and instructions about behavior when arrested. Al Qaeda appears to have a working knowledge of the rights of prisoners in Western justice systems.

White (2004, p.98) also describes the three-tiered model of al Qaeda terrorist attacks using sleeper cells. A **sleeper cell** is a group of terrorists who blend into a community.

 The three-tiered model of al Qaeda terrorist attacks consists of sleeper cells attacking in conjunction with the group's leaders in Afghanistan, sleeper cells attacking on their own apart from centralized command and individuals supported by small cells.

The centralized attacks such as those on 9/11 are the most effective. White notes: "In late 2001 the United States launched a devastating offensive against al Qaeda, destroying its central command. . . . The second and third tiers of al Qaeda are alive and well, surviving on every continent except Antarctica." The key is identifying its members.

Mariana (pp.22–23) notes that racial profiling has been used in law enforcement for decades and suggests the following typical appearance of an al Qaeda terrorist: a young (20 to 30) Middle-Eastern appearing male of average height and weight with prominent facial hair and a foreign accent. Not typical features include shoulder-length hair or a ponytail; flashy clothing and jewelry, business suits, dress shirts and ties, sports jackets, blazers, designer clothes, wing tip shoes, head gear; and use of alcohol or cigarettes. He (p.24) cautions: "Unfortunately, terrorist operatives are believed to have been instructed by a surviving bin Laden aide to do whatever is necessary to avoid detection (e.g., shave their beards, use cologne, wear western style clothing, etc.)."

## *Intelligence Gathering and Sharing*

Many of the day-to-day duties of local law enforcement officers bring them into proximity with sources of information about terrorism. Runge (2002, p.96), administrator of the National Highway Traffic Safety Administration (NHTSA), for example, stresses the role of traffic law enforcement in homeland security: "Patrol operations—and specifically traffic law enforcement—provides a way to track down information related to terrorism. . . . If they are properly trained in what to look for and what questions to ask when interacting with citizens, they can be a tremendous source of intelligence for their state and federal homeland security counterparts."

Heinecke (2004, p.80) describes what she calls "another layer to the security blanket"—Behavior Pattern Recognition (BPR): "BPR is a security methodology based on two components: observation of irregular behaviors for the environment and targeted conversations with suspects. . . . BPR is an extension of trained observation. Officers, whether they are in an airport, sports arena or convention center, need to look for behaviors that are irregular for that location."

The community can also be instrumental in providing information, especially those communities in which community policing is used, as discussed later in the chapter. Figure 9.3 illustrates a model to help local police implement their new antiterrorism responsibilities.

Hoover (2002, p.1) describes four challenges to local police participation in intelligence effectiveness.

 Four obstacles to intelligence effectiveness are technological, logistical, political and ethical.

Hoover (p.1) says: "The technological issue that most challenges state and local participation in any national anti-terrorism intelligence effort can be summarized by one word—*interoperability* [the ability to exchange information seamlessly]. The inability to exchange information on a regional and statewide level is overwhelmingly the primary issue." Logistical obstacles include data entry. "If intelligence officers spend all day entering data, they are not doing very much intelligence analysis" (Hoover, p.4).

Political obstacles include finances, roles, relationships with the FBI and with the state police. According to Hoover (p.4): "By far the most serious impediments to establishing a national interconnected anti-terrorism database are political. . . . First and foremost. . . . is the issue of 'who pays for this.' " The ethical obstacles include the issue of profiling and open records legislation.

**Withholding Information**   As Pilant (2004, p.34) explains: "Counterterrorism and anti-terrorism are difficult tasks made even harder by the operational style that exists at almost every level of policing and in nearly every agency—that of withholding, rather than sharing, intelligence." A report by the Senate Governmental Affairs Committee (Lieberman, 2003, pp.38–41) states:

> The frontline "first preventers" in the war against terrorism lack simple, streamlined access to the federal databases that are most valuable in the effort to identify and apprehend terrorists. . . .

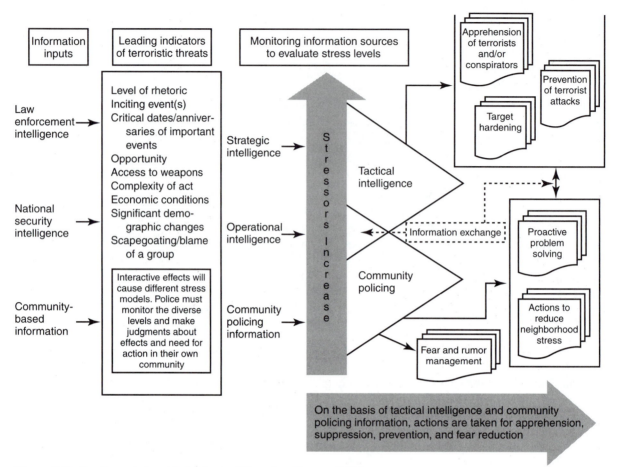

**Figure 9.3** Implementation Model for Anti-Terrorism Responsibilities

SOURCE: David L. Carter and Richard N. Holden. "Terrorism and Community Security." *Local Government Police Management*, 4th ed. Edited by William A. Geller and Darrel W. Stephens. Washington, DC: International City/County Management Association, 2003, p.307. Reprinted by permission.

States and localities still operate far too much as information islands, in relative isolation from their neighbors. Cities, counties and states also have few resources to learn what their counterparts around the country are doing to effectively protect their localities. . . .

Many state and local officials who need high-level information access lack the necessary federal security clearances to do what their job—and our safety—demands. . . .

States lack a single point of contact for both receiving "downstream" information needs and pushing intelligence and other information "upstream."

According to White (2004, p.17): "On the surface it seems simple: Defense and intelligence communities gather information concerning possible terrorist activities in the United States. . . . Under the surface, however, a complex network of interagency rivalries, laws, security clearance issues and turf protection reduces the possibility of shared information." Polisar (p.8) also asserts: "For far too long efforts to combat crime and terrorism have been handicapped by jurisdictional squabbles and archaic rules that prevented us from forging cooperative working relationships with our counterparts in local, regional, tribal and federal law enforcement. This must end."

Weiss and Davis (2002, p.80) note some sharing problems and limitations: "Sometimes information received by an agency such as the FBI is classified. . . . Rules of federal procedure and Grand Jury classified material are two other limitations to what or how much information can be shared." Voegtlin (2002, p.9) reports: "In response to these concerns, the FBI has launched the State and Local Law Enforcement Executive Clearance Initiative. This initiative, which is based on a long-running FBI program, is designed to help state and local law enforcement executives obtain security clearances that will allow them to receive classified information." This initiative might help avoid local law enforcement officers interfering with a terrorism investigation.

Savelli (p.43) observes: "The last thing any law enforcement officer wants to do is compromise a terrorism investigation. The best way to avoid compromising an existing investigation, or conducting conflicting cases, is to develop a local networking module with local, state and federal law enforcement agencies to discuss investigative and enforcement endeavors to combat terrorism. . . . These networking modules should have built-in deconfliction protocol. **Deconfliction**, in essence, means avoiding conflict. Deconfliction can be deployed with declassified and confidential investigations."

**The National Criminal Intelligence Sharing Plan (NCISP)**   A subtitle of the Homeland Security Act of 2002, called the Homeland Security Information Sharing Act, required the president to develop new procedures for sharing classified information as well as unclassified but otherwise sensitive information with state and local police. This charge was fulfilled in May 2002 when the International Association of Chiefs of Police (IACP), the Department of Justice, the FBI, the Department of Homeland Security and other representatives of the federal, state, tribal and local law enforcement communities endorsed the National Criminal Intelligence Sharing Plan (NCISP). In releasing the plan, Attorney General John Ashcroft said: "The NCISP is the first of its kind in the nation, uniting law enforcement agencies of all sizes and geographic locations in a truly national effort to prevent terrorism and criminal activity. By raising cooperation and communication among local, state and federal partners to an unprecedented level, this groundbreaking effort will strengthen the abilities of the justice community to detect threats and protect American lives and liberties" ("Justice Dept. Announces Plan for Local Police Intelligence Sharing," 2004, p.5).

**Intelligence Reform and Terrorism Prevention Act of 2004**   In December 2004 President Bush signed into law the Intelligence Reform and Terrorism Prevention Act to enhance public safety communication operability at all levels of government. It requires the president to facilitate sharing of terrorism information among all appropriate federal, state, local, tribal and private security entities through the use of policy guidelines and technology.

## Crucial Collaborations—Partnerships and Communication

The importance of partnerships between law enforcement agencies at all levels cannot be overstated as it applies to the war on terrorism.

 A key to combating terrorism lies with the local police and the intelligence they can provide to federal authorities.

As stressed earlier, communication should be the number one priority in any preparedness plan, and it is also number one in collaboration among local, state and federal law enforcement agencies. Strandberg (2002, p.12) stresses: "Communication and cooperation are huge issues in dealing with the terrorist threat." Berger (2001, p.6) comments:

> The initial response of law enforcement and other public safety agencies in New York, Virginia, and Pennsylvania and throughout the United States to the terrible events of September was outstanding. Millions around the world watched in admiration and astonishment as police officers, firefighters, and EMS technicians raced to assist the victims of these attacks with little apparent regard for the danger they faced.
>
> On a broader scale, federal, state and local law enforcement agencies immediately began working together in a massive effort to respond to the attack and to prevent additional attacks. In fact, the response of law enforcement agencies around the world to the attacks was truly impressive.
>
> However, since September 11, it has become apparent that the crucial partnership between federal, state and local law enforcement is being hindered by difficulties in cooperation, coordination and information sharing. This is unacceptable.

Nichols (2002, p.17) believes that at the heart of the communication problem is that the FBI refuses to share information in many instances because law enforcement officers lack security clearances. However, FBI Director Mueller (2001, p.12) has publicly stated the desire of the FBI to work with local agencies: "I want to let you know how deeply committed the FBI is to working with you to ensure the safety and security of your communities now and in the future."

Strandberg (p.13) cautions: "It's not just local law enforcement—the FBI and other federal law enforcement agencies must be willing to share information as well. It has to be a two-way street or communication is going to break down." He (p.15) says one tool already being used by law enforcement is facial recognition cameras and software. The system automatically captures faces, translates them into a mathematical code called a face print, and then matches them against a database. If a match occurs, the technology has an alarm that alerts local security. The process takes one to two seconds. Being able to identify people who pose a threat to public safety and to prevent their actions is key in the fight against terrorism.

## Investigating Terrorist Crimes

Fortunately investigating terrorist acts is very similar to investigating other crimes: "The good news is that the investigation of terrorism is not really any different from the investigation of any other kind of criminal activity" (Strandberg, p.13).

Bridges (p.35) suggests: "Suspected terrorist crimes will require investigations to determine suspects' identifications and possible links to crime networks. Disposable cell phones, Internet cafes, public library computers and even a Kinko's copy store were some of the instruments of communications used by terrorists associated with the terrorist acts committed on September 11, 2001."

## Initiatives to Assist in the Fight against Terrorism

Several initiatives have been undertaken to help in the fight against terrorism. One such initiation is production of the *FBI Intelligence Bulletin,* a weekly online publication containing information related to terrorism in the United States. Recipients include duly authorized members of all law enforcement agencies who have registered with a law enforcement network.

Another initiative that indirectly supports the fight against terrorism is passage of the Community Protection Act.

 The Community Protection Act gives off-duty as well as qualified retired police officers the right to carry their concealed firearms in all 50 states.

According to Garrett (2004b, p.6): "The men and women of law enforcement who can now carry the tools of their trade will help make America more secure." Rutledge (2004, p.108) cautions: "Federal laws affecting possession of firearms still apply. For example, firearms are restricted on the grounds of federal prisons, courthouses and other government buildings."

Other initiatives include increased security at our borders, the Community Vulnerability Assessment Methodology, the National Memorial Institute for the Prevention of Terrorism, the Center for Food Protection and Defense and the National Incident Management System.

### Increased Border Security

Moreno (2004) describes the Department of Homeland Security's program, US-VISIT (U.S. Visitor and Immigrant Status Indicator Technology program). One goal of the program is "to enhance the security of our citizens and visitors; facilitate legitimate travel and trade; and ensure the integrity of our immigration system." The program requires visitors to submit to inkless finger scans and digital photographs to allow Customs and Border Protection officers to determine whether the person applying for entry is the same one who was issued a visa by the State Department. Biometric and biographic data will also be checked against watch lists of suspected foreign terrorists and databases of sexual predators, criminals wanted by the FBI and people deported previously from the United States. The program was implemented in January at 115 airports and 14 seaports. It will be expanded to all 165 land ports of entry by December 31, 2005.

### Community Vulnerability Assessment Methodology

Goldsmith et al. (2004, p.100) describe this initiative: "One tool available to police departments and sheriff's offices across the country is the Community Vulnerability Assessment Methodology (C-VAM). Its back-to-basics approach identifies a community's weaknesses by using a detailed and systematic analysis of the facilities and their relationship to each other. By looking at a community as a whole instead of just looking at individual structures, a department will be able to focus its resources and funds on the areas where they are most needed. . . . Using a realistic approach to security, this performance-based system calculates how effective the current physical protection systems are against likely threats."

### The National Memorial Institute for the Prevention of Terrorism (MIPT)

McDonald and McLaughlin (p.15) describe this initiative: "The Memorial Institute (www.mipt.org) grew out of the desire of the survivors and families of the Murrah Federal Building bombing to have a living memorial. The result is an online, national network of best practices and lessons learned."

### The Center for Food Protection and Defense

In July 2004 the University of Minnesota was awarded a $15 million grant for a national Center for Food Protection and Defense. It won the grant because it is one of only a few universities in the country with experts in agriculture, public health, veterinary medicine and medicine on the same campus. The university will partner with General Mills, Cargill, 3M and Hormel. Frank Busta, professor emeritus of food science and nutrition, will direct the grant. According to Busta: "Our charge is to protect and defend safe food from intentional contamination. The vulnerability of food is immense. . . . We hope we can make it sufficiently difficult [so] if and when terrorists decide to look at [attacking the food supply], they will say, 'We'll try something else' " (Smetanka, 2004b, p.A4).

In announcing the new Center for Food Protection and Defense, Homeland Security Secretary Ridge noted: "Government can't do it alone. . . . Partnerships between government and our great research universities, businesses and scientists will produce together what would be impossible individually" (Smetanka, 2004a, p.B1).

### The National Incident Management System

"In October 2003 Homeland Security Secretary Tom Ridge approved the Initial National Response Plan (INRP), an interim plan designed to help develop a unified approach to domestic incident management across the nation" ("Initial National Response Plan," 2004, p.19). As Hamilton (2003, p.11) explains: "The events of September 11, 2001, and subsequent development of the DHS has necessitated a change in the response and management of major domestic incidents."

On March 1, 2004, Secretary Ridge announced the approval of the National Incident Management System (NIMS), the country's first standardized management approach unifying federal, state and local governments for incident response. NIMS establishes standardized incident management processes, protocols and procedures that all responders—federal, state, tribal and local—will use to coordinate and conduct response action ("DHS Secretary Ridge Approves National Incident Management System [NIMS]," 2004, p.14).

## The Role of the Media in the War on Terrorism

According to White (2003, p.256): "One of the most controversial current topics of terrorism analysis is the way print and electronic media cover terrorist acts. Police and other government forces operate with a set of objectives diametrically opposed to the goals of reporters covering an event. In addition, experts have heatedly debated the effects of electronic coverage on terrorism, and there are several competing schools of thought on the effectiveness and impact of newspaper coverage. Regardless of which side one favors, reporting terrorism will remain controversial because the media has become part of the terrorist event."

The Terrorism Research Center suggests: "Terrorism and the media have a symbiotic relationship. Without the media, terrorists would receive no exposure, their cause would go ignored, and no climate of fear would be generated. Terrorism is futile without publicity, and the media generates much of this publicity."

White (2003, p.257) points out: "Members of the media have two competing and often contradictory roles. They control the flow of information while simultaneously making the news entertaining enough to 'sell.' " White (p.259) raises the question of the **contagion effect,** that is, the coverage of terrorism inspires more terrorism. It is, in effect, contagious. This controversial issue leads to discussions about censorship in the war on terrorism.

Emerson (2002, p.35) contends: "The media need not become a tool of terrorism, by inadvertently spreading misinformation and escalating panic. Instead, state and local governments should learn to look at the mass media as partners in responding effectively to an attack."

## Concerns Related to the War on Terrorism

Two concerns related to the "war on terrorism" are that civil liberties may be jeopardized and that people of Middle Eastern descent may be discriminated against or become victims of hate crimes.

### *Concern for Civil Rights*

Civil libertarians are concerned that valued American freedoms will be sacrificed in the interest of national safety. For example, the Justice Department has issued a new regulation giving itself the authority to monitor inmate-attorney communications if "reasonable suspicion" exists that inmates are using such communications to further or facilitate acts of terrorism. However, criminal defense lawyers and members of the American Civil Liberties Union (ACLU) have protested the regulation, saying it effectively eliminates the Sixth Amendment right to counsel because, under codes of professional responsibility, attorneys cannot communicate with clients if confidentiality is not assured. The ACLU has vowed to monitor police actions closely to see that freedoms protected under the Constitution are not jeopardized.

According to Melekian (2002, p.1): "In the post-September 11 world, our greatest challenge is not dealing with terrorists. Rather it is finding the balance between enhancing security and maintaining liberty." Bulzomi (2003, p.26) stresses: "The government must use its new tools in a way that preserves the rights and freedoms guaranteed by America's democracy, but, at the same time, ensure that the fight against terrorism is vigorous and effective."

A difficult challenge facing law enforcement is balancing the need to enhance security with the need to maintain freedom.

### *Retaliation or Discrimination against People of Middle Eastern Descent*

Another concern is that some Americans may retaliate against innocent people of Middle Eastern descent, many of whom were either born in the United States or are naturalized citizens. According to Peed and Wexler (p.vii): "America's multicultural neighborhoods, particularly Arab and Muslim communities, were initially affected by backlash violence and hate crimes following the terrorist attacks." Davies and Murphy (2004, p.1) likewise note: "Within hours of the Twin Towers' collapse and the attack on the Pentagon, U.S. residents and visitors, particularly Arabs, Muslims and Sikhs, were harassed or attacked because they shared—or were perceived to share—the terrorists' national background or religion. . . . Law enforcement's challenge since then has been to maintain an appropriate balance between the security interests of our country and the constitutional rights of every American." We must remember the Japanese internment camps during World War II and make sure we do not repeat that mistake.

Closely related concerns are the rights of citizens detained as enemy combatants and the rights of detained foreign nationals. In *Hamdi v. Rumsfeld* (2004) the Supreme Court ruled that a citizen detained in the United States as an enemy combatant must be afforded the opportunity to rebut such a designation. Petitioner Hamdi was captured in an active combat zone in Afghanistan following the September 11, 2001, attack on America and surrendered an assault rifle. The U.S. District Court found that the declaration from the Defense Department did not support Hamdi's detention and ordered the government to turn over numerous materials for review. The U.S. Court of Appeals for the Fourth Circuit reversed, stressing that, because it was undisputed that Hamdi was captured in an active combat zone, no factual inquiry or evidentiary hearing allowing Hamdi to rebut the government's assertions was necessary. A 6–3 Supreme Court vacated and remanded, concluding that Hamdi should have a meaningful opportunity to offer evidence that he was not an enemy combatant.

In *Rasul v. Bush* (2004) the Supreme Court ruled that U.S. courts have jurisdiction to consider challenges to the legality of the detention of foreign nationals captured in Afghanistan in a military campaign against al Qaeda and the Taliban regime that supported it. The petitioners, two Australians and 12 Kuwaitis, were being held in Guantanamo Bay, Cuba, without charges. These and other legal issues regarding civil rights will be debated as the country seeks to balance the need for security with civil rights.

## Community Policing and Homeland Security

Griffith (2004, p.6) points out: "Real Homeland Security can only come from an alert, aware and vigilant public." According to C. Wexler (2001, p.vii): "The events of September 11, 2001, have changed the role of local police in America—perhaps forever. Local law enforcement faces the challenges of assuming more responsibility in countering domestic terrorism threats while continuing to address crime and disorder. Success will depend on their ability to build on strong community policing networks for information exchange and to maintain a collaborative problem-solving approach to crime amid high anxiety and crisis. Now more than ever, departments need to adhere to community problem-solving principles to decrease crime and disorder in their communities, increase their departments' efficiency and strengthen their relationships with citizens."

Bucqueroux and Diamond (2002, p.6) suggest that some departments are using the current focus on terrorism to "jettison" community policing. They explain: "Few people outside the field know about the pitched battle for the heart and soul of policing that has raged over the past decade [the military model versus community policing]. It is said that people get the police they deserve. If we are to maintain recent reductions in violent crime and uncover the terrorists living among us, while preserving the civil rights that make our society special, we must insist on community policing now more than ever."

Nislow (2001, p.1) contends: "Any remaining doubts about the efficacy of community policing should have been dispelled last month [September 2001] when such programs provided law enforcement not only with a vehicle for communicating a reassuring message to fearful residents, but a means for gathering information that may yet help further the federal investigations into the terrorist attacks on the World Trade Center and the Pentagon." She concludes: "I believe that even from a national security standpoint, community policing could well be our number-one line of defense."

"In order to truly protect our communities from terrorism we must enlist them as partners in our fight to prevent the next attack. If we are to be successful, it is imperative that we have the full cooperation of the communities we are trying to serve. The onus is on law enforcement to expand our community policing capabilities and continue to build relationships with our citizens, so that we can work together to reduce crime, violence and fear" (C. Wexler, 2003, p.2).

Olin (2002, p.28) likewise urges: "Every law enforcement agency in the United States should continue with its community-policing emphasis to strengthen the connections between citizens and the government." Carter and Holden (p.293) point out: "Community policing activities help police departments observe factors that could contribute to terrorism, identify individuals who may pose a threat or have information about terrorists' plans and lessen citizens' fears associated with terrorism."

## Being Proactive

Sims (2004) reports: "Americans are closely divided on whether they think the United States is prepared to deal with another terrorist attack, but the overwhelming majority has done nothing to prepare for such an attack themselves, according to a recent *New York Times* poll." In addition, according to Savage (2004): "Large numbers of Americans say they would probably ignore official instructions for how to respond to a terrorist attack involving a radiological dirty bomb or a smallpox attack according to a new study." Clearly, community policing officers can do much to educate citizens in their jurisdiction on preparedness plans, including a meeting place in case of a terrorist attack.

"Homeland Security Funding Sources" (2004, p.27) describes Citizen Corps, a component of the USA Freedom Corps focusing on opportunities for people across the country to participate in a range of measures to make their families, homes and communities safer from the threats of terrorism, crime and disasters of all kinds. In addition, Citizen Corps brings together a community's first responders, firefighters, emergency health care providers, law enforcement and emergency managers with its volunteer resources.

The New York City police are providing antiterrorism training to building supers and doormen to be the eyes and ears of the department. Plans call for training 28,000 building employees through 2005 (Butler, 2004, p.A7). Giannone and Wilson (2003, p.37) describe the CAT Eyes Program, the Community Anti-Terrorism Training Initiative, designed to enlist community members in the fight against terrorism: "The CAT Eyes program was designed to help local communities combat terrorism by enhancing neighborhood security, heightening the community's powers of observation, and encouraging mutual assistance and concern among neighbors."

Scheider et al. (no date, p.162) contend: "In the 21st century the community policing philosophy is well positioned to take a central role in preventing and responding to terrorism and in efforts to reduce citizen fear. Law enforcement agencies should realize that community policing is more important than ever in pro-actively dealing with and responding to terrorism in their jurisdiction." They (p.160) explain: "An officer in a department that fully embraces the community policing philosophy would know of potential terrorist targets in his jurisdiction because he has been assigned a regular patrol area and given the responsibility and authority to protect it."

### SUMMARY

The threat of terrorism has become a reality in America. Most definitions of terrorism have common elements, including the systematic use of physical violence, either actual or threatened, against noncombatants to create a climate of fear to cause some religious, political or social change. Three elements of terrorism are: (1) it is criminal in nature, (2) targets are typically symbolic and (3) the terrorist actions are always aggressive and often violent. The FBI classifies terroristic acts as either domestic or international. It is the lead agency for responding to terrorism. Most terrorist acts result from dissatisfaction with a religious, political or social system or policy and frustration resulting from an inability to change it through acceptable, nonviolent means. Domestic terrorist groups include white supremacists, black supremacists, militia groups, other right-wing extremists, left-wing extremists, pro-life extremists, animal rights activists and environmental extremists. Terrorists may use arson; explosives and bombs; weapons of mass destruction (biological, chemical or nuclear agents); and technology.

As a result of 9/11 the Department of Homeland Security was established, reorganizing the departments of the federal government. The Federal Emergency Management Agency (FEMA) is the lead agency for consequence management (after an attack). The Department of Homeland Security facilitates collaboration between local and federal law enforcement to develop a national strategy to detect, prepare for, prevent, protect against, respond to and recover from terrorist attacks within the United States.

The USA PATRIOT Act significantly improves the nation's counterterrorism efforts by:

- Allowing investigators to use the tools already available to investigate organized crime and drug trafficking.
- Facilitating information sharing and cooperation among government agencies so they can better "connect the dots."
- Updating the law to reflect new technologies and new threats.
- Increasing the penalties for those who commit or support terrorist crimes.

The first line of defense against terrorism is the patrol officer in the field.

The three-tiered model of al Qaeda terrorist attacks consists of sleeper cells attacking in conjunction with the group's leaders in Afghanistan, sleeper cells attacking on their own apart from centralized command and individuals supported by small cells. A key to combating terrorism lies with the local police and the intelligence they can provide to federal authorities. The Community Protection Act gives off-duty as well as qualified retired police officers the right to carry their concealed firearms in all 50 states.

Four obstacles to intelligence effectiveness are technological, logistical, political and ethical.

Two concerns related to the "war on terrorism" are that civil liberties may be jeopardized and that people of Middle Eastern descent may be discriminated against or become victims of hate crimes. A difficult challenge facing law enforcement is balancing the need to enhance security with the need to maintain freedom.

### APPLICATION

As your department's emergency management officer, you have been directed to establish a policy and procedure to respond to terrorist threats in your jurisdiction. Include the roles of local, state and federal agencies in your policy and procedure.

### DISCUSSION QUESTIONS

1. Which is the greater threat—domestic or international terrorism? Why?
2. Does your police department have a counterterrorism strategy in place? If so, what?
3. What type of terrorist attack do you fear most? Why?
4. Do you feel Americans have become complacent about terrorism?
5. What provisions of the PATRIOT Act do you think are most important?
6. What barriers to sharing information among the various local, state and federal agencies do you think are most problematic?
7. Does media coverage of terrorist acts lead to more terrorism, that is, do you think the contagion effect is in operation?
8. Should Americans expect to give up some civil liberties to allow law enforcement officers to pursue terrorists?
9. Do you think a terrorist sleeper cell could operate in your community? What signs might indicate that such a cell exists?
10. What means might terrorists use to attack the United States in the future? Are we more or less vulnerable at home or at our interests abroad?

### INFOTRAC COLLEGE EDITION ASSIGNMENTS

- Use InfoTrac College Edition to help answer the Discussion Questions as appropriate.
- Terrorism as seen in the United States on September 11, 2001, is a new phenomenon. Use InfoTrac College Edition to determine how many countries in the world have been exposed to terrorism and the specific nature of terrorist acts, if any distinguishing trends are noted. Be ready to discuss your results with the class.
- Use InfoTrac College Edition to read and outline one of the following articles to share with the class:

- "Confronting Terrorism on the State and Local Level" in the *FBI Law Enforcement Bulletin*
- "Fighting Terrorism in the 21st Century" by John F. Lewis, Jr.
- "'Baseline' Training for Terrorism" by Gary J. Rohen
- "Understanding the Terrorist Mind-Set" by Randy Borum
- "Foreign Intelligence Surveillance Act: Before and after the USA PATRIOT Act" by Michael J. Bulzomi
- "Hunting Terrorists Using Confidential Informant Reward Programs" by Douglas A. Kash
- "Amnesty Boxes: A Component of Physical Security for Law Enforcement" by Charles Mesiah, Mark Henych and Randy Mingo
- "Responding to Terrorism" by Robert S. Mueller, III
- "World Destruction: A Cultural Analysis of a Threat Communique" by Mitchell R. Manner
- "Weapons of Mass Destruction and Civil Aviation Preparedness" by Robert Raffel

### INTERNET ASSIGNMENTS

Select two assignments to complete.

- Go to the websites of the DEA (www.dea.gov), the FBI (www.fbi.gov), the Department of Justice (www.usdoj.gov) and the Department of the Treasury (www.ustreas.gov) and note how the different agencies are addressing the issue of *terrorism*. How do their focuses differ? Be prepared to share your findings with the class.
- Search for *USA PATRIOT Act* (2001). List specific applications of the act to law enforcement practices and explain how they might differ from conventional practices. Do you believe the phrase "extraordinary times demand extraordinary measures" justifies "bending the rules," so to speak, in the war on terrorism? In other words, do the ends justify the means? Should law enforcement be permitted to use roving wiretaps and breach privileged inmate-attorney communications in the name of national security, or is this the beginning of the end of our civil liberties? Be prepared to discuss your answers with the class.
- Go to the Department of Justice website devoted to the PATRIOT Act and list the myths the site dispels.
- Go to www.policeforum.org and find "Local Law Enforcement's Role in Preventing and Responding to

Terrorism." Read and outline the article. Be prepared to share your outline with the class.

- To learn what the U.S. Department of Homeland Security is doing to keep America safe go to http://www.ready.gov/.
- Go to the Terrorism Research Center's website, http://www.terrorism.com/ and select one of the links related to the U.S. Homeland Attack on 9/11.
- Go to the Counterterrorism Training and Resources website at http://www.counterterrorismtraining.gov and outline what resources are available for local police departments.
- Go to http://www.fbi.gov/publications/terror/terror99.pdf and outline the information on terrorist incidents and counterterrorist tactics and achievements in the United States in 1999. Be prepared to share your outline with the class.
- Go to www.fbi.gov/publications/terror/terrorism.htm and find "Terrorism in the United States." Outline either the past 30 years of terrorism in the United States, notable cases, trends, emerging threats or the development of the FBI response to terrorism, and be prepared to discuss your outline with the class.
- Go to the Office for Domestic Preparedness website at http://osldps.ncjrs.org and outline the information presented on *weapons of mass destruction*. Be prepared to discuss your outline with the class.
- Go to the Police Executive Research Forum website at www.policeforum.org and find their report *Local Law Enforcement's Role in Preventing and Responding to Terrorism*. Outline a section of the report that interests you, and be prepared to share it with the class.

 **BOOK-SPECIFIC WEBSITE**

The book-specific website at http://cj.wadsworth.com/wobleski_Hess_police_op4e hosts a variety of resources for students and instructors. Many can be emailed to the instructor. Included are extended activities such as Concept Builders - the 3 step learning module that reinforces key chapter concepts, followed by a real-world applications and critical thinking questions. InfoTrac College Edition exercises; Discussion Questions; interactive key-term FlashCards; and a collection of chapter-based Web Links provide additional information and activities to include in the curriculum.

### REFERENCES

Barakat, Matthew. "Muhammad Sentenced to Death in Sniper Killings." Associated Press as reported in (Minneapolis/St. Paul) *Star Tribune*, March 20, 2004, p.A3.

Baveja, Alok. "War on Illicit Drugs May Offer Lessons in Fight against Terrorism." *The Police Chief*, March 2002, pp.30–36.

Berger, William B. "IACP Actions in Response to September 11." *The Police Chief*, September 2002, p.6.

Berger, William B. "Uniting Law Enforcement to Fight Terrorism." *The Police Chief*, December 2001, p.6.

Berkow, Michael. "The Internal Terrorists." *The Police Chief*, June 2004, pp.25–30.

"Bioterrorism." *Security Management*, July 2003, pp.24–25.

Bodrero, D. Douglas. "Law Enforcement's New Challenge to Investigate, Interdict and Prevent Terrorism." *The Police Chief*, February 2002, pp.41–48.

Boyter, Jennifer. "Attorney General Ashcroft Defends Patriot Act." *The Police Chief*, September 2003, p.17.

Bridges, Dennis. "It's a Police Problem: The Terrorist Threat's Impact on State and Local Law Enforcement." *The Police Chief*, February 2002, pp.35–38.

Brinkley, Larry. "Present Threats." *The Law Enforcement Trainer*, November/December 2003, pp.30–35.

Brinkley, Larry. "Present Threats: Part II." *The Law Enforcement Trainer*, January/February 2004, pp.43–48.

Bucqueroux, Bonnie and Diamond, Drew. "Community Policing Is Our Best Bet against Terror." *Subject to Debate*, January 2002, pp.1, 6.

Bulzomi, Michael J. "Foreign Intelligence Surveillance Act: Before and after the USA PATRIOT Act." *FBI Law Enforcement Bulletin*, June 2003, pp.25–32.

Butler, Desmond. "Building Supers Standing Watch." Associated Press as reported in the (Minneapolis/St. Paul) *Star Tribune*, June 23, 2004, p.A7.

Carter, David L. and Holden, Richard N. "Terrorism and Community Security." In *Local Government Police Management*, Washington, DC: International City/County Management Association, 2003, pp.291–311.

Choudhury, Jayanto N. "Asymmetric Warfare: The 21st Century Challenge to U.S. Law Enforcement Executives." *The Police Chief*, April 2002, pp.183–188.

Cid, David. "Preventing Terrorism: The Intelligence Dimension." *The Police Chief*, March 2003, pp.30–35.

"Cities Pondering Wide Array of Physical Security Needs." *Homeland Security and Defense*, February 6, 2002, p.6.

"Confronting the Suicide-Bomber Threat." *Security Management*, November 2003, p.16.

"Congress Debates Terror Bill's Effects on Criminal Justice." *Criminal Justice Newsletter*, October 30, 2001, pp.1–4.

Czarnecki, Fabrice. "NBC's of 1st Response." *American Police Beat*, January/February 2002, pp.1, 12–13.

Davies, Heather J. and Murphy, Gerard R. *Protecting Your Community from Terrorism: The Strategies for Local Law Enforcement Series Vol. 2: Working with Diverse Communities*. Washington, DC: The Office of Community Oriented Policing Services and the Police Executive Research Forum, 2004.

DeMuro, Joseph G. "Terrorism and Extremist Training: The Rationale for Focused Terrorism Awareness Training for Law Enforcement." *The Law Enforcement Trainer*, January/February 2003, pp.32–33.

Devanney, Joe and Devanney, Diane. "Homeland Security and Patriot Acts." *Law and Order*, August 2003, pp.10–12.

"DHS Secretary Ridge Approves National Incident Management System (NIMS)." *NCJA Justice Bulletin*, March 2004, pp.14–16.

Emerson, Peter Van D. "Utilizing the Mass Media." In *Beyond the Beltway: Focusing on Hometown Security: Recommendations for State and Local Domestic Preparedness Planning a Year after 9-11.* A Report of the Executive Session on Domestic Preparedness, John F. Kennedy School of Government, Harvard University, September 2002.

Esposito, Tony. "On the Case, 24/7." *American Police Beat*, January/February, 2002, p.58.

Gardner, Gerald W. "Getting Ready for the Big One: Terrorism Can Happen Anywhere, at Any Time." *Police*, October 2003, p.6.

Garrett, Ronnie. "Terrorism on the Homefront." *Law Enforcement Technology*, July 2002, pp.22–26.

Garrett, Ronnie. "Tree Huggers with Hand Grenades?" *Law Enforcement Technology*, September 2004a, pp.88–95.

Garrett, Ronnie. "'V' Is for Victory." *Law Enforcement Technology*, September 2004b, p.6.

Garrett, Ronnie. "The Wolf Is at the Door: What Are We Waiting For?" *Law Enforcement Technology*, March 2004c, p.6.

Giannone, Donald and Wilson, Robert A. "The CAT Eyes Program: Enlisting Community Members in the Fight against Terrorism." *The Police Chief*, March 2003, pp.37–38.

Gips, Michael A. "Secondary Devices a Primary Concern." *Security Management*, July 2003, pp.16–20.

Goldsmith, Michael; Weiss, Jim; and Davis, Mickey. "Community Vulnerability Assessment Methodology." *Law and Order*, May 2004, pp.100–103.

Griffith, David. "Watching the Neighborhood." *Police*, April 2004, p.6.

Guida, Joseph F. "Enviroterrorism: A Long-Range View." *Security Products*, October 2002, p.54.

Hamilton, Randy C. "The Implementation of a National Incident Management System (NIMS)." *The Law Enforcement Trainer*, May/June 2003, pp.11–12.

Hanson, Doug. "Ricin Toxin: What Law Enforcement Needs to Know." *Law Enforcement Technology*, August 2003, pp.16–22.

Hanson, Doug. "Bacteria Viruses: The Terrorist's Bioweapons Arsenal." *Law Enforcement Technology*, August 2004a, pp.10–16.

Hanson, Doug. "The Nation's Food and Water Supply: A New Target for Terrorists?" *Law Enforcement Technology*, January 2004b, pp.18–24.

Heinecke, Jeannine. "Adding Another Layer to the Security Blanket." *Law Enforcement Technology*, March 2004, pp.78–85.

Hickman, Matthew J. and Reaves, Brian A. "Local Police and Homeland Security: Some Baseline Data." *The Police Chief*, October 2002, pp.83–85.

"Homeland Security Funding Sources." *The Police Chief*, February 2004, pp.23–27.

Hoover, Larry T. "The Challenges to Local Police Participation in the Homeland Security Effort." *Subject to Debate*, October 2002, pp.1, 3–10.

Hughes, Shawn. "How to Start a WMD Unit." *Police*, September 2003, pp.20–24.

Hughes, Shawn. "Anxiety Attack." *Police*, September 2004, pp.32–36.

"Initial National Response Plan." *The Police Chief*, February 2004, pp.19–21.

Jackman, Tom. "Teen Sniper Gets Life without Parole for Virginia Shooting." *Washington Post*, as reprinted in the (Minneapolis/St. Paul) *Star Tribune*, March 11, 2004, p.A3.

"Justice Dept. Announces Plan for Local Police Intelligence Sharing." *Criminal Justice Newsletter*, June 1, 2004, p.5.

Kash, Douglas A. "Hunting Terrorists Using Confidential Informant Reward Programs." *FBI Law Enforcement Bulletin*, April 2002, pp.26–31.

Lasky, Steve. "Confronting an Enemy with No Face." *Security Technology & Design*, January 2002, p.4.

Lesce, Tony. "WMD Training." *Law and Order*, December 2001, pp.99–103.

Levine, Samantha. "The Car Bomb Conundrum: Trying to Stop the Terrorists' Low-Tech, Lethal Weapons of Choice." *U.S. News & World Report*, August 16/August 23, 2004, p.30.

Lieberman, Senator Joseph I. *State and Local Officials: Still Kept in the Dark about Homeland Security.* Washington, DC: A Report by the Senate Governmental Affairs Committee, August 13, 2003.

Mariani, Cliff. *Terrorism Prevention and Response: The Definitive Law Enforcement Guide to Prepare for Terrorist Activity.* Flushing, NY: Looseleaf Law Publications, Inc., 2003.

McDonald, Kathleen and McLaughlin, W. Sean. "First Responders: Ready or Not?" *The Law Enforcement Trainer*, May/June 2003, pp.13–19.

McVey, Philip M. "Homeland Defense: An Effective Partnership." *The Police Chief*, April 2002, pp.174–180.

Melekian, Bernard. "Balancing Act: Security vs. Liberty." *Subject to Debate*, June 2002, pp.1, 4.

Moore, Jeffrey. "Car Bomb Security." *Law Enforcement Technology*, August 2003, pp.24–33.

Moreno, Sylvia. "Border Security Measures to Tighten Next Month." *Washington Post*, October 15, 2004.

Mueller, Robert S., III. "Responding to Terrorism." *FBI Law Enforcement Bulletin*, December 2001, pp.12–14.

Nason, Randall R. "Chemical Agent Terrorism: A Refresher in Strategic Approach." *Security Technology & Design*, February 2003, pp.44–46.

Nichols, Mark. "FBI Still Won't Share Crucial Information." *American Police Beat*, January/February 2002, p.17.

Nilson, Chad and Burke, Tod. "Environmental Extremists and the Eco-Terrorism Movement." *ACJS Today*, January/February 2002, pp.1–6.

"9/11 Report: Excerpts." Reported in the (Minneapolis/St. Paul) *Star Tribune*, July 21, 2004, p.A14.

Nislow, Jennifer. "Secret Weapon against Terrorism? Chiefs Say Community Policing Is an Ace in the Hole." *Law Enforcement News*, October 15, 2001, pp.1, 11.

Oldham, Scott. "Close UP: Counter-Terrorist. Scott Swat-Pak, A New Level in Tactical Protection." *Law and Order*, December 2001, pp.94–97.

Olin, W. Ronald. "Why Traditional Law Enforcement Methods Cannot Win the War on Terrorism." *The Police Chief*, November 2002, pp.27–31.

Page, Douglas. "Law Enforcement Renaissance: The Sequel." *Law Enforcement Technology*, March 2004, pp.86–90.

Pedersen, Dorothy. "What Police Departments Need to Know." *WMD Journal* (Insert in *Law Enforcement Technology*), January 2002, pp.6–7.

Peed, Carl R. and Wexler, Chuck. "Foreword." In *Protecting Your Community from Terrorism: The Strategies for Local Law Enforcement Series Vol. 2: Working with Diverse Communities*, edited by Heather J. Davies and Gerard R. Murphy, Washington, DC: The Office of Community Oriented Policing Services and the Police Executive Research Forum, 2004, pp.vii–viii.

Pilant, Lois. "Strategic Modeling: Los Angeles County's Counterterrorism Program Is Being Duplicated Nationwide." *Police*, May 2004, pp.34–38.

Pitcavage, Mark. "Domestic Extremism: Still a Potent Threat." *The Police Chief*, August 2003, pp.32–35.

Polisar, Joseph M. "The National Criminal Intelligence Sharing Plan." *The Police Chief*, June 2004, p.8.

Raffel, Robert. "Weapons of Mass Destruction and Civil Aviation Preparedness." *FBI Law Enforcement Bulletin*, May 2003, pp.1–5.

*Report from the Field: The USA PATRIOT Act at Work*. Washington, DC: Department of Justice, July 2004.

Reuland, Melissa and Davies, Heather J. et al. *Protecting Your Community From Terrorism: Strategies for Law Enforcement, Volume 3: Preparing for and Responding to Bioterrorism*. Washington, DC: COPS and PERF, 2004.

Rohen, Gary J. "WMD Response: Integrating the Joint Operations Center and Incident Command System." *The Police Chief*, October 2001, pp.148–163.

Runge, Jeffrey W. "The Role of Traffic Law Enforcement in Homeland Security." *The Police Chief*, October 2002, pp.90–98.

Rutledge, Devallis. "'Borderless' Concealed Carry." *Police*, November 2004, pp.106–108.

"Safety on the Scene." *First Responder Forum*, April 2002, pp.6–7.

Sanow, Ed. "Vandalism? Terrorism." *Law and Order*, May 2002, p.5.

Savage, Charlie. "Terror Response Study Spurs Concern: Many Americans Would Disobey." *Boston Globe*, September 15, 2004.

Savelli, Lou. *A Proactive Law Enforcement Guide for the War on Terrorism*. Flushing, NY: LooseLeaf Law Publications, Inc. 2004.

Scheider, Matthew C.; Chapman, Robert E.; and Seelman, Michael E. "Connecting the Dots for a Proactive Approach." *BTA America*, no date, pp.158–162.

Schweid, Barry. "Corrected Terror Report Shows More Attacks, More Injured." The Associated Press as reported in the (Minneapolis/St. Paul) *Star Tribune*, June 23, 2004, p.A1.

Scoville, Dean. "The Enemies Within." *Police*, September 2003, pp.44–50.

"The Shape of Things to Come." *Security Management*, March 2003, p.20.

Sims, Calvin. "Poll Finds Most Americans Have Not Prepared for a Terror Attack." *The New York Times*, October 28, 2004.

Smetanka, Mary Jane. "'U' Center Safeguards Food Supply." (Minneapolis/St. Paul) *Star Tribune*, July 7, 2004a, pp.B1, B4.

Smetanka, Mary Jane. "'U' Studies Terrorism at Your Table." (Minneapolis/St. Paul) *Star Tribune*, July 6, 2004b, pp.A1, A4.

Stanton, John J. "Is the U.S. Prepared for Nuclear Terrorism?" *Security Management*, March 2002, pp.154–156.

Strandberg, Keith. "Protecting the People: Law Enforcement's Role in the War against Terrorism." *Law Enforcement Technology*, January 2002, pp.12–16.

"Suicide Terrorism." *Security Management*, August 2003, pp.20–22.

Symonds, Daniel R. "A Guide to Selected Weapons of Mass Destruction." *The Police Chief*, March 2003, pp.19–29.

*Terrorism and International Victims Unit*. OVC Fact Sheet, January 2002. (FS-000276)

The Terrorism Research Center. http://www.terrorism.com/index.html

Uner, Eric. "Cyber Terrorism: Count on It." *Security Products*, February 2003, pp.26–28.

Voegtlin, Gene. "FBI Offers Security Clearances to State and Local Law Enforcement Executives." *The Police Chief*, March 2002, p.9.

Weiss, Jim and Davis, Mickey. "Information Partnering and the FBI." *Law and Order*, January 2002, pp.80–81.

Wexler, Chuck. "Foreword." In *Solving Crime and Disorder Problems: Current Issues, Police Strategies and Organizational Tactics*, edited by Melissa Reuland, Corina Sole Brito and Lisa Carroll. Washington, DC: Police Executive Research Forum, 2001, p.vii.

Wexler, Chuck. "Policing a Multicultural Community." *Subject to Debate*, July 2003, p.2.

Wexler, Sanford. "Homeland Security: Think Locally." *Law Enforcement Technology*, January 2003, pp.30–35.

White, Jonathan R. *Terrorism: An Introduction*, 4th ed. Belmont, CA: Wadsworth Publishing Company, 2003.

White, Jonathan R. *Defending the Homeland: Domestic Intelligence, Law Enforcement and Security*. Belmont, CA: Wadsworth Publishing Company, 2004.

## CASES CITED

*Hamdi v. Rumsfeld*, No.03-6696, U.S. June 28, 2004
*Rasul v. Bush*, No. 03-334, U.S. June 28, 2004

# SPECIALIZED POLICE OPERATIONS

The previous section described the basic police operations within any law enforcement agency: patrol; traffic; dealing with crime and disorder; dealing with violence at home, in school and on the job; dealing with emergencies; and fighting the war on terrorism—protecting the homeland. In addition to these basic functions, law enforcement agencies also perform highly specialized operations. In smaller departments these specialized operations are performed by the patrol officer. In larger departments they may be assigned to specific officers or even to specialized departments.

This section discusses the specialized operations that may be required of law enforcement agencies, including investigation (Chapter 10), dealing with juveniles (Chapter 11) and dealing with the gang and drug problem (Chapter 12). Even when the specialized operations are performed by nonpatrol officers, they still will require patrol officers' input and cooperation and, indeed, that of the entire community for maximum effectiveness.

# Criminal Investigation

## DO YOU KNOW . . .

■ How realistic fictionalized detectives are?

■ What the primary goals of a criminal investigation are?

■ What the most critical phase in the majority of criminal investigations is?

■ What AFIS is and how it helps solve crimes?

■ What two forms of positive identification may be available in criminal investigations?

■ What the major violent crimes are, their elements and what special considerations might be involved in each?

■ What the major property crimes are, their elements and what special considerations might be involved in each?

■ What problems might be encountered when investigating crimes against children?

■ What may be involved in computer-related crime?

■ What victimless crimes are?

■ When surveillance, undercover assignments and raids might be necessary?

■ What entrapment is and how it can be avoided?

## CAN YOU DEFINE?

| | | | |
|---|---|---|---|
| accelerants | computer-related crimes | fraud | parallel proceedings |
| arson | contamination | hate crime | phishing |
| assault | covert investigations | homicide | premeditation |
| Automated Fingerprint Identification System (AFIS) | DNA fingerprinting | identity theft | proxy data |
| | entrapment | igniters | robbery |
| burglary | environmental crimes | larceny/theft | sexual assault |
| | equivocal death investigation | motor vehicle thefts | victimless crimes |
| | | overt investigations | |

## Introduction

One of the most important functions of law enforcement agencies is criminal investigation. This is carried out largely by detectives, and everyone knows what a detective is because of television programs like *NYPD Blue, CSI* and *Cold Case*. To the public, detectives and criminal investigation are the "glamour jobs" within law enforcement. In fact, this same view is held by many officers who, at some point in their careers, want a promotion to the detective division.

The glamorous, exciting, action-packed fictionalized detective presents an exaggerated, unrealistic picture that differs greatly from the reality of detective work.

This chapter describes the real-life challenges of criminal investigation, an exceedingly complex field that can be only briefly introduced here. The chapter begins by discussing the primary goals, the investigation process, the preliminary investigation and the follow-up. This is followed by a brief look at *who* is responsible for investigating crimes. Next, the types of evidence to look for and the role of computer technology in criminal investigations are examined. Then the discussion turns to investigating specific crimes, including the violent and property crimes classified as Part I Index offenses and other serious crimes, as well as the special considerations involved in each type of investigation. This is followed by a quick look at the problem of false reports and the challenges of investigating so-called victimless crimes. Next surveillance, undercover assignments and raids are explored, including the issues of entrapment and the use of informants. The chapter concludes with a look at the relationship between criminal investigation and community policing, including problem solving.

## Goals of Criminal Investigation

Bennett and Hess (2004, p.5) observe: "The goal of criminal investigation would obviously seem to be to solve cases; to discover 'whodunit.' In reality, the goals of criminal investigation are not quite so simple."

 The primary goals of criminal investigation are to:
- Determine whether a crime has been committed.
- Legally obtain information and evidence to identify the responsible person.
- Arrest the suspect.
- Recover stolen property.
- Present the best possible case to the prosecutor.

An investigation can be considered successful if it follows a logical sequence and legally obtains all available physical evidence and available information from witnesses and suspects, if all leads are thoroughly developed and if all details of the case are accurately and completely recorded and reported. The overriding goal in a criminal investigation is to determine the truth regarding a specific crime.

Recall from Chapter 3 the critical importance of developing operational skills to perform police duties within the law. To operate outside of the law or violate someone's constitutional rights can cause irreparable damage to a case and can result in evidence not being admitted at trial under the Exclusionary Rule.

## The Investigative Process

Williams (2003, p.181) describes the typical process involved in a criminal investigation (Table 10.1). This chapter examines the initial investigation and the follow-up investigation.

## The Preliminary Investigation

Most criminal investigations have two phases: the preliminary investigation and the follow-up investigation. Chapter 6 stressed the importance of the preliminary investigation and outlined the duties and responsibilities typically encountered.

**Table 10.1** An Overview of the Investigative Process

| Stage | Police Personnel | Official Reports | Victim's Role |
|---|---|---|---|
| Reporting crime to the police | Operators, dispatchers | Tape of initial communication | Reporting the crime |
| Initial investigation: determining basic facts of the case and arresting suspects, if present | Patrol officers (sometimes an evidence technician and detectives) | Crime reports (sometimes physical-evidence reports or arrest report) | Providing information |
| Case screening: deciding whether to continue with the investigation | Investigations supervisor (sometimes a patrol supervisor) | Note on crime report, or screening form (some departments notify victims) | Sometimes notified about decisions |
| Follow-up investigation: pursuing leads developed earlier | Detective (sometimes a patrol officer for some crimes) | Supplemental report and perhaps an arrest report | Verifying information |
| Case preparation: presenting case to the prosecutor | Detective (sometimes a patrol officer) | Arrest report | No role (some departments may notify victim of an arrest) |
| Prosecution: attempting to get a conviction | Patrol officers and detectives to present evidence in court | Prosecutor's reports, court records | Providing testimony, if the case goes to trial; otherwise, little role |

SOURCE: Gerald L. Williams. "Criminal Investigation." In *Local Government Police Management*, 4th ed. Edited by William A. Geller and Darrel W. Stephens. Washington, DC: International City/County Management Association, 2003, p.181. Reprinted by permission.

 The most critical phase in the majority of criminal investigations is the preliminary investigation.

A brief review of the typical steps of a preliminary investigation is warranted:

- Attend to any existing emergencies, such as an injured person or a fleeing suspect.
- Secure the scene.
- Measure, photograph, videotape and sketch the scene.
- Search for evidence.
- Identify, collect, examine and process physical evidence.
- Question victims, witnesses and suspects.
- Record all statements and observations in notes to be later transformed into a report.

The order in which these tasks are performed will depend on the specific circumstances. The last task, recording all information into notes or onto tape, is vital. Many believe that the initial and follow-up report preparations are critical aspects of the investigative process.

Securing the crime scene includes excluding the media. According to Savelli (2004a, p.36): "Maintaining strict perimeters around the scene will insure that unauthorized persons, such as the media, will be kept out. First officers who are not the responsible investigators for the crime scene should never discuss the crime or the crime scene with the media. Some media persons are relentless in asking questions and have a knack for extracting information from inexperienced officers."

One responsibility not discussed in Chapter 6 is the neighborhood canvass. Fuller (2003, p.36) asserts: "This [the neighborhood canvass] is the nuts and bolts of most preliminary investigations, and should be done on every criminal offense that is reported to your officers—no exceptions; this should be a procedural must! Basically the neighborhood canvass is just what its name implies: going house-to-house and knocking on doors in the immediate vicinity of the offense, and along any known escape route to determine if anyone observed the offense and/or the suspect."

As mentioned in Chapter 6, exactly *who* is responsible for the preliminary and follow-up investigations varies by department, although most officers are expected to be trained and competent in performing basic investigative operations.

## Who Investigates?

The majority of local police departments lack special criminal investigative units, with line personnel bearing responsibility for crime scene duty. However, some departments, particularly those in larger jurisdictions, staff specialized teams to perform investigative functions. Whether the investigation is conducted by a generalist or a specialist, Colaprete (2004, p.86) suggests: "An investigator's critical skills consist of developing a strategy for case investigation, interviewing victims, testifying competently in a court setting and, most important, interrogating a suspect."

Davis and Clayton (2003, p.58) point out: "Processing crime scenes can be time-consuming and drain not only resources but manpower. If patrol currently handles basic CSI, it may be time to expand into a specialized unit equipped to specifically handle crime scenes."

### Crime Scene Investigators

The popular television series *CSI* has brought the role of the crime scene investigator and the importance of forensic evidence into the limelight. As Strandberg (2001a, p.21) points out: "The search for facts is what's behind forensic technology. And new technologies are making the investigator's quest for truth a bit easier. From DNA analysis to hair samples to 3D ballistics comparisons, things have never been better in the forensic world."

The basic function of a crime scene investigator (CSI) is to detect, collect, evaluate and preserve crime scene evidence, including taking photographs in most instances (Weissberg, 2001, p.45). Wade (2001, p.10) describes a publication of the FBI, the *Handbook of Forensic Services*, which gives detailed information on searching a crime scene as well as submitting evidence and what kinds of examinations can be done on the evidence. Geberth (2003a, p.46) asserts: "The search of the crime scene is the most important phase of the investigation conducted at the scene."

Regardless of who is charged with conducting a criminal investigation, the types of evidence to look for remain the same, and maintaining the integrity and subsequent admissibility of such evidence is as vital a role for the line officer as it is for the special crime scene investigator.

## Evidence

The successful resolution of a criminal investigation most often hinges on the availability of irrefutable, relevant and admissible evidence. Even when a suspect confesses, evidence is still required because the confession may later turn out to be untrue, it may later be denied, or there may be claims it was coerced or involuntary and is, therefore, inadmissible. As Bennett and Hess (p.151) stress: "A confession is only one part of an investigation. Corroborate it by independent evidence."

Houck (2004, p.126) explains that criminal investigators and forensic scientists work most often with proxy data. **Proxy data** are not seen as they are created but are only the remnants of an event left behind. Houck notes that this is based on the theory of transfer developed by Edmund Locard, a French forensic microscopist in the early twentieth century: When two things come into contact, information is exchanged. The results of such a transfer are proxy data. According to Houck (p.138): "Once criminal activity has stopped, any transfers that take place may be considered **contamination,** that is, an undesired transfer of information between items of evidence."

Hanson (2004b, p.139) points out: "Even the smallest piece of evidence can be of importance in solving a crime." Kanable (2004, p.52) suggests: "DO sweat the small stuff. Trace evidence can make a big difference." Trace evidence is often microscopic, such as fibers and hairs. "Without a Trace? Advances in Detecting Trace Evidence" (2003, p.8) reports: "Advances in technologies for detecting and distinguishing trace evidence are finding their way to police precincts and forensic labs. These improvements do not guarantee courtroom success of course, but they do hold great promise for speeding up evidence collection, limiting contamination and easing analysis." Among the advancements are a variety of alternative light sources (ALS) being used to enhance evidence.

### Kinds of Evidence

Evidence found at crime scenes may include fingerprints, blood, hair, bite marks, shoe and tire impressions, soil, tool fragments, glass, paint, safe insulation, fibers, documents and firearms.

*Fingerprints* are among the most common and useful types of evidence found at crime scenes because they are a positive form of identification. Finding latent prints has become especially important since the availability of *Automated Fingerprint Identification Systems* (*AFIS*). If latent prints are found, they can be entered into either the FBI's system, which contains millions of prints, or a city's or state's system.

 The **Automated Fingerprint Identification System (AFIS)** drastically reduces the time needed to identify latent fingerprints by selecting a limited number of likely matches for the latent prints.

Kanable (2003, p.50) notes: "More and more the power of automated fingerprint technology is being realized, and it's being used to solve more cases." According to Burger (2002, p.34): "Fingerprint technology has developed more in its past 15 years than it did in the first 100 years." He (p.36) suggests: "The product with the greatest potential to impact officers in the short-term is IBS, a revolutionary mobile identification system that captures forensic quality fingerprints and photographs."

In addition, palm print technology is making advances. This is important because between 25 to 30 percent of the latent impressions at a crime scene are palm prints or partial palm prints (Kanable, 2001, p.42). Savvy burglars often use their palms to push open windows, believing the AFIS cannot compare the palm prints. However, recent advancements in biometrics have made it possible for automated palm print systems to complement the standard AFIS, providing a more complete identification solution.

AFIS technology is continuously being enhanced through the introduction of new services and features. For example, the Integrated Automated Fingerprint Identification System (IAFIS) provides to local, state and federal criminal justice agencies combined, nationwide access to electronic ten-print identification services, latent fingerprint databases, subject search and criminal history databases, document and image services and remote search service (Figure 10.1). Figure 10.2 illustrates the submission of an electronic ten-print.

*Blood* may be valuable as evidence in assaults, homicides, burglaries, hit-and-run cases and rape. It is classified as A, B, AB or O. Although blood cannot be used to identify a particular individual's race or sex, it can help *eliminate* suspects.

*Hair* from victims and suspects can be found on clothing, weapons, blankets, sheets, seat covers and the undercarriage of vehicles. Microscopic examination can identify hair as human or animal, but it cannot be identified as coming from a specific person. Microscopic examination of hair can usually identify the person's race, but not the person's sex or age, except in the case of infants. Microscopic examination can also tell if the hair was pulled out forcibly and which part of the body it is from.

Blood, hair and other body tissues and fluids can also be used in **DNA fingerprinting.** This technique analyzes the genetic sequence of DNA—the "blueprint of life." Whereas other tests of human tissues and secretions can only eliminate suspects, DNA can positively identify an individual, except for identical

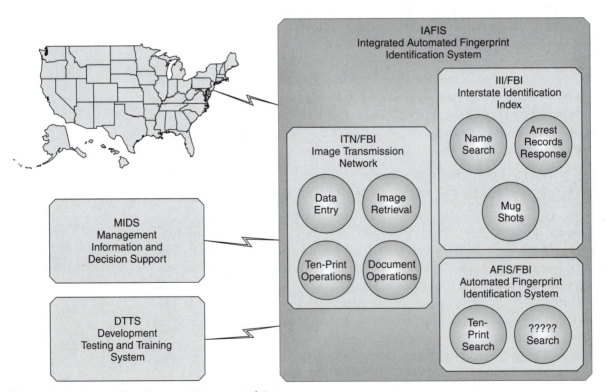

**Figure 10.1** Twenty-First Century ID Automated Systems

SOURCE: J. Van Duyn. "The FBI's 21st Century Integrated Computer System—'IAFIS.'" *Law Enforcement Technology,* April 1993, p.40. Reprinted by permission.

twins. Figure 10.3 illustrates how DNA analysis is conducted. Figure 10.4 shows how the A, G, C and T nucleotides are paired in a complementary, double-strand structure, held together in a zipper- or ladderlike fashion by hydrogen bonds.

Researchers have used DNA fingerprinting to make identifications from a four-year-old bloodstain and from semen stains that were several weeks old. While DNA fingerprinting has been heralded as a major breakthrough for criminal investigation, it is still not accepted by some courts. In *California v. Simpson* [O.J.] (1995), DNA played a pivotal role. The defense focused on procedures rather than the scientific validity of DNA analysis to discredit and have thrown out the DNA evidence.

According to Jones (2004, p.94): "All states have legislatively mandated the establishment of DNA data bases for law enforcement purposes." Investigators need to know where DNA evidence is likely to be located. Table 10.2 describes the possible location and source of DNA evidence.

Even with no suspect, DNA can be helpful as it can be entered into the FBI's Combined DNA Index System (CODIS), allowing agencies to match DNA profiles with other profiles entered into local, state and national databases ("DNA Evidence: What Law Enforcement Officers Should Know," 2003). This national database and searching mechanism has approximately 300,000 profiles from convicted felons and expects to have more than 1 million by 2005. More than 100 crime laboratories have installed the CODIS system.

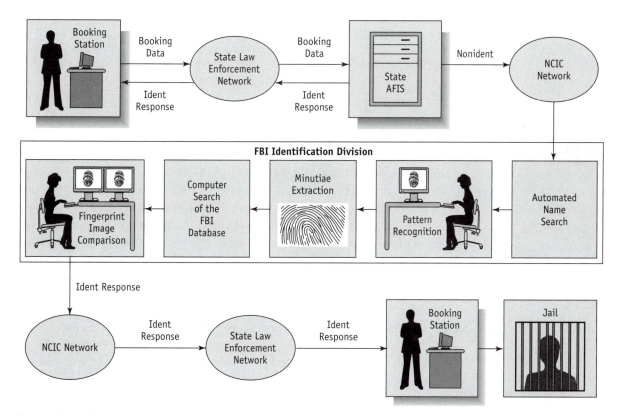

**Figure 10.2**  Electronic Ten-Print Submission

SOURCE: J. Van Duyn. "The FBI's 21st Century Integrated Computer System—'IAFIS.'" *Law Enforcement Technology,* April 1993, p.41. Reprinted by permission.

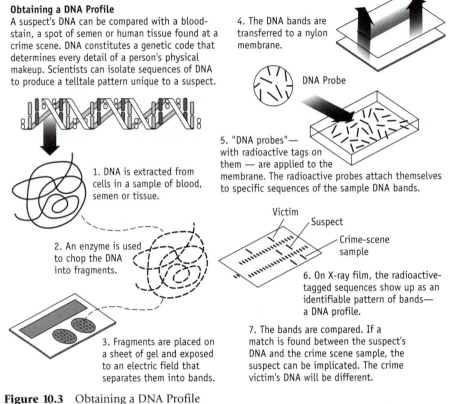

**Obtaining a DNA Profile**

A suspect's DNA can be compared with a blood-stain, a spot of semen or human tissue found at a crime scene. DNA constitutes a genetic code that determines every detail of a person's physical makeup. Scientists can isolate sequences of DNA to produce a telltale pattern unique to a suspect.

1. DNA is extracted from cells in a sample of blood, semen or tissue.

2. An enzyme is used to chop the DNA into fragments.

3. Fragments are placed on a sheet of gel and exposed to an electric field that separates them into bands.

4. The DNA bands are transferred to a nylon membrane.

DNA Probe

5. "DNA probes"— with radioactive tags on them — are applied to the membrane. The radioactive probes attach themselves to specific sequences of the sample DNA bands.

Victim

Suspect

Crime-scene sample

6. On X-ray film, the radioactive-tagged sequences show up as an identifiable pattern of bands— a DNA profile.

7. The bands are compared. If a match is found between the suspect's DNA and the crime scene sample, the suspect can be implicated. The crime victim's DNA will be different.

**Figure 10.3**  Obtaining a DNA Profile

SOURCE: Minnesota Bureau of Criminal Apprehension. (Minneapolis/St. Paul) *Star Tribune*, graphic by Ray Grumney, October 19, 1994, p.E1. Reprinted by permission.

As Turman (2001, p.8) notes: "The importance of the role forensic DNA evidence plays in solving sexual assault and homicide cases cannot be overstated. DNA evidence is a crucial tool used in effective police work to solve violent crimes." Hanson (2004a, p.16) predicts: "In the near future, characteristics such as hair color, skin tone and others will be added to the DNA profile" giving investigators a "fuzzy photograph" of a criminal.

Using DNA evidence does have its critics, however. Legal challenges have been *unsuccessfully* raised in several states that DNA collection constitutes an invasion of an individual's right to privacy. Nonetheless, it will remain a powerful investigative tool.

 Physical fingerprints and DNA fingerprinting are the two forms of positive identification available to investigators.

Turner (2004, p.5) observes: "DNA is such a popular tool that most states continue to take samples from suspects even as the states' labs fall farther behind in their analysis. The U.S. Department of Justice reports that more than 350,000 DNA samples remain unanalyzed nationally and that 90 percent of DNA evidence may be under law enforcement custody, not subject to the stringent protection common in crime labs. Moreover, as technology improves, police are turning to older, smaller degraded DNA samples to help solve cold cases."

*Bite marks* are sometimes significant in child and adult abuse cases. Bite marks have individual characteristics that match the size and configuration of the teeth.

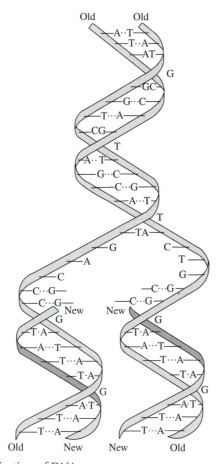

**Figure 10.4** The Replication of DNA

SOURCE: *Forensic DNA Analysis and Issues.* Washington, DC: U.S. Department of Justice, 1991, p.3.

Bite marks helped convict Ted Bundy in Florida. The key is successfully preserving the tissue. Marks on the body may last for several weeks. Bite marks sometimes also are found in partially eaten food.

*Shoe* or *tire impressions* often are found where suspects have entered or left a crime scene hastily. Shoe and tire prints are of two types: contamination prints and impressions. Contamination prints are left when a shoe or tire has on it a substance such as dirt or blood, which then leaves a print on a hard surface. Impressions are imprints left in soft surfaces such as mud or sand. Shoe or tire impressions can place a suspect at a crime scene.

*Soil* is also analyzed in some cases. Finley (2004, p.3) reports: "Evidence value rests upon the fact that soil varies from point to point on the surface as well as between the earth's surface."

*Tool fragments* also may be found at a crime scene and later matched to a broken tool in the possession of a suspect. *Tool marks* are found most often in burglaries and in malicious-destruction-of-property crimes. They may be found on windowsills and frames, doors and frames, cash register drawers, file cabinets and cash boxes. Tool marks often are left when windows have been forced open with screwdrivers or pry bars; when locks have been snipped with bolt cutters or when safes have been opened with hammers, chisels or punches. These tools leave marks that often can be identified as definitely as fingerprints.

**Table 10.2** Location and Sources of DNA Evidence

| Evidence | Possible Location of DNA on the Evidence | Source of DNA |
| --- | --- | --- |
| Baseball bat | Handle | Skin cells, sweat, blood, tissue |
| Hat, bandanna or mask | Inside surfaces | Sweat, hair, skin cells, dandruff, saliva |
| Eyeglasses | Nose or ear piece, lens | Sweat, skin cells |
| Facial tissue, cotton swab | Surface | Mucus, blood, sweat, semen, ear wax |
| Dirty laundry | Surface | Blood, sweat, semen, saliva |
| Toothpick | Surface | Saliva |
| Used cigarette | Cigarette butt (filter area) | Saliva |
| Used stamp/envelope seal | Moistened area | Saliva |
| Tape or ligature | Inside or outside surface | Skin cells, sweat, saliva |
| Bottle, can or glass | Mouthpiece, rim, outer surface | Saliva, sweat, skin cells |
| Used condom | Inside/outside surface | Semen, vaginal or rectal cells |
| Bed linens | Surface | Sweat, hair, semen, saliva, blood |
| "Through and through" bullet | Outside surface | Blood, tissue |
| Bite mark | Surface of skin | Saliva |
| Fingernail/partial fingernail | Scrapings | Blood, sweat, tissue, skin cells |

Note: When reviewing evidence, it is important to maintain chain of custody, consult with laboratory personnel, and take all appropriate precautions against contamination, including wearing gloves and changing them between handling of different pieces of evidence.

SOURCE: *Using DNA to Solve Cold Cases.* Washington, DC: NIJ Special Report, July 2002, p.21.

*Glass* from windows, automobiles, bottles and other objects often is used as evidence in assaults, burglaries, murders and many other crimes. When a person breaks a window, tiny pieces of glass are usually found in the clothing, pant cuffs or pockets, or on the clothing's surface. Glass is excellent evidence because two different pieces of glass rarely contain the same proportions of sand, metal oxides or carbonates. In addition, police usually can determine whether the glass was broken from inside or outside a building by observing the fracture marks and the location of the fragments.

*Paint* frequently is transferred from one object to another during the commission of a crime. During burglaries, it may be chipped off surfaces. During hasty getaways, it may flake off automobiles. Paint has provided a strong link in the chain of circumstantial evidence because it can associate an individual with the crime scene. It also can eliminate innocent suspects.

*Safe insulation* can be identified microscopically by composition, color, mineral content and physical characteristics. Particles of safe insulation or fireproof insulation on a suspect's clothing or shoes is a strong indication of guilt.

*Fibers* from clothing are often found where burglars have crawled through a window or opening. Clothing fibers are also often found adhering to the fenders, grill, door handles or undercarriage of hit-and-run vehicles. Fingernail scrapings and weapons also may contain fiber evidence. Examination of the fibers can identify the type of fabric: wool, cotton, rayon, nylon and so on. Sometimes the type of garment from which the fibers came can be identified.

**How bullets and casings receive a signature**
When a weapon is fired, it leaves unique markings—much like fingerprints—on bullets and casings.

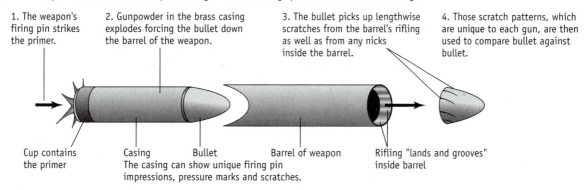

1. The weapon's firing pin strikes the primer.

2. Gunpowder in the brass casing explodes forcing the bullet down the barrel of the weapon.

3. The bullet picks up lengthwise scratches from the barrel's rifling as well as from any nicks inside the barrel.

4. Those scratch patterns, which are unique to each gun, are then used to compare bullet against bullet.

Cup contains the primer

Casing
The casing can show unique firing pin impressions, pressure marks and scratches.

Bullet

Barrel of weapon

Rifling "lands and grooves" inside barrel

**Linking weapons to shootings**
Here are two ways the FBI's DrugFire system and the ATF's Integrated Ballistics Identification System (IBIS) databases can use the markings to link weapons to shootings.

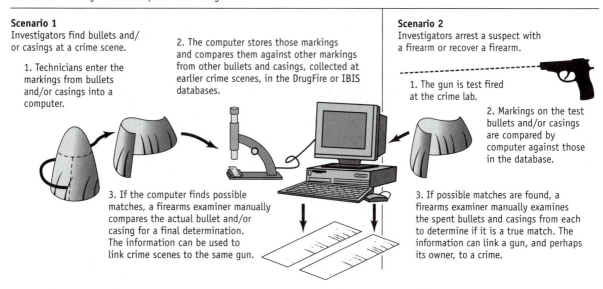

**Scenario 1**
Investigators find bullets and/or casings at a crime scene.

1. Technicians enter the markings from bullets and/or casings into a computer.

2. The computer stores those markings and compares them against other markings from other bullets and casings, collected at earlier crime scenes, in the DrugFire or IBIS databases.

3. If the computer finds possible matches, a firearms examiner manually compares the actual bullet and/or casing for a final determination. The information can be used to link crime scenes to the same gun.

**Scenario 2**
Investigators arrest a suspect with a firearm or recover a firearm.

1. The gun is test fired at the crime lab.

2. Markings on the test bullets and/or casings are compared by computer against those in the database.

3. If possible matches are found, a firearms examiner manually examines the spent bullets and casings from each to determine if it is a true match. The information can link a gun, and perhaps its owner, to a crime.

**Figure 10.5**   How Bullets and Casings Receive a Signature and Linking Weapons to Shootings
SOURCE: Chris Graves. "Linking Guns, Crime Is No Longer a Shot in the Dark." (Minneapolis/St. Paul) *Star Tribune*, February 19, 1996, p.A8. Data from Minneapolis Police, Minnesota Bureau of Criminal Apprehension. Reprinted by permission.

*Documents* may contain fingerprint evidence and may also be examined for handwriting characteristics or for typewriter or printer characteristics. If a document has been handwritten, experts can do a side-by-side comparison of the document and samples of the suspect's handwriting to determine if both were done by the same person. Testimony of handwriting experts has been accepted in our courts for several years. Documents produced on a typewriter or printer can be examined to determine the manufacturer, make, model and age of the machine.

*Firearms* left at a crime scene may be traced to their owner through the serial number, the manufacturer's identification or the dealer who sold the gun. Firearms also may contain fingerprints or other marks that could lead to identification. The weapon's make usually is determined by the barrel rifling, spiral grooves cut into the gun barrel in its manufacture. The rifling varies considerably from manufacturer to manufacturer. Figure 10.5 illustrates how bullets and casings receive a signature and how investigators can link weapons to shootings.

Since the 1990s, the ATF and the FBI had competing systems with the FBI being interested in cartridge cases through its DrugFire program and the ATF interested in bullets through its Integrated Ballistics Information System (IBIS). In 1999, however, the directors of the ATF and the FBI signed a memorandum of understanding to create a unified ballistics evidence system, using the basic technology of the IBIS machine and combining it with functions specific to the DrugFire system, creating the National Integrated Ballistics Information Network (NIBIN). According to Budden (2001, p.101): "The system makes it possible to search an entire database of firearms evidence in minutes, and the searches provide detectives with significant investigative leads, some of which would be available by no other means."

As Shaker and Shaker (2001, p.103) contend: "The advent of automated ballistic identification system has enabled forensic examiners to move the state of the technology beyond its focus as a tool through which to obtain convictions, to one through which to solve crimes." They (p.107) conclude:

> Bullets from crime scenes around the country can be compared to thousands of murder weapons, thus allowing the matching of previously unrelated bullets and weapons. Indeed, it is through such technology that the goal articulated in the President's State of the Union address on January 27, 2000, can be achieved in which he stated that: "we must give law enforcement the tools to trace every gun—and every bullet—used in a crime in America."

An often overlooked tool in discovering ballistic evidence is the metal detector. Investigators using standard search pattern with a metal detector can ensure that the crime scene is completely covered.

As seen, computers have assumed a vital role in the detection and analysis of evidence. Computer technology is being used in other ways to aid criminal investigations.

## Using Computers in Criminal Investigation

Before computers investigators relied upon pin maps, wall charts and other such devices to analyze facts related to a crime. This has changed considerably with the advent of the computer. Chapter 6 discussed several computerized crime mapping tools, including Geographic Information Systems (GIS), ReCAP and CompStat.

Use of computers in identifying fingerprints has been discussed. Computers also assist in other important ways. A department's own case information can be made immediately available to officers in the field through Mobile Display Terminals (MDTs). These same terminals also can access national databases such as those of the National Crime Information Center (NCIC) in a matter of seconds.

Computers are being used to track stolen vehicles as well. Dealing effectively with auto theft is a major concern of most law enforcement agencies because the crime is so prevalent.

Automatic vehicle locators (AVLs) use satellites and small transmitters. Cars are equipped with high-tech tracking devices that can be traced by police cars with special computers. In some systems, if a person drives off without deactivating the system, an alarm is sent. In other systems, the owner must notify police that the car has been stolen before they begin tracking it. Some systems include an alert service that allows motorists to signal police in case of an emergency. One system even allows police to shut off a stolen car's engine by remote control, a feature that would eliminate high-speed pursuit.

Computers have also become an integral part of report writing and are increasingly used in creating crime scene sketches through computer-aided drafting (CAD) programs. Figure 10.6 illustrates a computer-generated crime scene.

Furthermore, computers are being used to determine where to focus investigative resources. Artificial intelligence (AI) programs being used in several police departments help structure investigations by using software to help determine which cases are most likely to be cleared by arrest.

## Geographic Profiling

Chapter 6 introduced crime mapping as a way to identify hot spots of crime. Rich (2001, p.1) notes: "Crime mapping has become increasingly popular among law enforcement agencies and has enjoyed high visibility at the federal level, in the media and among the largest police departments in the nation." Geographic pro-

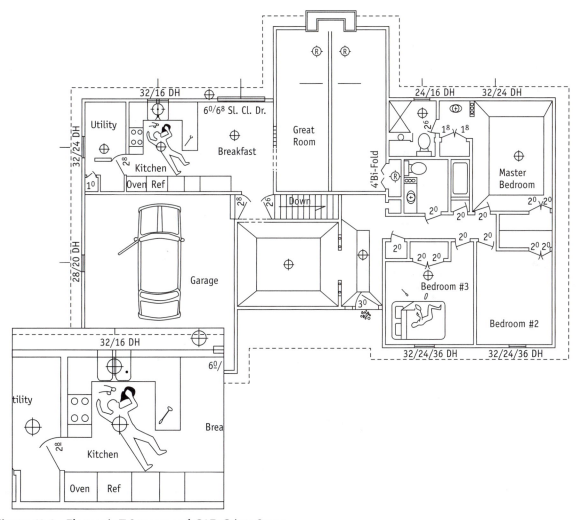

**Figure 10.6**   Electronic T-Squares and CAD Crime Scene

SOURCE: Paul R. Laska. "The Investigator and Electronic T-Squares." *Law Enforcement Technology,* June 1995, p.50. Reprinted by permission.

filing takes crime mapping techniques and turns them inside out. Geographic profiling can help prioritize suspect lists, direct patrol saturation and stakeouts and conduct neighborhood canvasses.

Regardless of the highly sophisticated technologies available to criminal investigators, to respond effectively and appropriately to a crime, officers must first know what defines the crime.

## Investigating Specific Crimes

Some actions and activities may seem "wrong" and unjust but are not technically criminal. Someone took something? Was it robbery, burglary, larceny/theft or simply a misunderstood "borrowing"? Following is a brief examination of some specific crimes and how they are generally investigated. This section begins with the eight Part I Crime Index offenses and their general definitions, including the specific elements of each offense that must be proven during a criminal investigation. Then investigating other serious crimes is discussed, including crimes against children, bias/hate crimes, computer-related crimes and environmental crimes.

### Violent Crimes

Investigating violent crimes is difficult because of the emotionalism usually encountered, not only from the victim and the victim's family, but also from the public. Generally, however, investigating crimes against persons results in more and better information and evidence than investigating property crimes because, in violent crimes, the victim is often an eyewitness, an important source of information and a key to identifying the suspect. The victim and other witnesses can often provide important information on how and by what means the attack was made; what the attacker's intent or motive was; descriptive information about the attacker, weapon and any getaway vehicle; and what words may have been spoken. Weapons may provide physical evidence, as may any injuries suffered by the victim. Typically, violent crimes yield much physical evidence, with the type of evidence to anticipate directly related to the type of crime committed. Officers could expect to find such evidence as a weapon, blood, hair, fibers, fingerprints, footprints and the like, depending on the specific crime. Therefore, the arrest rate for violent crimes is high.

Violent crime investigations have been enhanced by the establishment of the Violent Crime Apprehension Program (VICAP) at the FBI National Police Academy in Quantico, Virginia. The goal of this program is to coordinate major violent crime cases, regardless of their location, in the United States. Information considered viable is published in the FBI's *Law Enforcement Bulletin*. If the case merits interagency cooperation, a Major Case Investigation Team of investigators from all involved agencies may be formed.

 The major violent crimes are homicide, rape, robbery and assault.

**Homicide**    **Homicide** is the killing of one person by another. Litwin (2004, p.327) states: "Homicide consistently receives extensive criminological and public attention. It also commands intensive police attention. This diligence in homicide investigation may be reflected in the fact that the clearance rates for homicide in the United States are consistently higher than those for any other index crime."

Homicide investigations are challenging and frequently require all investigative techniques and skills. A primary requirement is to establish that death was caused by a criminal action. The four basic types of death are death by natural causes, accidental death, suicide and homicide. Although technically officers are concerned only with homicide, frequently they do not know at the start of an investigation what type of death has occurred. Therefore, any of the four types of death may require investigation.

 Homicide is classified as criminal (felonious) or noncriminal. The various degrees of murder and manslaughter are criminal homicide, noncriminal homicide (which includes excusable homicide, the unintentional, truly accidental killing of another person) and justifiable homicide (killing another person under authorization of law).

The elements present in a criminal homicide determine whether the act is charged as murder in the first, second or third degree, or as voluntary or involuntary manslaughter. A common element in every charge is "causing the death of another human being." Other elements in homicide include premeditation, malicious intent, adequately provoked intent resulting in heat of passion, while committing or attempting to commit a crime that is not a felony, when forced or threatened, culpable negligence or depravity or simple negligence. **Premeditation,** the deliberate, precalculated plan to cause death, is the essential element of first-degree murder, distinguishing it from all other murder classifications.

Geberth (2003b, p.38) points out: "The homicide crime scene is, without a doubt, the most important crime scene an officer or an investigator will be called upon to respond to." The first priority in a preliminary homicide investigation is to determine that death has occurred—provided the suspect is not at the scene. Signs of death include lack of breathing, lack of heartbeat, lack of flushing of the fingernail bed when pressure is applied and then released and failure of the

*Actors William Petersen (left), Marg Helgenberger and Paul Guifoyle investigate a bombing in the CBS television series "CSI: Crime Scene Investigation," photographed on January 29, 2001, in Los Angeles, California.*

CBS/Landov

eyelids to close after being gently lifted. In some instances, police can enter a premise without a warrant if they believe a person is in need of medical assistance or if they believe the premises may contain a victim or a killer, as established in *Flippo v. West Virginia* (1999). The Supreme Court "acknowledged that police may make warrantless entries onto premises if they reasonably believe that a person is in need of immediate aid or may make a prompt warrantless search of a homicide scene for other victims or a killer on the premises."

 After priority matters are completed, the focus of the homicide investigation is to identify the victim, establish the time of death, establish the cause of death and the method used to produce it and to develop a suspect.

Homicide victims are identified by their relatives, friends or acquaintances; by personal effects, fingerprints, DNA analysis, skeletal studies including teeth, clothing and laundry marks; or through missing-persons files.

Determining the time of death is one important part of any homicide investigation. General factors used to estimate time of death are body temperature, rigor mortis, postmortem lividity, appearance of the eyes, stomach contents, stage of decomposition and evidence suggesting a change in the victim's normal routine.

Currently, if a body is found within a day, investigators can determine the time of death quite accurately based on lividity, appearance of the eyes, rigor mortis and the like. After a day has passed, it becomes much more difficult to determine time of death. A project at the Oak Ridge National Laboratory is developing a tricorder-like device to wave over a body to determine how long a person has been dead. The project is based on the fact that as a body decomposes, proteins break down into amino acids and progressively smaller molecules. By studying whether there is a constant rate at which the large molecules of the body break down, researchers can develop a computer program to correlate the percentage of larger molecules to small ones within a number of days (Page, 2001, p.98).

Another aid in homicide investigations comes from forensic entomology, as Mulzac (2001, p.90) explains: "With the onset of death, insects are usually the first on the scene. . . . Insects, particularly flies, are attracted to the nose, eyes, ears and mouth of the victim. The flies lay eggs, which emerge or 'hatch' into maggots." He (p.88) notes: "Evaluation and interpretation of entomological evidence at a crime scene can address time of death, season of death, geographic location of death, movement or storage of the remains following death, specific sites of trauma on the body, sexual molestation and even the use of drugs." In addition, says Mulzac: "In certain forensic cases, the extraction of human DNA and/or mitochondrial DNA from the contents of an insect's stomach has the ability to link a perpetrator to the victim." He (p.92) further notes: "Blood-sucking insects such as mosquitoes, crab lice and bed bugs are a particular boon to the crime scene investigator because all can yield the perpetrator's DNA."

Among the most common causes of unnatural death are gunshot wounds; stabbing and cutting wounds; blows from blunt instruments; asphyxia induced by choking, drowning, hanging, smothering, strangulation, gases or poisons; poisoning and drug overdoses; burning; explosions; electric shock; and lightning.

A medical examination or autopsy provides legal evidence as to the cause and time of death and corroborates information obtained during the investigation. It may also reveal evidence that may otherwise have gone undetected and which may link the victim to a suspect. Suspects are developed by determining a motive for the killing and by circumstantial evidence.

Physical evidence in a homicide includes a weapon, a body, blood, hairs and fibers. The type of evidence available will depend on the nature of the homicide and the type of scene involved. For example, a hit-and-run crime scene may have numerous kinds of physical evidence, including hairs, fibers, blood and other biological fluids.

The initial police response to a homicide call and their subsequent degree of involvement and thoroughness in the follow-up investigation directly affect the outcome of the case and whether it is cleared. Some homicide investigations are relatively straightforward and free of complication. Others, however, pose one or more challenges.

 Special problems in homicide investigations include pressure by the public and the media; difficulty in establishing that it is homicide, rather than suicide or an accidental or natural death; handling serial murders; and, in some cases, locating the body.

An **equivocal death investigation** may have two or more meanings and may be presented as either a homicide or a suicide, depending on the circumstances. The facts may be purposefully vague or misleading or appear suspicious or questionable. Any weapon tightly clutched in the victim's hand as the result of cadaveric spasm indicates suicide rather than murder, but this cannot always be assumed. The victim's background also provides information as to whether the death was accidental, suicide or homicide. This background and evidence on the victim's body often provide leads to a suspect.

Occasionally, investigators find themselves handling multiple homicide cases with key similarities. Such cases may be linked merely by coincidence or may be the signature of a serial killer. The FBI classifies serial killers into two categories: organized and disorganized (Baker, 2001a, p.45): "The disorganized killer generally has a mental disorder and commits a delusional-related homicide. This offender's crime scenes are spontaneous, chaotic and unplanned. . . . A disorganized killer leaves significant evidence at the crime scene. . . . This offender lives near the scene of the crime and stands out in the community because of his eccentric or bizarre behaviors. He has limited intelligence, operates within a limited geographical area, and is therefore vulnerable to planned surveillance. In contrast, the organized killer's crime scene will be 'pristine' and will yield few clues. This type of killer plans intelligently and uses stealth and cunning. He is usually educated, has a job and is a respected member of the community."

As the result of advances in DNA analysis, many cold cases are being reinvestigated. Nyberg (2004, p.44) notes: "The nation's first official cold case squad teaches the bad guys that there's no statute of limitations on murder." According to Wexler (2004a, p.18): "Over the past decade, several metropolitan police agencies have created squads dedicated to investigating cold cases. . . . Several years ago, it would be almost impossible to solve these old homicide cases. Now, thanks to new technology and resources, an increasing number of cold murder cases are being cracked."

**Sexual Assault**   Sexual assault (rape) is sexual intercourse with a person against the person's will. It is classified as forcible (by use or threats of force) or statutory (with a minor, with or without consent).

Most states have in common the following elements for the crime of rape or sexual assault: (1) an act of sexual intercourse, (2) committed without the victim's consent, (3) against the victim's will and by force.

A survey funded by the U.S. Justice Department and the Centers for Disease Control and Prevention found that one out of every six U.S. women has been the victim of an attempted or completed rape, and most occurred before the woman reached age 18 ("1 in 6 Women . . .," 2001, p.6). A study conducted by Schwartz et al. (2001, p.624) found that college men who drank two or more times a week and had male peers who supported both emotional and physical violence were nearly 10 times as likely to admit to being sexual aggressors as men who had none of these three traits.

Special problems in investigating rape include the sensitive nature of the offense, social attitudes and the victim's embarrassment and feelings of shame. A rape investigation requires great tact. Modus operandi factors important in investigating sex offenses include type of offense, words spoken, use of a weapon, method of attack, time of day, type of location and the victim's age. Physical evidence commonly found in rape cases includes stained or torn clothing; scratches, bruises and cuts; evidence of a struggle; and semen and bloodstains. A particular challenge to law enforcement is drug-facilitated sexual assault, with the most common date rape drugs being rohypnol and gamma hydroxybutyrate or GHB. A timely response is necessary as such drugs may, over the course of only a few hours, be metabolized and rendered undetectable in the victim's bloodstream, or eliminated in the victim's urine.

Another challenge to law enforcement is the serial rapist. Baker (2001b, p.229) notes the FBI's four primary typologies of rapists—power-reassurance, exploitative, anger and violent sadistic—and how personality profiling and crime analysis may provide leads on suspects to interrupt their cycle of violence.

Strandberg (2001b, p.20) suggests using a team approach in rape investigations, partnering with a rape crisis advocate and a nurse examiner. The sexual assault response team (SART) provides victims with information on their medical, legal and psychological options. Wilson (2002, pp.14–15) describes two types of team models: (1) hospital-based programs and (2) community-based programs.

Other tools in dealing with sexual assault are sex offender registration and community notification programs. After Jacob Wetterling was abducted in October 1989 and never found, Congress, in 1994, passed the Jacob Wetterling Crimes against Children and Sexually Violent Offender Registration Act. The act required states to create sex offender registries within three years or lose 10 percent of their funding. The act also gave states the option of releasing information about registered sex offenders to the public, but did not require it.

Although registries gave police valuable information to identify, monitor and track sex offenders, they did little to protect the public. Then, in 1994, seven-year-old Megan Kanka was raped and murdered by a paroled sex offender living across the street. In 1996 Congress amended the Wetterling Act to require states to disclose information about registered sex offenders.

Given that each year about 24,000 sex offenders are released to the community after serving an average six-year prison sentence, a registration and notification system seems logical and, in fact, necessary. It would also seem to strike a balance between the public's right to be informed and the offender's right to privacy.

However, not everyone agrees. In fact, a federal court in the District of Columbia struck down that district's "Megan's Law," saying it deprived sex offenders of their Fifth Amendment due process rights without giving them a hearing. District Judge Huvelle wrote: "While it may well be that many of the sex offenders registered under the [D.C. Megan's Law] statute do pose a risk of recidivism and can lawfully be subjected to public notification, they are still entitled to the procedural rights guaranteed by the Constitution" ("Court Invalidates Megan's Law . . .," 2001, p.6).

**Robbery**    **Robbery** is the felonious taking of another's property from his or her person or in his or her presence through force or intimidation. Robberies are classified as either residential, commercial, street or vehicle-driver robberies or carjacking, the taking of a motor vehicle by force or threat of force. A relatively new type of residential robber is the home invader. Home invaders are young Asian gang members who travel across the country robbing Asian families, especially business owners.

The elements of the crime of robbery are (1) the wrongful taking of personal property, (2) from the person or in the person's presence, (3) against the person's will by force or threat of force.

The rapidity of a robbery, its potential for violence and the taking of hostages, and the usual lack of evidence at the scene pose special problems in robbery investigations. Officers responding to a robbery-in-progress call should proceed rapidly but cautiously. They should assume the robber is at the scene unless otherwise advised, and be prepared for gunfire; look for and immobilize any getaway vehicle discovered; avoid a hostage situation if possible; and make an immediate arrest if the situation warrants.

*Officer dusting for fingerprints in a carjacking case.*

Each element of robbery must be proven separately. To prove that personal property was wrongfully taken, the legal owner of the property must be identified and the property and its value described completely. To prove that property was taken from the person or in the person's presence, the exact words, gestures, motions or actions the robber used to gain control of the property must be recorded. To prove the property was removed against the victim's will by force or threat of force, a complete description of the robber's words, actions and any weapon used or threatened to be used must be obtained.

Information about the suspect's general appearance, clothing and disguises, weapon(s) and vehicle(s) used should be obtained. Important modus operandi information includes type of robbery, time (day and hour), method of attack (threatened or real), weapon, object sought, number of robbers, voice and words, vehicle used and any peculiarities. Physical evidence that can connect the suspect with the robbery includes fingerprints, shoe prints, tire prints, restraining devices used, discarded garments, fibers and hairs, a note and the stolen property.

Commercial bank robberies are jointly investigated by the FBI, state and local law enforcement personnel. A bank in Chicago has three cameras installed that are connected directly to the city's police dispatch center. Byers (2004) explains: "The cameras allow dispatchers to see what's going on inside the bank as it happens while giving instructions to officers."

**Assault**    **Assault** is unlawfully threatening to harm another person, actually harming another person or attempting unsuccessfully to do so. Simple assault is intentionally causing another to fear immediate bodily harm or death or intentionally inflicting or attempting to inflict bodily harm on another. It is usually a misdemeanor. Aggravated assault is an unlawful attack by one person on another to inflict *severe* bodily injury. It often involves use of a dangerous weapon and is a felony. In specified instances, teachers, people operating public conveyances and law enforcement officers use physical force legally.

The elements of the crime of simple assault are (1) intent to do bodily harm to another, (2) present ability to commit the act and (3) commission of an overt act toward carrying out the intent. An additional element in the crime of aggravated assault is that the intentionally inflicted bodily injury results in (1) a high probability of death, (2) serious, permanent disfigurement or (3) permanent or protracted loss or impairment of the function of any body member or organ or other severe bodily harm. Attempted assault requires proof of intent and an overt act toward committing the crime.

Special problems in investigating assaults include distinguishing the victim from the suspect, determining if the matter is civil or criminal and determining if the act was intentional or accidental. Obtaining a complaint against simple assault also is sometimes difficult.

To prove the elements of the offense of assault, the intent to cause injury, the severity of the injury inflicted and whether a dangerous weapon was used must be established. Physical evidence in an assault includes photographs of injuries, clothing of the victim or suspect, weapons, broken objects, bloodstains, hairs, fibers and other signs of an altercation.

Domestic abuse, stalking and elder abuse all are candidates for categorization as separate crimes, rather than being lumped in the general category of assault for reporting—and thus research—purposes.

## *Property Crimes*

Many property crimes are difficult to investigate because they typically have little evidence and no eyewitnesses. Physical evidence in property crimes is often similar to that found in violent crimes: fingerprints, footprints, tire impressions, hair, fibers, broken glass and personal objects left at the crime scene. Other important evidence in property crimes includes tools, tool fragments, tool marks, safe insulation, disturbance of paint and evidence of forcible entry. The modus operandi of a property crime often takes on added importance because other significant leads are absent. Further, property crimes tend to occur in series, so solving one crime may lead to solving an entire series of similar crimes.

 The major property crimes are burglary, larceny/theft, motor vehicle theft and arson.

**Burglary**   **Burglary** is the unlawful entry of a structure to commit a crime. It differs from robbery in that burglars are covert, trying to remain unseen, whereas robbers confront their victims directly. Burglary is a crime against property; robbery is a violent crime against a person.

 Burglaries are classified as residential or commercial. The elements of the crime of burglary include (1) entering a structure (2) without the consent of the person in possession (3) with the intent to commit a crime therein. Additional elements of burglary that may be required include (1) breaking into (2) the dwelling of another (3) during the nighttime. A burglary's severity is determined by the presence of dangerous devices in the burglar's possession or by the value of the property stolen. Attempted burglary and possession of burglary tools are also felonies. The elements of the crime of possessing burglary tools include (1) possessing any device, explosive or other instrumentality (2) with intent to use or permit their use to commit burglary.

Officers responding to a burglary call should proceed to the scene quietly, being observant and cautious. They should search the premises inside and outside for the burglar.

Special considerations in investigating burglary include the problem of false alarms, determining the means of entry into a structure, as well as into such objects as safes or vaults and recovering the stolen property. Jimmying is the most common method to enter a structure to commit burglary. Attacks on safes and vaults include punching, peeling, pulling or dragging, blowing, burning, chopping and, for safes, hauling them away.

Physical evidence at a burglary scene often includes fingerprints, footprints, tire prints, tools, tool marks, broken glass, safe insulation, paint chips and personal possessions. Important modus operandi factors include the time, the types of premises, the type of victim, point and means of entry, type of property taken and any peculiarities of the offense.

Mapping can be especially effective in dealing with burglaries, given the fact that burglars often live or work within a two-mile residential radius. Mapping plus modus operandi information can often effectively zero in on suspects. Burgled houses are likely to be burgled again. Therefore, the most important use of data is to facilitate preventive measures such as target hardening after an initial victimization.

Fences, pawnshops, secondhand stores, flea markets and informants should be checked for leads in recovering stolen property. In fact, Fass and Francis (2004, p.156) report: "Recent research argues that because markets for stolen goods act as incentives to steal, police and criminologists should shift attention from thieves to methods of disrupting demand for the goods."

**Larceny/Theft**   **Larceny/theft** is the unlawful taking, carrying, leading or riding away of property from another's possession. It is synonymous with theft. Both larceny and burglary are crimes against property, but larceny, unlike burglary, does not involve illegally entering a structure. Larceny differs from robbery in that no force or threat of force is involved. The two major categories of larceny/theft are grand larceny, a felony based on the value of stolen property (usually over $100), and petty larceny, a misdemeanor based on the value of the property (usually under $100).

 The elements of the crime of larceny/theft are (1) the felonious stealing, taking, carrying, leading or driving away of (2) another's personal goods or property (3) valued above or below a specified amount (4) with the intent to permanently deprive the owner of the property or goods. In most states, taking found property with the intent to keep or sell it is also a crime.

Among the common types of larceny are purse-snatching, picking pockets, theft from coin machines, theft from motor vehicles, theft from buildings, jewelry theft, bicycle theft and shoplifting (including altering the price of an item). (See Figure 10.7.) Closed circuit television (CCTV) is one effective way to detect not only shoplifters but dishonest employees as well.

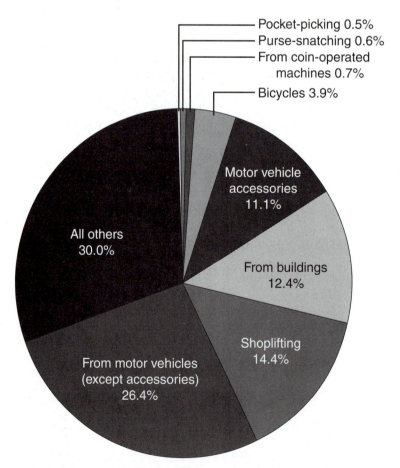

**Figure 10.7**   Larceny/Theft Distribution

One of the most frequent thefts is that of bicycles. More than 1 million U.S. residents have their bicycles stolen each year. In other words, a bicycle is lost or stolen about every 1.2 minutes. With the average cost of $300 a bike, this form of theft costs Americans over $300 million a year. The FBI Uniform Crime Reports puts the annual cost at between $800 million and $1 billion. Although police nationwide recover nearly 50 percent of lost and stolen bikes, less than 5 percent ever make it back to their rightful owners. This could be rectified if bike owners would register with the National Bike Registry at www.nationalbikeregistry.com.

Credit card theft is another challenge facing criminal investigators. According to Ballezza (2003, p.8): "Beginning in the early to mid 1990s, those law enforcement agencies principally involved with investigations of criminal activity inside casinos began noticing an increase in the use of stolen credit cards to obtain cash from the cash-advance merchants in the casinos. The interesting common denominator in these investigations was that many of the credit cards used in the scam had been stolen from health club lockers." Ballezza (p.13) concludes: "As more health clubs open and as additional states begin licensing casinos, health club credit card thieves will continue to have ample opportunity to perpetrate their interstate fraud."

While jewelry and art theft may be committed by those merely acting on opportunity, professional thieves or organized rings may also be responsible for these crimes. Given the enhanced security usually afforded such items of great monetary value, those who commit jewel or art theft have typically invested more time in planning their heist and may go to greater extremes to protect themselves and their loot, meaning they may be heavily armed. The FBI and Interpol are commonly involved in thefts of fine art. Officers investigating jewelry theft should also inform the FBI of the theft, even without immediate evidence of interstate operations.

As with burglary investigations, officers investigating cases of larceny/theft should check with fences, pawnshops, secondhand stores, flea markets and informants for leads in recovering stolen property.

 The elements of the offense of receiving stolen goods are (1) receiving, buying or concealing stolen or illegally obtained goods (2) knowing them to be stolen or illegally obtained.

**Fraud** is intentional deception to cause a person to give up property or some lawful right. It differs from theft in that fraud uses deceit rather than stealth to obtain goods illegally. Fraud is committed in many ways, including the use of checks, credit cards, confidence games and embezzlement. Common types of check fraud are insufficient-fund checks, issuing worthless checks and forgeries.

Unfortunately, as Cauthen (2001, p.13) points out, those who engage in fraud are rarely prosecuted because the courts traditionally regard fraud cases as civil rather than criminal. In addition, difficulty in establishing criminal intent needed for conviction is challenging.

Closely related to the preceding types of fraud are debit and credit-card fraud. Retailers and credit card companies incur tens of millions of dollars in losses each year due to credit-card fraud (Craft et al., 2001, p.71).

 Elements of the crime of larceny by credit card include (1) possessing credit cards obtained by theft or fraud (2) by which services or goods are obtained (3) through unauthorized signing of the cardholder's name. Bank embezzlements are investigated jointly by the local police and the FBI.

White-collar or business-related crime includes (1) securities theft and fraud, (2) insurance fraud, (3) credit-card and check fraud, (4) consumer fraud, illegal competition and deceptive practices, (5) bankruptcy fraud, (6) computer-related fraud, (7) embezzlement and pilferage, (8) bribes, kickbacks and payoffs and (9) receiving stolen property. Piquero and Benson (2004, p.161) suggest: "In a number of ways, white-collar crime is different from ordinary street crime. Involvement in it occurs at a different point in the life course. It has a dramatically different opportunity structure. Those who participate in it are drawn from a different sector of the American social structure. Finally, it may have significantly different motivations from those who engage in street crime."

Scuro (2003, p.20) notes: "Economic or white collar crimes do not involve violent acts associated with traditional criminal activity, but do result in victims who often are robbed of life savings, pension benefits and other assets accumulated through decades of hard work, saving and planning for the future. White collar criminals often steal from their victims their future hopes and dreams by betraying a trust earned and then utilized for selfish and illegal personal gains."

A problem of increasing concern is **identity theft,** which, in simple terms, is "the unlawful use of another's personal identifying information" (Bellah, 2001b, p.222). Barry (2001, p.25) contends that identity theft is America's fastest-growing financial crime. It is estimated that 10 million Americans were victimized by identity theft in 2003 at a cost of $50 billion ("Bush Signs Identity Theft Bill," 2004, p.A9).

Testimony given to Congress by an expert panel stated that identity theft has reached crisis proportions because for less than $40 a thief can purchase someone's social security number on the Internet (Brown, 2001, p.1). In addition, Myers (2001a, p.227) notes that the Internet has hundreds of websites that sell fake driver's licenses, ID cards, police ID and birth certificates on CDs.

Another reason identity theft has increased so dramatically is that there are over 200 valid forms of ID or drivers' licenses issued in the United States. Further, many ID cards are of extremely poor quality (Myers, 2001b, p.49). Bellah (2001b, p.391) offers yet another reason: "In today's high-tech world with sophisticated photocopy methods and computer equipment, almost any document can be easily altered or counterfeited. In some instances the counterfeit document may appear to be of better quality than a genuine document."

Identity theft can be devastating. As Craft et al. (p.71) describe: "Increasingly, unsuspecting law-abiding individuals are finding their lives thrown into turmoil when crooks steal citizens' very identities, using their names and social security numbers to take over existing credit accounts and open fraudulent new ones. . . . It is a crime against people. We live in a society where we depend upon our credit rating and credit cards to do our daily business. This type of crime causes tremendous problems that reduce the quality of people's lives and destroy their sense of security." Often identity theft goes undetected for a long time. On average it takes 14 months for a victim to discover that his or her identity has been stolen. Some thefts go undetected for years (Del Grosso, 2001, p.74).

Identity theft is a federal crime, becoming so in 1998 when then-President Clinton signed the Identity Theft and Assumption Deterrence Act. Although this looks good on paper, it does not cover thefts below the $50,000 to $100,000 threshold most attorneys use to determine if federal prosecution should occur.

In addition, as Barry (p.25) suggests: "Terrorism gives it [identity theft] a new twist. . . . All 19 of the September 11 hijackers had social security numbers (SSN), including several that were stolen. . . . A purloined SSN is as useful a tool for terrorists as it is for identity thieves." In July 2004, President Bush signed into law a sentence imposing mandatory prison terms for criminals who use identity theft to commit terrorist acts and other offenses.

Savelli (2004b, p.28) points out: "Identity theft is a crime that leaves a paper trail. Yes, it is quite different from other crimes, but the paper trail left behind will undoubtedly lead to the perpetrator(s). The trail may be mail, loan applications, credit cards, bank accounts or even e-mails. Also, most identity criminals will have to meet someone from a store, a delivery company or other contact, at some point, to receive their benefit or profit as a result of the identity theft. This means that there will be witnesses somewhere." Savelli (p.29) also contends: "Questions asked in such a tricky investigation as identity theft should be carefully formulated. Identity thieves are usually cautious people and have probably taken steps to hide evidence, cover their tracks and prepare for an interview or interrogation by the authorities."

**Motor Vehicle Theft**    **Motor vehicle thefts** take much investigative time, but they can provide important information on other crimes under investigation. The vehicle identification number (VIN), critical in motor vehicle thefts, identifies the specific vehicle in question and is the primary nonduplicated, serialized number assigned by the manufacturer to each vehicle.

 Categories for motor vehicle theft based on the offender's motive include (1) joyriding, (2) transportation, (3) stripping for parts and accessories, (4) use in committing another crime and (5) reselling for profit.

Although referred to as "motor vehicle theft," most cases are prosecuted as "unauthorized use of a motor vehicle" because a charge of theft requires proof that the thief intended to deprive the owner of the vehicle permanently, which is often difficult or impossible to establish. The elements of the crime of unauthorized use of a motor vehicle are (1) intentionally taking or driving (2) a motor vehicle (3) without the consent of the owner or the owner's authorized agent. Motor vehicles include cars, trucks, buses, motorcycles, motor scooters, mopeds, snowmobiles, vans, self-propelled watercraft and aircraft. Embezzlement of a motor vehicle occurs if the person who took the vehicle had consent initially and then exceeded the terms of that consent.

False motor vehicle theft reports are often filed because a car has been taken by a family member or misplaced in a parking lot, to cover up for an accident or a crime committed with the vehicle or to provide an alibi for being late. The FBI and the National Auto Theft Bureau provide valuable help in investigating motor vehicle theft.

To apprehend car thieves, many departments are using bait cars. Says Mertens (2003, p.36): "Whether watch-and-wait, radio or GPS tracking, bait vehicle programs are being deployed by police departments to catch criminals." Chu (2003, pp.109–110) explains one such program:

> The concept of a bait car is simple. Select a vehicle that is of a make and
> model and that has a high theft rate, and equip it with monitoring and

communications equipment. Place the vehicle in a high crime area, then sit back and wait for the vehicle to be stolen. There is no need to have officers physically monitor the car, as the technology devices in the bait car will alert the law enforcement agency when an intrusion and theft is taking place. If the supporting technologies are sophisticated enough, the vehicle can be tracked and instantly pinpointed for the responding police units.

In addition, locking mechanisms can be installed to prevent car thieves from running from the car, and vehicle engine shutoff systems can be in place in case the thief attempts to start a car chase or starts to drive erratically. The icing on the cake is video and audio monitoring equipment that records the suspect's activities, which then provides strong evidence for the criminal court prosecution. In fact, the Minneapolis [Minnesota] Police Department still maintains a 100 percent success rate in terms of suspects caught on videotape that plead guilty.

Pasquale (2004, p.34) notes: "Numerous high-tech gadgets are now being deployed by law enforcement to catch or stop car thieves. . . . These have led to arrests of entire car theft rings and the seizure and shuttering of chop shops. As such they get a lot of press, but they can't take the place of the best auto-theft recovery tool ever created, the well-educated patrol officer. Patrol officers have always been the backbone of the police department, and they play a crucial role in the fight against auto theft."

To improve the ability to recognize stolen vehicles, officers should keep a list of stolen vehicles in their cars, develop a checking system for rapidly determining if a suspicious vehicle is stolen, learn the common characteristics of stolen vehicles and car thieves, take time to check suspicious people and vehicles and learn how to question suspicious drivers and occupants. Numerous motor vehicle thefts can be prevented by effective educational campaigns and by manufacturer-installed security devices. The Dyer Act made interstate transportation of a stolen motor vehicle a federal crime and allowed for federal help in prosecuting such cases.

Bailer (2004, p.28) suggests to police departments: "Make time for proactive work, such as surveillance at hot spots or of known local thieves; obtain timely intelligence on repeat offenders or hot spots; work with local prosecutors for tough plea bargains and sentencing; and partner with state task forces and other agencies. They are working the same bad guys."

**Arson**   Arson is the malicious, willful burning of a building or property. Fires are classified as natural, accidental, criminal (arson), suspicious or of unknown origin. They are presumed natural or accidental unless proven otherwise.

The elements of the crime of arson include (1) the willful, malicious burning of a building or property (2) of another, or of one's own to defraud (3) or causing to be burned, or aiding, counseling or procuring such burning. Attempted arson is also a crime. Some states categorize arson as either aggravated or simple. Aggravated arson is intentionally destroying or damaging a dwelling or other property by means of fire or explosives, creating an imminent danger to life or great bodily harm, which risk was known or reasonably foreseeable to the suspect. Simple arson is intentional destruction by fire or explosives that does not create imminent danger to life or risk of great bodily harm. Other states use the Model Arson Law, which divides arson into four degrees: first-degree involves the burning of dwellings; second-degree involves the burning of buildings other than dwellings; third-degree involves the burning of other property; and fourth-degree involves attempts to burn buildings or property.

Martin (2004, p.122) notes: "In policing, it seems as if there is one crime that seems to be pushed to the side by the rank and file, DA's offices and the courts; that crime is arson." Logic suggests that the fire department should work to *detect* arson and determine the point of origin and probable cause, whereas the police department should *investigate* arson and prepare the case for prosecution. Special problems in investigating arson include coordinating efforts with the fire department and others, determining if a crime has been committed, finding physical evidence and witnesses and determining if the victim is a suspect.

An administrative warrant is issued when it is necessary for the agent to search the premises to determine the cause and origin of the fire. A criminal warrant is issued on probable cause when evidence of a crime is found on the premises. Entry to fight a fire requires no warrant. Once in the building, fire officials may remain a reasonable time to investigate the cause of the blaze. After this time, an administrative warrant is needed, as established in *Michigan v. Tyler* (1974).

Although the fire department is responsible for establishing when arson has occurred, law enforcement investigators must be able to verify such findings. To do so requires understanding what distinguishes an accidental fire from arson. Basic to this understanding is the concept of the fire triangle, which consists of three elements necessary for a substance to burn: air, fuel and heat. In arson, at least one of these elements is usually present in abnormal amounts for the structure. Evidence of **accelerants,** substances that promote burning, at an arson scene is a primary form of evidence. The most common accelerant used is gasoline. Also important as evidence are **igniters,** articles used to light a fire. These include matches; candles; cigars and cigarettes; cigarette lighters; electrical, mechanical and chemical devices; and explosives.

Burn indicators that provide important information include alligatoring (blistering), crazing, depth of char, lines of demarcation, sagged furniture springs and spalling. The point of origin is established by finding the area with the deepest char, alligatoring and (usually) the greatest destruction. Fires normally burn upward, are drawn toward ventilation and follow fuel. Arson is likely in fires that:

- Have more than one point of origin.
- Deviate from normal burning patterns.
- Show evidence of trailers.
- Show evidence of having been accelerated.
- Produce odors or smoke of a color associated with substances not normally present at the scene.
- Indicate that an abnormal amount of air, fuel or heat was present.
- Reveal evidence of incendiary igniters at the point of origin.

Officers investigating vehicle fires should look for evidence of accelerants and determine whether the vehicle was insured. It is seldom arson if there is no insurance. Officers investigating explosions and bombings should pay special attention to any fragments of the explosive device as well as to any powder present at the scene and attempt to determine a motive. If a computer is found at an arson scene, it is likely that the data on the hard drive is intact, surviving the heat and flames as well as the water and steam from the firefighting efforts.

The National Institute of Justice has published *Fire and Arson Scene Evidence: A Guide for Public Safety Personnel,* available online at www.ojp.usdoj.gov/nij/pubs-sum/181584.htm.

Arson investigations might also be made more effective and efficient if police officers are cross-trained with firefighters. As Miller (2004, p.86) contends: "Learning how the other works is beneficial to both agencies and the community they serve."

## Other Crimes

Beyond the eight Part I Index crimes, officers commonly investigate other offenses, such as crimes against children, hate or bias crimes, computer-related crimes and environmental crimes. Many of these offenses involve one or more elements of one or more of the Index crimes. For example, crimes against children may include assault, rape or murder. Bias crimes may be directed at a person (assault, homicide) or property (arson). Computer-related crimes may involve various forms of theft, including identity theft, and computers have been increasingly used to perpetrate crimes against children and distribute pornography. Finally, environmental crimes may involve theft of a commodity (for example, lumber) or, in some instances, homicide, as was the case when lethal acid was left on the street with the regular garbage and someone exposed to the chemical died.

**Crimes against Children**   Crimes against children were introduced in Chapter 7. They include physical, emotional and sexual abuse; neglect; abandonment; exploitation; and kidnapping. Such crimes can result in permanent and serious damage physically, mentally and emotionally.

Generally, reports of child neglect or abuse are made by third parties such as teachers, neighbors, siblings and parents. Seldom does the victim report the offense. When such reports are received, if the possibility of present or continued danger to the child exists, the child must be placed in protective custody.

 Problems in investigating crimes against children include the need to protect the child from further harm, the possibility of parental involvement, the difficulty in interviewing children and the potential need to involve other agencies.

In the vast majority of child abuse cases, children tell the truth to the best of their ability. Investigators should listen carefully to children and should look at indicators of neglect or abuse. These indicators may be physical or behavioral or both.

Investigators should also be aware of pedophiles, adults who have either heterosexual or homosexual preferences for young boys or girls of a specific, limited age range. Many pedophiles are members of sex rings, and many have moved from prowling the playgrounds to searching for their victims in cyberspace. To counter such activity, proactive law enforcement agencies go undercover online to develop a relationship with cyber sex offenders that allows collection of information about the offender's activities and location. This can lead to the eventual arrest of such offenders.

Pedophiles' reactions to being discovered usually begin with complete denial and progress through minimizing the acts, justifying the acts and blaming the victims. If all else fails, they may claim to be sick.

The Child Protection Act prohibits child pornography and greatly increases the penalties for adults who engage in it. Child abuse can be prevented by educating children about it and by keeping the channels of communication with them open.

**Bias/Hate Crimes**   A **hate crime,** according to the FBI, is "a criminal offense committed against a person, property or society which is motivated, in whole or in part, by the offender's bias against a race, religion, disability, sexual orientation or ethnicity/national origin" (Bouman, 2003, p.21). According to Steen and Cohen (2004, p.91): "Hate crime has emerged over the past 15 years as a distinct category within criminal law." Race was a motive for over half of the nation's 7,400 reported hate crimes in 2003 ("Race Was Motive . . .," 2004, p.A05). FBI statistics indicate that race is the most frequent motivation of hate crime (52.5 percent) followed by religion (16.4 percent), sexual orientation (16.4 percent), ethnicity (14.2 percent), disability (0.5 percent) and multiple bias (less than 1 percent). (See Figure 10.8.) According to Strom (2001, p.3), the majority of hate crimes are not reported to the police. In 2000 just under half of violent crimes and just over a third of property crimes were brought to the attention of the police.

A report by the Southern Poverty Law Center ("Hate Crime Statistics . . .," 2001, p.5) states: "The overall hate crime statistics are virtually useless. While the published hate crime totals have been running at about 8,000 a year, the real figure is probably closer to 50,000. And these numbers are critically important.

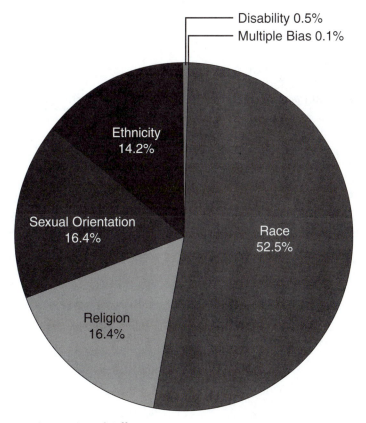

**Figure 10.8**   Bias-Motivated Offenses

Only when we know the level and nature of hate crime in the United States will we be able to allocate resources in an effective way to combat it." The IACP has developed a hate crime continuum depicting what can happen if a community ignores racial epithets or hate symbols (Figure 10.9).

Hate crimes differ from nonhate-based crimes in several other important ways, as summarized in Table 10.3.

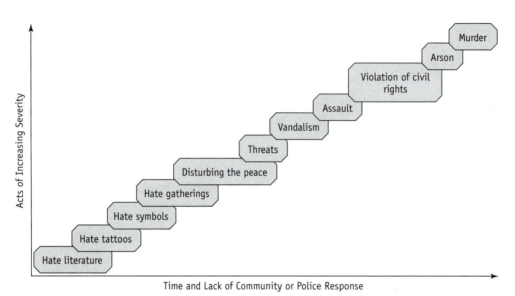

**Figure 10.9** Hate Crime Continuum

SOURCE: Adapted from the International Association of Chiefs of Police.

**Table 10.3** Hate-Based Crime versus Nonhate-Based Crime

| *Characteristics* | *Nonhate-Based Incidents* | *Hate-Based Incidents* |
|---|---|---|
| Relationship of victim to perpetrator | Most assaults involve two people who know each other | Assaults tend to be "stranger" crimes |
| Number of perpetrators | Most assaults have one perpetrator and one victim | Involve an average of four assailants for each victim |
| Nature of the conflict | Tends to be even | Tends to be uneven—hate crime perpetrators often attack younger or weaker victims, or arm themselves and attack unarmed victims |
| Amount of physical damage inflicted | Not typically "excessive" | Extremely violent, with victims being three times more likely to require hospitalization than "normal" assault victims |
| Treatment of property | In most property crimes, something of value is taken | More likely that valuable property will be damaged or destroyed |
| Perpetrator's personal gain | Attacker settles a score or profits from the crime | In most, no personal score is settled and no profit is made |
| Location of crime | No place with any symbolic significance | Frequently occur in churches, synagogues, mosques, cemeteries, monuments, schools, camps, and in or around the victim's home |

SOURCE: Adapted from Christina Bodinger-deUriarte. "Hate Crime: The Rise of Hate Crime on School Campuses." Research Bulletin No. 10 of Phi Delta Kappa, Center for Evaluation, Development, and Research, December 1991, p.2.

The Anti-Defamation League has launched a website to serve as a database for law enforcement officers investigating hate groups: http://www.adl.org/learn. The site identifies and monitors extremist groups and allows police to search for symbols they might find on literature or tattoos. It also tracks hate group meetings and rallies on a state-by-state calendar.

Bune (2004, p.44) suggests: "Photographs of graffiti, epithets and symbols should be taken immediately to preserve the evidence. Police should then see to it that the offending graffiti, epithets or symbols are removed quickly to avoid continued victimization."

**Computer-Related Crimes**    Mercer (2004, p.32) asserts: "The computer age dramatically has changed how people relate to each other, but not their basic human nature. A minority of individuals who believe there exists a shortcut to riches, or who invade the privacy or innocence of others, continue to carry out their criminal agendas. However, now they more likely use a computer or other digital device to store information about their actions or to commit their crimes." Rantala (2004, p.1) reports on the results of a 2001 Computer Security Survey (CSS) looking at cybercrimes against business. Ninety-five percent of the 198 businesses responding used computers. Seventy-four percent reported being a victim of cybercrime.

Bloomberg (2001, p.38) suggests: "The Internet creates a whole new source of confusion for law enforcement. Con-men can now sit at home in another state, or even another country, and defraud more people than ever using the same tried and true scams. . . . Most criminals can defraud hundreds of people around the country using the same type of scam and rake in tens of thousands of dollars, without really worrying about any local police departments."

According to Griffith (2003, p.18): "The computer crime hit parade includes distribution of child pornography, credit card fraud, industrial espionage, harassment, breaking and entering (hacking), solicitation of prostitution, conspiracy, child molestation, malicious mischief and property destruction (viruses), and that barely scratches the surface."

A relatively recent form of computer crime is phishing. **Phishing** is the use of fraudulent e-mails and websites to fool recipients into divulging personal information. According to Alexander (2004, p.D1): "In an online scheme called 'phishing,' consumers lost an estimated $1.2 billion last year to fraud perpetrators who sent fear-inspiring bogus e-mails that tricked people into disclosing personal information, such as bank account details and Social Security and credit card numbers."

Computer crimes are relatively easy to commit and difficult to detect. Most computer crimes are committed by insiders, and few are prosecuted.

 **Computer-related crimes** may involve input data, output data, the program itself or computer time. The most common types of computer crime are misuse of computer services, program abuse and data abuse. Investigating such crimes often requires a team approach.

People involved in computer-related crimes are usually technical people such as data entry clerks, machine operators, programmers and systems analysts. Common motivators for such crimes are personal gain, ignorance, misguided playfulness and maliciousness or revenge.

Jacobia (2004, p.30) describes the four phases of a computer forensic investigation: collection, examination, analysis and reporting:

The collection phase involves the search for, recognition, collection and documentation of electronic evidence. This phase would normally be accomplished by the first responder.

The examination phase helps make the evidence visible and explains its origin and significance. It should document the content and state of the evidence in its totality. Also included in this phase is the search for any information that may be hidden or obscured.

The analysis phase looks at the results of the examination for its significance and probative value to the case.

The report phase results in a written report that outlines the examination process and pertinent data recovered. Examination notes must be preserved for discovery or testimony.

Evidence in computer-related crimes is often contained on tapes or disks, not readily discernible and highly susceptible to destruction. In addition to information on tapes and disks, evidence may take the form of data reports, programming or other printed materials based on information from computer files.

Investigators who handle computer tapes and disks should avoid contact with the recording surfaces. They should never write on affixed computer disk labels and should never use paper clips on or rubber bands around computer disks. To do so may destroy the data they contain. Computer tapes and disks taken as evidence should be stored vertically, at approximately 70°F and away from bright light, dust and magnetic fields.

The FBI and the Department of Justice have created the Internet Fraud Complaint Center (IFCC) which, in its first three-and-a-half days, logged 3,700 complaints. The site (www.ifccfbi.gov) allows consumers and small businesses nationwide to file Internet fraud complaints online. The difficulty in dealing with computer crime is pointed out by Goodman (2001, p.10): "Unfortunately, the absence of a standard definition for computer crime, a lack of reliable criminal statistics on the problem, and significant underreporting of the threat pose vexing challenges for police agencies."

To help local law enforcement agencies obtain electronic evidence in computer crime investigations, the Department of Justice has published a manual, "Searching and Seizing Computers and Obtaining Electronic Evidence in Criminal Investigations." The manual is available on the Internet at www.cybercrime.gov/s&smanual2002.htm ("DOJ Publishes Guide . . .," 2001, p.7). The IACP also has a guide, *Best Practices for Seizing Electronic Evidence*, available on the Internet at www.theiacp.org ("IACP Issues Guide . . .," 2001, p.3). Another valuable website is www.cybercrime.gov, which is maintained by the Computer Crime and Intellectual Property Section of the U.S. Department of Justice. The site is a collection of documents and links to other sites and agencies that may assist in preventing, detecting, investigating and prosecuting computer-related crime (Dees, 2001, p.27).

**Environmental Crime** **Environmental crimes** range from people littering to those illegally disposing of used tires, used oil, biohazardous waste and other hazardous substances. In some states property owners can be civilly fined up to $500 a day if the cleanup is not completed within the required time.

When both civil and criminal proceedings are instituted against a violator, it is known as **parallel proceedings.** The courts have ruled that taking both criminal and civil actions against a violator is not considered double jeopardy. Unfortunately, many law enforcement agencies consider polluting the environment a civil matter and do not devote resources to finding and prosecuting those who break the laws concerning protecting the environment.

## False Reports

Whether officers are investigating violent crimes or property crimes, they should always be aware of the possibility of a false report.

People may claim to have been burglarized to collect money for the stolen items from their insurance companies. Or they may set a friend up to "rob" them while they are at work alone and in control of a large amount of cash.

## Victimless Crimes

A great amount of investigative time is spent on the so-called **victimless crimes,** such as prostitution, gambling, pornography and dealing/doing drugs. Such crimes are sometimes assigned to a division called Vice Investigations.

 Victimless crimes include prostitution, pornography, gaming and drug dealing/using.

Opinion polls indicate that the majority of the public is not all that upset about victimless crimes. However, a crime is a crime, even if the victim does not recognize or acknowledge it. This section addresses the "victimless" crimes of prostitution, gambling and pornography. Chapter 11 discusses investigating crimes involving drugs.

### Prostitution and Pornography

How aggressively police deal with prostitution depends to a great extent on public expectations. According to Parker (n.d.): "Prostitution, pornography and other forms of commercial sex are a multibillion dollar industry. They enrich a small minority of predators, while the larger community is left to pay for the damages." He further notes: "People used in the sex industry often need medical care as a result of the ever-present violence. They may need treatment for infectious diseases, including AIDS. Survivors frequently need mental health care for posttraumatic stress disorder, psychotic episodes and suicide attempts. About a third end up chronically disabled and on social security." Further problems are that the sex trade plays an active role in promoting alcohol and drug abuse and that pimps also may use their prostitutes in forgery and credit-card fraud.

Although streetwalking prostitutes are the most visible sign of a problem, escort services should not be overlooked. Because escort services advertise in local newspapers or telephone directories, these sources can be reviewed to reveal their presence. Researchers Surratt et al. (2004, p.55) report that nearly 45 percent of those in [their] sample of prostitutes were homeless, the majority had limited education, and very few possessed any sort of social or professional ties with the larger community. They also report: "Virtually all of the women encountered in this project indicated that prostitution is not a chosen career. Rather for most it is *survival sex,* and for almost all it is the result of a drug habit, combined with the lack of other skills or resources."

One common strategy to address prostitution is to focus on the "johns," exposing them to public humiliation. Undercover operations may also be successful in breaking up organized prostitution. In some instances, officers wait outside suspected establishments and talk with exiting customers. However, police tactics often result in charges of entrapment, discussed later in the chapter.

Pornography presents its own unique challenges because of the subjective nature of what is considered "offensive" and the various interpretations allowed of the First Amendment right to freedom of expression. Defining what is *pornographic* is problematic—given the graphic sex scenes on television and in movies, what are the standards today? Most citizens cannot agree. The Internet has also added a new dimension to pornography. Some countries are banning American online services, claiming they are pornographic.

## *Gaming*

Note that the term *gaming* has replaced the older term *gambling* among those who are involved in this activity. In years past, gaming was a focus of law enforcement, with raids on gaming establishments making headlines. Legal gaming includes charitable gaming, paramutual betting, casino gaming and lotteries. Moffett and Peck (2001, p.16) caution: "Gambling and gamblers attract many of the traditional vices (e.g., prostitution, pornography, loan-sharking and extortion)." They (p.17) note: "Officials must realize that legal gambling will attract an unsavory element that can jeopardize the safety and well-being of the city's residents and the many visitors who come to gamble." They (p.16) also suggest that police departments might expect an increase in robberies, check and credit-card fraud, property crimes, domestic abuse and alcohol-related violations. Researchers Stitt et al. (2003, p.253) report somewhat different results: "Crime rates increased significantly in some casino communities, some remained relatively stable, and others decreased."

The most significant forms of illegal gaming are numbers, betting with bookmakers or bookies and sports pools or sports cards. The Internet is responsible for a large growth in gaming with over 300 gaming-related sites, some of which have set up operations offshore. Many investigations, including those of victimless crimes, make use of surveillance, undercover assignments and raids.

## Surveillance, Undercover Assignments and Raids

"Follow that car!" "Don't lose her." "I've been made." "My cover's blown." "It's a raid." Fictionalized detective work frequently portrays the glamorous side of surveillance, undercover assignments and raids. In reality, however, such assignments often involve days, weeks, even months of tedious yet dangerous watchfulness.

 Surveillance, undercover assignments and raids should be used only when all other investigative alternatives have failed.

Because they are expensive and potentially dangerous, these investigative techniques are not routinely used.

## Surveillance

The purpose of surveillance is to gather information about people, their activities and associates that may help solve a crime or protect a witness. Surveillance can be designed to serve several functions (Bennett and Hess, pp.173–174):

- Gain information required for building a criminal complaint.
- Determine an informant's loyalty.
- Verify a witness' statement about a crime.
- Gain information required for obtaining a search or arrest warrant.
- Gain information necessary for interrogating a suspect.
- Identify a suspect's associates.
- Observe members of terrorist organizations.
- Find a person wanted for a crime.
- Observe criminal activities in progress.
- Make a legal arrest.
- Apprehend a criminal in the act of committing a crime.
- Prevent a crime.
- Recover stolen property.
- Protect witnesses.

A common type of surveillance is the stakeout, a stationary surveillance in which officers set up an observation post and monitor it continuously. Other forms of surveillance include aerial surveillance and audio surveillance, or wire-tapping. Before a judge will approve an application for electronic surveillance, those requesting it must show why surveillance is necessary, for example, standard techniques have been tried and failed or standard investigative techniques are too dangerous to try. Nason (2004, p.5) cautions: "During surveillances, participants must remain vigilant and alert to the possibility of countersurveillance techniques being employed against them."

Davis (2004, p.38) points out: "Since September 11, 2001, the development of new electronic surveillance techniques and equipment has been in overdrive. Fueled by a national desire to make our homeland safe for our citizens, the surveillance industry has sprung to life to supply agencies with an almost endless array of electronic gadgets."

Huntington (2001, p.30) describes the newest generation of on-site video: "We have the technology in place that allows a police agency to access real-time, seamless streaming video at remote sites. It's installed on school campuses now. This video is delivered at up to 24 frames per second and allows responding officers to be advised of what's happening, where and how, all at real time, with, at most, an 8 second delay."

"CCTV: Constant Cameras Track Violators" (2003, p.16) reports: "The use of closed-circuit television (CCTV) cameras to monitor public spaces is increasing, both in the United States and abroad. . . . Many people are wary about the government watching and recording their movements as they pass through parks, streets and other public areas. Yet despite the controversy, CCTV use by criminal justice personnel in the United States may be increasing."

Before leaving the topic of surveillance, consider the words of Davis (p.43): "Terrorists or not, we still live in a free society. Just because the Patriot Act has loosened the rules for the federal government, your local jurisdiction still needs to be aware of, and obey, local or state regulations when conducting surveillance.

Finding the balancing point between legal electronic surveillance and an individual's right to privacy will be something our nation's courts will tackle in the future."

## Undercover Assignments

An investigation can be overt or covert. **Overt investigations** are conducted openly, usually with officers either in uniform or introducing themselves as officers. **Covert investigations,** in contrast, are done secretively, for example, using surveillance and undercover personnel. Most people are aware of undercover (UC) operations from the television programs and movies in which detectives take on false identities and infiltrate groups engaged in illegal activity. However, undercover operations have been criticized by some as having no place in a free society such as ours.

 Undercover assignments are used to obtain information and evidence about illegal activity when it can be obtained in no other way.

Undercover work usually serves one of four functions (Miller, 2001, p.26): (1) to net fugitives from justice, (2) to establish probable cause to arrest or search, (3) to access a person or property without use of force during warrant execution or (4) to interview a subject who might otherwise be uncooperative. The undercover work itself may be light or deep.

*Light cover* involves deception, but the officer usually goes home at night. While on assignment the officer may pose as a utility worker or phone company repair person to obtain access to a suspect's home or workplace. Other covers may include that of a writer or member of the news media or a phony photographer.

*Deep cover* is much more dangerous but can be very effective. Rutledge (2004, p.78), for example, notes: "Police officers posing as inmates can get key information from suspects." The officer lives an assumed identity in an attempt to infiltrate a group or organization. No identification other than the cover identification is carried. Communication with the police department is risky and carefully planned. Plans also are made for what the undercover officer is to do if the criminal operation is "busted" and for how the officer will end the relationship. Wexler (2004c, pp.88–89) describes the essential traits of an undercover officer: "UCs have to be very disciplined yet able to function on their feet. They have to be able to blend into any environment. They have to be able to make conversation with people who are strangers. They have to be very personable and likeable. They also have to be able to have an extremely good memory because they have to document information."

Undercover operations may even extend into cyberspace. Malcolm and Girardi (2004, p.12) note: "The same anonymity used by criminals can be used by law enforcement investigators to conduct investigations." According to Cornell (2001, p.55): "The FBI has seen its cyber crime caseload increase 1200% over the past five years and estimates that computer losses equate to ten billion dollars annually." According to one expert, Sgt. John McLean, Director of Training at Internet Crimes, the applications of undercover operations in cyberspace are limitless and "the use of undercover investigative approaches online can be used in nearly every aspect of criminal activity" (Cornell, p.57). However, he cautions: "No matter what the approach, there are investigative concerns such as entrapment issues, undercover involvement with criminal activity, and the use of informants and secure/protective undercover methods." He suggests the following steps to developing an online undercover response (Cornell, p.57):

- Develop an undercover operations plan.
- Set nontraceable payment methods.
- Set systems (telephone, hardware, software) to support undercover operations.
- Ensure that the machines activate a log to capture the investigative process.
- Use tested anonymous servers (set firewall rules for outgoing—no ActiveX, Java).
- Check attachments for hidden/embedded ID code that could compromise your investigation.
- Have undercover profiles for a range of offenders/victims.
- Do not give up the UC identity to anyone (maybe trusted L.E./Corporate Security).
- Rotate/change and adjust the undercover identity on a case-by-case basis.
- Test the undercover profiles/methods.

Malcolm and Girardi (p.12) offer additional guidelines to establish an online cover:

> (1) Obtain a nonattributable credit card, one not tied to either the department or the officer's home address. (2) Obtain an Internet service account through a large, reputable provider and pay for it with the nonattributable credit card. (3) Choose an ambiguous username. (4) Purchase or obtain "clean" computers. (5) Do not use the computer for personal use.

Undercover operations can offer information not otherwise available. No question, the police cannot be everywhere. They must rely on inside information or tips where highly skilled criminal activities are involved, particularly lacking identifiable victims or witnesses. Audio recording or video filming a crime is often feasible in undercover operations. This is a surer form of evidence and is more difficult to manipulate than verbal testimony. Undercover practices are costly and susceptible to abuse and unintended consequences. Therefore, they should be used only for serious offenses when alternative means are not available, and then only under careful monitoring.

One danger of using undercover operations is that officers may become what they start out only pretending to be. Another danger of using undercover operations is the potential for a charge of entrapment.

**Entrapment**    *Sorrells v. United States* (1932) was the first time the Supreme Court recognized the entrapment defense. In this case, a federal prohibition agent, undercover as a tourist, engaged Sorrells in conversation. After gaining the defendant's confidence by sharing common war experiences, the agent asked for some liquor and was twice refused. The third time he asked, however, Sorrells gave in and was then arrested and subsequently prosecuted for violating the National Prohibition Act. Speaking for the Court, Chief Justice Hughes said the defendant should have had the defense of entrapment available. This defense prohibits law enforcement officers from instigating a criminal act by those "otherwise innocent in order to lure them to its commission and to punish them."

 **Entrapment** is an action by the police (or a government agent) persuading a person to commit a crime that the person would not otherwise have committed.

Several key Supreme Court decisions further define entrapment. In *Sherman v. United States* (1958), a government informant and Sherman were both being treated by the same doctor for narcotics addiction and had met several times, coincidentally, at the clinic. During one of these chance encounters, the informant asked Sherman for a narcotics supplier, saying he was not responding to treatment and was beginning to suffer. The defendant tried avoiding the issue but eventually relented after continuous pressure by the informant for a dealer. The Court reversed Sherman's conviction, saying the informant "not only enticed the defendant into carrying out an illegal sale but also to returning to the habit of use" and that this was entrapment.

In *United States v. Russell* (1973), an undercover narcotics agent worked his way into a "speed" manufacturing group by offering to supply them with an essential yet hard to obtain ingredient. After seeing the established drug lab and supplying the essential ingredient, the agent received half the finished batch of speed as payment. A month later, another batch of speed was made, and the agent obtained a search warrant. Defendant Russell's sole defense was entrapment, but the Supreme Court ruled the narcotics agent's participation was not entrapment: "The illicit manufacture of drugs is not a sporadic, isolated criminal incident, but a continuing, though illegal, business enterprise. In order to obtain convictions for illegally manufacturing drugs, the gathering of evidence of past unlawful conduct frequently proves to be an all but impossible task."

In drug-related offenses, law enforcement officers have turned to one of the only practicable means of detection: infiltrating drug rings. And courts have consistently upheld such law enforcement tactics, stating they can hardly be said to violate "fundamental fairness" or [be] "shocking to the universal sense of justice."

 Entrapment charges can be avoided by not enticing a person to do something illegal. Simply witness the illegal acts committed.

Public agents and informants acting on behalf of the police also may commit entrapment. However, use of such agents and informants can contribute greatly to the success of criminal investigations. Notably these have been used over time in narcotics trafficking and sting operations to recover stolen property and apprehend burglars, petty crooks engaged in shoplifting and car prowlers.

**Informants** Because of the information informants can provide, many crimes have been solved that would not have been without their assistance. Sometimes informants are paid, but more often their motives for assisting the police are to receive a reduced sentence for a pending criminal matter. Other common motives include concern for the public safety and revenge. Hendrie (2003, p.10) suggests: "It is reasonable to believe that an informant has a motive to be truthful when he is expecting some leniency for pending charges."

Police informers who operate in undercover roles may be involved only in passive observation. They can be used to vouch for and introduce sworn police undercover agents to a suspected person or group and then should be dropped from the investigation. They may also play an active role in the criminal activities of those on whom they are informing. Only a small fraction of informers ever testify in court, although the information they provide may be offered to the judge to obtain warrants for arrests, searches, wiretaps or electronic surveillances.

Some informers go beyond giving information obtained in their natural environment and use disguises and infiltrations. The environment is deceptively shaped to elicit information. For example, an informant is placed in a suspect's cell as a cellmate in the hope that confidences will be transmitted. Other examples are an agent posing as an employee to infiltrate a factory in response to problems such as employee thefts or the police posing as reporters seeking comments from political and social activists.

Known tactics whose legality are questionable include planting informers in a group organized for the legal defense of an activist facing serious criminal charges or having a police officer dressed as a clergyman visit an arrested person in jail. Another common, and often significant, tactic is the "front," such as a cocktail lounge or a neighborhood used-property store set up for a sting operation or specifically created by the police for intelligence purposes.

Once a person has begun to inform, the threat of exposure becomes a factor. Allegiances may shift or become more intense. A criminal who becomes overzealous and tries to play the role of super cop may jeopardize a whole operation. Or, informants may become double agents—that is, clever informants experienced in deception who manipulate and control their police contact, rather than the reverse. Because undercover work is complex, it has both positive and negative aspects. Assessing them is difficult. Little research can be done because of the work's covert nature and the courts' and civil rights advocates' suspiciousness.

## *Raids*

The errors involved in the raid in Waco in 1993 underscore the criticality of planning and timing. Although the planners of the raid knew that they had probably lost the element of surprise, rather than rethinking the plan for the raid, they speeded up their activities, with the result a deadly blaze on April 19 and much public criticism. Raids are discussed further in Chapter 12.

## Investigation and Community Policing

Singh (2001) describes the transformation of the investigative division at the North Miami Beach Police Department (NMBPD). In the mid-1990s the department added a community policing unit, but they had a problem in that their detective squad was a "unit of prima donnas." Poor intradepartmental communication and a case-by-case approach to crime made it hard to do good detective work.

The deputy chief helped devise a plan to shift investigation work from a reactive to a proactive model, in keeping with the community policing philosophy. To start, a new investigative structure was designed that centered around developing integrated major crime problem-solving task forces. According to Singh (p.3): "Detectives assumed new roles as task force coordinators responsible for providing leadership in identifying major crime problems, arriving at solutions, coordinating task force efforts and training task force members."

Attitudes started to change as detectives developed stronger ties with the community and discovered new avenues for their dedication. The greatest boost to the investigations unit came from the community. Singh (p.4) explains:

> Growing trust for police among residents became an ally in investigative work, because detectives were able to rely on residents for cooperation and intelligence. [Detective] Friedman recalled a homicide investigation in which a homeless man had been murdered.

"By this time, the detective working the case knew most of the homeless people in the area," said Friedman. "He saw one of his homeless acquaintances at the crime scene, questioned him onsite, was led to a suspect, and got a full confession on the same day."

A shift to community-oriented investigations is an acknowledgment that crime is a complex phenomenon that requires a balanced response. Adopting a balanced approach means that detectives must collaborate better among themselves and with other community stakeholders. . . .

Today, detectives no longer have to be told to form a needed task force. Nor do they need to be told to collaborate with the crime prevention unit, community policing unit, businesses, the community, or anyone else. These behaviors have become second nature.

Wexler (2004b, p.90) describes how Los Angeles Police Chief Bratton is taking a proactive and decentralized approach to reducing crime and gang-related violence in Los Angeles: "Bratton credits the significant drop in crime to drawing upon community policing techniques and establishing working relationships with various federal law enforcement agencies."

## Problem-Oriented Policing and Investigation

The use of problem solving in investigation may seem to be a stretch. Criminal investigation is, by its nature, concerned with solving crimes that have already occurred. Following is the 2003 Goldstein Award Winner for excellence in problem-oriented policing, The Oakland Airport Motel Program—The Oakland Police Department Beat Health Unit.

### Scanning

In September 2000, the recurring nuisance and criminal activity at a major motel, which is part of an international chain, located near the Oakland International Airport, came to the attention of Officer Brad Gardiner of the Oakland Police Department's Beat Health Unit. Problems included inordinate calls for police service, prostitution, illegal drug activity, abandoned cars, illegal auto repair business in the motel parking lot and renting of rooms to minors.

### Analysis

Data checks, site visits, interviews, undercover surveillance and comparisons of management practices to other nearby motels led police to conclude that it was the poor management practices at the motel that allowed crime and nuisances to flourish at this motel.

### Response

After meetings with on-site motel managers and corporate executives failed to result in improvements at the motel, Beat Health Unit officers and city attorneys filed a drug nuisance abatement lawsuit against the parent corporation. Eventually, through intense negotiations, the parent corporation agreed to improve its management practices and to post a $250,000 performance bond covering a two-year monitoring period to guarantee reductions in crime and nuisance at the motel. It further agreed to pay the City of Oakland about $35,000 to cover the costs of its investigation. Numerous specific improvements were made to the physical environment and management practices at the motel.

## Assessment

Two years after the agreement was signed, there have been few calls for police service at the motel and the property has been returned to productive use. The stipulated two-year monitoring period concluded in March 2003.

## Judge's Commentary

The Oakland Airport Motel project exemplifies the practice of problem-oriented policing in several significant ways. First, it illustrates the importance of careful documentation of the conditions that give rise to a problem. Particularly when dealing with sophisticated corporate executives, the Oakland police officials and city attorneys took great care to compile irrefutable evidence that a significant amount of crime and nuisance activity was occurring at the motel, that the amount of such activity was greatly disproportionate to that experienced by similarly situated motels, and that the poor management practices at the motel were largely to blame for the problems. Second, the project exemplifies the value of a systematic approach to addressing problems. The Beat Health Unit carefully followed its own step-by-step procedure for building a case against a problem property. This deliberate approach ensured that the investigating officers gathered the necessary information and drew the right conclusions from it before settling on a course of action. Third, and perhaps most significantly, this project exemplifies how police can, with proper documented evidence and careful analysis, shift the ownership of crime and disorder problems away from the police and local government alone, back to those individuals and groups whose actions create the problems and who have the capacity to address them. (Source: "The Oakland Airport Motel Program." *Excellence in Problem-Oriented Policing: The 2003 Herman Goldstein Award Winner and Finalists.* Washington, DC: The Office of Community Oriented Policing Services and the Police Executive Research Forum, November 2003.)

 **SUMMARY**

The glamorous, exciting, action-packed fictionalized detective presents an exaggerated, unrealistic picture that differs greatly from the reality of detective work. The goals of criminal investigation are to determine if a crime has been committed, legally obtain information and evidence to identify the person(s) responsible, arrest the suspect(s), recover stolen property and present the best possible case to the prosecutor. The most critical phase in the majority of criminal investigations is the preliminary investigation.

The successful resolution of a criminal investigation most often hinges on the availability of irrefutable, relevant and admissible evidence. The Automated Fingerprint Identification System, AFIS, drastically reduces the time needed to identify latent fingerprints by selecting a limited number of likely matches for the latent prints. Physical fingerprints and DNA fingerprinting are the two forms of positive identification available to investigators.

Detectives must be familiar with techniques to investigate specific crimes. The major violent crimes are homicide, rape, robbery and assault. Homicide is classified as criminal (felonious) or noncriminal. The various degrees of murder and manslaughter are criminal homicide, noncriminal homicide (which includes excusable homicide, the unintentional, truly accidental killing of another person) and justifiable homicide (killing another person under authorization of law). After priority matters are completed, the focus of the homicide investigation is to identify the victim, establish the time of death, establish the cause of death and the method used to produce it and to develop a suspect. Special problems in homicide investigations include pressure by the public and the media; difficulty in establishing that it is homicide, rather than suicide or an accidental or natural death; handling serial murders; and, in some cases, locating the body.

Most states have in common the following elements for the crime of rape or sexual assault: (1) an act of sexual intercourse, (2) committed without the victim's consent, (3) against the victim's will and by force. The elements of the crime of robbery are (1) the wrongful taking of personal property, (2) from the person or in the person's presence, (3) against the person's will by force or threat of force.

The elements of the crime of simple assault are (1) intent to do bodily harm to another, (2) present ability to commit the act and (3) commission of an overt act toward carrying out the intent. An additional element in the crime of aggravated assault is that the intentionally inflicted bodily injury results in (1) a high probability of death, (2) serious, permanent disfigurement or (3) permanent or protracted loss or impairment of the function of any body member or organ or other severe bodily harm. Attempted assault requires proof of intent and an overt act toward committing the crime.

The major property crimes are burglary, larceny/theft, motor vehicle theft and arson. Burglaries are classified as residential or commercial. The elements of the crime of burglary include (1) entering a structure (2) without the consent of the person in possession (3) with the intent to commit a crime therein. Additional elements of burglary that may be required include (1) breaking into (2) the dwelling of another (3) during the nighttime. A burglary's severity is determined by the presence of dangerous devices in the burglar's possession or by the value of the property stolen. Attempted burglary and possession of burglary tools are also felonies. The elements of the crime of possessing burglary tools include (1) possessing any device, explosive or other instrumentality (2) with intent to use or permit their use to commit burglary.

The elements of the crime of larceny/theft are (1) the felonious stealing, taking, carrying, leading or driving away of (2) another's personal goods or property (3) valued above or below a specified amount (4) with the intent to permanently deprive the owner of the property or goods. In most states, taking found property with the intent to keep or sell it is also a crime. The elements of the offense of receiving stolen goods are (1) receiving, buying or concealing stolen or illegally obtained goods (2) knowing them to be stolen or illegally obtained. Elements of the crime of larceny by credit card include (1) possessing credit cards obtained by theft or fraud (2) by which services or goods are obtained (3) through unauthorized signing of the cardholder's name. Bank embezzlements are investigated jointly by the local police and the FBI.

Categories for motor vehicle theft based on the offender's motive include (1) joyriding, (2) transportation, (3) stripping for parts and accessories, (4) use in committing another crime and (5) reselling for profit.

The elements of the crime of arson include (1) the willful, malicious burning of a building or property (2) of another, or of one's own to defraud (3) or causing to be burned, or aiding, counseling or procuring such burning. Attempted arson is also a crime. Some states categorize arson as either aggravated or simple. Aggravated arson is intentionally destroying or damaging a dwelling or other property by means of fire or explosives, creating an imminent danger to life or great bodily harm, which risk was known or reasonably foreseeable to the suspect. Simple arson is intentional destruction by fire or explosives that does not create imminent danger to life or risk of great bodily harm. Other states use the Model Arson Law, which divides arson into four degrees: first-degree involves the burning of dwellings; second-degree involves the burning of buildings other than dwellings; third-degree involves the burning of other property; and fourth-degree involves attempts to burn buildings or property.

Other crimes officers must investigate include crimes against children, bias/hate crimes, computer-related crimes and environmental crimes. Problems in investigating crimes against children include the need to protect the child from further harm, the possibility of parental involvement, the difficulty in interviewing children and the potential need to involve other agencies. Computer-related crimes may involve input data, output data, the program itself or computer time. The most common types of computer crime are misuse of computer services, program abuse and data abuse. Investigating such crimes often requires a team approach. Investigations may also involve so-called victimless crimes, such as prostitution, pornography, gaming and drug dealing/using.

Many investigations, including those of victimless crimes, make use of surveillance, undercover assignments and raids. These methods should be used only when all other investigative alternatives have failed. Undercover techniques may result in charges of entrapment, which is an action by the police (or a government agent) persuading a person to commit a crime that the person would not otherwise have committed. Entrapment charges can be avoided by not enticing a person to do something illegal. Simply witness the illegal acts that are committed.

## APPLICATION

To provide better service to the community, the department has decided to add a detective division to its organization. The chief has asked you to develop a policy and procedure for turning cases over to this division, after a patrol officer has conducted the preliminary investigation.

### INSTRUCTIONS

Using the form in the Appendix, write a policy on what specific types of cases will be assigned to the detective division. Then write the procedure(s) for assigning cases to this division. Be sure to consider a smooth transition in the investigation from the patrol officer who conducted the preliminary investigation to the detective assigned to handle the case.

### EXERCISES IN CRITICAL THINKING

A. Mary Jones, an 18-year-old high school girl, quarreled with her boyfriend, Thomas Smith. At 3 A.M. following the evening of their quarrel, Mary went to Smith's home to return his picture. Smith stated that after receiving the picture, he went to his room, went to bed and awoke about 8 A.M. When he looked out his window, he saw Mary's car parked out front. Looking into the car, he discovered Mary sitting erect behind the steering wheel, shot through the chest, a .22 revolver lying beside her on the front seat. She was dead—apparently a suicide. The revolver had been a gift to Mary from her father. Smith called the police to report the shooting.

Mary had been shot once. The bullet entered just below the right breast, traveled across the front of her body and lodged near her heart. The medical examiner theorized that she did not die immediately. When found, she was sitting upright in the car, her head tilted slightly backward, her right hand high on the steering wheel, her left hand hanging limp at her left side.

When questioned, Smith steadfastly denied any knowledge of the shooting. Mary's clothing, the bullet from her body and the gun were sent to the FBI Laboratory for examination. An examination of her blouse where the bullet entered failed to reveal any powder residues. The bullet removed from her body was identified as having been fired from the gun found beside her body.

1. Is the shooting likely to be a suicide or a homicide? What facts support this?
2. How should the investigation proceed?

B. Ten-year-old Denise was playing in a school parking lot with her nine-year-old stepbrother, Jerry. A car pulled up to the curb next to the lot, and the man driving the car motioned for Denise and Jerry to come over. When the man asked where they lived, Denise described their house. The man then asked Denise to take him to the house, saying he would bring her right back to the lot afterward. Denise got into the car with the man, and they drove away. When they did not return after an hour, Jerry went into the school and told a teacher what had happened. Denise did not return home that evening. The next day the police received a report that a body had been found near a lover's lane. It was Denise, who had been stabbed to death with a pocketknife.

1. What steps should be taken immediately?
2. Where would you expect to find leads?
3. What evidence would you expect to find?
4. Specifically, how would you investigate this murder?

### DISCUSSION QUESTIONS

1. What are some motivations for citizens to become informants?
2. Do the police commit entrapment when they make a "target of opportunity" by placing wrapped packages in an unlocked car in a shopping center parking lot?
3. What was the purpose of establishing the Violent Crime Apprehension Program (VICAP) at the National Police Academy in Quantico, Virginia?
4. What does a successful entrapment defense by a defendant in a narcotics case need to negate a government case?
5. What are some dangers of undercover operations?
6. What are some purposes of a surveillance? When would a surveillance be useful?
7. How does the general public view the police detective? Where do these images come from?

### InfoTrac College Edition Assignments

- Use InfoTrac College Edition to help answer the Discussion Questions as appropriate.
- Use InfoTrac College Edition to locate and outline one of the following articles to share with the class:
  - "Investment Fraud" by John Cauthen
  - "Electronic Surveillance: A Matter of Necessity" by Thomas D. Coldbridge
  - "Labeling Automobile Parts to Combat Theft" by Peter Finn
  - "Making Computer Crime Count" by Marc Goodman
  - "Basic Investigative Protocol for Child Sexual Abuse" by William P. Heck
  - "Working with Informants: Operational Recommendations" by James E. Hight

- "When Casino Gambling Comes to Your Hometown: The Biloxi Experience" by Tommy Moffitt and Donald L. Peck
- "Sex Offender Registration Enforcement: A Proactive Stance to Monitoring Convicted Sex Offenders" by Bernard Parks and Diane Webb
- "The Qualified Privilege to Protect Sensitive Investigative Techniques from Disclosure" by Jayme S. Walker
- "Geologic Material as Physical Evidence" by Joseph A. Finley, Jr.
- "Police and the Sexual Assault Examination" by Craig R. Wilson
- "Health Club Credit Card Theft: A National Crime Problem" by Richard A. Ballezza
- "Best Practices of a Hate/Bias Crime Investigation" by Walter Bouman
- "When an Informant's Tip Gives Officers Probable Cause to Arrest Drug Traffickers" by Edward M. Hendrie
- "Computer Forensics: Characteristics and Preservation of Digital Evidence" by Loren D. Mercer
- "Conducting Surveillance Operations: How to Get the Most Out of Them" by John T. Nason
- "The Hate Model" by John R. Schafer and Joe Navarro
- "Major Case Management: Key Components" by Brian P. Carroll
- "FBI Laboratory Publications" by Colleen Wade
- "Obtaining Admissible Evidence from Computers and Internet Service Providers" by Stephen W. Cogar
- "Surveillance Optics" by Carlyle Poindexter

### INTERNET ASSIGNMENTS

- Type in keyword *criminal investigation*. This will take you to many informative and educational abstracts, beneficial not only to students but also to practicing police officers. Select one abstract to review and outline. Be prepared to share your outline with the class.
- DNA is especially pertinent today because of the rising use in fingerprinting as evidence in court cases. Using keyword *DNA*, scroll through the topics until you find "Basics of DNA Fingerprinting." Read and outline the article, and be prepared to discuss your outline with the class.
- Select two of the following assignments to complete. For each assignment, be prepared to share and discuss your work with the class.
  - Find the article "Working with Informants" by James E. Hight and outline the main points of the article.
  - Learn about the International Crime Scene Investigators Association by going to its website:

www.icsia.com. Write a brief report on the goals of this association and what it offers its members.

- Find the article "Basic Investigative Protocol for Child Sexual Abuse" by William P. Heck, and describe the members of the multidisciplinary team he suggests.

- Go to the IACP's website at www.theIACP.org and find their pamphlet, *Responding to Hate Crimes: A Police Officer's Guide to Investigation and Prevention.* Outline the areas covered by this guide.

- Go to the FBI's website at www.fbi.gov to obtain the most recent statistics on hate crimes. Record the most relevant statistics for law enforcement.

- Go to the Anti-Defamation League's website at www.adl.org/learn, and see if any hate group meetings or rallies are planned for your state in the next 12 months.

- To learn more about identity theft go to www.identitytheft.org, www.privacyrights.org, or www.futurecrime.com. Write a brief report on what new information you learned about this crime.

 **BOOK-SPECIFIC WEBSITE**

The book-specific website at http://cj.wadsworth.com/wobleski_Hess_police_op4e hosts a variety of resources for students and instructors. Many can be emailed to the instructor. Included are extended activities such as Concept Builders - the 3 step learning module that reinforces key chapter concepts, followed by a real-world applications and critical thinking questions. InfoTrac College Edition exercises; Discussion Questions; interactive key-term FlashCards; and a collection of chapter-based Web Links provide additional information and activities to include in the curriculum.

### REFERENCES

Alexander, Steve. "Angling for Easy Money." (Minneapolis/St. Paul) *Star Tribune,* June 3, 2004, p.D1.

Bailer, Bryn. "Grand Theft Arizona." *Police,* October 2004, pp.26–32.

Baker, Thomas E. "Hunting Serial Killers: Understanding and Apprehending America's Most Dangerous Criminals." *Law and Order,* May 2001a, pp.43–48.

Baker, Thomas E. "Serial Rapists." *Law and Order,* October 2001b, pp.229–233.

Ballezza, Richard A. "Health Club Credit Card Theft: A National Crime Problem." *FBI Law Enforcement Bulletin,* November 2003, pp.8–13.

Barry, Patricia. "Sept. 11 Terrorism Puts Spotlight on Identity Theft." *AARP Bulletin,* December 2001, p.25.

Bellah, John L. "Fraudulent Identification Documents." *Law and Order,* February 2001a, pp.391–395.

Bellah, John L. "Identity Theft: Ruining Credit and Creating Criminal Records." *Law and Order,* October 2001b, pp.222–226.

Bennett, Wayne W. and Hess, Kären M. *Criminal Investigation,* 7th ed. Belmont, CA: Wadsworth Publishing Company, 2004.

Bloomberg, David. "Cons Hit the Internet: Same Scams, New Medium." *Law and Order,* June 2001, pp.38–40.

Bouman, Walter. "Best Practices of a Hate/Bias Crime Investigation." *FBI Law Enforcement Bulletin,* March 2003, pp.21–25.

Brown, Cynthia. "ID Theft Skyrockets." *American Police Beat,* September 2001, pp.1, 20.

Budden, Jennifer. "ATFs NIBIN Program." *Law and Order,* November 2001, pp.101–106.

Bune, Karen L. "Law Enforcement Must Take Lead on Hate Crimes." *The Police Chief,* April 2004, pp.41–44.

Burger, Dan. "New Fingerprint Technology IDs Bad Guys Faster than Ever." *Police,* January 2002, pp.34–39.

"Bush Signs Identity Theft Bill." Associated Press as reported in the (Minneapolis/St. Paul) *Star Tribune,* July 16, 2004, p.A9.

Byers, Christine. "Camera System Links Bank with Police." *Chicago Daily Herald,* October 19, 2004.

Cauthen, John. "Investment Fraud." *FBI Law Enforcement Bulletin,* May 2001, pp.13–17.

"CCTV: Constant Cameras Track Violators." *NIJ Journal,* July 2003, pp.16–21.

Chu, Jim. "Bait Cars: Reducing Auto Thefts with Telematics." *Law and Order,* March 2003, pp.109–111.

Colaprete, Frank. "Knowledge Management in the Criminal Investigation Process." *Law and Order,* October 2004, pp.82–89.

Cornell, Susan E. "Cybercrime Summit." *Law and Order,* June 2001, pp.55–60.

"Court Invalidates Megan's Law in District of Columbia." *Criminal Justice Newsletter,* October 15, 2001, pp.6–7.

Craft, Charles; Nelson, Chris; and Power, Patti. "May the Task Force Be with You: Forging an Alliance to Combat Credit Fraud." *The Police Chief,* March 2001, pp.71–73.

Davis, Becci and Clayton, Joe. "Equipping Your CSI Unit." *Law and Order,* May 2003, pp.58–61.

Davis, Bob. "Spy Gear: Modern Surveillance Tools Use the Newest Technology to Catch Crooks on the Sly." *Police,* October 2004, pp.38–43.

Dees, Tim. "Cyber Crime." *Law and Order,* May 2001, pp.27–28.

Del Grosso, Robert J. "How to Avoid an Identity Crisis." *Security Management,* December 2001, pp.72–79.

"DNA Evidence: What Law Enforcement Officers Should Know." *NIJ Journal,* July 2003, pp.10–15.

"DOJ Publishes Guide on Searching and Seizing Computers and Electronic Surveillance on the Internet." *NCJA Justice Bulletin,* January 2001, p.7.

*Excellence in Problem-Oriented Policing: The 2003 Herman Goldstein Award Winner and Finalists.* Washington, DC: The Community Oriented Policing Services Office and the Police Executive Research Forum, November 2003.

Fass, Simon M. and Francis, Janice. "Where Have All the Hot Goods Gone? The Role of Pawnshops." *Journal of Research in Crime and Delinquency*, May 2004, pp.156–179.

Finley, Joseph A. "Geologic Material as Physical Evidence." *FBI Law Enforcement Bulletin*, March 2004, pp.1–6.

Fuller, John. "A Training Dilemma: The Patrol Officer and the Preliminary Investigation." *The Law Enforcement Trainer*, May/June 2003, pp.34–37.

Geberth, Vernon J. "Legal Considerations for Crime Scene Investigation." *Law and Order*, May 2003a, pp.46–51.

Geberth, Vernon J. "The Homicide Crime Scene." *Law and Order*, November 2003b, pp.38–44.

Goodman, Marc. "Making Computer Crime Count." *FBI Law Enforcement Bulletin*, August 2001, pp.10–17.

Griffith, David. "How to Investigate Cybercrime." *Police*, November 2003, pp.18–22.

Hanson, Doug. "One More Piece of the DNA Puzzle." *Law Enforcement Technology*, June 2004a, pp.10–17.

Hanson, Doug. "Shining Light on Fingerprints to Fibers to Fluids." *Law Enforcement Technology*, October 2004b, pp.134–140.

"Hate Crime Statistics Are 'in Shambles,' Rights Group Says." *Criminal Justice Newsletter*, November 29, 2001.

Hendrie, Edward M. "When an Informant's Tip Gives Officers Probable Cause to Arrest Drug Traffickers." *FBI Law Enforcement Bulletin*, December 2003, pp.8–21.

Houck, Max. "The Nature of Physical Evidence." *Law Enforcement Technology*, October 2004, pp.124–133.

Huntington, Roy. "Streaming Video: A Cop's New Best Friend?" *Police*, October 2001, pp.30–32.

"IACP Issues Guide to Seizure of Computers and Other Evidence." *Criminal Justice Newsletter*, July 13, 2001, p.3.

Jacobia, Jack. "Computer Forensics: Duties of the First Responder." *Law Enforcement Technology*, April 2004, pp.28–30.

Jones, Phillip. "DNA Profiling." *Law and Order*, August 2004, pp.92–96.

Kanable, Rebecca. "Palmprint Technology Catches Up to Fingerprint Technology." *Law Enforcement Technology*, March 2001, pp.42–45.

Kanable, Rebecca. "Fingerprints Making the Case." *Law Enforcement Technology*, March 2003, pp.48–53.

Kanable, Rebecca. "DO Sweat the Small Stuff: Trace Evidence Can Make a Big Difference." *Law Enforcement Technology*, March 2004, pp.52–57.

Litwin, Kenneth J. "A Multilevel Multivariate Analysis of the Factors Affecting Homicide Clearances." *Journal of Research in Crime and Delinquency*, November 2004, pp.327–351.

Malcolm, Mark and Girardi, Brian. "Protecting Your Anonymity Online." *Law Enforcement Technology*, November 2004, pp.8–14.

Martin, Richard. "Combating Arson." *Law and Order*, July 2004, pp.122–126.

Mercer, Loren D. "Computer Forensics: Characteristics and Preservation of Digital Evidence." *FBI Law Enforcement Bulletin*, March 2004, pp.28–32.

Mertens, Jennifer. "Thieves Tempted by Bait." *Law Enforcement Technology*, April 2003, pp.36–43.

Miller, Christa. "The Art of the Ruse: Does Winning a Battle Mean Losing a War?" *Law Enforcement Technology*, November 2001, pp.26–32.

Miller, Christa. "The Value of Police/Fire Cross-Training." *Law Enforcement Technology*, August 2004, pp.86–92.

Moffett, Tommy and Peck, Donald L. "When Casino Gambling Comes to Your Hometown: The Biloxi Experience." *FBI Law Enforcement Bulletin*, January 2001, pp.12–18.

Mulzac, Henry. "The Worms Crawl in: Forensic Entomology for Crime Scene Investigations." *Law Enforcement Technology*, November 2001, pp.88–94.

Myers, David. "The Power of Plastic: How Fake IDs Can Steal Lives." *Law and Order*, October 2001a, p.227.

Myers, David. "Tackling the Problem of Counterfeit IDs." *American Police Beat*, February 2001b, p.49.

Nason, John T. "Conducting Surveillance Operations: How to Get the Most Out of Them." *FBI Law Enforcement Bulletin*, May 2004, pp.1–7.

Nyberg, Ramesh. "Justice Served Cold." *Police*, October 2004, pp.44–52.

"The Oakland Airport Motel Program." In *Excellence in Problem-Oriented Policing: The 2003 Herman Goldstein Award Winner and Finalists*. Washington, DC: The Community Oriented Policing Services Office and the Police Executive Research Forum, November 2003.

"1 in 6 Women Reports Being Raped, Usually Before 18, Study Finds." *Criminal Justice Newsletter*, February 26, 2001, pp.6–7.

Page, Douglas. "Determining Time Since Death: Tricorder-Like Device or Electronic Nose Might Sniff Out the Answer." *Law Enforcement Technology*, June 2001, pp.98–100.

Parker, Joe. "How Prostitution Works." *Prostitution Research and Education*, no date. http://www.prostitutionresearch.com/parker-how.html

Pasquale, Dan. "Be on the Lookout." *Police*, October 2004, pp.34–36.

Piquero, Nicole Leeper and Benson, Michael L. "White-Collar Crime and Criminal Careers." *Journal of Contemporary Criminal Justice*, May 2004, pp.148–165.

Rantala, Ramona R. *Cybercrime against Businesses*. Washington, DC: Bureau of Justice Statistics Technical Report, March 2004. (NCJ 200639)

"Race Was Motive for Over Half the Hate Crimes in 2003, FBI Reports." Associated Press as reported in the *Washington Post*, November 23, 2004, p.A05.

Rich, Thomas. *Crime Mapping and Analysis by Community Organizations in Hartford, Connecticut*. Washington, DC: National Institute of Justice Research in Brief, March 2001.

Rutledge, Devallis. "Under Cover Interrogation." *Police*, August 2004, pp.78–80.

Savelli, Lou. *Basic Crime Scene Investigation*. Flushing, NY: Looseleaf Law Publications, Inc., 2004a.

Savelli, Lou. *Identity Theft*. Flushing, NY: Looseleaf Law Publications, Inc., 2004b.

Schwartz, Martin D.; DeKeseredy, Walter S.; Tait, David; and Alvi, Shahid. "Male Peer Support and a Feminist Routine Activities Theory: Understanding Sexual Assault on the College Campus." *Justice Quarterly*, September 2001, pp.623–649.

Scuro, Joseph, Jr. "White Collar Crime." *Law and Order*, May 2003, pp.20–22.

Shaker, Steven and Shaker, Stephanie. "A New Dimension in Forensics Imaging." *Law and Order*, June 2001, pp.103–107.

Singh, David. *Community-Oriented Investigation at the North Miami Beach Police Department*. BJA Practitioner Perspectives, April 2001. (NCJ 185367)

Steen, Sara and Cohen, Mark A. "Assessing the Public's Demand for Hate Crime Penalties." *Justice Quarterly*, March 2004, pp.91–124.

Stitt, B. Grant; Nichols, Mark; and Giacopassi, David. "Does the Presence of Casinos Increase Crime? An Examination of Casino and Control Communities." *Crime & Delinquency*, April 2003, pp.253–284.

Strandberg, Keith W. "The Facts Don't Lie." *Law Enforcement Technology*, June 2001a, pp.20–24.

Strandberg, Keith W. "A Team Approach to Rape Investigations." *Law Enforcement Technology*, August 2001b, pp.20–24.

Strom, Kevin J. *Hate Crimes Reported in NIBRS, 1997–99*. Washington, DC: Bureau of Justice Statistics Special Report, September 2001. (NCJ 186765)

Surratt, Hilary L.; Inciardi, James A.; Kurtz, Steven P.; and Kiley, Marion C. "Sex Work and Drug Use in a Subculture of Violence." *Crime & Delinquency*, January 2004, pp.43–59.

Turman, Kathryn M. *Understanding DNA Evidence: A Guide for Victim Service Providers*. Washington, DC: Office for Victims of Crime Bulletin, April 2001. (NCJ 185690)

Turner, Lisa M. "State Labs Face Increasing Backlog of DNA Analysis." *Community Links*, August 2004, pp.5–6.

Wade, Colleen. "FBI Laboratory Publications." *FBI Law Enforcement Bulletin*, December 2001, pp.10–11.

Weissberg, Michael W. "Recent Directions in Crime Scene Investigations." *The Law Enforcement Trainer*, March/April 2001, pp.43–48.

Wexler, Sanford. "Cold Cases Are Getting Hot." *Law Enforcement Technology*, June 2004a, pp.18–23.

Wexler, Sanford. "Remaking the Los Angeles Police Department." *Law Enforcement Technology*, October 2004b, pp.86–94.

Wexler, Sanford. "Working Undercover." *Law Enforcement Technology*, November 2004c, pp.86–93.

Williams, Gerald L. "Criminal Investigation." In *Local Government Police Management*, 4th ed. Edited by William A. Geller and Darrel W. Stephens. Washington, DC: International City/County Management Association, 2003, pp.169–205.

Wilson, Craig R. "Police and the Sexual Assault Examination." *FBI Law Enforcement Bulletin*, January 2002, pp.14–17.

"Without a Trace? Advances in Detecting Trace Evidence." *NIJ Journal*, July 2003, pp.2–9.

### CASES CITED

*California v. Simpson*, No. BA097211 (Cal. Super Ct. 1995)
*Flippo v. West Virginia*, 120 S.Ct. 7 (1999)
*Michigan v. Tyler*, 417 U.S. 433 (1974)
*Sherman v. United States*, 356 U.S. 369 (1958)
*Sorrells v. United States*, 287 U.S. 435 (1932)
*United States v. Russell*, 411 U.S. 423 (1973)

# CHAPTER 11

# Responding to Children and Juveniles: Our Nation's Future

**DO YOU KNOW . . .**

- Below what age most states consider a person a juvenile?
- What the primary difference between the adult criminal justice and the juvenile justice system is?
- What the child welfare model and the juvenile justice model are?
- What reforms have been proposed for the juvenile justice system?
- What categories of children are included in the juvenile justice system's jurisdiction?
- What predelinquent indicator often goes unnoticed?
- What special challenge is posed by a missing child report?
- What conduct is included in status offenses?
- What factors enter into the disposition of status offenders?
- How much discretion officers have with status offenders?
- What dispositions are available to officers when dealing with status offenders and what the most common disposition is?
- Who usually enters juveniles into the justice system?
- What rights *In re Gault* guarantees juveniles involved with the juvenile justice system?
- What two programs are widely used throughout the United States to combat the drug and gang problem?

**CAN YOU DEFINE?**

| | | |
|---|---|---|
| Amber Alert | GREAT | *parens patriae* |
| child welfare model | juvenile | raves |
| DARE | juvenile delinquents | status offenses |
| decriminalization | juvenile justice model | street justice |
| diversion | one-pot jurisdictional | thrownaways |
| 8% problem | approach | |

## Introduction

Each professional working with children must understand children, their behavioral patterns and psychological development, and their changing emotional needs as they mature, seek independence, and acquire sexual appetites," says Juvenile Judge Emeritus Lindsay G. Arthur (2004, p.xxii). Just who is a juvenile? This is determined by the legal age set in state statutes.

All states have specified an age below which individuals are subject to the juvenile justice system. This age varies from state to state and even within parts of the justice system itself in some states. For example, some state statutes specify that their juvenile courts have jurisdiction over all individuals under 18 years of age, but that the juvenile correctional facilities have jurisdiction over all those under the age of 21 who were committed to a correctional facility before their 18th birthday.

 A **juvenile** is a person not yet of legal age. In three-fourths of the states, juveniles are defined as youths under age 18.

According to *America's Children* (2004), in 2002 there were 72.9 million children under age 18 in the United States, making up 25 percent of the population. The ethnic diversity of our children continues to increase with 60 percent white, non-Hispanic; 18 percent Hispanic, 15 percent black, non-Hispanic; 4 percent Asian/Pacific Islander; and 1 percent Native American/Alaska Native. Twenty-eight percent of children live with only one parent.

According to the Uniform Crime Reports for 2003, nearly a third (30.9 percent) of those arrested were under 21 years of age (*Crime in the United States 2003*, p.268). The media, however, often presents a very distorted picture of the amount of crime juveniles are involved with. Dorfman and Schiraldi (2001, p.6) note: "Few studies examine portrayals of youth on the news. Those that do find that youth rarely appear in the news but when they do, it is connected to violence. . . . Relatively few youth are arrested each year for violent crimes, yet the message from the news is that this is a common occurrence. . . . An analysis of Hawaii's major dailies over 10 years showed a 30-fold increase in coverage of youth crime, despite declining rates of youth crime." They (p.7) also report on a study examining stories on youths in the Los Angeles, Sacramento and San Francisco papers: "Violence stories made up 25% of all youth coverage, when only three young people in 100 perpetrated or became victims of violence. . . . Nearly seven in 10 news stories (68%) on violence in California involved youth, whereas youth made up 14.1% of violence arrests in California that year."

The dual role of protecting both children and the public and investigating behavioral facts is a great challenge facing not only juvenile officers, but any police officer who interacts with juveniles in any way. The aspect of protection in dealings with juveniles has its roots in the common law of England.

This chapter begins with a brief overview of our juvenile justice system. This is followed by a discussion of law enforcement's response to children in need of help as well as other law enforcement/youth encounters. Next, status offenders and the law enforcement response to them as well as violent juvenile offenders are presented. This is followed by an explanation of legal procedures when dealing with youths. The chapter concludes with a discussion of programs aimed at youths and juvenile justice and community policing, including a problem-oriented approach.

## An Overview of Our Juvenile Justice System

In English common law, the king, through his chancellor, was a substitute parent for abandoned, neglected and dependent children under a doctrine called *parens patriae*. In the United States, each individual state replaced the king in this responsibility. The doctrine of **parens patriae** allows the state to assume guardianship of abandoned, neglected and "wayward" children.

Under this doctrine, the state is to act toward the children entrusted to its care as a loving parent would. This is very different from the punitive thrust behind the adult justice system, which removed youths from homes and placed them in lock-ups and jails. To return to the principle of *parens patriae,* the Illinois Juvenile Court Act of 1899 established the first juvenile court in the United States. This court's primary purpose was to "save" children from becoming criminals.

 The juvenile justice system, under *parens patriae,* is intended to help children, not to punish them as is the intent of the adult criminal justice system.

With a juvenile justice model emphasizing the welfare of the child and the *In re Gault* (1967) decision granting youths the due process guaranteed in the adult justice system, some critics feel the juvenile justice system has gone too far. Our juvenile judges are placed in an impossible situation when they are asked to diagnose the "problem" of some young offender, when often it is obvious the criminal youth does not *have* a problem—he or she *is* the problem.

## The Welfare Model versus the Justice Model

The concept of "helping" youths who are members of violent gangs and who engage in heinous crimes is very difficult for police officers and others within the juvenile justice system to accept. It has, in fact, led to a call for reform of the juvenile justice system, revising state statutes to make juvenile court operate under a justice model rather than a welfare model.

 In a **child welfare model,** the courts operate with the best interests of the youths as the main consideration. In a **juvenile justice model,** the courts hold youths responsible and accountable for their behavior.

The states vary in where they place their emphasis, with some stressing prevention and treatment, others punishment and still others a balanced approach, as shown in Table 11.1.

To adopt a justice model is not to rule out or diminish the importance of rehabilitative measures employed by juvenile courts. Disapproval of, and punishment for, the wrongful act is probably the single most important rehabilitative measure available to the court.

 Our current juvenile system is treatment or welfare focused. Some argue it should be replaced with a juvenile justice system whereby youths who commit serious crimes are held accountable and punished for those acts.

In many states, the justice model has replaced the welfare model. This is not the only aspect of the juvenile justice system being challenged. Another problematic area is the juvenile justice system's jurisdiction.

## The "One-Pot" Jurisdictional Approach

Our juvenile justice system's evolution, from the beginning, was designed to deal not only with "wayward" children—that is, **juvenile delinquents,** whose "crimes" could range from talking back to their parents to murder—but also with children who were abandoned, abused or neglected. Early laws, in effect, equated being poor with being criminal.

**Table 11.1**  Philosophical Goals in Juvenile Codes

Some juvenile codes emphasize prevention and treatment goals, some stress punishment and others seek a balanced approach.

**Philosophical Goals Stated in Juvenile Code Purpose Clauses, 1997**

| Prevention/ Diversion/Treatment | Punishment | Both Prevention/Diversion/ Treatment and Punishment | |
|---|---|---|---|
| Arizona* | Arkansas | Alabama | Nevada |
| Dist. of Columbia | Georgia | Alaska | New Hampshire |
| Kentucky | Hawaii | California | New Jersey |
| Massachusetts | Illinois | Colorado | New Mexico |
| North Carolina | Iowa | Connecticut | New York |
| Ohio | Louisiana | Delaware | North Dakota |
| South Carolina | Michigan | Florida | Oklahoma |
| Vermont | Missouri | Idaho | Oregon |
| West Virginia | Rhode Island | Indiana | Pennsylvania |
| | | Kansas | Tennessee |
| | | Maine | Texas |
| | | Maryland | Utah |
| | | Minnesota | Virginia |
| | | Mississippi | Washington |
| | | Montana | Wisconsin |
| | | Nebraska | Wyoming |

- Most States seek to protect the interests of the child, the family, the community, or some combination of the three.
- In 17 States, the purpose clause incorporates the language of the balanced and restorative justice philosophy, emphasizing offender accountability, public safety, and competency development.
- Purpose clauses also address court issues such as fairness, speedy trials, and even coordination of services. In nearly all States, the code also includes protections of the child's constitutional and statutory rights.

*Arizona's statutes and court rules did not contain a purpose clause: however, the issue is addressed in case law.

Adaptation of Torbet and Szymanski's *State Legislative Responses to Violent Juvenile Crime 1996–97 Update* [unpublished background research].

SOURCE: *Juvenile Justice: A Century of Change.* Washington, DC: National Report Series, Juvenile Justice Bulletin, December 1999, p.3.

 The juvenile justice system includes children who are neglected or abused, those who are status offenders and those who commit serious crimes, in what is called the **one-pot jurisdictional approach.**

Many contend that situations involving children who are neglected or abused should be dealt with in a civil court.

## Children in Need of Help

Not all youths police officers deal with are breaking the law. A great many need help or protection, including not only those who are poor, deprived or neglected, but also those who are missing, runaways or thrownaways.

*Charles Andrew Williams (center/front), the 15-year-old student at Santana High School who allegedly opened fire and killed two people and wounded 13, appears in the State of California Superior Court in El Cajon March 7, 2001, surrounded by his attorneys Randy Mize (R) and Ron Bobo (L).*

© Reuters/CORBIS

## Children Who Are Poor, Neglected or Abused

Recall from Chapter 7 that an estimated four or five million children are neglected or physically abused each year, with an additional two million vulnerable as runaways or missing children. In addition, the percentage of children under age 18 who were related to the householder and living in poverty increased from 15.8 percent in 2001 to 16.3 percent in 2002 (*America's Children* . . .).

"Millions of children are abused each year, with 1,100 dying in a single statistical reporting year in the United States alone" (Glasscock, 2001, p.6). When police are called to deal with a child neglect or abuse case, their primary responsibility is the immediate protection of the child. In many cases, the child is taken into protective custody and placed in a foster home, as discussed in Chapter 7.

## Children Who Are Missing, Runaways or Thrownaways

The National Incidence Studies of Missing, Abducted, Runaway, and Thrownaway Children in America (NISMART) has five categories of missing children: (1) runaways, (2) thrownaways, (3) nonfamily abducted children, (4) family abducted children and (5) lost, injured or otherwise missing children.

**Missing Children**   When police are called to deal with a missing-child report, their responsibility is less clear. Many departments lack specific procedures to deal with missing-children calls. In addition, significant variation exists in the initial response to such calls. Officers might obtain a physical description, description of clothing and jewelry, amount of money carried, possible destination and places frequented and why the person filing the report thinks the child is missing. A picture should also be obtained.

Many jurisdictions also have policies as to when the information must be entered into the National Crime Information Center (NCIC) system. In California, for example, the law requires that a child's name be entered into the NCIC system within four hours if the child is under the age of 12.

**Runaways**    Running away is leaving home without parental permission. Usually, however, police are more interested in locating and returning the runaway than in entering the youth into the juvenile justice system. Often no police investigation, social service inquiry or school inquiry is conducted to determine why these children left home, were truant because of this absence or why they continue to run away.

 Running away is a predelinquent indicator, but its importance often is not recognized by the parents, police, school, social agencies or the courts.

If police dispositions are to be effective, the family must recognize the early signs of maladjustment in children. Running away is the most visible indicator of a possible future victim (assaulted, murdered) or involvement in criminal activity to support individual needs (prostitution, pornography, burglary, theft, robbery).

**Missing Children: Runaway or Abducted?**    According to Domash (2002, p.53): "The vast majority (74 percent) of abducted children who are murdered are dead within three hours."

 A special challenge in cases where a child is reported missing is determining if the child has run away (a status offense) or has been abducted.

If it is determined that the child has been abducted, law enforcement officers should know that the most frequent type of abduction is parental abduction. Lord et al. (2001, p.3) report: "Research and investigative experience have shown that family abductions, motivated by domestic discord and custody disputes, overwhelmingly represent the most frequent type of child abduction."

Grasso et al. (2001, p.12) note: "Parental abduction can be a form of serious child maltreatment and is a crime in all 50 states and the District of Columbia." They (p.10) suggest that police departments: "Develop and implement written policies and procedures addressing the handling of parental abduction cases."

Johnston et al. (2001) identify factors that predict parental abduction. In some instances one parent, usually the mother, believes, correctly or incorrectly, that the other parent is physically or sexually abusing or neglecting the child. The risk of abduction increases if the parents making the allegations of child abuse were themselves victims of abuse or neglect as children. The risk also increases if the suspecting parent has a network of family members, friends, or an "underground network" of supporters who help the abducting parent obtain a new identity and find a new home.

One valuable resource in missing children cases is the National Center for Missing and Exploited Children (NCMEC). The NCMEC provides two services to law enforcement agencies investigating missing children cases. The first is an age progression program that creates photographs of a child that approximate what the child would look like at the present time. The greatest age difference they have created is from age 6 to age 31. The second service is called Project KidCare, provided in collaboration with Polaroid Corporation. This service consists of an educational packet and a high-quality photo in a form the NCMEC and law enforcement consider ideal.

Another valuable resource is the Amber (America's Missing Broadcast Emergency Response) Alert Program. **Amber Alert** plans are voluntary partnerships between law enforcement agencies and public broadcasters to notify the public when a child has been abducted. According to Rasmussen (2002, p.43): "The Amber Plan was created in the Dallas-Fort Worth region after the murder of Amber Hagerman, a nine-year-old girl who was abducted from her home. . . . Amber Alert is an early-warning network that law enforcement can use to quickly convey key information to the general public via television and radio soon after a child has been abducted." It is not intended to be a federal program.

Krainik (2002, p.84) describes three criteria that should be met before an alert is sent: "(1) law enforcement should confirm that a child 17 or under has been abducted; (2) law enforcement should believe that the circumstances surrounding the abduction indicate that the child is in danger of serious bodily harm or death; and (3) there is enough descriptive evidence about the child, abductor or vehicle to believe an immediate broadcast alert will help." According to Garrett (2004, p.70): "To date, there are 46 statewide plans, 60 regional plans and 31 local plans across the United States."

Yet another resource for law enforcement is a telephone notification system called A Child Is Missing (ACIM). Based in Fort Lauderdale, Florida, ACIM can mobilize an entire community to aid in the search for a missing person. As Spratley (2004, p.60) explains: "Once the officer at the scene verifies that the child is, in fact, missing, he immediately contacts ACIM using the toll-free number on the wallet card supplied by ACIM. The officer gives basic descriptive information to the ACIM technician—name, age, physical and clothing details, and address with zip code where the child was last seen. This is the information that ACIM will give to the public. A technician at ACIM's offices in Florida enters the information into a database and discusses with the officer the radius surrounding the child's last known location to determine what size geographic area should be alerted. . . . Using a unique telephone system, ACIM's recorded message can be delivered to a thousand phones in 60 seconds. . . . The message ACIM sends out not only describes the missing person, but also asks recipients to look out their windows or step outside and check the vicinity in case the missing person is nearby." According to Spratley: "Since its inception, ACIM has assisted in over 6,000 missing persons cases and has made more than 4.3 million telephone alert notifications."

**Thrownaways**   According to Hess and Drowns (2004, p.131), **thrownaways** face one of four situations: they were told to leave, were not allowed back after having left, ran away and no one tried to recover them, or were abandoned or deserted. Hammer et al. (2002) report that the number of runaway/thrownaway children is estimated at nearly 1.7 million. Runaway/thrownaway children may band together and join other youths who are just "hanging out." Such youths may also pose a problem for law enforcement if they become disorderly.

## Other Law Enforcement/Youth Encounters

Law enforcement officers are also expected to deal with disorderly youths who are just "hanging out," those who violate curfew laws and those who are truant.

## Disorderly Youths Who Are "Hanging Out"

"Hanging out" behavior is well known to most police officers. It is an important part of youths' development. To most adolescents, peers become all-important. Parents, teachers and other authority figures have less influence on adolescents' development and behavior. "Hanging out" is often an indication of lack of direction or purpose and may lead to delinquent behavior, which may be seen as offering excitement. If youths congregate in large numbers inside or outside business establishments, business people and their customers may complain to the police. Some communities have enacted antiloitering laws to discourage groups of youths "hanging out."

Sometimes the youths have been drinking and are belligerent and unreasonable, making the problem even more difficult. How police officers deal with such situations can make the difference between a peaceful resolution of the problem or a violent confrontation.

Scott (2001, pp.13–14) suggests three general approaches to addressing problems of disorderly youths in public places:

1. A *pure control* approach that views the youths as offenders whose conduct is to be controlled and prohibited coercively.
2. A *developmental* approach that views youths more neutrally and adopts methods that, in addition to controlling misconduct, seek to improve the youths' general welfare.
3. An *accommodation* approach that balances the youths' needs and desires against the complainants' needs and desires.

Scott (p.14) notes that the police response to youth disorder might use all three approaches by (1) establishing and enforcing rules of conduct for youths, (2) cre-

*June 2002: Teenagers hanging out at Barnes and Noble at the Bluesprings Mall.*

© Scott Houston/CORBIS

ating alternative legitimate places and activities for youths and (3) modifying public places to discourage disorderly behavior. Scott (p.24) contends: "Merely increasing uniformed police officers' presence around locations where youths gather is expensive, inefficient and usually ineffective." In some instances among youths who are behaving disorderly, a runaway will be discovered.

## Curfew Violators

When youths' behavior is such that the community wants them off the streets at night, a curfew may be established for the public good. The 1990s popularity of curfews as a response to youth crime is simply the most recent revival of a delinquency control measure that has waxed and waned across urban America several times during the last century.

Curfew ordinances must demonstrate a compelling state interest and be narrow in interpretation to meet constitutional standards. For example:

> The curfew applies to youths under age 17 and between 11 P.M. to 6 A.M., Sunday through Thursday, and midnight to 6 A.M. on Friday and Saturday. Exemptions include juveniles accompanied by an adult, traveling to or from work, responding to an emergency, married, or attending a supervised activity.

Curfews may face resistance from police officers, who see them as baby-sitting detail and an infringement on crime fighting efforts. Further, many agencies lack adequate personnel to enforce a curfew law. If an officer picks up a child and transports him or her to the station, waits for a parent and does the necessary paperwork, it could take several hours, taking the officer off the street. Curfew programs should include such strategies as:

- Creating a dedicated curfew center or using recreation centers and churches to house curfew violators.
- Staffing these centers with social service professionals and community volunteers.
- Offering referrals to social service providers and counseling classes for juvenile violators and their families.
- Establishing procedures—such as fines, counseling or community service—for repeat offenders.
- Developing recreation, employment, antidrug and antigang programs.
- Providing hot lines for follow-up services and intervention.

In some instances daytime curfews have been implemented to curb truancy.

## Truants

When children skip school habitually, they miss some very valuable lessons, not only academically but socially. They also tend to engage in delinquent or criminal activity while on these unsanctioned leaves. For these reasons truancy is a major problem in many school districts. Antitruancy ordinances enacted in some cities have met with varied success.

Santoro (2001, p.34) describes the Monrovia, California, anti-truancy ordinance as "one giant step toward keeping kids in school and out of trouble." Santoro (p.37) notes: "In Monrovia, city officials believe the daytime curfew/anti-truancy ordinance, amended in 1999 to provide exceptions to the regulations, has resulted in a 'win-win-win' situation. Parents are happy because their kids are in school instead of running the streets during school hours. School officials are pleased in part because improved attendance has increased the amount of average-daily-attendance (ADA) money the school district receives from the state. And the Monrovia police are delighted because there has been a significant reduction in daytime crime, which they see as a direct result of the curfew/truancy program.

Although law enforcement is responsible to investigate cases of child abuse/neglect and missing children, much more of their time is involved in responding to status offenders.

## Status Offenders

A special category of offenses has been established for juveniles, designating certain actions as illegal for any person under the age specified by the state.

 **Status offenses** are violations of the law applying only to those under legal age. They include curfew violations, drinking alcoholic beverages, incorrigibility, smoking cigarettes, running away from home and truancy.

Status offenses are considered illegal acts simply because of the age of the person committing them. *Sourcebook of Criminal Justice Statistics 2003* (Table 3.58) reports the following changes in high school students' use of cigarettes, alcohol and marijuana from 1993 to 2003:

Lifetime cigarette use down from 69.5 percent to 58.4 percent
Current cigarette use down from 30.5 percent to 21.9 percent
Frequent cigarette use down from 13.8 percent to 9.7 percent
Current use of alcohol down from 48.0 percent to 44.9 percent
Episodic heavy drinking down from 30.0 percent to 28.3 percent
Lifetime marijuana use up from 32.8 percent to 40.2 percent
Current marijuana use up from 17.7 percent to 22.4 percent

Frequently, it is status offenses that bring young people into contact with police officers, often in a very negative manner. Sometimes the consequences of negative labeling and perhaps confinement with more criminally inclined youths can result in status offenders becoming involved in crime. Several states and the American Bar Association have made a case for **decriminalization** of status offenses, that is, for not treating them as criminal offenses.

Whether states decriminalize status offenses or not, police officers should clearly differentiate between simple delinquent behavior (status offenses) and criminal delinquent behavior (crimes regardless of age) when they are dealing with juveniles. Underage drinking and use of drugs are especially serious status offenses because youths who are drinking or doing drugs may commit illegal acts while under their influence. White et al. (2002, p.131), for example, studied the illegal acts committed by adolescents under the influence of alcohol and drugs. They found: "Participants reported committing offenses against persons more often than general theft under the influence of alcohol or drugs. Aggressive acts were more often related to self-reported acute alcohol use than to marijuana use."

### *Underage Drinking*

Johnson (2004, p.2) notes: "Underage drinkers experience a wide range of alcohol-related health, social, criminal justice and academic problems." Johnson (p.5) points out several other problems related to underage drinking: drunken driving, speeding in residential areas, cruising, disorderly conduct in public places, assaults in and around bars, acquaintance rape, vandalism and noise complaints. However, as with curfews, some officers see underage drinking as a low priority because of the perceived legal obstacles in processing juveniles; unpleasant, tedious paperwork; special detention procedures required for minors; lack of juvenile detention facilities or centers already above capacity; lack of significant punishment for underage drinking; and personal disagreements regarding underage drinking laws, particularly as they apply to people age 18 to 20. Despite the objections officers may have, serious and valid reasons exist for making the enforcement of underage drinking laws a higher priority.

Scialdone (2001, p.61) describes a program to reduce underage drinking in Fontana, California: "DRY2K is a comprehensive program designed to help and encourage minors to remain alcohol-free in the new millennium." The program uses five distinct strategies to address the problem (pp.61-62):

■ Minor Decoy Program—uses underage minors to conduct compliance checks on liquor-licensed stores—targeting availability of alcohol to minors.
■ Shoulder Tap Program—places minors outside a store to ask customers to buy them beer—targets adults furnishing alcohol to minors.
■ Cops in Shops Program—places officers posing as clerks inside licensed locations to look for alcohol violations.
■ LEAD Program—offers free training for owners and employees of stores with liquor licenses.
■ Educational Program—45-minute multimedia interactive portion takes students on an emotional roller coaster entertaining and educating with cartoon characters.

Geier (2003) describes the Party Patrol as the approach to underage drinking enforcement used in Albuquerque, New Mexico: "In addition to such offenses by minors as possession and consumption of alcohol, the Party Patrol officers enforce ordinances designed to deal with noise violations and premise liability." Officers have a planned, coordinated approach to handling party calls involving a "wolf pack response." They respond as a group, surrounding the target home and blocking off potential exit routes to ensure that no one drives from the scene after drinking alcohol. They thoroughly investigate and check the sobriety of all those in attendance. In addition to acting on tips about parties with alcohol involved, the Party Patrol also periodically checks parks, arroyos, parking lots and other hangouts where alcohol may be consumed.

Geier (p.103) reports: "The results of this underage drinking enforcement program have been remarkable. In a three-month period, officers issued 190 traffic citations and 1,284 misdemeanor citations. The unit responded to 174 actual party calls and wrote over 380 police reports.

In conjunction with the Harvard study of binge drinking on college campuses, a survey at Louisiana State University (LSU) was taken regarding alcohol policies at LSU *(LSU Campus-Community Coalition for Change)*. Support or strong support was indicated for making alcohol rules clearer (94 percent), offering alcohol-free dorms (89 percent) and providing more alcohol-free recreational and cultural opportunities such as movies, dances, sports and lectures (86 percent).

The National Institute on Alcohol Abuse and Alcoholism (NIAAA) *(Alcohol Alert*, 2002, pp.2–3) studied various strategies for preventing alcohol-related problems on college campuses. It reports: "Strong evidence supports the effectiveness of the following strategies: (1) simultaneously addressing alcohol-related attitudes and behaviors (e.g., refuting false beliefs about alcohol's effects while teaching students how to cope with stress without resorting to alcohol); (2) using survey data to counter students' misperceptions about their fellow students' drinking practices and attitudes toward excessive drinking; and (3) increasing students' motivation to change their drinking habits.

The NIAAA also reports on strategies that have proven successful in populations similar to those found on college campuses: (1) increasing enforcement of minimum legal drinking age laws; (2) implementing, enforcing and publicizing other laws to reduce alcohol-impaired driving; (3) increasing the prices or taxes on alcoholic beverages; and (4) instituting policies and training for servers of alcoholic beverages to prevent sales to underage or intoxicated patrons. A closely related problem is that of rave parties.

## Rave Parties

Scott (2004, p.1) explains: "Rave parties—or, more simply, **raves**—are dance parties that feature fast-paced, repetitive electronic music and accompanying light shows." Winton and Hayasaki (2004) state: "Word of the parties usually starts on campuses, where slick, lurid handbills, often promising sex, illicit drugs and alcohol, are distributed. Raves are the focus of rave culture, a youth-oriented subculture that blends music, art and social ideals (e.g., peace, love, unity, respect, tolerance, happiness). Rave culture also entails the use of a range of licit and illicit drugs. Drug use is intended to enhance ravers' sensations and boost their energy, so they can dance for long periods." Scott (p.7) points out: "Ecstasy is the drug most closely associated with the rave scene. . . . Two of ecstasy's common side effects are jaw clenching and teeth grinding. Ecstasy users at raves often suck on baby pacifiers to cope with these effects."

According to Scott (p.2): "The principal rave-related concerns for police are:
- Drug overdoses and associated medical hazards.
- Drug trafficking and the potential for violence associated with it.
- Noise (from rave music, crowds and traffic).
- Driving under the influence.
- Traffic control and parking congestion."

Approaches law enforcement might use when faced with a rave problem include using nuisance abatement laws, prosecuting rave operators or property owners for drug-related offenses and educating ravers about the dangers of drug use and overexertion. Winton and Hayasaki report that the Los Angeles Police Department is considering confiscating the equipment used at rave parties. After four people were shot and police were forced to kill the shooter at a rave party attended by over 200 people, Chief Bratton was considering this new tactic: "The quickest way to shut down the parties is to seize the equipment. It costs hundreds of thousands of dollars. Without the equipment, there can't be a party" (Winton and Hayasaki).

According to Scott (pp.26–27), responses with limited effectiveness include banning all raves, providing anonymous drug-testing services to raves, deploying off-duty police officers at raves, having uniformed police officers conduct random patrols at raves, and conducting roadblocks and vehicle searches before and after raves.

# Police Dispositions of Status Offenses

Police dispositions range from taking no action to referring the children to social service agencies or to the juvenile court. For status offenses the police have many alternatives that are guided by the community, the local juvenile justice system and individual officer discretion.

 In the disposition of matters related to status offenders, how police resolve cases often depends on the officers' discretion, the specific incident and the backup available.

Whether the police actually arrest a juvenile usually depends on several factors, the most important being the seriousness of the offense. Other factors affecting the decision include character, age, gender, race, prior record, family situation and the youth's attitude.

The decision may also be influenced by public opinion, the media, available referral agencies and the officer's experience. Officers' actions usually reflect community interests. For example, conflict may occur between the public's demand for order and a group of young people wanting to "hang out." How police respond to such hanging out is influenced by the officer's attitude and the standards of the neighborhood or community, rather than rules of the state. Each neighborhood or community and the officer's own feelings dictate how the police perform in such matters.

Sometimes police may "roust" and "hassle" youths who engage in undesirable social conduct, but they probably will not report the incident; in this case, street justice is the police disposition. **Street justice** occurs when police decide to deal with a status offense in their own way—usually by ignoring it.

## *Police Discretion and the Initial Contact*

Between 80 and 90 percent of youths commit some offense for which they could be arrested, yet only about 3 percent of them are. This is in large part because they do not get caught. Further, those who are caught have usually engaged in some minor status offense that can, in many instances, be better handled by counseling and releasing. Although the "counsel and dismiss" alternative may be criticized as being "soft" on juveniles, this approach is often all that is needed to turn a youth around.

 Police officers have considerable discretionary power when dealing with juveniles.

Law enforcement officers have a range of alternatives to take:
- Release the child, with or without a warning, but without making an official record or taking further action.
- Release the child, but write up a brief contact or field report to juvenile authorities, describing the contact.
- Release the child, but file a more formal report referring the matter to a juvenile bureau or an intake unit, for possible action.
- Turn the youth over to juvenile authorities immediately.
- Refer the case directly to the court, through the district or county attorney.

 Police officers who deal with juveniles may warn them, with or without an official report; turn them over to their parents, with or without an official report; refer them to a social agency; or refer them to juvenile court.

In some instances youths engaging in delinquent acts are simply counseled. In other instances they are returned to their families, who are expected to deal with their child's deviant behavior. Sometimes they are referred to social services agencies for help. And sometimes they are charged and processed by the juvenile justice system.

 The most common procedure is to release the child, with or without a warning, but without making an official record or taking further action.

If police officers refer youths to a community agency, this is known as **diversion.** Whether a youth is diverted will depend on department policy, the availability of appropriate programs and police awareness of community resources. Typical police referrals are to youth service bureaus, special school programs, boys clubs, the YMCA, community mental health agencies and drug programs.

 Of all youth referrals to court, the great majority are from law enforcement.

Remaining referrals to court come from parents, relatives, schools, probation officers, other courts, social services and other services. The options open to police officers when it comes to serious, violent juvenile offenders are much more limited.

## Violent Offenders

A report by the surgeon general ("Surgeon General Warns . . .," 2001, p.4) states: "For every youth arrested in any given year in the late 1990s, at least 10 were engaged in some form of violent behavior that could have seriously injured or killed another person. . . . Confidential surveys find that 13 to 15 percent of high school seniors report having committed an act of violence in recent years. The best available evidence from multiple sources indicates that youth violence is an ongoing national problem, albeit one that is largely hidden from public view."

One problem behavior associated with youth violence is animal abuse. Ascione (2001, p.1) suggests that the relationship between cruelty to animals and serious violent behavior, especially among youthful offenders, is strong. In a study of nine school shootings in the United States, 5 of the 11 perpetrators, or 45 percent, had histories of animal abuse.

Other factors are also associated with serious delinquent offending. Baron et al. (2001) studied 125 homeless male youths and found that these youths came to the street from backgrounds where violence was used as discipline, teaching them that violence is "an appropriate method for gaining compliance and settling disputes." Brutality in the home leads to departure for the streets and with it homelessness and poverty as well as a predisposition to anger. These youths seek each other out and spend significant time together, reinforcing each other's violent behavior as socially accepted. They (p.781) conclude: "Life on the street provides the opportunity to engage in violence, and it appears that the successful use of violence as a conflict management strategy makes youths more likely to adopt values that favor violence."

Cottle et al. (2001) conducted research to identify risk factors for juvenile recidivism. The most powerful predictors of recidivism were demographic factors—males and juveniles of low socioeconomic status were at higher risk—and offense history—those with earlier contact with the law, greater numbers of prior arrests/commitments and more serious prior crimes were also at higher risk.

Other family and social variables were also found to be predictive of recidivism. Juveniles who had been physically or sexually abused, were raised in a single-parent family, had a higher number of out-of-home placements or had experienced significant family problems were at higher risk of recidivism. Juveniles who did not use their leisure time effectively and those with delinquent peers were also at higher risk (recall the discussion of "hanging out"). A history of being in special education classes or having lower standardized achievement test scores, lower full scale IQ scores and lower verbal IQ scores were also predictive of reoffending. Race was not a significant predictor.

The classic long-term studies of delinquent youths conducted by Marvin E. Wolfgang found that 6 to 8 percent of male juveniles accounted for over 60 percent of serious offenses committed by juveniles and that by the third arrest, a juvenile delinquent was virtually guaranteed to continue in a life of crime.

Similar conclusions are reported in *The 8% Solution* (2001). The Orange County (California) Probation Department tracked a small group of first-time offenders for three years and found that a small percentage (8 percent) of the juveniles were arrested repeatedly (a minimum of four times within a three-year period) and were responsible for 55 percent of repeat cases. According to the report (p.1):

> The characteristics of this group of repeat offenders (referred to as "the **8% problem**") were dramatically different from those who were arrested only once. These differences did not develop after exposure to the juvenile justice system, as some might expect; they were evident at first arrest and referral to juvenile court, and they worsened if nothing was done to alleviate the youth's problems. Unfortunately, in wanting to "give a break" to first-time offenders, the juvenile justice system often pays scant attention to those at greatest risk of becoming chronic offenders until they have established a record of repeated serious offending [emphasis added].
>
> The good news is that most of the small group of potentially serious, chronic offenders can be identified reliably at first contact with the juvenile justice system. The 8% offenders enter the system with a complex set of problems or risk factors, which the study identified as (1) involvement in crime at an early age and (2) a multiproblem profile including significant family problems (abuse, neglect, criminal family members, and/or a lack of parental supervision and control), problems at school (truancy, failing more than one course or a recent suspension or expulsion), drug and alcohol abuse, and behaviors such as gang involvement, running away and stealing.

## Legal Procedures When Dealing with Youths

 *In re Gault* (1967) established that juveniles have the right to counsel, the right to be notified of the charges against them, the right to confront and examine witnesses and the privilege against self-incrimination.

These rights must be respected as police officers interact with children and youths.

## Custody and Detention

Police can take children into custody by court order if they have reasonable grounds to believe that the child is suffering from illness or injury or is in immediate danger from his surroundings or believe the child has run away or because he has no parent, guardian, custodian or other person able to supervise and care for him and return him to the court when required.

A landmark Supreme Court case affecting law enforcement is *Schall v. Martin* (1984), which upheld the state's right to place juveniles in preventive detention. Writing for the majority, Associate Justice Rehnquist cited two reasons for upholding the New York statute for preventive detention. The first was that of "protecting a juvenile from the consequences of his criminal activity." The second was protecting the public. In other words, preventive detention fulfills the legitimate state interest of protecting society and juveniles by temporarily detaining those who might be dangerous to society or to themselves.

After police have taken a juvenile into custody, they should either release the juvenile to their parent or guardian, take them before a judge, take them to a detention home or shelter or take them to a medical facility if needed. The parent or guardian and the court are to be notified in writing with all reasonable speed.

Delinquents are *not* to be put into a jail or other adult detention facility unless no other option is available. They are put into a room separate from the adults when their detention in an adult facility is necessary for their own safety or that of the public.

Being taken into custody and locked up can be a turning point for many youths. Is this young girl headed for a lifetime of crime, or can she be rehabilitated?

*An Implementation Guide for Juvenile Holdover Programs* (2001, p.1) explains: "A juvenile holdover program (JHP) is both an old and a new concept. The old concept—the creativity of law enforcement officers, social workers and probation officers has always been called upon to decide what to do with a juvenile in need of a safe, and perhaps secure, place to wait until a parent can be located or while the system mobilizes to respond to the needs of a child or youth. . . . The new concept—communities have developed a variety of different responses to meet the need for a short-term, temporary holding program for juveniles that can be called upon when the need arises." Among the key elements of a JHP are that it is integrated into a network of services for youths, is a short-term alternative, is easily accessible and has a trained staff. It should also be able to respond to a youth's immediate needs, to provide comfortable facilities with minimum services for an overnight stay and can respond to and de-escalate the immediate situation if necessary. It should have screening and assessment capacity and referral expertise and be able to coordinate postrelease services to the youth and family.

## Police Records and Files

Law enforcement records and files concerning a child should be kept separate from those of adults. Unless a charge of delinquency is transferred for criminal prosecution, the interest of national security requires, or the court otherwise orders in the interest of the child, the records and files should not be open to public inspection or their contents disclosed to the public. Juvenile records may be sealed in these cases:

- Two years have elapsed since the final discharge of the person.
- Since the final discharge the juvenile has not been convicted of a felony, or of a misdemeanor involving moral turpitude, or adjudicated a delinquent or unruly child, and no proceeding is pending seeking conviction or adjudication.
- The juvenile has been rehabilitated.

## Fingerprinting and Photographing Children

In most jurisdictions, law enforcement officers can take fingerprints of children 14 years and older involved in the crimes of murder, nonnegligent manslaughter, forcible rape, robbery, aggravated assault, burglary, housebreaking, purse snatching and automobile theft. However, children's fingerprint files usually must be kept separate from adult files. The fingerprints are to be removed from the file and destroyed if the youth is adjudicated not delinquent or if the youth reaches age 21 and has not committed a criminal offense after becoming 16.

If police officers find latent fingerprints during a criminal investigation and have probable cause to believe a particular youth committed the crime, they may fingerprint the youth, regardless of the youth's age. If the comparison is negative, the youth's fingerprint card should be destroyed immediately.

## Law Enforcement Programs Aimed at Youths

It should be stressed that the great majority of children and youths are *not* in trouble with the law. Programs should be provided that foster positive relations between such individuals and the juvenile justice community. Law enforcement programs aimed at youths take varied approaches. Some approach delinquency

Myrleen Ferguson Cate, PhotoEdit

*A community service officer is fingerprinting a youngster. The fingerprints are to be removed from the file and destroyed if the youth is adjudicated not delinquent or if the youth reaches age 21 and has not committed a criminal offense after becoming 16.*

with aggressive enforcement and sometimes referrals. Some provide volunteer opportunities through Explorer posts described shortly. Some are educational school-based programs aimed at preventing drug abuse and gang involvement, two major problems discussed in Chapter 12. Some are aimed at specific problems. And some are aimed at youths who have gotten into trouble.

## Aggressive Enforcement

The North Miami Beach Police Department took aim at another status offense: truancy. Its PET Project, Police Eliminating Truancy, is intended to tackle the underlying causes of truancy and, at the same time, reduce the criminal behavior that resulted when juveniles spent their day on the street instead of in school. About 20 percent of the students admitted to committing crimes while truant.

Crime analysis identifies "hot spots" where a high number of Part I Index crimes took place. The PET Project assigns two officers to patrol in those hot spots during regular school hours. Truants are taken by officers to the Truancy Evaluation Center (TEC) located in an off-campus classroom. TEC shares space with the department's Alternate to Suspension Program (ASP), whose intensive learning environment and disciplined approach helps many students rededicate themselves to school. A counselor evaluates the truants and then one of three things usually happens. If students have no history of truancy, PET officers take them back to school. Suspended students take part in ASP. Students who seem to be making truancy a habit meet with their parents and the counselor to discuss possible solutions to the problem.

Another positive aspect of aggressive enforcement programs is that youths who are not seriously delinquent can be referred to other programs for help in staying out of trouble in the future.

### Referrals

Sanchez (2004, p.51) stresses: "Law enforcement, social services agencies, community-based organizations and schools all can play a role in helping a young person to develop and keep from entering the juvenile justice system. Prevention and intervention programs can address risk factors for troubled youths or provide services that give young people choices other than criminal activity." Although each community will have different resources available, ideally they will have a youth services center that is knowledgeable of the programs available to help children and youths. Sanchez (p.55) describes a continuum of juvenile justice programs in Figure 11.1. Ideally prevention programs and early intervention programs can lessen the need for judicial programs, allowing those programs to concentrate on the more serious problem offenders.

Sanchez also describes the process for making referrals to the appropriate program in Figure 11.2. Note that the referral process usually begins with a police officer encountering an at-risk youth.

### Explorer Posts

According to Bamberger (2003, p.116): "In a society where violence, drugs and crime are a way of life for many kids, there is a flip side where others are starting to fight back. One program that helps youths fight back is the Police Explorer Program. This program is exactly as the name says: it is an opportunity for youths

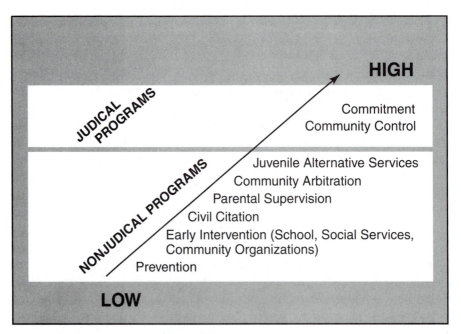

**Figure 11.1** Juvenile Justice Continuum of Programs.

SOURCE: Tom Sanchez. "Youth Referral System." *The Police Chief,* September 2004, p.55. Reprinted by permission.

to explore police work." Explorer posts are extensions of the Boy Scouts of America and allow young men and women a chance to volunteer their services to their local police department. The minimum age for most programs is 15. Cadets usually undergo three to six months of intensive training covering such areas as first aid, traffic control, firearms safety, fingerprinting, community relations and the like. After thorough training they work with sworn officers in numerous capacities.

The Multnomah County (Oregon) Sheriff's Office sponsors two Explorer posts, intended to allow youths to explore certain career fields. One post is dedicated to the usual explorer activities; the second is dedicated to search and rescue. As Boertien (2001, p.130) contends: "The youths involved in these Explorer programs benefit greatly from the training and experience they receive, the community benefits from the service provided, and the agency benefits from the positive publicity and the dedicated work of the volunteers."

The Portsmouth (New Hampshire) Police Department created a special project for their Explorers, helping with cutting down speeders and other traffic

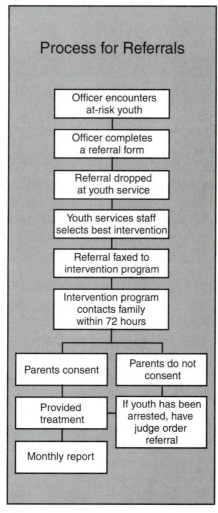

**Figure 11.2**    Process for Referrals

SOURCE: Tom Sanchez. "Youth Referral System." *The Police Chief*, September 2004, p.55. Reprinted by permission.

problems: Cadets Assisting Neighborhoods to Identify Driving Violations (CAN ID). As Giordano (2001, p.148) explains: "After a brief training in traffic monitoring practices, including the use of handheld digital radar detectors, the students or cadets who sign up for CAN ID take to the streets in teams of two to watch for moving violations, which range from 'people who blow through stop signs' to those who ignore pedestrians in crosswalks." One cadet calls out the speed or violation, license number and make of the car, and the other cadet records the information in a log book. They take the logs back to the department and with the help of an officer run the license to identify the drivers. These drivers are sent warning letters that future violations will probably result in a ticket.

The New Britain (Connecticut) Police Department came up with a solution to what to do with the recovered bicycles piling up. Many needed repair, so they decided to set up a bike shop, teach volunteers how to repair the recovered bikes and then distribute them to various organizations. One of the first recipients was the Police Explorers Post. Says Sencio (2001, p.8): "The Explorers now are on routine bike patrol, helping police keep a watch on the city."

## *Educational Programs*

 Two educational programs widely used across the country to combat drugs and gangs are DARE (Drug Abuse Resistance Education) and GREAT (Gang Resistance Education and Training)

Probably the best-known school-based educational program is **DARE,** the Drug Abuse Resistance Education program. According to Schennum (2001, p.103): "Today DARE is taught in more than 80% of all U.S. school districts, benefiting over 26 million students. DARE is an excellent program to assist parents and society as a whole in the fight against the influences of drugs, alcohol and tobacco on children and young adults."

However, DARE came under fire in the late 1990s: "More than a decade of research studies have pointed to the program's failure to live up to supporters' claims. Federal education officials, who distribute about $500 million in drug prevention grants each year, said last year that they would no longer allow schools to spend money from the Office of Safe and Drug Free Schools on DARE because it did not consider the program to be scientifically proven ("Truth, DARE & Consequences," 2001, p.1).

A study by the University of Illinois tracked 1,800 students over six years and found that by the end of high school any impact of the program had worn off. According to Brown (2001, p.76): "DARE has been the subject of 30 other studies over the past several years and all of them have arrived at the same conclusion—any effect that the program has to deterring drug use disappears by the time students are seniors in high school." As noted by Zernike (2001, p.A16): "DARE organizers have long dismissed criticism of the program's approach as flawed or the work of groups that favor decriminalization of drug use. But the body of research had grown to the point that the organization could no longer ignore it." In response, the curriculum was revised and will be tested in 80 high schools and 176 middle schools across the nation ("Drug Abuse Resistance Education . . .," 2001, p.2). One key change in the new version is that police officers are used more as "facilitators" and less as "instructors."

Another school-based education program is **GREAT,** the Gang Resistance Education and Training program. This is a proactive approach to deter violence before it begins. The program builds a foundation focused on teaching children the life skills needed to avoid violence and gang membership. Research on the benefits of this program conducted by Esbensen et al. (2001) found that the program was beneficial: "Beneficial program effects emerged gradually over time so that there was, on average, more pro-social change in the attitudes of GREAT students than the non-GREAT students four years following program exposure."

A five-year study by the National Institute of Justice ("NIJ: G.R.E.A.T. Improves Adolescents' Attitudes . . .," 2004, p.15) also found the program to have modest positive effects on youths. A small percent had lower levels of victimization, more negative attitudes towards gangs, more positive attitudes towards police, had less involvement in risk-seeking behaviors and were involved in more prosocial activities with their peers. The study also found, however, that the G.R.E.A.T. program did not reduce gang membership.

## Camps

Many police departments sponsor camps for youths, some for at-risk youths and some for youths who have gotten into trouble with the law.

Respect and Responsibility (R&R) is a camp sponsored by the Winnooski (Vermont) Police Department and the National Guard. Its emphasis is on building self-esteem and enhancing young people's ability to work as a team. Activities at the one-week camp include land navigation, wilderness survival, first aid and CPR certification and a rope course. As noted by Fuller (2001, p.10): "All campers have gone the distance. No dropouts. Campers are admitted regardless of family background or individual risk factors."

Camp Turning Point, as the name implies, is for first-time juvenile offenders to have a second chance to turn around their situations. Leverette-Sanderlin (2001, p.123) explains: "All participants must be enrolled in school (Adult Education or a GED program), may be required to attend group or individual counseling with at least 20 hours of community service, and attend Camp Turning Point or Camp Turn Around. Restitution must be paid in full." Designed as an intervention for young men ages 13 to 16, the camp has the usual activities of swimming, fishing and horseback riding, but it also teaches campers about working as a team. By the time Camp Turning Point entered its third year, the nonrepeater success rate remained close to 90 percent.

## Other Programs

Several other programs whose orientations are less educational also have been instituted by police departments to help deal with problem youths. One of the most common programs is a school resource officer (SRO) program, described in Chapter 7. Other well-known programs found throughout the country are the Officer Friendly program and the McGruff police dog ("Take a bite out of crime") program. The McGruff program not only focuses on crime prevention and safety, but also helps youths contribute positively to the community.

## The Juvenile Justice System and Community Policing

Dorsey (2004, p.71) describes Memphis, Tennessee's, Juvenile Violence Abatement Project (JVAP) using prevention, intervention and law enforcement: "The project takes advantage of the agency's community policing resources and enlists the help of parents, schools and community organizations of all types to reach and teach local youth. . . . The prevention component addresses youth violence by attempting to repress delinquency before youths have an opportunity to commit illegal acts or advance to more serious offenses. The program addresses known risk factors for crime, violence and substance abuse."

Table 11.2 describes risk factors found in the community, the family, the school and the individual and the association of the risk factors with behavior problems. Among the problems associated with the community that the community might address are the availability of drugs and guns.

Robertson et al. (2001, p.265) state: "Recent empirical research indicates that for juvenile offenders various community-based intervention techniques result in significantly greater positive effects when compared to more traditional approaches [probation and supervision]. . . . The results indicate that relative to those on probation participants in the CB program imposed significantly fewer costs on the justice system during the investigative period . . . a net savings of $1,435 in justice system expenditures per youth offender served for the sample period. Such findings would also support the use of problem-oriented policing to address problems involving youths."

## Juvenile Justice and Problem-Oriented Policing

A finalist in the Excellence in Problem-Oriented Policing Awards in 2003 was the "Underage Drinking: More than a Minor Issue" project of the Plano Police Department.

### Scanning

Officer Richard L. Glenn had noticed that an increasing number of calls for service in his area involved minors in possession of and/or consuming alcohol. These calls included juvenile problems, noise, party disturbances and others. The minors involved in the incidents advised Glenn that they could easily walk into a beer store in Plano and purchase alcohol.

### Analysis

Officer Glenn observed that this problem involved not only the subjects that he caught in violation, but also the store clerks who sold the alcohol, the police department, and the residents of the City of Plano. The harm this caused to the residents was demonstrated in police calls for service involving juvenile problems, party disturbances, noise complaints and alcohol-related traffic accidents. His goal was to reduce the number of stores in Plano selling alcohol to minors.

**Table 11.2**  Risk Factors and Their Association with Behavior Problems in Adolescents

| Risk Factors | Adolescent Problem Behaviors | | | | |
| --- | --- | --- | --- | --- | --- |
| | Substance Abuse | Delinquency | Teen Pregnancy | School Drop-Out | Violence |
| **Community** | | | | | |
| Availability of drugs | ✓ | | | | |
| Availability of firearms | | ✓ | | | ✓ |
| Community laws and norms favorable toward drug use, firearms, and crime | ✓ | ✓ | | | ✓ |
| Media portrayals of violence | | | | | ✓ |
| Transitions and mobility | ✓ | ✓ | | ✓ | |
| Low neighborhood attachment and community disorganization | ✓ | ✓ | | | ✓ |
| Extreme economic deprivation | ✓ | ✓ | ✓ | ✓ | ✓ |
| **Family** | | | | | |
| Family history of the problem behavior | ✓ | ✓ | ✓ | ✓ | |
| Family management problems | ✓ | ✓ | ✓ | ✓ | ✓ |
| Family conflict | ✓ | ✓ | ✓ | ✓ | ✓ |
| Favorable parental attitudes and involvement in the problem behavior | ✓ | ✓ | | | ✓ |
| **School** | | | | | |
| Early and persistent antisocial behavior | ✓ | ✓ | ✓ | ✓ | ✓ |
| Academic failure beginning in elementary school | ✓ | ✓ | ✓ | ✓ | ✓ |
| Lack of commitment to school | ✓ | ✓ | ✓ | | ✓ |
| **Individual-Peer** | | | | | |
| Alienation and rebelliousness | ✓ | ✓ | | ✓ | |
| Friends who engage in a problem behavior | ✓ | ✓ | ✓ | ✓ | ✓ |
| Favorable attitudes toward the problem behavior | ✓ | ✓ | ✓ | ✓ | |
| Early initiation of the problem behavior | ✓ | ✓ | ✓ | ✓ | ✓ |
| Constitutional factors | ✓ | ✓ | | | ✓ |

SOURCE: J. David Hawkins. "Controlling Crime Before It Happens: Risk-Focused Prevention." *National Institute of Justice Journal,* August 1995, p.12. Reprinted by permission.

## Response

Officer Glenn implemented a plan for conducting special enforcement details to increase enforcement, obtain specific data on which stores were selling alcohol to minors and to educate violators. He utilized confidential informants under the age of 18 to purchase alcohol under very controlled circumstances. Finding that the problem was pervasive throughout the City of Plano, he identified four main reasons that store clerks sell alcohol to minors. He then utilized this information to educate the community and violators about this problem.

## *Assessment*

Officer Glenn has continued to conduct special enforcement details and the number of stores selling alcohol to minors in Plano has significantly decreased during the time that he has been working on this project.

## *Judge's Commentary*

Several features of Plano's underage drinking project deserve note. The city is surrounded by dry jurisdictions, making its 159 package stores magnets for an entire region. The problem of underage drinking was particularly significant in Plano because the city prides itself on its quality of life, especially for children. After a beat officer sensed an increasing problem of minors in possession of and consuming alcohol, he was stymied in his attempt to gather conclusive data about the problem. This turned out to be one of those problems that fell through the police department's data system's cracks. Specific cases of underage possession were often handled informally, resulting in no reports and no data. Underage drinking was not a specific code on police reports, so he had no way of determining what proportion of loud parties, noise complaints, juvenile problems, or traffic accidents involved minors in possession. The officer persevered, however, eventually creating his own database to document the scope and seriousness of the problem.

After getting cleared to address the problem citywide, the officer implemented a systematic enforcement campaign of multiple attempted underage buys at every package store in Plano. This served both as a response to the problem and as a continuation of problem analysis. Offending clerks and their managers were interviewed to determine why underage purchases could be made in their stores. This line of inquiry yielded valuable information that led to additional responses of a nonenforcement nature. The data issues that limited initial problem analysis also made it difficult to demonstrate that this project reduced the impact of underage drinking on noise, disorder or traffic accidents in Plano. However, the officer's careful and systematic efforts did clearly affect the behavior of store clerks and managers, making it harder for minors to purchase alcoholic beverages in the city.

### SUMMARY

The doctrine of *parens patriae* allows the state to assume guardianship of abandoned, neglected and "wayward" children. The juvenile justice system, under *parens patriae*, is intended to help children, not to punish them as intended by the adult system.

In a child welfare model, the courts operate with the best interests of the youth as the main consideration. In a juvenile justice model, the courts hold youths responsible and accountable for their behavior. Our current juvenile system is treatment or welfare focused. Some argue it should be replaced with a juvenile justice system whereby youths who commit serious crimes are held accountable and punished for those acts. The juvenile justice system is responsible for children who are neglected or abused, those who are status offenders and those who commit serious crimes, in what is called the "one-pot" jurisdictional approach.

Running away is a predelinquent indicator, but its importance often is not recognized by the parents, police, school, social agencies or the courts. A special challenge in cases where a child is reported missing is determining if the child has run away (a status offense) or been abducted.

Some youths get into trouble with the law for minor status offenses. Status offenses are violations of the law applying only to those under legal age. They include curfew violations, drinking alcoholic beverages, incorrigibility, smoking cigarettes, running away from home and truancy. In the disposition of cases related to status offenders, how police resolve matters often depends on the officers' discretion, the specific incident and the backup available. Police officers have considerable discretionary power when dealing with juveniles.

Police officers who deal with juveniles may warn them, with or without an official report; turn them over to their parents, with or without an official report; refer them to a social agency; or refer them to juvenile court. The most common procedure is to release the child, with or without a warning, but without making an official record or taking further action. Of all youth referrals to court, 84 percent are from law enforcement.

*In re Gault* (1967) established that juveniles have the right to counsel, the right to be notified of the charges against them, the right to confront and examine witnesses and the privilege against self-incrimination. Two educational programs widely used across the country to combat drugs and gangs are DARE (Drug Abuse Resistance Education) and GREAT (Gang Resistance Education and Training).

### APPLICATION

As an officer with the Mytown Juvenile Bureau, you have noted some inconsistent handling of juvenile offenders that has caused the juvenile court authorities to worry about youngsters not receiving due process when taken into police custody. You call together a group, including citizens and youths, to rectify the situation by making a statement of need for juveniles and the ultimate purpose in their apprehension. Based on that group discussion, establish a policy to standardize procedures for handling juveniles.

### INSTRUCTIONS

Use the form in the Appendix to formulate a policy that provides guidelines to police officers in handling juveniles. Include in the policy those guidelines necessary for processing juveniles taken into custody for various reasons. The policy and procedure should include searching, questioning and transporting juveniles, as well as public release of information. Necessary reports should be highlighted and dispositions clearly specified. A visit to the local police department or sheriff's office may help determine what to include in the policy and procedure.

### AN EXERCISE IN CRITICAL THINKING

D.F.B.'s parents and two younger siblings were killed with an axe on February 18. D.F.B., age 16, was a sophomore in high school and had discussed killing his family with friends. D.F.B. and several friends also had prepared a "hit list" of others to be terminated. Several friends testified, however, that this list was merely a joke.

D.F.B. had no history of delinquent behavior. He had, however, been depressed for several years. D.F.B. expressed fear of his father, but masked the depression with jokes and quick wit at school. Some school reports indicate D.F.B. was depressed when his brother left home (or was ousted) in the fall. Two good friends moved away in the same year. D.F.B. twice attempted suicide, once in June and again in September.

There were 22 wounds on D.F.B.'s father's body, 19 on his mother's body, 8 on his sister's body and 9 on his brother's body.

After his family was killed (sometime around 3:00 A.M. on February 18), D.F.B. obtained cash and purchased groceries. He cut and dyed his hair and then slept in a culvert. He was arrested the following day at the post office while talking on the telephone with a friend. D.F.B. was placed in the custody of the county sheriff.

1. Should D.F.B. be referred for adult prosecution?
   a. Yes, for there is probable cause to believe D.F.B. committed first-degree murder, and there is evidence that D.F.B. is not amenable to treatment.
   b. No, because D.F.B. is only 16 years old.
   c. No, because D.F.B. has no history of prior delinquent acts.
   d. No, because although these acts were criminal, they were actions that came from extreme emotional disturbance during puberty when a body is not matured, and such acts will not be repeated as D.F.B. has now run out of family (which was the singular focus of his anger).
   e. No, because police should always use the least restrictive alternative for dealing with any type of juvenile problem.

2. If the county sheriff had known of D.F.B.'s disturbed emotional state of mind prior to the murders, what action might the police have taken?

a. Initiate a treatment program (patterned along the lines of informal probation).

b. Attempt a deterrence program (athletic, recreational and club activities).

c. Make a voluntary referral to appropriate community agencies.

d. Establish a counseling service to give one-on-one talks to youths.

e. Only deal with mandatory referral to mental or public health agencies under statutory authorization to make such referrals (e.g., to detoxification programs).

3. Because of the vulnerability of juveniles, greater safeguards are needed, such as these:

a. Greater intrusions than are normally allowed under the Fourth Amendment for adults should be allowed to protect juveniles from damaging home environments.

b. Stronger mandates must be allowed for juvenile treatment programs.

c. Juveniles should not be permitted to waive constitutional rights on their own.

d. More restrictive means should be allowed to protect juveniles from themselves (in the instance of suicide).

e. Juveniles should receive a set of safeguards totally different from those of adults in preliminary investigations (e.g., stop and frisk), questioning, search and seizure and the arrest process.

## DISCUSSION QUESTIONS

1. What are the advantages and disadvantages of a separate system of justice for juveniles?

2. A major principle of English common law is *parens patriae*. Is this philosophy viable in today's society?

3. Should the police be responsible for status offenses, or should some other agency such as the welfare department be given the options of dealing with youths who commit these offenses?

4. Would our society be better off if we treated juveniles like adults in the justice system? Explain. Should a child's criminal record follow him or her into adulthood?

5. Is the status offender similar to or different from the delinquent? Do status offenders "get worse"; that is, do their offenses escalate into more serious offenses?

6. Should juvenile offenders be subjected to capital punishment?

7. Does your department have a juvenile division? If so, how many officers are involved?

## INFOTRAC COLLEGE EDITION ASSIGNMENTS

- Use InfoTrac College Edition to help answer the Discussion Questions as appropriate.

- Use InfoTrac College Edition to find the article "The Common Thread: Diversion in Juvenile Justice" by Franklin E. Zimring. Outline the development of the juvenile court. Be prepared to share your outline with the class.

- Use InfoTrac College Edition to find the article "Arrest My Kid" by Anne-Marie Cusac. After reading the article do you agree that arrest may be the only means for parents to get proper mental health care for their children? In a brief report, state your position, including information from the article to support your position, and be prepared to discuss your report with the class.

- Use InfoTrac College Edition to read and outline one of the following articles to share with the class:

  - "Violent Crimes among Juveniles" by William B. Berger and Susan Wind

  - "The Advent of the Computer Delinquent" by Arthur L. Bowker

  - "Violent Crimes among Juveniles: Behavioral Aspects" by William Andrew Corbitt

  - "Operation Linebacker: Using Status Offenders to Reduce Crime in Communities" by Robert J. Girot

  - "Protecting Children on the Electronic Frontier: A Law Enforcement Challenge" by Matt Parsons

  - "Runaway or Abduction? Assessment Tools for the First Responder" by Andre B. Simons and Jeannine Willie

## INTERNET ASSIGNMENTS

Select two assignments to complete. For each, be prepared to discuss your findings or conclusions with the class.

- Find and outline the article "The Advent of the Computer Delinquent" by Arthur L. Bowker.

- Find and read *Youth Violence: A Report of the Surgeon General* at www.surgeongeneral.gov and determine whether the report is pessimistic or optimistic. Give quotes to support your opinion.

- Find *Juvenile Justice: A Century of Change* at www.ojjdp.ncjrs.org. Write down for your state (1) what transfer provisions to criminal court exist, (2) what offenses and minimum age criteria are for transfer, (3) if your state has concurrent jurisdiction and, if so, what the offense and minimum age criteria for waiver are and (4) whether your state has a minimum age for judicial waiver and, if so, what that age is.

- Go to the National Center for Juvenile Justice website at www.ncjj.org and find the publication *Juvenile Justice with Eyes Open*. Outline the portion of that publication describing legal barriers to information sharing.

- Using the keywords *Uniform Crime Reports*, find and outline the types of crimes predominantly committed by juveniles.

## REFERENCES

*Alcohol Alert.* Bethesda, MD: National Institute on Alcohol Abuse and Alcoholism, October 2002.

*America's Children: Key National Indicators of Well-Being, 2004.* Federal Interagency Forum on Child and Family Statistics. http://www.childstats.gov/americaschildren/index.asp

Arthur, Lindsay G. "Foreword." pp.ix–xi. In *Juvenile Justice,* 4th ed., by Kären M. Hess and Robert W. Drowns. Belmont, CA: Wadsworth Publishing Company, 2004.

Ascione, Frank R. *Animal Abuse and Youth Violence.* Washington, DC: Office of Juvenile Justice and Delinquency Prevention, Juvenile Justice Bulletin, September 2001.

Bamberger, Lauren. "Exploring Police Explorer Programs." *Law and Order,* June 2003, pp.116–119.

Baron, Stephen W.; Kennedy, Leslie W.; and Forde, David R. "Male Street Youths' Conflict: The Role of Background, Subcultural, and Situational Factors." *Justice Quarterly,* December 2001, pp.759–789.

Boertien, Robert. "Multnomah County Volunteers." *Law and Order,* October 2001, pp.127–131.

Brown, Cynthia. "DARE Officials Responding to Critics, Come Up with New Program." *American Police Beat,* April 2001, p.76.

Cottle, Cindy C.; Lee, Ria J.; and Heilbrun, Kirk. "The Prediction of Criminal Recidivism in Juveniles: A Met-Analysis." *Criminal Justice and Behavior,* Vol. 28, No. 3, 2001.

*Crime in the United States 2003.* Washington, DC: Federal Bureau of Investigation, 2004.

Domash, Shelly Feuer. "Protecting the Innocent." *Police,* October 2002, pp.52–56.

Dorfman, Lori and Schiraldi, Vincent. *Off Balance: Youth, Race & Crime in the News.* Building Blocks for Youth, April 2001.

Dorsey, Rita. "Reducing Juvenile Violence through Prevention, Intervention and Law Enforcement Practices." *The Police Chief,* June 2004, pp.71–73.

"Drug Abuse Resistance Education Plans Test of a New Curriculum." *Criminal Justice Newsletter,* February 26, 2001, pp.2–3.

*The 8% Solution.* Washington, DC: OJJDP Fact Sheet #39, November 2001. (FS 200139)

Esbensen, Finn-Aage; Osgood, D. Wayne; Taylor, Terrance J.; Peterson, Dana; and Freng, Adrienne. "How Great Is G.R.E.A.T? Results from a Longitudinal Quasi-Experimental Design." *Criminology and Public Policy,* November 2001, pp.87–118.

Fuller, James R. "Challenge by Choice." *Community Links,* March 2001, pp.9–11.

Garrett, Ronnie. "Looking beyond Amber Alert: Technologies to Supplement Amber Alert Systems Can Save Lives." *Law Enforcement Technology,* February 2004, pp.68–74.

Geier, Michael. "Party Patrol: A New Approach to Underage Drinking Enforcement." *Law and Order,* March 2003, pp.96–103.

Giordano, Alice. "Teen Drivers Turn into Speed Busters." *Law and Order,* July 2001, pp.148–149.

Glasscock, Bruce D. "The Child Protection Summit: Exploring Innovative Partnerships." *The Police Chief,* August 2001, p.6.

Grasso, Kathi L.; Sedlak, Andrea J.; Chiancone, Janet L.; Gragg, Frances; Schultz, Dana; and Ryan, Joseph F. *The Criminal Justice System's Responses to Parental Abduction.* Washington, DC: OJJDP Juvenile Justice Bulletin, December 2001. (NCJ 186160)

Hammer, Heather; Finkelhor, David; and Sedlak, Andrea J. *Runaway/Thrownaway Children: National Estimates and Characteristics.* Washington, DC: NISMART Bulletin, October 2002.

Hess, Kären M. and Drowns, Robert W. *Juvenile Justice,* 4th ed. Belmont, CA: Wadsworth Publishing Company, 2004.

*An Implementation Guide for Juvenile Holdover Programs.* Washington, DC: National Highway Traffic Safety Administration, Office of Juvenile Justice and Delinquency Prevention and American Probation and Parole Association, June 2001. (DOT HS 809260)

Johnson, Kelly Dedel. *Underage Drinking.* Washington, DC: Office of Problem Orientated Policing Services Problem-Oriented Guides for Police Problem-Specific Guides Series, Guide No. 27, September 2004.

Johnston, Janet R.; Sagatun-Edwards, Inger; Blomquist, Martha-Elin; and Girdner, Linda K. *Early Identification of Risk Factors for Parental Abduction.* Washington, DC: OJJDP Juvenile Justice Bulletin, March 2001. (NCJ 185026)

Krainik, Peggy Wilkins. "Amber Alert: America's Missing: Broadcast Emergency Response." *Law and Order,* December 2002, pp.84–85.

Leverette-Sanderlin, Anne. "Camp Turning Point." *Law and Order,* October 2001, pp.122–124.

Lord, Wayne D.; Boudreaux, Monique G.; and Lanning, Kenneth V. "Investigating Potential Child Abduction Cases: A Developmental Perspective." *FBI Law Enforcement Bulletin,* April 2001, pp.1–10.

"NIJ: G.R.E.A.T. Improves Adolescents' Attitudes But Does Not Reduce Gang Membership." *NIJ Justice Bulletin,* July 2004, p.15. http://www.ncjrs.org/pdffiles/nij/198604.pdf.

Rasmussen, Janell L. "Amber Alert: Working to Curb Child Abductions." *Minnesota Police Chief,* Summer 2002, pp.43–49.

Robertson, Angela A.; Grimes, Paul W.; and Rogers, Kevin E. "A Short-Run Cost-Benefit Analysis of Community-Based Interventions for Juvenile Offenders." *Crime and Delinquency,* April 2001, pp.265–284.

Sanchez, Tom. "Youth Referral System." *The Police Chief,* September 2004, pp.51–55.

Santoro, Joseph A. "Monrovia's Anti-Truancy Ordinance: One Giant Step toward Keeping Kids in School and Out of Trouble." *The Police Chief*, March 2001, pp.34–39.

Schennum, Tim. "Unfair Rap for DARE." *Law and Order*, August 2001, pp.103–104.

Scialdone, Frank J. "DRY2K: A Program to Reduce Underage Drinking." *The Police Chief*, October 2001, pp.57–64.

Scott, Michael S. *Disorderly Youth in Public Places*. Washington, DC: Office of Community Oriented Policing Services Problem-Oriented Guides for Police Series No. 6, September 2001.

Scott, Michael S. *Rave Parties*. Washington, DC: Office of Community Oriented Policing Services Problem-Oriented Guides for Police Problem-Specific Guides Series, Guide No. 14, August 2004.

Sencio, William. "Young Mechanics." *Community Links*, March 2001, pp.8–9.

*Sourcebook of Criminal Justice Statistics 2003*. Washington, DC: Bureau of Justice Statistics, 2003.

Spratley, Lynnette. "Telephone Notification Finds Missing Children." *Law and Order*, August 2004, pp.58–62.

"Surgeon General Warns of 'Hidden' Violence by Youths." *Criminal Justice Newsletter*, February 9, 2001, pp.4–5.

"Truth, DARE & Consequences." *Law Enforcement News*, February 28, 2001, pp.1, 10.

"Underage Drinking: More than a Minor Issue." *Excellence in Problem-Oriented Policing: The 2003 Herman Goldstein Aware Winner and Finalists*. Washington, DC: Office of Community Oriented Policing Services and the Police Executive Research Forum, 2003, pp.37–44.

White, Helene Baskin; Tice, Peter C.; Loeber, Rolf; and Stouthamer-Loeber, Magda. "Illegal Acts Committed by Adolescents under the Influence of Alcohol and Drugs." *Journal of Research in Crime and Delinquency*, May 2002, pp.131–152.

Winton, Richard and Hayasaki, Erika. "LAPD Considers New Tactics to Combat Rave Parties." *Los Angeles Times*, November 30, 2004.

Zernike, Kate. "Criticized as Ineffective, DARE Program to Change Strategy for Drug Prevention." *New York Times*, as reprinted in the (Minneapolis/St. Paul) *Star Tribune*, February 16, 2001, p.A16.

## CASES CITED

*In re Gault*, 387 U.S. 1 (1967)

*Schall v. Martin*, 467 U.S. 253 (1984)

# Gangs and Drugs: Two National Threats

### Do You Know . . .

- Whether the gang problem is increasing or decreasing?
- How criminologists have categorized street gangs?
- What activities gang members frequently engage in?
- What the first step in dealing with a gang problem usually is?
- How gang members might be identified?
- How gang problems might be dealt with?
- If drugs and crime have been proven to be related?
- What approaches have been suggested to address the drug problem?
- What three stages are involved in a drug buy?
- What the critical elements in an illegal drug buy are?
- Why the sale and use of illegal drugs is difficult for police to investigate and prosecute?
- How to avoid a charge of entrapment?
- What the predominant approach to the drug problem in the 1980s was? In the 1990s? Currently?
- What drug abatement statutes do?

### Can You Define?

| | | | |
|---|---|---|---|
| cultural gangs | hedonistic/social | nystagmus | scavenger gangs |
| designer drug | gangs | organized/corporate | serious delinquent |
| drug gangs | horizontal | gangs | gangs |
| flashroll | prosecution | party gangs | territorial gangs |
| gang | instrumental gangs | predatory gangs | turf |
| graffiti | moniker | pulling levers | vertical prosecution |

## Introduction

Shelden et al. (2004, p.123) state: "There is little question that drug usage and violent crime are closely related. What is still in doubt, however, is the relationship between drugs (both usage and sales) and gangs. Research on this issue has produced conflicting findings. . . . Gang members are about twice as likely as nongang members to use drugs and to use them more often." Because there are drug gangs, the two problems are presented together in this chapter.

The gang problem is exceedingly complex. Not all gangs deal with drugs, and not all who use drugs commit other crimes. Law enforcement officers must maintain objectivity and refrain from stereotyping gang members and drug users and

pushers. They must know how to deal with gangs effectively and how to do their part in the war on drugs. Keep in mind, however, that many gangs are not involved in drugs, either using or selling. The chapter first focuses on the gang problem.

Miethe and McCorkle (2002, p.191) suggest: "By all indications, gang activity in large metropolitan areas has become a major social problem. Driveby shootings, carjackings, drug trafficking and other predatory offenses by active gang members and their associates are common occurrences in urban areas." The gang problem is not restricted to metropolitan areas. Researches Weisheit and Wells (2004, p.2) report that gangs are increasingly becoming a problem in rural areas. They (p.5) also report that most gangs in rural areas are homegrown.

This chapter begins with some definitions of gangs and a description of the current gang problem. This is followed by a discussion of the types of gangs in the United States, their characteristics and activities. Next is an explanation of why people join gangs and their characteristics and activities. Then are discussions of how to recognize a gang problem, how to identify gang members and how to investigate illegal activities of gangs. The exploration of the gang problem concludes with a look at approaches to the gang problem other than investigation, including community policing.

The chapter then focuses on the drug problem in the United States and the drugs involved. This is followed by a description of approaches to combating the drug problem, including the drug buy, undercover operations and drug raids. Next, recognizing people on drugs is discussed, followed by a discussion of legislation as a tool in the war on drugs. The chapter concludes with a description of prevention efforts and on how community policing and problem-oriented policing can enhance efforts to deal with both the gang and the drug problems.

## Gangs Defined

Weisel (2003, p.175) points out: "The police and the public use the term [*gang*] to refer to organized groups of young adults engaged in a wide variety of criminal behavior, including drug dealing, assaults, drive-by shootings and a host of other violent and property crimes." Esbensen et al. (2001, p.105) note: "The least restrictive definition includes all youths who claim gang membership at some point in time. The most restrictive definition includes only those youths who are current core gang members who indicate that their gang has some degree of organizational structure and whose members are involved in illegal activities."

The Chicago Police Department (*Gang Awareness*, n.d., p.1) defines a gang as "a group which has an organizational structure, leadership and . . . exists or benefits substantially from the criminal activity of its members." A **gang** is a group of individuals with a recognized name and symbols who form an allegiance for a common purpose and engage in unlawful activity.

A definition commonly accepted by law enforcement is that a gang is any group gathering continuously to commit antisocial behavior. But as Esbensen et al. (p.124) caution: "Obviously the definition used greatly affects the perceived magnitude of the gang problem. By restricting gang membership status to gangs that are involved in delinquent activity and have some level of organization, we reduce the size of the gang problem substantially." According to Weisel (2003, p.175): "Although increasingly defined by statute, the terms 'gang,' 'gang member' and 'gang-related crime' mean different things to different police departments. The selection of definitions may result in over- or underestimation of the nature and extent of the local gang problem."

*The Growth of Youth Gang Problems in the United States: 1970–1999* (Miller, 2001, pp.7–8) suggests: "The definition problem is not trivial. How to define a youth gang is one of the most contentious issues in the field of youth crime. Policymakers, law enforcement personnel, social service agencies, researchers and other groups have not been able to reach consensus on this issue over the past 25 years, and current efforts to reach this goal have thus far met with only limited success. . . . Few are willing to relinquish and replace the definitions that have become established within their agencies and are intimately related to agency operations." Langston (2003, p.8) urges: "Adoption of a uniform [definition] would benefit the entire law enforcement community in several ways." In addition to differing definitions for gangs, understanding the threat of gangs is made more complex because of the numerous categories that have been established, to be discussed shortly. First, consider the extent of the gang problem.

## The Extent of the Gang Problem

The *gang* label has been applied to various groups, from the "Spanky and Our Gang" little rascals of the 1920s to the leather-clad, violent, drug-using outlaw motorcycle gangs of the 1950s and 1960s. People often talk about getting their "gang" together. Belonging to a gang is certainly not a crime. Most people belong to groups or organizations. But when a gang engages in violence or crime, it is a law enforcement problem.

The last quarter of the twentieth century saw significant growth in gang problems across the country. In the 1970s, less than half the states reported youth gang problems, but by the late 1990s, every state and the District of Columbia reported gang activity. During that same period, the number of cities reporting youth gang problems mushroomed nearly tenfold—from fewer than 300 to more than 2,500 in 1998. The good news is that an analysis of the growth rates of gangs provides support for a prediction that the rate of growth prevailing during the later 1990s will decrease in the early 2000s and that the actual number of gang localities in the United States will also decrease (Miller, pp.iii, x).

This contention is supported by the *2002 National Youth Gang Survey* (Egley and Major, 2004, p.1), which reported that approximately 731,500 gang members and 21,500 gangs were active in the United States in 2002. According to the report: "The estimated number of gang members between 1996 and 2002 decreased 14 percent and the estimated number of jurisdictions experiencing gang problems decreased 32 percent."

 The youth gang problem appears to be decreasing but is still of concern.

## Types of Gangs

Shelden et al. (pp.42–43) describe the major types of gangs identified in various studies by different researchers nationwide:

- **Hedonistic/social gangs**—With only moderate drug use and offending, these gangs are involved mainly in using drugs (getting high) and having a good time; with little involvement in crime, especially violent crime.

- **Party gangs**—A group with relatively high use and sale of drugs, but with only one major form of delinquency (vandalism).
- **Instrumental gangs**—Those whose main criminal activity is that of committing property crimes (most members use drugs and alcohol but seldom engage in the selling of drugs).
- **Predatory gangs**—Those heavily involved in serious crimes (robberies and muggings) and seriously involved in the abuse of addictive drugs such as crack cocaine; some with much lower involvement in drug use and drug sales than the party gang, some may engage in selling drugs, although in an organized fashion.
- **Scavenger gangs**—Loosely organized groups of youths who are described as "urban survivors," preying on the weak in the inner cities; engaging in rather petty crimes but sometimes violence, often just for fun. The members have no greater bond than their impulsiveness and need to belong. They have no goals and are low achievers, often illiterate with poor school performance.
- **Serious delinquent gangs**—With heavy involvement in both serious and minor crimes, but much lower involvement in drug use and drug sales than the party gang.
- **Territorial gangs**—Those gangs associated with a specific area or turf and who, as a result, get involved in conflicts with other gangs over their respective turfs.
- **Organized/corporate gangs**—Heavy involvement in all kinds of crime and heavy use and sales of drugs; they may resemble major corporations, with separate divisions handling sales, marketing, discipline, and so on. Discipline is strict, and promotion is based on merit.
- **Drug gangs**—These gangs are smaller than other gangs; are much more cohesive; are focused on the drug business; and have strong, centralized leadership with market-defined roles.

Table 12.1 summarizes the common differences between street gangs and drug gangs.

**Table 12.1**  Common Differences between Street Gangs and Drug Gangs

| Street Gangs | Drug Gangs |
|---|---|
| Versatile ("cafeteria-style") crime | Crime focused on drug business |
| Larger structures | Smaller structures |
| Less cohesive | More cohesive |
| Looser leadership | More centralized leadership |
| Ill-defined roles | Market-defined roles |
| Code of loyalty | Requirement of loyalty |
| Residential territories | Sales market territories |
| Members may sell drugs | Members do sell drugs |
| Intergang rivalries | Competition controlled |
| Younger on average, but wider age range | Older on average, but narrower age range |

SOURCE: M. W. Klein. *The American Street Gang.* New York: Oxford University Press, 1995, p.132. Reprinted by permission.

Weisel (p.170) categorizes different types of gangs according to which groups and the criminal activity they typically engage in, for example, drug-trafficking gangs include the Bloods, Crips, Gangster Disciples, Latin Kings and many others. They engage in trafficking of heroin, cocaine, crack and other drugs; violence; arson; indirect prostitution; and the like. (see Table 12.2).

Criminologists have classified gangs as cultural or instrumental.

 **Cultural gangs** are neighborhood-centered and exist independently of criminal activity. Instrumental gangs are formed for the express purpose of criminal activity, primarily drug trafficking.

Police conflicts with most cultural gangs center around turf. The youth gangs mark out a specific territory using **graffiti,** symbols and slogans written on walls and sides of buildings. They defend this territory ferociously, even to the death. Certain gangs that began as cultural gangs, especially such gangs as the Bloods and the Crips, have evolved into instrumental gangs.

Prison gangs are also of concern to law enforcement. Fraser (2001, p.11) reports that gangs are proliferating in the [New York City Department of Corrections] system: "The violence with which they continued to conduct their business while in jail contributed to exorbitant overtime costs of $100 million per year." In addition, they were experiencing over 100 stabbings and slashings a month. The department's response was the formation of a Gang Intelligence Unit (GIU) to gather information on names, gang affiliations, gang ranks, aliases, enemies, associates, weapons carried, intended contraband recipients and prior arrests, as well as physical characteristics and photos of scars, markings and tattoos.

Valdez (2001, p.46) questions whether cyber gangs might also be forming: "It is almost like the Internet is becoming the 'electronic turf' for many gangs. Reading the messages can help determine the insults, greetings and challenges issued by the hosting gang or rival gang members. Gang members also create Web sites to display their colors and symbols or to warn off enemies. E-mailing has become a form of electronic graffiti for many gang members. The Internet is a way to communicate with each other, spread the gang culture and gives the ability to recruit nationwide."

Female gangs have also become more prevalent. Shelden et al. (p.142) report: "There are three types of female gang involvement: (1) membership in an independent gang, (2) regular membership in a male gang as a coed, and (3) as female auxiliaries of male gangs. Most girls are found within the third type."

Moore and Hagedorn's (2001) research found that most female gangs are either African-American or Latina, with a small but increasing number of Asian and white female gangs (p.6). In general, female gang members commit fewer violent crimes than males and are more inclined to property crimes and status offenses. Drug offenses are among the most common offenses committed by female gang members (p.5). Female gangs are somewhat more likely to be found in small cities and rural areas than in large cities (p.2). One aspect of female gang life appears to be constant—the gang is a refuge for young women who have been victimized at home (p.3).

**Table 12.2**   Criminal Organizations

| Type of Group | Groups | Criminal Activity |
|---|---|---|
| Chinese street gangs, Tongs, and Triads | Ghost Shadows, Flying Dragons, Wah Ching, United Bamboo, Ping On, Fuk Ching, White Tigers, Taiwan Brotherhood | Heroin distribution, smuggling of humans and exploitation of new immigrants; extortion of Chinese businesses, street taxes; gambling. |
| Drug-trafficking gangs | Bloods, Crips, Gangster Disciples, Latin Kings, and many others | Trafficking of heroin, cocaine, crack, and other drugs; violence; arson; indirect prostitution; vandalism, property crime; strong-arm robbery. African-American gangs known for crack; Chicano gangs known for heroin and crack. |
| Graffiti or tagger crews (also tagger posses, mobs, tribes, and piecers) | Known by three-letter monikers such as NBT (Nothing But Trouble) or ETC (Elite Tagger Crew) | Graffiti vandalism; tag-banging in which violence occurs. |
| Hate groups (Terrorist groups, including militias, are closely related to hate groups. All share a focus on ideology.) | Aryan Nation, Ku Klux Klan, skinheads (White Aryan Resistance), American Nazi Party, Christian Defense League | Violence; counterfeiting; bombings; loan fraud, armored car and bank robberies; theft rings. |
| Japanese gangs (Yakuza or Boryokudan) | Yamaguchi Gumi, Kumlai, Sumiyoshi Rengo | Gambling: prostitution and sex trade; trafficking in weapons and narcotics; management of foreign criminal investments in American corporations; money laundering. |
| Jamaican posses | Shower posse, Spangler posse | Trafficking of cocaine, crack, and marijuana; weapons trafficking; known for gratuitous violence, trafficking green cards. |
| Korean gangs | Flying Dragons, Korean Power, Junior Korean Power, AB (American Burger), KK (Korean Killers) | Prostitution, massage parlors, exploitation of women for nude and topless bars; extortion of Korean businesses, especially green grocers, produce markets, and restaurants; gambling; loansharking. |
| La Cosa Nostra | Families such as Bonnano, Gambino, and Genovese | Gambling, loansharking, corrupting public institutions and officers; money laundering; theft of precious metals, food, and clothing; fencing stolen property; labor racketeering; stock manipulation; murder; securities fraud. |
| Latin American gangs (Cuban, Mexican, Colombian, Peruvian, El Salvadoran, and others) | Medellin, Cali cartels; Arellano-Felix organization, Amazcua Contreras brothers, Amado Carillo Fuentes group, Caro Quintero organization | Trafficking of cocaine, crack, heroin, marijuana; counterfeiting; pickpocketing; murder; money laundering into real estate. |
| Nigerian gangs | NCE (Nigerian Criminal Enterprise) | Use of mules for heroin smuggling and heroin dealing, infiltrate private security; planned bankruptcy of companies; credit card fraud; exploitation of other Africans. |
| Outlaw motorcycle gangs | Hell's Angels, Outlaws, Pagans, Bandidos | Trafficking in methamphetamine (crank), speed, ice, PCP angel dust, LSD; chop shops; massage parlors; strip bars; prostitution; weapons trafficking; arson. |
| Prison gangs | Mexican Mafia, Nuestra Familia, Consolidated Crip Organization, Aryan Brotherhood, Black Guerilla Family, Texas Syndicate | Drug trafficking; prostitution; extortion; protection, murder for hire. |
| Russian (or Soviet) gangs | Odessa Mafia, Evangelical Russian Mafia, Malina/Organizatsiya, Gypsy gangs | Theft of diamonds, furs, gold and fencing stolen goods; extortion; insurance fraud; export and sale of stolen Russian religious art and gold; counterfeiting; daisy chain tax evasion schemes; credit card scams; smuggling illegal immigrants; drug trafficking; money laundering. |
| Street gangs (African-American, Hispanic, Caucasian, and others) | Variants of Bloods/Crips such as Westside or Rolling Crips, Latin Kings, Disciples, Vice Lords, Dog Pound, and many others | Motor vehicle theft; drug sales (especially crack and marijuana); weapons trafficking; assaults; drive-by shootings; robbery; theft and fencing stolen property; vandalism; graffiti; and burglaries. |
| Vietnamese gangs | Born to Kill (BTK) | Strong arm and violent crimes related to business extortion; home invasion for theft of gold, jewelry, and money coupled with rape to deter reporting; prostitution. |

Note: Although nationality and ethnicity are often unifying characteristics of criminal organizations and used to identify them, this view is overly narrow and promotes ethnic stereotypes. The organization of criminal groups by nationality and ethnicity in this table is not intended to suggest that criminal behavior is characteristics of any group; ethnicity, however, is often a marker to police.

SOURCE: Deborah Lamm Weisel. "Criminal Investigation." In *Local Government Police Management*, edited by William A. Geller and Darrel W. Stephens. 2003. p.270. Washington, DC: International City/County Management Association. Reprinted with permission of the International City/County Managment Association, 777 North Capitol Street, NE, Suite 500, Washington, DC 20002. All rights reserved.

## Why People Join Gangs

Many factors contribute to the development of delinquent gangs including dropping out of school, unemployment, family disorganization, neighborhood traditions of gang delinquency and ethnic status. Gangs provide acceptance and protection to inner-city youth. Allender (2001, p.4) suggests that young people join gangs for some combination of five reasons:

1. *Structure:* Youths want to organize their lives but lack the maturity to do so on their own. The gang provides rules to live by and a code of conduct.
2. *Nurturing:* Gang members frequently talk of how they love one another.
3. *Sense of belonging:* Because humans require social interaction, some young people find that the gang fulfills the need to be accepted as an important part of a group.
4. *Economic opportunity:* Gang members motivated by this consideration alone probably would become involved in criminal activity anyway.
5. *Excitement:* This often represents a motivation for suburban and affluent youths.

Shelden et al. (p.223) focus on the fourth reason, stating: "Unemployment, poverty, and general despair lead young people to seek out economic opportunities in the growing illegal marketplace, often done within the context of gangs." They contend: "It does not take much of a leap in logic to conclude there exists a strong correlation between the growth of gangs in the inner cities on the one hand and the growth in the gap between the rich and the poor on the other." The title of Chapter 7 in their book illustrates this emphasis: "Gangs in Context: Inequality in American Society."

Shelden et al. (p.174) also note: "What emerges from a review of research on girl gangs is a portrait of young women who, just like their male counterparts, find themselves trapped in horrible social conditions characterized by widespread poverty and racism." They (p.175) conclude: "There is general consensus in the research literature that girls become involved in gang life for generally the same reasons as their male counterparts—namely, to meet basic human needs, such as belonging, self-esteem, protection, and a feeling of being a member of a family." Table 12.3 lists numerous factors placing an individual at risk for becoming a gang member.

## Characteristics and Activities of Gangs

Some gang experts talk about the three Rs of the gang culture: reputation, respect and revenge. Reputation is of prime concern to the gang, both individually and collectively. They expect, indeed demand, respect. And they are required to show disrespect for rival gang members, called a *dis* in gang slang. Disrespect inevitably leads to the third R—revenge. Every challenge must be answered, often in the form of a drive-by shooting.

Many people believe that joining a gang leads youths into criminal activity. However, some studies show that most youths were delinquent before joining a gang, but that their delinquency increases as a result of joining. Research by Gordon et al. (2004, p.56) reports: "We find more evidence than has been found in prior studies that boys who join gangs are more delinquent before entering the gang than those who do not join. Even with such selective differences, however,

**Table 12.3** Risk Factors for Youth Gang Membership

| *Domain* | *Risk Factors* |
|---|---|
| Community | Social disorganization, including poverty and residential mobility |
| | Organized lower-class communities |
| | Underclass communities |
| | Presence of gangs in the neighborhood |
| | Availability of drugs in the neighborhood |
| | Availability of firearms |
| | Barriers to and lack of social and economic opportunities |
| | Lack of social capital |
| | Cultural norms supporting gang behavior |
| | Feeling unsafe in neighborhood: high crime |
| | Conflict with social control institutions |
| Family | Family disorganization, including broken homes and parental drug/alcohol abuse |
| | Troubled families, including incest, family violence and drug addiction |
| | Family members in a gang |
| | Lack of adult male role models |
| | Lack of parental role models |
| | Low socioeconomic status |
| | Extreme economic deprivation, family management problems, parents with violent attitudes, sibling antisocial behavior |
| School | Academic failure |
| | Low educational aspirations, especially among females |
| | Negative labeling by teachers |
| | Trouble at school |
| | Few teacher role models |
| | Educational frustration |
| | Low commitment to school, low school attachment, high levels of antisocial behavior in school, low achievement test scores and identification as being learning disabled |
| Peer group | High commitment to delinquent peers |
| | Low commitment to positive peers |
| | Street socialization |
| | Gang members in class |
| | Friends who use drugs or who are gang members |
| | Friends who are drug distributors |
| | Interaction with delinquent peers |
| Individual | Prior delinquency |
| | Deviant attitudes |
| | Street smartness: toughness |
| | Defiant and individualistic character |
| | Fatalistic view of the world |
| | Aggression |
| | Proclivity for excitement and trouble |
| | *Locuro* (acting in a daring, courageous, and especially crazy fashion in the face of adversity) |
| | Higher levels of normlessness in the context of family, peer group and school |
| | Social disabilities |
| | Illegal gun ownership |
| | Early or precocious sexual activity, especially among females |
| | Alcohol and drug use |
| | Drug trafficking |
| | Desire for group rewards, such as status, identity, self-esteem, companionship and protection |
| | Problem behaviors, hyperactivity, externalizing behaviors, drinking, lack of refusal skills and early sexual activity |
| | Victimization |

SOURCE: James C. Howell. *Youth Gangs: An Overview.* Washington, DC: Office of Juvenile Justice and Delinquency Prevention, August 1998, pp.6–7. (NCJ 167249)

we replicate research showing that drug selling, drug use, violent behavior and vandalism of property increase significantly when a youth joins a gang."

Negative gang activities vary widely, ranging from underage drinking, truancy and vandalism to burglary, assault, extortion and homicide. The gang survey by Gordon et al. (p.xv) showed that the percentage of respondents reporting involvement of "most or all" gang members was largest for drug sales (27 percent), followed by larceny/theft (17 percent), burglary/breaking and entering (13 percent), aggravated assault (12 percent), motor vehicle theft (11 percent) and robbery (3 percent). More than one-half (53 percent) said gang members in their jurisdiction used firearms in assault crimes "often" or "sometimes." Only 16 percent said their gang members did not use firearms in conjunction with assaults. One-third (34 percent) of all youth gangs were drug gangs, that is, gangs organized specifically to traffic in drugs.

Researcher Weisel (2002, p.35) notes that police reported a great deal of criminal versatility among their serious gangs: "Assaults, crack cocaine sales, graffiti, intimidation, vandalism, violence as a means of discipline and violence as a means of retaliation were the most common activities of gangs as reported by police respondents." Table 12.4 summarizes criminal activity by gang type reported to Weisel.

 Gang members often engage in vandalism, drug dealings, larceny/theft, burglary/breaking and entering, aggravated assault, motor vehicle theft and drive-by shootings.

Weisel (p.39) also reports: "Like the police respondents . . . gang members report that their gang is extensively involved in a wide range of criminal activity. Indeed gang members reported much greater participation of their gang in specific criminal activities than police attributed to specific serious gangs. In the interviews, gang members reported about two to three times as much criminal activity as did police."

## Recognizing a Gang Problem

Many communities are blind to local gang activity. However, according to Fraser (p.11): "The presence of gangs can be seen everywhere. Gang members do not represent an invisible empire; they thrive on attention and recognition, constantly seeking ways to make their presence felt. They go unseen only when law enforcement personnel, as well as educators and parents, fail to recognize the signs of gang activity." Such failure to recognize or acknowledge the existence of gang activity, whether willingly or through the lack of gang identification training, dramatically increases a gang's ability to thrive and develop a power base.

 The first step in dealing with a gang problem is to recognize it.

### Warning Signs of a Gang Problem

Identifying gangs is difficult, but a school or community can be aware of warning signs of a gang problem: graffiti, obvious colors of clothing, tattoos, initiations, hand signals or handshakes, uncommon terms or phrases and a sudden change in behavior.

**Table 12.4**   Criminal Activity by Gang Type

| Crime | Percent of Police Who Report That Violent Gangs Commit the Offense Very Often or Often (n = 223) | Percent of Police Who Report That Drug-Dealing Gangs Commit the Offense Very Often or Often (n = 148) | Percent of Police Who Report That Entrepreneurial Gangs Commit the Offense Very Often or Often (n = 75) |
|---|---|---|---|
| Motor Vehicle Theft | 25 | 25 | 44 |
| Arson | 1 | 1 | 1 |
| Assault | 87 | 69 | 57 |
| Burglary | 36 | 25 | 37 |
| Driveby Shooting | 42 | 49 | 32 |
| Crack Sale | 55 | 80 | 39 |
| Powder Cocaine Sale | 23 | 46 | 29 |
| Marijuana Sale | 35 | 54 | 33 |
| Other Drug Sale | 17 | 26 | 25 |
| Graffiti | 67 | 50 | 38 |
| Home Invasion | 10 | 11 | 27 |
| Intimidation | 81 | 72 | 74 |
| Rape | 7 | 4 | 8 |
| Robbery | 33 | 30 | 36 |
| Shooting | 37 | 41 | 38 |
| Theft | 49 | 37 | 52 |
| Vandalism | 57 | 38 | 37 |

Note: Reflects aggregation of police estimates of participation in criminal activity by a gang of that type in the jurisdiction.

SOURCE: Deborah Lamm Weisel. "The Evolution of Street Gangs: An Examination of Form and Variation." In *Responding to Gangs: Evaluation and Research*, edited by Winifred L. Reed and Scott H. Decker. Washington, DC: National Institute of Justice, July 2002, p.36. (NCJ 190351)

## Criteria for Qualifying as a Gang

Pennell and Melton (2002, p.101) suggest that to qualify as a gang, a group had to meet all of the following criteria:

- Have a name and identifiable leadership
- Claim a territory, turf, neighborhood or criminal enterprise
- Associate on a continuous or regular basis
- Engage in delinquent or criminal behavior

Table 12.5 shows the criteria used by some departments for identifying gangs.

# Identifying Gang Members

Pennell and Melton (p.202) suggest that to be documented as a gang member, an individual should meet at least one of the following criteria:

- Admit gang membership
- Have tattoos or wear or possess clothing or paraphernalia associated with a specific gang

**Table 12.5**  Criteria for Defining Gangs

| Criteria Used | Large Cities* (Percent) | Smaller Cities* (Percent) |
|---|---|---|
| Use of Symbols | 93 | 100 |
| Violent Behavior | 81 | 84 |
| Group Organization | 81 | 88 |
| Territory | 74 | 88 |
| Leadership | 59 | 48 |
| Recurrent Interaction | 56 | 60 |

*Of the cities surveyed, 70 (89 percent) of the large cities and 25 (58 percent) of the smaller cities indicated the criteria used to define gangs.

SOURCE: G. David Curry et al. *Gang Crime and Law Enforcement Recordkeeping.* Washington, DC: National Institute of Justice Research in Brief, August 1994, p.7. Data from NIJ Gang Survey.

*Gang members proudly displaying their sign.*

- Be observed participating in delinquent or criminal activity with known gang members
- Be known to the police as having a close association with known gang members
- Be identified by a reliable informant as a gang member

According to Weisheit and Wells (p.3), with rural gangs the most frequent indicator was self-identification by youths. They note: "Respondents also frequently used the presence of graffiti and tattoos, the wearing of gang colors and the judgment of criminal justice official that some youths were gang members."

Gang members take pride in belonging to their specific gangs and will make their membership known in various ways. Many gang members have a street name, called a **moniker.** Often more than one gang member has the same moniker. They frequently use hand signals. The color and type of clothing can also indicate gang membership. For example, Bloods are identified by red or green colors. Crips are associated with blue or purple bandanas or scarves. Many also have tattoos.

Stephen Wilkes/The Image Bank/Getty Images

*Gang graffiti marks the gang's turf.*

 Gang members identify themselves by their names, clothing, sign language and graffiti.

Most gangs establish a specific area, their **turf,** which they mark with graffiti and will defend to the death. They control their turf through intimidation and violence. Police officers can learn much about gang activity if graffiti appears in their jurisdiction. Graffiti may list gang members' names, often in order of authority. The most graffiti will appear in the center of the turf area. Graffiti crossed out or overwritten is often the challenge of a rival gang. If gang symbols are written upside down, this graffiti is usually written by a rival gang and is a great insult to the gang it depicts. Gang members caught crossing out a rival's graffiti are usually severely beaten or even killed.

The Vice Lords use the following symbols in their graffiti:

- Cane—staff of strength.
- Circle—360 degrees of knowledge that blacks ruled the world in the past and will again do so.
- Crescent moons—the splitting of the Black Nation into two parts, one West, one East.
- Fire—the Black Nation's true knowledge being suppressed and their inability to reach knowledge because of the fire's heat.
- Gloves—purity.
- Hat—shelter.
- Pyramid—the mystery of the pyramid constructed by black people. The three corners represent physical, mental and spiritual knowledge.
- Rabbit—swiftness.
- Star—the eye of Allah, watching over his people.
- Sun—the rising of truth in the Black Nation.

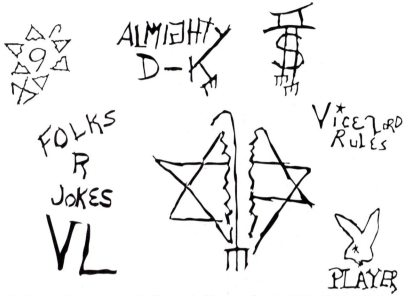

Typical Vice Lord markings documented in Minneapolis, Minnesota. Bear in mind that these markings are often personalized and may appear in various combinations. Watch for repeated code and image patterns.

**Figure 12.1** Typical Graffiti

These symbols are often personalized and may appear in various combinations (see Figure 12.1).

## Investigating Gangs' Illegal Activities

The same procedures used in investigating any other kind of illegal activity apply to investigating gangs' illegal activities. Information and evidence must support the elements of specific offenses and link gang members to those offenses.

It is often difficult to obtain information about a gang's illegal activities because the gang members stick together and will intimidate the people living and working within their turf. Businesspeople and residents alike are usually fearful of telling the police anything, believing the gang will cause them great harm if they do.

If a neighborhood canvass is conducted and information is received, it is important that the canvass not stop at that point. This would implicate the house or business at which the canvass was terminated as the source of information. In addition, more information might be available from a source not yet contacted during the canvass.

Crime scenes that involve gangs are unique. Often the crime scene is part of a chain of events. When a gang assault occurs, for example, often a chase precedes the assault, considerably widening the crime scene. If vehicles are involved, the assault is probably by a rival gang. If no vehicles appear to have been involved, the suspects are probably local, perhaps even members of the same gang as the victim. This frequently occurs when narcotics, girlfriends or family disputes are involved. Evidence obtained in gang investigations is processed in the same way as evidence related to any other crime.

## Reading Graffiti

Savelli (2004, p.9) suggests: "The key to understanding gang graffiti is being able to analyze the symbols, indicators and terminology used by gangs. Simply, gangs use graffiti to send messages."

The purposes of these messages are:

■ To mark the gang's turf (territory).
■ To disrespect a rival gang or gang member.
■ To memorialize a deceased gang member.
■ To make a statement.
■ To send a message.
■ To conduct business.

Savelli (p.15) notes: "While it is important to read the writing on the walls, it is equally important to cover it over as soon as possible. Don't give the gang a chance to claim your community as their turf by allowing their graffiti to stay intact. . . . When dealing with graffiti, it is recommended to:

■ Photograph it (the whole piece and in sections).
■ Analyze it while it is intact.
■ Remove it (paint over it, sandblast it, etc.).
■ Keep an archive of the photo.
■ Document the colors used.
■ Document the gang "Tag" names.
■ Document the indicators of "beef" or violence.
■ Get involved in, or create, an antigraffiti program to cover over all graffiti. Get the youths involved!

## Gang Impact Teams

Collins (2004, p.12) describes the gang problem facing Los Angeles: "More than 400 gangs, comprising 52,000 members are known to operate in Los Angeles, population 4 million. . . . Of the 516 homicides in the city last year 263, or 41 percent, were gang-related, costing the city nearly $875 million per homicide. Intangible costs cover quality-of-life issues, such as revenue loss due to fear or crime or declining property values, and are estimated at more than $2.16 million per homicide. And that's just for homicide. Add to that the dollar costs for rape, robbery and aggravated assault and you're looking at a $946 million price tab." One approach to this problem was the formation of gang impact teams and strategic targeting. Collins (p.13) explains:

> In L.A., where gangs are so pervasive, the police department has formed gang impact teams to manage investigations. Previously, LAPD's narcotics work was handled in a separate, centralized division. However, when it was recognized that gang activity and drug activity went hand in hand, narcotics officers and gang officers were assembled into teams that operate out of each of the city's 18 precincts. This arrangement gives the teams autonomy to address neighborhood gang problems as they see fit, but the teams also meet once or twice monthly to coordinate a centralized strategy. . . .
>
> [According to the overseer of the teams] Given the totality of our resources against the magnitude of the problem, we like to concentrate on the 10 percent factor—that is, the concept that 10 percent of suspects are responsible for 50 percent of crime and that 10 percent of locations account for 60 percent of all crime scenes.

**Table 12.6**    Methods Used for Gathering Information on Gangs,
Ranked by "Often Used" Category

|  | Never Used | Sometimes Used | Often Used |
|---|---|---|---|
| Internal contacts with patrol officers and detectives | 1 | 22 | 64 |
| Internal departmental records and computerized files | 4 | 22 | 62 |
| Review of offense reports | 2 | 25 | 60 |
| Interviews with gang members | 5 | 26 | 56 |
| Information obtained from other local police agencies | 1 | 35 | 51 |
| Surveillance activities | 6 | 37 | 44 |
| Use of unpaid informants | 2 | 44 | 42 |
| Information obtained from other criminal justice agencies | 3 | 43 | 42 |
| Information obtained from other governmental agencies | 3 | 47 | 37 |
| Provision of information by schools | 2 | 50 | 35 |
| Reports from state agencies | 11 | 63 | 14 |
| Use of paid informants | 28 | 46 | 13 |
| Reports from federal agencies | 16 | 62 | 9 |
| Information obtained from private organizations | 27 | 51 | 9 |
| Infiltration of police officers into gangs or related groups | 75 | 11 | 2 |

SOURCE: James W. Stevens. "Youth Gangs' Dimensions." *The Encyclopedia of Police Science*, 2nd ed., edited by William G. Bailey. New York: Garland, 1995, p.832. Reprinted by permission.

## *Obtaining and Recording Information*

The most common way to gather information about gangs is internal contacts with patrol officers and detectives, followed by internal departmental records and computerized files and then by review of offense reports.

An effective records system is critical in dealing with any gang problem. Information is an essential tool for law enforcement and should include the following: type of gang (street, motorcycle, etc.), ethnic composition, number of active and associate members, territory, hideouts, types of crimes usually committed and method of operation, leadership and members known to be violent. Table 12.6 shows the methods used for gathering information on gangs.

Meeker et al. (2003, p.291) describe the Gang Incident Tracking System (GITS) used in Orange County, California, developed to obtain an accurate, unbiased picture of gang activity in the county: "The GITS has made it possible to use GIS [geographic information system] technology to create computerized maps that analyze the spatial and temporal distribution of gang activity." Says Meeker et al.: "The GITS above all demonstrated the usefulness of multijurisdictional efforts to understand and ultimately prevent gang crime."

## Approaches to the Gang Problem

Four general strategies are being used to deal with gang problems: (1) suppression or law-enforcement efforts, (2) social intervention, (3) opportunities provision and (4) community organization.

Tony Freeman/PhotoEdit

*A total community effort is needed to combat gangs and drugs. All segments of the community can find a way to become involved as evidenced by the public service message on this truck.*

The most effective approach is probably a combination of prevention, intervention and suppression strategies. More specific strategies might include not tolerating graffiti, targeting hard-core gang leaders and consolidating major gang-control functions. Table 12.7 shows the law enforcement strategies being used, with what frequency and with what perceived effectiveness if used.

Although in-state information exchange was the most used strategy, it was also among those judged least effective. Street sweeps and other suppression tactics were used by less than half the departments, but their effectiveness was judged high.

### Suppression

As might be expected, law enforcement agencies view suppression tactics, such as street sweeps, intensified surveillance and hotspot targeting; crime prevention activities and community collaboration—in that order—as most effective in preventing and controlling gang crime.

Fritsch et al. (2003, p.267) point out: "Suppression tactics include tactical patrols by law enforcement, vertical prosecution by district attorneys and intensive supervision by probation departments. Generally, suppression involves the arrest, prosecution and incarceration of gang members. Although suppression is the primary strategy used in many jurisdictions, it is also frequently viewed as the least effective."

Boston used suppression to attack the problem of gang-related youth homicides, with an average of 44 people under age 25 being murdered annually, with 60 percent being gang-related. In addition, 15 percent of the city's junior high school students said they had stayed home from school within the last month because they were afraid ("Boston Program . . .," 2001, pp.5–7). Their program, Operation Ceasefire, began with the creation of the Youth Violence Strike Force (YVSF).

**Table 12.7**   Law Enforcement Strategies and Perceived Effectiveness*

| Strategy | Used (Percent) | Judged Effective (If Used) (Percent) |
|---|---|---|
| Some or a lot of use | | |
| Targeting entry points | 14 | 17 |
| Gang laws | 40 | 19 |
| Selected violations | 76 | 42 |
| Out-of-state information exchange | 53 | 16 |
| In-state information exchange | 90 | 17 |
| In-city information exchange | 55 | 18 |
| Federal agency operational coordination | 40 | 16 |
| State agency operational coordination | 50 | 13 |
| Local agency operational coordination | 78 | 16 |
| Community collaboration | 64 | 54 |
| Any use | | |
| Street sweeps | 40 | 62 |
| Other suppression tactics | 44 | 63 |
| Crime prevention activities | 15 | 56 |

*Percentage of cities *n* = 211. The number of cities responding to each question varied slightly.

SOURCE: James C. Howell. *Youth Gang Programs and Strategies.* Washington, DC: OJJDP, August 2000, p.46. (NCJ 171154)

This strike force reviewed what had been done in the past and found one program mentioned over and over: the Wendover Street operation. In that operation police disrupted gang violence by cracking down on any type of criminal activity and by telling gang members that the crackdown would continue until the violence stopped. The YVSF decided to take this approach, calling **pulling levers,** telling gang members: "We're here because of the shooting. We're not going to leave until it stops. And until it does, nobody is going to so much as jaywalk, nor make any money, nor have any fun. The plan involved pulling every legal lever the police could, which was not difficult as many gang members were on probation, selling drugs or otherwise chronically offending." Tita et al. (2003, p.115) list several other levers police can use, including property (vehicle, housing) ownership, vehicle licensure, child support payments, children's truancy, asset forfeiture and warrants.

## Gang Units

Many departments have established gang units, which use a combination of prevention, suppression and intervention. The suppression component involves collaboration between police, probation and prosecution, targeting the most active gang members and leaders. The intervention component includes giving gang members the chance to finish high school or obtain a GED, to have tattoos removed, to obtain gainful employment and legal assistance. The prevention component includes conflict resolution skills and peer counseling.

Webb and Katz (2003, p.25) note: "Police gang units generally engage in one or more of four principal functions: intelligence, enforcement/suppression, investigations and prevention." Collins (pp.11–12) describes the efforts of a gang unit formed in Loudoun County, Virginia, after an alert from a neighboring county that MS-13, a gang with roots in El Salvador, was becoming active in the area. A gang unit of five full-time investigators was formed. According to the county sheriff, "We got very aggressive at going out and identifying gang members, finding the hotspots where they were hanging out and doing business. This was important to us because we started gathering statistics and could see where we stood, what was going on throughout the county."

### Civil Gang Injunctions and Ordinances

As Maxon et al. (2003, p.239) explain: "Civil gang injunctions (CGIs) are a legal tool for addressing the hold that entrenched gangs have on urban neighborhoods. Unlike some law enforcement gang intervention strategies that focus on individuals or gangs without regard to place, CGIs are spatially based, neighborhood-level interventions intended to disrupt gang's routine activities. . . . The injunction targets specific individuals (and often other unnamed gang members) who affect the daily lives of residents through intimidation and public nuisances and restricts their activities within the boundaries of a defined geographic area."

Another approach to the gang problem in some cities is to pass a gang ordinance. Santa Clara, California, recently passed such an ordinance and as O'Rourke (2004) states: "Gang members bent on intimidating others by loitering in public places have been put on notice by the city that they are breaking the law. An ordinance adopted [recently] empowers the Sheriff's Department to arrest gang members who loiter in public areas with the intent to mark their domain or to conceal illegal acts."

### Vertical Prosecution and Special Prosecution Units

"**Vertical prosecution** can be defined as one assistant prosecutor or small group of assistant prosecutors handling the criminal complaint from start to finish through the entire court process" (Bynum and Varano, 2003, p.227). This is in contrast to **horizontal prosecution,** where different assistant prosecutors are responsible for specific phases of the court proceedings. In some jurisdictions, a few assistant prosecutors specialize in gang-related cases. Miethe and McCorkle (p.171) note: "Special prosecution units can be an important arena for processing and adjudicating gang cases, although the decision to establish them will depend on the gravity of the gang problem and the expertise of the district attorneys."

The other strategies, social intervention, opportunities provision and community organization can be seen in the Office of Juvenile Justice Delinquency Prevention's (OJJDP) five-pronged approach to gang reduction.

## A Five-Pronged Approach to Gang Reduction

In introducing the OJJDP's program to support community antigang efforts, then–Attorney General Ashcroft stated:

> We must focus on the immediate priority of safeguarding the public, while at the same time attacking the underlying causes that attract young people to gangs in the first place. We must work to offer our youths a viable alternative to gangs by providing opportunities for success as productive citizens, and we

must also prepare those young people who have been held in confinement to return to their communities—not to their gangs ("New Program Supports Community AntiGang Efforts," 2003, p.l).

The OJJDP's Gang Reduction Program (GRP) uses a five-pronged approach:

1. *Primary prevention* targets the entire population in high-crime, high-risk communities. The key component is a one-stop resource center that makes services accessible and visible to community members. Services include prenatal and infant care, afterschool activities, truancy and dropout prevention, and job programs.
2. *Secondary prevention* identifies young children (ages 7 to 14) at high risk and, drawing on the resources of schools, community-based organizations and faith-based groups, intervenes with appropriate services before early problem behaviors turn into serious delinquency and gang involvement.
3. *Intervention* targets active gang members, close associates and gang members returning from confinement and involves aggressive outreach and recruitment activity. Support services for gang-involved youths and their families help youths make positive choices.
4. *Suppression* focuses on identifying the most dangerous and influential gang members and removing them from the community.
5. *Reentry* targets serious offenders who are returning to the community after confinement and provides appropriate services and monitoring. Of particular interest are "displaced" gang members who may cause conflict by attempting to reassert their former gang roles.

As can be seen, this program meshes well with community policing.

## Gangs and Community Policing

Allender (2001, p.7) stresses: "The gang problem is not an exclusive law enforcement problem, nor can police deal with it in a vacuum." He notes: "Society must provide young people with meaningful alternatives that will draw them away from the gang lifestyle. These alternatives should vary and include educational programs, social interaction, recreational activities, and employment opportunities. Obviously, the provision of these services will take cooperation among families, local schools, government-funded social services, area businesses, religious organizations, and other neighborhood resources." One valuable resource available to all communities is the National Gang Crime Research Center website: http://www.ngcrc.com. The community and other law enforcement agencies are also now becoming more involved in dealing with the drug problem, often closely associated with gang problems.

## The Drug Problem

Gangs are not the only faction involved in dealing drugs. Organized crime is also heavily into this area, as are some "reputable" businesspeople. Ericson (2001, p.1) reports: "Research has long shown that the abuse of alcohol, tobacco and illicit drugs is the single most serious health problem in the United States, straining the health care system, burdening the economy and contributing to the health problems and death of millions of Americans every year." In addition: "By

**Table 12.8** Unavailable Costs of Illegal Drug Use

| Criminal Justice Expenditures on Drug-Related Crime | Health-Care Costs | Lost Productivity Costs | Other Costs to Society |
|---|---|---|---|
| ■ Investigating robberies, burglaries and thefts for drug money and adjudicating and punishing the offenders<br><br>■ Investigating assaults and homicides in the drug business (or by a drug user who has lost control) and adjudicating and punishing the offenders | ■ Injuries resulting from drug-related child abuse/neglect<br><br>■ Injuries from drug-related accidents<br><br>■ Injuries from drug-related crime<br><br>■ Other medical care for illegal drug users, including volunteer services and outpatient services, such as emergency visits<br><br>■ Resources used in non-hospital settings | ■ Of drug-related accident victims<br><br>■ Of drug-related crime victims<br><br>■ Time away from work and homemaking to care for drug users and their dependents<br><br>■ Drug-related educational problems and school dropouts<br><br>■ Offenders incarcerated for drug-related or drug-defined crimes | ■ Loss of property values due to drug-related neighborhood crime<br><br>■ Property damaged or destroyed in fires, and in workplace and vehicular accidents<br><br>■ Agricultural resources devoted to illegal drug cultivation/production<br><br>■ Toxins introduced into public air and water supplies by drug production<br><br>■ Workplace prevention programs such as drug testing and employee assistance programs<br><br>■ Averting behavior by potential victims of drug-related crime<br><br>■ Pain and suffering costs to illegal drug users and their families and friends |

SOURCE: *Drugs, Crime, and the Justice System: A National Report from the Bureau of Justice Statistics.* Washington, DC: Bureau of Justice Statistics, December 1992, p.127.

the 8th grade, 52 percent of adolescents have consumed alcohol, 41 percent have smoked cigarettes, and 20 percent have used marijuana. By the 12th grade, about 80 percent have used alcohol, 63 percent have smoked cigarettes and 49 percent have used marijuana."

A three-year study by Columbia University's National Center on Addiction and Substance Abuse (CASA) ("Substance Abuse Costs . . .," 2001, p.5) found that state governments spent $81.3 billion on services to deal with alcohol and other drug problems, surpassing spending on Medicaid or transportation and equaling the amount spent on higher education. Of the $81.3 billion, only $3 billion went toward research, prevention and treatment of substance abuse. Table 12.8 shows the unavailable costs of illegal drug use.

Alcohol and drug abuse has other equally serious consequences. Drugs and drug-using behavior have been linked to crime in many ways: "It is a crime to use, possess, manufacture or distribute drugs classified as illegal. The effects of drug-related behavior—violence as the effect of drug use, robberies to get money to buy drugs, violence against rival traffickers—influence society daily" (*Drug Treatment in* . . ., 2001, p.1).

 Research supports the link between street-level drug hot spot activity, disorder and serious crime.

The use of illicit drugs and alcohol is a major cause of the soaring rate of incarceration, with an estimated two-thirds of federal and state prisoners and probationers characterized as drug involved.

**Figure 12.2**   National Snapshot of the 25 Cities Included in *Pulse Check*

SOURCE: *Pulse Check: Trends in Drug Abuse 2004.* Washington, DC: Office of National Drug Control Policy, January 2004, p.3. (NCJ 201398)

## The Drugs Involved

The primary drugs being abused include heroin, cocaine, marijuana, metham-phetamine, club drugs and prescription drugs. *Pulse Check* reports on trends in drug abuse based on data derived from 25 major cities shown in Figure 12.2. *Pulse Check* reports that of the cities included in their survey, 77 percent considered the problem of drug abuse as very serious; 23 percent considered it somewhat serious. According to *Pulse Check* (2004, p.5):

- Marijuana remains the country's most widely abused illicit drug.
- Crack remains a serious problem.
- Methamphetamine is reported as an emerging or intensifying problem.
- Heroin is the drug associated with the most serious consequences.
- Marijuana and crack are the illicit drugs most easily purchased by users and undercover police across the country (see Figure 12.3).

The *National Drug Threat Assessment 2004* reports that the majority of state and local law enforcement agencies identified either powder or crack cocaine (37.0 percent) or methamphetamine (36.7 percent) as their greatest drug threat. Other drugs named were much further behind, including marijuana (13.1 percent), heroin (8.7 percent) and MDMA or Ecstasy (0.9 percent). Cocaine and methamphetamine are the drugs believed to contribute most to violent crime.

According to Strong (2001, p.56): "The growing popularity and expansion of the rave culture and the criminal activity that surrounds it pose a continuing threat to America's youth." Says Strong: "The dramatic increases in the availability and use of club drugs, especially MDMA [Ecstasy] and GHB (gamma-hydroxybutyrate), and the array of hallucinogens and other illegal drugs available at raves and dance clubs indicate that the full impact of the rave culture has not yet been felt."

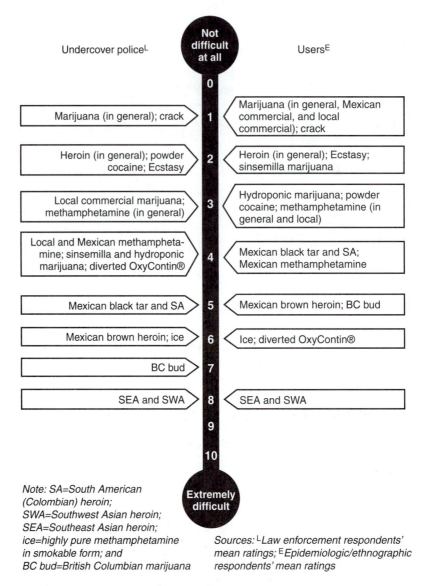

**Figure 12.3** Difficulty in Buying Illicit Drugs

SOURCE: *Pulse Check: Trends in Drug Abuse 2004.* Washington, DC: Office of National Drug Control Policy, January 2004, p.5. (NCJ 201398)

Ecstasy is a **designer drug,** a drug created by altering the chemical makeup of one or more existing drugs. In the case of Ecstasy amphetamines, methamphetamines and hallucinogens are altered. Taken orally by pill or capsule or swallowed, snorted or injected as a powder or liquid, it produces both stimulant and psychadelic effects. Streit (2001, p.24) notes: "When on the drug, a user's energy levels go through the roof. 'You can dance, talk, drink, whatever, all night long,' says a user." Unlike many other drugs, Ecstasy is not easily detected in a user.

Burke (2004, p.17) contends: "Conservative estimates are that prescription drug abuse represents approximately 25 to 30 percent of the overall drug problem in America." He (p.21) stresses: "The small percentage of physicians engaging in true criminal behavior can be responsible for causing and/or maintaining hundreds or thousands of addicts in a single jurisdiction. They are nothing less

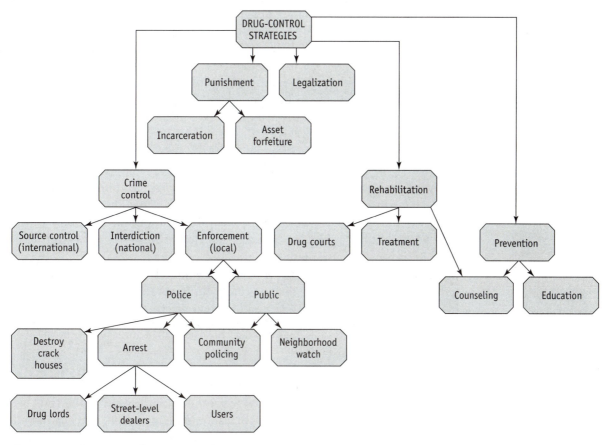

**Figure 12.4** Overview of Drug-Control Strategies

than drug dealers, regardless of the license or shingle they hang over their office door. These offenses typically involve an exchange of prescriptions for sex, street drugs or money." These operations exist across the country. One of the most popular drugs is OxyContin, which can sell for up to $80 a pill on the street.

## Approaches to the Drug Problem

In February 2002, President Bush set a goal of cutting drug abuse by 25 percent in five years through greater efforts toward prevention, treatment of addicts and improved law enforcement ("Bush Goal . . .," 2002, p.A7). Other approaches are also available.

 Approaches that have been suggested to address the drug problem include:
- Crime control.
- Punishment.
- Rehabilitation.
- Prevention.
- Legalization.

Figure 12.4 provides an overview of drug-control strategies.

The approaches being suggested should help support the three priorities of the *National Drug Control Strategy* (2004, p.1): (1) stopping use before it starts—education and community action, (2) healing America's drug users—getting treatment resources where they are needed and (3) disrupting the market—attacking the economic basis of the drug trade.

Steffen and Candelaria (2004, p.40) point out: "The illicit drug market in the United States is one of the most profitable in the world. It attracts aggressive and sophisticated drug traffickers and organizations." Efforts at international source control and national interdiction are beyond the scope of this text. However, local enforcement efforts are of great importance in the efforts to address the drug problem. These efforts often involve drug buys, undercover operations and raids.

## The Drug Buy

Many police departments use plainclothes police officers or informants to make drug buys, which are watched by a surveillance team. Often these buys are taped to provide further evidence of illegal activity. In addition, the surveillance team can step in if trouble develops and the plainclothes officer or informant needs help. Such buys are also useful because they can provide leads to the suspect's other customers and associates, as well as to where the supply is coming from. Often it is best to simply watch and wait, continuing to make buys and to gather information, rather than to make an immediate arrest.

 Buy operations occur in three well-defined stages: preparations for the buy, the buy itself and actions needed after the buy to process evidence and information.

**Preparations for the Buy**    Officers need to learn all they can about the entire situation. Security is vital. The slightest leak can ruin the operation and endanger the agent. All bills to be used for the buy should be recorded. A backup surveillance team is highly desirable to protect the agent and secure additional evidence. A plan needs to be devised that attempts to cover every contingency. Thorough briefing is essential, but only on a need-to-know basis. When a surveillance team is involved, a set of signals must be arranged. Just before the buy, the officer or informant and vehicle should be searched.

**The Actual Buy**    During the buy, any deviation from the plan increases the risk and decreases the chance of obtaining admissible evidence. The agent should control the situation and refuse to accept suggestions made by the seller. The agent should make the buy himself rather than let the informant do it. Sellers should be advised of their rights as soon as they are arrested. They should then be searched to recover the buy money and any other evidence.

**After the Buy**    The drugs should be weighed and tested. Every precaution should be taken to protect their integrity and to maintain the chain of custody as they are checked into the evidence room. All participants should be debriefed. An operational report should be written. Sometimes drug buys are much more sophisticated and complex. Such buys often involve carefully planned undercover operations.

## Undercover Operations

One primary approach to dealing with the drug problem is through undercover operations. In such operations, police officers assume a fictitious identity and attempt to infiltrate a drug ring or a drug-dealing gang or to pose as a buyer of drugs.

Steve Starr/Corbis

*Many police departments use plainclothes police officers or informants to make drug buys, which are watched by a surveillance team. Such buys are useful because they can provide leads to the suspect's other customers and associates, as well as to where the supply of drugs comes from.*

The negotiations conducted by an undercover narcotics officer are similar to those used by a hostage negotiator and require similar communication skills. In the case of the undercover agent, however, the innocent victim whose life may be saved is the agent. To successfully negotiate, undercover agents need as much *information* as possible about the sellers and their needs. Agents often consider that money is the main objective of drug dealers, but security is often even more important. This can be seen in drug dealers' insistence on controlling all aspects of the transaction, especially the location.

Another critical factor in undercover negotiations is *time.* Most drug dealers want to conduct their business as rapidly as possible, keeping the amount of time they have the drugs in their possession to a minimum. Undercover agents also can give the impression of being in a hurry to conduct business, perhaps by having an airline ticket with an impending departure time printed on the envelope jutting from a pocket. Despite the time press to conduct the transaction, it must also be remembered that the passage of time builds trust.

Information and time are critical elements in an illegal drug buy.

Another crucial aspect of the buy is how the **flashroll,** the buy money, is managed. Many undercover narcotics officers who are injured or killed while on assignment usually have mismanaged the flashroll. The most dangerous time is when the drugs and money are in the same place. Grave risks also occur when the flashroll is *not* present. In such instances, undercover agents may not be as on guard as they should be because they feel they are not at that much risk.

If the flashroll is present, agents should allow the dealer to count the money. There is little point in having it on hand if this is not part of the plan. If the agent cannot come up with the full amount requested, it is sometimes a good tactic to simply explain to the dealer that cash is temporarily short. Such an admission can do much to strengthen the agent's cover.

 The sale and use of illegal drugs is difficult to investigate and prosecute because sellers and buyers are willing participants.

**Entrapment—Revisited**   Whether a sophisticated undercover operation or a simple drug buy is involved, care must be taken to avoid a charge of entrapment. Entrapment, as stated in Chapter 10, occurs when a police officer (or other government official or person acting on behalf of the police or government) entices someone to commit a crime the person would not normally commit. Repeated requests to buy drugs are sometimes considered entrapment.

In *Hampton v. United States* (1976), Hampton was convicted of selling heroin to DEA agents. The question before the Court was: If a government informant supplies heroin to a person who then sells it to government agents, is this entrapment? The Court said No; Hampton was "predisposed" to deal in drugs. This view agrees with the majority opinion on entrapment, focusing on the defendant's behavior rather than on that of the officers involved. States vary, however, as to whether they support the majority or the minority view. The minority view focuses on how officers or their agents conduct themselves.

To avoid charges of entrapment, those making the buy, be they plainclothes officers, informants or undercover agents, should make more than one buy. The more buys made, the weaker the entrapment defense.

 Making several drug buys will protect against a claim of entrapment.

Among the other actions to be avoided are pressure such as badgering or coaxing, creating an unusual motive such as sympathy or making the crime unusually attractive. For example, it might be entrapment if officers said the crime would not be detected or that it was not illegal. Police may create an opportunity for someone to commit crime. It is presumed a law-abiding person would resist the temptation. They may also originate the criminal plan. As the California Supreme Court said: "We are not concerned with who first conceived or who willingly, or reluctantly, acquiesced in a criminal project." It is also not entrapment for an officer to take reasonable steps to gain the suspects' confidence.

## *Proving Guilty Knowledge*

Another area police officers involved in drug investigations must consider is the need to prove the person in possession of a package containing illegal substances knew of their presence. This frequently arises in vehicle courier and package delivery cases. Among the facts the courts have found relevant to proving knowledge are: (1) inconsistent statements, (2) implausible stories, (3) a large quantity of valuable contraband, (4) nervousness, (5) failure to ask any questions regarding the nature of a trip, (6) more contraband or drug paraphernalia found in the subject's possession, (7) lack of surprise upon discovery of the contraband, (8) scanning for police surveillance, (9) accepting a package without question or surprise,

(10) hiding a package once it is delivered and (11) inquiring about the status of a package in anticipation of its delivery.

## Drug Raids

During the 1980s, drug raids made frequent headlines. Tanklike vehicles, SWAT teams and sophisticated weaponry all have been involved in drug raids. During such raids, communication is usually critical. Such raids can be highly successful.

Ellement (2004) reports on a raid of a multistate OxyContin drug ring involving "mobsters, violent street gang members, pharmacists and college students working together. At its height the alleged drug ring, based in New Jersey, generated $160,000 a week from the illegal sale of thousands of pills." The investigation and ensuing raids, dubbed Operation Dr. Feelgood, included the Massachusetts State Police, police from several communities, the federal DEA and agencies in New Jersey and other states. Nearly 20 suspects were rounded up and hundreds of pills were seized.

Johnson (2001) describes in detail how to conduct a successful rave raid. His suggestions would also apply to most other types of drug raids. A briefing should first provide the target location to the officers, including an exact street address as well as nearby cross streets. Pictures of the popular rave drugs should be available at the briefing as well as special rave clothing designed with hidden compartments where rave drugs can be found. The raiding party should be aware that rave promoters frequently conduct counter surveillance by listening to police scanners, so such communication should not occur. Video cameras, binoculars and listening devices are needed for surveillance teams. It is also advisable to have a narcotic K-9 on standby.

Cohen et al. (2003, p.257) researched the effects of drug raids and report: "Results indicate that the police intervention suppresses levels of drug dealing during periods of active enforcement, but the effects largely disappear when the intervention is withdrawn."

 In combating the drug problem, law enforcement in the 1980s focused on undercover operations and sophisticated raids. In the 1990s, law enforcement focused on enlisting and educating the public and targeting street-level sales. That emphasis continues into the twenty-first century.

## Combating Prescription Drug Diversion

Burke (p.21) suggests: "Although prescription drug abuse is not commonly associated with street violence, the deaths and destruction that surround pharmaceutical diversion often exceeds that of illicit substances. The abuse and diversion of prescription drugs remains a very healthy criminal enterprise. To reduce this criminal behavior and loss of lives, it is essential that law enforcement agencies become more aggressive in their pursuit of these offenses. Two organizations have been formed to help law enforcement tackle the problem: RxPATROL and the National Association of Drug Diversion Investigation (NADDI)."

RxPATROL (Pattern Analysis Tracking Robberies and Other Losses) helps law enforcement solve pharmacy robberies, burglaries and other major crimes committed in health care facilities through its national computer database. NADDI is a nonprofit organization that provides prescription drug abuse education to law enforcement, regulatory agents and health care professionals.

## Dealing with Meth Labs

"Meth labs are a danger to all who encounter them" says an Evansville (Indiana) police sergeant (Garrett, 2004, p.38). Common signs of a meth lab include the following ("Additive Might Help Police Catch Meth Cooks," 2004, p.37):

- Chemical odor (especially ammonia, brake cleaner or ether)
- Coffee grinders and blenders with white residue
- Coffee filters with red stains
- Large quantities of matches, acetone, lithium batteries, antifreeze, engine starting fluid, camping fuel, drain cleaners, plastic baggies and glass jars
- Small propane tanks
- Exhaust fans in constant use
- Chemical containers and tubing
- Thermoses and plastic liter pop bottles
- Filthy living conditions
- People coming and going at all hours of the day and night
- Excessive traffic, often with a short stay

Surveillances and raids are options for law enforcement. A more proactive approach to shutting down meth labs is to educate retailers about the ingredients and hardware needed for manufacturing methamphetamine. Wuestewald and Adcock (2004, p.2) describe how the Broken Arrow (Oklahoma) Police Department approached the growing problem of meth labs:

> The Broken Arrow Police Department responded with an educational and intelligence-gathering program called Operation Don't Meth Around. As we analyzed the problem, it became evident that business owners and the community knew little about methamphetamine. Retailers were unaware that they were selling over the counter the ingredients and hardware for manufacturing methamphetamine—paint thinner, aluminum foil, lighter fluid, iodine, drain cleaner, battery acid, kerosene, cold medication, glassware and lithium batteries. They also were unaware of the characteristics of hard-core meth users, the dangers created by meth labs and the devastating impact of the drug.
>
> Therefore, in early 2001, our Special Investigations Unit initiated Operation Don't Meth Around to educate the public and business community. We worked to bring the public into the fold with:
>
> - An extensive media campaign—print and electronic—to alert and educate the public on the medical dangers, the manufacturing process and the clandestine labs associated with meth. As part of the strategy to promote news stories, we allowed reporters to accompany Special Investigations Unit detectives on raids of meth labs.
> - Blanket distribution of a methamphetamine informational brochure.
> - Large color posters for local businesses of methamphetamine ingredients.
> - Seminars at schools, businesses and civic halls.
> - An anonymous 24-hour Crimeline for tips on meth trafficking.
>
> The results were immediate and dramatic. Tips started rolling in faster than investigators could follow them up. Retailers started notifying detectives about suspicious purchases. . . . Raids of clandestine labs initially more than doubled, going from 16 to 33; arrests jumped to more than 25 percent; search warrants by 56 percent; and we seized huge quantities of methamphetamine

and other drugs. . . . Many traffickers are now in the penitentiary; others have been driven out of the city.

Iowa, Missouri and Oklahoma have approached the meth problem by restricting the sale of cold tablets containing pseudoephedrine, a key ingredient in methamphetamine. Such cold tablets must be locked up and their sale requires identification and a signature ("A Sinus of the Times . . .," 2004, pp.1, 15).

Another approach being used in some areas is to add GloTell to anhydrous ammonia fertilizer, often stolen to be used in meth labs. The chemical additive stains the hands and clothes of a fertilizer thief bright pink. It is visible under a black light for up to 72 hours even after being scrubbed off and no longer visible to the naked eye ("Additive Might Help Police Catch Meth Cooks," p.37).

## Combating Street-Level Narcotics Sales

Citizens know where drug dealing is going on. If they can be encouraged to report these locations, police can concentrate their efforts on those locations receiving the most complaints. Often police officers want to go higher than the street pusher, but should avoid this temptation. If information regarding someone higher up is obtained, it should be given to the narcotics unit for follow-up. The main purpose of the street-level raids is to respond to citizen complaints and to let them see their complaints being acted on—arrests being made. Officers should know where to search a person being detained on suspicion of possession of drugs. The variety of hiding places for illegal drugs is limited only by the violators' ingenuity. Common hiding places include body orifices, boots, chewing gum packages, cigarettes, coat linings, cuffs, false heels, hair, hatbands, inside ties, lighters, pants, pens and pencils, seams, shoes, shoulder pads, sleeves and waistbands.

Smith (2001) describes the Richmond, Virginia, police-led crackdowns and cleanups "Blitz to Bloom" initiative. The program targeted the many drug hot spots located throughout Richmond. During and after the crackdown, the targeted areas received other civic services aimed at enhancing the quality of life, including code enforcement, litter removal and street light repair. The Blitz part of the program was not designed to reduce crime long term, but rather to provide a crime-free area where social programs could be implemented. According to Smith, there was a significant reduction in reported crime over the month-long crackdown, with only one serious crime (a larceny) reported, a decrease of 92 percent from the preintervention period.

### Public Housing and the Drug Problem

To deal with the drug problem in public housing projects, police officers need to understand the workings of their local public housing authorities or agencies (PHAs) managing these complexes. Officers need to work at establishing a relationship with the PHAs and at overcoming the occasional disbelief of management and residents that the police truly want to help. Once this is accomplished, a fact-finding mission should identify key players, provide information about each organization and determine what programs exist and the participation level. Next the problem should be identified: What is the problem and for whom? Police, residents, housing personnel, the mayor? Does one problem mask another problem? Then a dialogue should be undertaken with key players to enlist support and mobilize the housing project's residents. After that a strategy should be developed, including goals, objectives and tactics that might be used. Next the strategy should be implemented, coordinating all available resources, specifying roles for each key player and determining a time frame. The final step is to evaluate progress. Was the problem improved or changed?

Various specific strategies have been used to tackle the drug problem in public housing. Often efforts focus on improving the physical environment: limiting entrances, improving lighting, erecting fences, requiring a pass card to gain entrance to the housing and keeping trash collected.

Efforts may also focus on removing offenders, strengthening enforcement and prosecution efforts, enforcing lease requirements and seizing assets. Or they may focus on reducing the demand, focusing on the buyers of the drugs rather than the sellers either through sting operations or through educational programs, youth diversion programs or treatment programs. Another strategy is to work on improving communications by using community surveys and tip lines and by improving communications between narcotics investigators and patrol officers.

In addition to being concerned with those who deal in drugs, police officers need to be prepared to manage those who use them.

## Recognizing Individuals Using Illegal Drugs

Police officers must be able to recognize when a person is probably under the influence of drugs and must also be aware of the dangers the person might present. Table 12.9 summarizes the primary physical symptoms, what to look for and the dangers involved in the most commonly used drugs, including alcohol.

Police officers must be able to recognize individuals who might be on angel dust, or PCP. One symptom always present in an individual high on PCP is **nystagmus,** an uncontrollable bouncing or jerking of the eyes when an intoxicated individual looks to the extreme right or left and up or down. Individuals on PCP may display superhuman strength.

Some agencies have drug recognition experts (DREs). As Hayes (2003, p.103) explains: "The drug recognition expert's main focus is the detection and recognition of drug-impaired drivers. But DREs have used, and continue to use, their specialized training and skills to assist in many other areas of public safety."

### An Alternative to Arrest

Wayne, Illinois, is taking a different approach with first-time drug violators. Police and village officials are dealing locally with those caught drinking or possessing small amounts of marijuana, sitting down with them and their parents or lawyers to work out a punishment that will fit the crime. As the chief said: "I would rather that these first-time offenders work their fannies off doing community service—preferably alongside a police officer" ("Taking a Different Road . . .," 2001, p.5).

## Legislation as a Tool in the War on Drugs

The government has the power to finance the war on drugs by seizing the drug traffickers' illegally obtained assets. This includes cars and weapons as well as cash. Among items that have been seized are airplanes, vehicles, radio transmit-

**Table 12.9**   Common Symptoms, What to Look for and Dangers of Commonly Abused Drugs

| Drug Used | Physical Symptoms | Look For | Dangers |
|---|---|---|---|
| Alcohol (beer, wine, liquor) | Intoxication, slurred speech, unsteady walk, relaxation, relaxed inhibitions, impaired coordination, slowed reflexes. | Smell of alcohol on clothes or breath, intoxicated behavior, hangover, glazed eyes. | Addiction, accidents as a result of impaired ability and judgment, overdose when mixed with other depressants, heart and liver damage. |
| Cocaine (coke, rock, crack, base) | Brief intense euphoria, elevated blood pressure and heart rate, restlessness, excitement, feeling of well-being followed by depression. | Glass vials, glass pipe, white crystalline powder, razor blades, syringes, needle marks. | Addiction, heart attack, seizures, lung damage, severe depression, paranoia (see Stimulants). |
| Marijuana (pot, dope, grass, weed, herb, hash, joint) | Altered perceptions, red eyes, dry mouth, reduced concentration and coordination, euphoria, laughing, hunger. | Rolling papers, pipes, dried plant material, odor of burnt hemp rope, roach clips. | Panic reaction, impaired short-term memory, addiction. |
| Hallucinogens (acid, LSD, PCP, MDMA/Ecstasy, psilocybin mushrooms, peyote) | Altered mood and perceptions, focus on detail, anxiety, panic, nausea, synaesthesia (e.g., smell colors, see sounds). | Capsules, tablets, "microdots," blotter squares. | Unpredictable behavior, emotional instability, violent behavior (with PCP). |
| Inhalants (gas, aerosols, glue, nitrites, Rush, White Out) | Nausea, dizziness, headaches, lack of coordination and control. | Odor of substance on clothing and breath, intoxication, drowsiness, poor muscular control. | Unconsciousness, suffocation, nausea and vomiting, damage to brain and central nervous system, sudden death. |
| Narcotics Heroin (junk, dope, Black tar, China white) Demerol, Dilaudid (D's), Morphine, Codeine | Euphoria, drowsiness, insensitivity to pain, nausea, vomiting, watery eyes, runny nose (see Depressants). | Needle marks on arms, needles, syringes, spoons, pinpoint pupils, cold moist skin. | Addiction, lethargy, weight loss, contamination from unsterile needles (hepatitis, AIDS), accidental overdose. |
| Stimulants (speed, uppers, crank, Bam, black beauties, crystal, dexies, caffeine, nicotine, cocaine, amphetamines) | Alertness, talkativeness, wakefulness, increased blood pressure, loss of appetite, mood elevation. | Pills and capsules, loss of sleep and appetite, irritability or anxiety, weight loss, hyperactivity. | Fatigue leading to exhaustion, addiction, paranoia, depression, confusion, possibly hallucinations. |
| Depressants Barbiturates, sedatives, tranquilizers (downers, tranks, ludes, reds, Valium, yellow jackets, alcohol) | Depressed breathing and heartbeat, intoxication, drowsiness, uncoordinated movements. | Capsules and pills, confused behavior, longer periods of sleep, slurred speech. | Possible overdose, especially in combination with alcohol; muscle rigidity; addiction, withdrawal and overdose require medical treatment. |

SOURCE: *1991 Drug Education Guide*. The Positive Line #79930. Positive Promotions, 222 Ashland Place, Brooklyn, NY 11217. Reprinted by permission.

ters with scanners, telephone scramblers, paper shredders, electronic currency counters, assault rifles and electronic stun guns. Asset forfeiture is another form of punishment. Hartman (2001, p.6) states: "Asset forfeiture remains a powerful tool for law enforcement agencies. It remedies many of the problems that often slip through the criminal justice system, such as addressing the issue of allowing a criminal to profit from crime, and it provides a remedy for the victim. In short, asset forfeiture deprives the subject of ill-gotten gains [punishment], compensates the victim and serves the community."

Similar to legislation aimed at the gang problem, recent legislation, such as drug abatement statutes, is also helping in the war on drugs. Such legislation makes it much easier to shut down crack houses and clandestine drug laboratories.

Drug abatement statutes declare any property where illegal drugs are used or sold to be a public nuisance.

Areas in which new legislation would be of help include drive-by shootings, witness protection programs, recruitment of gang members, rural gang prevention laws, lowering age on juvenile offenses, vehicle forfeiture, brandishing a weapon, continuing criminal enterprise, loitering, automatic adult/juvenile certification for gang-related crimes and pointing a weapon from a vehicle.

# Prevention

Just as it is always preferable to prevent physical illness rather than treating it when it occurs, so it is always preferable to prevent a drug problem rather than treating it after the fact. One problem associated with drug abuse is the transmission of HIV infections when drug addicts share needles. Needle exchange programs (NEPs) have been found to significantly decrease the spread of HIV infections among intravenous drug users.

One effective way to approach prevention is to focus on known risks. The same factors placing youths at risk for joining gangs can also make them at risk for using drugs or alcohol. *Community risk factors* include extreme economic deprivation; low neighborhood attachment and community disorganization; transitions and mobility; community laws and norms favorable toward drug use, firearms and crime; availability of firearms; and media portrayals of violence. *School risk factors* include early and persistent antisocial behavior, academic failure beginning in elementary school and lack of commitment to school. *Family risk factors* include family history of problem behaviors, family management problems, family conflict and favorable parental attitudes and involvement. *Individual and peer risk factors* include alienation and rebelliousness, early initiation of problem behaviors, friends who engage in problem behaviors and favorable attitudes toward problem behaviors.

It is not enough to simply identify risks, however. Programs must also be put into place to keep youths from abusing drugs.

## *Educational Programs*

Educational programs such as DARE were discussed previously. A booklet, *The Coach's Playbook against Drugs,* published by the Office of Juvenile Justice and Delinquency Prevention, is aimed at the coaches in youth athletic programs. Most coaches have special relationships with their athletes and can influence their thinking and behavior. The booklet provides a list of "do's and don'ts," as well as how the game will be affected and team spirit will suffer.

Another approach might be to address what many see as flaws in current drug education programs. One such flaw is to equate drug use with drug abuse, using the terms interchangeably. But teenagers know the difference. Another flaw is the "gateway" theory, a mainstay of drug education, that use of marijuana leads to use of harder drugs such as cocaine. There is no research evidence to support this. These flaws conflict with what students observe and experience. Many prevention programs involve community partnerships.

# Community Policing and the Drug Problem

Simonson (2001, p.1) describes the Drug-Free Communities Act of 1997, which provides grants of up to $100,000 to community coalitions that mobilize their communities to prevent youth alcohol, tobacco, illicit drug and inhalant abuse. The grants support coalitions of youths; parents; media; law enforcement; school officials; faith-based organizations; fraternal organizations; state, local and tribal government agencies; health-care professionals; and other community representatives. The Drug-Free Communities Support Program has two major goals:

1. To reduce substance abuse among youths and, over time, adults, by addressing the factors in a community that increase the risk of substance abuse and enhancing factors that reduce that risk.
2. To establish and strengthen community collaboration—including their working with federal, state, local and tribal governments and private, nonprofit agencies—and to support local coalition efforts to prevent and reduce substance abuse among youths.

Simonson and Maher (2001, pp.1–2) provide summaries of a variety of innovative strategies among the 307 projects currently being funded by the Promising Practices: Drug-Free Communities Support Program.

## Adolescent Counseling Exchange (ACE), Denver, Colorado

The ACE coalition provides services to a majority Hispanic population at risk for substance use/abuse, gang involvement, gun violence, low school achievement, dropping out of school and teenage pregnancy. This charter school serves 100 at-risk, hard-to-reach middle school students. It has integrated its substance abuse and violence prevention curriculum into the school's educational structure and provides a daycare center for young children so teen parents can attend classes and participate in afterschool activities. The coalition has also intervened in and mediated conflicts between two rival gangs to substantially reduce the number of drive-by shootings in the community.

## Troy Community Coalition (TCC), Troy, Michigan

This coalition has successfully raised funds to support a number of drug abuse prevention activities, such as a prayer breakfast to recognize the importance of the religious community in prevention programming and to celebrate its diversity. It also held a basketball shooting contest, sponsored in part by the Detroit Pistons professional basketball team, to provide a drug-free family activity. The coalition's alcohol-free celebrity dinners and silent auctions feature speakers with national and local reputations and draw more than $100,000 in business support.

## North Central Community Based Services (NCCBS), Chama, New Mexico

The majority of the population served is Hispanic and Native American. The NCCBS coalition has developed a unique approach to address the area's graffiti problem, which is often an indication of substance abuse and gang activity. The coalition partners, including schools, businesses, the faith community and youth-serving organizations, supervise area youths in a mural creation project.

The youths create murals expressing their lives and experiences on the walls of schools, private businesses and public areas. Almost immediately, the graffiti problem has stopped.

### Together! Youth Violence, Alcohol, Drug Prevention, Lacey, Washington

The neighborhood centers project of Together! provide a targeted drug abuse prevention program to children and families living in low-income apartment complexes. Together! rents an apartment in each complex and offers afterschool and summer programs that promote a drugfree climate for children. Activities range from homework assistance and computer availability to skills building, conflict resolution and peer pressure resistance training. Girl Scout meetings, arts and crafts and field trips are offered. Drug abuse information, in addition to information about employment and community resources, is disseminated to parents at family potluck dinners and informal coffee hours. Programs for preschool children are also sponsored at the neighborhood centers.

## Problem-Oriented Policing, Gangs and Drugs

Public housing often poses a problem for both gangs and drugs. The SARA model has been successfully used to address such problems, as illustrated in the following case study from "Ridding Public Housing of Organized Drug Gangs" by Ron W. Glensor.*

---

### *Case Study 12.1*

#### Scanning

John Hope Homes and University Homes are two large Atlanta public housing complexes adjacent to one another and to the Clark-Atlanta University Center that essentially comprise one community of more than 1,200 units and house about 2,100 residents. The Atlanta Police Department, the Atlanta Housing Authority and the residents identified the community as a problem site for drug trafficking, as street gangs were selling drugs in and around the housing units. Drug-related violence also increased, including reports of gunfire.

Police believed most of these incidents resulted from turf battles between rival drug gangs. While shootings had usually ceased by the time police arrived, spent shell casings collected by officers at the scene indicated that semiautomatic and automatic weapons were being used. Questioning of residents and suspects helped police identify three groups involved—locals operating independently, a local gang known as the Terry White Boys and a third group known as the Miami Boys.

The Miami Boys were quickly identified as the most dangerous of the three groups because, unlike neighborhood-based gangs, the Miami Boys' operation appeared similar to that of organized crime. They ran a citywide criminal enterprise composed of several different factions, which operated essentially independent of one another but were loosely linked and known to cooperate on occasion. Seven factions of the gang were identified as operating in the Atlanta area.

Intelligence data provided by Atlanta narcotics officers revealed that each faction was organized in a hierarchical, military fashion. A captain served as the liaison between each faction and the supply source, which was presumed to be in south Florida. Two lieutenants were responsible for distributing drugs and collecting monies. Each lieutenant controlled two sergeants, who in turn controlled street workers who fell into one of four categories—lookouts, couriers, enforcers or dealers. Members were recruited from neighborhoods in southern Florida and relocated to Atlanta.

The Miami Boys were considered particularly violent—weapons of choice were the Ingram MAC 11 machine pistol and the Intratec automatic rifle. Within a short time, they had come to dominate the drug market at John Hope and University Homes. Their success was achieved by intimidating competitive drug dealers, including murder if necessary. Murders were usually

---

*SOURCE: *Problem-Oriented Drug Enforcement: A Community-Based Approach for Effective Policing.* Washington, DC: Bureau of Justice Assistance, October 1993, pp.38–40.

carried out by members of one of the factions not operating out of the John Hope and University Homes complexes. Because the shooters did not originate from the neighborhood, they were almost impossible to identify.

## Analysis

Officer T., assigned to the neighborhood evening watch, began gathering information on the Miami Boys. He talked with area residents; questioned arrestees and suspected dealers; and conducted surveillance by hiding in bushes, trees or vacant apartments and videotaping his suspects. Officer T. discovered that the gang openly displayed firearms (including machine guns) to intimidate residents and other rival narcotics dealers while they conducted sales of crack cocaine, 24 hours a day in 12-hour shifts. Gang members gained access to apartments to sell and stash their wares through several methods—by supplying users living in the buildings with cocaine, through romantic liaisons with tenants and by force. Higher-level gang members even paid residents to let the group store large amounts of cocaine in their apartments.

Because the gang was a tightly knit group, it was difficult to gather information about its inner workings, particularly about higher-ranking members. In addition, the gang controlled area residents, who became visibly nervous when officers approached them. Residents were threatened and often too frightened to even come out of their apartments because they feared gang retaliation. As a result, they rarely provided any information about the gang.

## Response

In response to increased street-level drug dealing and associated violence, the Atlanta commissioner of public safety established a new street-level strike force, the Red Dog Squad. Officer T. was assigned to the squad, where he continued to work on the Miami Boys' case. Based on his analysis of the gang's operations, he devised a two-part plan to break them up. The first part of his plan called for gathering information. Officer T. and the Red Dog Squad wanted to determine who was controlling the Miami Boys' operation at the complex. Because they hoped this information could be secured from the gang's underlings and from those residents whose apartments the gang used, they decided to make strategic arrests of gang members and collaborating tenants. The plan's second phase involved seizing control of the community from the drug dealers through numerous arrests. By disrupting the drug dealing and ridding the complex of some of the dealers, he hoped to send a message to the gang that they did not own the community. Even more importantly, visible police presence in the area would show residents that the Miami Boys were not as fearsome as they appeared.

Officer T. and his partner conducted military-type reconnaissance missions in the community. At times they would lie in the bushes for hours, waiting for an opportunity to move into an abandoned apartment to conduct direct surveillance of the group. When it rained, they would take advantage of the weather to move undetected around the area and position

themselves to observe the dealer's operation and literally "appear from nowhere" to make surprise arrests of group members. These tactics accounted for some attrition among group members and psychologically demoralized gang members because they were unaccustomed to losing members through arrest.

Arrests and seizures also resulted from undercover buys, informant buys and search warrants. Most low-level dealers arrested could not make bail and consequently remained off the street. Others returned to Florida as part of a plea agreement. Officer T.'s tactics were depleting the Miami Boys' Florida-born labor pool.

A break came when a dealer identified as G. P. was arrested for narcotics violations. Originally thought to be a low-level dealer, interrogations of Miami Boys and local suspects revealed that G. P. was, in fact, the Miami Boys' leader. Local suspects revealed that G. P. had been selling only because of the arrests of his street workers. Officer T. also learned through a Florida records check that G. P. had only recently been released from prison.

The apartment in John Hope Homes where G. P. stored his crack cocaine shipments was identified through surveillance and intelligence. G. P. paid the resident $75 a day for use of the apartment. After a search warrant was issued, police seized a large amount of money and more than two ounces of narcotics. Faced with a long jail sentence, the tenant provided information that not only confirmed that G. P. was an upper-level member of the Miami Boys, but also enabled prosecutors to obtain a grand jury indictment against him for trafficking in cocaine. Out on bond, G. P. and the few left in his operation moved their business from John Hope Homes into two other apartment complexes in northwest Atlanta. However, G. P. was followed by police and later arrested on the indictment warrant while he was transporting 15 bags of crack cocaine.

## Assessment

Due to successful enforcement activities, the Miami Boys gang in John Hope and University Homes was completely shut down. Residents, housing authority staff and police officers noted a subsequent decline in street-level drug dealing at the complex.

Resident fear was also substantially reduced. Tenants began to walk through the complex at night, and children began to play in the playgrounds during the day, unheard of occurrences when the Miami Boys were in charge.

During the latter part of the Miami Boys' crackdown, residents began to demonstrate visible support for the police. For example, during police raids, residents came outside and praised the officers and offered words of encouragement. They also began providing information about the drug situation in their area, which surfaced initially in the form of whispers and confidential telephone calls. Eventually, as trust grew, residents began to openly volunteer information and gave their names freely.

Partially because area residents began to understand their role in ridding the area of drug dealers, no other Miami Boys factions or other organized drug gangs were able to establish a foothold. Officer T. and his partner continued to monitor the situation at the complex.

## SUMMARY

The youth gang problem appears to be decreasing but is still of concern. A cultural gang is neighborhood-centered and exists independently of criminal activity. An instrumental gang is formed for the express purpose of criminal activity, primarily drug trafficking. Gang members often engage in vandalism, drug dealings, larceny/theft, burglary/breaking and entering, aggravated assault, motor vehicle theft and drive-by shootings. The first step in dealing with a gang problem is to *recognize* it. Once the problem is recognized, police need to identify gangs and their members. This is not difficult as most gang members identify themselves by their names, clothing, sign language and graffiti.

Four general strategies are being used to deal with gang problems: (1) suppression or law enforcement efforts, (2) social intervention, (3) opportunities provision and (4) community organization.

Frequently, gangs and drugs are integrally related. Research supports the link between street-level drug hot spot activity, disorder and serious crime. Approaches that have been suggested to address the drug problem include crime control, punishment, rehabilitation, prevention and legalization.

Police often use simple drug buys, undercover operations and raids to combat the drug problem. Buy operations occur in three well-defined stages: preparations for the buy, the buy itself and actions needed after the buy to process evidence and information. Information and time are critical elements in an illegal drug buy. The sale and use of illegal drugs is difficult to investigate and prosecute because sellers and buyers are willing participants. Making several drug buys will protect against a claim of entrapment.

In the 1980s, law enforcement focused its efforts in dealing with the drug problem on undercover operations and sophisticated raids. Law enforcement's focus in the 1990s was on enlisting and educating the public and targeting street-level sales. Legislation may also help, such as drug abatement statutes, which declare any property where illegal drugs are used or sold to be a public nuisance.

## APPLICATION

The chief wants you, the new commander of the narcotics squad, to establish some policies and procedures regarding drug buys. The present guidelines are obsolete. He instructs you to look at the previous general orders, policy and procedure bulletins, and to upgrade the operations.

### INSTRUCTIONS

Use the form in the Appendix. Identify the problems and needs. Specify what the policy is, why it is needed and what the police department's responsibility is. In this set of policies and procedures, concentrate on only drug *buy* procedures. Include the preparation, intelligence, surveillance, the buy money procedures, what to do during and after the buy, what to do when making arrests and processing evidence, and what the report should contain.

### AN EXERCISE IN CRITICAL THINKING

On July 8 Mike O'Brien came to an apartment building with five minors to purchase marijuana from a minor who lived in the complex. A group of minors (gang members) was also present in the parking lot for the same purpose. A number of the youths congregated around O'Brien's car, a classic 1966 Chevrolet Impala that O'Brien was in the process of restoring.

Fred Fidel (a member of a rival neighborhood gang) pulled into the parking lot and attempted to pull his vehicle partway into the limited space next to O'Brien's car, almost hitting it. Although none of the building's tenants were assigned designated parking spaces, Fidel habitually parked in the spot directly adjacent to the spot in which O'Brien had parked and in which many of the youths were standing. Although other parking spaces were available, Fidel pulled up to the spot where the youths were standing and repeatedly honked his horn. At that time, O'Brien told Fidel, "If you scratch my car, I'll kick your ass."

Fidel got out of his car, entered into an altercation with O'Brien, and pulled out a knife, brandishing it back and forth in front of O'Brien. O'Brien initially backed away as Fidel walked toward him. Fidel got back into his car and attempted to pull further into the parking space. Fidel then got out of his car, leaving it in such a position that O'Brien would be unable to move his car to leave.

As Fidel walked toward the building, O'Brien went toward him, advising Fidel that he was blocking O'Brien's car and offering to move it for him. During this second confrontation, Fidel again pulled out his knife. O'Brien told him to "back off; everything is cool." Fidel, however, grabbed O'Brien by the shirt with one hand as O'Brien tried to remove himself from Fidel's grasp and thrust the knife into O'Brien's chest with his other hand.

O'Brien was interviewed by police on the scene, but he bled to death before medical care could be administered. When Fidel was questioned by police, he at first denied possessing a knife or knowing anything about the stabbing. After a few minutes, he changed his account of the event and claimed self-defense.

1. Given the conflicting testimony between the members of the gang and Fidel, is there sufficient evidence to arrest Fidel for second-degree felony murder?
    a. Numerous witnesses give probable cause to believe that Fidel committed felony murder, and therefore, Fidel should be arrested.
    b. Because the only witnesses are juvenile gang members whose testimony is suspect, prosecution will be nearly impossible; therefore, Fidel's testimony should be recorded, but he should not be arrested.
    c. As Fidel clearly was outnumbered and likely felt insecure, he probably wanted only to intimidate O'Brien; so there is insufficient cause to arrest Fidel for second-degree felony murder.
    d. Because of the intended purchase of drugs, Fidel can be arrested for first-degree intentional murder.
    e. Because it is Fidel's word against the gang's, both negate each other, leaving insufficient evidence for arresting and convicting Fidel of second-degree felony murder.

### DISCUSSION QUESTIONS

1. How might possible changes in the juvenile justice system be a deterrent to juveniles joining gangs?
2. Does your community have a gang problem? If so, describe it.
3. What role can citizens and community groups usefully play in coping with the drug problem?
4. What must officers consider when establishing a fictitious past for a cover story as an undercover agent?
5. As an undercover agent, if someone asks you if you are a "narc," how do you respond? What attitude will protect your safety?
6. Is drug dealing a problem in your educational institution? Your community?
7. What are some unobtrusive signals surveillance team members can use to cover such various situations as when the buy has been completed, when help is needed and so on?

### INFOTRAC COLLEGE EDITION ASSIGNMENTS

- Use InfoTrac College Edition to answer the Discussion Questions as appropriate.

- Using InfoTrac College Edition, find and outline one of the following articles and be prepared to share the outline with the class:
    - "Preventing Street Gang Violence" by Allen L. Hixon
    - "Gangs in Middle America: Are They a Threat?" by David M. Allender
    - "Drugs and the Legal System" by Kevin Burke
    - "Implementing an Asset Forfeiture Program" by Victor E. Hartman
    - "The Gangs behind Bars" by Tiffany Danitz
    - "The Violence of Hmong Gangs and the Crime of Rape" by Richard Straka
    - "Connecting Drug Paraphernalia to Drug Gangs" by Robert D. Sheehy and Efrain A. Rosario

 ### INTERNET ASSIGNMENTS

Select two of the following assignments to complete.

- Go to fortunecity.com/meltingpot/oltorf/1024 and outline the history and profiles of the 18th Street gang or any of the other L.A.-based Hispanic street gangs. This site also has photographs of gang graffiti which may be of interest to you. Be prepared to discuss your findings with the class.
- Go to the Florida Department of Corrections website www.dc.state.fl.us/pub/index.html and write a description of three gangs of interest to you. Be prepared to discuss your gang descriptions with the class.
- Go to the website Gangs or Us at www.gangsorus.com. Find your state and list the information provided, comparing it to the information provided for a state in a different part of the country. Be prepared to share your findings with the class.
- Go to the Department of Justice website at www.ojp.usdoj.gov/nij and find the report, *Reducing Gun Violence: The Boston Gun Project's Operation Ceasefire*. Write a brief summary detailing the specific strategies used and the results obtained by Operation Ceasefire. Be prepared to share your summary with the class.
- Go to the Vera Institute website at www.vera.org/ssc and find their report "Do Drug Courts Save Jail and Prison Bed Space?" Cite statistics they provide to support their finding that drug courts do save jail and prison beds. Be prepared to share your findings with the class.
- Use the Internet to locate information on the drug *Ecstasy* and see what effects it may have on the person using it. Be prepared to share your information with the class.
- Go to the Office of National Drug Control Policy at www.whitehousedrugpolicy.gov/drugfact/pulsechk/midyear2000/midyear2000.pdf. Write a two- to three-page report on what the emerging drugs are and the distribution patterns. Be prepared to share and discuss your report with the class.

## BOOK-SPECIFIC WEBSITE

The book-specific website at http://cj.wadsworth.com/ wobleski_Hess_police_op4e hosts a variety of resources for students and instructors. Many can be emailed to the instructor. Included are extended activities such as Concept Builders - the 3 step learning module that reinforces key chapter concepts, followed by a real-world applications and critical thinking questions. InfoTrac College Edition exercises; Discussion Questions; interactive key-term FlashCards; and a collection of chapter-based Web Links provide additional information and activities to include in the curriculum.

## REFERENCES

"Additive Might Help Police Catch Meth Cooks." *Minnesota Police Chief*, Autumn 2004, p.37.

Allender, David M. "Gangs in Middle America: Are They a Threat?" *FBI Law Enforcement Bulletin*, December 2001, pp.1–9.

"Boston Program Said to Show Problem-Solving Policing Works." *Criminal Justice Newsletter*, December 13, 2001, pp.5–7.

Burke, John. "Prescription Drug Diversion." *Law Enforcement Technology*, May 2004, pp.16–21.

"Bush Goal: Cut Drug Abuse 25% in Five Years." Associated Press, as reported in the (Minneapolis/St. Paul) *Star Tribune*, February 13, 2002, p.A7.

Bynum, Timothy S. and Varano, Sean P. "The Anti-Gang Initiative in Detroit: An Aggressive Enforcement Approach to Gangs." In *Policing Gangs and Youth Violence*, edited by Scott M. Decker. Belmont, CA: Wadsworth Publishing Company, 2003, pp.214–238.

*The Coach's Playbook against Drugs*. Washington, DC: Office of Juvenile Justice and Delinquency Prevention, no date. (NCJ 173393)

Cohen, Jacqueline; Gorr, Wilpen; and Singh, Piyusha. "Estimating Intervention Effects in Varying Risk Settings: Do Police Raids Reduce Illegal Drug Dealing at Nuisance Bars?" *Criminology*, May 2003, pp.257–292.

Collins, Geneve. "Fighting Gangs: Strategic Targeting vs. Kitchen Sink Model." *Community Links*, August 2004, pp.11–13.

Decker, Scott H., ed. *Policing Gangs and Youth Violence*. Belmont, CA: Wadsworth Publishing Company, 2003.

*Drug Treatment in the Criminal Justice System*. Washington, DC: Office of National Drug Control Policy, Fact Sheet, March 2001. (NCJ 181857)

Egley, Arlen, Jr. and Major, Aline K. *Highlights of the 2002 National Youth Gang Survey*. Washington, DC:OJJDP Fact Sheet #01, July 2004.

Ellement, John. "Police Thwart OxyContin Drug Ring." *The Boston Globe*, November 12, 2004.

Ericson, Nels. *Substance Abuse: The Nation's Number One Health Problem*. Washington, DC: Office of Juvenile Justice and Delinquency Prevention, Fact Sheet #17, May 2001. (FS-200117)

Esbensen, Finn-Aage; Winfree, Thomas L., Jr.; He, Ni; and Taylor, Terrance J. "Youth Gangs and Definitional Issues: When Is a Gang a Gang, and Why Does It Matter?" *Crime and Delinquency*, January 2001, pp.105–130.

Fraser, William J. "Getting the Drop on Street Gangs and Terrorists." *Law Enforcement News*, November 30, 2001, pp.11, 14.

Fritsch, Eric J.; Caeti, Tory J.; and Taylor, Robert W. "Gang Suppression through Saturation Patrol and Aggressive Curfew and Truancy Effectiveness." In *Policing Gangs and Youth Violence*, edited by Scott M. Decker. Belmont, CA: Wadsworth Publishing Company, 2003, pp.267–284.

*Gang Awareness*. Chicago: City of Chicago, Department of Human Services, no date.

Garrett, Ronnie. "Turning Up the Heat on Meth Cooks." *Law Enforcement Technology*, May 2004, pp.36–42.

Gordon, Rachel A.; Laheu, Benjamin B.; Kawai, Eriko; Loeber, Rolf; Stouthamer-Loeber, Magda; and Farrington, David P. "Anti-Social Behavior and Youth Gang Membership: Selection and Socialization." *Criminology*, February 2004, pp.55–84.

Hartman, Victor E. "Implementing an Asset Forfeiture Program." *FBI Law Enforcement Bulletin*, January 2001, pp.1–7.

Hayes, Chuck. "Drug Recognition Experts: A Public Safety Resource." *The Police Chief*, October 2003, pp.103–106.

Johnson, Matt. "Successful Rave Operations." *Law and Order*, October 2001, pp.184–188.

Langston, Mike. "Addressing the Need for a Uniform Definition of Gang-Involved Crime." *FBI Law Enforcement Bulletin*, February 2003, pp.7–11.

Maxon, Cheryl L.; Hennigan, Karen; and Sloane, David C. "For the Sake of the Neighborhood: Civil Gang Injunctions as a Gang Intervention Tool in Southern California." In *Policing Gangs and Youth Violence*, edited by Scott M. Decker. Belmont, CA: Wadsworth Publishing Company, 2003, pp.239–266.

Meeker, James W.; Parson, Katie J. R.; and Vila, Bryan J. "Developing a GIS-Based Regional Gang Incident Tracking System." In *Responding to Gangs: Evaluation and Research*, edited by Winifred L. Reed and Scott H. Decker. Washington, DC: National Institute of Justice, July 2003, pp.289–329. (NCJ 190351)

Miethe, Terrance D. and McCorkle, Richard C. "Evaluating Nevada's Antigang Legislation and Gang Prosecution Units." In *Responding to Gangs: Evaluation and Research*, edited by Winifred L. Reed and Scott H. Decker. Washington, DC: National Institute of Justice, July 2002, pp.169–185. (NCJ 190351)

Miller, Walter B. *The Growth of Youth Gang Problems in the United States: 1970–1998*. Washington, DC: Office of Juvenile Justice and Delinquency Prevention, April 2001. (NCJ 181868)

Moore, Joan and Hagedorn, John. *Female Gangs: A Focus on Research*. Washington, DC: Office of Juvenile Justice and Delinquency Prevention, Juvenile Justice Bulletin, March 2001. (NCJ 186159)

*National Drug Control Strategy, 2004 Annual Report.* Washington, DC: Office of National Drug Control Policy, 2004. http://www.whitehousedrugpolicy.gov/publications/policy/ndcs04/

*National Drug Threat Assessment 2004.* Washington, DC: National Drug Intelligence Center, April 2004.

"New Program Supports Community AntiGang Efforts." *OJJDP News @ a Glance,* September/October 2003, pp.1–2.

O'Rourke, Judy. "City Passes Gang Ordinance." *TheSignal.com,* October 14, 2004.

Pennell, Susan and Melton, Roni. "Evaluation of a Task Force Approach to Gangs." In *Responding to Gangs: Evaluation and Research,* edited by Winifred L. Reed and Scott H. Decker. Washington, DC: National Institute of Justice, July 2002, pp.169–185. (NCJ 190351)

*Pulse Check: Trends in Drug Abuse 2004.* Washington, DC: Office of National Drug Control Policy, January 2004. (NCJ 201398)

Reed, Winifred L. and Decker, Scott H., editors. *Responding to Gangs: Evaluation and Research.* Washington, DC: National Institute of Justice, July 2002. (NCJ 190351)

Savelli, Lou. *Gangs across America and Their Symbols.* Flushing, NY: Looseleaf Law, 2004.

Shelden, Randall G.; Tracy, Sharon K.; and Brown, William B. *Youth Gangs in American Society,* 3rd ed. Belmont, CA: Wadsworth Publishing Company, 2004.

Simonson, James M. *The Drug-Free Communities Support Program.* Washington, DC: Office of Juvenile Justice and Delinquency Prevention, Fact Sheet #08, April 2001. (FS-200108)

Simonson, James M. and Maher, Pat M. *Promising Practices: Drug-Free Communities Support Program.* Washington, DC: Office of Juvenile Justice and Delinquency Prevention, Fact Sheet #11, April 2001. (FS-200111)

"A Sinus of the Times: Drug Stores Ordered to Restrict Key Meth Ingredient." *Law Enforcement News,* July 2004, pp.1, 15.

Smith, Michael R. "Police-Led Crackdowns and Cleanups: An Evaluation of a Crime Control Initiative in Richmond, Virginia." *Crime and Delinquency,* Vol. 47, No. 1, 2001.

Steffen, George and Candelaria, Samuel. "Currency Seizures during Interdiction Investigations." *Law and Order,* March 2004, pp.40–48.

Streit, Corinne. "The Increasingly Popular Club Drug: Ecstasy." *Law Enforcement Technology,* May 2001, pp.24–28.

Strong, Ronald L. "The National Drug Intelligence Center: Assessing the Drug Threat." *The Police Chief,* May 2001, pp.55–60.

"Substance Abuse Costs States $81 Billion Annually." *NCJA Justice Bulletin,* March 2001, pp.5–6.

"Taking a Different Road with First-Time Drug Violators." *Law Enforcement News,* February 28, 2001, p.5.

Tita, George; Riley, K. Jack; and Greenwood, Peter. "From Boston to Boyle Heights: The Process and Prospects of a 'Pulling Levers' Strategy in a Los Angeles Barrio." In *Policing Gangs and Youth Violence,* edited by Scott M. Decker. Belmont, CA: Wadsworth Publishing Company, 2003, pp.102–130.

Valdez, Al. "Cyber Gangs? Is the Reality of www.crips.com Here?" *Police,* March 2001, p.46.

Webb, Vincent J. and Katz, Charles M. "Policing Gangs in an Era of Community Policing." In *Policing Gangs and Youth Violence,* edited by Scott M. Decker. Belmont, CA: Wadsworth Publishing Company, 2003, pp.17–49.

Weisel, Deborah Lamm. "The Evolution of Street Gangs: An Examination of Form and Variation." In *Responding to Gangs: Evaluation and Research,* edited by Winifred L. Reed and Scott H. Decker. Washington, DC: National Institute of Justice, July 2002, pp.25–65. (NCJ 190351)

Weisel, Deborah Lamm. "Criminal Investigation." In *Local Government Police Management,* edited by William A. Geller and Darrel W. Stephens. Washington, DC: International City/County Management Association, 2003, pp.169–206.

Weisheit, Ralph A. and Wells, L. Edward. "Youth Gangs in Rural America." *NIJ Journal,* July 2004, pp.2–5. (NCJ 204516)

Wuestewald, Todd and Adcock, Gayla. "Retailers Were Unaware That They Were Selling Over the Counter the Ingredients and Hardware for Manufacturing Methamphetamine." *Community Links,* May 2004, pp.2–3.

**CASE CITED**

*Hampton v. United States,* 425 U.S. 484 (1976)

# THE PERSONAL SIDE OF POLICE OPERATIONS

Section I described the basic skills needed to perform the functions of today's law enforcement agencies legally and in the context of a changing society, while using discretion wisely. The need to protect the constitutional rights of all citizens, including those who commit crimes, was emphasized throughout Section I, as was the need to act professionally.

Sections II and III examined the basic police operations as well as specialized functions of police, still emphasizing the importance of respecting individual rights, of acting within the law and of using discretion professionally.

This section examines the personal side of police operations even as it continues to stress the needs for protecting the rights of others and for acting professionally. Today's officers face more stresses than ever before, so it is incumbent upon them to be physically and mentally fit. The stresses of the job can be every bit as hazardous as a gun-wielding criminal (Chapter 13). The text concludes with two critical areas in law enforcement, avoiding civil liabilities and doing what is moral and right. Given the great amount of discretion officers have, it is crucial that they select alternatives that are legally and morally acceptable to themselves, their colleagues and the public they serve (Chapter 14).

# CHAPTER 13

# Physical and Mental Health Issues: Keeping Fit for Duty

## Do You Know . . .

- What the prime factor in physical fitness is?
- What police-specific physical skills are important?
- What job-related factors detract from police officers' physical fitness?
- What constitutes an effective fitness program?
- What bloodborne pathogens police officers should protect against?
- What the concept of universal precaution recommends?
- What the greatest threat to officers' mental fitness is?
- What the major categories of stressors for police officers are?
- What the effects of stress might include?
- What the awareness spectrum is and where in that spectrum police officers should try to be?
- What the three sides of the border patrol's survival triangle are?
- What the five Cs of basic tactics for survival are?

## Can You Define?

| | | | |
|---|---|---|---|
| acute stress | burst stress | mental fitness | stress |
| aerobic training | chronic stress | physical fitness | survival triangle |
| anaerobic training | cross-training | split-second | universal precaution |
| awareness spectrum | depression | syndrome | |
| burnout | | | |

## Introduction

"Cops kill themselves three times more often than other Americans. They suffer more depression, divorce more, and drink more—As many as one in four police officers have alcohol abuse problems" (Fox, 2003, p.9). Police work has been characterized as long periods of devastating boredom punctuated by sporadic, relatively brief periods of utter terror. Vila et al. (2002, p.4) describe it this way: "Police work often swings unpredictably from monotonous routine and numbing boredom to dynamic, fact-starved, and confusing situations that make extreme physical, mental and emotional demands on officers." Much about the job, unfortunately, allows officers to become less physically and mentally fit than they were when they passed the rigorous pre-employment screening. Physical and mental fitness are fundamentally related: mental discipline is needed to

maintain or improve physical fitness, and mental alertness requires physical fitness. Physical and mental fitness also affect stress levels and officers' responses to stress. Furthermore, physical fitness, mental fitness and adaptability to the stresses of police work are all correlated with officers' safety on the job—in effect, their very lives may depend on such physical and mental preparedness.

Although this chapter discusses physical fitness, mental fitness, stress and officer safety as separate topics, their interrelationship must be kept in mind. The chapter begins with a discussion of physical fitness. This is followed by discussions of physical fitness training programs and the threats posed by bloodborne pathogens and biological and chemical agents. Next, mental fitness is explored, including an explanation of stress, sources of stress, the effects of stress, reducing stress and mental fitness programs. The chapter concludes with a discussion of officer safety.

## Physical Fitness

The United States has become fitness conscious. Visit almost any city and you can see joggers and runners, bikers and rollerbladers. Health clubs do a brisk business. Weight-loss programs have proliferated. Even fast food chains are now offering reduced-fat and fat-free items. People strive to be fit. **Physical fitness** is the body's general capacity to adapt and respond favorably to physical effort.

The demands of police work require officers to be in top physical condition. Physical fitness may make the difference between success and failure on the job and sometimes may even make the difference between life and death. Furthermore, officers who are not physically fit are not prepared to adequately discharge their duties and may, as a result, be sued. In *Parker v. District of Columbia*, the jury awarded nearly half a million dollars to a man shot twice by a DC police officer during an arrest. The jury reasoned: "Had the officer been physically fit, . . . he might have overpowered the suspect instead of reaching for his gun. The officer 'simply was not in adequate physical shape' to do his job." This is not an isolated case.

Many people evaluate fitness on the basis of appearance alone. Although personal appearance can give certain indications of fitness levels, what is going on inside is more important. The prime indicators of physical fitness are endurance, balance, agility, flexibility, strength, power and body composition.

 Although many factors contribute to a well-conditioned body, the prime factor is the condition of the circulatory (cardiovascular) system, upon which endurance or stamina depends.

Many police departments are now using body composition rather than height/weight charts in setting their physical standards. Excessive body fat not only hinders physical motion; it is also a serious risk factor for heart disease, diabetes and stroke. In addition to the preceding factors involved in physical fitness, several other physical factors are related specifically to how well police officers perform.

 Motor skills important to police officers include coordination, speed and accuracy.

### Myths about Physical Fitness

People hold many misconceptions about physical fitness, sometimes as excuses to avoid getting back into shape.

*Physical fitness may make the difference between success and failure on the job and sometimes may even make the difference between life and death.*

**Too Far Gone**    Many people feel they either are too old or have physically deteriorated to such a degree it is impossible to get back into good physical shape. This is not true. Regardless of age or how "far gone" a person is, if the person is organically sound, he or she can become fit through a well-structured physical training program.

**Hard Work Will Kill You**    A rather common misconception is that the harder you work, the quicker you die. Not only is this false, but just the opposite is true. People need to exercise regularly or they deteriorate. People "rust out" from inactivity far more than they "wear out" from hard physical work.

**Any Kind of Exercise Is Good**    Again, this is not true. Different exercises and activities have varying degrees of value depending on their intensity, duration and frequency. Short-duration exercising such as stretching or isometrics offers limited benefits. Likewise, an hour of racquetball, tennis or softball every few weeks by a usually sedentary person not only offers limited benefits, but can be extremely dangerous. The most beneficial programs are those done regularly for at least 20 to 30 minutes and directed toward all aspects of total fitness.

**No Pain, No Gain**    Although when people first begin exercise programs they often experience some stiffness and soreness, usually such programs should not cause pain. This is not to imply, however, that getting and keeping physically fit is not hard work.

**The Quick and Easy Way to Fitness**    Despite hordes of advertisements to the contrary, getting and keeping physically fit is hard work and requires commitment and discipline. It also takes time—weeks or months—to get into shape. Unfortunately, it takes much less time to get out of shape.

Police work is often sedentary, boring, involves irregular hours and rotating shifts, and may promote poor diets, excessive cigarette smoking and consumption of alcohol, and great amounts of stress.

Because of these factors, it is important that police officers engage in some sort of physical fitness training program.

## Physical Fitness Training Programs

Because police officers often face situations involving physical restraint, self-defense or foot pursuit, many police departments have set up both mandatory and voluntary physical fitness programs for officers.

What kind of program is instituted varies from department to department. An effective program should include **aerobic training** aimed at the cardiovascular system. This can be biking, cross-country skiing, rowing, swimming or walking. It also can include treadmills, stationary cycles and rowing machines. Aerobic training should be done at least three times a week for a minimum of 15 to 20 minutes. It should be preceded by a light warm-up and followed by a brief cool down. Aerobic training can also incorporate **cross-training,** with an officer biking one day, running one day and swimming one day.

*Speed training* should be incorporated into the aerobic portion of the exercise. Police officers are often older than the suspects they chase and are further hindered by the 20 or more pounds of weight added by their gun belt and accessories. Although speed is usually needed in a foot chase, agility is often even more important. Agility can be practiced on an obstacle course or through drills such as those football players use. Jumping rope is another way to improve agility. Eye-hand coordination can be improved through racquetball, tennis, basketball and softball. Martial arts training can improve an officer's power, flexibility, speed and balance.

Another important part of an exercise program is *strength training,* or **anaerobic training.** Strength training helps maintain muscle tissue. Strength exercises can also help reduce low-back problems. Aerobic activities do little in this area.

In addition, an officer's physical abilities are frequently tested in such activities as restraining a violent suspect, pushing a disabled vehicle and lifting an injured person. Among the methods available for building strength are free weights and machines, which usually rely on "progressive resistance," and resistance against one's own body weight, which usually relies on "progressive repetition." Exercises using resistance against one's own body weight include push-ups, pull-ups, dips and sit-ups.

*Flexibility training* is also important. This can be done as stretching in the warm-up and cool down portions of aerobic or strength training. Stretching reduces muscle tension, improves coordination and can prevent injuries. Each stretch should be held for approximately 10 seconds. Breathing should be normal, and no bouncing should be done. It should *not* be painful. If a muscle is stretched to the point of pain, it is being stretched too far.

 An effective physical fitness training program that is varied and of interest to the officer should include aerobic, strength and flexibility training. It should be engaged in regularly for 20 to 30 minutes a day, at least three days a week.

Besides the obvious benefits to individual officers, physical fitness programs tend to reduce absenteeism and sick time as well as early retirement. Insurance premiums may go down, while productivity often goes up.

**Table 13.1**  Physical Factors and Tests

| Fitness Factor | Test |
|---|---|
| Absolute strength of the upper body | 1RM bench press raw score (pounds) <br> 1RM bench press ratio score (weight pushed divided by body weight) |
| Explosive leg strength | Vertical jump in inches |
| Dynamic strength | |
|    Abdominal muscular endurance | One-minute sit-up (number) |
|    Upper-body muscular endurance | Maximum push-up (number) |
| Trunk strength | One-minute sit-up (number) |
| Extent flexibility | Sit and reach (inches) |
| Endurance and aerobic power | 1.5-mile run (minutes and seconds) |
| Speed | 300-meter run (seconds) |
| Anaerobic power | 300-meter run (seconds) |
| Gross coordination agility | Illinois agility test (seconds) |

SOURCE: Thomas R. Collingwood, Robert Hoffman and Jay Smith. "Underlying Physical Fitness Factors for Performing Police Officer Physical Tasks." *The Police Chief,* March 2004, p.34.

Collingwood et al. (2004) researched physical fitness assessments for 15 years, with validation studies performed on more than 5,500 incumbent officers representing 75 federal, state and local law enforcement agencies. Their study was designed to assess the accuracy of a physical fitness test as a predictor of an officer's ability to perform physical job tasks. They (p.33) identified three basic events containing critical and frequent tasks:

1. Roadway clearance, involving lifting, carrying and dragging debris, and pushing a car
2. Victim extraction, involving sprinting to a disabled vehicle and lifting and dragging a dummy to safety
3. Sustained foot pursuit, involving running up stairs, dodging, jumping, climbing a fence, crawling, vaulting obstacles, striking and moving a dummy, and simulated cutting using resistance bands.

They then isolated fitness factors and tests that might measure them, shown in Table 13.1.

## Other Aspects of Physical Fitness

Nutrition plays an important role in a person's overall fitness. Low-cholesterol, low-fat foods can reduce the risks of coronary artery disease (CAD), sometimes called coronary heart disease (CHD). Farmer (2004, p.34) stresses: "Physical exercise and diet must be done together. Think of it as a positive and negative on a battery. If one end is not connected, you have no power."

Smoking and drug use should be eliminated. Alcohol should be used in moderation if used at all. In addition, officers should take precautions to protect themselves against bloodborne pathogens and other health hazards.

# Bloodborne Pathogens and Biological and Chemical Threats

 Bloodborne pathogens police officers should protect against include HIV infections and AIDS, hepatitis B and hepatitis C.

## HIV Infection and AIDS

HIV is typically transmitted from one person to another, usually during unprotected sex or by sharing needles during IV drug abuse. HIV may also be transmitted through blood transfusions. AIDS, or Acquired Immune Deficiency Syndrome, is the end stage of HIV infection.

The potential for exposure to HIV/AIDS in police work remains minimal. However, civil liability may result when officers deal with suspects who have AIDS. A police department can be vulnerable both to internal and external civil claims. For example, in *Jane Doe v. Borough of Barrington* (1990), a city was held responsible for failing to adequately train its officers about AIDS, resulting in privacy right violations to the family of an HIV-positive arrestee. Likewise, in *Woods v. White* (1990), the court ruled that individuals have a constitutional right to privacy in information relating to AIDS. Another issue is whether offenders with HIV should be isolated.

The main concerns involve including HIV information in police reports and having officers disclose their own HIV status to co-workers and supervisors. Including a suspect's HIV status in a police report may violate medical information laws, but not including it may raise issues of why an officer acted in a certain way.

## Hepatitis B Viral Infection

Hepatitis B viral infection affects the liver and poses a much greater risk than HIV. It can progress to chronic liver disease or liver cancer and death. Symptoms range from fever, aching muscles and loss of appetite to prolonged nausea and vomiting and yellowing of the skin (jaundice).

Fortunately, a vaccine is available whose protection lasts for nine years. Since 1992, OSHA has required law enforcement agencies to offer at no cost the vaccination against hepatitis B to all officers who may have contact with body fluids while on the job.

## Hepatitis C Viral Infection

Hepatitis C virus also attacks the liver and is much more treacherous than hepatitis B. Unfortunately, there is no effective treatment or protective vaccine for this disease.

## How Bloodborne Pathogens Are Spread

*Bloodborne Pathogens for Law Enforcement* (1998, p.4) explains:

> Hepatitis B, hepatitis C and HIV infection are spread in the same way. They are not spread through the air like cold and flu germs, so you won't get these viruses from working alongside someone who is infected or from touching, coughing, sneezing or a kiss on the cheek. Nor will you become infected from sharing things such as telephones, bathrooms, eating utensils, gym equipment, swimming pools or water fountains with an infected person.

These infections are spread through contact with blood, semen, vaginal secretions (sexual contact) and any other body fluid or tissue that contains visible blood. You can also get infected by contact with the fluid that surrounds an unborn child and the fluid around the heart, lungs or joints.

Body fluids such as sweat, tears, saliva, urine, stool, vomitus, nasal secretions and sputum have not been shown to transmit bloodborne diseases, unless they contain visible blood.

## Other Diseases

*Tuberculosis* is transmitted through the air by people who are coughing, hacking and wheezing. *Meningitis* is also spread by airborne transmission. It causes inflammation of the membranes that surround the brain and can result in headaches, fever, vomiting, stiff neck and light sensitivity.

## Protecting Oneself

OSHA has standards on bloodborne pathogens requiring employers to address employee protection in a written exposure control plan describing precautions employees can take to prevent exposures as well as steps to take if exposure does occur. Pedersen (2001b, p.52) cautions: "You are legally entitled to some protection from your agency, but the bottom line is that your health is in your hands." The following precautions may protect against bloodborne disease such as hepatitis B and C and HIV (Pedersen, 2001b, p.54):

- Get the hepatitis B vaccine.
- Treat all people, all of the time, as if they have a bloodborne disease.
- Treat all body fluids as infectious.
- Wear appropriate personal protection equipment (PPE) whenever contact with blood or body fluids is likely [PPE includes latex gloves, face mask or protective eyewear, gown or coveralls and resuscitation devices].
- Book contaminated items into evidence safely or dispose of them properly.
- Thoroughly wash your hands and other exposed parts of your body after every personal contact. [Wash for at least 10 to 15 seconds, including your rings, between your fingers and above your wrists.]
- Change contaminated clothing as soon as possible.
- Do not re-use personal protection equipment.
- Immediately follow your department's protocol after every exposure [e.g., get tested].
- Document and report all exposures.
- Never re-cap, bend or remove needles from syringes.
- It is also advisable to use an alcohol wipe if bitten.

 The concept of **universal precaution** recommends that all blood and potentially infectious materials other than blood must be treated as if infected.

Cuts, scrapes and puncture wounds can all get infected and should be thoroughly washed and bandaged as soon as possible. The *tetanus shot* is an important safeguard against infections and should be repeated every 10 years. If, however, a deep or dirty wound is sustained, a tetanus shot should have been given within the last five years. Officers can also become infected from human bites. An officer who is bitten by a human should wash the wound immediately and then see a doctor for the appropriate antibiotics. An officer who is bitten by an animal should impound the animal if possible and have it tested for rabies.

### Biological and Chemical Threats

According to Sweet (2001, p.49): "As the potential threat of chemical, biological and other unconventional weapons grows on the local, state and federal levels, preparation for a catastrophic event is rapidly becoming a significant issue."

The Environmental Protection Agency is working to improve its ability to detect biological agents in the water supply, and the Food and Drug Administration is enhancing surveillance methods for detecting disease outbreaks in humans and animals ("Are the Feds Doing Enough . . .," 2001, p.16).

Sweet (p.53) stresses: "Advance preparation is always the key to any successful disaster response or preventive plan." Responding to HAZMAT incidents was discussed in Chapter 5. In addition to being physically fit, it is crucial that officers also be mentally fit.

## Mental Fitness

Mental fitness is not as easily perceived or analyzed, but it is equally as important as physical fitness. **Mental fitness** refers to a person's emotional well-being, the ability to feel fear, anger, compassion and other emotions and to express them appropriately. It also refers to a person's alertness and ability to make decisions quickly.

 The greatest threat to officers' mental fitness is stress.

## Stress

Most people have a general idea of what **stress** is. Most people also perceive stress as negative, but this is not necessarily true. A certain amount of stress keeps people alert and functioning. Too much stress, or *distress,* however, can be incapacitating. In ancient China, the symbol for stress included two characters—one symbolizing danger, the other opportunity.

Stress may be acute or chronic. **Acute stress** is temporary and may result in peak performance. Adrenaline rushes through the body; heart rate increases; blood pressure, brain activity, breathing rates and metabolic rates increase—adapting the body for fight or flight. Thousands of years before we became "civilized," our bodies were faced with simple survival, for which either a "fight or flight" response was appropriate. Table 13.2 presents an explanation of the anatomy of stress: what physical and psychological changes occur, how they were previously advantages and how they now have become disadvantages.

**Chronic stress,** in contrast, is ongoing, like being under a state of constant siege. This can lead to severe psychological problems. In his classic work *The Stress of Life* (1956), Dr. Hans Selye suggested that humans subjected to excessive stress undergo a "general adaptation syndrome" consisting of three distinct stages: alarm reaction, resistance and exhaustion. In the first stage, *alarm reaction,* individuals perceive a threat to their safety or happiness. They recognize their inability to reach their personal/professional goals. The body releases stress hormones. In the second stage, *resistance,* individuals try to cope with the problem. The amount of resistance to the stressors increases, and bodily defense mechanisms

**Table 13.2**   The Anatomy of Stress

| Natural Response | Original Benefit | Today's Drawback |
|---|---|---|
| ■ Release of cortisone from adrenal glands. | ■ Protection from an instant allergic reaction or from a dustup with an attacking foe. | ■ If chronically elevated, cortisone destroys the body's resistance to the stresses of cancer, infection, surgery and illness. Bones are made more brittle by cortisone. Blood pressure can be elevated. |
| ■ Increase of thyroid hormone in the bloodstream. | ■ Speeds up the body's metabolism, thereby providing extra energy. | ■ Intolerance to heat, shaking nerves to the point of jumpiness, insomnia, weight loss and ultimately exhaustion or burnout. |
| ■ Release of endorphin from the hypothalamus. | ■ Identical to morphine, a potent pain killer. | ■ Chronic, relentless stresses can deplete levels of endorphin, aggravating migraines, backaches, and the pain of arthritis. |
| ■ Reduction in sex hormones—testosterone in the male and progesterone in the female. | ■ Decreased fertility. In wartime, decreased libido made both partners' lives more bearable. | ■ Obvious anxieties and failures when intercourse is attempted. Premature ejaculation in male; failure to reach orgasm in female. |
| ■ Shutdown of the entire digestive tract. Mouth goes dry to avoid adding fluids to the stomach. Rectum and bladder tend to empty to jettison any excess load prior to battle. | ■ Acts as a vital "self-transfusion" allowing person to perform superordinary feats of muscular power. | ■ Dry mouth makes it difficult to speak with authority. The drawback of the "jettison response" is obvious. |
| ■ Release of sugar into the blood, along with an increase in insulin levels to metabolize it. | ■ Quick, short-distance energy supply. | ■ Diabetes can be aggravated or even started. |

SOURCE: Adapted from Peter G. Hanson. *The Joy of Stress.* Kansas City, MO: Universal Stress Syndicate Company, 1995, pp.19–27.

are activated. In the third stage, *exhaustion,* individuals feel helpless and hopeless. Bodily resources are also exhausted, and people cannot adequately defend against the stressors.

## Sources of Stress

Many lists of stressors have been generated, including stressors specific to the police profession. Most of the stressors fall into four main categories, although some overlap exists.

Sources of stress for police officers include:
- Internal, individual stressors.
- Stressors inherent to the police job.
- Administrative and organizational stressors.
- External stressors from the criminal justice system and the citizens it serves.

### Internal, Individual Stressors

Internal stressors vary greatly and can include officers' worries about their competency to handle assignments as well as feelings of helplessness and vulnerability. An especially pertinent source of stress today is that generated by an officer's racial or gender status among peers.

### Stress Related to Police Work

Moore (2004, p.146) suggests: "Between mandatory training, court, call duty and shifts that ricochet an officer from his or her usual eight or 10 hours into overtime, police often find themselves trapped in a profession that doesn't allow room for family and recreational pursuits. Duty-related tasks occupy so much of their time, their home lives suffer. They miss anniversaries, their kids' concerts and school open houses. This dearth of time for personal development can translate into divorce, suicide, alcoholism or burn-out."

The police role itself is often vague and contradictory. Many people become police officers to fight crime, not to do social work. They are surprised to see how much "service" is actually involved in police work. They are also surprised to learn that their efforts are often not appreciated and that, in fact, their uniform is an object of scorn and derision.

The media often presents a distorted view of police work and police officers, resulting in unrealistic expectations by many citizens. Further, the distorted image is displayed over and over. Approximately one-third of regular television programming deals with some aspect of the criminal justice system. If a TV cop can solve three major crimes in an hour, why can't the local police at least keep prostitutes off the street or find the person who vandalized the school?

The police badge may weigh only a few ounces, but it carries a heavy weight to those who wear it. They need to be in constant emotional control. And they experience what is referred to as **burst stress,** that is, having to go from relative calm to high intensity, sometimes life-threatening activity. This is closely related to what Fyfe (1986) refers to in his classic **split-second syndrome** that affects police-decision making in crisis. In such situations, all that can reasonably be asked is that officers respond quickly and that a high percentage of inappropriate decisions should be expected and accepted. The split-second syndrome asserts that if a person has intentionally or unintentionally provoked or threatened a police officer, at that instant the provoker rather than the police should be viewed as the cause of any resulting injuries or damages.

Lindsey and Kelly (2004, p.3) note: "Each day officers grid themselves for the dangers and rigors of the job. When they go off duty, the process of 'coming down' begins to take effect on the body and mind. Having been hypervigilant for the duration of the shift, the body demands downtime to preserve itself. However, family life and the day-to-day activities of living require the body to continue pushing. Officers constantly face the inability to come down from a hypervigilant state, causing their bodies to deteriorate further and faster." A common result is fatigue.

**Fatigue** A former police sergeant (Pedersen, 2001a, p.130) contends: "The challenges in the police environment are shift work and overtime. . . . Our bodies weren't made to do shift work. Working overtime, covering for sick leave and special details, constitute additional physical challenges." She argues: "The dangers associated with lack of sleep are astounding. Fatigue is strongly associated with traffic accidents." In fact: "Twenty-four hours without sleep proved equivalent to a 0.1 percent blood alcohol level" (p.132).

Rodriguez (2004, pp.9–10) also comments: "As a police officer myself, I have worked the midnight shift, the overtime, the court time and the extra duty days while trying to juggle a 'normal' life with my family at home. It is not easy. As a general rule, no single factor is solely responsible for police officer fatigue; it is typically the result of a combination of factors, along with the stresses of police work itself."

According to Vila (2002, p.44): "Fatigue is a critical issue . . . for two reasons: (1) it diminishes the ability of officers to learn and (2) excess fatigue has a detrimental effect on officers' performance, safety on the job and overall health."

In addition to fatigue, shift work is associated with other complicating factors. Shift work may contribute to isolation from family and friends and contribute to the "blue wall" and "code of silence" perceptions some have. Studies indicate that officers who work overtime have a greater number of complaints filed against them. Further, as Cochrane (2001, p.22) notes: "A growing concern exists over sleep problems related to shift work and the increased liability law enforcement agencies face."

Monthly shift rotations necessitate not only physical adaptations such as getting used to sleeping different hours, but also adaptations in officers' social and personal lives. Other stressors inherent in police work include constant threat to safety; entering dark buildings in which armed suspects are believed to be hiding; high-speed pursuits; continual exposure to victims in pain as well as unsavory criminals; the immense responsibilities of the job; the authorization to take a life; the ability to save a life; and the need to remain detached yet be empathetic.

## Administrative and Organizational Stressors

Many management practices and organizational factors can cause stress specific to law enforcement. Stress frequently arises from having to operate from a set of policies and procedures drawn up by individuals who do not have to carry them out. Seldom is the on-line officer's opinion on operational policies and procedures sought, even though it is the individual officer who must carry out these policies and procedures.

Lack of support from an administration when a questionable action is taken, the unavailability of needed resources or the poor condition of equipment also causes stress for officers. Other stressors include excessive paperwork, adverse work schedules, unfair discipline, lack of promotional opportunities and the autocratic quasi-paramilitaristic model. Scott (2004, p.237) studied stress among rural and small town patrol officers and found that the strongest predictor of stress stemmed from a change in the department's top management positions.

## Stressors Related to the Criminal Justice System and Society

The criminal justice system and society at large also can induce stress in police officers. Officers are often faced with the court's scheduling of police officers for appearances, prosecutors' decisions not to prosecute a case, defendants "getting off" because of a loophole in the law, the court's perceived leniency, the early release of offenders on bail or parole, corrections' failures to rehabilitate criminals resulting in "revolving door" justice, the exclusion of police officers when plea bargaining is used and the perceived lack of appreciation for the role of law enforcement. One police officer put it this way: "I think the crowning blow was to see that it's almost futile to go out there and do anything about it. You keep putting 'em away, and they keep letting 'em out. And then new people come along, and it just doesn't stop, and it will never stop."

## The Interplay of Stressors

Garcia et al. (2004) studied stressors during a period of decreasing crime and found similar stressors to those already discussed. They (p.43) report: "The top ranked stressor—concern for a fellow officer being injured or killed—is consistent with similar findings in the literature and reinforces the frequent perceived potential for crisis situations, even during a period of low crime. This aspect continues to differentiate police work from most other occupations." They (pp.45–46) also found:

- Public criticism is indicative of the contemporary stressors experienced by police officers.
- Family demands for personal time and involvement continue to be a significant stressor for police officers.
- Organizational stressors are less of a factor for officers in the early (less than 5 years) and later (more than 20 years) stages of their career. Officers with more than 20 years of experience are also significantly less susceptible to job-related and overall stressors than those with fewer years on the job.
- Working the late shift results in more job-related stress than other shifts.
- There is no statistically significant difference in the stress levels evidenced by male and female officers.

## Effects of Stress

Chronic stress can result in high blood pressure, heart disease, chronic headaches and gastric ulcers. Other physical effects of stress are chronic back pain, tension headaches, neck pain, gastrointestinal distress, chest pain, skin rashes and hives. Some disorders such as constipation, heartburn, irritable bowel syndrome and stomach ulcers can be made worse by stress. In fact, an estimated 70 percent of physician visits are stress-related ("You Can Reduce . . .," 2001, p.2). Stress can also lead to severe depression, alcohol and drug abuse, aggression and suicide.

 Police officers tend to have high rates of alcoholism and divorce, often related to the stress of the job.

Whether police divorce and alcoholism rates are higher than such rates for people in other professions is open to question. It is known, however, that the police job does seriously interfere with officers' social and home lives, that many officers take their jobs home with them, that spouses worry about the officers' safety and that rotating shifts make normal social life difficult. Some authorities feel that police suicides are underreported because fellow officers are usually the first on the scene and may cover up the suicide to save the family further pain or embarrassment or for insurance purposes. Police suicide is discussed shortly. It is also clear that stress usually results in other forms of behavior changes. The Dallas Police Department has developed a list of 15 common warning signs for stress (see Table 13.3).

 Devastating psychological effects of stress include posttraumatic stress disorder, burnout, depression and suicide.

### Posttraumatic Stress Disorder (PTSD)

Cross and Ashley (2004, p.24) contend: "Law enforcement officers face traumatic incidents daily. These events, typically unexpected and sudden, fall well beyond the bounds of normal experiences; hence, they can have profound physical, emotional and psychological impacts—even for the best trained, experienced and seasoned officers." They (p.30) also contend: "Similar to military combat veterans, law enforcement officers experience a plethora of treacherous, violent stresses on

**Table 13.3** The 15 Most Prevalent Stress Warning Signs

| Warning Signs | Examples |
|---|---|
| 1. Sudden changes in behavior (usually directly opposite to usual behavior) | From cheerful and optimistic to gloomy and pessimistic |
| 2. More gradual change in behavior but in a way that points to deterioration of the individual | Gradually becoming slow and lethargic, possibly with increasing depression and sullen behavior |
| 3. Erratic work habits | Coming to work late, leaving early, abusing compensatory time |
| 4. Increased sick time due to minor problems | Headaches, colds, stomach aches, etc. |
| 5. Inability to maintain a train of thought | Rambling conversation, difficulty in sticking to a specific subject |
| 6. Excessive worrying | Worrying about one thing to the exclusion of any others |
| 7. Grandiose behavior | Preoccupation with religion, politics, etc. |
| 8. Excessive use of alcohol and/or drugs | Obvious hangover, disinterest in appearance, talk about drinking prowess |
| 9. Fatigue | Lethargy, sleeping on job |
| 10. Peer complaints | Others refuse to work with the officer |
| 11. Excessive complaints (negative citizen contact) | Caustic and abusive in relating to citizens |
| 12. Consistency in complaint pattern | Picks on specific groups of people (youths, blacks, etc.) |
| 13. Sexual promiscuity | Going after everything all of the time—on or off duty |
| 14. Excessive accidents and/or injuries | Not being attentive to driving, handling prisoners, etc. |
| 15. Manipulation of fellow officers and citizens | Using others to achieve ends without caring for their welfare |

SOURCE: Reprinted with permission of the Psychological Services Unit, Dallas Police Department.

a daily basis." Posttraumatic stress disorder was introduced in Chapter 8 as a concern when dealing with emergencies. But it can also result from other aspects of police work. According to Reese (2001, p.14): "Police officers can and often do become vicarious victims—stressed, altered, and in some cases destroyed by the crimes they investigate" or by the events they witness.

Kates (2001, p.30) makes a distinction between posttraumatic stress and posttraumatic stress disorder: "Post-traumatic stress may include some PTSD symptoms such as nightmares and flashbacks, but it also features symptoms like depression, eating disorders, heavy drinking and gambling, which are not part of PTSD's roster of reactions. Post-traumatic stress symptoms are generally short-lived, unlike PTSD's symptoms. Post-traumatic stress often times if left alone, and not evaluated by a professional or some form of support, has the potential to develop into PTSD."

Clagett (2004, p.42), a police sniper, describes how after being forced to kill a suicidal subject, he found himself "snared in a web of legal proceedings and personal guilt." For example, when he went to shave: "I try to look in the mirror. I realize I can't look myself in the eye. Nothing like this has ever happened to me before, and I don't like it" (p.46). He (p.49) says: "Let me sum up by saying that surviving as a police sniper involves two problems. Problem number one is properly making the shot so an innocent life is saved. Problem number two is surviving everything that comes after that shot. Please trust me when I tell you that problem number two is much tougher than problem number one."

Kureczka (2002, p.18) recounts his life and death battle with an armed robber and the struggle during which Kureczka was shot in the leg, and he shot and killed the robber. His initial reaction: "I had been a member of the department for 2 1/2 years and had just survived the ultimate test as a police officer, or so I thought. I soon realized, however, that the ultimate test would be to survive the psychological battle that had just begun." He describes the lack of department support and embarrassment he felt seeking outside counseling, the trauma of being civilly sued and the emotional turmoil he endured for several years as the lawsuit dragged on. He was cleared, and gradually he was able to put the incident behind him. He (p.21) urges: "While it took strength, courage and the will to live to survive my physical battle, it took far more moral fortitude and emotional resolve to survive the aftermath. If anything could be construed as brave or heroic as a result of my incident, it would be that I broke through the 'image armor' and triumphed over tragedy by honestly confronting and resolving my psychological battle, the ultimate test."

According to Cross and Ashley (pp.24–25): "Regardless of an officer's personal experiences with traumatic incidents, avoiding, ignoring or hurrying the emotional aftermath of a traumatic event can lead to serious short- and long-term consequences. Sadly, however, some officers believe that substance use and abuse may offer the best way to cope with their otherwise unbearable feelings. Certainly, not every officer deals with stress and trauma by abusing chemicals, and not every officer who chooses to abuse chemicals does so to numb the effects of trauma. However, overwhelming evidence suggests that the two factors often *are* linked, particularly in the high-stress environment of police work." They (p.26) believe: "Alcohol and other drug abuse are maladaptive behaviors associated with stress and trauma."

### Burnout

When stress continues unremittingly for prolonged periods, it can result in the debilitating condition referred to as *burnout*. **Burnout** has occurred in a person who is "used up or consumed by a job," made listless through overwork and stress. The person experiences a persistent lack of energy or interest in his or her work. Hawkins (2001, p.343) defines burnout as "a syndrome of emotional exhaustion, depersonalization and reduced personal accomplishment. . . . An important aspect of the burnout syndrome is increased feelings of emotional exhaustion."

Unfortunately, burnout happens only to those who are initially "on fire"—that is, too enthusiastic, highly productive workers. As one officer said: "I just couldn't go on. It seemed that there was nothing inside of me to keep me going. I couldn't look at one more dead body, one more abused child, or handle one more domestic fight. I'd just had it." Officers who are burned out are at extremely high risk of being injured or killed on duty because they are usually not safety conscious. They are also at risk for depression or suicide.

### Depression

As Hoofnagle (2002, p.84) explains: "Although **depression** may be regarded as a character weakness or personality flaw by some, it is actually a serious and life-threatening medical illness. Anyone can be affected, and police officers are no exception. . . . Our society places a tremendous stigma on having depression or seeking help for it" (bold added).

Because depression is a medical illness, an imbalance of chemicals in the brain, medication can often be prescribed to treat it. But often people do not recognize the symptoms. Hoofnagle reports that if a person has five or more of specific symptoms for more than two weeks, they may be suffering from depression. These symptoms include significant changes in appetite and sleep patterns; irritability, anger, worry, agitation, anxiety; loss of energy, persistent lethargy, unexplained aches and pains; feelings of guilt, worthlessness and/or hopelessness; inability to concentrate, indecisiveness; inability to take pleasure in former interests, social withdrawal, pessimism, indifference; prolonged sadness or unexplained crying spells; excessive consumption of alcohol or use of chemical substances; and recurring thoughts of death or suicide.

The difficulty lies in getting people to recognize the symptoms and to seek treatment. Depression must be treated because it is one of the leading causes of suicide. According to Hoofnagle: "For every police officer who is killed in the line of duty, there are at least two who take their own lives. In fact, it is estimated that one officer takes his or her life every 24 hours. In at least 90 percent of all suicides, untreated depression is believed to be the major factor."

## Officer Suicide

- "Police kill themselves at twice the rate that they are killed in the line of duty" (Nislow, 2004, p.1).
- "Suicide in law enforcement is three times greater than the national average" (Lindsey and Kelly, p.1).
- "More law enforcement officers are slain by their own hands than any other cause" (Hamilton, 2003a, p.18).
- "Why do police officers kill themselves with their sidearms? Because they can" (Hamilton, 2003b, p.24).

Alcohol, family problems, the breakup of relationships and stress all contribute to the high rate of police suicide, about 30 percent higher than what is found in the general population. Czarnecki et al. (2002, p.22) report: "Suicide is the quiet killer in law enforcement. Many officers and many agencies consider suicide a sign of weakness, 'the coward's way out.' The stigma attached to suicide can be so great that friends and family members of the person who committed suicide are embarrassed or ashamed to discuss it. So suicide isn't talked about, but every law enforcement officer, trainer, supervisor and executive needs to know about it."

Czarnecki et al. (pp.22–23) say that although a suicidal person may give little indication that he or she plans to commit suicide, officers should know the signs to watch for: depression; talking about or threatening suicide; making plans for the care of children; giving away valued possessions or pets; saying goodbye; sudden interest in insurance, wills, burial plots and the like; sudden calmness: the calm before the storm; hopelessness; use of alcohol and/or drugs; divorces, breakups and the like; being investigated on charges of crime or serious misconduct; and separation from family or friends.

According to Hamilton (2003c, p.25): "One of the main reasons cops murder themselves is because they are under investigation. While many see the suicide as an admission of guilt, experts say it's more likely caused by an officer's fear of losing his or her badge, his or her identity as a cop."

Help for those at risk of suicide within the department includes counseling units, peer counseling groups and police chaplains. Outside the department help might be sought from physicians, priests, ministers, rabbis, attorneys, family and friends. Czarnecki et al. (p.22) describe a new organization to help prevent suicide by law enforcement officers, the Police Suicide Prevention Center, part of the National Institute of Ethics. The Center's website, www.policesuicide.com, features information about suicide, suicide prevention and related subjects, as well as links to suicide prevention and mental health sites.

## Reducing Stress

Many books and articles deal with stress reduction. Good nutrition and exercise can help. So can taking time for oneself, relaxing, meditating, going for a walk or finding a hobby. Officers should anticipate the stressors involved in police work and, when possible, avoid them. They should prepare in advance for those that may be unavoidable. They should also be physically fit and active and get adequate sleep. Stress management is taking care of yourself. You can't take care of others unless you take care of yourself first!

## Mental Fitness Programs

Although seldom called *mental fitness programs*, many police departments have established programs geared to helping their officers combat emotional problems. Such programs are absolutely essential.

The following problems are often included in stress programs: postshooting trauma, alcoholism, drug abuse, marital or other family difficulties, difficult relationships with fellow officers or supervisors, trauma associated with the catastrophic death of a child or spouse, debt management, gambling, issues associated with layoffs due to budget cuts and adjustment to retirement.

Law enforcement departments should be as concerned with their officers' mental health as they are with their physical health and should offer some sort of employee assistance program for those officers needing help in this area. Professional counseling, peer counseling, police-spouse support groups and the like can do much to improve the mental fitness of a law enforcement agency. A physically and mentally fit officer is a much safer officer. However, officers can do even more to ensure their safety on the job.

## Officer Safety

A physically and mentally fit officer is in a much better position to perform effectively and to stay alive, but another aspect of officer safety sometimes comes into play. After being in police work for a few years, officers often come to feel invincible, having what is called the "it won't happen to me" syndrome. Although they see people all around them being victimized, such police officers refuse to believe they can become victims themselves. This attitude lulls them into a false sense of security.

Most officers injured or killed in the line of duty could have either avoided the confrontation or minimized the injury had they been mentally prepared for the danger, alert and trained in the proper survival techniques.

 The **awareness spectrum** describes an officer's level of awareness, ranging from environmental unawareness, to panicked/blacked out/perhaps dead. Ideally, officers will be between these two stages, alert but relaxed.

Rayburn (2004, p.62) also emphasizes assessing personal threat levels. He uses the example of a traffic light with its three colors: "Green means go; everything is OK so proceed on with your life. Condition green is when you are in a safe environment." In contrast, Rayburn (p.63) says: "Condition red means you have recognized a threat and are prepared to deal with it. Condition red is the highest state of awareness, just like it is the highest light of the three on a traffic light." In the middle of condition red and green is the yellow light. Rayburn (p.62) explains: "Understand that condition yellow is not a state of paranoia. It is a state of awareness. In condition yellow, you are prepared for what could happen. You are prepared for when that light might turn red."

A Bureau of Justice Statistics study ("Police Officer Tops List . . .," 2001, p.5) found that law enforcement officers are at a higher risk of encountering violence in the workplace than people in any other occupation. On average, 261 out of every 1,000 police officers are victims of violent crime on the job, compared to the second most violent occupation, correctional officers at 156 violent victimizations per 1,000 officers annually. The third most dangerous occupation was taxicab drivers.

A press release by the National Law Enforcement Officers Memorial Fund (2004) reports 148 law enforcement officer fatalities in 2003, making it the second year in a row that the number has been well below the decade-long average of 166 annual police deaths. The 142 male and six female officers who died worked in 38 of our nation's 50 states, as well as Puerto Rico and one federal agency. Automobile accidents and shootings were the leading causes of death. The release also reported: "Dating back to the first known law enforcement fatality in 1792, there have been more than 16,000 federal, state and local officers killed." "Law Enforcement Fatalities on the Rise" (2004, p.54) reports that 82 peace officers were killed during the first half of 2004, up 7 percent from the same period in 2003.

Among officers' survival skills is the ability to recognize the indicators of aggression—so as to be prepared for an attack before it happens. Among the common indicators of aggression are the folded arm stance, hands on hips, an invasion of personal space, finger pointing, wandering attention, ignoring verbal commands, pacing, standing with fists clenched and talking through clenched teeth.

Part of being alert is being aware of objects that can pose a danger to police officers. Many everyday items can be used as dangerous weapons, for example, a ball point pen or a plastic straw can serve as a knife; a tightly rolled newspaper or magazine can serve as a baton; a set of keys firmly locked between the fingers and raked across exposed skin can serve as brass knuckles. Another part of being alert is suggested by the Border Patrol's "survival triangle" illustrated in Figure 13.1.

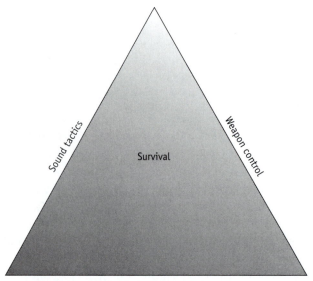

**Figure 13.1**   Survival Triangle

 The border patrol's **survival triangle** consists of these components:
- Mental and physical preparedness.
- Sound tactics.
- Weapon control.

## *The Warrior Attitude*

Nowicki (2003, p.6) points out: "[Officers] need to know how to release the beast from within in order to survive and win. There's a time to talk and a time to fight. There are times when your nice guy Mr. Rogers community-policing personality needs to be replaced by Godzilla." Norcross (2003, p.20) refers to this as being a "modern warrior":

> Being a law enforcement officer carries an awesome responsibility, and only those with the strongest character will succeed. In the law enforcement profession, there is no other option but success. The strength of character needed lies within everyone; learning to harness it is the key to developing the law enforcement officer's warrior mentality.
>
> Having the warrior mentality does not mean that officers are prepared to "kill" their enemy nor does it mean that they are prepared to die for their cause. Instead, for them, the words *warrior* and *survivor* are interchangeable. Because of this, these officers are prepared to accomplish their mission—to protect the public from the menace of those who violate the law—with honor and to the best of their abilities while overcoming any obstacle by any means. They can apply this mind-set to an armed encounter, to a hand-to-hand altercation, or even to a search for a suspect who stole a small child's bicycle. Warriors/survivors are determined to succeed and will not be distracted from accomplishing the task at hand. In essence, they enter every situation mentally prepared to do what it takes to win.

*In our society today, it is mandatory that officers maintain their weapons skills through constant training.*

This determination to win surfaced in research conducted on law enforcement officers who survived serious, life-threatening assaults. Although the study could not provide a definitive answer as to why some officers lived and others did not, it did find that an uncommon "will to survive" existed in many of the surviving officers. These officers related that they attributed their survival to their determination to "win," which they believed was ingrained in them through concentrated training.

## Responding to an Emotionally Disturbed Person Call

One of the most dangerous calls police officers respond to is an emotionally disturbed person (EDP) call. Grossi (2004b, p.72) gives four rules for officers to survive EDP calls:

- Rule #1 Officers should understand what their job is: to control the EDP's behavior and get them to someone who can help. Officers should get backup immediately, never taking on an EDP alone.
- Rule #2 Officers should use time to their advantage, slowing things down, talking slowly using simple terms.
- Rule #3 Officers should keep their distance and let them ramble until backup or the Crisis Intervention Team (CIT) arrives.
- Rule #4 Officers should be ready to use force if necessary. If forced to resort to deadly force, officers should keep the universal concepts of verbalization, center-of-mass and shooting until the threat stops firmly in mind.

Pinizzotto et al. (2004, p.16) stress Rule #4 for any encounter requiring deadly force: "Realistic and regular law enforcement training must counterbalance and mentally and emotionally override the fallacy of the one-shot drop." They (p.21) point out: "The perpetuation of the one-shot drop by movies and television programs has no place in the real world of violent criminals bent on their destructive mission. Officers must realize that they have to continually hone their survival skills, always expect the unexpected and never give up; they must protect themselves to protect their communities." Sometimes the threat comes from a canine.

## Countering a Canine Attack

Rayburn (2003, p.64) outlines how to stop an attacking dog. Officers should:
- Lower their center of gravity by bending their knees.
- Yell at the dog.
- Spray it with OC.
- If they can do so safely, shoot the dog before it bites them.
- When they can't shoot the dog before it bites them, control the attack by making the dog bite their weak side arm.
- Do everything they can to stay on their feet.
- Shoot the dog in the chest or shoulder until it releases them.

Grossi (2004a, p.63) elaborates on the last recommendation, saying if a canine is locked onto an officer's arm, the officer should shoot the dog in the chest, *not* the head. He gives two reasons: (1) the officer might shoot himself in the arm or hand. And (2) the dog's head will be moving fast back-and-forth and is protected by a lot of thick bone. Grossi recommends that officers dealing with a canine attack think "center-of-mass" and remember double-taps or even trip-taps if they suspect they're dealing with "Rin-Tin-Tin's illegitimate grandson."

## The Other Two Sides of the Survival Triangle

The focus of this chapter has been on the base of the survival triangle, physical and mental preparedness. The second side of the survival triangle is sound tactics, which consist of the five "Cs": cover, concealment, control, containment and communications. Effective, constant communications is the single thread that stitches all the pieces together.

 The five Cs for survival tactics are cover, concealment, control, containment and communications.

The third side of the survival triangle is weapons control. This is addressed in the following checklist:
1. Do you know the capabilities and limitations of yourself and each of your weapons?
2. Are your weapons clean and functional?
3. Are they loaded? How are they loaded? What type of ammunition are they loaded with? Does your partner know the answers to these questions?
4. Are your weapons immediately accessible to you? Or are they on the seat next to you where they might slide out of reach under your leg, or in the trunk, or the back seat? Close to you is not the same as accessible in a dynamic confrontation!
5. Do you practice constant forearm contact with your sidearm? (This is an excellent habit to acquire.)
6. Have you mastered a good technique for weapon retention?
7. Can you practice fire discipline?
8. Have you mentally prepared yourself to use your weapons? Lag time is a killer.

Witness reports of officers who were shot indicated some made no attempt to draw or use their weapons once they were down. Other reports stated that officers were shot by assailants while lying on the ground pleading, with arms raised to deflect gunshots. Even though they had full use of their arms and hands, they made no attempt to use their weapon for protection. Officers should also take safety precautions for keeping their service revolvers at home as well as carrying them when off duty.

## Advice from Veteran Officers

Huntington (2004, p.58) suggests that if officers want to make it home alive at the end of their shift, they should heed the advice of veteran cops. Officers should (pp.58–62):

- Not believe suspects. Crooks always lie. Always. And they'll look officers right in the eye when they do it and smile and be all serious and such, and officers will be tempted to believe them, but they shouldn't.
- Watch suspects' hands. If a suspect is going to try to kill an officer, they'll do it with their hands. Officers should handcuff anyone they feel uncertain about, even if the suspect gets upset about it.
- Search and search again. If an officer takes someone from another officer, the second officer should search the suspect again himself.
- Carry a backup gun and a folding knife where they can get to them.
- Don't drive fast. If a pursuit gets crazy, stop it.
- Have a good flashlight. Officers should also keep a small, high-intensity light on their belt as a backup. They should carry their flashlights in their off-hand, not their gun hand so they do not have to pass the flashlight to their off-hand if they need to draw their guns.
- When in doubt, point their guns if they think someone might try to kill them.
- When contacting someone, especially a bad guy, use at least two officers or hold the situation still until cover is there.

Stay safe!

## SUMMARY

Physical fitness is the body's general capacity to adapt and respond favorably to physical effort. Although many factors contribute to a well-conditioned body, the prime factor is the condition of the circulatory (cardiovascular) system, upon which endurance or stamina depends. Motor skills important to police officers include coordination, speed and accuracy.

Police work is often sedentary, involves irregular hours and constantly changing work shifts and may promote poor diets, excessive cigarette smoking and consumption of alcohol, and great amounts of stress. These factors can be offset by physical fitness training programs. An effective physical fitness training program that is varied and of interest to the officer should include aerobic, strength and flexibility training. It should be engaged in regularly for 20 to 30 minutes a day, at least three days a week.

Bloodborne pathogens that present a risk to police officers and that they should protect against include HIV infections and AIDS, hepatitis B and hepatitis C. The concept of universal precaution recommends that all blood and potentially infectious materials other than blood must be treated as if infected.

Mental fitness is as important as physical fitness. The greatest threat to officers' mental fitness is stress. Sources of stress for police officers include internal, individual stressors; stressors inherent to the police job; administrative and organizational stressors; and external stressors from the criminal justice system and the citizens it serves. The effects of stress may include high rates of alcoholism and divorce, posttraumatic stress disorder, burnout, depression and suicide.

Officer safety is another important aspect of keeping prepared for duty. The awareness spectrum describes an officer's level of awareness, ranging from environmental unawareness, to panicked/blacked out/perhaps dead. Ideally, officers will be somewhere in between these two extremes, alert but relaxed. The border patrol's survival triangle, useful for all police officers, consists of mental and physical preparedness, sound tactics and weapon control. The five Cs for survival tactics are cover, concealment, control, containment and communications.

## APPLICATION

You have noticed that many of your fellow officers are stressed out, and the department has no program to assist them. You approach your supervisor and offer to discuss this with your colleagues and then develop a policy dealing with stress management. The policy should point out various types of stressors officers must cope with and various services available to help officers. It also should bring employee assistance programs to the attention of the officers. It should include how to contact an individual or a group for help. Consider such programs as Alcoholics Anonymous, marriage counseling, financial advisors, psychological counseling and any other services locally available. It should stress that officers may keep their contacts confidential and that no department interference will be generated that might impair or threaten an officer's job because that officer seeks assistance.

## AN EXERCISE IN CRITICAL THINKING

One morning at approximately 9:00 A.M., a state trooper received a message from the dispatcher that a probable drunken driver was traveling south on Highway 61 in a white Cadillac. The dispatcher did not know the identity of the person who called in the tip. Shortly thereafter while driving north, the trooper saw a white Cadillac southbound on Highway 61, approximately 200 yards from his squad car. The Cadillac was traveling about 15 miles per hour with at least half the width of the car on the shoulder of the road. The trooper walked over to the southbound lane and held up his hand to stop the driver of the Cadillac for investigation.

The Cadillac stopped for approximately five seconds, then made a U-turn into a driveway, and entered the northbound lane of Highway 61. While this turnaround was happening, several drivers passed by the trooper and told him that the Cadillac had been driving all over the road. The trooper ran to intercept the Cadillac, which by then had crossed over the centerline and was headed for the ditch. The Cadillac continued, traveling about 10 miles per hour, into the ditch and headed for a steep embankment (a drop-off of about 30 feet) about 50 yards away.

1. If the trooper is in good shape, what should he do?
   a. Continue to hold up his hand to stop the Cadillac.
   b. Let the Cadillac continue in the ditch—sooner or later it will come to rest.
   c. Run alongside the Cadillac, try to reach in and turn off the ignition, or at least steer the vehicle in a safe direction.
   d. Shoot out the tires to make it impossible for the vehicle to continue.
   e. Try to verbally communicate with the driver in a nonthreatening, calming voice to help the driver become cooperative, and only as a last resort attempt to physically stop the vehicle.
2. The trooper discovers that the driver of the Cadillac is fellow trooper Vernon Francis. After being successfully stopped, Francis takes an alcohol concentration test, which yields a result of more than .10. What are the appropriate actions for the state trooper on duty?
   a. An arrest for aggravated drinking is appropriate.
   b. Both an arrest and a recommendation for counseling should be made.
   c. Francis needs to be shocked into understanding that his career is jeopardized, so the kindest treatment is to be as harsh with him as possible.
   d. In addition to the arrest, Francis should be dismissed from duty.
   e. Criminal indictment of a fellow officer should be avoided out of loyalty, but a verbal warning (no written report) does need to be given.

## DISCUSSION QUESTIONS

1. Is peer counseling—"cops working with cops"—better for helping troubled officers than outside professional counseling? Is it better for short-term or long-term impact?
2. Is there one best way to handle officers who have drinking problems? Explain.
3. One reason police officers are reluctant to seek therapeutic services is that they fear their careers will be jeopardized. How can this obstacle be overcome?

4. Is it a good idea for every police department to have its own police psychologist? What are the advantages of in-house versus outside psychological assistance?

5. Are police officers confronted with the same stressful problems faced by everyone in society, such as firefighters, construction workers, business people and military personnel?

6. Do the media create unnecessary stress for police officers in your community? If so, how?

7. How do police administrations contribute to the stresses of police officers? What role does the department play in dealing with the stress faced by an officer's spouse/family? Why should it become (or not become) involved?

### InfoTrac College Edition Assignments

■ Use InfoTrac College Edition to help answer the Discussion Questions as appropriate.

■ Use InfoTrac College Edition to find and outline one of the following articles to share with the class:
   ■ "The Effects of Sleep Deprivation" by Glory Cochrane
   ■ "HIV/AIDS in Law Enforcement: 'What-If' Scenarios" by John Cooley
   ■ "Law Enforcement Physical Fitness Standards and Title VII" by Michael E. Brooks
   ■ "Surviving Assaults: After the Physical Battle Ends, the Psychological Battle Begins" by Arthur W. Kureczka
   ■ "Issues in Small Town Policing: Understanding Stress" by Dennis Lindsey and Sean Kelly
   ■ "Police Trauma and Addiction: Coping with the Dangers of the Job" by Chad L. Cross and Larry Ashley
   ■ "The 'Modern Warrior': A Study in Survival" by Richard H. Norcross
   ■ "One-Shot Drops: Surviving the Myth" by Anthony J. Pinizzotto, Harry A. Kern and Edward F. Davis
   ■ "Accidentally Dead: Accidental Line-of-Duty Deaths of Law Enforcement Officers" by Anthony J. Pinizzotto, Edward F. Davis and Charles E. Miller III

### Internet Assignments

Select two of the following assignments. For each, be prepared to share your work with the class.
   ■ Go to the FBI's website at www.fbi.gov and outline how the officers who were not shot were killed.
   ■ Go to Shering Corporation's website at www.hepatitisinnovations.com and outline the information contained in "About Hepatitis."
   ■ Go to Coastal Training Technologies Corp.'s website at www.coastal.com. Select the video "Anthrax Awareness," "Fear and Stress" or "Biological and Chemical Threats" and preview it (at no cost) and outline the main points.

   ■ Go to The Police Suicide Prevention Center's website at www.policesuicide.com and click on *myths about suicide*. List the myths.

   ■ On the Internet, use the keyword *stress* and see how the various segments of society deal with stress. Write a two- to three-page essay summarizing what you find.

### Book-Specific Website

The book-specific website at http://cj.wadsworth.com/wobleski_Hess_police_op4e hosts a variety of resources for students and instructors. Many can be emailed to the instructor. Included are extended activities such as Concept Builders - the 3 step learning module that reinforces key chapter concepts, followed by a real-world applications and critical thinking questions. InfoTrac College Edition exercises; Discussion Questions; interactive key-term FlashCards; and a collection of chapter-based Web Links provide additional information and activities to include in the curriculum.

### References

"Are the Feds Doing Enough for Bioterror Defense?" *Security Management*, December 2001, p.16.

*Bloodborne Pathogens for Law Enforcement.* Virginia Beach, VA: Coastal Training Technologies, Corp., 1998.

Clagett, Russ. "After the Echo." *Police*, March 2004, pp.42–49.

Cochrane, Glory. "The Effects of Sleep Deprivation." *FBI Law Enforcement Bulletin*, July 2001, pp.22–25.

Collingwood, Thomas R.; Hoffman, Robert; and Smith, Jay. "Underlying Physical Fitness Factors for Performing Police Officer Physical Tasks." *The Police Chief*, March 2004, pp.32–37.

Cross, Chad L. and Ashley, Larry. "Police Trauma and Addiction: Coping with the Dangers of the Job." *FBI Law Enforcement Bulletin*, October 2004, pp.24–32.

Czarnecki, Fabrice; Kasanof, Adam; and Trautman, Neal. "Preventing Police Suicide: What You Can Do to Help." *The Law Enforcement Trainer*, January/February 2002, pp.22–25.

Farmer, Mark. "Fit at 40." *Law and Order*, June 2004, pp.34–37.

Fox, Robert A. "The Blue Plague of American Policing." *Law Enforcement News*, May 15/31, 2003, p.9.

Fyfe, James J. "The Split-Second Syndrome and Other Determinants of Police Violence." In *Violent Transactions*, edited by Anne Campbell and John Gibbs. New York: Basic Blackwell, 1986.

Garcia, Luis; Nesbary, Dale K.; and Gu, Joann. "Perceptual Variations of Stressors among Police Officers during an Era of Decreasing Crime." *Journal of Contemporary Criminal Justice*, February 2004, pp.33–50.

Grossi, David. "Surviving Canine Threats." *The Law Enforcement Trainer*, January/February 2004a, pp.62–63.

Grossi, David. "Surviving Emotionally Disturbed Person (EDP) Calls." *The Law Enforcement Trainer*, Third Quarter, 2004b, pp.70–72.

Hamilton, Melanie. "Cop Killer." *Police*, May 2003a, pp.18–32.

Hamilton, Melanie. "Eating a Gun." *Police*, May 2003b, p.24.

Hamilton, Melanie. "Losing Yourself." *Police*, May 2003c, p.25.

Hawkins, Homer C. "Police Officer Burnout: A Partial Replication of Maslach's Burnout Inventory." *Police Quarterly*, September 2001, pp.343–360.

Hoofnagle, Laura. "Recognizing Depression and Raising Awareness among Law Enforcement Professionals." *The Police Chief*, February 2002, pp.84–89.

Huntington, Roy. "Old Cops Know 'Stuff.'" *Police*, October 2004, pp.58–63.

Kates, Allen R. "Post-Traumatic Stress Disorder: Hoax or Reality?" *The Associate*, January/February 2001, pp.29–31.

Kureczka, Arthur W. "Surviving Assaults: After the Physical Battle Ends, the Psychological Battle Begins." *FBI Law Enforcement Bulletin*, January 2002, pp.18–21.

"Law Enforcement Fatalities on the Rise: 82 Peace Officers Killed during First Half of 2004." *The Law Enforcement Trainer*, Third Quarter 2004, p.65.

Lindsey, Dennis and Kelly, Sean. "Issues in Small Town Policing: Understanding Suicide." *FBI Law Enforcement Bulletin*, July 2004, pp.1–7.

Moore, Carole. "Never Enough Time." *Law Enforcement Technology*, September 2004, p.146.

The National Law Enforcement Officers Memorial Fund. "Law Enforcement Officer Fatalities Reach 148 for 2003." Press release, January 5, 2004.

Nislow, Jennifer. "An Alarming Body Count? Questions Surround Data on Police Suicides." *Law Enforcement News*, October 2004, pp.1, 15.

Norcross, Richard H. "The 'Modern Warrior': A Study in Survival." *FBI Law Enforcement Bulletin*, October 2003, pp.20–26.

Nowicki, Ed. "Unleashing the Warrior Spirit." *Police*, March 2003, p.6.

Pedersen, Dorothy. "Sleepy Heads on Patrol." *Law Enforcement Technology*, July 2001a, pp.130–138.

Pedersen, Dorothy. "Don't Forget to Wash Your Hands: Protecting Yourself from Other People's Illnesses." *Law Enforcement Technology*, November 2001b, pp.52–56.

Pinizzotto, Anthony J.; Kern, Harry A.; and Davis, Edward F. "One-Shot Drops: Surviving the Myth." *FBI Law Enforcement Bulletin*, October 2004, pp.14–21.

"Police Officer Tops List of Most Dangerous Jobs." *Criminal Justice Newsletter*, December 24, 2001, p.5.

Rayburn, Michael T. "Countering Canine Attacks." *Police*, March 2003, pp.64–69.

Rayburn, Michael T. "Personal Threat Levels." *Police*, February 2004, pp.62–63.

Reese, James T. "6 Keys to Stress-Free Living." *The Associate*, January/February 2001, pp.14–17.

Rodriguez, Dennis. "When Police Ethics Is Spelled with a Zzzz. . . ." *Law Enforcement News*, October 2004, pp.9–10.

Scott, Yolanda M. "Stress among Rural and Small-Town Patrol Officers: A Survey of Pennsylvania Municipal Agencies." *Police Quarterly*, June 2004, pp.237–261.

Selye, Hans. *The Stress of Life*. New York: McGraw-Hill, 1956.

Sweet, Kathleen M. "The Biological Threat: No Longer Just a Federal Issue." *Minnesota Police Chief*, June 2001, pp.49–53.

Vila, Bryan. "Cops: Learn Your A, B, Zzzzzz." *The Law Enforcement Trainer*, September/October 2002, pp.44–47.

Vila, Bryan; Morrison, Gregory B.; and Kenny, Dennis J. "Improving Shift Schedule and Work-Hour Policies and Practices to Increase Police Officer Performance, Health and Safety." *Police Quarterly*, March 2002, pp.4–24.

"You Can Reduce the Stress in Your Life." *Discover*. Minneapolis, MN: HealthPartners, Spring 2001, pp.2–5.

### CASES CITED

*Jane Doe v. Borough of Barrington*, 729 F.Supp. 376, (D.N.J.) (1990)

*Parker v. District of Columbia*, 850 F.2d 708, 109 S.Ct. 1339

*Woods v. White*, 899 F.2d 17 (7 Cir.) (1990)

# CHAPTER 14

# Liability and Ethics: Is It Legal? Is It Moral?

## DO YOU KNOW . . .

- Under what three types of state liability (tort) law officers may be sued?
- On what basis most civil lawsuits are brought?
- What the most common civil actions brought against the police involve? What the most common defenses used against civil liability police officers are?
- What can protect against civil liability?
- How to minimize lawsuits?
- Whether officers can countersue?
- Whether ethical issues are usually absolute or relative?
- According to conventional wisdom, what the defining characteristics of the police culture are and what the result is?
- What two areas in discussions of law enforcement ethics are controversial?
- What the key elements in corrupt behavior are?
- What the most important factor in police officers becoming corrupt is?
- What other factors may cause officers to become corrupt?
- If scandals are caused by "bad apples" or "bad barrels"?
- What basic ethics tests can be used to assess behavior?
- What maxim should guide ethical decisions?
- How ethical behavior can be promoted?
- Who is most responsible for the ethics of a law enforcement agency?

## CAN YOU DEFINE?

| | | | |
|---|---|---|---|
| absolute issue | discretionary acts | malicious | Section 1983 |
| blue lie | ethics | prosecution | slander |
| civil actions | gratuities | ministerial acts | slippery slope |
| Civil Rights Act | integrity | moral principles | solidarity |
| code of ethics | intentional tort | negligence | strict liability |
| collective deep pocket | libel | nonfeasance | tort |
| conscience | litigious | police placebo | vicarious liability |
| corruption continuum | malfeasance | relative issue | |

## Introduction

Law enforcement officers must act within the law. If they do not, they may be found criminally liable for misconduct under Title 18, Section 242, U.S.C.A., as well as under state criminal law. Most lawsuits against law enforcement officers, however, deal with civil matters and are filed under Title 42, Section 1983 USC. In carrying out their official duties, law enforcement officers must protect the constitutional rights of their public. The consequences of violating such rights in a criminal investigation were discussed in Chapter 3. Actions in violation of a suspect's constitutional rights can cost a favorable decision. In addition, the suspect can sue the police. Police operations also involve considerable discretion. This, too, can result in actions viewed as conduct "not becoming a police officer" and thereby subject officers to civil lawsuits. The United States has been called a **litigious** society—that is, its citizens are very likely to sue over any perceived wrong.

Law enforcement officers must not only act legally, they must also act ethically. Ethics has become a "hot topic" in business, education, medicine *and* law enforcement. **Ethics** refers to standards of fair and honest conduct. It involves **integrity,** doing what is considered just, honest and proper. Ethics looks at human conduct in the light of **moral principles,** that is, set ideas of right and wrong. Moral principles can be established by individuals, set forth by a particular society or culture, laid down by a religious body or doctrine or established by a given subculture. In most instances, an individual's moral principles derive from a combination of all of these. Further, in our pluralistic country, many differences exist in what is considered right and wrong.

This chapter begins with an overview of civil liability and Section 1983, the Civil Rights Act. This is followed by common charges brought against police officers. Next is a discussion of defenses in civil lawsuits, of ways to reduce their occurrence and of the possibility of countersuits. The discussion of legal liability ends with a look at legal liability and community policing.

The chapter then changes its focus from what is legal to what is moral or ethical. This discussion begins with an overview of ethics and of ethics in law enforcement. This is followed by a discussion of the police culture and of how this culture might encourage unethical conduct, including some gray areas in police ethics and outright unethical behavior. Next, corruption in policing is discussed and basic ethics tests are presented. The chapter concludes with the role of the police department in fostering ethical behavior and ethics, community policing and problem solving.

## Civil Liability: An Overview

A person who feels wronged by someone, even though the action may not be a crime, can sue. Such lawsuits are called **civil actions.** In civil law, the wrongdoing itself is called a **tort.** Sometimes an action is considered both a tort and a crime. For example, a person who strikes someone could be charged with assault (a crime) and sued for the assault (a tort). An individual found guilty of a crime is *punished* by paying a fine and/or serving a jail or prison sentence. An individual found guilty of a tort is made to make *restitution,* usually in the form of a monetary payment.

An estimated 30,000 civil actions are filed against the police every year, with between 4 and 8 percent resulting in an unfavorable verdict. According to Stevens

(2001, p.105): "Police officers are more likely to be defendants in a civil liability suit today than at any other time in American history." He (p.106) suggests: "The threat of civil liability is a major component of an arrest decision for most officers today."

The threat of a lawsuit may also influence other officer decisions. Chudwin (2003, p.10) provides this example: "In a case in the Northwest, an officer reported that he and his partner did not fire on an offender pointing two pistols at the officers because they were afraid of liability if the pistols were not real. The offender shot and murdered one of the officers. The officers were more fearful of a lawsuit than being murdered." As Daniels and Spratley (2003, p.54) suggest: "In today's litigious society, departments can easily fall victim to the Catch 22 . . . sued if you do and sued if you don't."

According to Means (2004, p.10): "Civil lawsuits against police are common; million dollar judgments are not rare." A New York man who was struck by a police officer's nightstick was awarded $3 million. A youth shot by the Detroit police in a looted store was awarded $1 million. In Richmond, California, the city, the police department and two officers were ordered to pay $3 million to the families of two men the officers had shot and killed.

Law enforcement officers can be sued in just about every phase of police operations. Each time officers are sued, it exposes them to personal embarrassment in the community and on the job. It may result in possible job loss. It may mean financial ruin. Equally damaging is the undermining of respect for the rule of law when officers are found guilty. Although the increase in lawsuits is alarming, it is still true that few lawsuits against police officers can be traced to extremely poor judgment or malicious acts by one or more officers. The responsible behavior of officers is a definite deterrent to any action against them.

 Officers may be sued under three types of state liability (tort) laws: strict liability, intentional tort and negligence.

**Strict liability** refers to an act where the injury or damage is so severe and the harm should have been foreseen so that intent or mental state need not be proven, for example, reckless operation of a vehicle. **Intentional tort** refers to an act where the officer's intent to engage in the behavior must be proven, for example, wrongful death or false arrest. **Negligence** refers to an act where intent or mental state does not matter. What must be proven is if some inadvertent act or failure to act created an unreasonable risk to another person, for example, speeding resulting in a traffic accident or not responding to a 911 call.

## Section 1983, The Civil Rights Act

 Most civil lawsuits brought against law enforcement officers are based on Statute 42 of the U.S. Code, **Section 1983,** also called the **Civil Rights Act.**

This act, passed in 1871 after the Civil War, was originally part of the Ku Klux Act of 1871, one part of which is now called the Civil Rights Act of 1871. The act was designed to prevent the abuse of constitutional rights by officers who "under color of state law" deny defendants those rights. The act states:

> Every person who, under color of any statute, ordinance, regulation, custom, or
> usage, of any State or Territory, subjects, or causes to be subjected any citizen of

the United States or other person within the jurisdiction thereof to the deprivation of any rights, privileges, or immunities secured by the Constitution and laws, shall be liable to the party injured in an action at law, suit in equity, or other proper proceeding for redress.

In other words, Section 1983 says that anyone acting under the authority of the law who violates another person's constitutional rights can be sued. This includes law enforcement officers. It now may also include their supervisors, their departments and even their municipalities. Such lawsuits may involve First Amendment issues like freedom of speech, religion and association; Fourth Amendment matters like arrest and detention, search and seizure, and use of force; Fifth Amendment issues in interrogation and confessions; Sixth Amendment concerns regarding the right to counsel and Fourteenth Amendment claims of due process violations. It is important for law enforcement officers to understand Section 1983 because, as Means (p.10) points out, it has "become the preferred tool for suing police."

Griffith (2002, p.6) contends: "In the American system of justice, you're innocent until proven guilty unless you carry a badge. . . . A law enforcement officer tried by the media in a racially charged case has as much chance of a fair trial as a Wiccan priestess in Old Salem."

According to Means (p.10): "Even when police win such lawsuits, they often lose in other significant ways. Civil lawsuits are aggravating, stressful and time-consuming at best. At worst they threaten careers, personal finances and health. Other costs, as described by the Supreme Court, 'include the expenses of litigation, the diversion of official energy from pressing public issues and the deterrence of able citizens from acceptance of public office.'"

## Vicarious Liability

**Vicarious liability** makes others specifically associated with a person also responsible for that person's actions. The vast majority of lawsuits naming supervisory officers are attempts to get to more, wealthier and better-insured defendants through vicarious liability. Suing every possible individual and agency involved creates a **collective deep pocket** from which astronomical judgments can be collected.

# Common Charges Brought against Police Officers

As noted, most cases being tried are based on Section 1983, alleging police violation of constitutional rights. More recently, several lawsuits have been brought for failure to protect or investigate. Two important distinctions determine personal liability of city officers and employees for acts committed while on duty: discretionary versus ministerial acts and malfeasance versus nonfeasance.

**Discretionary acts** are those actions officers perform using their own judgment. Policies and procedures for the acts leave decisions up to the officers. If police officers are carrying out a duty requiring judgment, they cannot be liable for damages unless they are willfully or grossly negligent. Making an arrest is an example of a discretionary act. **Ministerial acts** have to do with the way the duty is to be performed. If officers fail to perform the duty as prescribed, they can be sued. If, for example, a department has a policy against shooting a gun from a moving squad car and an officer does so and injures someone, the officer can be sued.

**Malfeasance** refers to acts of misconduct or wrongdoing, while **nonfeasance** refers to failure to take action. In the infamous Rodney King incident, officers participating in the beating might be charged with malfeasance in civil proceedings. Those who stood by and did nothing to interfere might be charged with nonfeasance.

 The most frequent civil lawsuits against police involve false arrest or imprisonment, malicious prosecution, use of unnecessary or excessive force, brutality, wrongful death, failure to protect and negligent service.

## False Arrest or Imprisonment

The largest number of lawsuits, accounting for about 50 percent of all lawsuits filed, is for false arrest and imprisonment. False arrest and false imprisonment are exceptionally vulnerable to lawsuits because such suits are filed with ease and can be filed as group actions. False arrest and false imprisonment are almost synonymous under the law. Both are usually alleged against the officer.

Arrest is broadly defined as taking an individual into custody by physical or constructive restraint with the intention of charging the individual in a court of law. Physical force need not be used to accomplish arrest or imprisonment. The assertion that would be brought to the court's attention in such a lawsuit is that the officer lacked probable cause to arrest. An absolute defense in such a case is that probable cause *did* exist. The courts look at two important factors when examining liability for false arrest: (1) the information known to the police officer at the time the arrest was made and (2) the reasonableness of the officer's action given all the circumstances at the time of the arrest.

A common problem occurs when police officers respond to retail stores' calls for assistance in arresting people suspected of shoplifting. Most agencies have standardized procedures requiring the apprehending store employee to make a formal citizen's arrest. In this case, a claim of false imprisonment may be filed against both the store and the police officer.

Many other false-arrest suits result from drunk and disorderly arrests and from warrantless arrests under proarrest domestic violence statutes.

## Malicious Prosecution

An area of liability closely associated with false arrest and imprisonment is malicious prosecution. **Malicious prosecution** is a proceeding instituted in bad faith without any probable cause in the belief that the charges against the defendant can be sustained. The cause of action in the civil suit is usually for damages suffered. This type of civil action arises most frequently when one citizen formally charges another citizen and the defendant is not successfully prosecuted.

## Excessive Force or Brutality

The second largest numbers of civil actions against police officers are filed in the areas of excessive force or brutality. Such a suit can be the result of lawful or allegedly unlawful arrest and will usually name a supervisor as a defendant along with the officer(s) actually involved.

The specific allegations may be civil assault and battery. Assault refers to conduct that may result from a well-founded fear of imminent peril. Battery is the unlawful, hostile touching or shoving of another, no matter how slight. Some states have combined the two into a single charge of assault. In some instances, criminal charges may be brought as well. For example, if a police officer were to strike a handcuffed prisoner with a nightstick hard enough to shatter the bones in the prisoner's face, the prisoner could bring a civil action *and* press criminal charges against the officer.

Courts have held an officer liable for assault and battery if that officer strikes a suspect or uses an aerosol irritant on the suspect for talking back, or if an officer continues to beat a defendant who has stopped resisting. Almost every state now has statutes that define the extent to which police officers can use physical force in specific situations. All officers should become thoroughly familiar with their states' statutes in this area.

Most states allow officers to use some physical force short of deadly force to make an arrest or prevent an escape. Officers may also use physical force, short of deadly force, to defend themselves. Recall that *Graham v. Connor* (1989) established that police officers could be held liable for using excessive force, with the test for liability being "objective reasonableness."

Lawsuits are also likely when use of deadly force is involved. As stated in Chapter 3, the use of *deadly force* to make an arrest or prevent an escape is generally permitted only when:

- The crime committed was a felony involving the use or threatened use of imminent physical force against a person.
- The crime committed was an inherently dangerous felony such as kidnapping, arson or burglary in a dwelling.
- The officer's life or personal safety was endangered in the particular circumstances involved.
- The person was an escapee from a correctional facility.

It is doubtful the court would uphold the use of deadly physical force in cases involving property crimes unless there was imminent danger to the officer or other individuals.

The use of physical force by police officers to prevent destruction of evidence is controversial. Generally, the force used must be reasonable under all circumstances. Deadly physical force is *never* permitted in preventing the destruction of evidence. The swallowing of drugs in an arrest is an issue for which courts have not given police any guidelines. Cases have included everything from officers sticking their fingers down suspects' throats to officers taking suspects to hospitals to have emergency personnel give them enemas. Handcuffing an arrested person who is resisting arrest also has been deemed excessive force in some instances, as discussed in Chapter 3.

## Wrongful Death

Closely related to excessive force and brutality complaints is the area of wrongful death actions. Wrongful deaths can be caused either by intentional or negligent acts or by omissions of police officers. Intentionally inflicting fatal injuries causes the greatest number of wrongful death actions. Circumstances that lead to wrongful death suits include shooting an unarmed, fleeing misdemeanant; a fleeing felon when the felon could have been subdued without deadly force; any misdemeanant to effect an arrest; and shooting in self-defense of an actual or threatened attack when the attacker did not use great bodily force.

Negligent killings account for a much smaller number of deaths and usually arise in the following situations:

- Shooting to halt a motor vehicle and striking a passenger. (Most police departments have regulated this practice by forbidding firing at a moving vehicle.)
- Accidentally shooting a bystander.
- Reckless firing of warning shots. (Many police departments forbid the firing of warning shots.)
- Poor aim when shooting to wound a suspect. (This includes accidentally striking a hostage or accidentally discharging a firearm, wounding or killing an innocent person.)

Officers participating in raiding parties, such as those making drug arrests, must act reasonably. Any lawsuits that may emanate from their actions will encompass all officers participating in the raid. The lawsuit can extend to the supervisors, the department and the city itself. Some wrongful death suits arise from police pursuits or negligent operation of squad cars.

## Negligent Operation of a Vehicle

Another area of specific liability is the operation of a police vehicle. Liability in this particular area has increased dramatically in recent years. Police officers are charged with the same standard of care as the general public and are found liable under a straight negligence theory for the negligent operation of vehicles. Statutes allowing police officers to disregard stop signs and other traffic laws and cautions are now being interpreted by the courts to require officers to use reasonable care under existing circumstances. The requirement of reasonable care is particularly critical when "hot pursuit" is involved and the police vehicle is unmarked and lacks a siren and red lights.

## Failure to Protect

Another broad area of officer liability involves lawsuits alleging "failure to protect." This can take several forms, including failure to answer calls for help, failure to arrest, failure to investigate and so on. Some "special relationships" have been found to exist in certain circumstances, and failure to protect can involve several types of situations.

**General Failure to Protect**   One of the most common situations occurs when a victim assumes the police will provide protection and then relies on that assumption. Publishing a 911 number, according to some courts, implies that the police will protect those who call that number.

Failure to protect also occurs when the police tell a victim they will let the victim know when someone is released from custody or from prison and fail to do so. Failure to protect witnesses who have cooperated with police and whose cooperation brings them into contact with the suspects also has resulted in lawsuits.

**Failure to Arrest or Restrain People Committing or About to Commit Violent Crimes**   This is usually classed as an act of negligence. For example, an officer failed to get a drunken motorist off the road before causing a serious accident. Failure to arrest a person known to be dangerous when probable cause exists can also lead to suits for damages subsequently done by that person.

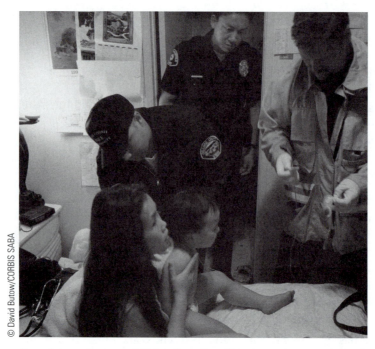

*One of the main responsibilities of a police officer is to administer first aid to victims.*

**Failure to Respond to Calls for Assistance**   If police officers have reason to believe someone is in imminent danger, they must take action or face the possibility of a lawsuit. In *Thurman v. City of Torrington* (1984) the victim, an estranged wife who was beaten by her husband, received a $2.3 million award because the police had refused to act on her complaints.

## Failure to Identify

At times, failure to identify oneself as a police officer before making an arrest can lead to liability on negligence theory. The liability would be for incurred damages or injuries that might have been avoided if the officer had given proper identification.

## Negligent Service

The past decades have seen an increase in civil lawsuits claiming negligence by police officers, departments and municipalities in providing traffic services. Police officers or agencies may be liable if they know of a potentially dangerous condition and fail to take reasonable action to correct the existing hazard. They may also be liable if they fail to warn oncoming traffic of an existing hazard.

Some courts do hold police officers responsible for providing assistance at a crash scene. Other courts, however, contend that although the police have a duty to help at a crash scene, officers become liable only after establishing a special relationship with the victim.

Traffic-related incidents are not the only area in which charges of negligent service can be made. Some cases suggest that the negligent administration of first aid by police officers can be the basis for an action in negligence in which an officer's act or omission becomes the cause for complaint. In addition, some lawsuits have been filed in attempts to make officers liable for not recognizing existing medical impairments. Though these cases are rare, officers should be aware of them. Most have not been successful, and many have centered around individuals who appeared to be drunk and were treated as being drunk, but who in actuality were suffering heart attacks or having epileptic seizures.

## Other Areas of Civil Liability

Although the next areas to be discussed have produced limited litigation against police officers to date, officers should be aware of these possibilities for lawsuits.

**Libel and Slander**   An action in this area usually is based on written **(libel)** or spoken **(slander)** false statements that tend to humiliate and degrade a person in the esteem of others. These usually are known as *defamation of character* suits. These suits often pivot around statements made during arrests because much of the court process and testimony are privileged communications and should not be repeated by the police officers. Proving the statement's truth is a defense to such actions.

The normal defenses used by police officers, departments and municipalities being sued are that:
- They did not intend to deprive the plaintiff of constitutional rights.
- They acted in good faith.
- They acted with what was considered reasonable judgment at the time and with valid authority.

## Reducing the Occurrence of Civil Lawsuits

Police officers and agencies can expect more rather than fewer lawsuits unless specific steps are taken. Ultimately, the risk of civil liability rests upon the individual actions of each police officer. Police departments can develop extensive policies and procedures to help assure that their officers act in a way that will deter civil lawsuits.

Protection against lawsuits includes:
- Effective policies and procedures clearly communicated to all.
- Thorough and continuous training.
- Proper supervision and discipline.
- Accurate, thorough police reports.

At the heart of protecting against lawsuits are the department's *policies and procedures.* A department's procedures manual should clearly state that a fundamental mission of the department is to protect everyone's civil rights and that officers and supervisory personnel have an affirmative duty to intervene if they witness the violation of civil rights by anyone, including fellow officers.

*Training* should include the basic rookie training as well as ongoing in-service training and specialized training. Training must include the policies and procedures of the department. It also must include continual updating on changes in laws that affect police operations.

*Proper supervision and discipline* are also vital to avoiding lawsuits. Discipline can be viewed both positively and negatively. On the positive side, police departments should foster professional discipline within their officers; that is, they should encourage an atmosphere in which officers act according to established policies and procedures. They should be able to say of their personnel that they are well-disciplined officers. On the negative side, officers who do not act according to established policies and procedures should be reprimanded (disciplined).

Another key area in preventing lawsuits is *thorough, accurate police reports* establishing the reasonableness of officers' actions. According to Stine (2001, p.46): "The value of a properly written report detailing the circumstances surrounding an incident cannot be overstated. When a lawsuit is filed a thorough and complete accounting of the actions of those involved in the police action is invaluable." Close (2001, p.27) adds: "Report writing plays a key role in any determination of liability. Mistakes and oversights in a police report are a gift to the plaintiff's attorney. Departments should give the plaintiff as little as possible to work with. This means that supervisors should be accountable for the completeness and accuracy of police reports."

To minimize lawsuits at a more personal level, law enforcement officers should:
- Know and follow their department's guidelines.
- Stay in the scope of their duties.
- Always act professionally.
- Know and respect their constituents' rights.
- Seek advice if in doubt.
- Carefully document their activities in their reports.
- Maintain good community relations.
- Keep current on civil and criminal liability cases.

The importance of documentation cannot be emphasized enough. Comprehensive incident reports are vital to defenses against civil suits. Videotaping traffic stops also provides officers with documentation of their actions, especially in cases involving DWI arrests.

## Countersuits

In many instances, civil suits brought against law enforcement officers either have no basis or are frivolous. Some people consider the best defense to be a good offense and, therefore, sue the officer who arrested them, thinking it might put them in a better bargaining position.

Law enforcement officers and agencies can countersue if they are falsely accused of a civil offense.

In one case a deputy sheriff responded to a public drunkenness complaint at a convenience store. When he arrived, the deputy approached the suspect and asked that he come outside with him to discuss the problem. The suspect filed a brutality complaint against the deputy, claiming the deputy grabbed him by the throat and physically dragged him out of the store. The evidence obtained from the convenience store security camera showed that the deputy did not grab the suspect by the throat, but even held the door open for him when they left the store. The trial judge awarded the deputy sheriff $25,000 in damages as a result of the false accusations.

Law enforcement officers also can sue even if they have not been sued. Prosecutors, police and sheriff's deputies are entitled to the same right to recover for wrongful injury as any other citizen.

## Legal Liability and Community Policing

If community policing becomes a reality in a jurisdiction, citizens will better understand why the police do what they do. Citizens should also be less likely to bring suit against officers if they view them as partners. Likewise, police officers operating under a community policing philosophy will have a service orientation and will be much less likely to infringe on the constitutional rights of those with whom they work. This may also lead to officers policing in a more ethical manner.

## Ethics: An Overview

Ethics usually involves what is often referred to as the **conscience,** the ability to recognize right from wrong and to follow one's own sense of what is right. Some believe conscience is an innate moral sense; people are either born with it or not. Others believe it is a power acquired by experience—that is, it can be taught or consciously ignored. Cline (2003, p.61) supports the latter view: "Training time and resources are spent showing officers how to stay alive in confrontations, but little or nothing is being spent on how to stay alive in confrontations with themselves."

A complexity in ethical behavior is whether the issues addressed by ethics are absolute or relative. For example, is killing a human being always "bad" (absolute) or is it even "good" at times (relative)?

 An **absolute issue** is one with only two sides; the decision is between "black" and "white." A **relative issue** is one with a multitude of sides, that is, varying shades of "gray" between the two absolute positions. Ethical issues are usually relative.

Ethics, then, involves looking at moral rules recognized by individuals with a conscience and held to be either absolute or relative. What one individual considers ethical behavior may be considered highly unethical behavior by another individual. An example of this is the Hmong practice in which adult males marry very young girls. To Hmong people this is moral and right. To many Americans, this is immoral and wrong. Ethics *is* complex and presents serious challenges to those who seek to behave ethically. Consider, for example, which of the following ethical principles are behind your behavior:

- Do unto others as you would have them do unto you.
- Do what will accomplish your goal/vision in the most efficient manner.
- Do whatever you please so long as it does not cause harm to anyone else.
- Might makes right.

Ethics includes integrity, that is, doing right when no one is watching. Figure 14.1 illustrates the dynamics of integrity in a police career, including the personal, departmental and external forces affecting an officer's behavior.

One departmental force influencing police officers is often a **code of ethics** that sets forth accepted standards of behavior for a profession. Conditt (2001, p.19) notes: "Every organization has an official, or formal, code of conduct that sets forth the responsibilities of its employees and the rules and regulations governing employee conduct." The code of ethics is usually framed and hanging on the wall. Such codes usually have at least three important themes:

- Justice or fairness is the single most dominant theme. Officers are not to take advantage of people or accept gratuities.
- The importance of the law and the police as tools of the Constitution is a second theme. Police behavior must be totally within the bounds set by the law.
- Police must at all times uphold a standard of behavior consistent with their public position.

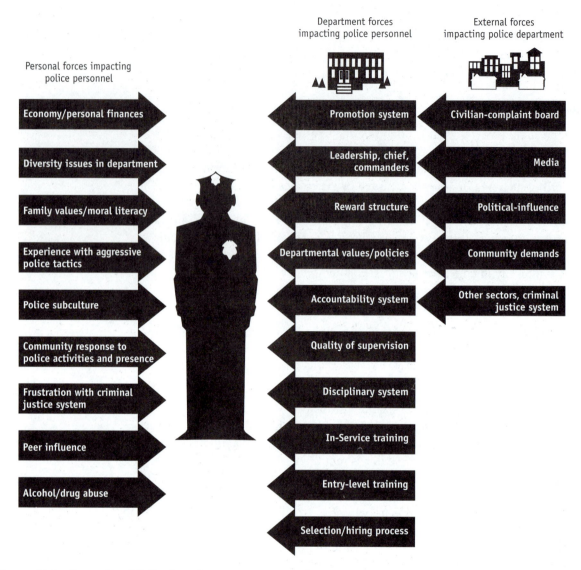

Personal forces impacting police personnel

- Economy/personal finances
- Diversity issues in department
- Family values/moral literacy
- Experience with aggressive police tactics
- Police subculture
- Community response to police activities and presence
- Frustration with criminal justice system
- Peer influence
- Alcohol/drug abuse

Department forces impacting police personnel

- Promotion system
- Leadership, chief, commanders
- Reward structure
- Departmental values/policies
- Accountability system
- Quality of supervision
- Disciplinary system
- In-Service training
- Entry-level training
- Selection/hiring process

External forces impacting police department

- Civilian-complaint board
- Media
- Political-influence
- Community demands
- Other sectors, criminal justice system

**Figure 14.1** Dynamics of Police Integrity

SOURCE: *Police Integrity: Public Service with Honor.* Washington, DC: National Institute of Justice, January 1997, p.92.

The Law Enforcement Code of Ethics, shown in Figure 14.2, was adopted unanimously at the 98th Annual IACP Conference in 1991. This conference also adopted unanimously the Police Code of Conduct for police officers, shown in Figure 14.3.

Often, however, the police department's formal code of ethics and its informal code of ethics are entirely different. The informal code of ethics results from what is commonly referred to as the police culture.

## The Police Culture

In most police departments new officers recite the Oath of Honor, which stresses integrity: "On my honor, I will never betray my badge, my integrity, my character or the public trust. I will always have the courage to hold myself and others accountable for our actions. I will always uphold the Constitution and the com-

As a law enforcement officer, my fundamental duty is to serve the community; to safeguard lives and property; to protect the innocent against deception, the weak against oppression or intimidation and the peaceful against violence or disorder; and to respect the constitutional rights of all to liberty, equality and justice.

I will keep my private life unsullied as an example to all and will behave in a manner that does not bring discredit to me or to my agency. I will maintain courageous calm in the face of danger, scorn or ridicule; develop self-restraint; and be constantly mindful of the welfare of others. Honest in thought and deed both in my personal and official life, I will be exemplary in obeying the law and the regulation of my department. Whatever I see or hear of a confidential nature or that is confided to me in my official capacity will be kept ever secret unless revelation is necessary in the performance of my duty.

I will never act officiously or permit personal feelings, prejudices, political beliefs, aspirations, animosities or friendships to influence my decisions. With no compromise for crime and with relentless prosecution of criminals, I will enforce the law courteously and appropriately without fear or favor, malice or ill will, never employing unnecessary force or violence and never accepting gratuities.

I recognize the badge of my office as a symbol of public faith, and I accept it as a public trust to be held so long as I am true to the ethics of police service. I will never engage in acts of corruption or bribery, nor will I condone such acts by other police officers. I will cooperate with all legally authorized agencies and their representatives in the pursuit of justice.

I know that I alone am responsible for my own standard of professional performance and will take every reasonable opportunity to enhance and improve my level of knowledge and competence. I will constantly strive to achieve these objectives and ideals, dedicating myself before God to my chosen profession . . . law enforcement.

**Figure 14.2** Law Enforcement Code of Ethics (from the International Association of Chiefs of Police)

SOURCE: Reprinted from *The Police Chief*, Vol. LIX, No. 1, January 1992, p.17. Copyright held by the International Association of Chiefs of Police, Inc., 515 N. Washington Street, Alexandria, Virginia 22314. Further reproduction without express written permission from IACP is strictly prohibited.

munity I serve." Anderson (2003, p.104) describes the indoctrination of an individual into policing: "The recital of the oath is often marked with ceremony and witnessed by one's family, friends, peers and colleagues. It is understandably a proud rite of passage into a profession steeped in tradition." Anderson (p.105) notes: "The act [of taking the oath] bonds an individual to a fraternal order." The newcomers soon become part of the police culture.

Paoline (2004, p.205) contends: "The police culture has been a topic of study for well more than 40 years." The police culture usually includes at least the following beliefs: The police are the only real crime fighters. Loyalty counts more than anything. It is impossible to win the war on crime without bending the rules. The public is demanding and nonsupportive. Working in patrol is the least desirable job in the police department.

 Conventional wisdom holds that the defining characteristics of the police culture are social isolation and group loyalty, resulting in a code of silence.

Dees (2001, p.214) says: "The officer has to decide where his *first loyalty* lies. Is it to his fellow officer, or to enforce the law?" He contends: "The answer to this question is in the oath every officer takes upon accepting the call to the badge. The officer promises to support, protect and defend the Constitution of the United States, the constitution and laws of his state and possibly the laws and ordinances of his county or city. Note there isn't anything in the oath about his fellow officer, his chief or sheriff." Nonetheless, many times officers will put loyalty to their colleagues above loyalty to the public or even to the department, often by abiding by the code of silence. This loyalty to colleagues is often referred

All law enforcement officers must be fully aware of the ethical responsibilities of their position and must strive constantly to live up to the highest possible standards of professional policing.

The International Association of Chiefs of Police believes it important that police officers have clear advice and counsel available to assist them in performing their duties consistent with these standards, and has adopted the following ethical mandates as guidelines to meet these ends.

### Primary Responsibility of a Police Officer

A police officer acts as an official representative of government who is required and trusted to work within the law. The officer's powers and duties are conferred by statute. The fundamental duties of a police officer include serving the community, safeguarding lives and property, protecting the innocent, keeping the peace and ensuring the rights of all to liberty, equality and justice.

### Performance of the Duties of a Police Officer

A police officer shall perform all duties impartially, without favor or affection or ill will and without regard to status, sex, race, religion, political belief or aspiration. All citizens will be treated equally with courtesy, consideration and dignity.

Officers will never allow personal feelings, animosities or friendships to influence official conduct. Laws will be enforced appropriately and courteously and, in carrying out their responsibilities, officers will strive to obtain maximum cooperation from the public. They will conduct themselves in appearance and deportment in such a manner as to inspire confidence and respect for the position of public trust they hold.

### Discretion

A police officer will use responsibly the discretion vested in his position and exercise it within the law. The principal of reasonableness will guide the officer's determinations, and the officer will consider all surrounding circumstances in determining whether any legal action shall be taken.

Consistent and wise use of discretion, based on professional policing competence, will do much to preserve good relationships and retain the confidence of the public. There can be difficulty in choosing between conflicting courses of action. It is important to remember that a timely word of advice rather than arrest—which may be correct in appropriate circumstances—can be a more effective means of achieving a desired end.

### Use of Force

A police officer will never employ unnecessary force or violence and will use only such force in the discharge of duty as is reasonable in all circumstances.

The use of force should be used only with the greatest restraint and only after discussion, negotiation and persuasion have been found to be inappropriate or ineffective. While the use of force is occasionally unavoidable, every police officer will refrain from unnecessary infliction of pain or suffering and will never engage in cruel, degrading or inhuman treatment of any person.

### Confidentiality

Whatever a police officer sees, hears or learns of that is of a confidential nature will be kept secret unless the performances of duty or legal provision requires otherwise.

Members of the public have a right to security and privacy, and information obtained about them must not be improperly divulged.

### Integrity

A police officer will not engage in acts of corruption or bribery, nor will an officer condone such acts by other police officers.

The public demands that the integrity of police officers be above reproach. Police officers must, therefore, avoid any conduct that might compromise integrity and thus undercut the public confidence in a law enforcement agency. Officers will refuse to accept any gifts, presents, subscriptions, favors, gratuities or promises that could be interpreted as seeking to cause the officer to refrain from performing official responsibilities honestly and within the law. Police officers must not receive private or special advantage from their official status. Respect from the public cannot be bought: it can only be earned and cultivated.

*continued*

**Figure 14.3**    Police Code of Conduct

SOURCE: Reprinted from *The Police Chief*, January 1992, p.15. Copyright held by the International Association of Chiefs of Police, Inc., 515 N. Washington Street, Alexandria, Virginia 22314. Further reproduction without express written permission from IACP is strictly prohibited.

Cooperation with Other Police Officers and Agencies

Police officers will cooperate with all legally authorized agencies and their representatives in the pursuit of justice.

An officer or agency may be one among many organizations that may provide law enforcement services to a jurisdiction. It is imperative that a police officer assist colleagues fully and completely with respect and consideration at all times.

Personal-Professional Capabilities

Police officers will be responsible for their own standard of professional performance and will take every reasonable opportunity to enhance and improve their level of knowledge and competence.

Through study and experience, a police officer can acquire the high level of knowledge and competence that is essential for the efficient and effective performance of duty. The acquisition of knowledge is a never-ending process of personal and professional development that should be pursued constantly.

Private Life

Police officers will behave in a manner that does not bring discredit to their agencies or themselves.

A police officer's character and conduct while off duty must always be exemplary, thus maintaining a position of respect in the community in which he or she lives and serves. The officer's personal behavior must be beyond reproach.

---

**Figure 14.3**  Continued

to as **solidarity**—a togetherness that binds officers to each other rather than to the department, the community and sometimes ethical principles.

A survey by the National Institute of Ethics (NIE), with 1,116 officers participating, found that 46 percent of the officers stated they had witnessed misconduct by another employee but had not taken action (Trautman, 2001, p.68). Of those officers, 47 percent said they had felt pressure to take part in the code of silence from the officers who committed the misconduct. According to Trautman (p.69), head of the National Institute of Ethics: "Anger was the most frequent incident for which the code of silence was used; 41 percent were excessive use of force circumstances." Trautman (p.70) concludes that a code of silence does exist and that it breeds, supports and nourishes other forms of unethical actions. In addition, he (p.71) suggests: "The Us vs. Them mentality is usually present within the minds of those who participate in the code of silence."

 The code of silence and the Us vs. Them mentality often bond. Loyalty becomes more important than integrity.

McErlain (2001, p.87) contends: "Those who would suggest that some law enforcement officers today no longer hide behind the banner of loyalty are either naïve or concealing reality, contributing to the problem and enabling others to do the same." According to Trautman (2002, p.18): "The development of loyalty and the code of silence is a totally natural phenomenon among people who spend significant time together."

According to Nowicki and Punch (2003, p.330): "To some officers, the most serious aspersion that can be cast upon another officer is to say that he or she breached the code of silence and provided information to internal affairs investigators." Griffith (2003, p.74) suggests: "Police loyalty known as the 'blue wall' or the 'code of silence' has forced many officers to jeopardize their careers and their liberty to cover up another officer's misconduct. The results are often tragic." Griffith quotes Trautman as saying: "Misconduct and the code of silence are the most destructive forces in law enforcement. It is far more likely that an officer's career will be cut short by these things than by a bad guy with a knife in the alley" (2003, p.74). Quinn (2004) also cautions:

> As terrible as it is, there is no escaping the Code. It is as inevitable as your childhood diseases and just as necessary. Each stinging battle with the Code will be either an inoculation of the spirit and an opportunity to grow stronger or a crippling injury to your integrity. Regardless of the outcome there will be vivid images you can't erase from your memory. There will always be the mental and physical scars to remind you of your battles.
>
> But, each encounter can leave you better prepared both physically and mentally for the tough challenges ahead, if you are willing to admit you're not superman, and you recognize your "dark side" for what it is. Because only when we know the Code of Silence for what it is can we gain some control over it. Either way, you won't escape unscathed because at some point in time you are going to "Walk with the Devil" in order to get the job done (p.27).
>
> Every day is a new challenge and ethical police conduct is often an uphill battle. Even the best of cops have days when they want to give up and do whatever it takes to put a child molester, baby murderer, or other lowlife in prison. When you sit inches away from these scum and they brag about the truly horrific things they have done to an innocent it's easy to abide by the Code—if that's what it takes. When the evidence isn't perfect, you just use a little creative report writing and this guy will never harm another person again. Illegal searches, physical abuse, or even perjury, you know you will be in the company of many good cops who have done the same. But are they really good cops? (pp.13–14).
>
> The choice of being a "Peace Officer" means there will be many battles in solitary combat with other cops and with yourself. You will not win them all—you cannot—the cards are stacked against you. There will be no medals, awards ceremonies or cheering crowds for the battles you do win. But there will be honor and integrity—in your life and in your work.

### The Police Culture and Use of Force

Researchers Terrill et al. (2003, p.1003) studied the relationship between police culture and coercion: "The findings indicate that those officers who closely embody the values of the police culture are more coercive compared with those that differentially align with the culture." Excessive use of force, as previously discussed, is usually clearly unethical. But many areas of policing are not so clear.

## Gray Areas in Police Ethics

 Two areas in discussions of law enforcement ethics are controversial: police use of deception and police acceptance of gratuities.

### Police Use of Deception

As Klockars (1995, p.552) comments: "At the core of the ethical life of the officer is a profound moral dilemma. On the one hand, the officer's obligations to the values of civilized society oblige him or her to coerce people effectively. On the other hand, the officer's obligation to coerce people effectively requires that he or she suspend the very values that civilized society treasures.

Klockars (p.552) describes two types of lies commonly used by police officers in doing their duties. The first is the **police placebo** (sometimes referred to as the "little white lie"): "Police officers find it ethically defensible to lie when the lie is told to benefit the person lied to and no more effective means of dealing with the problem is available." Klockars gives as an example two mentally ill brothers well known to police who believed they were being pursued by invisible agents from outer space. The officers told the brothers that they had reported the so-called invasion to Washington and were sending out a squad of equally invisible investigators to protect them.

The second type of lie is the **blue lie** (p.553): "'Blue lies' are different from police placebos in that they are not told to help or comfort the person lied to but, rather, to exert control." Klockars gives as an example a police officer attempting to remove an abortion protestor from an abortion clinic waiting room. She insisted they'd have to carry her out. The officer told her he had just had a hernia repaired and was afraid if he lifted her he would tear out his stitches. He even offered to show her, but his lie was sufficient to get her to leave peacefully.

Noble (2003) describes two types of lies: those justified by investigative necessity and those that are malicious:

> In the performance of their duties, police officers frequently engage in a significant amount of deceptive conduct that is essential to public safety. Consider lying to suspects, conducting undercover operations and even deploying unmarked cars. Presenting a suspect with false evidence, a false confession of a crime partner or a false claim that the suspect was identified in a lineup are but a few of the deceptive practices that police officers have used for years during interrogations. These investigatory deceptive practices are necessary when no other means would be effective, when they are lawful, and when they are aimed at obtaining the truth. . . (p.95).
>
> Malicious lies are the true evil of officer misconduct. For example, a police officer may be tempted to testify falsely to imprison a criminal. The officer's intent may be a worthy objective to the public; removing a criminal from society and the officer may validate his intent in his own mind by believing that he is engaging in a greater good. But this lie would violate the standard by which we would say the lie was reasonable and appropriate under the circumstances given the status obligations of the person engaging in the lie. Although the intent may be legitimate, the actions are malicious. This malice is the motive by which any sense of limits or constraint or fidelity to law and policy is destroyed. It is important to understand that motive or intentions can be mixed, so that a person may deceive in order to pursue some worthwhile, utilitarian goal (such as public safety) and at the same time have a malicious disregard for the rights of the suspect and for the laws, policies, and limits that apply to policing (p.97).

Noble (p.99) suggests: "Perhaps it is easier to assess intentional deceptive conduct on a continuum. At one end is intentional, malicious, deceptive conduct that will take one of three forms:

1. Deceptive action in a formal setting, such as testifying in court or during an internal affairs investigation [testilying]
2. Failure to bring forward information involving criminal action by other officers, also known as observing the so-called code of silence
3. Creation of false evidence that tends to implicate another in a criminal act

*Accepting gratuities such as free coffee can be the first step toward becoming corrupt.*

Intentional, malicious, deceptive conduct in any of these three areas will permanently destroy an officer's credibility. . . .

At the other end of the continuum are lies justified by necessity, which may be defended, based on the circumstances. These types of deceptions are at least excusable if not acceptable. Deceptive conduct at either end of the continuum can be dealt with easily. At one end, the conduct does no harm and no action is necessary. At the other end, there is great harm and there is no option other than the termination of the officer's employment. The problem is not the conduct at the ends of the continuum, but rather the conduct that falls somewhere in between.

Another gray area is the acceptance of gratuities.

## *Gratuities*

The formal law enforcement code of ethics disapproves of **gratuities,** material favors or gifts given in return for a service. However, many citizens feel there is nothing wrong with a business giving freebies, such as gifts or free admission, to a police officer. Many officers believe these are small rewards for the difficulties they endure in police work.

White (2002, p.21) notes: "The payment of free coffee and discounted meals or services from businesses to police officers is a widespread, traditional practice in many jurisdictions. Free coffee is perhaps the most commonly received gratuity." The question becomes: What gratuities are acceptable and under what circumstances, if any? Certainly gratuities are acceptable in many other professions. But in a profession involving great discretion, gratuities can be extremely problematic. They can give the appearance of preferential treatment, even if such preferential treatment does not exist.

Withrow and Dailey (2004, p.159) point out: "Very few issues cause more heated debate among police scholars and practitioners than gratuities. Some

## Allowing Gratuities

- They help create a friendly bond between officers and the public, thus fostering community-policing goals.

- They represent a nonwritten form of appreciation and usually are given with no expectation of anything in return.

- Most gratuities are too small to be a significant motivator of actions.

- The practice is so deeply entrenched that efforts to root it out will be ineffective and cause unnecessary violations of the rules.

- A complete ban makes officers appear as though they cannot distinguish between a friendly gesture and a bribe.

- Some businesses and restaurants insist on the practice.

## Banning Gratuities

- The acceptance violates most departments' policies and the law enforcement code of ethics.

- Even the smallest gifts create a sense of obligation.

- Even if nothing is expected in return, the gratuity may create an appearance of impropriety.

- Although most officers can discern between friendly gestures and bribes, some may not.

- They create an unfair distribution of services to those who can afford gratuities, voluntary taxing, or private funding of a public service.

- It is unprofessional.

**Figure 14.4**   Arguments For and Against Gratuities

SOURCE: Mike White. "The Problem with Gratuities." *FBI Law Enforcement Bulletin*, July 2002, p.21.

argue the police should never, under any circumstances, receive any gratuity, tip or extra recognition for doing their job. Others question the rigidity of such a position. In their view, tips, gratuities and even expensive gifts are normal gestures of appreciation for exemplary or dedicated service and serve to forge positive community relationships, an important component of contemporary policing strategies."

Some officers take a very strong stand on this issue. Fuller (2001, p.6), for example, contends: "The average street cop is expected to conduct his or her personal and professional life with more integrity and decorum than most other citizens, however unrealistic and difficult that may seem at times." So what if an officer is offered free coffee or half-price lunches? What's the harm in that? Fuller (p.7) reminds officers: "One of the occupational attributes of the veteran street cop is not accepting things at face value. Always ask yourself what people have in mind when they offer you something for nothing. There is almost always an ulterior motive or hidden agenda." As O. W. Wilson was fond of saying: "Nobody ever gave a cop something for nothing" (Fuller, p.7). Figure 14.4 summarizes the arguments for and against accepting gratuities.

As noted, accepting gratuities may be the first small step on the road to more unethical behaviors and eventually to corruption.

# Unethical Behavior

Son (2004, p.179) contends: "Police misconduct has been a social issue in the United States for much of the 20th century." This interest continues into the twenty-first century. Police misconduct involves a broad spectrum of behavior including mistreatment of offenders, discrimination, illegal searching and seizures, violation of suspects' constitutional rights, perjury, evidence planting and other forms of corruption. Concern has always existed about controlling the powers granted by the government to the police to use force. Where power exists, the potential to abuse that power also exists. Unethical behavior, which in its extreme form results in corruption, is an exceedingly complex problem.

Police routinely deal with the seamier side of society, not only drug addicts and muggers, but middle-class people involved in dishonesty and corruption. The constant displays of lying, hiding, cheating and theft create cynicism and threaten even the strongest code of ethics, especially when these behaviors are carried out by judges, prosecutors, superiors and politicians. The following are some rationales police might easily use to justify unethical behavior:

- The money is there—if I don't take it, someone else will.
- I'm only taking what's rightfully mine; if I got a decent wage, I wouldn't have to get it on my own.
- I need it—it's a good cause—my wife needs an operation.
- I put my life on the line every day—I deserve it.

According to Griffith (2003, p.69): "Since 1993 major cities nationwide, including Los Angeles, Miami, Detroit and New Orleans have been rocked by revelations of officer misconduct. Internal and external investigations of these departments led to lurid evidence of officers dealing drugs, stealing evidence, hiring themselves out for contract killings, planting guns on suspects after police-involved shootings and covering up for fellow officers."

Green (2001, p.90) stresses: "The administration needs to help when the decision is between what the officer knows is legally right, but morally bad or what is illegal but morally the right thing to do." He gives as an example an individual stopped for speeding, clearly a violation, but the person driving is a doctor on his way to an emergency. Should the officer write a citation? Or an officer stops someone for a crime and finds narcotics. It is a small amount, and the officer decides nothing will happen when it comes to court, so he destroys the evidence and lets the person go. Green asks: "At what point do these acts of omission escalate to acts of commission as officers begin to rationalize their behavior?"

One way to help officers facing ethical decision making is to help them understand what might be tempting to them. He (p.88) describes the formula used by the FBI to explain temptation:

Attraction + Proximity + Perceived Availability = Temptation

For example, if a person liked money, was placed in situations where money was readily available and if there were little chance of being caught, temptation would be high. But even in high temptation situations, most officers do not act unethically. Why? This is explained by another formula delineating consequences (p.89):

Temptation – Perceived Consequences = Action

Without any perceived consequences, unethical behavior is much more likely to occur. The FBI defines perceived consequences by yet another formula:

Perceived Consequences = Rules, Enforcement of Consequences, Reality

To help officers avoid unethical behavior, Green (p.89) suggests that management make sure officers are aware of the temptation process. Officers need to know what might be tempting to them. If the proximity or availability of the desired object cannot be changed, thus removing or reducing temptation, the consequences must be equally high or greater.

# Corruption

Corruption is not a twenty-first century police problem. Much police corruption is drug related, for example, stealing money and/or drugs from drug dealers, selling stolen drugs, planting drugs on suspects and protecting drug operations. A police officer making a modest salary may be greatly tempted by easily gaining the equivalent of two years' salary by making one "favorable" decision for the drug trafficker. Other corrupt behaviors may or may not be drug related, such as conducting unconstitutional searches and seizures, providing false testimony and submitting false crime reports. Although examples of police corruption vary, they all have key elements in common.

 The key elements in corrupt behavior are (1) conduct prohibited by law (2) involving misuse of position (3) resulting in a reward or personal gain for the officer.

## *Why Do Officers Become Corrupt?*
Several factors contribute to becoming corrupt, such as ego, sex or the exercise of power; tolerance of the behavior by the community; socialization from peers and/or the organization; inadequate supervision and monitoring of behavior; lack of clear accountability of employees' behavior; and no real threat of discipline or sanctions.

 Perhaps the most important factor in police officers becoming corrupt is the extraordinary amount of discretion they have.

"Chief Justice Warren Burger stated: 'The officer working the beat makes more decisions and exercises broader discretion affecting the daily lives of people everyday and to a greater extent than a judge will exercise in a week'" (Strong, 2004, p.65). This discretion in ethical decision making connects strongly with the ends versus means dilemma.

**The Ends versus Means Dilemma**   The "ends" of policing are noble: keep the peace, bring criminals to justice, serve and protect the public. Some officers come to believe that the ends justify the means by which they are accomplished. They resort to unlawful behavior in the name of justice. A classic example of this is the behavior of fictional Detective Andy Sipowicz in *NYPD Blue*, a no-nonsense cop who will "bend" the rules to get a confession out of a "scumbag." Dees (p.213) suggests: "Police officers in television and the movies frequently display behavior that would result in discipline or termination in the real world, but they usually get away with it. A common theme is the guy who does bad things for good reasons."

**The Slippery Slope**   Another theory on why good cops turn bad is that something seemingly insignificant, such as accepting free coffee or meals, can put an officer on a **slippery slope,** leading to major crimes. According to Trautman (2000, p.65): "Research repeatedly confirms that most scandals start with one employee doing relatively small unethical acts and grow to whatever level the leadership allows." He calls this the **corruption continuum.**

**Being above the Law**   Another explanation for police officers becoming corrupt is that they are taught in the academy that in many areas they may break the law; for example, they can exceed speed limits, go through red lights and carry concealed weapons.

Bayley (2002, p.133) suggests that there is a common presumption among police officers that "circumstances often justify cutting legal corners in the interests of public safety." He (pp.141–143) asserts: "Violating the rule-of-law impairs crime control by alienating the public. This occurs in two ways. First, violating the rule-of-law lessens the willingness of the public to assist the police in carrying out their assigned role. Research has shown again and again that the police are almost wholly dependent on the public to provide the information needed to provide safety and deter crime. . . . Second, when the police violate the rule-of-law, they not only forfeit the cooperation they need, but they also raise the likelihood that encounters with the public will generate hostility and violence." Bayley (p.145) also thinks violating the rule-of-law places police officers at risk: "Most obvious of all, the personal cost to officers who are caught violating the rule of law can be catastrophic."

Thompson (2001, p.77) asserts: "Policing practices that have been taught and encouraged by administrators have reinforced, beyond any doubt, that the police are not subject to the laws that they enforce and sometimes impose on others." This is detrimental, however, because, as Thomspon (p.79) stresses: "Equality under the law is the foundation of American criminal justice. If law enforcement officers believe they are above the law, then this subverts the very essence of law enforcement and criminal justice in our society."

**The Code of Silence**   The code of silence introduced earlier in this chapter also can be viewed as a form of corruption. Pedersen (2001, p.138) contends: "The code of silence encourages people not to speak up when they see another officer doing something wrong."

 In addition to the existence of discretion, officers may become corrupt because they believe the ends justify the means, they begin with accepting gratuities and progress to larger indiscretions, they believe they are above the law or they engage in the code of silence.

Although corruption begins with individual officers, controversy exists over whether a rotten apple spoils the barrel or the other way around.

## Rotten Apples versus Rotten Barrels

It is commonly thought that a few "bad apples" can cause a whole department's reputation to suffer when a scandal is uncovered. Some scandals, such as the Rodney King incident, can cause the whole profession's reputation to suffer.

Trautman (2000, p.65) says: "The 'rotten apple' theory that some administrators propose as the cause of their demise is usually nothing more than a self-serving, superficial façade, intended to draw attention away from their own failures." Swope (2001, p.80) also suggests: "Yes, a few who should not be part of policing will always find their way into police agencies no matter how rigorous selection procedures are. But these few are generally effectively dealt with. They will never crush a police agency. It is the unethical breeding environment of the barrel that generates the major difficulties. It is the barrel, the culture of the police organization, that can cause the most shaking scandals that periodically face some police departments." Swope (p.83) explains: "An officer's behavior is influenced more directly by the actions or lack of actions in response to ethical shortcomings of his superiors than by the stated directives or written ethical code of an organization."

 It is the culture of the police department (the barrel) that can allow or eliminate corrupt behavior (bad apples).

Perry (2001, p.23) suggests three organizational failures that can lead to individual and collective acts of corruption:

1. Little or ineffective discipline and deselection of trainees (a commitment to fairly but firmly graduate only those individuals who truly demonstrate performance and integrity standards).
2. Ignorance of the nature and effects of the goal-gradient phenomenon (the farther away individuals remain from their goal, the less the tendency to remain passionately interested in its attainment).
3. The allowance of a double standard within the organization, thereby decreasing moral accountability as professional responsibility increases.

Perry (p.24) states: "Corrupt police officers are not natural-born criminals, nor morally wicked men, constitutionally different from their honest colleagues. The task of corruption control is to examine the barrel, not just the apples, the organization, not just the individual in it, because corrupt police are made, not born."

## Basic Ethics Tests

Some questions, such as the question of gratuities, might appear to be black-and-white (absolute) issues to most, but many other ethical decisions police officers must make are not black and white at all, but are instead varying shades of gray (relative issues). To arrest or not? To inform on someone or not? To lie to suspects to build a case or not? In such instances, the answer is seldom obvious. How do police officers decide what is and is not ethical behavior?

 Some basic ethics tests include asking oneself: Am I doing the right thing? At the right time? In the right way? For the right reason? What if it were to be made public?

Many people believe all behavior should be guided by the Golden Rule, Do unto others as you would have them do unto you. Other, less positive people have coined the Silver Rule, Do unto others before they do unto you. A simple maxim set forth by Blanchard and Peale (1989, p.9) might guide police officers when they wrestle with ethical decisions:

 There is no right way to do a wrong thing.

Police officers have awesome powers over other people's lives. They must act legally and ethically to be true professionals and to be true to themselves as individuals. It has been said that there is no pillow so soft as a clear conscience.

## The Role of the Police Department

Arnold (2001, pp.80–81) suggests that departments establish an Early Warning System (EWS) to provide a "heads up" about behavioral problems with police officers and to allow the agency to take remedial action. Warning signs include poor performance, hostility and anger, unnecessary risk-taking, increases in use of force and insubordinate conduct. "Intervention is usually triggered when a certain number of complaints of a particular type are filed within the specified time frame." Arnold (p.85) concludes: "Proactive approaches must be explored and expanded where some type of intervention is introduced prior to misconduct."

An important way to promote ethical behavior is to incorporate it into every aspect of training. McNeff (2001, p.10) stresses: "In today's police environment, the incorporation of ethics into all aspects of police agency training and operations may yield wide-ranging benefits, including reduced exposure to liability."

To maintain integrity departments must:
- Hire selectively.
- Ensure that all officers understand the importance of integrity in policing.
- Create an anticorruption environment.

The public demands that the integrity of police officers be above reproach. The dishonesty of any police officer may impair public confidence and cast suspicion upon the entire department. Succumbing to even minor temptations can destroy an officer's effectiveness and contribute to the corruption of others. An officer must avoid any conduct that might compromise his or her own integrity, or that of fellow officers or of the department.

Just as each officer is responsible to maintain the highest level of personal integrity, the department must develop and foster an environment where honesty will thrive.

Ethical behavior within a law enforcement agency is ultimately the responsibility of each individual officer within that agency.

## Ethics and Community Policing and Problem Solving

The roots of community policing can be found in Sir Robert Peel's instructions to the Metropolitan Police in 1829:

> The primary objective of an efficient police department is prevention of crime: the next that of detection and punishment of offenders if crime is committed. . . . In attaining these objectives, much depends on the approval and cooperation of the public, and these have always been determined by the degree of the esteem and respect in which the police are held.

As police officers get involved with the community and work together to solve problems, they may change the way they think and, more importantly, the way they behave.

## *Integrating Ethics into the SARA Model*

The Boston Police Department established a task force to integrate ethics analysis into the SARA problem-solving model by using the Dilemmas-Options-Consequences (DOC) method as well. As Romano et al. (2000, p.98) explain: "The DOC method puts moral decision making in the day-to-day realm of an officer's professional and personal life. The DOC method challenges officers to carefully consider their decisions, as well as the short- and long-term consequences of those decisions."

Romano et al. (p.99) say if a decision maker is facing a dilemma that "feels" wrong, he or she should ask questions such as:

- What feels unsatisfactory? What feels wrong?
- Who or what is presenting a choice to me?
- Is there a moral or ethical threat to me or someone else?
- Will I, or someone in the community, be affected or hurt physically or emotionally?
- Will I, or someone in the community, be treated disrespectfully or without dignity?
- Is my quality of life, or the quality of life of someone in the community threatened?

Once the dilemma is defined, the action or response phase involves the following questions:

- What are my options?
- What are the extreme options?
- Am I considering all options?
- Am I being open-minded and creative about my options?
- Do my options rely only on me, or could I use a resource or someone's help? What are those resources? Whose help could I use?

For each option, the consequences must be assessed by asking questions such as the following:

- What happens because of my choice? What happens if I do nothing?
- Who is affected by what I do? How will they be affected? How will I be affected?
- Will I be preserving and protecting the quality of life and the dignity of others?
- Will I be preserving my moral and ethical integrity? Will I be preserving the moral and ethical integrity of my organization?
- What are the short-term effects? What are the long-term effects?

As Romano et al. (p.102) suggest: "Ethical problem solving incorporates values, human dignity and respect into the problem-solving process. It encourages officers to include stakeholders, rather than exclude stakeholders. This method raises the standards in the community and will ultimately positively affect the qualify of life in that community."

## SUMMARY

Officers may be sued under three types of state liability (tort) laws: strict liability, intentional tort and negligence. Most civil lawsuits brought against law enforcement officers are based on Statute 42 of the U.S. Code, Section 1983, also called the Civil Rights Act. This act says that anyone acting under the authority of the law who violates another person's constitutional rights can be sued. The most frequent civil lawsuits against police involve false arrest or imprisonment, malicious prosecution, use of unnecessary or excessive force, brutality, wrongful death, failure to protect and negligent service.

The normal defenses used by police officers being sued are that they did not intend to deprive the plaintiff of constitutional rights, that they acted in good faith and that they acted with what was considered reasonable judgment at the time and with valid authority. Protection against lawsuits includes effective policies and procedures clearly communicated to all, thorough and continuous training, proper supervision and discipline, and accurate, thorough police reports.

To minimize lawsuits at a more personal level, law enforcement officers should know and follow their department's guidelines; stay in the scope of their duties; always act professionally; know and respect their constituents' rights; seek advice if in doubt; carefully document their activities in their reports; maintain good community relations; and keep current on civil and criminal liability cases. Law enforcement officers and agencies can countersue if they are falsely accused of a civil offense.

Police officers should be concerned not only with acting legally so as to avoid civil lawsuits, but also with acting ethically. Ethics deals with standards of honesty, fairness and integrity in behavior. An absolute issue is one with only two sides—the decision is black and white. A relative issue is one with many sides, that is, varying shades of gray between the two absolute positions. Ethical issues are usually relative and are affected by the police culture. Conventional wisdom holds that the defining characteristics of the police culture are social isolation and group loyalty, resulting in a code of silence. The code of silence and the attitude of Us versus Them often bond. Loyalty becomes more important than integrity.

Two areas in discussions of law enforcement ethics are controversial: police use of deception and police acceptance of gratuities. Accepting gratuities may be the first step on the way to corrupt behavior. The key elements in corrupt behavior are (1) conduct prohibited by law (2) involving misuse of position (3) resulting in a reward or personal gain for the officer. Perhaps the most important factor in police officers becoming corrupt is the extraordinary amount of discretion they have. In addition to the existence of discretion, officers may become corrupt because they believe the ends justify the means, they begin with accepting gratuities and progress to larger indiscretions, they believe they are above the law, or they engage in the code of silence. It is the culture of the police department (the barrel) that can allow or eliminate corrupt behavior (bad apples).

Basic ethics tests include asking oneself: Am I doing the right thing? At the right time? In the right way? For the right reason? How would I feel if it were made public? There is no right way to do a wrong thing. To maintain integrity, departments must hire selectively, ensure that all officers understand the importance of integrity in policing and create an anticorruption environment. Ethical behavior within a law enforcement agency is ultimately the responsibility of each officer within that agency.

## APPLICATION

The chief of police has been concerned about officers coming to him wanting advice about what to do when business people give them gratuities such as boxes of candy, children's toys, bottles of liquor and other items useful to an officer and the officer's family. The officers are concerned as to how much they can take, when they can take it and whether they should report to the administration upon receipt. The chief asks a committee, of which you are chair, to develop a policy and procedure to clarify how officers are to respond to such offers.

### INSTRUCTIONS

Write a policy and procedure specifying the need for uniformity in accepting gratuities and gifts and if they are to be accepted at all. Include what can be accepted and under what circumstances.

## TWO ETHICAL CHALLENGES

Scenarios 14.1 and 14.2 present two hypothetical cases to promote thoughtful consideration of common situations police officers encounter and the ethical issues involved in each.

### EXERCISES IN CRITICAL THINKING

A. In the early morning hours, Jacqueline McKone stepped outside her apartment and witnessed what she said was the uncalled-for arrest and beating of a young black man, 21-year-old Dennis Cherry. McKone was a legal assistant in an attorney's office, completing course work to become a court reporter. She reported that four police officers held Cherry, and one, whom she identified as Ed Nelson, hit him. Cherry, she reported, had done nothing to attract the police or to resist their efforts to arrest him. The incident occurred more than a block away from the Convention Center to which police had come to close down a dance.

Several officers, including Ed Nelson, tried to intimidate McKone as she stood watching the scene. She said this to herself, however: I can't stop it, but I will watch this whole thing and report it. When Lieutenant Bruce Jones arrived on the scene, she approached him to report what she had witnessed.

1. When Lieutenant Bruce Jones arrived at the scene, what should have been his treatment of McKone?
   a. To tell McKone that the police were simply following arrest procedure and that because she was not present at the beginning of the incident or close enough to hear all that Cherry said to police, she could not be expected to understand what actually happened.
   b. First, to ask if she had been harmed, second, to apologize for what she had witnessed and then, to provide her with the information needed to contact civilian review.
   c. First, to interview the police officers who conducted the arrest, then to interview McKone and then to explain to McKone that although Cherry denied it, the police said he tried to hit them, which justified their treatment of Cherry.

   d. To ignore McKone other than to tell her that she could bring her views and testimony to the Police Civilian Review Authority.
   e. To gently remind McKone that it was not wise to offend local police, especially well-liked officers such as Ed Nelson, and to point out that if she called the news media and filed a complaint, she would get a series of hateful, racist responses accusing her of having a black boyfriend or of being a "nigger lover."

B. In June, a police officer received information from a confidential, reliable informant. He had observed a film depicting a 16-year-old girl engaging in sex with a Rottweiller dog while at the home of Robert Bonynge. The officer applied for a search warrant for Bonynge's residence. The affidavit accompanying the application reiterated the information received from the informant and stated that the officer sought the search warrant "to seize any film involving child pornography and bestiality." The warrant permitted seizure of the following:

> Pornography films involving female juveniles and a Rottweiller dog and any contraband that would violate the state statute governing the pornography laws. Any filming equipment and duplicating equipment.

The affidavit was attached to the warrant. The police executed the search warrant at Bonynge's residence. A police lieutenant observed the Rottweiller dog on the premises and numerous video cassettes, 8-millimeter movies, photographs and magazines depicting sexual scenes involving young females, possibly juveniles. The officers seized hundreds of films and photographs including several commercial videotapes of popular motion pictures. The officer stated that it was his experience that "obscene material is planted in the middle of what appears to be a commercial tape to make it difficult to locate."

2. Were the videotapes seized in violation of Bonynge's Fourth Amendment rights?
   a. Yes, because the Fourth Amendment gives individuals the right to be free from unreasonable search and seizure and declares that warrants shall particularly describe the place to be searched and the person or things to be seized, and not all the videotapes were of pornographic subjects.
   b. Yes, because a warrant limits the discretion of the executing officers as well as gives notice to the party searched, and the materials seized were not described with sufficient particularity.
   c. No, because a warrant to search a residence gives rights to search all parts of that residence and seize any evidence found.
   d. Yes, because pornography is an ethical issue that must be left to individual discretion—no law or police action is appropriate.
   e. No, because the officers who swore out the affidavit also executed the search; they had the benefit of the more specific language of the affidavit.

This scenario and others like it serve as useful discussion starters for experienced police officers attempting to identify the standards of conduct to which they have committed and personally clarifying the values that generate acceptable police behavior. The use of such scenarios by a knowledgeable and skilled instructor invariably results in lively, illuminating group analysis.

The dispatcher sends you to the scene of a single-car accident. When you arrive, you determine that the driver needs an ambulance and that the car is disabled. You ask the dispatcher to get you an ambulance and to send a wrecker to tow the car.

When the wrecker arrives, it is driven by the owner of a nearby garage. He starts to make friendly conversation as he hooks up the car. As he finishes hitching it and is about to drive off, he says to you, "Thanks for calling me on this one. I really appreciate it. Why don't you bring your own car to my place for a tune-up one of these days? I'll be real glad to give you one—on the house."

*What should you do?*

From the following list of possible responses, check the one(s) that would meet the ethical standards of good police work.

_____1. Tell him, "Thanks. I'll have to take you up on that as soon as I've got the time," but never take him up on the offer.

_____2. Tell him, "You're under arrest for trying to bribe an officer for future considerations."

_____3. Tell him, "That's really nice of you to offer, but I can't take credit for calling you. The dispatcher issued the call."

_____4. Accept his offer courteously in order not to alienate local business people.

_____5. Tell him that you are not his business partner and that you resent the suggestion that you work for him.

_____6. Report the offer to your supervisor.

_____7. Other _____

*What if the situation were different?*

1. Suppose that instead of a free tune-up, the garage owner offered you a "business proposition" of $15 for each call you referred to him? Review responses 1–7. Which one(s) meet the ethical standards of good police work in this situation?

2. Suppose that instead of a free tune-up, the garage owner said nothing but dropped a $20 bill on the seat of your cruiser? Review responses 1–7. Which one(s) meet the ethical standards of good police work in this situation?

*In the original example, the most important ethical consideration is:*

_____The size of the offer.

_____The fact that an offer was made.

_____The way the officer responds to the garage owner.

_____The fact that the garage owner wants special access to the police.

*The ethical standard most applicable to this example is:*

_____Fair access.

_____Public trust.

_____Safety and security.

_____Teamwork.

_____Objectivity.

**Scenario 14.1**   Offer of a Gratuity

SOURCE: Howard Cohan and Michael Feldberg. "Ethics for Professional Policing." Reprinted from *The Police Chief*, Vol. LVIII, No. 1, January 1991, p.49. Copyright held by the International Association of Chiefs of Police, Inc., 515 N. Washington Street, Alexandria, Virginia 22314. Further reproduction without express written permission from IACP is strictly prohibited.

You have been assigned to a special drunk-driving enforcement unit, and have been specially trained in administering the field sobriety test and in the use of the breathalyzer. Your state has also recently adopted a mandatory drunk-driving loss of license statute: If a driver is convicted of operating with a blood alcohol content of .1 percent, he is considered to be driving while legally intoxicated and must lose his license for three months.

While patrolling around 11:00 P.M. on a clear, dry night along a main but lightly traveled road, you spot a vehicle pulling out of a restaurant parking lot that begins to weave across the road, changes speeds erratically, and even stops in the middle of the road for a moment although there are no other cars around. You decide to stop the vehicle on probable cause to suspect operation by a drunk driver. You turn on your flashing lights, and when the driver finally stops, you ask him to step out of the car. He stumbles, falls, gets up again, and hands you what you think is his wallet. To your discomfort it is a case containing his shield, and you recognize the driver as a fellow officer with whom you graduated from the academy. He is off-duty, and tells you with slurred speech that his wife has just left him and is threatening to leave town with his three-year-old son. He starts to cry.

*What should you do?*

From the following list of possible responses, check the one(s) that would meet the ethical standards of good police work.

_____1. Administer the field sobriety test: arrest him if he fails.

_____2. Follow him home, since he lives less than a mile from the scene.

_____3. Put him in a taxi and tell him he can pick up his car keys at headquarters tomorrow.

_____4. Do not arrest him; drive him home, but report him to his immediate superior tomorrow.

_____5. Tell him he has put you in a terrible position, and that you will arrest him if you catch him driving drunk again.

_____6. Other _____

*What if the situation were different?*

1. Suppose that the officer in the original example is abusive to you instead of apologetic. He tells you to mind your own business and butt out of his personal life. He also tells you that in his book, cops don't hassle other cops. Review responses 1–6. Which one(s) meet the ethical standards of good police work in this situation?

2. Suppose that instead of a fellow officer from your academy days, the officer you stopped was a high-ranking official in your department who makes it clear that your career is on the line if you report him. Review responses 1–6. Which one(s) meet the ethical standards of good police work in this situation?

*In the original example the most important ethical consideration is:*

_____The offending officer's attitude.

_____The mandatory arrest provision of the law.

_____Loyalty to fellow officer.

_____Equal treatment of all violators.

_____The reaction of your fellow officers if you arrest your colleague.

_____The seriousness of the offense.

_____The consequences of the arrest for the officer himself.

_____The consequences of the arrest for you.

*The ethical standard most applicable to this example is:*

_____Fair access.

_____Public trust.

_____Safety and security.

_____Teamwork.

_____Objectivity.

## Scenario 14.2  The Drunk Officer

SOURCE: Howard Cohan and Michael Feldberg. "Ethics for Professional Policing." Reprinted from *The Police Chief*, Vol. LVIII, No. 1, January 1991, p.49. Copyright held by the International Association of Chiefs of Police, Inc., 515 N. Washington Street, Alexandria, Virginia 22314. Further reproduction without express written permission from IACP is strictly prohibited.

3. Which of the following would be unethical?
   a. The temporary seizure of constitutionally protected material (in this case, of every film and videotape regardless of content).
   b. Providing a prior adversary hearing before authorizing the seizure of allegedly obscene material for the purpose of destroying it.
   c. Accepting gratuities from bookstores or commercial theaters involved in the distribution or exhibition of pornographic materials and being loyal to fellow officers who accept gratuities.
   d. Varying the times when you take breaks, eating meals at different times and places, filling out reports at irregular times and places to protect yourself from temptation and blowing the whistle on colleagues who routinely bend rules.
   e. Exercising discretion while extending due process to criminal suspects and victims alike (such as withholding the identity of the 16-year-old girl).

## DISCUSSION QUESTIONS

1. Have any misconduct lawsuits been filed against local police officers? Check with your police department to see what their history of civil lawsuits has been.

2. How much training is enough to avoid lawsuits under Section 1983? Explain your reasoning in the areas of firearms, search and seizure, and laws of arrest.

3. How could a Section 1983 action be brought where an officer in the locker room preparing for duty accidentally discharged his revolver, striking a custodian? What would be the justification for a lawsuit in this case?

4. In what areas of law enforcement should police officers be exempt from lawsuits, if any?

5. What are some temptations that lead to police misconduct or corruption?

6. Can ethical standards that apply to police officers be circumvented when it comes to apprehending drug dealers? If so, to what extent?

7. Do you feel there is value in civilian review boards?

### INFOTRAC COLLEGE EDITION ASSIGNMENTS

Use InfoTrac College Edition to answer the Discussion Questions as appropriate.
- Select three of the following assignments:
  - Use InfoTrac College Edition to find and outline the article "Getting Along with Citizen Oversight" by Peter Finn. Be prepared to share your outline with the class.
  - Use InfoTrac College Edition to find the article "Law Enforcement Accreditation: One Department's Experience" by Robert J. Falzarano. List the tangible benefits attributed to accreditation and

then summarize the impact of accreditation on the Long Hill Township and the conclusion drawn by the author. Be prepared to discuss your summary with the class.
- Use InfoTrac College Edition to find and outline the article "Managing for Ethics: A Mandate for Administrators" by Timothy J. O'Malley. Be prepared to share your outline with the class.
- Use InfoTrac College Edition to find the article "Institutional Integrity: The Four Elements of Self-Policing" by John H. Conditt, Jr. List and briefly explain what the four elements of self-policing are according to Conditt. Be prepared to discuss your findings with the class.
- Use InfoTrac College Edition to research *police liability*. Note why officers are sued, what cities are most vulnerable to lawsuits and what some awards have been. Outline your findings, and be prepared to discuss your outline with the class.
- Use InfoTrac College Edition to find the article "Ethics and Police Integrity" by Stephen J. Vicchio. Summarize the story the author begins with and why. Then list the seven core virtues required of police officers and the answers the author gives to the questions: Can integrity be taught? And can integrity be measured? Be prepared to discuss your answers with the class.

### INTERNET ASSIGNMENTS

- Go to the CALEA website at www.calea.org and read their most recent newsletter. Write a one- to two-page summary of the most important articles, and be prepared to discuss your summaries in class.
- Go to the Police Complaint Center at www.policeabuse .org and click on "Caught on Tape." View and describe five or six examples of police abuse. Be prepared to share your examples and thoughts with the class.
- Use the Internet to research some approaches police administrators use to help their officers adopt ethical standards. Outline your findings, and be prepared to discuss them in class.

### BOOK-SPECIFIC WEBSITE

The book-specific website at http://cj.wadsworth.com/ wobleski_Hess_police_op4e hosts a variety of resources for students and instructors. Many can be emailed to the instructor. Included are extended activities such as Concept Builders - the 3 step learning module that reinforces key chapter concepts, followed by a real-world applications and critical thinking questions. InfoTrac College Edition exercises; Discussion Questions; interactive key-term FlashCards; and a collection of chapter-based Web Links provide additional information and activities to include in the curriculum.

## REFERENCES

Anderson, Jonathan. "The Oath." *Law and Order,* November 2003, p.104.

Arnold, Jon. "Ethics: Early Misconduct Detection." *Law and Order,* August 2001, pp.80–86.

Bayley, David H. "Law Enforcement and the Rule of Law: Is There a Tradeoff?" *Crime and Public Policy,* November 2002, pp.133–154.

Blanchard, Kenneth and Peale, Norman Vincent. *The Power of Ethical Management.* New York: Fawcett Crest, 1989.

Chudwin, Jeff. "Lawsuits, Training and Officer Safety." *Tactical Response,* Spring 2003, p.10.

Cline, Thomas J. "Tough and Most Dangerous Battles." *Law and Order,* January 2003, pp.60–64.

Close, Dale H. "How Chiefs Should Prepare for Nine Liability Risks." *The Police Chief,* June 2001, pp.16–27.

Conditt, John H., Jr. "Institutional Integrity: The Four Elements of Self-Policing." *FBI Law Enforcement Bulletin,* 2001, pp.18–22.

Daniels, Wayne and Spratley, Lynnette. "Lawsuit Defense: Protecting the Department from Litigation." *Law and Order,* June 2003, pp.54–59.

Dees, Tim. "First Loyalty." *Law and Order,* October 2001, pp.213–214.

Fuller, John J. "Street Cop Ethics." *The Law Enforcement Trainer,* May/June 2001, pp.6–7.

Green, Don. "Calculating Ethics." *Law and Order,* August 2001, pp.87–90.

Griffith, David. "Swimming the Witch." *Police,* October 2002, p.6.

Griffith, David. "Cracking Down on Bad Cops." *Police,* October 2003, pp.68–74.

Klockars, Carl B. "Police Ethics." In *The Encyclopedia of Police Science,* 2nd ed., edited by William G. Bailey, New York: Garland, 1995, pp.549–553.

McErlain, Ed. "Acknowledging the Code of Silence." *Law and Order,* January 2001, p.87.

McNeff, Michael. "One Agency's Effort to Reduce Liability Risk through Emphasis on Ethics." *The Police Chief,* August 2001, p.10.

Means, Randy. "The History and Dynamics of Section 1983." *The Police Chief,* May 2004, p.10.

Noble, Jeff. "Police Officer Truthfulness and the *Brady* Decision." *The Police Chief,* October 2003, pp.92–101.

Nowicki, Dennis E. and Punch, Maurice E. "Fostering Integrity and Professional Standards." *Local Government Police Management,* 4th ed., William A. Geller and Darrel W. Stephens, editors. Washington, DC: International City/County Management Association, 2003, pp.315–352.

Paoline, Eugene A., III. "Shedding Light on Police Culture: An Examination of Officers' Occupational Attitudes." *Police Quarterly,* June 2004, pp.205–236.

Pedersen, Dorothy. "Rising Above Corruption: How to Put Integrity at the Forefront in Your Department." *Law Enforcement Technology,* October 2001, pp.136–142.

Perry, Frank L. "Repairing Broken Windows: Preventing Corruption within Our Ranks." *FBI Law Enforcement Bulletin,* February 2001, pp.23–26.

Quinn, Michael W. *Walking with the Devil: The Police Code of Silence (What Bad Cops Don't Want You to Know and Good Cops Won't Tell You).* Minneapolis, MN: Quinn and Associates, 2004.

Romano, Linda J.; McDevitt, Jack; Jones, Jimmie; and Johnson, William. "Combined Problem-Solving Models Incorporate Ethics Analysis." *The Police Chief,* August 2000, pp.98–102.

Son, In Soo. "The Prevalence and Visibility of Police Misconduct: A Survey of Citizens and Police Officers." *Police Quarterly,* June 2004, pp.179–204.

Stevens, Dennis J. "Civil Liability and Selective Enforcement." *Law and Order,* May 2001, pp.105–107.

Stine, Joseph J. "A Ballistic Vest against Lawsuits: Protecting Yourself and Your Department against Civil Liability." *The Police Chief,* June 2001, pp.44–47.

Strong, Paul. "Ethics." *Law and Order,* January 2004, p.65.

Swope, Ross. "Bad Apples or Bad Barrel?" *Law and Order,* January 2001, pp.80–85.

Terrill, William; Paoline, Eugene A., III; and Manning, Peter K. "Police Culture and Coercion." *Criminology,* November 2003, pp.1003–1034.

Thompson, David. "Above the Law?" *Law and Order,* January 2001, pp.77–79.

Trautman, Neal. "How Organizations Become Corrupt: The Corruption Continuum." *Law and Order,* May 2000, pp.65–68.

Trautman, Neal. "Truth about Police Code of Silence Revealed." *Law and Order,* January 2001, pp.68–76.

Trautman, Neal E. "The Code of Silence Antidote: If Successful, Systemic Corruption Will Seldom Occur." *The Law Enforcement Trainer,* March/April 2002, pp.16–21.

White, Mike. "The Problem with Gratuities." *FBI Law Enforcement Bulletin,* July 2002, pp.20–23.

Withrow, Brian L. and Dailey, Jeffrey D. "A Model of Circumstantial Corruptibility." *Police Quarterly,* June 2004, pp.159–178.

## CASES CITED

*Graham v. Connor,* 490 U.S. 396 (1989)

*Thurman v. City of Torrington,* 595 F. Supp. 1521 (D. Conn. 1984)

## A Look Ahead

Police organizations do not stand still. They are undergoing continuous, often unnoticeable, change. The police culture itself is changing. The first noticeable change is in the department structure. Next is a change in attitude as the community policing philosophy emerges and citizens experience a sense of hope as they connect personally with law enforcement officers and their efforts to contain crime and violence. In the twenty-first century, the two ideologies of community-based and problem-oriented policing are reshaping the way most police organizations operate.

Police departments must look ahead with confidence and trust that they can undertake the tremendous challenges of change that confront them: worldwide terrorism that has attacked the United States, internal strife that political foes generate against the government and violence erupting in our schools and workplaces. Law enforcement is the first line of defense to keep peace in this country. Their cooperative efforts with other agencies throughout the country will be needed more than ever. In addition to keeping the peace, fighting crime, protecting constitutional rights and serving the public, police must deal with the various cultures in our society and the many cultural and language barriers that immigration and diversity have brought to this country. It is now more than ever that law enforcement needs the utmost cooperation of the citizens and agencies throughout the country. United we must stand.

# Appendix

## Policies and Procedures Sample Form

| | |
|---|---|
| Name of Agency: | Date Issued: |
| Procedure Directive No.: | Page _____ of _____ |
| Effective Date: | |
| Subject: | |
| Goal: | |
| | |
| | |
| Policy: | |
| | |
| | |
| | |
| | |
| | |
| | |
| | |
| | |

(Continued)

| | |
|---|---|
| Policy No.: | Page _____ of _____ |

Procedures:

 

 

 

 

 

 

 

 

 

 

 

_____
Chief of Police

# Glossary

*Numbers in (parentheses) indicate the chapter in which the term can be found.*

**absolute issue**—An issue with only two sides, viewed as either/or, black or white. (14)

**absolute privilege**—Information or testimony that cannot be received; there are no exceptions (see *privileged information*). (2)

**accelerants**—Substances that promote burning; at an arson scene are a primary form of evidence. The most common accelerant used is gasoline. (10)

**acute stress**—Temporary stress that may result in peak performance; body adapts for fight or flight. (13)

**admission**—Statement containing some information concerning the elements of a crime, but falling short of a full confession. (2)

**aerobic training**—Physical training aimed at strengthening the cardiovascular system. (13)

**Amber Alert**—Voluntary partnerships between law enforcement agencies and public broadcasters to notify the public when a child has been abducted. (11)

**anaerobic training**—Physical training aimed at strengthening the muscles of the body. (13)

**arrest**—The official taking of a person into custody to answer criminal charges. Arrest involves at least temporarily depriving the person of liberty and may involve the use of force. (3)

**arson**—The malicious, willful burning of a building or property. (10)

**assault**—Unlawfully threatening to harm another person, actually harming another person or attempting unsuccessfully to do so. (10)

**asymmetric war**—One in which a much weaker opponent takes on a stronger opponent by refusing to confront the stronger opponent head on. (9)

**Automated Fingerprint Identification System (AFIS)**—Computerized database maintained by the FBI used to identify a limited number of likely matches for a latent fingerprint. (10)

**awareness spectrum**—Framework for describing officer's level of awareness, ranging from condition white, environmental unawareness, to condition black, panicked/blacked out/perhaps dead. Ideally, officers will be at condition yellow: alert but relaxed. (13)

**battered woman syndrome**—Defense used by women who have been beaten by their husbands and who then kill those husbands, apparently while completely sane and in control. (7)

**battering**—The use of physical, emotional, economic or sexual force to control another person. (7)

**bifurcated society**—Divided into two distinct socio-economic groups, upper and lower. (1)

**bioterrorism**—Involves such biological weapons of mass destruction (WMD) as anthrax, botulism and smallpox. (9)

**blood-alcohol concentration (BAC)**—The weight of alcohol in grams per milliliter of blood. (5)

**blue lie**—A lie told not to help or comfort the person lied to but, rather, to exert control. (14)

**broken windows metaphor**—Broken windows in a neighborhood make a statement that no one cares enough about the quality of life in the neighborhood to bother fixing little things that need repair. (1)

**bullying**—Intentional, repeated hurtful acts, words or behavior. (7)

**burglary**—The unlawful entry of a structure to commit a crime. (10)

**burnout**—Condition experienced by a person who is "used up or consumed by a job," made listless through overwork and stress. The person lacks energy or has little interest in work. (13)

**burst stress**—Having to go from relative calm to high intensity, sometimes life-threatening, activity. (13)

**chain of custody**—Documented account of who has had control of evidence from the time it is discovered until it is presented in court. Also called *chain of possession*. (6)

**chain of possession**—See *chain of custody*. (6)

**child abuse**—Any physical, emotional or sexual trauma to a child for which no reasonable explanation, such as an accident, can be found. Includes neglecting to give proper care and attention to a young child. (7)

**child welfare model**—Society's attempt to help youths who come in conflict with the law. (11)

**chronic stress**—Ongoing, continuous stress; like being under a state of constant siege; can lead to severe psychological problems. (13)

**civil actions**—Lawsuits for perceived wrongs against individuals for which restitution is sought in civil court. (14)

**civil disobedience**—Intentional breaking of a law to prove a point or to protest something. (6)

**Civil Rights Act**—States that anyone acting under the authority of the law who violates another person's constitutional rights can be sued. See also *Section 1983*. (14)

**closed-ended question**—Limits the amount or scope of information that a person can provide, for example, what color was the car? (the opposite of an open-ended question). (2)

**code of ethics**—A statement setting forth accepted standards of behavior for a profession. (14)

**cognitive interview**—Interviewing method that puts witnesses mentally back at the scene of an incident and encourages them to tell the whole story without interruption. (2)

**collective deep pocket**—A pool of defendants from which astronomical financial judgments can be collected; created by suing every possible individual and agency involved in an incident. (14)

**collective efficacy**—Cohesion among neighborhood residents combined with shared expectations for informal social control of public space that inhibits both crime and disorder. (6)

**community policing**—Involves empowering citizens to help local law enforcement provide safer neighborhoods. It usually includes an emphasis on foot patrol, partnerships and problem solving. (1)

**compliance**—A complete lack of physical resistance. (3)

**computer-related crimes**—Offenses involving input data, output data, a program itself or computer time. (10)

**conditional privilege**—The official information privilege; that is, the information can be received but the source of the information can be protected. (2)

**confession**—Information supporting the elements of a crime that is provided and attested to by any person involved in committing the crime. Can be oral or written. (2)

**conscience**—The ability to recognize right from wrong and to follow one's own sense of what is right. (14)

**contagion effect**—Coverage of terrorism inspires more terrorism. It is, in effect, contagious. (9)

**contamination**—An undesired transfer of information between items of evidence. (10)

**continuum of contacts**—Almost limitless variations of contacts between the public and the police, ranging from no contact to incarceration or even the death penalty. (3)

**corruption continuum**—Most scandals begin with one employee doing relatively small, unethical acts and grow to whatever level the leadership allows. Also referred to as the slippery slope. (14)

**covert investigations**—Those done secretively, for example, using surveillance and undercover personnel. (10)

**Crime Index**—Term identifying the FBI's Uniform Crime Report program (UCR); includes the violent crimes and the property crimes. (6)

**critical-incident stress debriefing (CISD)**—Officers who experience a critical incident, such as a mass disaster or large accident with multiple deaths, are brought together as a group for psychological debriefing soon after the event. (8)

**cross-training**—Alternating between different forms of exercise. (13)

**cruising**—Driving around and around a predetermined, popular route, usually through the heart of a town or city; a social activity of teenagers. (5)

**cultural gangs**—Neighborhood-centered groups of youths that exists independently of criminal activity. (12)

**curtilage**—A house and the area immediately surrounding it. (3)

**cyberterrorism**—Terrorism that initiates, or threatens to initiate, the exploitation of or attack on information systems. (9)

**DARE**—Drug Abuse Resistance Education, a school program aimed at teaching fourth- and fifth-grade students to say no to peer pressure to use drugs. (11)

**de facto arrest**—A detention without probable cause that is factually indistinguishable from an arrest. (3)

**deconfliction**—Avoiding conflict. (9)

**decriminalization**—Making status offenses noncriminal matters. (11)

**depression**—A serious and life-threatening medical illness. (13)

**designer drug**—A drug created by altering the chemical makeup of one or more existing drugs. (12)

**differential police response strategies**—Practice of varying the rapidity of response as well as the responder, based on the type of incident and the time of occurrence. (4)

**directed patrol**—Use of officers' discretionary patrol time to focus on specific department goals. (4)

**discovery crimes**—Offenses that have been completed and whose scenes have been abandoned before the crimes are noticed. In contrast to *involvement crimes*. (4)

**discretion**—The freedom to act or decide a matter on one's own. (1)

**discretionary acts**—Those actions officers perform using their own judgment. Policies and procedures for the acts leave decisions up to the officers. (14)

**diversion**—Referring a juvenile out of the justice system and to some other agency or program. (11)

**DNA fingerprinting**—Use of the unique genetic structure of an individual for identification. Blood, hair and other body tissues and fluids may be used in this process. (10)

**dog shift**—Typically the shift from 11 P.M. to 7 A.M. (1)

**drug gangs**—Smaller than other gangs; much more cohesive; focused on the drug business; strong, centralized leadership with market-defined roles. (12)

**drug recognition expert (DRE)**—Specially trained individual who can determine if someone is under the influence of drugs. Also called *drug recognition technician.* (5)

**drug recognition technician (DRT)**—See *drug recognition expert.* (5)

**dual motive stop**—A stop in which the officer is stopping a vehicle to investigate not only a traffic violation but also the fact that the driver looks suspicious. Also called a *pretext stop.* (5)

**due process of law**—The fundamental principle of American justice. It requires notice of a hearing or trial that is timely and that adequately informs the accused persons of the charges; it also gives the defendant an opportunity to present evidence in self-defense before an impartial judge or jury and to be presumed innocent until proven guilty by legally obtained evidence. (3)

**ecoterrorism**—Seeks to inflict economic damage to those who profit from the destruction of the natural environment. (9)

**8% problem**—50–60 percent of juvenile crime is committed by 8 percent of juveniles. (11)

**elder abuse**—The physical and emotional trauma, financial exploitation and/or general neglect of individuals over 65 years of age. (7)

**emergency operations center (EOC)**—The location from which personnel operate during a natural disaster or other type of emergency. (8)

**enforcement index**—Standard suggesting that for each fatal and personal injury crash, between 20 and 25 convictions for hazardous moving violations indicates effective traffic enforcement. (5)

**entrapment**—An action by the police (or a government agent) persuading a person to commit a crime that the person would not otherwise have committed. (10)

**environmental crimes**—Range from people littering to those illegally disposing of used tires, used oil, biohazardous waste and other hazardous substances. (10)

**equivocal death investigation**—May have two or more meanings and may be presented as either a homicide or a suicide, depending on the circumstances. (10)

**ethics**—The study of human conduct in the light of moral principles. It deals with standards of honesty, fairness and integrity in behavior. (14)

**Exclusionary Rule**—Courts cannot accept evidence obtained in illegal searches and seizures, regardless of how relevant the evidence is to the case (*Weeks v. United States*, 1914). (3)

**exigent circumstances**—Conditions surrounding an emergency situation in which no time is available to secure an arrest or search warrant. (3)

**expressive violence**—That resulting from hurt feelings, anger or rage. (7)

**felony syndrome**—Obtaining complete information on only felony cases, deeming them to be the only "real" police work. (2)

**FEMA**—The Federal Emergency Management Agency, an independent federal agency charged with building and supporting the nation's emergency management system. Its mission is to reduce loss of life and property and protect our nation's critical infrastructure from all types of hazards through a comprehensive, risk-based, emergency management program of mitigation, preparedness, response and recovery. (8)

**field inquiry**—The unplanned questioning of a person who has aroused a police officer's suspicions. (2)

**firewall**—A security measure intended to prevent unauthorized Internet users from accessing private networks connected to the Internet. (8)

**flashbangs**—Devices that explode with a loud bang and emit brilliant light; used by police as a diversion. (6)

**flashroll**—Buy money in a drug deal. (12)

**fraud**—Intentional deception to cause a person to give up property or some lawful right. (10)

**frisk**—A brief patdown following a stop to determine if a person is armed. (3)

**functional equivalent**—Refers to places other than actual borders where travelers frequently enter or exit the country, such as international airports. (3)

**gang**—A group of individuals with a recognized name and symbols who form an allegiance for a common purpose and engage in unlawful activity. (12)

**geographic information systems (GIS)**—Creating, updating and analyzing computerized maps. (6)

**goals**—Broad, general purposes. (1)

**good faith**—Belief that one's actions are just and legal. (3)

**graffiti**—Symbols and slogans written on walls and sides of buildings, often by gang members to mark their turf. (12)

**grapevine**—A network of informal, internal channels of communication. Also called the *rumor mill*. (2)

**gratuities**—Material favors or gifts in return for service, such as a tip for service in a restaurant. (14)

**GREAT**—The Gang Resistance Education and Training program. (11)

**hate crime**—A criminal offense committed against persons, property or society that is motivated, in whole or in part, by an offender's bias against an individual's or group's race, religion, ethnic/national origin, gender, age, disability or sexual orientation. (10)

**HAZMAT incident**—An incident involving hazardous materials. (8)

**hedonistic/social gangs**—Only moderate drug use and offending, involved mainly in using drugs and having a good time; little involvement in crime, especially violent crime. (12)

**homicide**—The killing of one person by another person. (10)

**horizontal prosecution**—Different assistant prosecutors are responsible for specific phases of the court proceedings. (12)

**hot spots**—Clusters of crime in certain geographic areas. (6)

**identity theft**—The unlawful use of another's personal identifying information, often to achieve monetary gain. (10)

**igniters**—Articles used to light a fire. (10)

**implied consent law**—A law stating that those who request and receive driver's licenses agree to take tests to determine their ability to drive. Refusal will result in revocation of the license. (5)

**"in the presence"**—Perceived by an officer through the senses (does not refer to proximity). (3)

**incivilities**—Subtle signs of a community not caring about disorder, including rowdiness, drunkenness, fighting, prostitution and abandoned buildings. (6)

**informant**—A human source of information in a criminal action whose identity must be protected. (2)

**informational probable cause**—Communications from official sources, statements from victims and information from informants that lead an officer to suspect that a crime has been, or is about to be, committed. (3)

**instrumental gangs**—Groups formed for the express purpose of criminal activity, primarily drug trafficking. (12)

**instrumental violence**—That used to exert control. (7)

**integrity**—Doing what is considered just, honest and proper. (14)

**intentional tort**—An act where the officer's intent to engage in the behavior must be proven, for example, wrongful death or false arrest. (14)

**interoperability**—The ability of public safety officials to communicate with each other seamlessly in real time over their wireless communications network either by voice or through data transmissions. (2)

**interrogation**—The questioning of suspects from whom officers try to obtain facts related to a crime as well as admissions or confessions related to the crime. (2)

**interview**—The planned questioning of a witness, victim, informant or other person with information related to an incident or a case. (2)

**involvement crimes**—Offenses in which the victim and the suspect confront each other. In contrast to *discovery crimes*. (4)

*jihad*—A holy war. (9)

**juvenile**—A person not yet of legal age, usually under the age of 18. (11)

**juvenile delinquents**—Young people who violate the law. (11)

**juvenile justice model**—A judicial process in which young people who come in conflict with the law are held responsible and accountable for their behavior. (11)

**larceny/theft**—The unlawful taking, carrying, leading or riding/driving away of property from another's possession; synonymous with theft. (10)

**leading question**—One that suggests an answer, for example, when did you leave the house?—Implying that the person did leave the house. (2)

**libel**—Written defamation of another's character; false statements that tend to humiliate a person and degrade that person in the esteem of others. (14)

**litigious**—Highly likely to sue. (14)

**lockdowns**—Periods when students are detained in classrooms while police and dogs scour the building searching for contraband or any danger to a safe educational environment. (7)

**malfeasance**—Acts of misconduct. (14)

**malicious prosecution**—A proceeding instituted in bad faith without any probable cause, in the belief that the charges against the defendant can be sustained. (14)

**mental fitness**—A person's emotional well-being, the ability to feel fear, anger, compassion and other emotions and to express them appropriately. This also refers to a person's alertness and ability to make decisions quickly. (13)

**mere handcuff rule**—A policy stating that in the interest of officer safety, all persons arrested and transported shall be handcuffed. It disregards the fact that handcuffing is a form of force and should be used only if the situation warrants. (3)

**ministerial acts**—Duties prescribed by law as some of the tasks of an administrative office. (14)

*Miranda* **warning**—A statement of a suspect's rights when that suspect is being questioned: the rights to remain silent, to talk to an attorney and to have an attorney present during questioning, the attorney to be provided free if a suspect cannot afford one. (2)

**mission**—An organization's reason for existence, its purpose. (1)

**mission statement**—Written statement of an organization's reasons for existence or purpose. (1)

**moniker**—A gang member's street name. (12)

**moral principles**—Set ideas of right and wrong that form the basis for ethical behavior. (14)

**motor vehicle thefts**—Intentionally taking or driving a motor vehicle without the consent of the owner or the owner's authorized agent. (10)

**Munchausen's syndrome by proxy (MSBP)**—A psychiatric ailment that leads a person to fabricate a child's illnesses to fulfill their own needs for attention and sympathy. (7)

**negligence**—An act where intent or mental state does not matter; what must be proven is if some inadvertent act or failure to act created an unreasonable risk to another person, for example, speeding resulting in a traffic crash or not responding to a 911 call. (14)

**nonfeasance**—Failure to take action, with the result being injury or damage to another person. (14)

**nystagmus**—An uncontrollable bouncing or jerking of the eyes when an intoxicated individual looks to the extreme right or left and up or down. (12)

**objectives**—Specific activities to accomplish a goal. (1)

**observational probable cause**—What an officer sees or hears that makes that officer reasonably believe that a crime has been or is about to be committed. It includes suspicious conduct, being high on drugs, associating with known criminals, having a criminal record, running away, presence in an unusual place or at an unusual time, presence in a high-crime area, presence at a crime scene, failure to answer questions, failure to provide identification, providing false information and physical evidence. (3)

**one-pot jurisdictional approach**—Use of the same system to deal with youths who are neglected or abused, those who are status offenders and those who commit serious crimes. (11)

**open-ended question**—One that allows for an unlimited response from the witness in his/her own words, for example, "what can you tell me about the car?" (the opposite of a closed-ended question). (2)

**organized/corporate gangs**—Heavy involvement in all kinds of crime, heavy use and sale of drugs; may resemble major corporations, with separate divisions handling sales, marketing, discipline and so on; discipline is strict, and promotion is based on merit. (12)

**osteogenesis imperfecta**—A medical condition characterized by bones that break easily; also called *brittle bone disease.* (7)

**overt investigations**—Those conducted openly, usually with officers in uniform or introducing themselves as police officers. (10)

**parallel proceedings**—When both civil and criminal proceedings are instituted against a violator; a frequent occurrence in environmental crimes. (10)

*parens patriae*—A doctrine allowing the state to assume guardianship of abandoned, neglected and "wayward" children. (11)

**Part I (Crime Index) Offenses**—FBI's classification for serious crimes, which includes arson, assault, auto theft, burglary, larceny/theft, murder, rape and robbery. (6)

**Part II offenses**—FBI's classification for less serious crimes. (6)

**participatory leadership**—Allows officers to influence decisions affecting them and seeks to form a cohesive team. (1)

**party gangs**—Commonly called "party crews"; relatively high use and sale of drugs, but only one major form of delinquency—vandalism; may contain both genders or may be one gender; flexible turf called the "party scene." (12)

**patdown**—A brief feeling of a person's outer clothing to determine if a weapon is present. Also called a *frisk.* (3)

**phishing**—Use of fraudulent e-mails and websites to fool recipients into divulging personal information. (10)

**physical fitness**—The general capacity to adapt and respond favorably to physical effort. (13)

**plain view**—Term describing evidence that is not concealed, that is easily seen by officers while performing their legal duties. (3)

**police operations**—Those activities conducted in the field by law enforcement officers as they "serve and protect." They usually include patrol, traffic, investigation and general calls for service. (1)

**police placebo**—A lie told by the police when the lie benefits the person lied to and when no more effective means of dealing with the problem is available. Also known as a *white lie.* (14)

**policy**—A guiding principle or course of action. (1)

**positional asphyxia**—A type of strangulation that results if a person's body position interferes with breathing. (3)

**posttraumatic stress disorder (PTSD)**—A reaction to a violent event that evokes intense fear, terror and helplessness; a debilitating stressful reaction to a trauma that may last for months or years. It can be experienced not only by victims, but also by those who help the victims. (8)

**predatory gangs**—Heavily involved in serious crimes (robberies, muggings) and the abuse of addictive drugs such as crack cocaine; may engage in selling drugs but not in an organized fashion. (12)

**predisaster plans**—Preparing for anticipated and unanticipated emergencies before they occur. (8)

**preliminary investigation**—The on-the-scene interviews of victims and witnesses, interrogations of suspects and search of the crime scene itself. (6)

**premeditation**—The deliberate, precalculated plan to act; the essential element of first-degree murder, distinguishing it from all other murder classifications. (10)

**pretext stop**—A stop in which the officer is stopping a vehicle to investigate not only a traffic violation but also the fact that the driver looks suspicious. Also called a *dual motive stop.* (5)

**primary victim**—One who actually is harmed. (2)

**privileged information**—Data that does not need to be divulged to the police or the courts because of the existence of a special relationship, such as that between spouses or between lawyers and their clients. (2)

**probable cause**—The fact that it is more likely than not that a crime has been committed by the person whom a law enforcement officer seeks to arrest. An officer's probable cause to conduct an arrest depends on what the officer knew *before* taking action. (3)

**problem-oriented policing (POP)**—A proactive approach to patrol and policing that focuses on problems to be solved rather than incidents to be responded to. (4)

**procedural law**—Deals with process, or how the law is applied. (3)

**procedures**—Step-by-step instructions for carrying out department policies. (1)

**property crimes**—Offenses in which no physical contact with the victim occurs, including arson, auto theft, burglary and larceny/theft. (6)

**proportionate assignment**—Determination of area assignments by requests for service based on available data. No area is larger than the time it takes a car to respond in three minutes or less. (4)

**proximate**—Closely related in space, time or order. Very near. (4)

**proxy data**—Evidence not seen as they are created but are only the remnants of an event left behind. (10)

**pulling levers**—Cracking down on any type of criminal activity and telling gang members that the crackdown will continue until the violence stops. (12)

**pursuit**—An active attempt by a law enforcement officer on duty in a patrol car to apprehend one or more occupants of a moving motor vehicle, providing the driver is aware of the attempt and is resisting apprehension by maintaining or increasing his speed or by ignoring the law enforcement officer's attempt to stop him. Can also refer to a foot chase. (5)

**racial profiling**—Inconsistent, discriminatory enforcement of the law; an officer uses a person's race to assess the likelihood of criminal conduct or wrongdoing. (1, 5)

**rave**—A form of dance and recreation held in a clandestine location with fast-paced, high-volume music, a variety of high-tech entertainment and often the use of drugs. (11)

**reader-friendly writing**—Avoids police jargon and communicates in plain, simple language. It is written as it would be spoken, and it considers who the audience is. (2)

**regulations**—Rules governing the actions of employees of the city, including police department personnel. (1)

**relative issue**—An issue with a range of morally acceptable options, which are of several shades of gray rather than either black or white. (14)

**response time**—The time elapsed from when the need for police arises and when they arrive on the scene. (4)

**road rage**—An assault with a motor vehicle or other dangerous weapon by the operator or passenger(s) of one motor vehicle on the operator or passenger(s) of another motor vehicle and is caused by an incident that occurred on the roadway. (5)

**robbery**—The felonious taking of another's property from his or her person in his or her presence through force or intimidation. (10)

**scavenger gangs**—Loosely organized groups described as "urban survivors"; prey on the weak in inner cities; engage in rather petty crimes but sometimes violence, often just for fun; members have no greater bond than their impulsiveness and need to belong; lack goals and are low achievers; often illiterate with poor school performance. (12)

**scofflaws**—Drivers with at least three unpaid parking tickets. (5)

**secondary victim**—One who is not actually harmed but who suffers along with the victim—a spouse or parent, for example. (2)

**Section 1983**—The Civil Rights Act; it states that anyone acting under the authority of the law who violates another person's constitutional rights can be sued; the legal authority for most lawsuits against law enforcement officers and agencies. (14)

**selective enforcement**—Assignment of officers to areas identified as having high crime or crash rates. (1, 5)

**serious delinquent gangs**—Heavy involvement in both serious and minor crimes, but much lower involvement in drug use and drug sales than party gangs. (12)

**sexual assault**—A crime including (1) an act of sexual intercourse (2) committed without the victim's consent (3) against the victim's will and by force. (10)

**slander**—Spoken defamation of another's character; false oral statements that tend to humiliate a person and degrade that person in the esteem of others. (14)

**sleeper cell**—A group of terrorists who blend into a community. (9)

**slippery slope**—One small indiscretion can lead to more serious misbehavior and finally to actual corruption. See also the *corruption continuum*. (14)

**solidarity**—A unique sense of identity, belonging and cohesion that one develops as part of a group of colleagues who share common social roles, interests, problems, concerns and even lifestyles. (14)

**split-second syndrome**—In some circumstances, officers have very little time to think through decisions. A high percentage of inappropriate decisions should be expected and accepted because the officer must act quickly. (13)

**stake-in-conformity variables**—Include marital status, employment, residential stability and age—all variables offenders might lose if convicted for a repeat offense. (7)

**statement**—A legal narrative description of events related to a crime. (2)

**status offenses**—Violations of the law applying only to those under legal age. Includes curfew violations, drinking alcoholic beverages, incorrigibility, smoking cigarettes, running away from home and truancy. (11)

**Stockholm syndrome**—In a hostage situation, the process of transference, with the hostages feeling positive toward their captors (and negative toward the police) and the captors returning these positive feelings. (6)

**stop**—Brief detention of a suspicious person by law enforcement officers for questioning. (3)

**stop-and-frisk situation**—One in which law enforcement officers briefly detain a suspicious person for questioning and pat the person's outer clothing to assure that they are not armed. (3)

**street justice**—Decision of police officers to deal with an offense in their own way—usually by ignoring it. (11)

**stress**—Strain; physical, cognitive and/or emotional response to a situation that is perceived to greatly affect future health, happiness or security. It can be positive or negative. (13)

**strict liability**—Refers to an act where the injury or damage is so severe and the harm should have been foreseen so that intent or mental state need not be proven. (14)

**substantive law**—Deals with the content of what behaviors are considered crimes; defines the elements of crimes and the punishments for them. (3)

**survival triangle**—Model for police survival; consists of mental and physical preparedness, sound tactics and weapon control. (13)

**synchrony**—In harmony or in sync. (2)

**territorial gangs**—Associated with a specific area or turf and, as a result, get involved in conflicts with other gangs over their respective turfs. (12)

**terrorism**—The use of force or violence against persons or property in violation of U.S. criminal laws for purposes of intimidation, coercion or ransom. (9)

**thrownaways**—Youths who were either told to leave, were not allowed back after having left, ran away and no one tried to recover them, or were abandoned or deserted. (11)

**tort**—A civil wrong, the equivalent to a crime in criminal law. (14)

**totality of circumstances**—All relevant variables in an arrest, including an individual's age, mentality, education, nationality and criminal experience, as well as the reason for the arrest and how it was explained to the individual being arrested. During an interrogation, it also includes whether basic necessities were provided and the methods used during the interrogation. (2)

**traffic calming**—Describes a wide range of road and environment design changes that either make it more difficult for a vehicle to speed or make drivers believe they should slow down for safety. (5)

**triage**—Prioritizing, sorting out by degree of seriousness, as in medical emergencies. (8)

**turf**—The territory claimed by a gang, often marked by graffiti. (12)

**Uniform Crime Reports (UCRs)**—The FBI's national crime reporting system, published annually as *Crime in the United States*. (6)

**universal precaution**—All blood and potentially infectious materials other than blood must be treated as if infected. (13)

**vertical prosecution**—Where one assistant prosecutor or small group of assistant prosecutors handle the criminal complaint from start to finish through the entire court process. (12)

**vicarious liability**—Responsibility for a person's actions or others specifically associated with that person. (14)

**victimless crimes**—Offenses in which there are no complainants. Includes prostitution, pornography, gaming and drug dealing/using. (10)

**violent crimes**—Offenses in which physical contact with the victim occurs, including assault, murder, rape and robbery; sometimes called *crimes against persons*. (6)

**zero-tolerance policies**—School policies that mandate predetermined consequences or punishments for specific offenses, for example, suspension or expulsion for possession of drugs or a weapon. (7)

# Index

# Credits